RIGIDITY OF BEHAVIOR

*

RIGIDITY
OF BEHAVIOR

A VARIATIONAL APPROACH TO THE
EFFECT OF EINSTELLUNG

ABRAHAM S. LUCHINS

Professor of Psychology
University of Miami, Coral Gables, Florida

and

EDITH HIRSCH LUCHINS

Research Associate in Mathematics
University of Miami, Coral Gables, Florida

*

UNIVERSITY OF OREGON BOOKS

Eugene, Oregon, 1959

UNIVERSITY OF OREGON MONOGRAPHS
Studies in Psychology No. 3

In Memory of
Anne Rissa Y. Luchins

1891-1935

Habit is thus the enormous fly-wheel of society, its most precious conservative agent. It alone is what keeps us all within the bounds of ordinance,
and saves the children of fortune from the envious uprisings of the poor. It
alone prevents the hardest and most repulsive walks of life from being
deserted by those brought up to tread therein. It keeps the fisherman and
the deck-hand at sea through the winter; it holds the miner in his darkness,
and nails the countryman to his log-cabin and his lonely farm through all
the months of snow; it protects us from invasion by the natives of the desert
and the frozen zone. It dooms us all to fight out the battle of life upon the
lines of our nurture or our early choice, and to make the best of a pursuit
that disagrees, because there is no other for which we are fitted, and it is
too late to begin again. It keeps different social strata from mixing. Already
at the age of twenty-five you see the professional mannerism settling down
on the young commercial traveller, on the young doctor, on the young
minister, on the young counsellor-at-law. You see the little lines of cleavage
running through the character, the tricks of thought, the prejudices, the
ways of the 'shop,' in a word, from which the man can by-and-by no more
escape than his coat-sleeve can suddenly fall into a new set of folds.

WILLIAM JAMES, *The Principles of Psychology*, vol. 1, p. 121

PREFACE

THIS publication marks the twenty-third anniversary of a research project on rigidity of behavior. The first phase of the project (1936-1938), a report of which has been published elsewhere (Luchins, 1942), was primarily concerned with discovering factors that increase or decrease the tendency to become habituated when the same method of solution is used in a series of similar problems. The second phase began during World War II, when, as a clinical psychologist in army hospitals, I investigated the use of these problems and other materials as tests of rigidity of behavior. In order to systematize the use of the tests, in 1948, while director of training at the Mental Hygiene Clinic of the New York Regional Office of the Veterans' Administration, I prepared a manual setting forth the procedure for conducting each test. Repeated requests for the manual led to a revised edition in 1950. The revised manual, entitled *An Examination for Flexibility-Rigidity*, included, in the appendices, data on the theoretical and methodological background of the tests. Since the manuals foreshadowed the present book, it is appropriate here to thank those who made them possible: Dr. Richard H. Payntner, chief clinical psychologist, Mental Hygiene Clinic, New York Regional Office, Veterans' Administration, who saw to it that I had time to write the manuals and who arranged the distribution of the 1948 manual; Dr. Seymour G. Klebanoff, chief clinical psychologist, Franklin D. Roosevelt Veterans' Administration Hospital, Montrose, New York, who arranged for the printing and distribution of the 1950 manual; the late James Holsopple and Dr. Harry V. McNeill, chief clinical psychologists, Veterans' Administration Branch No. 2, and Dr. Harold M. Hildreth, chief, Clinical Psychology Division, Veterans' Administration, who encouraged the preparation of the manuals.

For almost two decades, my wife, Dr. Edith H. Luchins, has shared in the formulation of research on rigidity of behavior, in the analysis of data, and in the writing of reports. In 1950-51, we completed a 1,500-page manuscript that included elaborations of the appendices contained in the 1950 manual. It dealt primarily with the methodology of science in general and psychology in particular, and large use was made of experimental work on mechanized behavior for the exposition of ideas on theory and methodology. Because of difficulties in getting such a long manuscript published, and because of the increased interest in rigidity, we revised the manuscript in 1954-55. The present text is the result of that revision. In it we are concerned primarily with rigidity of behavior and only incidentally with methodology. We hope, in the future, to publish a volume that will include the methodological sections of the earlier manuscript.

Some of the experiments dealt with herein have been described in other reports (e.g., Luchins, 1942; Luchins and Luchins, 1950), to which we refer the reader interested in the early phase of the research. However, the results of many of the experiments described have not been published before. The writings of others on rigidity of behavior have also been surveyed, but with no pretense at inclusiveness.

Our research has been guided by a phenomenon-centered variational approach. Since this approach is described later, it suffices to note here that it involves centering on a specific phenomenon of behavior and attempting to vary systematically the conditions under which it is studied. An aspect of the approach involves a multitheoretical orientation wherein different theories are focused on the phenomenon. Helping to crystallize this approach and orientation was the fact that our research was viewed from different frames of reference arising from the different professional interests of my wife and myself; my wife's interest in her field of specialization, mathematics, and my interest in the behavioral sciences.

Our methodological ideas were influenced by many stimulating lectures on mathematics and mathematical physics delivered by Professor Richard Courant, with whom my wife studied at New York University. Also contributing to the approach and orientation were the opportunities I had to study with teachers who, although they represented different disciplines and diverse theoretical points of view, even with respect to the same topic, yet shared a profound respect for the concrete living phenomena of human behavior. Among these teachers were the late Isadore Kayfetz, professor of education at Brooklyn College, who introduced me to psychology and education in my undergraduate days and encouraged my research in these areas; Professor Hadley Cantril, then at Teachers College, Columbia University, and now with the Institute for International Research, Princeton, whose stimulating teaching led to my decision to become a psychologist and whose continuing friendship has reinforced this decision; the late Max Wertheimer, whose research assistant I was from 1936 to 1942 and whose sympathetic reception of the early phases of the research project has sustained me ever since; and the late Paul R. Radosavljviech, who introduced me to traditional experimental pedagogy and comparative education and who sponsored my doctoral dissertation (Luchins, 1939).

It is customary to acknowledge financial support for research. However, we neither asked for nor accepted grants for the research projects reported herein. It has been our conviction that financial assistance is not always necessary or sufficient for productive research and we feel strongly that at least some of the research that a scientist does should be done for its own sake. The tendency to associate research with grants involves the dangers that research for its own sake may become a thing of the past in universities, that graduate students (and their instructors) may come to believe that one does not do research unless he is paid for it, and that there may even be a slackening of research when grants are no longer readily available.

How then was the research conducted and sustained? Through 1950 we did the research ourselves; since then, students have assisted with some of the research, particularly with the collection of data. I was fortunate to find students who, because of their scientific curiosity, did research eagerly when there was no monetary reward or a course or thesis requirement (although some experiments developed into the bases for theses). Mention of the students' names, in appropriate places in the text and Bibliography, is a small token of gratitude for their companionship in this research experience.

Grateful acknowledgment is also made to the thousands of subjects, children and adults, in New York City, the state of Oregon, and Montreal, Canada, who participated in the experiments and to the instructors who permitted their pupils to serve as subjects.

We take this opportunity to thank Professors Ernest R. Hilgard and Theodore M. Newcomb, who read parts of the earlier manuscript and made suggestions which proved helpful in its revision.

We are grateful to Beverly Houghton, departmental secretary at McGill University, and to Mary Engelstein, our Canadian friend, for typing the early 1,500-page manuscript. We shall long remember their helpfulness and kindness in finding time to do this extra chore. To Karen Arendt and Mary Robertson, departmental secretaries at the University of Oregon, we are indebted for typing portions of the present manuscript.

Without the cooperation and flexibility shown by our children, David, Daniel, Jeremy, Anne, and Joseph, it would not have been feasible to write this book and to maintain both a household and a research program.

Finally, thanks are due to the Publications Committee of the University of Oregon, which accepted the book in 1955, and especially to John E. Bailey, assistant University editor, for the editorial services he rendered in making the book more readable and understandable.

ABRAHAM S. LUCHINS

University of Miami
Coral Gables, Florida

TABLE OF CONTENTS

LIST OF TABLES

INTRODUCTION

WHY DO PEOPLE persist in behavior when it is no longer useful? Why do they hold on to their accustomed patterns of behavior when other more efficient ones are available? Why do they sometimes repeatedly manifest behavior which is destructive and self-defeating? Such problems are of fundamental importance to students of human behavior.

Persistence in a pattern of behavior, when it is uncalled for, may have humorous and ludicrous effects. The reader may recall the scene in the moving picture *Modern Times* in which Charles Chaplin, after spending his working hours in making one type of hand movement to bolt a part on an automobile assembly line, persists in making the same hand movement during his nonworking hours. In his attempt to eat his lunch, the coffee and sandwich miss his mouth more often than reach it. After work, all boltlike and protruding objects, including the top of a hydrant and the prominent bosom of a woman passer-by, attract his attention and result in an attempt at manipulation by the same type of hand movement. In actual life, the consequences are, of course, often less humor-provoking and spectacular, perhaps entailing only some small inconvenience or slight embarrassment. We may cuss a bit as, plodding our accustomed way through the living room, we stumble over furniture which has been rearranged, or as we keep on looking for a wallet, a light switch, or a tool in its former place after we ourselves have changed its location. But there are consequences which are far more profound. Serious maladjustment may result from carrying over into adulthood childlike behavior, mannerisms, or fears. Mental hospitals are filled with patients who repeatedly manifest certain behavior even though it brings tragedy in its wake. The stereotypy of psychotics; the compulsive repetitious behavior of neurotics; the alcoholic's persistence in drinking despite the misfortune it brings to him and to his family; the drug addict's insistence on his drug even when use of it leads him to crime; the inability of the individual to give up smoking when he knows it is injurious to his health; the mulelike "pigheadedness" of some individuals which makes life difficult for themselves and for others—all these are striking illustrations of behavior that is continued despite being maladaptive. Examples are legion of man acting through force of habit, of his mastering a habit so well that it in turn masters him.

The social scene offers ample evidence of persistence in customs and ways of behaving that are inadequate in the light of the existing situation. Consider the rivalries and feuds that continue long after their original causes no longer exist, the set habits of voting of certain families or certain regions, the prevalency of rituals and social customs. Sociologists have coined the term "cultural lag" to describe the resistance to change of social institutions, the discrepancy between technological and other advances, on the one hand, and cultural standards and behavior, on the other. Social reformers have decried the deadwood of custom that encrusts behavior and hinders social progress.

Social scientists are concerned with the deleterious effects of habits and past experiences. One of the objectives of modern education is so to educate the individual that, while he has a repertoire of certain habits, he does not become a mechanized robot, but instead is flexible enough in his behavior to meet the needs of a changing, dynamic world. The industrial psychologist in his human-engineering efforts must make provision for the hampering, negative effects of past experience and for the tendency to resist change. Psychiatrists and clinical psychologists who are attempting to produce therapeutic changes come face to face with the patient's resistance to change and his tendency to cling to inadequate, maladaptive behavior patterns. Social psychologists and others concerned with changing attitudes and reducing social tensions, with "unfreezing" certain situations in the community, know only too well about the need for recognizing and coping with factors which foster one kind of attitude or behavior and hinder change.

Psychologists concerned with the field of learning have dealt with the hampering and interfering influences of past experiences on present behavior under the rubrics of set, retroactive inhibition, proactive inhibition, negative transfer with positive effect, and similar headings. Interfering influences of learned behavior have been interpreted as illustrating a very strong habit or as illustrating "overlearning." The concept of perseveration has also been invoked to account for the persistence of behavior.

In short, both for theoretical and practical reasons, psychologists are interested in the manifestation of behavior that is similar to or decidedly influenced by behavior manifested at a previous time, but that is inadequate in the present situation. Such behavior has been described as habituated, mechanized, resistant to change, inflexible, rigid, and by related terms. For convenience of exposition, we use the terms "rigid behavior" or "rigidity of behavior." The aim of this monograph is to collate existing knowledge about rigid behavior and to attempt to add to this knowledge.

The first portion of the monograph surveys outstanding approaches to and theories of rigidity, describes their experimental and conceptual foundations, and, where feasible, submits them to critical evaluation.

The remaining portion focuses on one specific case of rigid behavior and subjects it to intensive experimental investigation. The history of science reveals that it is not unusual to select one case of a phenomenon for concentrated study. Classical illustrations are Galileo's investigations of the motion of a pendulum and of motion on an inclined plane; Ehrlich's 606 experiments with the germ of syphilis which culminated in the discovery of the drug salvarsan; and, to turn to psychology, Wertheimer's investigations of the Phi phenomenon and Köhler's study of figural aftereffects. Yet, in recent years there have been few investigations devoted to a concentrated attack on one specific case of a psychological phenomenon. This may be a sign of the times. Psychology, in recent years, has been strongly theory-centered rather than phenomenon-centered. The aim generally has been to promulgate, defend, or refute a theory; hence, it is customary for the theory to be of central concern while the phenomenon under investigation may be of interest only insofar (or mainly insofar) as it pertains to a hypothesis suggested by the theory.

In contrast to this contemporary theory-centered orientation, ours is more of an empirical, phenomenon-centered or phenomenological orientation. We are interested in the selected case of rigid behavior for its own sake and not for the sake of defending or refuting a theory. We do not start with a theory or a hypothesis suggested by a theory; rather, we first look at the phenomenon for clues concerning its structure and dynamics; the phenomenon is allowed to speak for itself. Nor is the goal the promulgation of a broad theory; rather, the goal is to obtain empirical relationships that reveal the crucial variables involved in this specific case of rigid behavior.

Pleas for a phenomenon-centered approach recently have been heard from some philosophers, psychologists, and other students of man and of society. Contemporary existentialist philosophers call for a phenomenological approach (cf. Blackham, 1952, p. 161); a psychologist strongly advocates a phenomenological approach in dealing with social phenomena (MacLeod, 1947); and such an approach has also been called for in the study of the behavior of the individual (Snygg and Combs, 1949). We have noted elsewhere (Luchins, 1952) that one who adopts a phenomenon-centered approach need not accept the philosophical implications of phenomenology as promulgated, for example, by Husserl (1952) and Heidigger (1950).

Critics of an empirical, phenomenon-centered orientation have also been heard from. It has been charged that empirical fact finding that does not test a deduction from a theory or a hypothesis belongs to the prescientific era (Blake and Ramsey, 1951). Empirical studies, not guided by theories, have been called mere busywork rather than scientific investigations (Dallenbach, 1953). In short, empirical study of a concrete case of behavior is regarded by some psychologists as having little or no scientific value.

One of the objectives of this monograph is to demonstrate the scientific value of empirical study of a particular case. Moreover, it is hoped that the particular mode of attack used may serve as a model for others interested in concentrated study of a specific phenomenon, as a model for phenomenon-centered experimentation.

What was studied, and how it was studied, will be presented later in our explorations of rigidity of behavior. We now ask the reader to join us in our survey of the outstanding approaches to and explorations of rigidity.

CHAPTER I

PSYCHOANALYTIC APPROACHES
TO RIGIDITY

CONTEMPORARY clinical and experimental work on rigidity is
replete with psychoanalytic concepts. This is not surprising since
most psychoanalysts, while not necessarily using the term "rigidity,"
have been concerned with the kind of maladaptive, repetitive behavior
that may be described as rigid behavior. What we shall attempt to do in
this chapter is to outline the basic tenets of the various psychoanalytic
theories, and, at the same time, high-light the aspects which seem most
germane to the subject of rigidity.

SIGMUND FREUD

The Repetition Compulsion

Observations of rigid, repetitive behavior led Freud to alter his formulation of psychoanalytic theory. Basal to his early formulation was
the pleasure principle—the dictum that human behavior is regulated
by a propulsion to seek pleasure, especially sexual satisfactions, and
to avoid pain or dissatisfactions. Gradually, Freud became convinced
that a tendency to repeat was stronger than the pleasure principle.

The inadequacy of the pleasure principle was revealed during World
War I when "shell-shocked" soldiers frequently relived disturbing
traumatic experiences in their dreams. "What conative impulse could
possibly be satisfied," Freud asked (1933, p. 44), "by this reinstatement of a most painful traumatic experience?" His conclusion was that
the reoccurring dreams were the manifestation of an automatic tendency
to repeat earlier experiences and situations, pleasant as well as un-
pleasant ones. This repetition compulsion—"a principle powerful
enough to overrule the pleasure principle" (1953, vol. 4, p. 391)—
manifested itself in forms other than reoccurring dreams. As early as
1905 Freud reported on the "transference phenomenon" occurring during analysis—the patient's transference to the analyst of feelings and
reactions he had once had to an important figure in his childhood, usually his father or mother—and the acting out or reliving of forgotten
incidents from his past, both pleasant and painful. Many of his patients
repeatedly recounted certain experiences, real or phantasies, or showed
rigid adherence to various behavioral patterns. Repeated washing of
the hands, elaborate rituals before going to bed, and other compulsive
acts seemed to occur automatically, as if the patients were powerless

[5]

to prevent them. The lives of certain individuals, Freud noted, revealed
a repeated pattern, such as repeatedly making sacrifices for others without thanks or repeatedly entering into unsuccessful friendships and
marriages. Freud also noted a tendency in "normal" adults and children
to relive and recount previous experiences and to indulge in repetitive
behavior, although the tendency was not so marked in them as it was
in neurotics. All these observations supported the thesis that

there really exists in psychic life a repetition-compulsion which goes beyond the
pleasure principle ... and this seems to us more primitive, more elementary, more
instinctive than the pleasure principle which is displaced by it. (1922, pp. 24-25.)

Freud explicitly mentioned that his formulation of the repetition
compulsion was influenced by certain principles in physics and biology.
He related the repetitive tendency to "an attempt on the part of the
psychic apparatus to keep the quantity of excitations present as low as
possible, or at least constant," and saw this as "a special case of Fech-
ner's principle of the tendency toward stability" (1922, p. 4). The influence of physical principles, particularly the principle of inertia, is
clearly revealed in Freud's formulation of the relationship between instincts and the repetition compulsion.

In what way is the instinctive connected with the compulsion to repetition? At
this point the idea is forced upon us that we have stumbled on the trace of a general and hitherto not clearly recognized—or at least not expressly emphasized—
characteristic of instinct, perhaps of all organic life. According to this, an instinct
would be a tendency innate in living organic matter impelling it toward the reinstatement of an earlier condition, one which it had to abandon under the influence
of external disturbing forces—a kind of organic elasticity, or put it another way,
the manifestation of inertia in organic life. (1922, pp. 44-45.)

Carrying through to its ultimate conclusion this tendency to repeat
former psychic experiences, to achieve a former state, Freud was led
to postulate that a fundamental instinct in all living matter was the
death instinct: the tendency of living matter to return to its original
inorganic state.

The Death Instinct

The relation of rigidity to the concept of the death instinct
warrants tracing the history of the concept. Freud's first instinct
theory had been the duality of sex instincts and self-preservation
instincts, with instinctual life ruled by the pleasure principle. Dissatisfaction with the latter seemed to be coupled with a realization of
the need to revise the concepts of the basic instincts, and resulted in
Freud's second (and final) instinct theory. Many of the phenomena

attributed to the repetition compulsion apparently did not satisfy either the sex or the self-preservation urge. On the contrary, they seemed to be self-destructive. Moreover, World War I had vividly revealed the strength of man's aggression toward others. These and other considerations, including biological considerations, led Freud to postulate a destructive instinct, also called the death instinct or Thanatos since "the final aim of the destructive instinct is to reduce living things to an inorganic state" (1949, p. 20). The death instinct is

the urge toward effortlessness, inertia and disintegration, the mental correlate of the tendency of non-living energy to dissipate itself to the lowest possible level, and of the energy of organic life to fall back to "the peace of the inorganic world" and "restore conditions to what they were before life by its emergence upset them." Every backward trend, every destructive or aggressive impulse, whether directed toward oneself or outward, is an expression of the Death instinct. (Kallen, 1934, p. 582.)

The other basic instinct is Eros, also called the life, love, or sex instinct; it is the constructive and combining urge that preserves the organic substance. Every particle of living substance is said to contain Death and Eros, although in differing proportions. Freud considers all the phenomena of life as "explicable from the interplay of the two and their counteracting effect on each other" (1930, p. 97). That life persists despite the death instinct can be accounted for on the grounds that the death instinct is sometimes directed outward and that Eros fuses with the death instinct to mitigate its effect. "Some portion of self-destructiveness remains permanently within, until it at length succeeds in doing the individual to death" (1949, p. 23).

The polarity of Eros and Thanatos may be interpreted as a broadening of Freud's early theory that the aim of life is to relieve sexual tension. Life itself is seen as a state of tension and its ultimate aim as death, the final release of tension.

Freud notes that the formula that instincts tend toward a return to an earlier state (cf. the repetition compulsion) can be applied to the death instinct but not to Eros. The implication is that the repetition compulsion is an exponent of the death instinct, so that phenomena attributed to this compulsion may be interpreted as manifestations of the death instinct.

The energy associated with Eros is referred to as "libido" but there is no analogous term for the energy associated with the destructive instinct. Freud implies that people differ in the amount of energy available to each of these basic instincts as well as in the proportions one bears to the other, and that the differences may be due to constitutional or developmental factors.

Personality Divisions

The same years (1918-1922) that witnessed the explicit formulation of the repetition compulsion and the final instinct theory, also saw the formulation of the tripartite personality organization of id, ego, and superego. "Id" is the primordial, instinctual psyche, devoid of morals or logic, the "reservoir" of passions and destructive impulses. "Ego," which represents sanity and intelligence, is just a part of the id developed through a more direct relation with the external world. "Superego," representing claims of morality, society, and tradition, is a special portion of ego that incorporates the attitudes of parents (and of others in authority) toward libidinal gratifications. These attitudes in turn stem from the superegos of parents (and other authorities). Hence, the child's superego is built upon the model of the parents' superegos: "it takes over the same content, it becomes the vehicle of tradition and of all the age-long values which have been handed down in this way from generation to generation" (1933, p. 95).

Thus, the superego is extremely influential in determining rigid adherence to the past, representing as it does the hoary hand of tradition; failure to obey its sanctions is paid for with guilt and feelings of tension. Energy utilized by the superego is said to derive ultimately from the death instinct and directs aggressive impulses inward rather than against society.

The ego must try to achieve equilibrium in the face of the irrational impulses of the id, the stern demands of the superego, and the changing requirements of the external world. If the ego is unable to stand the strain of the conflicting demands, there may develop a neurosis or, in extreme cases, a psychosis.

Archaic Heritage

Freud maintained that at birth the infant id possesses fragments from the past heritage of mankind, individual recapitulations of the experiences of former generations. Moreover, each individual in his development is said to go through characteristic stages (including the oral stage, the anal stage, and the phallic stage in which the Oedipus and castration complexes are central). These stages are regarded as repetitions of outstanding events in the development of the human race and of society (1918). Thus, the very pattern of individual development is regarded by Freud as a repetition (or symbolic repetition) of the past.

The Unconscious, Repression, and Resistance

The unconscious is the locus of psychic processes of which the individual has never been conscious, as well as those which he has repressed (pushed out of consciousness) because he did not want to be conscious of them. The repetition compulsion compels the pent-up energy of a repressed process to seek reinstatement of its earlier nonrepressed state. Forces that gave rise to the repression also resist reinstatement. There ensues a conflict in which a repressed impulse (e.g., the infantile sexual impulse) may wholly or partly be kept in the unconscious or may became conscious. The repressed impulse may find direct expression (e.g., as in perversions) or indirect expression (as in dreams, jokes, mistakes, forgetting, free associations, and neurotic symptoms). Thus, the operation of the repetition compulsion in the unconscious constitutes an even more potent influence on psychic events than does its operation with respect to conscious processes.

Freud asserts that anything that can create a psychic disturbance was once conscious and then repressed. Psychotherapy aims to make the patient aware of the unconscious forces contributing to his difficulties. But therapy runs into resistance against bringing these forces into awareness, an outstanding example of resistance being transference. By transferring repressed childhood experiences and attitudes to the therapist, the patient circumvents his becoming conscious of them; that is, the associated pent-up energy is displaced, the repetition compulsion is given an outlet. Transference may hinder therapy but, if properly managed, is an essential therapeutic factor since it can be used dramatically to reveal, both to the analyst and patient, just what parts of the patient's repressed past are at the core of his psychic disturbance.

Fixations and Other Ego Defenses

A fixation is defined as "a peculiar psychic inertia hostile to change or progress" (Freud, 1953, vol. 2, p. 160). Fixations occur when there is a particularly strong attachment of the libido to an object or to a stage of development so that some or all of the libido remains permanently bound to the object or developmental stage. Fixations are induced by constitutional predisposing tendencies and/or accidental occurrences in childhood. The tendency of the libido to be bound to certain objects or stages is sometimes called its adhesiveness; in contrast, the ease with which the libido passes from one object or stage to another is called its plasticity or mobility.

Corresponding to the two kinds of fixation, there are two kinds of regression: a flowing back of libidinal energy to objects or to pregenital stages of development. Regression is fostered by anxiety (fear of danger to the ego) and is more likely to occur if there have been fixations. But, if the anxiety is sufficiently strong, there may be regressions despite a "normal" constitution and development.

Each stage of development is considered to have its own dangers, its characteristic conditions for anxiety. One of the features of the neurotic is that he is still afraid of a childhood danger or that he has substituted a childhood danger for the actual dangers confronting him.

A neurosis is always accompanied by a history of fixation and by regression to a point of fixation. A neurotic is said to be tied to his childhood past and hence to be alienated from present and future; he is, to use Freud's apt expression, "wrecked by his rigidity" (1953, vol. 2, p. 116). Neurotic symptoms, formed for the purpose of escaping anxiety, are described as disguised repetitions of infantile sexual experiences.

Fixations and regressions are examples of ego defenses of which there are at least seventeen different kinds. Ego defenses are part of the normal adjustment process but in the neurotic they become permanent or rigid, leading Freud to comment on the element of permanency in the neurotic's reactions to danger. The more normal, the more flexible person, can give up a particular ego defense when it is no longer adequate, but the neurotic rigidly adheres to his particular ego defenses to the point where maintaining and repeating them may become sources of anxiety. For example, compulsive washing of the hands (an example of the defense termed "undoing") may have developed originally to counteract an imaginary or real dirtying act, but the need to wash may become so frequent and so obsessional as to generate considerable anxiety. Herein lies the crux of what has been called the neurotic paradox, the paradox of behavior which is at one and the same time self-defeating and yet perpetuated (Mowrer, 1948). The answer, as implied in Freud's writings, is that the repetition compulsion, and concomitantly the death instinct and the superego, are extraordinarily powerful in the neurotic who has "given himself up to the compulsion to repeat" (Freud, 1953, vol. 2, p. 371).

Characterology

According to Freud's ideas on character, as elaborated and developed by Karl Abraham, character types correspond to stages of libidinal development. When part or all of the libido becomes fixated at a certain stage, a person will maintain characteristics throughout life that are related to this stage. The particular impulses that predominated at this stage (e.g., sucking impulses at the oral-sucking stage, biting impulses at the oral-biting stage) may continue unchanged, may be turned into other channels (sublimated), or may lead to the formation of conscious ideas and actions opposite in nature to the original impulses (reaction formations). In Freud's words, an individual's "permanent character traits are either unchanged perpetuations of the original impulses, sublimation of them, or reaction-formations against them" (1953, vol. 2,

p. 50). Individuals whose character traits reflect the predominant influence of the oral or anal stage are called archaic character types because they constitute recapitulations of primitive stages of development of the human race. The final stage of character development, marked by a friendly, well-wishing attitude toward others, requires attainment of the genital stage. And so Freud sees an individual's character as essentially a repetition or disguised repetition of his own and mankind's past.

OTHER PSYCHOANALYTIC APPROACHES TO RIGIDITY

Repetition compulsion and the death instinct are among the most controversial of psychoanalytic concepts. The thesis of a death instinct has been accepted by some psychoanalysts (e.g., K. Menninger) but rejected by others (e.g., W. Reich, Fenichel). An innate compulsion to repeat has been accepted by some (e.g., Alexander, Anna Freud) but rejected by others (e.g., Horney, Sullivan). Doubts have been raised about whether rigid, repetitive behavior is (1) due to an inherent compulsion, (2) related to destructiveness, and (3) necessarily an expression of a death instinct. What is in dispute is Freud's explanation of rigid, repetitive behavior; his observations as to the occurrence and frequency of such behavior have been widely corroborated.

Analysts vary in their opinions as to the nature of basic character types, and as to whether or not they are libidinal in origin, but there is high accord that character structure involves habitual attitudes which are reflected in neurotic symptoms. It has been said: "The term character, in psychoanalysis, is used only for habitual attitudes developed as reactions to life situations ... Symptoms might be considered special aspects of character trends in that symptoms are consistent with the character" (Thompson, 1950, p. 64).

While there are divergent opinions as to the mechanisms producing ego defenses, there is general agreement that an individual does develop defenses, that his character structure or personality structure is itself a kind of defense system, and that the individual tends rigidly to maintain these defenses. It has been recognized that a major task of therapy is to overcome this rigidity. As Fenichel (1945) puts it, "in therapy it is particularly urgent that the personality first be released from" its rigidity (p. 472).

We shall now survey some of the ideas germane to rigidity that have been offered by other psychoanalysts.

Franz Alexander

"Individual development proceeds on the principle of economy by which energy is as far as possible conserved and the necessities of life secured with the minimum expenditure of energy" (Alexander, 1951, p. 175). This economy (inertia, energy-saving) principle is said to underlie (1) the trend toward habit formation: the tendency to replace flexible adjustments by automatisms; (2) resistance to change: unwillingness of the organism to make new adjustments; and (3) regressive tendencies: attempts to revert to earlier forms of behavior and emotional attitudes when a new adjustment is difficult. Throughout life the ego is seen as having two basic tasks: to consciously determine, by trial and error (by "experimentation"), suitable means for gratifying its subjective needs, and to repeat this behavior until it becomes automatic. Learning is defined by Alexander as consisting in experimentation and repetition leading to automatic (habituated) behavior. Advantages of automatic behavior are its swiftness and effortlessness, which conserve energy. "Its disadvantage is its rigidity" (p. 124). Automatic behavior is adapted to a definite situation and is not easily modified even when changed conditions call for modification. To change or replace a performance that was satisfactory in the past requires effort, and the organism disposed to save its energy resists the change. Difficulties associated with weaning furnish an example of habit formation, rigidity of automatic behavior, and resistance to change.

Resistance to change is found not only in individual development but also in the social scene; e.g., in cultural lag, the rigid adherence to outworn social attitudes in a changed social order. But even cultural change and progress may be motivated by the energy-saving principle. Thus, machines are invented to conserve our energy, and the ideal of a world in which the necessities and comforts of life are secured with minimum exertion has long been a great social force.

Inertia plays a major role in morbid (pathogenic) phenomena, whether individual or social, since these are traceable to disharmony between existing conditions that call for change and habitual attitudes and behavior that resist change. Regressive trends are strong in an emotionally ill individual who is unable or unwilling to adjust his needs and desires to each other, to the existing external conditions, and to the actual stage of biological development. He vainly tries to evade new, necessary adaptations by adhering or regressing to older behavioral patterns that do not fit present conditions. Repetitive, compulsive, and ritualistic behavior manifested by patients, and all other neurotic and psychotic symptoms, are considered to be regressive. A neurosis is taken as a sign of succumbing to inertia and a psychosis as complete yielding to it.

Even a normal individual may show regressive tendencies under conditions of frustration and hostility, for these create anxiety, which hinders adaptability and prompts the return to earlier forms of adaptation. Regression is indeed part of the rhythm of life. Thus, sleep is said to represent regression (regression to a rough approximation of intra-uterine conditions). Sleep, with the accompanying low expenditure of energy, reflects the economy principle, as do dreams which aim to protect sleep. "Many habits of everyday life such as smoking, chewing, alcoholism, and all kinds of hobbies and games are intelligble as signs of a deep-seated need of the organism to return to earlier irresponsible pleasures of life" (p. 165). Furthermore, folklore reveals an almost universal sentimental attachment to the past.

Is the inertia principle sufficiently broad in scope to account for all mental life? Is the main thing in life to save energy so that man expends effort only when necessary? Does a man work only so that he can eventually retire and conserve energy? Must we accept the paradoxical conclusion that the expenditure of energy serves the organism's ruling tendency: to save energy? If so, then the inertia principle would suffice as the sole explanatory concept. But, Alexander contends, this principle seems inadequate to account for certain expenditures of energy—the infant's spontaneous and playful physical exercise, the spontaneous impulse to learn rather than to stick to what one has already mastered, scientific curiosity, the creative aspects of inventions apart from the utilitarian aspects, and, more generally, the urge toward maturation and reproduction. To account for such phenomena, Alexander introduces a second fundamental explanatory concept: the principle of surplus energy. This is a progressive urge distinct from the tendency to save energy and to regress. It is strikingly manifested in the mature sexual drive which is said to constitute the most powerful progressive tendency opposing the regressive desire to remain a child. Surplus energy is expressed in genital sexuality, reproduction, the desire for and care of children, in leadership, and in creative tendencies whether they constitute intellectual, artistic, or social productivity. In all creative activities (as opposed to those controlled by inertia), the emphasis shifts from self-centered aims to outside objects, from receiving to giving help and love, and from saving energy to creatively expanding it.

The principles of surplus energy and inertia are used to explain human development, emotional disturbances, political thought, and social systems and events. Alexander says that these principles can account for facts that Freud sought to account for with his Eros and death instincts, and that they have the advantage of being empirically derived, in strict accord with the biological process, and devoid of abstract metaphysical concepts. He regards the term "death instinct" as unfortunate because the organism "aims not at death but life with a minimum of exertion" (p. 168), and notes that Freud's concept of repetition compulsion is another name for habit formation and for the energy-saving principle.

It has been said (Szasz, 1952, p. 29) that Alexander "rediscovered" in the concept of the death instinct the principles of physics on which Freud rested this concept (inertia, tendency to stability). In short, if Eros is considered analogous to a surplus-energy principle and Death to an inertia principle, then it may be said that Alexander directly applied physical principles that had served Freud as analogies.

Wilhelm Reich

Reich accepts Freud's thesis of libidinal energy but rejects the death instinct. He holds that emotional disturbances reflect a disturbed libidinal economy. The capacity to regulate the libidinal (vegetative, organismic, orgastic) economy is measured in terms of "orgastic potency," which is defined as the ability to discharge an amount of sexual energy corresponding to the sexual tension. Sexuality and anxiety are considered to represent the basic antithesis in organic life, being identical excitations with opposite directions. The therapeutic goal is to make for a more satisfactory genital sex life by dissolving pregenital fixations, by analyzing defenses against repressed (unconscious) material, by overcoming resistances to genital activities, by freeing libidinal energy which is dammed up or distorted into anxiety, and by remobilizing energy so that it flows and remains in genital channels.

Character is described by Reich as a defense or an armor of the ego against both the outer world and inner libidinal strivings.

> The ego, the exposed part of the personality, under the continued influence of the conflict between libidinal needs and threatening outer world, acquires a certain rigidity, a chronic, automatically functioning mode of reaction, that which is called "character." It is as if the affective personality put on an armor, a rigid shell on which the knocks from the outer world as well as the inner demands rebound. (Reich, 1945, p. 310.)

Character is traceable to the infantile sex conflict, and different types of character reflect different ways of handling this conflict. The more rigid—the less mobile—the character armor, the more libidinal energy is bound and the lower is orgastic potency. The first step in character analysis, Reich maintains, is the breaking down of the rigidity of the character armor.

Another central concept in Reich's theory is that of rigidity (hypertension) of the musculature, which he describes as muscular armoring. The basic function of the muscular armor is to prevent the orgasm reflex from taking place; the individual holds back, instead of relaxing, and this results in the incapacity for plasmatic pulsation in the sexual act. Reich states that, since the excitations of the orgasm are produced along the body axis, the muscular blocks to the excitations work at right angles to the spine. He proposes that the muscular blocks are arranged in rings: (1) ocular (eyes and forehead), (2) oral (chin and throat), (3) neck muscles, (4) chest muscles, (5) diaphragm and the organs under it, (6) middle of the diaphragm, and (7) the pelvic region. Rigidity in any of these rings must be dissolved before the orgasm reflex can occur. Chronic muscular rigidity is said to represent an inhibition of every kind of excitation, of pleasure, anxiety, and hatred. "It is as if the inhibition of the vital functions (sexual, anxiety, destructive) took place by way of the formation of a muscular armor around the center of the biological person" (p. 315).

Reich notes that muscular rigidity may be found along with character rigidity or that one can take the place of the other; that is, energy may be bound in the form of muscular and/or character armor. The typical compulsive character is said to manifest a general muscular rigidity, while other patients (e.g., passive-feminine characters) combine physical rigidity in certain regions with flaccidity (hypotonus) in other regions. The complete muscular rigidity in the catatonic paranoid's stupor is said to correspond to complete character armoring. Postencephalitics manifest both strong muscular and character rigidity. Reich concludes that muscular and character armoring are functionally identical (p. 321), representing only different forms in which energy becomes bound.

Reich maintains that the armor (muscular or character) of the neurotic or psychotic is chronic and automatic, while the genital character (one who has a more orderly libidinal economy) has his armor at his disposal and can put it on or take it off at will. Reich asserts that the goal of mental hygiene is not to prevent the ability to form an armor, but to aim at the formation of an armor which is flexible, mobile. He holds that an essential part of analysis is reduction in the rigidity of the character and muscular armoring since this is a necessary prelude to remobilization of libidinal energy.

Carl Jung

Jung retains many Freudian concepts but arranges them within a different interpretative framework. The concept of the libido is broadened so that it is synonymous with undifferentiated psychic energy, of which the sexual is only one component; there is also an asexual, rather spiritual, component. Libidinal development is through three phases. The first, called presexual, goes up to about the third (or fourth or fifth) year of life, and its goals are growth and nutrition. The second phase, called prepubertal, extends to puberty. The third phase, the time of maturity, extends from puberty onwards. "Development consists in a continuous widening of the libido's range through critical points of struggle by the old against the new" (Kallen, 1934, p. 586). The forward flow of the libido from one stage of development to another is defined as "progression"; stoppage in the flow is "regression." Regression, which is the rigid adherence or fixation of the libido to a stage of development, is characterized by outward rigidity—stereotypy of conduct—as well as by irritability and a feeling that life is meaningless; these symptoms would disappear if the libido could be liberated from its rigidity so that it could flow continuously and flexibly. It is just this freeing of the libido from its rigidity that constitutes an important function of therapy in Jung's analytic psychology.

In general, it is only slowly and with considerable struggle that the libido detaches itself from the characteristics of one phase before going on to those of the next. Even in progressing to the next stage, the libido always carries with it traits of a former phase; this explains, for example, the close association between the nutritional function and the sexual function. For many adults, regressive, rigid forces have won out over the progressive ones, so that much of their libidinal energy is attached to early phases; and, instead of attaining mature development, they are essentially children all their lives. Those who are relatively more neurotic than others are those who have, to a greater degree, unconsciously retained childhood expectations and phantasies that do not fit present reality.

Character types are divided by Jung according to whether the libido turns outward to the world (extroversion) or withdraws inward (introversion). There are four fundamental mental processes: thinking, feeling, sensation, and intuition, the energy associated with each going in an introverted or extroverted direction. For each individual, one of the four processes and one of the two directions predominates in his consciousness. Thus, Jung speaks of the thinking introvert, the feeling extrovert, etc. The predominance is both a matter of inborn dispositions and of reinforcement by experiences which habituate the predominant mode of responding to the world.

Jung places more emphasis than Freud on man's archaic heritage. He postulates an inherited collective unconscious. Identical or similar for all people, it contains residues of mankind's development and traces of his animal ancestry. When these animal traces are reactivated, there is a tendency to regression in libidinal development. The collective unconscious also contains the untold wisdom of the ages and the unlimited potentialities of human imagination.

In addition to the collective unconscious, each individual has a personal unconscious, consisting of what he has forgotten, repressed, or only subliminally perceived, thought, and felt. The unconscious, personal and collective, "contains in concentrated form the entire succession of imprints, from time immemorial, that have determined the contemporary psychic structure" (1920a, p. 211).

The contents of the psychic structure are images. Corresponding to the division into individual and collective unconscious, there are personal images, peculiar to each person, and primordial images (world images, archetypes). The latter are the inherited, instinctive patterns of action and thought that form the collective unconscious. "Archetypes are systems of preparedness that are at the same time images and emotions. They are inherited with the structure of the brain of which they represent the psychic aspect" (1928, p. 118). They are revealed in mythology, folklore, and ritual and may function in dreams, in children's night terrors, in hallucinations and delusions of the insane, and in situations for which we are not prepared. Faced with a situation for which he has no ready conscious response, the individual falls back on archetypes, thinks animistically or in terms of primitive symbols. Thus, man may be rigidly tied to his ancient past.

Through a process of differentiation from the collective unconscious there can develop the unique personality, the true individuality. This requires that the person come to individual consciousness by becoming aware of the archetypes and integrating them with his conscious thoughts and actions. But this is a painful process which most people avoid like the plague. They take the less arduous path and forfeit their chance of achieving individuality by clinging to the trammels of the collective unconscious. Just as the infant is not yet aware of himself as a unique, differentiated personality but is essentially an appendage of the parents, so most adults are tied to their childhood past to the extent that they remain like children, lacking in true self-awareness and living as appendages of a group. They substitute submission to the group (nation, society, organized religion) for their unconscious submission to parental images. Just as the infant's life is predominantly instinctive and unconscious, bound by the rules set by his parents, so many adults live, for the most part, unconsciously and instinctively. They rely on the inherited, fixed patterns of thought and action (archetypes), and are bound by traditions and conventions. Theirs is a life run by automatic habits and rigid customs and rules, rather than by personal, conscious choice. As Jung words it: "The mechanism of convention keeps people *unconscious,* and then, like wild game, they can follow their customary runways without the necessity of conscious choice" (1939, p. 295). To live an independent, creative, mentally healthy life requires further differentiation, more crystallized individuality, than most people achieve.

In immersing himself in the collective psyche, the person develops a mask that hides his essential individuality. This is called the "persona," "a slice of the collective psyche." The persona refers to the role one plays, to the view of the personality presented to the world. It is a compromise between the individual and society based on what one appears to be rather than what one essentially is. The persona may be influenced by childhood impressions and by certain factors in one's education and occupation that set rigid bounds, lead to repression of positive facets of the personality, and divert the person from his search for his individuality.

In a well-adjusted person, the persona is elastic, allowing ready contact with the environment. But the danger lurks that the persona may stiffen, may become an automatic, habitual mode of adjustment, that it may become a tight mask behind which the actual ego shrivels. There may result a lack of correspondence between the attitudes of the true ego and those of the persona which can lead to personality disturbances, even severe neuroses or psychoses. Jacobi (1942) offers an illuminating analogy between healthy and dead skin, on the one hand, and a healthy and rigid persona, on the other. Healthy skin allows the tissues underneath to transpire through its pores, but, when it turns into a hardened, dead epidermis, it may cut off the life of the inner layers. Analogously, a healthy, properly "vascularized" persona serves as a mediator between the inner and outer worlds, whereas a rigid persona, having lost much of its elasticity and permeability, becomes a troublesome impediment and even a fatal barrier to the true individuality, to its development, and to the actualization of its potentialities.

Jung emphasizes that the person must be understood retrospectively and prospectively. "Psyche is transition, hence necessarily to be defined under two aspects. On the one hand the psyche gives a picture of the remnants and traces of the entire past, and, on the other, but expressed in the same picture, the outlines of the future" (1915a, p. 391). To understand any act of behavior or a trait, one must know how it is rooted in the past, what present function it serves, and what it indicates about the patient's striving for the future. Therapy must be concerned not only with the present conflict and its relation to the past but also with the future; there must be some constructive planning of the future to set the patient on a new road to developing his individual line of life.

Alfred Adler

Adler maintains that the principle of compensation holds in both the biological and mental realms. The basic drive in human behavior is taken to be a feeling of inferiority which begets a compensatory striving to overcome it, with the striving proportional to the strength of the inferiority feeling. To understand present behavior, one must look both to the past and to the future; behavior is directed by the individual's life goal or purpose. This life goal, which may not be explicitly known to the individual, will dictate the direction of his behavior and subordinate goals, usually from early childhood onwards. Running through a person's behavior is a rather consistent pattern which may be described as his scheme of orientation or his life style. This constitutes the individual's character and is a constellation of the guiding principles or "fictions" that he employs. Its prototype is usually established by the fifth year of life as the child's unified mode of reacting to the world. One's posture, habits, dreams, apperceptions, thinking, memory, every aspect of one's being, reflects the life goal and style. Thus, we "remember tendentiously," recalling only those experiences which fit our purpose and orientation; likewise, Adler notes, "we do not think objectively but in accordance with the goal and style of life we have formed" (1930, p. 5).

The style of life is conservative, and thereby permits recognition of it as a consistent trend. But, in the mentally healthy person, it is usually also a progressive tendency, a process of growth. The relatively normal person, when he realizes that his scheme is seriously in conflict with reality, is adaptable and modifies his orientation, abandoning what is patently false. But there are certain situations which work against flexibility and adaptability and favor rigid adherence to the guiding fictions. These are conditions in which the individual experiences exaggerated feelings of inferiority and psychological uncertainty, conditions that spell anxiety to him since anxiety is the sensation accompanying a strong, uncompensated inferiority feeling. Under such conditions even a normal person may cling to his guiding fictions despite their conflict with reality. There are some individuals who live quite constantly under such anxiety-inducing conditions; and so rigidly do they adhere to their guiding fictions that these become accentuated and create a rigid, hardened life style or character, an orientation out of tune with reality but nonetheless dogmatically maintained. Such people are referred to by Adler as "nervous" characters, a prime example being the neurotics.

In their chapter on Adler's individual psychology, Murphy and Jensen summarize the distinction between the character of the nervous individual and that of the healthier individual in the following words:

> ...the character of the relatively healthy is as rich in variation as life itself, elastic, adjustable, friendly to society. The nervous character, on the contrary, is always *narrow*, limited, rigid, self-conscious and anxious, schematic...inelastic, unbending, enmeshed by his fictions which blind him to reality. (1932, pp. 218-19.)

What brings about such a rigid mode of existence? The answer may often be found in childhood experiences that made for an exaggerated feeling of inferiority, that led the child to distrust his capability of coping with what appeared to be a hostile world. Contributory factors may be a constitutional defect (organ inferiority) or a "foolish" environment in which the child is neglected or ridiculed. Overpampering may also be a factor since it leaves the child not adequately prepared to cooperate with others and makes him the center of his regard. Adler stresses the importance of preparation and training for life that teaches the child to adapt to the demands of reality and to have a friendly, social outlook. Overpampering is poor training, and so is the requirement of blind, implicit obedience to a parent or other authority, for this does not give the child the opportunity to face and evaluate the demands of the situation; such blind obedience is a stereotyped, instead of an adaptive, reaction. An inferiority by itself, whatever its genesis and nature, does not suffice to produce the potential nervous character. It need only produce heightened compensatory striving. The nuclear conditions for a nervous character are those in which the striving proves unsuccessful, so that the child becomes increasingly discouraged and anxious, and stresses his inferiority and inadequacy in a difficult, unfriendly world. The exaggerated low self-esteem calls for heightened compensation, and so the child adopts a goal of unattainable personal superiority. Since he distrusts himself and others, this goal is a striving for power through dominance rather than through cooperation. In our culture, where the male is the symbol of superior, dominant status, the goal takes the form of the masculine protest, with the individual having as his purpose the attainment of his masculine ideal—an asocial goal of great personal power over others.

To Adler a nonsocial goal is necessarily a false goal since man is inextricably bound to humanity and can compensate for his own inferiority only through interaction with others. The individual's social or community feeling is an index of his will to be healthy. Every deviation from adequate sociality is a deficiency in the will to be healthy and is manifested in some emotional disturbance. When the life goal is actually incompatible with sociality, the striver is outside the bounds of normality. In short, the nuclear conditions for the development of a nervous character—and a rigid life style—are those that militate against the development of sufficient sociality.

All failures—neurotics, psychotics, criminals, drunkards, problem children, suicides, perverts and prostitutes—are failures because they are lacking in fellow-feeling and social interest. They approach the problems of occupation, friendship, and sex without the confidence that they can be solved by cooperation. The meaning they give to life is a private meaning; no one else is benefited by the achievement of their aims and their interest stops short at their own persons. (Adler, 1930, p. 8.)

The three "unavoidable problems of humanity" (Adler, 1938, p. 13) —occupation, friendship, and sex life—are those in which it is most difficult to tolerate inferiorities and in which an individual's character is most clearly revealed. It is in these areas that the nervous character most shirks his social responsibilities.

But why is a nonsocial goal concomitant with a rigid life style? The key to this riddle lies in the false, unattainable nature of the goal and in the individual's distrust of himself and others. He tries to make himself and reality conform to his false purpose and orientation—an impossible demand which is doomed to defeat. Defeat only strengthens the rigid adherence to his scheme of orientation by confirming his low self-esteem and anxiety, by showing him once more what a difficult thing is this business of living. All this makes him even more fearful of giving up his scheme and changing to a new orientation. The more life demonstrates the untenability of his scheme, the more he clings to it as the only stable anchorage in an unstable, difficult world.

The neurotic, considered to differ only in degree from normal individuals, has been described as chained to an artificial scheme which, for him more than most persons, is based on false premises, on sharp inconsistencies between guiding fictions and reality. So rigidly and dogmatically does he cling to this scheme that his will is robbed of its freedom and flexibility. His thinking, which tends to be in stereotypes, schematic categories, and either-or dichotomies, reflects this rigidity as do his extreme character traits. "Individual psychology says that whenever the mind is compressed into a rigid scheme it is neurotic. Every schematization, every stereotyping . . . is a neurotic war weapon" (Murphy and Jensen, 1932, p. 240). The neurotic's extreme inferiority calls for a goal of absolute, godlike power. With his customary dogmatism, he must attain absolute success or nothing at all. He may have a "hesitant attitude" toward life, vacillating in his thinking from one extreme attack on a problem to another, until he ends up by doing nothing. His neurosis helps him to evade social responsibilities in the three important areas of life. Thus, a compulsion to repeat a certain act, such as continual washing of the hands, leaves the neurotic little time for other tasks, and fits his false goal, which in this case may be one of extreme personal cleanliness. Whatever the compulsive act may be, it fits (as does any habit of any individual) the life purpose, so that, while it is rooted in the past, it always points toward the future. A compulsion has also been described as a mimic battle in which the neurotic, who is perpetually battling his conviction of extreme inferiority, seeks to prove himself stronger than himself. This inner battle has been substituted for outward adjustment. The conviction of inferiority and anxiety rob him of the courage to face reality and to adapt. Instead, he adheres tenaciously to his false scheme as a means of avoiding adaptation and change, as a defense against having to develop a new life style.

A major function of therapy, Adler believes, is to soften the rigid life style by strengthening social feeling and giving the individual experience in more satisfactory interpersonal relations, and by gradually substituting a more social goal for his false goal.

Karen Horney

Along with rejecting much of Freudian theory, Karen Horney rejects the repetition compulsion. She does not deny the observational phenomena on which Freud founded the repetition compulsion; rather, she offers an alternative interpretation.

That the past influences present behavior is not denied by Horney, but she differs from Freud with reference to the nature of its influence. Freud, she contends, regards childhood attitudes and experiences as largely predetermined, encapsuled, as not directly participating in the further growth and development of the individual, and as uninfluenced by further experiences. The early experiences remain isolated and unaltered in intensity and specific quality until, propelled by the repetition compulsion, they appear at some later stage. Freud's doctrine is compared with myths in which people remain unchanged for many years while life around them continues. Horney claims that, to Freud, "present manifestations are not only conditioned by the past but contain nothing except the past. They are, in other words, a repetition of the past" (1939, p. 133). In contrast, Horney believes that early attitudes and experiences are contributory factors in one's development and character structure, but that they may be added to and modified by subsequent experiences, particularly subsequent interpersonal relationships. Present manifestations must be understood as resultants of a developmental process, conditioned to a smaller or larger degree by past attitudes and experiences, but not mere repetitions of them.

The totality of childhood experiences starts the development of a certain character structure. The direction of development established in childhood often continues throughout life, but it may change, even drastically, if environmental factors and interpersonal relationships are radically altered.

To the question why childhood attitudes sometimes persist into adulthood, Horney answers that many people do grow out of them so that a repetition compulsion is not the answer. One must instead ask what there is in present reality that sometimes demands the persistence of such attitudes. When Freud said that childhood attitudes were later manifested when not warranted by reality, he overlooked an important aspect of reality—the patient's own character structure. This structure may make it inevitable for the patient to react with these attitudes. For example, hostility toward the analyst or toward the patient's husband is not traceable in one straight line to hostility toward a parent developed when the patient was four years old; but this earlier hostility—itself a product of environmental and interpersonal factors and not of an innate death instinct—may have helped to start a character structure in which hostility was a central factor, and, reinforced by subsequent experiences and itself contributing to these experiences, the character structure may have continued in the same direction. There may even be factors on the environmental side which foster persistence of childhood attitudes. Thus a child who developed extreme submissiveness to a dominating parent may continue to manifest behavior which invites other people to dominate her and may be attracted to domineering people, so that submissive behavior persists. But the hostility shown to the analyst or spouse, or the submissiveness displayed in later life, is not precisely the same as the child's hostility or submissiveness to the parent, and should not be described as the exact repetition or reliving of a past attitude or experience.

To cite other examples: A person who repeatedly worships idols that turn out to have clay feet may have a propensity for hero worship coupled with indiscriminate choice of heroes. An individual who enters into several unsuccessful marriages may have a character structure which makes it difficult to give or receive love and the selected mates may be unwilling or unable to alter this deficiency. A character with a strong masochistic trend may be led to repetition of painful experiences, not because of a repetition compulsion linked to a death instinct, but because of his present character. A person with a so-called obsessional or compulsion neurosis is seeking to measure up to certain standards of perfection, and the particular kind of perfection he emphasizes (e.g., cleanliness, orderliness) depends on cultural, personal, environmental, and interpersonal factors in the past and present, as well as on the kind of anxieties against which he has to protect himself by being perfect. In short, Horney claims that there is always something in the present reality (in the character structure and/or on the environmental side) to account for what may superficially appear to be a compulsive repetition of past experiences, attitudes, or patterns of behavior.

Horney emphasizes that behavior which is considered neurotic in one culture may be considered normal in another culture. What is considered normal not only varies from culture to culture, but within the same culture it varies with time and with the class to which one belongs.

Nonetheless, Horney maintains, there are at least two characteristics discernible in all neuroses: "a certain *rigidity in reaction* and a discrepancy between potentialities and accomplishments" (1937, p. 22, italics ours). By rigidity in reactions, Horney means a lack of that flexibility which enables individuals to react differently to different situations. While the healthier individual reacts differently in different circumstances, a neurotic has rigid modes of facing all situations involving people. Thus, the neurotic, whether or not he is aware of so doing, may invariably evince an attitude of suspicion or of spitefulness or of indecision, etc., or, more generally, may use methods of moving toward, away from, or against the world. According to Horney, rigidity is indicative of a neurosis only when it deviates considerably from the patterns and degrees of rigidity which prevail in the particular culture.

Rigid modes of reacting to the world are referred to as neurotic trends. A necessary (but not a sufficient) condition for the development of neurotic trends is "basic anxiety" during childhood—a feeling of weakness and helplessness in a world perceived as potentially hostile and dangerous. The basic anxiety, which stems from unfavorable interpersonal relationships, necessitates that the child search for ways with which to cope with life safely. Barring mitigating circumstances, such as the intervention of a devoted relative or teacher, the ways which he selects tend to become rigidified into neurotic trends and to form the basis of the neurotic character structure. This inflexibility occurs because the individual feels that only by rigidly adopting the modes of defense can he assert himself and avoid potential danger; other methods of adjustment seem to him to be replete with anxiety. While the neurotic trends originally developed as means of avoiding anxiety and as a basis for interpersonal relationships, they actually increase anxiety and impair human relations, for, whenever the neurotic trends are ineffective, anxiety is aroused, and the rigidity of the neurotic trends in turn increases because they are the sole methods the individual has of defending himself against anxiety, and this makes for further anxiety—and so on, in psychological "vicious circles." The individual's neurotic trends may also conflict with one another and make for further anxiety. Moreover, his dealings with people are extremely difficult because throughout all his dealings he must not give up his neurotic trends. And, so, neurotic trends which arose as means of defense, in turn develop a compulsive character which requires that they be defended. Increasing his anxiety and insecurity, the neurotic trends alienate the individual from himself. This, together with his rigidity, impairs his productivity. His real, spontaneous self is choked by the rigid hold which the neurotic trends have on him.

One of the tasks of therapy, Horney believes, is to loosen this rigidity and to help the person to be flexible and to change, the underlying thesis being that "man can change and go on changing as long as he lives" (1945, p. 19).

Erich Fromm

Fromm's central thesis is that certain factors in modern culture make for the development of a personality which feels powerless and isolated. Psychological isolation beyond a certain degree produces anxiety. There have developed certain mechanisms of escape from this isolation and anxiety. Fromm contends that the one most frequently employed is that of "automaton conformity": "a mechanism of escape, of overcoming the feeling of insignificance in comparison with the overwhelming power of the world outside" in which the individual "adopts entirely the kind of personality offered to him by cultural patterns; and he therefore becomes exactly as all others are and as they expect him to be" (1941, p. 186). This conformity rests on the assumption that the person who gives up his individual self to become an automaton identical with the millions of other automata about him, no longer need feel isolated and anxious. Actually, the conformity leads to the renouncing of the individual's autonomous strength, and thus only increases his insecurity, helplessness, and powerlessness.

Because of the loss of autonomous strength, the individual seeks constantly to act according to what he thinks other people expect of him.

> In order to overcome the panic resulting from loss of identity he is compelled to conform, to seek his identity by continuous approval and recognition by others. Since he does not know who he is, at least the others will know—if he acts according to their expectations; if they know he will know too, if he only takes their word for it. (1941, p. 254.)

This results in the elimination of the feelings themselves, that is, in a lack of spontaneity. "Friendliness, cheerfulness, and everything that a smile is supposed to express, become automatic responses which one turns off and on like an electric switch" (1941, p. 242). More generally, the mechanism of automaton conformity leads the individual to adopt rigid conforming patterns of feeling, thinking, and behaving.

There are two main processes by which man relates himself to the world: assimilation, in which things are acquired and assimilated, and socialization, through which the individual relates to himself and to other people. Character structure is the form in which human energy is channelized in the processes of assimilation and socialization. Once energy is organized into a character structure, the person has a certain orientation to life, known as his character, which is extremely resistant to change. That is, the character structure and the concomitant character types tend to become inflexible and rigidified. Fromm notes that at birth the human infant has fewer fixed inherited patterns of action or instincts, and less completeness of structural development, than lower forms of life. The character structure which each individual develops, and which thereafter tends rather rigidly to be maintained, is regarded by Fromm as "the human substitute for the instinctive apparatus of the animal" (Mullahy, 1948, p. 259). It is the character structure that determines the quality of our experiences.

Harry S. Sullivan

Sullivan regards psychiatry as the study of communications between persons. Each person in a two-way relationship is regarded as part of an interpersonal field, participating in processes which affect and are affected by the field. The interviewer or therapist is therefore not simply an onlooking observer but is a *participant observer* who participates in creating the interpersonal field; he must be on the lookout for blocks to effective communication that are introduced by the patient or by himself.

Anxiety is considered to be the main disruptive factor in interpersonal relationships, the chief obstacle to adequate communication, and the principal factor in the development and perpetuation of mental disorders. The experience of anxiety has been variously described as a loss in euphoria (the state of well-being), as a reduction in self-esteem, self-respect, or security. In relatively adult life, anxiety "can often be explained plausibly as anticipated unfavorable appraisal of one's current activity by someone whose opinion is significant" (1953, p. 113).

The infant experiences anxiety, through a process of empathy, when anxiety is present in the mothering one. Gradually, the infant learns to distinguish increasing anxiety from diminishing anxiety (learning through the anxiety gradient). He develops rudimentary personifications of himself into a "good me," a "bad me," and a "not me," all related to the conception of "my body." The "good me" is the organization of experiences in which satisfactions have been enhanced by increased tenderness on the part of the mothering one; the "bad me," the organization of experiences marked by increasing degrees of anxiety; and the "not me" stems from experiences of intense anxiety which are therefore so intolerable that they are "disassociated" from the self, pushed out of conscious awareness. Such a tripartite cleavage in personifications is said to continue throughout life.

At first the infant has no capacity to attain relief from anxiety. Related to learning through the anxiety gradient and to the "good me," there "comes into being in late infancy an organization of experience which will ultimately be of nothing less than stupendous importance in personality, and which comes entirely from the interpersonal relations in which the infant is now involved" (1953, p. 165). This is the start of the anxiety system which is also called the self-system or the self-dynamism. A "dynamism" is defined as a relatively enduring pattern of energy transformation. All the other dynamisms that the individual develops are related to biological needs (e.g., hunger) ; only the self-system lacks a biological basis but stems entirely from experiential factors, from the impact of people.

The self-system has the function of avoiding anxiety or moving in the direction of diminishing anxiety, and thereby maintaining or enhancing the individual's self-esteem and security. The operations that the self-system employs are called security operations. An outstanding characteristic of the self-system is its extreme rigidity. "The self-system, unlike any of the other dynamisms ... is extraordinarily resistant to change by experience" (1953, p. 190). While other dynamisms are readily modified by recurring experiences, the self-system seems to continue unchanged or only slightly changed from year to year. Not only the structure of the self-system but also its operations or functional activity are marked by rigidity. When operations used by the other dynamisms are repeatedly unsuccessful, they are usually abandoned ; but "a person can go through a whole series of consistent failures of what we call security operations ... without learning much of anything" (1953, p. 190) ; that is, he may rigidly adhere to the particular security operations he developed despite their repeated failure to bring him relief from anxiety. Rigid maintenance of the self-system becomes a strong urge which is the source of further anxiety. As Thompson words it : "By the time the self-system is formed there is an emotional stake in maintaining it blindly and this forms a rigidity in the personality and increases potentialities for anxiety" (1950, p. 126).

Part of the explanation for the self-system's little profiting from experience is that intense anxiety is a most unfavorable condition for learning. Sullivan likens it to a severe blow on the head that results in amnesia covering the few minutes before the head was struck. Similarly, intense anxiety contributes no information about the provoking situation. Less severe anxiety does allow realization of the situation in which it occurs. But what happens is that the self-system gradually develops foresight of impending anxiety and becomes extremely agile at deflecting the person away from a situation which provokes or promises to provoke in him even a little anxiety. One of the security operations it uses to accomplish this is called "selective inattention."

Through selective inattention the person does not really "have" certain experiences from which he might have profited since he is not consciously aware of them or overlooks glaring implications. This is because the self-system exerts "continuous vigilance" lest one notice certain things. Any threat of the disassociated material to come into conscious awareness, promptly arouses the self-system, which acts against this threat. The result is that a person almost never grasps the character of situations that provoke anxiety for him. The nature of such situations varies considerably from person to person and is largely a matter of past experiences, traceable to the impact of significant people in one's past and the particular tripartite personifications of the self.

Another security operation used by the self-system is sublimation: "the unwitting (unconscious) substitution, for a behavior pattern which encounters anxiety or collides with the self-system, of a socially more acceptable activity which satisfies part of the motivational system that caused trouble" (1953, p. 193). Once a sublimation is formed, it persists, reoccurring throughout life. Sullivan regards the compulsive repetitions and rituals of obsessional neurotics as sublimations, as substitutive acts by which they attempt continually to ward off anxiety.

Another operation of the self-system is to nurture and maintain a false personification of the self as well as false personifications of others. Sullivan considers stereotypes as false personifications which are invariably related to limitations in one's personification of oneself and in the self-system. "Stereotypes reflect inadequate and inappropriate elements in one's own self-system" (1953, p. 303). To change stereotypes and the corresponding prejudices and intolerances requires changing one's self-concept and encounters the rigidity of the self-system. Stereotypes are "unescapable handicaps in becoming acquainted with strangers . . . chiefly effective in denying one any opportunity for spontaneous favorable change in the corresponding limitation in one's personification of oneself" (1953, p. 304).

False personifications are involved in "parataxic distortions," in which one endows people falsely with characteristics taken from significant persons in one's past or in which one member of an interpersonal relationship reacts not to another member but to a personage existing mainly in his phantasy. Sullivan considers the transference phenomenon during therapy to be a case of parataxic distortion.

The self-system makes for restrictions in freedom of living, restricted contact with others, and restricted interests. It may make for a narrower world and for rigid maintenance of its boundaries. Any interest moving toward areas which the self-system labels as restricted, immediately arouses anxiety which prohibits further movement in pursuit of information.

Sullivan divides development into six phases: infancy, childhood, juvenile, preadolescent, early adolescent, and late adolescent. Not only the earlier phases, but every phase can influence subsequent development. That individuals profit so little from experiences in various phases, and that they often remain so far from maturity, is explicable in terms of the rigidity of the self-system. The rigidity is considered to be somewhat lessened when the person is entering a new developmental phase, so that such a time is a most propitious one for changing the self-system. But the only time the rigidity really is markedly reduced is during sleep when security operations of the self-system are more relaxed than during waking hours. Depth of sleep is viewed as a rather direct function of the extent to which the activity of the self-system has been abandoned.

It is the rigidity of the self-system, its strong resistance to change, which makes it "the principal stumbling block to favorable changes in personality" (1953, p. 169). This is the case for so-called normals as well as for neurotics and psychotics. Sullivan, unlike many psychoanalysts, has undertaken therapy with schizophrenics, whom he considers to differ only in degree from normals and neurotics. Whether a person experiences only minor or very serious difficulties in living, depends on how vulnerable he is to anxiety; this vulnerability is based, to a large extent, on past experiences, on one's training for living, which went into the building and maintaining of the self-system. What happens in the case of serious difficulties is that the self-system, which came into being as a means of helping the person to come to grips with his anxiety, has instead gotten him into the rigid grips of anxiety. The therapist's task is to help loosen the rigid grip. This is a difficult but not an impossible task. It requires extensive and lengthy organization of therapeutic experience to help the patient to see what constitutes anxiety for him, when and how anxiety has intervened in his interpersonal relationships, and that the present way of life is unsatisfactory in the sense that it is not changing things for the better. Sullivan emphasizes that this calls for a flexible approach in therapy rather than for rigid adherence to particular therapeutic procedures.

We have seen that exponents of different psychoanalytic schools of thought offer diverse explanations for manifestations of rigidity. Critical evaluation of these explanations would require evaluation of the core of the corresponding psychoanalytic theory which is beyond the scope of this book. We shall return to psychoanalytic concepts pertinent to rigidity in subsequent chapters that discuss experimental work.

CHAPTER II

THREE THEORIES OF RIGIDITY

THREE THEORIES dominate contemporary discussions of rigidity: Goldstein's, Lewin's, and Werner's. That these theories are presented in one chapter is quite appropriate since their proponents have been interlocked in controversies, some rather vitriolic, over the nature of rigidity. We shall describe and evaluate each theory, compare and contrast them, and then consider the bases of the controversies.

GOLDSTEIN'S NEUROPATHOLOGICAL APPROACH

Rigidity is characterized by Kurt Goldstein (1943) as adherence to a performance that is inadequate for the present task; that is, an individual manfesting rigidity does not shift from one performance to another as required by the task to be fulfilled. "Rigidity is a phenomenon which we meet again and again in pathology, but which also plays a great role in normal behavior" (Goldstein, 1943, p. 209). Because he regards rigidity as especially pronounced in pathological states, Goldstein considers the findings of pathology to be particularly suited to bring about an understanding of the nature of rigidity.

Relationship Between Rigidity and Isolation

Observations of patients with neurological defects led Goldstein to conclude that such patients characteristically manifest rigidity. What the neurological defect does, according to Goldstein, is to isolate part of the central nervous system by severing its connections from the rest of the system, with rigidity a consequence of this isolation.

Observations of surgical experiments in animals and of pathological processes in men have shown that rigidity appears if a part of the central nervous system which is anatomically and functionally isolated from the rest of the system is exposed to stimulation, or, as I refer to it, if it is "isolated." (Goldstein, 1943, p. 209.)

Furthermore, rigidity occurs if "isolation takes place between the stratification of mental performances" (p. 209) ; that is, if one mental performance functions as an isolated unit, separated from other performances. Isolation is related by Goldstein to two kinds of rigidity : primary and secondary.

Primary Rigidity

Primary rigidity is defined as an inability to change from one set or Einstellung to another. It is observed especially in patients with subcortical lesions and is attributed to a defect in the "Einstellung mechanism." The patient is able to shift from one task to another when the same Einstellung is involved; but he is unable to shift voluntarily to a task which demands a new set or Einstellung. If a new set is demanded, either of two things may happen. The patient may persist abnormally in repeating the present (inadequate) activity and, indeed, may seem incapable of stopping. Or, if the new stimulus is very strong, his activity may be "brusquely interrupted" (Goldstein, 1943, p. 210). The result may be a "catastrophic condition" (shock) in which he is unable to respond to any stimulation. After a while he may gradually acquire a set for the new task, "which he then may perform normally, but indeed with the same rigidity as in any reaction" (1943, p. 211). In short, primary rigidity does not refer to rigidity of any single performance but, rather, to rigidity of an Einstellung once acquired.

Secondary Rigidity

While primary rigidity is considered to be independent of higher mental processes, secondary rigidity is regarded as directly due to a defect in the higher mental processes. This defect, which occurs in cortical damage and cortical malformation, has been characterized as an impairment of "the abstract attitude," an impairment which compels the individual to behave in accordance with "the concrete attitude." It becomes increasingly evident, Goldstein writes, that, for all acquired cortical damage, for schizophrenia, and for the mental changes due to malformation of the brain cortex, such as in feeble-mindedness, "the defect . . . consists first and mainly of an impairment of the abstract attitude" (1943, p. 213).

Abstract and Concrete Attitudes. Goldstein and Scheerer (1941) offer the following characterization of the abstract and concrete attitudes:

> The abstract and the concrete attitudes are not acquired mental sets or habits of an individual, or special isolable aptitudes, such as memory, attention, etc. They are rather capacity levels of the total personality. (P. 1.)

One can assume an abstract or a concrete attitude toward an inner experience or toward the outer world. In assuming either attitude, the individual as a whole gears himself toward a corresponding direction of activity which is called abstract or concrete behavior.

The abstract attitude implies conscious activity in the sense of reasoning, awareness, and a self-account of one's behavior. The individual transcends the immediately given situation and is oriented in his action by "a category, a class, or a general meaning" under which falls the particular object before him (1941, p. 4). The abstract attitude is regarded as the basis for the following conscious and volitional activities: detaching the ego from the outer world or from inner experiences; assuming a mental set willfully and consciously; accounting for acts to oneself; verbalizing the account; shifting reflectively from one aspect of a situation to another; holding in mind simultaneously various aspects; grasping the essential of a given whole; breaking up a given whole into parts; isolating and synthesizing them; abstracting common properties reflectively; forming hierarchic concepts; planning ahead ideationally; assuming an attitude towards the "mere possible"; and thinking or performing symbolically.

The foregoing are *not* characteristic of the concrete attitude. The concrete attitude does not involve conscious activity in the sense of reasoning, awareness, or a self-account of one's doing. While apprehension in concrete behavior may be by sense or percept, it is never brought about by discursive reasoning. Highly "realistic" in nature, the concrete attitude confines one to the immediate apprehension of the given thing, situation, idea, thought, or feeling "in its particular uniqueness" and leads one to respond unreflectively to the "immediate claims" of the object, situation, etc. (p. 3). These claims may constitute bonds between the responding individual and the stimulus from which the claims arise. Because of these "stimulus bonds," the individual cannot readily detach himself from the demands exerted by the experienced uniqueness of the object, so that it is difficult, or impossible, for him to conceive of the object as a representative of a general class or category.

The essential feat of abstract behavior is described as the appearance of the factor of conscious will. Any seeming abstraction which does not involve conscious will is regarded as not abstraction at all. Thus, so-called "involuntary abstraction" is described as essentially a concrete procedure, determined by an unreflective apprehension.

Goldstein and Scheerer recognize that there are various degrees of both concrete and abstract behavior. They maintain, however, that there is a pronounced line of demarcation between the concrete and abstract attitudes which does not represent a gradual ascent from more simple to more complex mental sets.

The greater difficulty connected with the abstract approach is not simply one of greater complexity, measured by the number of separate, subservient functions involved. It demands rather the behavior of the new emergent quality, generically different from the concrete.

From the evolutionary point of view, this behavioral quality would represent a recent achievement. Be this as it may, in any event we are dealing here with a "new" functional level, intimately connected with the intact working of the brain cortex (especially of the frontal lobes). (P. 22.)

Consequences of an Impairment of the Abstract Attitude. In the normal individual, abstract and concrete attitudes are interwoven in a fluid relation. Such an individual is therefore able to shift at will from one attitude to the other in accordance with the demands of the situation. But a patient with a brain disease is regarded as having his capacity for abstract behavior impaired to a greater or lesser degree. He is therefore more or less confined to concrete behavior.

If the individual suffering from an impairment of the abstract attitude is allowed to react in a concrete way, rigidity need not be manifested. He may shift passively from one part of a task to another, but only as long as there is no requirement of voluntary shifting, of which he is incapable because of his defect in abstraction. "The moment he is set for a task which demands active shifting, rigidity occurs" (Goldstein, 1943, p. 214). The rigidity here is called secondary rigidity because it is secondary to the impairment of abstract ability.

Thus, the individual suffering from a defect in abstract ability is able to behave normally in situations which call for a concrete attitude. But a task the performance of which requires an abstract attitude constitutes a catastrophic situation for him because he is helpless to cope with it. One important way by which he may attempt to escape the distress of such a catastrophic situation is to stick rigidly to performances which he can fulfill. Another means of attempting to escape the distress of a catastrophic situation lies in abnormal distractability. The individual reacts to a part of the task with which he is able to cope, but, instead of sticking to that part in a rigid manner, he may, under certain conditions, particularly when he feels (or is told) that he has not fulfilled the task correctly, become attached to another part of the situation, and then to still another part, and so on. This is not spontaneous shifting of attention; rather, the individual is being passively shifted or shunted from one situational part to another. Both rigidity of behavior and extreme distractability are interpreted as consequences of the defect in abstraction.

Secondary rigidity is described as always traceable to a discrepancy between the capacity for abstract behavior of the individual and the demands of the environment. Even normals may manifest secondary rigidity when confronted with a task which is beyond their capacities for abstract behavior. The rigidity of those with cortical defects is distinguishable from the rigidity of normals only by its more frequent occurrence; that is, for those with cortical defects, catastrophic conditions occur more frequently.

Comparison of Primary and Secondary Rigidity

The distinctions between primary and secondary rigidity may be sum-

marized in the following manner: Primary rigidity involves an abnormality of the Einstellung mechanism; secondary rigidity is secondary
to (a consequence of) a primary defect in the higher mental processes.
Primary rigidity affects all performances; secondary rigidity is manifested only when the individual is faced by a "catastrophic situation,"
one in which he is inadequate. A patient with primary rigidity shows
"rigid behavior" but not distractability; either rigidity or distractability
may be a sequel to the impairment of abstract ability. Primary rigidity
is observed especially in those having lesions of the subcortical apparatus; secondary rigidity is observed especially in those suffering from
cortical damage and cortical malformation, but it may also, under certain
conditions, occur in normals.

Comments

Relationship Between Rigidity and Isolation Is Vague. Goldstein
states that rigidity appears when a part of the central nervous system
which is anatomically and functionally separated from the system is
exposed to stimulation; that is, if it is isolated. Rigidity is also said to
occur when "isolation takes place between the stratification of mental
performances" (1943, p. 209). It would therefore seem that isolation is
a prerequisite for the occurrence of primary or secondary rigidity. But,
on the other hand, Goldstein states that isolation of the function of one
part of the nervous system can be caused by two conditions: primary
and secondary rigidity (1943, p. 210). Thus, rigidity is a prerequisite
for the occurrence of isolation while, oddly enough, isolation is a prerequisite for the occurrence of rigidity. Here we seem to be going around
in a circle. Clarification would seem to be in order (beyond that offered
in Goldstein's publications) as to the relationship between isolation and
rigidity and also as to the meaning of the term "isolation."

*Primary and Secondary Rigidity Do Not Include All Cases of Ri-
gidity.* There are normals and patients who manifest rigidity of Einstellung in some situations but not in others; since not all of their performances are affected, their rigidity cannot be described as primary,
as due to a primary defect of the Einstellung mechanism. Indeed, they
often do not show the other criteria of primary rigidity. Yet their behavior does not seem adequately characterized as secondary rigidity
when it is kept in mind that secondary rigidity occurs only when the
individual is presented with tasks with which he cannot cope. Behavioral
rigidity has been observed, both in patients and normals, even in tasks
with which they seem perfectly capable of coping, which are well within
their capabilities for abstraction, and which do not seemingly constitute
catastrophic or shock situations for them.

Inapplicability of the concepts of primary and secondary rigidity is particularly striking when we limit ourselves to the behavior of normal individuals suffering neither from lesions of the subcortical ganglia (associated with primary rigidity) nor from cortical damage or malformations (associated with secondary rigidity). The occasional behavioral rigidity which they manifest cannot be designated as primary rigidity, which is essentially a pathological type of rigidity affecting all performances. As a matter of fact, Goldstein does not refer to normal individuals when discussing primary rigidity, but he does mention that normal individuals may exhibit secondary rigidity in performances beyond their capacities for abstract behavior. However, behavioral rigidity has been shown by normals even in performances well within their capacities for abstraction. Nor can their behavioral rigidity be characterized as it is by Goldstein in the case of secondary rigidity, as due to a primary defect in the higher mental processes, a defect which he believes to be "an impairment of the abstract attitude," since they are capable of manifesting the abstract attitude in some situations.

In short, there is behavioral rigidity exhibited by both patients and normals which conforms to the definition of rigidity offered by Goldstein but which does not meet the criteria of either primary or secondary rigidity. These two concepts of rigidity would therefore seem inadequate to cover all cases of behavioral rigidity.

Relationship Between Rigidity and the Concrete Attitude Needs Clarification. Goldstein's thesis that secondary rigidity is a consequence of an impairment of the abstract attitude has been widely accepted by other psychologists and even broadened and generalized. In present-day literature the terms "rigid" and "flexible" are frequently employed as if they were synonymous with "concrete" and "abstract" respectively. "Rigidity," "the concrete attitude," and "concrete-mindedness" are terms which are often used interchangeably or as if one were necessarily a concomitant (or a prerequisite) of the other. What seems to be overlooked is that normal individuals who are apparently quite capable of assuming the abstract attitude nonetheless show rigid behavior in certain situations. A later chapter reports on our experimental attempts to study the relationship between rigidity and concreteness of thinking.

WERNER'S COMPARATIVE-DEVELOPMENTAL APPROACH

The construct of rigidity plays a central role in Heinz Werner's theory of mental development (1940). A principal tenet of this theory is that increasing development is marked by increasing differentiation of parts, progressive hierarchization of parts, and increasing differentiation between the organism and the outer world. This holds for both ontogenetic development, referring to the development of an individual, and phylogenetic development, referring to the development of a race, type, or species. A second tenet refers to rigidity, which Werner defines as a lack of variability in response or as a lack of adaptability in behavior. "Rigidity," he states, "decreases with ontogenetic as well as phylogenetic development" (1946b, p. 43). This implies that more rigid behavior should be exhibited by the young child than by the more mature individual, by the so-called primitive man than by the so-called civilized man who is regarded as higher on the developmental scale, and by lower species than by those higher on the evolutionary scale.

Abnormality due to underdevelopment or injury or disease of the brain is also associated with rigidity. "Evidence is accumulating which indicates that rigidity is a behavioral trait particularly characteristic of the subnormal mind . . . [It is] also conspicuously present in abnormal behavior" (1946a, p. 15). In short, rigidity as a behavioral trait is regarded by Werner as caused by various organismic conditions, outstanding among which are immaturity (including subnormality) and abnormality.

"Primitive" Behavior More Rigid than "Higher" Behavior

The less developed organism, according to Werner, is capable only of "primitive" activity or "primitive" behavior, whereas the more developed organism is capable not only of primitive activity but also of a "higher" activity. In particular, "primitive conceptual activity" (that engaged in by certain animals, young children, and individuals of primitive societies) is characterized as "primitive abstraction" or by its synonyms, "concrete abstraction" or "concrete thinking." Contrasted with this level of conceptual activity is the more advanced level on which the civilized normal adult is considered capable of operating, a level characterized as "true abstract thinking."

Werner asserts that higher activity is marked by a plasticity of outer form and inner content, the term "plasticity" being synonymous with "flexibility" and the conceptual opposite of "rigidity." Plasticity of inner content is subdivided by Werner into plasticity of acting subject (plasticity of motive) and plasticity of the object acted upon (plasticity of goal). "Primitive behavior is comparatively lacking in plasticity so far as *outer form* is concerned. . . . Both plasticity of motive and of goal are comparatively limited in primitive behavior" (1940, p. 210). Primitive behavior is therefore relatively more rigid than higher behavior.

In the last analysis, lack of plasticity of motive and goal are considered to be grounded in a comparative lack of polarity, a comparative lack of differentiation between the organism and the outer world. Thus, the greater rigidity of primitive behavior is related to the thesis that the

THREE THEORIES OF RIGIDITY   37

less developed organism does not differentiate as sharply between himself and the world as does the more developed organism.

Primitive behavior is also regarded as characterized by comparative instability since "stability of behavior requires a flexibility of response in order to preserve the functional equilibrium of the organism in the face of mutable situations" (1940, p. 55).

In summary: The more developed the organism (the more hierarchically integrated, the more differentiated the mental structure, the greater the differentiation between the organism and the world), then the less rigid (the more flexible or plastic) its behavior and, at the same time, the more stable its behavior.

Comments

Is Rigidity the Inverse of Variability? Werner defines "rigidity" as a lack of variability of response or as a "sluggishness in the variation of a response" (1946b, p. 43).

> In general, the more differentiated and hierarchically organized the mental structure of an organism, the more flexible (or plastic) its behavior. . . . if an activity is highly hierarchized, the organism, within a considerable range, can vary the activity to comply with the demands of the varying situation. (1940, p. 55.)

In short, the more variable the behavior, the lower is rigidity of behavior. We raise the problem whether variability is actually the inverse of rigidity, whether the individual who gives the more varied responses is necessarily less rigid in his behavior. A subsequent chapter reports on experimental evidence that is pertinent to this problem.

Does Rigidity Imply Lack of Adaptability? Consider also the definition of "rigidity" as a lack of adaptability (1946a, p. 15). There are times when men refuse to adapt to a situation but instead attempt to change the situation itself. Are they then manifesting rigid behavior? It should be noted in connection with this definition that Werner speaks of "the admirable adjustment of the aborigine [primitive man] to his surroundings" while noting that the "friction between individual and environment . . . is the very life and essence of higher, advanced cultures" (1940, p. 19). If rigidity is considered to be lack of adaptability, then it follows that the primitive man, with his "admirable adjustment," is less rigid than members of higher, advanced cultures. Yet the very opposite relationship is postulated by Werner; that is, primitive behavior is characterized as more rigid than the higher activity of which civilized man is assumed to be capable. Some clarification would seem to be required with reference to the relationship between rigidity and adaptability.

Is Rigidity a Negative Function of Development? It is Werner's thesis (1940, 1946b) that rigidity is a negative function of development, the less developed organism manifesting the most rigidity. Unfortunately, little experimental evidence is presented in support of this thesis.

Werner (1940, p. 239) cites a study by Usnadze showing that children of three and four years of age tended to group objects on the basis of one selected category (color or form) but not to shift from one category to another. Since older children (five-seven years) showed more shifting from one category to another, it was concluded by Werner that "young normal children display little capacity to shift; as they grow older this capacity increases" (1946b, p. 47). This is the extent of the cited experimental evidence. It can hardly be regarded as adequately supporting the contention that rigidity decreases with age.

To attest to the rigidity of primitives, Werner (1940, p. 142) refers to some examples of their "conservative persistence" in maintaining accustomed methods and folkways even when they recognize that civilized man's methods would be better. But each example cited from primitive societies could probably be matched by an illustration from our own society where a folkway, mode of behavior, institution, etc., persists in spite of having outlived its usefulness; "conservative persistence" and "cultural lag" are not limited to primitive societies.

To attest to the greater rigidity of the child, as compared to the adult, Werner cites some incidents regarded as indicating rigid behavior in the child and refers to the "well-known conservatism" of the child (1940, p. 130). But, when one realizes how readily children usually can shift their roles when at play, how readily they can shift from fantasy to reality; when one bears in mind, for whatever they are worth, the adages that the older person is more set in his ways, more conservative, less able to change or shift, less adaptable, that one cannot teach an old dog new tricks, then one begins to wonder whether there has not been some neglect of negative instances. "Proof" by examples leads neither here nor there. It should be possible to determine experimentally whether or not rigidity decreases with age even if it is not so simple a matter to test the more general contention that rigidity decreases with ontogenetic as well as phylogenetic development. A later chapter deals with experimental data bearing on the relationship of age to rigidity.

Is Alleged Egocentrism of the Child Supported by the Evidence? While there is little experimental evidence bearing on the supposed relationship between rigidity and development, there is considerable speculation concerning the theoretical relation between the two. The high rigidity of the less well-developed organism (e.g., the child or the primitive man) is attributed to his being less differentiated from the outer world. In particular, the young child is regarded as having his self, his ego, less differentiated from the outer world and, hence, as being more egocentric in his thinking and behavior. Werner characterizes egocentrism as "a low degree of differentiation between the individual and society" (1940, p. 440). Let us therefore evaluate some of the grounds on which there is deduced the alleged egocentrism of the young child.

Egocentrism Is Not Revealed by All Studies of Children's Speech. In discussing the nature of the child's language, Werner refers, among other studies, to a study by Piaget (1930). Piaget analyzed about 1,500 remarks recorded for each of two children, each about six and a half years of age, while they were at play in La Maison des Petites in Geneva. He classified the remarks into various categories, chief among them being egocentric speech, by which he meant speech which disregards the audience, and socialized speech, by which he meant speech in which the child addresses his hearer, considers his point of view, tries to influence him, or exchanges ideas with him. Piaget concluded that about 40 per cent of the young child's language falls into the egocentric category and implied that this egocentrism is a symptom of psychological immaturity which is outgrown with age, so that adult speech tends to be highly socialized.

Other investigations have not always corroborated this conclusion. McCarthy (1930) analyzed fifty consecutive reports of the speech of each of 140 children ranging in age from one and a half to four and a half years. The egocentric category averaged only 3.6 per cent for all age levels and did not exceed 6.5 per cent for any one age level. Johnson and Josey (1931), analyzing the language of fifty-five children, stated that their findings refuted many of Piaget's claims since they found their children to be socially minded "and in no manner dominated by an egocentric attitude." Huang and Chu (1936) analyzed a total of 1,500 sentences from twenty-one nursery-school children and found only 20 per cent egocentric while 80 per cent were socialized.

Other investigators have found varying percentages for remarks which they characterized as egocentric; a few are as high as the percentage reported by Piaget but the majority are considerably lower. McCarthy (1946) attempted to account for these discrepancies by pointing to the fact that the various investigations differed considerably with regard to definitions of the egocentric category, situations in which the responses were recorded, and individual differences among the observed children. In particular, she noted that investigators who looked for egocentric remarks tended to find them. Investigators, she said, often characterized as egocentric any remarks about the self, overlooking the possibility that such remarks may be regarded as socialized in so far as they are directed toward a hearer who is expected to understand and reply.

Not only is there little agreement as to whether or not children's speech is egocentric, but it is not even agreed that speech becomes increasingly socialized with age. It was implied by Piaget and others, but never demonstrated, that adult speech contains a high degree of socialization and a relatively low degree of egocentrism. As a matter of fact, when Henle and Hubble in 1938 classified remarks of college students and other adults, they found that 40.7 per cent of all the remarks fell into an "ego-related" category. Compare this with Piaget's conclusion that 40 per cent of the young child's language falls into the egocentric category. There would seem to be little conclusive evidence that egocentricity is an outstanding characteristic of childhood speech and that it is outgrown with increasing age.

Egocentrism Is Not Revealed by All Studies of Children's Causal Thinking. The young child's reasoning with reference to causality has been interpreted by Werner (and others) as testifying to the child's egocentric nature and to the lack of differentiation between the child and the external situation. Werner characterizes the child's causal reasoning as subjective, egomorphic, and anthropomorphic, with the outer world and inner experience constituting such an undivided unity "that the events of the surrounding world appear to be intimately linked with the ego and its needs" (1940, p. 319). He distinguishes, as does Piaget (1930), three successive fundamental stages of causal thinking. In the first, identified with very young children, physical events receive egomorphic, anthropomorphic explanations; in the second, explanations tend to be "based on the dynamistic principle that things behave as they do because of some force inherent in them"; the third stage is marked by realistic attitude toward the world (Werner, 1940, p. 320).

Division of causal reasoning into stages supposedly representing definite age levels (Piaget) or a general developmental trend (Werner) is open to criticism on the ground that the various stages may not be inherently characteristic of age levels or of a developmental trend; rather, the types of causal reasoning supposedly characteristic of the various stages may in reality be artifacts of the particular culture, the kind of education and training received by children, and the manner in which the investigator interprets the children's explanations. It has been said of Piaget's (1930) classification of types of causal thinking (e.g., magical causality, moral causality, animistic causality) that "the child's world is being interpreted in terms of the adult conception, and philosophical and logical implications are being read into the child's thoughts which may not be there at all" (Deutsche, 1943, p. 143).

On the basis of an extensive investigation of children's causal thinking, involving over 700 children who contributed approximately 12,000
answers, Deutsche concluded that all evidence in her study "points
against the validity of classifying causal reasoning into stages" (1943,
p. 143). While aware of deficiencies in Piaget's classification of types
of causal thinking (1930), Deutsche nonetheless applied it to her data.
The outstanding finding was that most types were obtained over the
entire age range (from eight to sixteen) and that no one type characterized children of a given age. Responses which Piaget would characterize as "pre-logical" and as belonging to the egocentric, anthropomorphic stage identified only with the very young child, were actually
found at the highest age levels; so-called logical, abstract answers, proceeding in terms of necessary causes, and supposedly yielded by only
the older child, were frequently found at the youngest age level. This
led Deutsche to conclude that causal reasoning does not develop in
definite stages with certain types of thought characteristic of children of
one age and not of another.

It is implied by Piaget and Werner that the child's answers to questions of causality reflect the stage of development which his thinking
has reached. Such an implication is not supported by Deutsche's findings. If the child has reached a certain stage in the development of causal
thinking, then it might be expected that his answers to the different
questions contained in the test would tend to be at about the same level;
yet correlations between the odd and even items in the test administered
by Deutsche, as well as correlations between two forms of the test
taken by the same subjects, revealed low coefficients. Moreover, it was
found that the content of the particular question appeared to influence
the type of response given to it, irrespective of the particular child or
particular age level.

In short, Deutsche's intensive study suggests that a particular type
or level of causal thinking is not typical of a given child and that there
are not successive stages of causal thinking associated with given ages
or with a developmental trend. Her findings further refute Werner's
contentions that "the contrast between the fortuitous and the necessary
[is] an idea which is foreign to a child's reasoning" (1940, p. 329),
and that the child "sees and thinks in terms of individual, concrete, and
non-divisive relationships where the adult would analyze the concrete
event by means of applying abstract, causal reasoning" (p. 324).

The Ego and Egocentrism May Be Functions of Conditions. What we
find when we examine the evidence bearing on the language and causal
thinking of children thus seems to constitute far from clear-cut support
for the thesis that the child is more egocentric than the adult, that he
has more difficulty in differentiating his ego from the outer world. Per-

haps the controversial nature of the evidence may in some measure be attributed to the possibility that it is not always the child who experiences difficulty in differentiating his ego from the external world; conceivably in some cases it is the investigator who cannot, on the basis of the child's response, distinguish what is supposed to constitute the child's ego or his ego's influence from the so-called external world.

There is involved the even broader issue of the genesis, development, and functioning of the ego. Underlying the thesis that the child is more egocentric than the adult, there seems to be the implicit assumption that the child's ego is a well-formed definite "thing" which persists in getting deeply entangled with external conditions. But this may not be the case. The "ego" may first be emerging, developing, and changing, with its genesis, nature, and functioning dependent on field conditions. It is known from experiments on perception (Wertheimer, 1937) that there are situations in which, even for an adult, the ego may serve as the center of the perceptual coordinate system and others in which perception tends to be determined more by external forces than by the ego. Perhaps the issue whether or not the child is more egocentric than the adult, whether or not the extent of egocentrism is a function of development, ought to be replaced by the problem of determining the conditions under which a given organism behaves as if the ego is at the center of his coordinate system and the conditions under which this is not the case. Intensive study of the individual case, including systematic variations of experimental conditions, may reveal that certain conditions are more conducive to ego-centered behavior than others. It may be that conditions which serve to induce ego-centered behavior in young children will not tend so readily to induce it in older individuals, or perhaps vice versa. But, until such experiments are actually conducted, it seems rather fruitless, particularly in view of the controversial evidence, to haggle over whether the child is *in vacuo* more egocentric than the adult.

Rigidity May Be a Function of Conditions. Egocentric behavior is related by Werner to the relative lack of differentiation between the organism and the outer world. He regards this degree of differentation as solely a function of the degree of phylogenetic and ontogenetic development. In line with the preceding paragraphs, we suggest that the degree of differentiation may not be dependent solely on the organism's development but on the conditions in which the organism finds itself. Thus, under certain conditions a child or a primitive man may evince a greater degree of differentiation between himself and the outer world than would the "civilized" adult.

If rigidity is actually grounded in the lack of differentiation between the organism and the world, and if the degree of differentiation is not solely a function of development but is rather a function of field conditions, then it follows that rigidity is itself a function of field conditions and that it cannot be regarded as simply a decreasing function of phylogenetic and ontogenetic development.

Lewin's Topological Approach to Rigidity

The Construct of Topological Rigidity

Rigidity, as used by Kurt Lewin (1935, 1936), is one of a series of interrelated constructs postulated in his "topological psychology." The person is regarded as structured and differentiated into various psychical regions and systems. Rigidity is a material property; that is, a factor determining the state of the region which is conceived of as a property of the region itself (1936, p. 218).

> The person, dynamically, is a totality of systems. First, one can distinguish the structure of the totality, that is, the *degree* of differentiation of the systems and the *kind* of differentiation of systems in this totality. The one-year-old child, for example, is dynamically not so differentiated into separate systems as a thirty-year-old man. ... Second, with the same structure the dynamic *material* of the systems may be different. The systems can be more or less rigid, more or less fluid, and so forth. ... The elasticity or the rigidity of the systems seems to be a very basic and important characteristic of the whole person. (1935, p. 187.)
>
> Diversities in structure (in degree of differentiation and in type of structure) do not exhaust the possible differences within the personality. Thus with identical structures, the *ease* with which they *change* may differ decidedly. Further, the shifting may occur suddenly or gradually. In this connection one may speak of a varying dynamic softness, elasticity, hardness, brittleness, or fluidity of the psychical material. (1935, p. 207.)

Rigidity has also been defined in reference to the boundaries of psychical systems. Thus, in the glossary of his text on topological psychology (1936), Lewin writes, "Rigidity: Boundaries (barriers, walls) are the more rigid the greater the forces necessary to overcome them" (p. 218). Referring to Lewin's construct of rigidity, Kounin defines it as "that property of a functional boundary which prevents communication between neighboring regions" (1941a, p. 254). But Lewin apparently does not regard rigidity as necessarily preventing communications since he writes: "Relative immobility [rigidity] of systems does not necessarily mean that these systems are not in communication with one another" (1935, p. 232).

Topological Rigidity and Behavioral Rigidity

As synonyms for the construct of rigidity of the psychical regions making up the person's structure, Lewin utilizes numerous expressions: "psychical rigidity," "dynamic rigidity," "structural rigidity," "functional rigidity," "material rigidity," "primary rigidity," "immobility of the topological system," or even the unmodified term "rigidity." We shall usually employ the phrase "topological rigidity."

While Lewin deals with "behavioral rigidity," he does not precisely define it or the numerous terms which he uses as synonyms for it: "phenomenological rigidity," "secondary immobility," "external rigidity," "external immobility." In his paper on feeble-mindedness (1935), he implies that behavioral rigidity includes stereotypy and pedantry, inflexibility in clinging to a fixed goal, rigidity of will and needs, and intellectual immobility (referring to difficulties in the restructuring of the field necessary for intellectual insights). In one instance (1935, p. 235), he refers to an increase in external mobility as corresponding to an increase in the wealth of possible varieties of behavior, thus apparently interpreting variability of behavior as an inverse index of behavioral rigidity.

Lewin and his students do not regard topological rigidity as equivalent to behavioral rigidity. Kounin states that "rigidity of overt behavior cannot be directly coordinated with rigidity of the boundaries of the regions making up a person's structure" (1941a, p. 252). Kounin, who at times uses the unmodified term "rigidity" to refer to topological rigidity, emphasizes that he is not defining (topological) rigidity as a behavioral trait, that he is not using it as a descriptive, phenotypical concept referring to behavior described as stereotypy, perseveration, fixity, pedantry, lack of variability, and so on; rather, he says, he uses the concept of (topological) rigidity as a genotypical construct referring to a property of personality structure.

Topological Rigidity May Have Consequences Other than Behavioral Rigidity. Topological rigidity is regarded by Lewin as influencing both the psychical person and the psychical environment. He states:

> In surveying the consequences of a person's dynamic material properties for experience and behavior, one must remember that these properties are characteristic not only of the internal psychical systems but equally of the psychical environment and of its changes, in so far as the latter are psychologically conditioned. ... Thus not only the content and momentary state of needs and interests, but all dynamic properties of the person, the rigidity and unchangeability of his systems, make themselves felt in the structure and changes of the psychical environment. (1935, p. 215.)

Topological rigidity is considered to have an effect on the formation of wholes or Gestalten, greater rigidity hindering the formation of weak Gestalten but favoring strong Gestalten, unities whose subordinate parts are closely bound together and which as wholes are relatively separated. Greater topological rigidity is also regarded as hindering the development and reorganization of Gestalten.

In so far as the "psychology of the will" is concerned, high topological rigidity is considered to make for difficulty of transformation or restructurization (*Umstrukturieng*) which "signifies a *deliverance* of the person to the mercies of the momentary situation" (Lewin, 1935, p. 216). This may have externally different effects according to the particular circumstances. The effects may appear as helplessness and incapacity to find a way out of a situation. Under certain circumstances, the small changeability and relatively strong segregation of the situation, which are concomitants of high topological rigidity, may result in considerable energy and persistence in the pursuit of a definite goal.

Lewin's writings suggest that topological rigidity may have various effects, some of which may be classed as rigidity of overt behavior, but some of which have no apparent relation to behavioral rigidity.

Behavioral Rigidity May Result from Factors Other than Topological Rigidity. While high topological rigidity is recognized by Lewin as working, under certain conditions, for behavioral rigidity, he does not consider it the sole cause of immobility in behavior. "Certainly the cause of behavioral rigidity may vary" (Lewin, 1935, p. 236). Recognized as a possible causal factor is the degree of differentiation of the person. A higher degree of differentiation is said to make possible a greater variety and richness in modes of behavior and to facilitate restructuring of the field required for intellectual insights, while a smaller degree of differentiation, other things being equal, tends to be associated with lower external mobility (greater behavioral rigidity). Lewin concludes from Dembo's work on anger (1931) that an increase in the state of tension may, under certain conditions, lead to greater momentary unity and primitiveness of the total behavior and may result in a certain fixation, i.e., behavioral rigidity.

Kounin (1941a, 1943) also notes that factors other than topological rigidity may operate to produce behavioral (phenomenological) rigidity. In addition to the degree of differentiation of the person as a whole, Kounin refers to the degree of differentiation of particular areas or regions of a person's structure. He points out that two persons may have the same total degree of differentiation, and yet one of them may behave in a more stereotyped manner in a particular situation because the psychical regions relevant to this situation are less differentiated in his case. Kounin also lists security and other motivational factors as possible causal factors of behavioral rigidity, including under this heading such factors in the psychological environment as the fear of failure, uncertainty as to consequences, and hesitancy to enter unfamiliar situations. "If an individual feels insecure, he may exhibit phenomenologically rigid behavior, not because of dynamic [topological] rigidity but because he is afraid of attempting the new and so clings to what he does know" (1941a, p. 253).

Thus, rigidity of overt behavior may be brought about by factors other than topological rigidity. According to Lewin, the problem whether particular behavior is attributable to topological rigidity is one which must be faced anew each time.

Topological Rigidity Tends to Increase with Age. Lewin hypothesizes that topological rigidity is small in the infant and young child but that it tends to increase with age.

> The great material plasticity of the normal small child gives way, generally at least, to greater firmness. That with increasing age this development may lead finally to decided rigidity, lack of mobility, and inelasticity scarcely demands extensive demonstration. (1935, p. 236.)

He assumes a gradual stiffening with age of the psychical system's material properties, a gradual decrease with age in the capacity for dynamic rearrangement. Kounin (1941a) offers an even more precise formulation of the relationship, postulating that topological rigidity is a positive monotonous function of chronological age; that is, it does not decrease with age.

Behavioral Rigidity Tends to Decrease with Age. Neither Lewin nor Kounin assumes that behavioral rigidity increases with age. Indeed, Lewin suggests the very reverse; namely, that behavioral rigidity tends to decrease with age (at least from infancy until the time of maturity). In order to understand this inverse relationship between topological rigidity and behavioral rigidity along the gradient of age, it is necessary to bear in mind the relationship between age and degree of differentiation.

The infant and young child are considered to be less differentiated in their various psychical regions and systems than the adult. "The fact that various life-spheres (profession, family, friendships with definite persons, and so on) as well as different needs are much more differentiated in the adult than in the one-year-old child scarcely demands extensive demonstration" (Lewin, 1935, p. 206). More generally, there is assumed to be an increasing differentiation of the total person, from infancy until maturity, at least in the cases of normal development.

Thus, it is hypothesized that the increase in topological rigidity with age is generally cut across by increasing differentiation. Now, greater topological rigidity may, but need not, lead to greater behavioral rigidity. A larger degree of differentiation tends to be related to smaller behavioral rigidity. Hence, the progressive increase in degree of differentiation from infancy to maturity may be regarded as tending to produce a decrease in behavioral rigidity.

Apparently assuming that the rate of advance of differentiation is in general faster than the rate of advance of topological rigidity, Lewin posits that external mobility should tend to increase with age or, in other words, that behavioral rigidity should tend to decrease with age, at least until senility sets in.

If our conception of a certain equivalence between higher degree of differentiation and external mobility be correct, then under certain conditions, even with the feeble-minded, a greater mobility of actual behavior should make itself noticeable with an increase in age. Even though the actual material properties do not change, or, indeed, though the change with age is in the direction of greater [topological] rigidity, yet a sufficiently faster advance of differentiation should increase the wealth of possible varieties of behavior. (1935, p. 235.)

Lewin makes it clear that the tendency of behavioral rigidity to decrease with age need not always prevail. In a particular individual the heightening of topological rigidity may outstrip the advance of differentiation. In some cases, particularly in the later years of life, there may be, instead of an increase of differentiation, a cessation of development or even a decrease in differentiation, "an impoverishment of structure, a loss of part systems" (1935, p. 237). Pointing to the great individual differences in the development of differentiation, as well as to the individual differences in the tempo and extent of stiffening of the psychical material, Lewin warns that in the concrete instance one must lay most weight upon how the different part systems of the individual behave and interact. Nonetheless, it is hypothesized that the general trend with age is a decrease in behavioral rigidity.

Summary. We have seen that the construct of topological rigidity, as utilized by Kounin and Lewin, is not identical with the construct of behavioral rigidity. That the distinction between the two is by no means a trivial one is seen in the fact that topological rigidity is posited to produce consequences other than behavioral rigidity, that behavioral rigidity is interpreted as capable of being brought about by factors other than topological rigidity, and that topological rigidity and behavioral rigidity are interpreted as varying inversely along the gradient of age. Failure to keep the distinctions in mind has led, as we shall see, to considerable controversy.

Topological Rigidity and Feeble-Mindedness

Lewin's most systematic and notable application of the construct of topological rigidity has been to the problem of feeble-mindedness (1935). He notes that he is considering only the most common type of feeble-mindedness. Most of the experiments he cites used young moron children as subjects.

From "the dynamic point of view," the feeble-minded child "is defined as a person who has a less differentiated structure, like that of a
younger child" (Lewin, 1935, p. 187) ; that is, he has less psychical
regions than the normal child of the same chronological age. But the
feeble-minded is not considered entirely similar in psychical structure
to a younger normal child possessing the same degree of differentiation.
Lewin conceives

the major dynamic difference between a feeble-minded and a normal child of the
same degree of differentiation to consist in a greater stiffness, a smaller capacity
for dynamic rearrangement in the psychical systems of the former . . . [so that]
on the whole the feeble-minded is to be characterized as dynamically more rigid,
less mobile. (1935, p. 210.)

This characterization is based upon experiments on satiation, will,
memory, attention, and intelligence in the feeble-minded. "For the most
common kind of moron, according to our experiments, it seems to be
typical that the psychological systems are comparatively *rigid*, not easily
flexible" (Lewin, 1935, p. 187). The theory that the systems of the
feeble-minded child are not so flexible as in the young normal child is
utilized by Lewin to account, wholly or partially, for the results of various experiments and also for many observations of the behavior and
development of the feeble-minded.

Feeble-Minded Manifest Inflexibility and Pedantry. Pedantry is defined by Lewin as "the tendency to insist upon strict regulations and
to develop inflexible habits to an unnecessary degree and under inappropriate circumstances" (1935, p. 210). Lewin refers to the striking
inflexibility, stereotypy, and pedantry with which feeble-minded children have been observed to cling to a habit. General observations suggest, he says, that pedantry in the feeble-minded goes significantly
beyond the occasional fixation observable in normal children of the
same chronological age or younger. The pedantry of the feeble-minded
is attributed in part to his greater helplessness in the world, his lesser
mastery of the world, his smaller intellectual capacity. Because mishaps
occur to him oftener, because he finds more frequently than the normal
child that he cannot trust the world in which he lives, he inclines to
cling to ways he can trust. But pedantry is often observed even when
the feeble-minded seems to feel neither helpless nor overwhelmed.
" . . . there seems to exist here a very deep and primary rigidity which
manifests itself not only in well-worn habits but also in new volitional
goals" (1935, p. 211). It would seem that this "deep and primary rigidity" is rigidity of psychical structures (that is, topological rigidity) but
the matter is not entirely clear. Lewin does explicitly relate fixation on
goals to topological rigidity. Referring to observations of daily life that

the feeble-minded child is often extremely stubborn and that it is relatively difficult for such a child to change his goal after he has set himself toward it, Lewin concludes that this "well-known stubbornness is a result of the rigidity of his psychological systems" (1935, p. 188).

Topological Rigidity Accounts for Certain Paradoxes in the Behavior of the Feeble-Minded. Lewin refers to the work of Rickers-Ovsiankina (1928) which showed that, if an individual is interrupted while engaged in an activity, there is a tendency to resume the interrupted activity. Studies by Köpke (reported in Lewin, 1935, pp. 185, 204) with retarded children of moron level, revealed that the frequency of resumption was greater for the retarded children than for the normal children. But, when the children were brought to a different situation after the interruption (e.g., if they were moved to another table), the frequency of resumption was much less for the feeble-minded than for the normal children. To account for these results, Lewin appeals to the thesis that topological rigidity is higher in the feeble-minded.

If we accept the theory that the systems [of the feeble-minded] are more rigid, then ... we can explain ... that the feeble-minded resume the interrupted task in 100 per cent of the cases. This abnormal frequency of resumption is a consequence of the fact that a tension system, once it is built up, stays unchanged without being diffusely discharged.... The reason for the nonresumption [when the child is brought to a different situation] is again the rigidity of the psychological systems. The new psychological situation is so rigid that it cannot be changed readily for a connection with the old situation to be brought about. (Lewin, 1935, p. 188.)

When another task intervened between the interrupted task and the opportunity to resume the interrupted task, the frequency of resumption was greater for the feeble-minded than for the normal children. The frequency of resumption was great even when the intervening task was similar to the interrupted task. These findings are interpreted by Lewin to mean that the substitute value of the intervening task was lower for the feeble-minded than for the normal children.

Lewin notes that these experimental results accord with certain observations of daily life which reveal the striking rigidity with which feeble-minded children insist on carrying out a definite action in precisely one way. "Thus the *will* of the feeble-minded often appears stronger, certainly more *rigid* than that of the normal child" (Lewin, 1935, p. 204). In contrast to these observations are others which seem to imply the opposite. Tricks and diversions are likely to be more effective with feeble-minded than with normal children. The feeble-minded is more readily satisfied with an incomplete solution of a task or even with a gesture rather than the real act (for example, he may be satisfied with the gesture of throwing a ball far). Moreover, the experimental findings of Gottschaldt (cited in Lewin, 1935, p. 205) suggest that,

when the original task is too difficult, the feeble-minded are more easily
satisfied with completing a simpler task at a lower level of aspiration
than are normal children.

Experimental results and observations of daily life thus testify with equal im-
pressiveness to an apparent contradiction: on the one hand the feeble-minded show
an especial rigidity and tendency toward fixation which makes the occurrence of
substitute actions, in the functional sense, very difficult; on the other, there is revealed a pronounced tendency toward substitute actions and a tendency to be
readily satisfied with them.... Both extremes are characteristic of one and the
same child. (Lewin, 1935, p. 205.)

In showing how topological rigidity can account for these apparent
contradictions, Lewin speaks of a psychological (tension) system corresponding to the first task and another such system corresponding to
the second task. If the completion of the second task is to have substitute value for the first system, the two systems must be so connected
that the discharge of the first (tension) system also discharges the second. In normal children, the dynamic systems are relatively more capable of rearrangements, so that the completion of the second task changes
the first system. There results a new system in which the first and second systems are now subsystems, divided by a dynamic wall or boundary. If one part is discharged, then, according to the strength of this
boundary, the second system is influenced. "If the systems are particularly rigid in respect to their material properties, such a differentiation
of one total system into two weakly divided parts would less easily
occur" (1935, p. 214). For the feeble-minded child the first system remains unchanged as a result of its rigidity, while a separate system is
established for the second task. Hence, the discharging of the second
system does not discharge the first; that is, the second task has no
substitute value. But, if the second task develops out of the original
system (as happens when the child spontaneously proceeds from the
original activity to the substitute, as in some of the experiments of
Gottschaldt and described observations), then there is only one system
and hence the substitute value tends to be very great. "From this dynamic rigidity of systems and its effect on the formation of differentiated total systems the paradoxes of substitute value may be derived
as necessary consequences" (1935, p. 214).

Topological Rigidity Fosters Strong Gestalten. A system that is differentiated into two or more weakly divided parts is called a weak
Gestalt by Lewin while a unified, undifferentiated system is called a
strong Gestalt. The relatively greater topological rigidity of the feeble-
minded, Lewin maintains, tends to foster strong dynamic Gestalten
and to work against the establishment of weak Gestalten. This state of
affairs makes clear, Lewin believes, not only the paradoxes of substitute

values and other apparent contradictions in the behavior of the feeble-minded but also the "either-or behavior so characteristic of the feeble-minded in a variety of fields" (1935, p. 214). The feeble-minded generally cannot do two things at one time; they tend to be either in one situation or in another rather than in overlapping situations. For example, Lewin found that in experiments on satiation normal children were able to carry on secondary activities without interrupting the main activity, while the feeble-minded more often stopped to rest and to interpose actions which completely interrupted the main activity.

The extreme sensitivity of the feeble-minded to distractions is also accounted for by their relatively high topological rigidity and the resulting tendency to establish strong Gestalten. Even a small change in the situation, resulting from an external influence, tends to constitute a more profound interference since "the changed situation must, in much higher degree, tend to appear completely closed, supplanting entirely the facts of the first situation" (1935, p. 217).

Similarly, the pronounced topological rigidity of the feeble-minded accounts for their reluctance to remain in conflict situations and for the extreme discomfort they experience when forced to remain in such situations. "The characteristic conflict situation before decision is a state of suspension in which situations corresponding to various possible decisions are sufficiently present but must at the same time be kept apart" (1935, p. 217). Maintenance of this state of suspension with its stratified situations is peculiarly difficult for the feeble-minded because of their difficulty in forming weak Gestalten and their tendency toward dynamically closed systems. The same difficulty in maintaining stratified situations makes it hard for the feeble-minded to play, make believe, or dissimulate.

Topological Rigidity Fosters Intellectual Defects. Not only does the feeble-minded manifest a relative lack of weak Gestalten but, because of his topological rigidity, he may encounter general difficulties in developing and in changing Gestalten. These difficulties are related by Lewin to the intellectual defects of feeble-mindedness. He notes that a sufficiently great rigidity of the psychical systems must hinder the occurrence of intellectual acts; that is, must lead to intellectual immobility.

Because of the slighter mobility [greater rigidity] of his psychical systems and his greater difficulty in developing and changing Gestalten, one is enabled to understand why the feeble-minded requires other conditions than the normal individual in order to achieve a reorganization of the field, an intellectual Aha-experience. (1935, p. 222.)

The slower intellectual development of the feeble-minded, and the smaller degree of differentiation of his psychical systems, are also attributed by Lewin to his pronounced topological rigidity.

...a high functional *rigidity* with respect to changes must *hinder differentiation* of the total system. If, then, the material properties of the feeble-minded are to be characterized as particularly immobile, the direct deduction may be made that his development must, other things being equal, be slower. (1935, p. 226.)

Topological Rigidity Fosters Concreteness of Thinking. Lewin refers to a tendency towards concreteness of thinking evinced by the feeble-minded and attributes it in part to the lack of dynamic differentiation, commenting that a tendency to concreteness and primitiveness of think-ing appears to be a general feature of the childlike or otherwise un-differentiated person. The concreteness of thinking of the feeble-minded is also considered to be related to specific properties of his psychical system other than the degree of differentiation. To begin with, concrete-ness of thinking is interpreted as implying that certain types of group construction are hindered, particularly those types of grouping which do not directly belong in the "levels of reality" but are sufficiently imag-inal, conceptual, and unreal to be regarded as belonging in the "levels of unreality." Lewin claims, citing as evidence a study by Brown (1933), that in the normal person the levels of unreality tend to be characterized by greater fluidity and less rigidity than do the levels of reality.

If now relatively small mobility [great rigidity] of psychical systems is charac-teristic of feeble-mindedness it is understandable that those psychical levels which in the normal individual are characterized by a particularly high fluidity will suffer particularly in the feeble-minded. Thus the consequence of a relative lack of development of the levels of unreality must be a lowered imaginativeness in total behavior, an increased concreteness of thinking. (Lewin, 1935, p. 224.)

Experimental Studies of Topological Rigidity

From Lewin's general theory of topological rigidity in relation to feeble-mindedness, Kounin (1941a and 1941b) attempted to derive logically various theses to be put to an experimental test. His studies had a twofold purpose: (1) to arrive at a dynamic theory of age and of feeble-mindedness and (2) to determine the predictive value of cer-tain topological and vector constructs.

Kounin, in accordance with Lewin's views, assumed that topological rigidity increases with chronological age or, more precisely, that it is a positive monotonous function of chronological age. In order to control the factor of degree of differentiation of the person, which was also postulated to increase with age, Kounin used subjects with about equal mental age, the assumption being that mental age is coordinated with the degree of differentiation. Since the degree of feeble-mindedness may be taken to be inversely proportional to the intelligence quotient—the ratio of mental age to chronological age—it follows that the degree of feeble-mindedness is directly proportional to chronological age when mental age is kept constant. Hence, he derived the following proposition: Topological rigidity is a positive monotonous function of the degree of feeble-mindedness.

Kounin also accepted two more postulates: the degree of communication between neighboring regions is inversely proportional to the degree of topological rigidity; the rigidity of personal regions parallels the degree of functional segregation of neighboring regions in the psychological environment.

From these postulates he derived the conclusions that the older and/ or more feeble-minded the individual (that is, the greater the topological rigidity), (1) the less effect a change of state in one region will have upon the state of neighboring regions; (2) the less likely he is to be in an overlapping situation; (3) the more difficulty he will have in the performance of a task which requires him to be influenced by more than one region; (4) the more likely he is to structure a new field which is perceptually ambiguous into a relatively large number of separate, independent regions (achieve a less integrated structure); (5) the less easily can he perform a task which requires that he restructure a given field.

These derivations are related to Lewin's contention that high topological rigidity tends to be associated with the formation of strong Gestalten and the corresponding tendency to be in either one situation or the other but not in overlapping situations.

Each of the five derivations was then tested by one experiment. Three groups of subjects of equal Binet mental ages (mean of about 81 months) but of differing chronological ages were used. These groups were characterized as old feeble-minded subjects (mean chronological age of 41.7 years), young feeble-minded subjects (mean chronological age of 14.5 years), and normal children (mean chronological age of 6.8 years).

Satiation-Cosatiation Experiment. Experiment 1, devised to test Derivation 1, was designed to study the influences of satiation in one region on satiation in a neighboring region. After some experience in drawing cats, bugs, turtles, and rabbits, each subject was asked to draw cats until he became "satiated" and would draw no more. He was then asked if he wanted to draw bugs. After becoming satiated with the drawing of bugs, he was asked if he wanted to draw turtles. Finally, after becoming satiated with the drawing of turtles, he was asked if he would draw rabbits.

Assume that satiation constitutes a change of state in a region (corresponding, say, to the cat-drawing activity); then it follows from Derivation 1 that the effects of this satiation on satiation in other regions (corresponding, say, to the drawing of bugs or turtles or rabbits) should be smaller the greater the topological rigidity. In other words, the older and/or more feeble-minded the subject, the less should satiation in one region "cosatiate" a neighboring region. Results were interpreted as substantiating the first derivation since cosatiation effects increased from the old feeble-minded group to the young feeble-minded to the normals.

Transfer-of-Habit Experiment. A transfer-of-habit experiment was devised to test Derivation 2. Each subject was given ninety trials in which he released a marble by depressing a lever. In the next sixty trials the instructions were to raise instead of to depress the lever. (The apparatus was so designed that either depressing or raising the lever would release the marble.) The more errors the subject made in the second series of trials (the more times he depressed the lever), the more he was considered to be influenced by the previous situation and, hence, the more he was considered to be in an overlapping situation. From Derivation 2 it followed that the old feeble-minded subjects would make the least number of errors—be least likely to be in an overlapping situation—and the normal subjects the most errors. This was substantiated by the trend of results.

Classification Experiment. We shall consider only one more experiment, that designed to test Derivation 5. Twenty-five cards were used, consisting of five different colors and five different forms. All subjects were able to classify the cards into five groupings either on the basis of color or form. They were then asked to change the method of classification. They were allowed a maximum of ten trials, coupled with the experimenter's increasingly stronger directions to change the classificatory scheme. If such a change is regarded as requiring restructuring of the field, then it can be predicted from Derivation 5 that the old feeble-minded subjects should least readily change from one to the other method of classification while the normal subjects should change most readily. Substantiating results were obtained. Moreover, the normal subjects required the least force to get them to change the method of classification, force being measured in terms of the number of trials necessary and the strength of the experimenter's directions.

Every one of the five experiments yielded results in line with the derivation to which it corresponded. The findings were therefore interpreted by Kounin as supporting the validity of the theory that topological rigidity is a positive monotonous function of both chronological age and the degree of feeble-mindedness, and as testifying to the predictive value of the construct of topological rigidity.

The Controversy over the Lewin-Kounin Theory

Much of the controversy which has arisen with regard to the Lewin-Kounin theory of rigidity can be traced, we think, to a failure to distinguish clearly between behavioral and topological rigidity. Consider some of the charges which have been made.

Werner's Critique of the Lewin-Kounin Theory. Lewin's theory of feeble-mindedness and Kounin's related reports have been criticized by Werner (1946b). Werner doubts the usefulness of the Lewin-Kounin concept of rigidity, claims that it does not take into account the "functional dynamics underlying behavior," refers to Kounin's experimental results as "illogical" and "contradictory," not only amongst themselves but also with relation to Lewin's results, accuses Kounin of confusing the concepts of rigidity and differentiation, and dubs the hypothesis that (topological) rigidity is a positive monotonous function of age as "too general," "surprising," and "erroneous." In his reply (1948), Kounin says that Werner's critique contains too many emotionally toned labels and authoritative pronouncements of opinions and conclusions without adequate and explicitly stated reasons for them.

That there is considerable confusion concerning the concept of rigidity is recognized by Werner (1946b). He attributes part of the confusion to the fact that some authors (including himself and Goldstein) have defined the concept functionally while others (notably Lewin and Kounin) have defined it structurally. Referring to Lewin's and Kounin's attempts to relate the concept of rigidity to a structural organization of personality, he states that he doubts the usefulness of their "novel definition" and claims that it does not sufficiently take into account the functional dynamics underlying behavior.

In his reply to Werner, Kounin (1948) retorts that he believes he is dealing with a functional concept, claims that he postulated the property of rigidity as a functional property underlying behavior, and says that he finds it hard to see how one can attach the label "structural" to a construct that is defined in terms of the amount of change produced in one region by a change in another. But elsewhere in his reply Kounin states that his construct of rigidity refers to a postulated property of personality structure.

Werner hypothesizes that rigidity decreases with development and, hence, that rigidity decreases with age. He then states that Kounin's hypothesis that rigidity is a positive monotonous function of age is exactly the opposite of his own contention. He further claims that Kounin's hypothesis contradicts the following view of Lewin: "a greater mobility of actual behavior should make itself noticeable with an increase in age" (1935, p. 235).

These apparent contradictions disappear when it is realized that Werner's hypothesis and the cited quotation from Lewin refer to behavioral rigidity while Kounin's hypothesis (which is also accepted by Lewin) refers to topological rigidity. Both Lewin and Kounin agree that behavioral rigidity tends to decrease with development and age, and hence they are here in agreement with Werner; both further agree that topological rigidity tends to increase with development and age, a point on which Werner has expressed no opinion. The contradictions and disagreements to which Werner refers therefore exist only so long as one insists upon erroneously equating the two constructs.

Similarly, Werner refers to findings by Usnadze and others which demonstrate that on various sorting tests young normal children displayed little capacity to shift but that as they grew older this capacity increased. He then states: "If Kounin were familiar with these well-known experiments, he hardly would have made the statement that rigidity increases with age" (1946b, p. 47). In his reply, Kounin (1948) staunchly maintains his position, claiming that Usnadze's finding is in no way contradictory to it. Again, the confusion is resolved when it is realized that Usnadze's finding implies that behavorial rigidity (or, at least, the ability to shift) tends to decrease with age while Kounin's statement refers to topological rigidity.

Confronted with the apparent contradiction between the hypothesis that (topological) rigidity increases with age and his own hypothesis that (behavioral) rigidity decreases with age, Werner seeks to resolve the difficulty by proposing that Kounin probably confused the concept of rigidity with the concept of differentiation. The explanation provides a neat way of accounting for Kounin's "surprising" hypothesis and resolves the contradiction to Werner's satisfaction since both he and Kounin happen to agree that differentiation (which, incidentally, does not mean precisely the same thing to both of them) does tend to increase with age.

> The surprising statement by Kounin, "... rigidity is a positive function of chronological age," is obviously based on the erroneous identification of the two concepts [rigidity and differentiation]. It is not difficult to see why a structural concept of rigidity might invite a mistake of this sort. Rigidity is here defined in terms of segregation of regions; the distinction between "segregation of regions" and "differentiation of regions" is easily obscured. (Werner, 1946b, p. 46.)

In his reply to Werner, Kounin (1948) denies that he confused the two concepts. The answer would again seem to be that Werner identified the concepts of behavioral and topological rigidity, for only in this way could he be led to regard his hypothesis as contradictory to Kounin's. In short, Werner seems to regard the Lewin-Kounin construct of topological rigidity as another definition, a "novel definition," to use his phrase, of the concept of behavioral rigidity, overlooking the fact—repeatedly pointed out, particularly by Kounin—that the construct of topological rigidity cannot be directly coordinated with the concept of behavioral rigidity.

Werner's Critique of Kounin's Experiments. Further evidence that Werner tends to equate the two concepts is found in his criticism of Kounin's experimental findings as contradictory and illogical. He refers to both the marble-releasing experiment (Kounin's Experiment 2) and the study on changing classification methods (Kounin's Experiment 5) as being concerned with the ability to shift. The marble-releasing experiment was designed to test the thesis that, the greater the individual's topological rigidity, the less likely he is to be in an overlapping situation; while the fifth experiment was designed to test the thesis that, the greater his topological rigidity, the less easily can the individual perform a task which requires that he restructure a given field.

Kounin in Experiment 2 found that the old feeble-minded subjects made the smallest number of errors (that is, fewer depressed the lever) when placed in the new situation (requiring the raising of the lever). He concluded that the old feeble-minded subject is least likely to be in an overlapping situation; he is either in the one situation, "pushing the handle down," or in the other situation, "pulling the handle up," but is rarely in both situations simultaneously. In Experiment 5, on changing the method of classification (from form to color or vice versa), it was found that the old feeble-minded subjects were least able to change from one to the other method of classification. Kounin's general conclusion, based on the thesis that the degree of communication between neighboring regions is inversely proportional to the degree of topological rigidity, is that any performance which requires a certain degree of communication between neighboring regions (as in the experiment on changing classifications) is, to the extent that greater communication is required, more difficult for the older and/or more feeble-minded individual; however, if a task is facilitated by a lack of communication between neighboring regions (as in the marble-releasing study), such a task will be more efficiently and accurately performed by an older and/or more feeble-minded individual. Thus, Kounin sees no contradiction between the results of the two experiments, but regards each as substantiating the thesis to which it is related.

Werner, however, sees the two experiments as measures of the ability to shift and finds their results contradictory; that is, the old feeble-minded showed the most ability to shift (more than the young feeble-minded and the normals) in the marble-releasing experiment and the least ability to shift in the classification experiment. He therefore concludes that the results of the classification experiment, but not of both experiments, can attest to a higher degree of rigidity in old feeble-minded persons. The rigidity to which Werner refers is behavioral rigidity and he uses ability to shift as a direct measure of this rigidity. But the rigidity which Kounin's experiments were designed to test is topological rigidity. In his reply to Werner, Kounin warns that "behaviors sometimes called 'rigidity' in the varied meanings of lack of variability, perseveration, stereotypy, external mobility, 'inability to shift', and so on, cannot be used as direct measures of dynamic [topological] rigidity" (1948, p. 163).

Goldstein's Criticisms. Goldstein (1943) also criticizes the Lewin-Kounin theory and states that he is opposed to the conception that rigidity is a positive monotonous function of chronological age. He discusses the symptoms of rigidity, apparently referring to behavioral rigidity, and he notes that the rigidity that feeble-minded children show may sometimes be so dominant that it seems to be the outstanding symptom of feeble-mindedness. He notes also that Lewin and Kounin have promulgated the idea that rigidity is the primary symptom in feeble-mindedness—an opinion with which he differs. Goldstein apparently attributes to Lewin and Kounin the idea that (behavioral) rigidity is the primary symptom in feeble-mindedness, whereas the primary characteristic of feeble-mindedness in the Lewin-Kounin theory is topological rigidity and not behavioral rigidity.

Comments

Confusion Is Fostered by the Use of the Term "Rigidity" Without Qualifications. Criticism of the Lewin-Kounin theory of rigidity advanced by Goldstein and Werner can be traced, in part, it seems to us, to misunderstandings, usually of a semantic nature. To some extent such misunderstandings are attributable to Lewin's and Kounin's frequent utilization of the unmodified term "rigidity" to denote their construct of "topological rigidity." While Kounin is aware that the term "rigidity" has been widely used to refer to behavior and the term "rigid" to describe individuals manifesting rigid behavior, he prefers to reserve the term for his "genotypical construct" of rigidity. Such preference is an open invitation for misunderstanding in view of the prevalent connotation of the unmodified term "rigidity." Indeed, the situation is strongly analogous to what would occur if a writer "preferred" to utilize the unmodified term "age" to denote "mental age" rather than its more common connotation of chronological age.

With the "genotypical nature" of a construct unrevealed in the printer's ink, it is not wholly unexpected that the Lewin-Kounin thesis "rigidity increases with age" should cause some eyebrow raising among psychologists supporting the apparent opposite: "rigidity decreases with age." That the former refers to topological and the latter to behavioral rigidity seems to be easily overlooked.

While the scientific writer is of course free to define his terms as he chooses, Lewin and Kounin might well have foregone some of this freedom, and utilized a term other than "rigidity," or suitably and consistently modified the term, in order to denote their construct. So doing might have decreased the chances of misinterpretation of their views and served to lessen semantic confusion. As it is, even in Lewin's writings the use of the unmodified term "rigidity" often leaves the reader in doubt as to just what construct is involved so that, for example, when Lewin refers to "rigid persons" (1936, p. 162), it is not at all clear whether these are persons who manifest much behavioral rigidity or persons characterized by a high degree of topological rigidity.

Meaning of Topological Rigidity Needs Clarification. While Lewin generally employs the unmodified term "rigidity" to denote topological rigidity, when he does use adjectives, he is more than generous in varying them. For instance, the construct of topological rigidity has a veritable galaxy of aliases: "dynamic rigidity," "functional rigidity," "structural rigidity," "material rigidity," etc. This may have supplied fuel for the flames of controversy since Lewin failed to indicate just what he meant by "dynamic," "functional," "structural," "primary," etc., and why all these adjectives were applicable to the same construct. Kounin (1943) adds to this list with "inner rigidity" and "inner-person rigidity."

Lewin is not entirely consistent in employing terms as apparent synonyms or antonyms for rigidity of psychical structures. There are instances in which he employs the terms "elasticity," "fluidity," "plasticity," and "dynamic softness" as if they were all synonyms, and opposite in meaning to "rigidity," "dynamic immobility," "dynamic firmness," and "dynamic stiffness." For example, he writes: "The elasticity or rigidity of the systems seems to be a very basic and important characteristic of the whole person" (1935, p. 187). In discussing the ease with which structures change, he notes that one may speak here "of a varying dynamic softness, elasticity, hardness, brittleness, or fluidity of the psychical material" (1935, p. 207). He speaks of the great material plasticity of the normal small child gradually giving way to greater firmness so that, with increasing age, there results "decided rigidity, lack of mobility, and inelasticity" (1935, p. 236).

But, in the glossary of his text on topological psychology (1936), he distinguishes somewhat among such terms as "elasticity," "fluidity," and "plasticity," noting, for example, that the "degree of elasticity can differ for regions of the same fluidity" (1936, p. 217). Nor does he make it clear that any of these terms is necessarily the obverse of rigidity which is defined as follows: "Rigidity: Boundaries (barriers, walls) are the more rigid the greater the forces necessary to overcome them. Rigidity of a region can differ for different types of processes" (1936, p. 218).

It is not evident that rigidity of a region is equivalent to (or necessarily measured by) rigidity of its boundaries; yet, in relation to feeble-mindedness, Lewin speaks of rigidity of regions and not of rigidity of boundaries. The glossary of the text on topological psychology notes that a boundary is considered with reference to its influence on communication, with a stronger wall corresponding to a smaller degree of communication. Hence the definition of rigidity given in the glossary, which we cited above, is essentially a definition in terms of degree of communication, and thus is similar to Kounin's definition. Yet Lewin has stated that relative immobility (rigidity) of systems does not necessarily mean that these systems are not in communication with one another (1935, p. 232). In short, there seems to be some ambiguity, even in Lewin's writings, concerning the meaning of his construct of rigidity.

Even the relationship between topological and behavioral rigidity is somewhat ambiguous in Lewin's writings. He offers the thesis that the young normal child is characterized by less topological rigidity than an older normal person or than a feeble-minded child. But theoretical difficulties arise, Lewin notes, because the young child appears in many respects to be more fixated and pedantic than an older child or even an adult. Citing instances of the behavioral rigidity of young children, Lewin concludes:

> Thus even though one wishes to continue holding to the thesis of greater mobility [less topological rigidity] of the child . . . it becomes apparent that behavior quite closely related to the fixation and rigidity of the feeble-minded may occur under circumstances in which an immobile material is not to be thought of. (1935, p. 228.)

As a way out of this theoretical difficulty, Lewin suggests (but not with enthusiasm) that one might attempt to dispense with the assumption of a difference in topological rigidity between a normal and a feeble-minded child. But if, as Lewin says, topological rigidity is not equivalent to behavioral rigidity, and topological rigidity can bring about consequences other than behavioral rigidity, and behavioral rigidity can be brought about by factors other than topological rigidity, then why does the behavioral rigidity of the young normal child constitute a theoretical difficulty for the thesis that the young normal child is characterized by low topological rigidity? Here too some clarification would seem to be in order. If a more clear-cut distinction had been drawn between topological and behavioral rigidity, some of the controversy we have been discussing might have been avoided.

Characterization of the Topological Rigidity of a Person Poses Difficulties. Lewin notes that the degree of rigidity of different regions within the same individual is by no means completely uniform (1935, p. 208). Yet both he and Kounin speak of the rigidity of a person as if it were of a uniform degree for all regions. Moreover, they attempt to compare the topological rigidity of one person (say, a feeble-minded individual) with the topological rigidity of another (say, a normal individual). Consider Kounin's justification:

> The rigidity of the boundaries of different regions of the same person varies. Nevertheless, it is possible to speak of the rigidity of a Person-1, R(P-1), as compared to the rigidity of a Person-2, R(P-2) when: (1) we compare equivalent regions (a) of the individuals, i.e., regions which correspond to activities of the same psychological meaning, and (2) we further assume that the rigidity of the boundary of region A is representative of the rigidity of the boundaries of other regions (B, C. D, ... X) of the person. (1941a, p. 254).

The first requirement refers to comparison of "equivalent regions" corresponding to "activities of the same psychological meaning." Just how is one to determine that an activity has the same psychological meaning for one person as for another? For example, how can it be ascertained that the drawing of cats (or the pressing of a lever or the classification of cards) had the same psychological meaning for the various groups of subjects who participated in Kounin's experiments or for the various members of each group? If similar meanings did not prevail—and there is no guarantee that they did—then the first requirement would not have been satisfied and comparisons of topological rigidity would therefore not have been permissible; but such comparisons were made in spite of the lack of evidence that "equivalent regions" were involved. Similarly, the thesis that topological rigidity increases with age or with the degree of feeble-mindedness implies that there are necessarily "equivalent regions" within the same person at different ages or, more generally, "equivalent regions" for older and younger persons, as well as "equivalent regions" for persons of different degrees of feeble-mindedness. Otherwise, the first requirement for comparisons of their topological rigidity would not be satisfied. But there is nothing in Lewin's theory of the psychical structure which implies that such equivalent regions must prevail.

The second requirement is the acceptance of the assumption that the rigidity of the boundary of one region of the person is representative of the rigidity of the boundaries of other regions of the person. Does this assumption not imply that the rigidity of the boundaries of different regions of the same person is rather uniform? Hence, does it not contradict Lewin's and Kounin's explicit recognition that this need not be the case, that the rigidity of the various boundaries varies and need by no means be uniform? If there is a general lack of uniformity, it is difficult to see on what basis the rigidity of any one region can be selected as typical or representative and can be used to characterize the rigidity of the person.

Indeed, even the degree of rigidity of any one boundary or region may vary. Lewin (1936, p. 217) has noted that the degree of resistance of a boundary can be different for different kinds of locomotion (or communication), for locomotion (or communication) in different directions (e.g., whether from Region A to Region B or the other way around), and at different points of the boundary. In short, one cannot speak of the degree of the rigidity of a boundary as if the boundary were completely homogeneous in the resistance it offers and as if the degree of rigidity were independent of the nature and direction of the communication between regions. Moreover, Lewin notes (1936, p. 218) that the rigidity of a region can differ for different types of processes.

The concept of the topological rigidity of a person implies either that all boundaries (or regions) in the personality structure have a uniform degree of rigidity, independent of the nature and direction of the communication between regions (or independent of the type of process), or that there is a "representative" boundary (or region) whose rigidity is of a uniform degree, independent of communication or type of process, and whose rigidity can be used to characterize the rigidity of the person. Similarly, any comparison of various degrees of topological rigidity rests on the assumption that there are fixed degrees of rigidity to be compared. Thus, the hypothesis that topological rigidity increases with age and with the degree of feeble-mindedness implies either that all boundaries (or all regions) become more rigid with increasing age and feeble-mindedness, or that there is a region, "equivalent" for persons of different ages and different levels of feeble-mindedness, the rigidity of whose boundary is representative of the topological rigidity of the person and is a positive function of age and/or degree of feeble-mindedness. The first possibility (that all boundaries or regions become more rigid) cannot be verified on a scientific basis. The second possibility requires the establishment of a basis for determining the representative "equivalent" boundary or region, if it exists. But there is nothing in the writings of Lewin or Kounin that tells how to determine the existence or nature of such a representative "equivalent" boundary or region.

These difficulties suggest that the construct of topological rigidity should perhaps remain limited to the degree of resistance offered by a boundary in relation to a specified kind of locomotion or communication (or to the degree of rigidity of a region in relation to a particular type of process), and should not be applied to characterize the topological rigidity of the person as a whole or to compare the topological rigidity of various persons. At present, the problem remains: Just what is meant by the topological rigidity of the person as a whole?

One-Way Relationship Between Topological Rigidity and the Environment Is Questioned. Lewin claims that the special properties of one's psychical material, including topological rigidity, "must constitute a very deep individual peculiarity of the person and play a decided role in heredity" (1935, p. 208). Rigidity of psychical regions is thus regarded as a property of the regions that is probably largely inherited and largely predetermined.

There seems to be overlooked the possibility that topological rigidity may be influenced by experiences of one kind or another or by situational factors of one kind or another—or, more generally, by the "field conditions" with which Lewin is concerned in his other writings. Thus, while topological rigidity is said to influence the psychological environment, the reverse relationship is not formulated or explored. Apparently the relationship between rigidity of boundaries and the environment is a one-way affair. Small wonder, then, that Goldstein (1943, p. 225) deplores Lewin's construct of rigidity as therapeutically futile, for, if topological rigidity is a characteristic of the person which cannot be changed by outside influences, just what can therapy hope to accomplish with reference to this rigidity?

Nowhere, it seems to us, does Lewin come more dangerously close to the concept of an "essence" of the person which is independent of field conditions—a concept which he has characterized (1935, p. 15) as belonging to an Aristotelian, pre-Galilean era—than he does in his construct of rigidity as it is formulated in his theory of feeble-mindedness (1935). Later, in the chapter dealing with the concept of rigidity as used in physics, we shall see that the "rigidity," "plasticity," and "elasticity" of such substances as steel and rubber may be altered if suitable forces are applied. With all due awareness of the possible pitfalls of reasoning by analogy, we raise the problem whether it is plausible to assume on an a priori basis, as Lewin seems to have done, that the rigidity of so complex a structure as a person is not susceptible to alteration—perhaps drastic alteration—if suitable forces are applied.

Concept of Topological Rigidity Holds Obstacles to Experimentation. While acknowledging the ingenuity of Kounin's experimental studies of rigidity, we submit that the construct of topological rigidity does not readily lend itself to experimental investigation. It has been defined by Kounin as "that property of a functional boundary which prevents communication between neighboring regions" (1941a, p. 254). In an actual experimental situation, just what are to constitute regions, neighboring regions, and boundaries, and with what gauge is one to measure communication or hindrance to communication?

In Lewin's writings the concept of a region seems to be undefined but it is to be understood to be analogous to the mathematical concept of a region. It is postulated that both the person and his psychological environment are structured into parts called regions. Most of Kounin's experiments refer to regions of the psychological environment and, in particular, to various activity regions, e.g., the region corresponding to the activity of releasing a marble. Since his theorems and deductions are concerned mainly with rigidity of boundaries in the structure of the person, he seeks to bridge the gap between rigidity of regions of the person and rigidity of regions of the environment by means of a bold assumption: namely, that the rigidity of the person parallels the rigidity of the boundaries in his psychological environment (Kounin, 1943, p. 186). (Since the latter rigidity may vary considerably, the problem again arises as to what is meant by the topological rigidity of the person.)

In his experiment on satiation and cosatiation (see p. 53), Kounin seems to be directly concerned with regions of the person. Thus, he makes the supposition that an old feeble-minded individual and a young normal individual are both equally differentiated in equivalent areas. He speaks of the Regions a, b, c, and d of each of these individuals, and presents diagrammatic sketches of the individuals depicting them to be structured into Regions a, b, c, and d (1941a, p. 256). But what are these regions of the personality structure? Why, they are the region of drawing cats, the region of drawing bugs, the region of drawing turtles, and the region of drawing rabbits. In another publication (1943), he refers to them as "need-regions." We confess that we lack the imagination necessary to conceive of personality as structured according to these regions: a drawing-cats region, a drawing-bugs region, etc., or even regions corresponding to the needs for drawing cats, bugs, etc. If there is a region of the person corresponding to each drawing activity, then presumably any activity in which an individual engages— from twitching his nose to planning a complex activity in the social field —may be regarded as having a corresponding inner-person region. If to every activity there is a corresponding region of the person, then differentiation (referring to the number of regions of the person), would increase at so phenomenal a rate, even for the infant, as to make Alice's sprouting while in Wonderland seem stationary by contrast.

We question the validity of the assumption that there is a region of the person corresponding to each drawing activity. Lewin has said (1936) that one should treat as environment, and not as regions of the person, everything in which, toward which, or away from which the person as a whole can perform locomotion, i.e., change of position. Based on this contention, the activity regions corresponding to the various drawing tasks should be represented as parts of the environment. Indeed, in the other experiments of his study Kounin regards regions corresponding to activities, e.g., the releasing of a marble, as belonging to the environment. That in the satiation-cosatiation experiment—where he had perforce to deal with regions of the personality structure and with communication between them—he allowed activity regions to represent regions of the person may be a reflection of the difficulties involved in attempting to cope experimentally with the construct of rigidity of the psychical structure.

Granted for the moment that drawing cats represents one region and drawing bugs (or turtles or rabbits) another, just why should one assume, as Kounin does, that these are neighboring regions? Regions are defined by Lewin as neighboring when they have a common boundary, with a "boundary" in topological psychology regarded as constituting "those points of a region for which there is no surrounding that lies entirely within the region" (1936, p. 215). This definition of boundary, taken directly from the corresponding mathematical concept, may be all right for mathematics, but is it relevant for psychology?

Lewin does not offer precise criteria for determining what psychological phenomena correspond to "points." With reference to "surrounding," he notes that it can be determined by "certain monotonous series of inclusion" (1936, p. 53), a carry-over from the related mathematical concept, which again does not seem to have direct psychological relevancy. The proffered definition of boundary does not allow for the experimental determination of its nature or presence since the points composing a boundary are not finite in number and, for any one point, there is no certainty that some surrounding—be its diameter as small as you please—does not lie entirely within the region. Perhaps in recognition of such difficulties, Lewin states that for purposes of psychological investigation the presence of a boundary within the environment or person can be determined by means of locomotions or communications. Supposedly, then, the problem is simple: if "movements" or communications between regions reveal an "obstacle," it may be interpreted as a boundary; if no such "obstacle" is revealed, it may be assumed that no boundary is present. Lewin acknowledges, however, that the problem is not so simple, noting, on the one hand, that not every obstacle is necessarily a boundary of a psychological region and, on the other hand, that a boundary "is not necessarily an obstacle to locomotion or communication" (1936, p. 215). Thus, the problem of determining whether regions are neighboring is not simplified by shifting to the problem of determining the presence of a common boundary.

Again we raise the problem why certain regions were regarded as neighboring in Kounin's study. Apparent "communication" or hindrances to "communication" between regions would not, we have seen, suffice to establish the presence or absence of a common boundary between the regions. Consider in this connection some experimental findings reported by Lewin with reference to the resumption of interrupted tasks. He reports (1935, p. 216) that results obtained with feeble-minded children depended on whether or not the second task was presented on the same table as the first interrupted task. When the same table was used, feeble-minded children resumed work on the first task more frequently than did normal children. But, when the second task was performed on another table, the frequency of resumptions was reduced almost to zero for the feeble-minded children but did not decrease as much for the normals. Lewin concluded that for the feeble-minded individual separate situations are to a higher degree "closed wholes" and he is in either one or the other situation.

In Kounin's satiation-cosatiation experiment, the four drawing activities were conducted at separate tables. May this not have tended to make separate, closed situations of them for the feeble-minded subjects, perhaps so separate that the regions corresponding to any two activities possessed no common boundary, that is, were not neighboring? On the other hand, they may have been neighboring regions for the normals. But then the experiment would in no way be able to test the derivation which it was intended to test (the derivation that, the older and/or more feeble-minded an individual, the less effect a change of state in one region will have upon the state of *neighboring* regions). Indeed, the fact that for the feeble-minded individuals, satiation in one drawing activity did not appreciably lower the satiation time in subsequent activities may be interpreted as resulting from the fact that the activity regions were completely separated, *nonneighboring* regions for them.

Our primary aim here is not to establish that the regions involved were nonneighboring but, rather, to demonstrate that there is not conclusive evidence that they were neighboring regions. More generally, it seems to us that it is a thorny problem to establish that one actually is dealing with phenomenological counterparts of the concepts of common boundary and of neighboring region. Because of the difficulties involved in ensuring that one is dealing experimentally with the various concepts of topological psychology which are intimately related to the construct of topological rigidity, as defined by Kounin, this construct—however interesting it may be theoretically—seems at present rather inaccessible to direct experimental investigation. Research is needed to determine whether and how these difficulties can be resolved. Also, it is of interest to determine whether topological rigidity can be characterized in ways that lend themselves more readily to experimental investigation.

Lewin's Use of the Concept of Topological Rigidity Is Limited. At this point it is interesting to note that, aside from the papers on topological rigidity in relation to feeble-mindedness, none of Lewin's writings in topological or vector psychology has dealt extensively with this construct. His book on topological psychology includes the term "rigidity" in the glossary but the text itself makes rather limited use of the construct. Rather, Lewin indicates in this text that the construct, involving as it does resistance of boundaries or regions to forces of communication or locomotion, is more properly the subject matter of vector (force) psychology. What we find, however, in thumbing through his later text on vector psychology (1938), is a well-nigh complete neglect of the construct of rigidity, with neither the term "rigidity" nor any of its numerous aliases appearing in the index. Are we to surmise from this that Lewin thought it advisable to abandon the construct of topological rigidity.

COMPARISON OF THE THREE APPROACHES

Views on Feeble-Mindedness

In comparing the approaches to rigidity promulgated by Lewin, Goldstein, and Werner, it seems appropriate to compare their views on feeble-mindedness since the Lewin-Kounin theory of feeble-mindedness has been criticized by both Werner and Goldstein while Goldstein's views have been criticized by Werner.

Lewin's Views. The central thesis in Lewin's formulation of the theory of feeble-mindedness is pronounced topological rigidity. Lewin attempts to deduce both the smaller degree of differentiation of the feeble-minded and his slower rate of development, from his assumed greater topological rigidity. Kounin hypothesizes that topological rigidity is a positive function of the degree of feeble-mindedness.

Goldstein's Views. To Goldstein the chief characteristic of feeble-mindedness is an impairment of the abstract attitude which he equates with a lack of differentiation in the organism. All the abnormalities of the feeble-minded are considered "understandable as secondary to the effect of the lack of differentiation, i.e., impairment of abstract attitude" (1943, p. 224). Goldstein claims that the feeble-minded lack

plasticity and hence manifest behavioral rigidity or distractibility only
in situations with which they cannot cope; that is, situations that cannot be dealt with in terms of the concrete attitude they possess but that
demand the abstract attitude they lack. Rigidity is thus a means of pro-
tection against catastrophic conditions.

Goldstein attributes to Lewin and Kounin the thesis that rigidity is
the primary symptom in feeble-mindedness and then proceeds to criti-
cize this thesis. He claims that a theory which considers rigidity as the
primary symptom can never explain the fact that not only abnormal
behavioral rigidity but also distractibility may be manifested by the
same patient. Both manifestations, he says, become intelligible under his
theory which considers rigidity as secondary to the impairment of the
abstract attitude. (Lewin does refer to the extreme distractibility sometimes manifested by feeble-minded individuals and seeks to account for
it in terms of the either-or behavior connected with the tendency toward
the formation of strong Gestalten.) Goldstein recognizes that there is
something one could call rigidity of boundaries and he attributes this
also to "abnormal concreteness" (1943, p. 223). Criticizing the Lewin-
Kounin theory for putting the "disturbance of relationships between
neighboring fields in the foreground" (1943, p. 219), he maintains that
the factor of mental set may determine what is neighboring and what is
not, and that the nature of the mental set may be affected by the impairment of the abstract attitude. In short, "the phenomena explainable by
abnormalities in the boundaries—and I think all the phenomena in
feeble-mindedness—become understandable from the central defect"
(Goldstein, 1943, p. 224), the defect in abstract ability.

An important consequence for therapy is developed by Goldstein
(1943, p. 224). He states that, if rigidity is assumed to be a special
abnormal phenomenon which cannot be changed (presumably referring
here to topological rigidity which Lewin appears to regard as immune
to situational conditions), then there is no possibility of helping the
feeble-minded. But from Goldstein's point of view, a definite kind of
therapy can be initiated. One can attempt to organize the outer world
of the individual in such a way that there occur as few catastrophies as
possible. Doing this, he believes, will make for less (behavioral) rigidity, allow the individual to utilize the mental capacity he does possess
to the highest degree possible, and foster his mental development.

Werner's Views. Werner (1946b) questions the assumption that
rigidity, as a behavior characteristic of feeble-minded persons, is a unitary trait. Experiments by Strauss and Werner (1942) and Werner
(1946a) are regarded as having demonstrated that "kinds of rigidity
can be distinguished, which vary in quantity and quality with organis-

mic conditions" (Werner, 1946b, p. 48). In particular, Werner distinguishes between subnormal and abnormal rigidity. Subnormal rigidity is regarded as particularly characteristic of feeble-mindedness of the familial type (endogenous, subnormal individuals) and also of primitive peoples, while abnormal rigidity is considered particularly characteristic of feeble-mindedness caused by injury to the brain (exogenous type). One of the differences between subnormal and abnormal rigidity is said to be revealed in remedial-reading situations. Subnormal children, Werner points out, often repeat a previously read word when presented with another of a similar shape, whereas the stereotypy shown by brain-injured children does not seem to depend on similarity in shape or visual form. Children with a brain injury often reiterate one particular word during the presentation of other, dissimilar words (repetitive perseveration), or, after having read correctly several words in succession, they repeat suddenly a previously read word not necessarily similar to the presented word (delayed perseveration). Repetitive and delayed perseveration, Werner claims, seldom occurs in the feeble-minded children of the familial type.

Subnormal rigidity is considered by Werner to be mainly the result of dedifferentiation or undifferentiation, both terms referring to a lack of sufficient differentiation in the organism. Inflexibility of response in the case of subnormal rigidity is regarded by him as related predominantly to "global" behavior, i.e., to perception or action organized as undifferentiated wholes. For individuals manifesting subnormal rigidity, situations which objectively are not sharply set apart from one another are considered to fuse easily, so that responses are stereotyped.

Abnormal rigidity is regarded by Werner as traceable not to a trend toward "global" behavior but to the opposite trend by which wholes are dissected into unrelated parts through disintegration or isolation: "a sensori-motor activity may become self-contained to an abnormal degree so that it may repeat itself irrespective of the incongruity of such behavior" (1946b, p. 50). He concludes: ". . . subnormality [subnormal rigidity] can be best described in terms of de-differentiation; the abnormality of brain-injured organisms, in terms of disintegration" (1946a, p. 23).

It is Werner's impression that the feeble-minded subjects used by Lewin and his coworkers were probably of the brain-injured type. In Werner's critical evaluation of the concept of rigidity, he attempts to apply the Lewin-Kounin conception of rigidity to brain-injured children; the attempt leads to conclusions which he describes as "absurd" (1946b, p. 45). Kounin objects to this treatment, noting that his publications have explicitly stated that the subjects he used had no history or signs of physiological or neurological pathology (1948, p. 165).

For Werner, the essential characteristic of feeble-mindedness (except when produced by brain injury) is a lack of differentiation. Here he differs sharply from Lewin who claims that "a theory [of feeble-mindedness] that would restrict itself to differences in degree of differentiation cannot be regarded as sufficient fundamentally" (Lewin, 1935, p. 228) since it would conceive of the feeble-minded as entirely similar to a younger person. Werner interprets concreteness of thinking as only one sign of undifferentiated behavior whereas Goldstein seems to equate the two as, for example, when he speaks of "the lack of differentiation, i.e., impairment of abstract attitude" (Goldstein, 1943, p. 224).

Werner raises the question whether Goldstein's distinction between primary and secondary rigidity can be applied profitably to the analysis of the behavior of feeble-minded children. He concludes that the application is probably unfeasible, noting that, since feeble-minded children of the brain-injured as well as of the familial type are both "lacking in abstract behavior," it is difficult to see how lack of abstraction can be responsible for the differences in rigidity manifested by them (1946b, p. 51).

Werner is in agreement with Goldstein that all feeble-minded individuals are highly concrete-minded and lacking in abstract behavior. However, he implies that they lack plasticity not only in situations demanding abstract behavior (not only in catastrophic situations) but even in situations of a "concrete-perceptual" kind (1946b, p. 51). He therefore prefers to define the cause of subnormal and abnormal rigidity as lack of differentiation of functions and as isolation of functions, respectively, rather than as lack of abstract behavior.

In short, the essential characteristic of feeble-mindedness is the nature of the topological rigidity for Lewin, impairment of the abstract attitude for Goldstein, and lack of differentiation or isolation of functions for Werner.

Comparison of Some Apparently Similar Terms

Both Lewin and Goldstein use the phrases "primary rigidity" and "secondary rigidity," but with decidedly different referents. To Lewin "primary rigidity" refers to rigidity of the boundaries of the regions of the personality structure, while "secondary rigidity" is synonymous with behavioral or phenomenological rigidity. Goldstein uses both phrases to refer to behavioral manifestations. "Primary rigidity," to him, denotes rigidity of the Einstellung mechanism which affects all performances, while "secondary rigidity" denotes behavioral rigidity which is secondary to (a consequence of) the impairment of the abstract attitude and which manifests itself only in situations calling for abstract behavior. In Goldstein's critique of the Lewin-Kounin theory, it is not always apparent whether the terms "primary rigidity" and "secondary rigidity" are to be interpreted à la Lewin or à la Goldstein.

Differentiation in Relation to Development and Concreteness of Thinking

In all three approaches, there is agreement that the infant and young child are "less differentiated" than the adult. All three accept differentiation as increasing with development and, more specifically, as tending to increase with age, at least from infancy until maturity (Goldstein, 1943, p. 221; Werner, 1940, p. 44; Lewin, 1935, p. 206).

Similarly, in all three approaches, there is agreement that the less developed, the less differentiated individual tends to think in a "concrete" or "primitive" manner. Lewin notes that "the tendency to concreteness and primitiveness appears to be a general feature of the childlike or otherwise undifferentiated person" (1935, p. 222). Werner writes: "Among primitive peoples, and also children, there is found a kind of thinking which, with great justification, may be termed 'concrete' thinking" (1940, p. 52). To Goldstein, the development of an abstract attitude is practically synonymous with increasing differentiation. He notes: "The feeble-minded does not develop according to age; he does not develop particularly the abstract attitude" (1943, p. 222). And: "The difference between the younger normal child and the older one . . . concerns particularly the development of the abstract attitude" (1943, p. 222). So intimate is the relationship between a small degree of differentiation and concreteness of thinking, as viewed by Goldstein, that, as we have already noted, he can write "lack of differentiation, i.e., impairment of abstract attitude" (1943, p. 224).

It is here that one must distinguish clearly between Goldstein's views, on the one hand, and those of Lewin and Werner, on the other. Goldstein regards concreteness of thinking as the chief characteristic of the "undifferentiated" individual; to Werner (and Lewin), "concreteness is only one of several signs of undifferentiated behavior" (Werner, 1946b, p. 51).

Behavioral Rigidity in Relation to Differentiation, Isolation, and Concreteness of Thinking

In all three approaches, there is agreement that behavioral rigidity may be produced by a lack of differentiation or a small degree of differentiation. Thus, Werner, in attempting to account for some of the results obtained by Kounin, writes: "Lack of differentiation, varying with the type of child and the type of task, can therefore be considered as

the basis of the rigidity" (1946b, p. 48). He describes a less differentiated activity pattern as a rigid pattern and a more differentiated pattern as a flexible one. From the thesis that the regions of personality
of an immature individual are little differentiated, he concludes that it
is to be expected that mutual interference, in the form of perseveration
and stereotypy, should occur frequently; from the thesis that the regions of a mentally growing organism become more differentiated, he
concludes that "a differentiated behavior emerges, varying with changes
of situation (functional stability and flexibility)" (1946b, p. 46).

Goldstein (1943, p. 222) writes of the feeble-minded child that he is
similar to the immature child in his responses; the feeble-minded, he
says, can differentiate only imperfectly and he therefore takes each
stimulation as a whole, with the result that he is rigid so far as a given
task as a whole is concerned. Goldstein attributes the behavioral rigidity
of the feeble-minded to a lack of differentiation considered synonymous
with an impairment of the abstract attitude.

Lewin has specifically stated that, under certain conditions and to a
certain extent, "there exists a functional equivalence between a higher
degree of differentiation of the total system and a greater mobility of
the person in the face of a given situation or task" (1935, p. 233). Kounin (1941a, 1948) has remarked that some of the factors which may
contribute to behavioral rigidity are the degree of differentiation of the
person and of the psychological environment as well as the degree of
differentiation of relevant areas. In his reply to Werner, Kounin reiter-
ates that he has previously "unequivocally stated that increasing degree
of differentiation leads to increasing variability of behavior and external
mobility" (1948, p. 162).

In short, all the approaches are in accord when it comes to viewing a
small degree of differentiation as a possible factor underlying behavioral rigidity. Disagreement arises, however, with reference to other
causes of behavioral rigidity.

With respect to the relationship of behavioral rigidity to isolation,
Goldstein (1943, p. 209) maintains that rigidity appears if a part of
the central nervous system which is anatomically and functionally separated from the rest of the system is exposed to stimulation or, as he calls
it, if it is "isolated." He notes that the "same formal changes occur if
isolation takes place between the stratification of mental performances"
(p. 209). Isolation of the function of one part of the nervous system is
said by him to be caused by either of two conditions, designated as
primary rigidity and secondary rigidity.

Werner (1946b, p. 50) claims that the repetitive perseveration and
delayed perseveration which he found to be characteristic of feeble-
minded children of the brain-injured type are probably the result of

isolation of a sensorimotor activity. Only in this particular pathological case, he states, does the concept of rigidity approach in meaning the construct of rigidity as used by Lewin and Kounin.

It seems to the present writers that isolation, as used by Goldstein and Werner, may be interpreted as a case of an extremely low degree of intercommunication between regions: the cessation of communication. Thus, it may be regarded as extremely high topological rigidity, in the sense in which Kounin defines the latter. Yet Goldstein and Werner do not specifically utilize the concept of topological rigidity. Indeed, we have seen that much of their criticism of the Lewin-Kounin theory and experimentation stems from their identification of topological rigidity and behavorial rigidity.

With regard to the relationship of behavioral rigidity to concreteness of thinking, Goldstein (1943) maintains that all secondary rigidity is due to an impairment of the abstract attitude and hence is associated with concrete thinking; in contradistinction, his concept of primary rigidity is interpreted as not involving any disturbance of the higher mental processes.

Werner recognizes concreteness of thinking as one possible cause of behavioral rigidity. Thus, he attempts to explain Kounin's finding that feeble-minded children showed less shifting from one classificatory scheme to another in the classificatory test than did normal children (Kounin's Experiment 5, discussed earlier) as

probably not due to rigidly bounded and segregated regions of personality, but the result of their concrete manner of thinking. Immature persons sort by means of perceptual concrete configurations rather than by means of abstract concepts such as color or form categories. (1946b, p. 47.)

In short, both Goldstein and Werner imply a causal relationship between behavioral rigidity and concreteness of thinking. Lewin, however, implies no such relationship. He regards concreteness of thinking as a general feature of the undifferentiated personality; behavioral rigidity, as we have noted before, he attributes to topological rigidity, low degree of differentiation, and various motivational factors—but not directly to concreteness of thinking.

Concluding Remarks

This chapter has reviewed three approaches to rigidity. We have seen that for both Goldstein and Werner rigidity refers to certain observable facts of behavior for which they offer explanations. The concept of (topological) rigidity, as used by Lewin and Kounin, does not refer directly to observable facts or to any act of behavior. In this connection it should be noted that, in the glossary of Lewin's text on topological psychology, the term "rigidity" is not included under the heading, "Concepts Mainly Concerned with Directly Observable Facts" (1936, p. 215) but, instead, is included under "Dynamic Concepts" (1936, p. 217). The Lewinian construct of rigidity is used to account for some behavior classified as rigidity as well as for other behavior. Thus, rigidity for Goldstein and Werner is an observable fact for which explanations are needed, whereas (topological) rigidity for Lewin and Kounin is an explanation for certain observable facts.

Some of the observable facts to which the Lewinian construct of rigidity is applied as an explanatory concept are identical with or similar to facts to which such concepts as impairment of the abstract attitude and relative lack of differentiation are applied by Goldstein and Werner, respectively. We have not attempted to reach a decision as to which of the three approaches accounts more adequately for these facts. There is not sufficient evidence at present to warrant such a decision. In part, this state of affairs is a result of the fact that the three approaches have not received sufficient attention from other psychologists. One of the aims of the review of the three approaches contained in this chapter is to awaken interest in them. This is also an objective of the analysis, undertaken in subsequent chapters, of the concepts involved in the three approaches, and of the application of these concepts to the instance of behavorial rigidity which we shall study.

It is hoped that a renewed interest in the three approaches will lead to exploration of the avenues of research opened up by each and to the development of methodological and experimental tools with which to assess the fruitfulness of each approach.

CHAPTER III

FACTOR-ANALYTIC APPROACHES TO RIGIDITY

NOT psychoanalysis, but factor analysis, led Charles Spearman to propose an answer to the question what brings about rigidity of behavior. Since then, many different answers have been proposed as a result of factorial studies of rigidity. The present chapter reviews the historical background of Spearman's proposal and surveys some of the other proposals concerning rigidity that have resulted from factor analysis. Since it is still popular at the present time, factor analysis constitutes one of the oldest and yet one of the most prevalent contemporary orientations to the study of rigidity.

THE FACTOR OF PERSEVERATION
OR MENTAL INERTIA

Factor analysis convinced Charles Spearman that there was a tendency toward inertia in human activities. This conviction arose from the attempts, by Spearman and his associates in the so-called English (or London) school of psychology, to account for correlations between certain test results. It seemed to Spearman that the g factor, the factor of intelligence which he had previously postulated, could not by itself explain the correlations. He therefore posited a p factor (1927), the factor of perseveration or mental inertia, with the g factor considered to represent the amount of mental energy and the p factor the degree of inertia of this energy. The g factor and p factor were regarded as varying independently of one another. All human beings were considered to possess the p factor but to vary in the amounts of it which they possessed. In any one individual the p factor was regarded as operating as a functional unity, pervading all behavior processes. In order to gain perspective from which to view this p factor or perseveration factor, let us turn to a brief review of the history and early experimentation relating to the perseveration concept.

Early History of the Concept

Coining of the Term. Perseveration, as a modern psychological concept, may be regarded as tracing at least as far back as the metaphysical psychology of Herbart. Herbart (1891) maintained that ideas possess an attribute or force by means of which they can thrust themselves into consciousness from time to time even when the original experience

which produced them is not repeated. The coining of the term "perseveration" is generally accredited to Neisser who in 1894 defined this
term as an abnormally persistent repetition or continuation of an activity after the activity has been once begun or recently completed.

Secondary Function. In 1902 Gross distinguished between a primary
and secondary function. He maintained that there was a primary process which was responsible for the occurrence of a stimulus in consciousness as well as a secondary process responsible for its unconscious
afterfunction. Specifically, he claimed that every nervous process which
gives rise to a mental content tends to persist for a time as an unconscious afterfunction which may influence subsequent associative activity. This unconscious afterprocess, designated by Gross as a secondary function, is seen to be related to the concept of perseveration of
processes.

Spontaneous Recurrence. It was also at about the turn of the century
that Müller and Pilzecker (1900) referred to the "spontaneous recurrence of ideas" as a perseveration phenomenon. In their investigation
of memory they noted that, when an individual was required to learn
an Item A in association with Item B, and then to establish a connection
between A and C, B was found to interfere with the establishment of
the latter connection. This "spontaneous recurrence" of B was referred
to as perseveration. Incidentally, the phenomenon of interference was
henceforth to be studied in many investigations of perseveration, the
underlying assumption being that the greater the interference of one
idea (or activity) with another, the greater the perseverative tendency
of the former.

Tests of Sensory Perseveration. Perseveration, in the sense of the
immediate aftereffects of sensation or "sensory lag," was studied by
the Dutch psychologist Wiersma in about 1906. His are believed to be
the earliest tests of perseveration. Concerned with what has been called
sensory perseveration, the tests included (1) flicker fusion: the speed
at which two rapidly alternating stimuli would fuse and appear unitary,
low speed of fusion being considered indicative of high perseveration;
(2) time of adaptation to a liminal threshold, low adaptation being
considered indicative of high perseveration; and (3) the time required
to return to normal sensitivity to a weak electric shock after a strong
shock, the criteria being the same as in (2). Wiersma administered his
tests to normal individuals as well as to mental patients, designated as
either "maniacs" or "melancholiacs," and found that maniacs had lower
average perseverative scores than normals while melancholiacs had
higher average scores than normals.

Motor Tests. Two other Dutch psychologists, Heymans and Brugmans (1913), are accredited with introducing the first motor tests of perseveration. Accepting Gross's notion of a "secondary function," they were particularly concerned with studying the interference effects of preceding mental processes upon present processes. One of the tests they utilized consisted in writing letters of the alphabet forward and then backwards, the rationale being that the first activity would interfere with the second so that the ratio of the number of letters written forward to the number written backwards would be a measure of perseveration.

Work of the English School

Coordination of Concepts. It seemed to Spearman and his associates that the various phenomena of recurrence of ideas, aftereffects, and interference effects, which had been studied under the guise of perseveration or of secondary function, might all be manifestations of the same basic phenomenon. Spearman notes: "Joining these two concepts (perseveration and secondary function) together, we get simply that, with some persons, there is a tendency for mental processes to persist in activity long after the cessation of the conditions to which they were originally due" (1927, p. 52).

The Study by Lankes. One of the earliest investigations of perseveration significant for the English school was conducted in 1915 by Lankes, a student of Spearman's. His tests were designed to measure what he regarded as the threefold nature of perseveration: (1) aftereffects of a sensory experience, (2) spontaneous recurrence to consciousness of an experience, and (3) unconscious or subconscious continuance of the effects of past experience. We shall discuss briefly the nature and rationale of the tests he employed since many of them appear again and again in subsequent test batteries of perseveration.

Test 1. Natural Rate of Tapping. S was asked to tap a pencil on the desk at a rate which seemed most natural to him. Rationale: Higher perseverators will be more susceptible to the interference caused by each tap on the successive tap and hence will have a slower rate.

Test 2. Alphabet Writing. Several letters of the alphabet were written in alphabetical order as many times as possible within the assigned time (thirty seconds). They were then written in reverse order as many times as possible within the same time limit. Rationale: If the first activity is perseverating, it will interfere with the second activity so that the ratio of the number of letters written in the first situation to the number written in the second will serve as an index of perseveration.

Test 3. Cancellation. A page of randomly arranged letters was presented to S who was to cross out certain prescribed letters. Rationale: The greater the number of correct cancellations, the lower the inertia.

Test 4. Color Disks or Fusion. A color-fusion wheel composed of two complementary colors was rotated, with increasing speed, until S reported that the colors had fused into a unified gray. Rationale: Low rate of fusion indicates high inertia.

Test 5. Drawings. A drawing was exposed for ten seconds and S was asked to reproduce it from memory. Two drawings were then presented simultaneously for twenty seconds and S was asked to reproduce them from memory. Rationale: Interference of one drawing upon the other in the simultaneous presentation is indicative of a perseverative tendency. Interference should result in errors in reproduction. Hence, the index of inertia is the number of errors in the first task divided by the average number of errors in the second task.

Test 6. Narratives. A short narrative was presented and S was questioned about it. Two narratives were then presented one immediately after the other and S was then questioned about both. The same number and kind of questions were asked with respect to each narrative. Rationale: As in Test 5, the index of inertia is the score in the first part divided by the average score in the second part.

Test 7. Associative Reaction. A list of words was read and S asked to respond to each with the first association he thought of. Many of the words in the list were repeated at various intervals. Rationale: Reaction time can serve as a measure of lag or inertia of response. The relation of the frequency of repetition of a stimulus word to the frequency of repetition of the associated response can serve as a second index of inertia.

Test 8. Essays. In the first part of the test, four minutes were allowed for writing an essay comparing two objects or persons; e.g., Napoleon and Wellington. In the second part, six short comparison essays had to be written in rapid succession within the same time limit; i.e., forty seconds were allowed for each. The number of "significant" comparisons was scored. Rationale: As in Test 6, the ratio of the scores obtained in part one to those obtained in part two serves as an index of inertia.

All tests in Lankes's investigation were administered to groups rather than to individuals. (Mass administration prevailed in most of the subsequent investigations of perseveration.) Each subject also completed a questionnaire pertaining to what were regarded as introspective criteria of perseveration. Included were such questions as these:

Does a tune, line of poetry, phrase, problem, etc., come back to your mind again and again without your intending it? How often in a week? In a day? At what time of the day? Do you, after a long rail journey or sea voyage, seem to hear the noise and feel the motion of the train or ship from time to time? Have you ever noticed them recurring in your dreams?

Lankes found that the inertia index on each test correlated positively with the "inertia score" determined on the basis of the questionnaire. Intercorrelations between test results also tended to be positive, although small, with none of the average intercorrelations exceeding $+0.29$. What was responsible for these consistently positive intercorrelations? A common factor, Lankes reasoned, must be revealed in all the tests. Since the tests were not designed to measure intelligence, the common factor must be other than the g factor. He designated it as the inertia, perseveration, or p factor, maintaining that it is common to perseveration of a sensory, motor, and associative nature and is present in every individual. In view of the small intercorrelations found between test results, Lankes admitted that "normally, with average, unselected subjects, this general factor, though present and operative, is not very strong" (1915, p. 418).

A Factor-Analytic Approach. The first application of Spearman's factor analysis to perseveration was carried out by Spearman in 1927 on data which had been obtained by Jones (1915, 1928, 1929). Jones had given seventy-seven children four motor tests:

(1) Writing the letter S forward for thirty seconds and then writing it backwards, i.e., as it would appear in a mirror.

(2) Writing digits forward for thirty seconds and then writing them in reverse order with backward strokes.

(3) Mirror drawing.

(4) Copying a unit of prose in the usual way and then copying it again without dotting the i's or crossing the t's (the "it" test).

Computing the tetrad differences from the table of intercorrelations, Spearman was satisfied that the intercorrelations could be attributed to the existence of a single operating factor which he described as the p factor.

On the basis of this analysis as well as analyses of data obtained by Bernstein (1924), Hargreaves (1927), and others, Spearman concluded that perseveration is a genuine group factor, possessed in various degrees by all individuals, which participates as a "functional unity" in all of the individual's behavior processes. He hailed the discovery of the p factor or mental inertia as "one of the latest and perhaps greatest conquests of experimental psychology" (1927, p. 30) and he even formulated a law of inertia: "Cognitive processes always begin and cease more gradually than their apparent causes" (1927, p. 291). Thus acclaimed, and with a law named in its honor, mental inertia or the p factor seemed well established as a broad group factor, as a characteristic of the human mind. And, yet, efforts to discredit it had already begun. Within a few years the p factor or mental inertia was to be dislodged from its throne and its power usurped by a relative newcomer, disposition rigidity.

Critiques of the Factor of Mental Inertia or Perseveration

Chance May Account for Positive Intercorrelations. The purported functional unity of mental inertia rested on the observation that positive intercorrelations were found between scores on various tests which were assumed to measure perseveration. The problem of determining the cause of these positive intercorrelations had apparently been solved by assuming that an underlying factor of inertia was responsible. But the critics—Kelley (1928), Burri (1934, 1935), Jasper (1930), Shevach (1936)—had another answer available: the intercorrelations, although positive, usually were so low as to be explicable on the basis of chance. For example, in Lankes's study none of the average intercorrelations was greater than +0.29. In Bernstein's research (1924) the average intercorrelation was +0.181 (P.E. of 0.081) for one group and +0.171 (P.E. of 0.086) for another group. And yet Spearman had leaned heavily on these investigations in attempting to establish the p factor. Jasper contends that it is meaningless to apply a factor analysis to very low intercorrelations, that factor analysis "has no significance if the actual intercorrelations are so low as to show practically negligible relationship" (1930, p. 42).

Incidentally, Jones's studies yielded the relatively high intercorrelation of +0.492—one of the highest obtained in research on perseveration—but his battery had been limited exclusively to motor tests, and mainly to tests involving "mirror writing," so that the underlying factor could hardly be regarded as justifying the functional unity of perseveration outside of the particular motor processes involved.

No Perseveration Factor. Criticism was leveled against the apparent gap between Spearman's method of analyzing the intercorrelations between the scores of a group of tests for a common factor and his formulation of the nature of the p factor. Burri (1935) writes that the demonstration of a common factor p does not prove that this "mysterious something" is a native quality of the nervous system and that it determines an individual's ability to alternate. Kelley (1928) contends that it is not necessary to postulate a *p* factor since the apparent operation of this factor can be accounted for in terms of the *g* factor, speed, or manual dexterity.

Possibly More Than One Perseveration Factor. Some of the investigations of perseveration had failed to indicate one common factor running through all the tests of perseveration. For example, Hargreaves (1927) had employed six tests presumed to measure perseveration, but he found, in studying the intercorrelations, that they fell into two distinct groups of three tests each. Since one of these groups of tests was found by Bernstein (1924) to correlate positively with estimates of perseveration given by teachers, Hargreaves assumed that this group actually measured perseveration while the other group of tests failed to do so. The common factor running through the accepted group was regarded as the *p* factor. But Shevach (1936a) noted that two of the tests in the rejected group, when used by other investigators, had positive correlations with assumed tests of perseveration and had been regarded as attesting to the presence of the *p* factor. Shevach raised the question : "Why should a test intercorrelate when used by one investigator and stand alone when used by another?" (1936a, p. 382).

Burri (1935) claimed that, even when it is possible to demonstrate that the intercorrelations from a series of perseveration tests can have a common factor, this does not prove that the intercorrelations are accounted for by only one factor, for there may be still other factors present. He demonstrated statistically that intercorrelations which led to the extraction of one common factor could also lead to the extraction of two or possibly three or four common factors. Were all these to be regarded as perseveration factors?

Reliability, Validity, and Administration of Tests. Thus far we have been concerned with intercorrelations between test scores and with statistical manipulations of these correlations. But what of the tests upon which these scores are based? Are they actually tests of perseveration? Shevach (1936a) noted that none of the tests used in the isolation of the *p* factor had ever been established as a valid or reliable indicator of perseveration; nor had the tests been at all standardized. Moreover, he claimed that most of the investigations were based upon small populations, inadequate samples, and insufficient numbers of tests. Mass administration of the tests, common to most of the investigations, was a further deficiency, Shevach claimed, particularly with respect to tests of sensory perseveration (e.g., color-disk or flicker-fusion tests) where the position of the subject and the angle of perception might contribute to variance of results. Retesting, a possible means of determining reliability, he said, had not been resorted to in the vast majority of investigations. The resulting scores, he concluded, need therefore not be at all indicative of perseveration; to resort to elaborate statistical procedures would in no wise enhance the meaning and significance of the data. The extracted common factors, Shevach emphasized, need not at all pertain to perseveration.

Jasper's Study. An important experimental attack was made by Jasper (1930). Employing a large number of sensory, motor, and ideational tests similar to those used by the English school, he obtained an average intercorrelation which was negative, —0.021, and which thus failed to support the hypothesis of a broad group factor of perseveration.

Shevach's Study. We have seen that Shevach criticized past experimental work on perseveration for its mass application of tests and its infrequent utilization of retesting. His own investigations of sensory perseveration, described in 1936, were characterized by administration of the tests to small groups of subjects and by two readministrations of the entire battery of tests to the same subjects. It was found that the same tests of perseveration might intercorrelate positively when applied to one group of subjects and yet yield a negative intercorrelation when applied to another group. In attempting to account for this result, Shevach postulated that perseveration manifests functional unity for some people whereas for others its functional unity is either very weak or nonexistent. He noted a general tendency for perseveration to vary according to the test situation but for the degree of perseveration manifested by specific sensory processes to be highly consistent in the tests and retests. In short, the perseverative tendency "is not consistent from situation to situation, but it is highly consistent for the same situation" (1936a, p. 427). Shevach's findings thus speak against a fixed characteristic of inertia operating as a functional unity in all behavior or even in all sensory experiences.

Scoring of Alternation Tests. Batteries of perseveration tests often included alternation tests. In such tests, a short period of time, say thirty seconds, was allotted for the performance of a certain task, e.g., writing the letter S; an equal period of time was then allowed for a related task, e.g., writing the letter Z. These two tasks, designated as Tasks A and B respectively, constituted the homogenous series of the test. Following them there was a mixed series in which Task A was alternated with Task B; e.g., the subject was required to write $SZSZ...$ Comparison of the score on the mixed series with the combined scores on the homogeneous series served to yield an index of inertia, the underlying assumption being that the greater the perseverative tendency of the tasks, the greater would be their interference effects when alternated. A poorer score on the alternation series as compared with the combined scores on the homogeneous series was therefore regarded as evidence of interference effects and, hence, of perseveration.

There exists considerable disagreement as to the proper formula to be utilized in order to obtain an index of perseveration from an alternation test. Some investigators utilize the simple difference formula $M -$ H, while others prefer the ratio $\frac{M}{H}$, where M is the score on the mixed series and H equals the combined scores on the homogeneous series. Cattell (1936) prefers the ratio formula, criticizing the difference formula on the ground that it correlates highly with speed and therefore yields a different measure of perseveration for a slow worker than for a faster one, even if both actually experience the same interfering effects.

But Walker, Staines, and Kenna (1943) claim that the ratio formula accurately portrays the interference effect only if the individual's speed of work on the two homogeneous tasks is equal; otherwise, it yields an interference effect even when none exists. For example, if the subject does 30 of Task A in the allotted time of thirty seconds and 15 of Task B in the same time, then he requires an average of one second for Task A and an average of two seconds for Task B. To do the two together, as in the mixed series, would then require an average of three seconds so that in thirty seconds he could do 10 units of A plus B, and, in one minute, 20 such units provided that there were no interference effects. In other words, in the one minute allowed for the mixed series he could be expected to do 20 units or 40 tasks while, in the one minute devoted to the combined homogeneous series, his combined scores would be 30 plus 15, or 45. Thus, even without any interference effects, the ratio $\frac{M}{H}$ or $\frac{40}{45}$ would show an interference effect.

To counteract the effects of unequal speed in the homogeneous series, Walker, Staines, and Kenna (1943) propose that the interference score be taken as $\frac{E}{M}$ where E is the score which would be expected in the mixed series provided that there was no interference effect and M is the actual score obtained. As we noted in the example, E would be obtained by dividing the time allotted to the mixed series by the average time required to do one unit (one Task A plus one Task B) ; for example, in the cited illustration E is 40.

Walker, Staines, and Kenna (1943) administered a battery of motor alternation tests to 205 college students, one of the largest samples used in research on perseveration. Utilizing the new scoring formula on the data, they failed to obtain a common factor of interference effects. They regarded their results as speaking strongly against the existence of a common factor of inertia.

Investigation by Kleemeier and Dudek. A new attempt to investigate the existence of a common factor of perseveration or, rather, of its assumed obverse, flexibility, was described by Kleemeier and Dudek (1950). For the purposes of their study, flexibility was treated as the ability to shift from one task to another. They included alternation tests (two homogeneous series followed by a mixed series) which involved numbers, single-digit numbers in some tests and two-digit ones in others, or which involved verbal material, or which were tests of perceptual speed. It was reasoned that, if the mixed series which required shifts of tasks appeared on an independent axis regardless of the type of ability represented (numerical, verbal, perceptual speed), then there would be evidence of a common factor of flexibility. While the investigators preferred not to use the term "perseveration" because of its confused connotations, the finding of a factor common to all the mixed series might well have been regarded as evidence of a factor of perseveration, considered as the obverse of flexibility.

The test battery was administered to 205 college students. Factor analysis revealed that the tests designed to measure flexibility (the mixed series) did not group themselves along an independent axis but could be accounted for in terms of number, perceptual, and verbal factors, depending upon the kind of material involved in the mixed series. The investigators extracted four factors identified as perceptual speed, verbal, single-digit number, and two-digit number. They concluded that, at the level of simplicity characterizing their tests, a common factor of flexibility does not exist.

Summary Statement. There seem to be well-founded doubts as to the feasibility of regarding mental inertia or perseveration either as a factor common to all tests of perseveration or as a general characteristic of the human mind which is possessed in various degrees by all individuals and which operates as a functional unity pervading all behavior processes. The simple formulation of mental inertia originally set forth by Spearman thus seems rather inadequate. Indeed, in 1929 Spearman admitted, apropos of the recent investigations pertaining to perseveration, that "the newest and most exact investigations have had their usual effect of showing the problem to be much more complicated than it appeared originally" (1929, p. 366). As we noted previously, the spot-

light of fame in the domain of rigidity has tended to shift from mental
inertia to disposition rigidity.

THE CONCEPT OF DISPOSITION RIGIDITY

In 1934 Stephenson concluded, from an analysis of motor tests employed to measure perseveration, that a common factor can be found
only in those tests involving the breaking away from or the modification of a habitual activity. Cattell (1935) observed that the motor alternation tests which seem to yield the best measurements of the p factor
are those in which one activity involves an old-established set whereas
the other activity involves a newly established set; he suggested that the
temporal relations of the two "interfering" performances are unimportant. In 1943 it was demonstrated, by Walker, Staines, and Kenna,
that perseveration tests involving an old, well-established behavioral
pattern, as well as a new activity, one to which the person is not accustomed, tended to give similar results whether the old activity preceded
or followed the new activity. Regardless of the order, the well-established behavior tended to interfere with the new activity whereas the
latter seemed to exert little influence on the habitual behavior. Rejecting
the notion that every cognitive activity has a perseverative tendency
(which was Spearman's contention), these investigators instead introduced the concept of disposition rigidity to refer to the interfering influence of a habitual activity on a new activity It has since been pointed
out that most of the tests which Spearman used as evidence for the perseveration factor involved both a well-established and a new activity
(for example, normal writing and mirror writing). Hence, the results
may be interpreted as attesting to perseveration of a habituated activity,
but not to perseveration of all cognitive activities. That is, Spearman
may unwittingly have been demonstrating the existence of disposition
rigidity. Some psychologists contend that disposition rigidity (and not
Spearman's perseveration factor) is a basic rigidity factor possessed
by all individuals but in different degrees.

Critique of Disposition Rigidity

Contradictory Evidence. While Cattell and other psychologists have
concluded that the only assured manifestation of perseveration is disposition rigidity, the case for disposition rigidity seems to have several
loopholes. Notcutt (1943), for example, found evidence of some interference effects even in the shifting back and forth between two tasks
presumed to be equally old or equally new. Such results would imply
that there may be interference other than that of an old activity on
a newer activity, that is, other than that attributable to disposition
rigidity.

Conflicting Definitions. Seeking to take into account results such as those of Notcutt, Cattell stated that the factor of disposition rigidity is "manifested, so far as we know, most clearly in motor performances, as a resistance to willed change of old established habits, but is *perhaps slightly manifested in interference with switching of any kind"* (1946, p. 437; italics ours). But the italicized phrase is in direct contradiction to definitions of disposition rigidity offered by Cattell. He has defined "disposition rigidity" as "difficulty in new tasks relative to old tasks when the new tasks are not difficult by reason of complexity" (1946, p. 436) and as "a difficulty (slowness) in turning from old to new responses to a situation when the new responses are clear to the individual's intelligence and he wills to make them" (1946, p. 329). Both of these definitions regard disposition rigidity as hinging on a difficulty in new relative to old tasks. But, then, how can this factor be assumed to operate when both tasks are equally old or equally new? These definitions seem to preclude the possibility suggested by Cattell that disposition rigidity may be manifested in interference with switching of any kind.

To complicate matters, Cattell has also given other, considerably broader definitions of disposition rigidity. Thus, he has defined it as "a relative resistance to changing to more rewarded paths" (1950, p. 176) and as "resistance to change of neural discharge paths" (Cattell and Tiner, 1949, p. 325). Cattell does not reconcile these broad definitions with the definition in terms of new versus old tasks. Does the writing of the letter *S* backwards, for example, constitute a "more rewarded path" than writing the letter forward, and what constitutes the reward?

In speaking of disposition rigidity as "resistance to change of neural discharge paths," Cattell notes that this rigidity is inherent in the individual. This formulation does not indicate whether the degree of resistance to change is the same for all neural discharge paths in an organism or whether the resistance may differ for different paths. Moreover, the formulation seems to overlook the possibility that resistance to change of a neural pathway may be influenced by past and present conditions in the cortical tissue and may not be solely a function of the individual's inherent disposition rigidity. Köhler and Wallach's experimental investigations of cortical satiation (1944) suggest that the "resistance to change" of a cortical region is not constant for the individual but may vary with variations in the conditions of the cortical region and its surroundings.

Relationship Between Disposition Rigidity and Classical Perseveration. There arises the problem of the relationship between disposition rigidity and perseveration as studied by Spearman, the latter sometimes being referred to by Cattell as "classical perseveration." Cattell at one time claimed that disposition rigidity was such that it required being considered "in complete detachment" from what had heretofore been called perseveration. But more recently he has stated that disposition rigidity may be referred to as "classical perseveration" (Cattell and Tiner, 1949, p. 329), has described it as the classical perseveration factor (p. 339), has identified it with the p factor (Cattell, 1950, p. 92), and has concluded that disposition rigidity almost certainly does exist "as a general characteristic, in the form of inertia" (p. 168). As such, disposition rigidity would be subject to much of the criticism which has been directed against inertia or perseveration as a general characteristic. But, even in the very reports where he explicitly identifies disposition rigidity and classical perseveration, Cattell, in some contexts, draws distinctions between them. For example, he distinguishes between "structural rigidity" and "process-momentum rigidity" (terms which we shall define later), and notes that disposition rigidity refers to the former while perseveration refers to the latter. Clarification is required to remove some of the confusion concerning the relationship between disposition rigidity and what has in the past been studied as perseveration or as mental inertia.

RELATION OF DISPOSITION RIGIDITY TO LEARNING AND CREATIVE EFFORT

Disposition rigidity has been intimately linked with learning. Cattell and Tiner write: "We cannot . . . be sure that differences in rate of learning are controlled solely by motivation, repetition, and time conditions. It is necessary to hypothesize individual differences in basic rigidity [disposition rigidity]" (1949, p. 325). This hypothesis overlooks the possibility that rate of learning may be influenced by the nature of the material learned, different methods of teaching and learning, various social atmospheres, various test conditions, attitudes and assumptions with respect to the task, etc. (cf. Hilgard, 1948; McGeoch and Irion, 1952). If rate of learning can be influenced by so many factors, not all of which are controlled in tests of disposition rigidity, it seems questionable to attribute differences in rate of learning to differences in disposition rigidity.

It is hypothesized that speed of learning is a negative function of disposition rigidity (Cattell and Tiner, 1949, p. 325). Conclusive evidence is not furnished for this hypothesis. That one individual writes relatively fewer S's backwards than another cannot be used both as evidence that he possesses more disposition rigidity and as evidence that he is a slower learner. Independent criteria are needed to measure rate of learning and disposition rigidity.

Cattell implies that learning involves changes in specific neural discharge paths. But there are some psychologists (cf. Morgan, 1951, p. 768) who do not accept such specificity as the neurological basis of learning. Moreover, forces which cause learning are equated by Cattell with forces which change a habit. But there are theories which conceive of forces that produce learning as not necessarily producing any changes in specific habits (cf. Koffka, 1935). Disposition rigidity is referred to as partly a "rigidity operating against the formation of new connections" and "a rigidity operating against the extinction of unrewarded responses" (Cattell and Tiner, 1949, p. 325). This implies a conception of learning which some psychologists do not accept as the prototype of all learning. The problem arises whether disposition rigidity is to be considered basic to all learning or only to the specific kind of learning implied in Cattell's writings.

Disposition rigidity is said to be measured best by "creative effort" tests. These are described as tests in which one activity is a well-established habit, e.g., writing S's, and the other activity involves creative effort: "a task of equal complexity but breaking new ground; e.g., writing capital S's backward" (Cattell, 1946, p. 435). Presumably, a person who can write S's backward with greater speed and fewer errors than another is manifesting more "creative effort." Actually, scores on such tests have never been shown to differentiate between those who are more creative, as measured by actual accomplishments, and those who are less creative; they have never been shown to differentiate scientists, mathematicians, philosophers, poets, artists from others who manifest less creativity. Why then should the writing of S's backwards and other tasks of this sort be considered as creative-effort situations?

The underlying assumption seems to us to be as follows: creative thinking, creative effort, consists simply in the establishment of new neural or stimulus-response connections and the extinction of "unrewarded" responses, so that creative effort can be equally well tested by any task which "breaks new ground," whether it be writing letters backwards or solving a difficult, hitherto unsolved, scientific problem. Such a conception of creativity has been seriously challenged by Wertheimer (1945).

Disposition Rigidity as a Functional Unity

To speak of "the disposition rigidity of an individual" implies that he has a fixed level of disposition rigidity. But it has not been shown that the measured extent of disposition rigidity remains the same for a person from day to day or from test to test. Yet it is implied that disposition rigidity operates as a functional unity, generally and consistently characteristic of an individual's habitual activities—a contention which is not at present experimentally established.

Similarly, Cattell speaks of "high perseverators" and "low perseverators," where perseveration refers to the factor of disposition rigidity "variously diluted" (1946, p. 438). The phrases seem to signify that there are individuals who consistently manifest extremes in perseveration. But it has not been established that an individual consistently scores high (or low) in perseveration tests of various kinds or that his score remains high (or low) when he is considered in another test population.

At our present level of knowledge, "the disposition rigidity of an individual," "high perseverators," and "low perseverators" are terms that represent fictional abstractions rather than demonstrable realities.

Personality Attributes

It has been said that the importance of measuring disposition rigidity resides not so much in the thing measured as in the personality traits found empirically to be associated with it. Cattell lists personality correlates of disposition rigidity (noting, for example, that it is negatively related to good character integration, to dominance, and to cheerfulness) and also lists differences in personality characteristics between high and low perseverators, where perseveration again refers to disposition rigidity "variously diluted." He describes the low perseverators as tempermentally more "high strung, less deeply emotional, of a more insistent temper, and in character more disciplined, integrated earlier, and with a more exacting superego" (1946, p. 442).

Many of the tests on which the correlates are based were not established as valid or reliable indicators of the personality trait in question or of disposition rigidity or perseveration. The resulting data has often failed to conform to accepted standards of statistical significance; and studies by different investigators have yielded rather conflicting findings in some cases. Of such deficiencies Cattell is aware, noting that substantiation of any one part of the nexus of qualities which go with the perseveration factor "is in general scientifically defective" (1946, p. 442). Since this is the case, the associations of personality characteristics with disposition rigidity had best, it seems to us, be accepted with many grains of salt.

One is tempted to point to the history of the assumed relationship between perseveration and the introversion-extroversion complex. For many years it was maintained—in spite of the absence of adequate confirming data—that "high perseveration" is linked with introversion while "low perseveration" goes with extroversion. The first experimental test of this assumption was made by Pinard in 1932. Patients in a mental hospital were studied intensively by the staff for traits generally regarded as belonging to the introvert type and were also given various motor tests of perseveration. On the basis of his findings, Pinard concluded that

the facts before us definitely explode the theory held so long and by such eminent psychologists, that introversion is synonymous with extreme perseveration, or that there is any significant correlation between perseveration and what was generally supposed to be the mental makeup of the introvert. (1932, p. 123.)

A little later Stephenson (1934) was led to conclude that, if the test situation was properly evaluated, it was the introvert who tended to show low-perseveration scores—a complete reversal of the belief prevailing prior to Pinard's study. Drawing an obvious moral, we point out that, when relationships between personality characteristics and perseveration, referred to in Cattell's writings, are put to adequate experimental tests, the results may well explode the delineated picture of the "high perseverator" and the "low perseverator."

Constitutional Basis and Racial Differences

In 1928 Jones wrote: "The quality of perseveration is a fundamental property of the germ plasm, inherited from our ancestors. It is thus probable that we can speak of national inertia. If so, future investigators may determine what are the peculiarities in the glandular make-up of the races which exhibit it" (1928, p. 282). More than a score of years later (1950) Cattell speaks of disposition rigidity as powerfully constitutionally determined, as possibly a property of the genes or of the body chemistry, and refers to "racial levels" of disposition rigidity. He writes:

Just what disposition rigidity means in terms of genetic units, or what the full extent of the association in this bundle of physical and mental traits is, remains to be discovered. Possibly there is only one gene at work, operating upon only a few of the physical characters that correlate to form the racial type. Possibly this temperamental trait of disposition rigidity will be traced to some difference of body chemistry, and be found to influence far more aspects of behavior than have yet been noticed. Obviously there are advantages and disadvantages in divergence from some central level of disposition rigidity—one can change ideas and way of life too rapidly or too slowly—and perhaps these racial levels indicate evolution towards adaptation to particular climatic and, especially, cultural conditions. Contingently, it seems a likely conclusion that a community of personalities of high disposition rigidity would show more conservatism in folkways than one formed of racial groups lower in this temperamental tendency. (1950, p. 139.)

Aside from the metamorphism of perseveration into disposition rigidity, there are strong resemblances between the citation from Jones and the more recent one from Cattell. Both statements are based on inadequate evidence. In support of the contention that disposition rigidity is "powerfully constitutionally determined" (1949, p. 330), Cattell and Tiner cite as evidence two investigations (Cattell and Malteno, 1940; Yule, 1935) in which, it seems to us, there was insufficient control of environmental factors to allow such a conclusion to be validly deduced. Among the evidence which Cattell and Tiner cite in support of the contention that disposition rigidity is "significantly higher for Mediterranean than other European races" (1949, p. 330) is the investigation by Rangachar (1932) comparing differences in perseveration among English and Jewish boys. Rangachar's study, probably inspired by the previously cited quotation from Jones, was concerned with perseveration or inertia, and not all of his tests could be regarded as measuring the influence of an old-established habit on a new activity; yet Cattell and Tiner apply his findings to disposition rigidity. This matter aside, let us consider whether Rangachar's investigation at all supports Cattell and Tiner's assertion.

Since Cattell and Tiner speak of Mediterranean and other European races while Rangachar deals with English (non-Jewish) and Jewish boys, the inference would seem to be that one of Rangachar's groups (presumably the Jewish boys) belongs to the Mediterranean race while the other group (presumably the English group) belongs to another European race. Yet the adjective English refers to a nation of peoples composed of many racial strains, the adjective Jewish to a religion to which belong members of different national and racial strains; that is, the two terms do not refer to distinct European races. Hence, Rangachar's investigation actually has no bearing on Cattell and Tiner's statement that disposition rigidity is higher for the Mediterranean race than for other European races.

In any event, it is interesting to note that Rangachar's finding that Jews are higher perseverators was not confirmed in a subsequent investigation. Administering a battery of ten tests of sensory perseveration to non-Jewish adults as well as Jewish adults, Shevach (1938) found that the differences between the groups tended not to be statistically significant. The Jewish group made higher perseveration scores in some tests while the non-Jewish made higher scores in other tests. Moreover, when nine of the tests were administered to a group of Jewish children, in seven tests the children showed lower perseverating scores than the adults, whether compared with adult Jews or adult non-Jews. Shevach concludes that his findings contradict Rangachar's research.

Far more study is required before it can be conclusively established whether or not disposition rigidity (or perseveration or inertia) is constitutionally determined and differs for different races.

In short, there seems to be little evidence to support the implicit assumption that there is a factor of perseveration or of disposition rigidity which is generally and consistently characteristic of an individual or of a race or which is genetically determined. To attempt to list the distinctive personality features of such fictional abstractions as "high perseverators" and "low perseverators" may constitute a fascinating game but it is one in which results are not well substantiated by scientific observations. Nor can the listed characteristics be regarded as justifiable on the ground that they may serve as leads for future research; rather, the implicit assumption that high and low perseverators exist and that the only problem is to distinguish between them in terms of temperament, character, or personality characteristics, may serve as a smoke screen to obscure the essential problems involved in the conceptualization of "high" and "low perseverators" or of "rigid" and "nonrigid persons."

Varieties of Rigidity and Rigidity Factors

Factor-analytic studies of rigidity have resulted in the "extraction" of a large number of "rigidity factors" to account for the intercorrelations among test scores. Combining the proposals of various studies, we find the following factors invoked to account for rigidity:

(1) Mental inertia or the classical perseveration factor

(2) Sensory or perceptual perseveration

(3) Motor perseveration

(4) Mental or cognitive perseveration

(5) Associative perseveration

(6) Conative perseveration

(7) Orectic perseveration (of a mood or a task)

(8) Structural rigidity

(9) Process-momentum rigidity

(10) Disposition rigidity

(11) Rigidity operating against formation of new connections

(12) Rigidity operating against the extinction of unrewarded responses

(13) Rigidity of innately preferred patterns contrasted with acquired habits

(14) Rigidity specific to particular drives such as hunger, fear, or sex

(15) Rigidity of the ego

(16) Rigidity of the superego

(17) Ideational inertia

(18) Spatial intelligence rigidity

(19) Fluency of association

(20) Goal-path rigidity

(21) Goal rigidity

(22) Ergic rigidity

(23) Ego-level rigidity

(24) Peripheral-level rigidity

(25) Effort factor in rigidity

(26) Motor-speed rigidity

(27) Rigidity for simple tasks   (31) Verbal rigidity
(28) Rigidity for complex tasks   (32) Perceptual rigidity
(29) Single-digit arithmetical rigidity   (33) Speed and strength of closure
(30) Two-digit arithmetical rigidity   (34) Flexibility of closure

RELATIONSHIPS AMONG FACTORS

While some psychologists still speak of rigidity as a unitary trait, others insist that it is a multiform trait, manifested in diverse forms. Thus, Cattell and Tiner propose two broad varieties of rigidity: process-momentum and structural, with the latter described as the resistance of a habit or personality trait to forces which might be expected to change it, and the former as "the tendency of a percept or an emotion or a motor activity to persist, when once activated totally or partially, despite substitution of new stimuli for the original one that produced the process" (1949, p. 322). They cite Factors 10, 17, 18, and 19 in the above list as examples of structural rigidity and suggest that disposition rigidity (Factor 10) may be further broken down into Factors 11-16. They imply a dichotomous as well as a hierarchical arrangement of rigidity factors.

Several other dichotomous arrangements of rigidity factors have been proposed. Fisher (1950) identifies factors of ego rigidity and of peripheral rigidity, the former operating in tasks central to the ego and the latter in tasks that are more peripheral, less vital to the ego. Scheier (1951) distinguishes between rigidity for simple tasks and rigidity for more complex tasks. Horwitz's intensive factorial study (1951) identifies one factor contributing to rigid behavior as low motor speed and another as high effort.

Thurstone (1943) conducted an extensive factorial study of perception, using a battery of sixty tests. Two factors which he identified pertain to rigidity. One is the factor of speed and strength of closure which includes "the strength with which a configuration is held against distractions" (p. 118). This factor is related to what "the Gestalt psychologists have called *Gestaltbindung*, which seems to refer to the rigidity of the perceived unity in a presentation" (p. 20). Another factor, identified as flexibility of closure, refers to flexibility (or rigidity) in manipulating several perceptual configurations.

As noted earlier in this chapter, Kleemeier and Dudek (1950), using perceptual, verbal, and numerical materials, found that one factor did not suffice to account for test intercorrelations; instead they "isolated" four distinct factors of rigidity: perceptual, verbal, single-digit numerical, and two-digit numerical.

The relationships among the listed factors are not clear. Even differ-

ences among factors "isolated" in the same study are sometimes ambiguous. Thus, in Fisher's study one does not know where ego rigidity
ends and peripheral rigidity begins. Nor do Cattell and Tiner differentiate adequately between disposition rigidity and ideational inertia.
Ideational inertia is said to be shown in inability to break with perceptual
habits and habits of thinking. "Whether it is to be considered primarily
a rigidity of old-established habits . . . or a lack of energy to establish
new sets . . . is a matter for further research" (1949, p. 338). The distinction between ideational inertia and disposition rigidity is beclouded
since the latter is also characterized as "essentially a rigidity of old-
established habits" (1949, p. 339) and is also said to be shown in inability to break with habits. Thus, while the factorial solution revealed
them as separate factors, there seems to be little in the content of the
interpretation which makes clear the grounds for the separation.

What is particularly confusing in the literature is that one investigator seldom relates the factors he promulgates to those in other studies.
Hence, to cite examples at random, one cannot know whether the ego
rigidity proposed in one study is the same as the rigidity of the ego
proposed in another, or whether perceptual rigidity is identical with
perceptual perseveration and how it relates to the perceptual factors
of rigidity found by Thurstone. In general, one does not know whether
factors with similar or identical names, isolated in different studies, are
actually similar or identical. One is tempted to ask whether the different
names are semantic facades to hide essential similarity or identity of
factors.

But, even taking into account possible duplication of factors, it nonetheless seems that one of the dramatic outcomes of factorial studies has
been the proposal of a plethora of rigidity factors. True, multiple factors have been proposed by workers who did not employ a factorial
approach; e.g., Werner has divided rigidity into abnormal and subnormal; Lewin, into topological and behavioral; and Goldstein, into
primary and secondary. The use of factorial methods, however, has
yielded, not two or four or six rigidity factors, but a veritable rash of
factors, and, with new factorial studies continuing to "identify" more
factors, it appears that the epidemic is by no means over. That the factorial method should have contributed to the multiplicity of rigidity
factors is thought-provoking and almost ironic, since factor analysis
has been described as "a branch of statistical theory concerned with
the resolution of a set of descriptive variables in terms of a small number of categories or factors . . . The chief aim is thus to attain scientific
parsimony or economy of description" (Holzinger and Harman, 1941,
p. 3). Why is it that the chief aim of factor analysis—economy of de-

scription—failed of accomplishment in the domain of rigidity? Why has it not made a greater contribution to our knowledge of rigidity? We shall examine some possible reasons for the failures in subsequent paragraphs. Although the discussion will be centered on factorial studies of rigidity, much of what we shall say will be relevant to factorial studies of other psychological phenomena.

CRITICAL EVALUATION OF FACTOR ANALYSIS

Fundamental Assumption

The fundamental assumption of factor analysis is that the variables under analysis are capable of being represented as linear functions of a finite number of numerical factors. This assumption has not been justified either for psychological phenomena, in general, or for rigidity, in particular. While the assumption may simplify the mathematical foundations of factor analysis, it has the disadvantage that the factorial solutions may be incorrect and misleading when they come from data in which the assumption does not hold, in which, say, the variables are not linearly related to the factors (for example, in which test scores are not linear functions of factor scores) or in which there are infinitely many numerical factors. No conclusive evidence is available concerning the nature of the relationship between test scores made by subjects in various studies of rigidity and their scores on the various extracted factors. As long as the fundamental assumption is not justified for any particular psychological phenomenon, it must be borne in mind that actual deviations from linearity and the finite assumption may exist and may contribute to the inaccurate picture yielded by the factorial solutions.

Fundamental Equations

Four kinds of factors have been recognized: a general factor common to all the tests in the battery under analysis, a group factor common to at least two of the tests in the battery, a specific factor involved in one and only one test of the battery, and an error factor pertaining to errors of measurement and other accidental factors involved in any one test. The term "common factor" covers both general and group factors, while the term "unique factor" has been used to designate the combination of specific and error factors involved in one test.

Designating the test score (or test performance) by the symbol T, the common factors by the symbol F, and the unique factor by the symbol U, we may express the fundamental assumption of factor analysis in the following algebraic form:

$$T_j = A_{1j}F_1 + A_{2j}F_2 + \ldots + A_{mj}F_m + A_jU_j.$$

Here Tj refers to performance in Test j; $F_1, F_2, \ldots F_m$ refer to the m common factors; U_j denotes the factor unique to Test j; and A_{1j}, A_{2j}, $A_{3j}, \ldots A_{mj}$, A_j, are the coefficients of the factors of Test j. These factor coefficients are often referred to as the "loadings" or "weight" of their corresponding factors; for example, A_{1j} represents the "loading" of Test j on Factor F_1. They represent the proportion of the factor that contributed to the test performance. The larger the factor coefficient, the more important is its corresponding factor in determining the test performance. There is assumed to be an equation such as the above for each of the n tests in the battery. Moreover, there is assumed to be one such equation for each individual who has taken the test, so that for Individual k the above equation takes the following form:

$$T_{kj} = A_{1j}F_{k1} + A_{2j}F_{k2} + \ldots + A_{mj}F_{km} + A_j U_{kj}.$$

Here T_{kj} denotes the score made by Individual k on Test j; F_{k1}, F_{k2}, $\ldots F_{km}$, U_{kj} denote the particular factor scores of this individual; that is, his particular amount of, or endowment on, each factor; e.g., the amount of disposition rigidity he possesses.

All scores in these equations, whether the test scores or the factor scores, are assumed to be expressed in standard form or to be standard scores, where these phrases refer to a score which has a mean of zero and a standard deviation of unity both for the studied sample group and for the total population.

It should be noted that factor analysis, at least in its present state of development, is not able to determine the specific and error factors but limits itself to common factors. In actual practice, then, the fundamental equations are modified so that the unique factors are ignored.

It is seen that the factor coefficients are assumed to be the same for all individuals taking the test. This implies that, if a Factor F_1 has a loading on Test j of 0.40 ($A_{1j} = 0.40$), then precisely 40 per cent of an individual's endowment on Factor F_1 contributes to his test score; that is, A_{1j} remains invariant for Test j regardless of the particular individual, the particular amount of the factor with which he is endowed (F_{k1}), and the particular score he makes on the test (T_{kj}). For example, if a factor of perceptual rigidity contributes to a test performance, then it is assumed that exactly the same proportion of a person's perceptual rigidity contributes to his score regardless of how much or how little perceptual rigidity he possesses; the proportion depends on the test and on the nature of the factor and not on the individuals tested.

This feature of the fundamental equations has been cogently criticized by Meunzinger (1955), who notes that there is no justification for such an arbitrary assumption. Individuals may conceivably differ in the proportion of a factor that contributes to the test performance; for example, a person with little mental ability may conceivably use a larger proportion of this ability on a test of intelligence than a person with more mental ability, or two people who are endowed with equal amounts of a certain rigidity factor may differ in the proportion of this factor that they use on a particular test.

Validity of Tests Employed

The extracted factors can be no more significant psychologically than the data on which they are based and the tests which yielded these data. In most investigations of rigidity, little attempt has been made, prior to the application of factorial methods, to confirm the validity of the various tests purporting to measure rigidity or perseveration. There is indeed no general agreement as to what tests best measure rigidity or perseveration. Some psychologists assume motor tests are the best measures, while others, for example, Cameron and Caunt (1933), speak strongly against motor tests as suitable measures of perseveration.

Shevach contends that tests of sensory perseveration "must serve as the basis for all further investigations [of perseveration]" (1936a, p. 386), while Cattell maintains that some of the tests Shevach used are those "which no careful student would have considered proved manifestations of perseveration" (1946, p. 434).

There is as yet little basis for determining what does or does not constitute a proved manifestation of rigidity; factor analysis cannot supply the basis. What seems to be needed, before factor-analytic methods are applied, is experimentation aimed at establishing fairly valid tests of rigidity. If the validity of the so-called tests of rigidity included in the battery is not first ascertained, by what logic may the extracted factors be described as rigidity factors? The presence of a positive correlation between test scores and the extraction of a factor, does not necessarily establish it as a factor of rigidity.

It may be thought that the repeated inclusion of certain tests in different investigations should yield some evidence as to whether or not these tests measure rigidity. If the same tests tend to correlate positively in various studies and to show similar loading patterns on one extracted factor, may that factor not be interpreted as a rigidity factor and the tests as tests of rigidity? The answer to this question seems to be negative. Even if the various tests do correlate positively in several studies, it does not follow that what they have in common is their measurement of rigidity. Moreover, as Cattell and Tiner point out, "the possession by factors, in two different researches, of a somewhat similar loading pattern is not sufficient ground for considering them identical" (1949, p. 337).

In any event, the argument is largely hypothetical since investigations of rigidity have not tended to include precisely the same tests employed in other investigations; when the same tests have been included, they have sometimes yielded a positive correlation when administered to one group or included in one battery, but failed to yield a positive correlation when the group or the battery was changed. Similar loading patterns have not been customary in the various investigations of rigidity. Actually, there is no a priori reason for assuming that the same tests, when included in different test batteries and/or when applied to different groups, should load the same factor.

Moreover, since most so-called tests of rigidity are not standardized tests, it is not unusual to find that, when the "same" test is included in various investigations, there are variations in the instructions given to subjects, in the methods of administration, or in the interpretation and scoring of responses. Such variations may affect the factorial outcome; e.g., Thurstone (1947, p. 326) indicates that the factorial composition of a test may be changed if the instructions are changed.

Reliability of Tests

Many of the tests which have been employed in investigations of perseveration and rigidity either have not had their reliability determined or have been found to show very low reliability. The reliability of a test is an important determinant of the loading it makes on various factors. Since factorial analysis cannot throw any light on the reliability of the employed tests, it seems advisable, prior to factorial studies, to investigate the reliability of existing tests and, if necessary, to direct research at the establishment of fairly reliable (and valid) tests of rigidity.

Interpretation of Factors

After extracting some factors, there remains the problem of interpreting them, a problem which has been characterized as the most important part of a factorial study. In Thurstone's words, "if the interpretation is foggy, then so is the whole study, no matter how elegant the statistical work may have been" (1947, pp. 337-38). The first step in interpreting a factor consists in determining which tests load the factor significantly. But the meaning of the word "significant" is usually arrived at subjectively. One investigator may decide that any loading of 0.40 or above is significant while all smaller loadings are to be discarded as insignificant. But another may decide that all loadings of 0.20 or more are significant. Still another investigator may decide that the four (or five or seven) largest loadings on a factor are significant.

Whatever may be the basis of selection of significant loadings, the researcher now is narrowed down to a factor which has various "significant" loadings on various tests. On the basis of the processes assumed to be involved in these tests, he proceeds to interpret or to christen the factor under consideration.

Consider a hypothetical case. Assume the battery consists of ten tests, five of which have been established as fairly valid and reliable measures of a process or an ability M while five others are not believed to measure M. Suppose that a factor is extracted which is significantly loaded (say, greater than 0.40) by all five tests assumed to measure M, but on which the remaining tests have loadings which are close to zero. With considerable assurance this factor might then be designated as representing process or ability M. To complete the orderliness of this example, suppose that there is extracted a second factor on which all the tests supposedly measuring M have loadings which are close to zero but on which the remaining tests have significant loadings. One might well designate this second factor as representing a process or ability L rather distinct from M. Unfortunately, actual factorial studies are not so clear-cut in nature. Yet the interpretation is often no less hesitant than in the cited hypothetical example.

Consider a recent factorial study which included ten tests, five of them described as tests of rigidity. A loading of 0.25 or higher was regarded as significant. On this basis, two of the extracted factors were loaded significantly by three of the five rigidity tests. And, yet, one of these two factors was "identified unambiguously as a rigidity or habit-interference factor" (Oliver and Ferguson, 1951, p. 58), while the other was described as "in no sense a pure factor." Whence the striking difference in interpretation?

Consider firstly the factor which emerged as the rigidity factor. As has already been indicated, three of the rigidity tests had significant loadings on this factor, but the other two rigidity tests had insignificant loadings. Moreover, this factor was sufficiently badly behaved to have a significant loading on a test of mental ability. The investigators decided that the two rigidity tests having poor loadings on this factor might after all not be tests of rigidity, commenting that a more thorough analysis of the nature of these tests might have revealed this beforehand. As for the significant loading on the test assumed to measure mental ability, it was dismissed on the ground that an analysis of the nature of the tasks comprising this test made such a finding plausible. Such was the evidence on the basis of which this factor was "unambiguously" identified as the rigidity factor.

Consider now the factor which was dismissed as impure. It also had insignificant loadings on two of the rigidity tests but not on the two on which the previous factor had missed out. It erred, however, in having significant loadings on two tests assumed to measure mental ability. No attempt was made to consider the tests of rigidity which this factor failed to load significantly as not truly testing rigidity. No plea was made that an analysis of the tests of mental ability which loaded this factor might have made such a finding plausible. Instead, the present factor was dismissed as in no sense a "pure factor" and no interpretation of it was attempted. Its virtue thus derided, remaining unidentified for all time, the factor came to an inglorious end. One might propose that it could at least have been a runner-up for the title. After all, the other factor was not quite so pure and unambiguous. This rather facetious treatment of the interpretation is not intended to reflect adversely on the study itself or to single it out, since many similar illustrations can be found in the literature. Nor do we intend to minimize the difficulties which are involved in interpreting the extracted factors. What we are trying to illustrate is that the interpretations are not always objectively determined. Yet one of the chief claims of enthusiasts of factor analysis is that it constitutes an objective means of dealing with psychological phenomena as opposed to older, subjective methods. It seems to us that, when it comes to interpretation of the factors—the most important part of a factorial study—objectivity is often thrown overboard.

Thurstone claims that "the severe restrictions that are imposed by the logic of factor analysis make it an arduous task to isolate each new mental faculty because it is necessary to prove that it is called for by the experimental observations" (1947, p. 70). Whatever may be "the logic" of factor analysis, it seems to us either that it is highly equivocal in nature or that factor analysts, in their interpretation of factors, have not necessarily heeded the logic and its "severe restrictions."

In brief, the gap between the offered interpretation and what can be objectively inferred from the test data and loading patterns seems, at least in some of the factorial investigations with which we are familiar, to be bridged less by severe restrictions of the logic of analysis and the dictates of experimental observations than by the ingenuity, imagination, and whimseys of those who are making the interpretation.

It would be of interest to give the same set of factorial data to different psychologists for interpretation of the factors. Would there result a uniformity of interpretations, guided by "the severe restrictions that are imposed by the logic of factor analysis" and stemming from strictly objective "operational definitions" of the factors? Or—as we suspect—would there result a diversity of interpretations depending upon the particular viewpoints of the particular interpreters?

Our objection to the identification or naming of the factors may seem rather naive, since a rose by any other name is still a rose. Perhaps the reader, if he is acquainted with the anecdote, is reminded of the gushing lady who rushed over to a famous astronomer after his lecture, exclaiming, "Oh, I just loved your lecture. I understood how you discovered the distance of the stars from the earth, and all that, but tell me, how did you ever find out their names?"

The question we direct to some of the investigators utilizing the factorial approach could be worded as follows: How did you ever find out the names of the factors? In particular, how do you know that these are rigidity factors? The situation is not at all akin to that confronting the astronomer for whom the naming of the stars is essentially an arbitrary affair. Giving the name Venus to a star does not attribute any Venus-like qualities either to the star or to the solar system to which it belongs. But, when factors are designated as perseveration, inertia, disposition rigidity, etc., it is assumed that they correspond to actual processes in behavior or actual characteristics of the personality. It is therefore extremely important to know whether the extracted factors are properly identified as rigidity factors or whether the labeling is essentially arbitrary and subjective.

Factor Scores

It will be recalled that the factor coefficients of any one test are assumed to be the same for all individuals participating in the test. Hence, once the factor coefficients are determined, since the test scores are known, it is theoretically possible to determine a given individual's factor scores. Proponents of factor analysis sometimes stress its ability to reveal the factor scores, claiming that the factor scores are indicative of an individual's status with respect to the corresponding factors, e.g., the amount of disposition rigidity he possesses. Yet in actual practice the factor analysis usually ceases after the computation of the loadings and the extraction and identification of factors, and does not go on to a consideration of factor scores. Moreover, the factor scores are subject to considerable error because specific and error factors enter into the equations involving the factor scores but are not taken into account in computing the latter and because the factor coefficients themselves involve approximations. It has been said (Thomson, 1939, c. VII) that the factor scores are not more revealing of information or better guides for prediction and guidance (but may be worse guides) than the original test scores from which they stem.

"The factor score is a characteristic of the individual and will have the same numerical value for that individual in all tests in which that factor occurs" (Thomson, 1939, p. 564). Neither a priori nor experimental grounds have been offered in support of this assumption. Comparisons have not been made of an individual's scores on one factor, as estimated from various tests, in order to see if the estimates were sufficiently similar to suggest identity within the margin of error. Nor is it made clear whether or not the factor score (say, the individual's status on a rigidity factor) is invariant for the individual, independent of training, education, or other experiences. It should prove of interest to attempt to study the influence on an individual's factor scores of different tests, different test conditions, and different patterns of past experiences.

Referents of the Extracted Factors

Since the factor analyst begins with test scores and then usually talks about the extracted factors as if they pertained to test performances, processes, or abilities, an implicit assumption would seem to be that the scores are adequate indices of performances, processes, or abilities. What seems to be overlooked is the possibility that similar scores may result from different performances or from different processes or abilities. Moreover, the processes or abilities underlying a subject's actual performance may differ from those which the investigator assumes are measured by the test. Hence, the extracted factors may not pertain to test performances or processes or abilities. Moreover, if the extracted factors pertain to one of these, it does not follow that they necessarily pertain to the others.

Another implicit assumption is that a given test constitutes the same task for all participants, so that differences in test scores are due to individual differences in factor scores. This assumption seems to neglect the possibility that two subjects may differ strikingly with regard to the interpretation of the instructions and the task, their attitudes toward the test and the experimenter, etc., and that the differences may not be entirely ascribable to differences in factor scores but may be the resultants of other, possibly momentary, conditions.

The fundamental equations of factor analysis imply that, for all individuals in the studied population, the test scores depend on the same factors. This rules out the possibility that different factors (and different behavioral conditions) may be determinants of the test scores for various members of the studied population. Moreover, the extracted factors are not usually restricted to the studied group but are assumed to be possessed, in various amounts, by all people. This assumption has been challenged by some psychologists, among them Stephenson (1936) and Jeffries (1948). As Loevinger writes, in discussing Jeffries' objection: "Why should all minds be organized in the same fashion? May people differ not only in amounts, not only in mental profiles, but in the whole pattern of mental organization?" (1951, p. 593.)

There is little agreement concerning the psychological meaningfulness of the factors. Holzinger and Harman (1941) claim that factor analysis does not necessarily attempt to discover the fundamental or basic categories in a given field of investigation such as psychology. Kelley states that there is no search for "timeless, spaceless, populationless truth in factor analysis," which seeks to solve a problem of description of a definite group functioning in definite manners, and that "he who assumes to read more remote verities into the factorial outcome is certainly doomed to disappointment" (1928, p. 120).

But Thurstone declares: "The factorial methods were developed primarily for the purpose of identifying the principal dimensions or categories of mentality" (1947, p. 55). He states that the objects of factor analysis are to discover the mental faculties or the primary abilities and to obtain a quantitative description of each fundamental ability in each individual by means of tasks that require these abilities in different amounts. Cattell notes that "the factors are likely to be structural and functional unities in personality" (1950, p. 42) and describes the factorial approach as "a search for the dimensions of personality, i.e., for the number of truly independent directions in which personality needs to be measured in order completely to describe it" (1950, p. 27).

If factorial studies of rigidity have actually revealed fundamental abilities and principal dimensions of personality or mentality, then we must conclude that there are a large number of such abilities and dimensions centering around rigidity. But one wonders why the same "fundamental abilities" were not more often found in different investigations. Doubt is cast on the likelihood of factorial solutions yielding the principal dimensions or even the number of truly independent directions in which rigidity of behavior or personality (or behavior or personality in general) needs to be measured in order completely to describe it. Thus, the number of common factors extracted (presumably corresponding to the number of dimensions) may vary with the particular factorial method employed or, within the same method, with the particular criterion as to when to stop extracting factors. This means that a search for the fundamental processes or forms or dimensions of rigidity via factor analysis, is likely to yield disagreement not only with reference to the nature of the dimensions but even with reference to the number of dimensions. This is attested to by the differing answers yielded by various factorial studies on rigidity, each of which hoped to reveal the principal underlying processes or forms of rigidity that exist.

The Factorial Solution as a Reference System

There are various factorial procedures, including the bifactor method, the centroid method, and the principal-axis method. Factor analysts often favor only one particular factorial procedure. They sometimes brand other factorial procedures as less objective than the procedure they prefer and as less likely to yield the genuine underlying factors. (Cf. the description of the disharmony among factor analysts given by Cureton, as cited in Holzinger and Harman, 1941, pp. 7-8.) Disharmony among proponents and opponents of various factorial solutions is uncalled for, Holzinger and Harman contend, since a set of factors yielded by one method of factorial solution can be transformed into a set of factors yielded by another method. They present mathematical formulas for certain transformations; these transformation formulas are based on a realization that factorial solutions are simply reference systems or coordinate systems.

Other psychologists have also recognized that the factorial solution represents a reference system or reference frame. For example, Thurstone states: "The test correlations define a configuration of test vectors without a reference frame. Since the factors are represented by the axis of this frame, it is necessary to locate a reference frame somewhere in the test configuration" (1947, p. vii). The apparent dilemma of why different factorial approaches may yield different outcomes is resolved, Holzinger and Harman point out, when any particular factorial method is viewed as an application of a particular coordinate or reference system. The problem of relating two factorial solutions, they note (p. 290), involves the determination of the relationships among the coordinates of the two systems.

A simple mathematical example may serve to make this clearer. In rectangular Cartesian coordinates, with the axes labeled x and y, a circle with its center at the origin and radius of length r has the equation $x^2 + y^2 = r^2$. In polar coordinates, the same circle has the equation $\rho = r$, where ρ is the radius vector; in this case, the distance from the origin to any point on the circle. The problem of relating two factorial solutions involves the determination of the relationship among the two systems of coordinates. In this case, the relationship is given by the formula $\rho^2 = x^2 + y^2$.

If a factorial method is recognized as involving the application of a particular coordinate system to the set of data, then championing any one factorial approach on the grounds that it is better than others is akin to a mathematician praising one coordinate system—say, the polar system—as better than all others. A coordinate system is not good in and of itself. It is true that there are curves whose equations can be expressed in a simplified form or whose properties can be more readily derived from the resulting equation, if one rather than another coordinate system is utilized. Analogously, a particular factorial method may be more directly applicable to a particular set of psychological data than other methods— but it does not follow that one factorial approach is generally more appropriate than other approaches.

If the close relationship between a factorial solution and the selection of a particular reference system were more generally recognized, it seems to us that there might be fewer claims that the extracted factors are necessarily fundamental and basic to the psychological data or to the phenomena on which the data are supposed to have a bearing. In every case, the extracted factors are necessarily dependent on the reference system, just as the particular form which an equation of a curve assumes is dependent on the reference system employed. Since the extracted factors may vary with changes in the reference system (changes in the factorial method), why should any one set of factors be regarded as fundamental or basic to the given data or related psychological phenomena, and why should the number of factors yielded by one factorial solution be considered as equivalent to the number of fundamental factors or properties underlying the data or the phenomena?

Apropos of the case of the circle which we have just considered, it might be mentioned that mathematicians do not argue about whether the true character of the circle is best expressed in three terms (equation in rectangular coordinates) or in two terms (equation in polar coordinates) or whether the circle possesses three or two fundamental or determining properties. The number of "determining properties" or "fundamental constants" which characterizes the given curve does not depend on the reference system. For example, for any circle the determining properties are (1) the location of its center and (2) the length of its radius. It should be noted that there are equations of a curve which do not explicitly reveal the determining properties of the curve.

Similarly, the fundamental factors involved in a set of data under analysis or in the underlying psychological phenomena may be independent of the particular reference system and may not necessarily be directly contained in the factorial outcome. That the number of extracted factors may vary with the particular method employed suggests that the number of factors extracted by any one method need not necessarily be a clue to the number of fundamental factors actually involved in the data or phenomena under analysis.

In brief, investigators who treat the number of common factors that they have extracted as necessarily equivalent to the number of common factors that underlie the data under analysis or that underlie the phenomena on which the data may have bearing, who proceed to instill these factors with psychological meaningfulness and to treat them as basic verities, might do well to remember the dependence of their obtained factorial solution on the particular reference system employed.

Factor Analysis and Experimentation

Some psychologists regard factor analysis as an experimental approach. For example, investigators have claimed that via factor analysis they will experimentally demonstrate the principal forms of rigidity (cf. Cattell and Tiner, 1949, p. 323); apparently they regard the factorial outcome as akin to an experimental demonstration. It seems to us that there are fundamental differences between the two.

In an experiment, one manipulates certain variables in a situation involving a subject, but, in a factorial study, one manipulates numerical variables (the test scores) in terms of the logic of a certain statistical procedure. Furthermore, the tests are not in any sense simultaneous variables involved in determining one function; the tests are given in succession, in serial manner. When a subject is taking one test of the battery, he is not being influenced by the other tests, particularly the subsequent ones, in the same way as he would be if certain variables were operating in a particular experimental situation. For the factor analyst the battery of tests and the resulting test scores may constitute a unified schema which, under statistical manipulation, reveals interrelations (correlations); but neither the unified schema nor the complex of interrelated variables existed for the subject.

An experimenter often manipulates the situation to study the apparent influence on his subject; e.g., he may vary the instructions, the assigned task, etc. Such control and manipulation of variables is not generally within the province of the factor analyst. He does not vary the variables (usually the tests or test scores); nor does he seek to vary the individual's attitude toward the task or toward the experimenter, or the conditions of testing, etc. The factor analyst usually deletes or adds variables by deleting or adding tests to the battery. For example, interested in the problem of the influence of speed on rigidity of behavior, the investigator decides to include a speed test in his battery in addition to tests of rigidity. If the speed test has a significant loading on an extracted factor identified as a rigidity factor, he will probably conclude that speed is a determinant of rigidity of behavior; if the speed test does not have such a loading, he will probably conclude that speed does not tend to influence rigidity. To introduce speed as a variable by including a speed test in the battery is not equivalent to administering the test battery under speed conditions. When the latter procedure is followed, the consequent speed conditions and the individual's reaction to these conditions may operate to influence rigidity of behavior in a manner—possibly a variety of manners—which may not be at all portrayed when scores on a speed test are correlated with scores on rigidity tests. More generally, a variable introduced statistically, in an "and-summative" manner, by either adding or deleting tests and test scores, need not at all accord with the influence of a presumably related variable which is introduced into and functions in the actual situation in which the subject is responding.

Other distinctions between the factorial solution and an experimental demonstration could also be cited. Our main contention is that factor analysis is not an adequate substitute for experimental investigation of a phenomenon.

Chapter IV

THE SELECTED CASE OF RIGID BEHAVIOR

WE have seen that the surveyed theories and approaches to rigidity have offered different, and sometimes apparently conflicting, answers to questions concerning the nature and determinants of rigidity. We now turn to another approach, one which selects a specific case of behavior and subjects it to intensive experimental investigation. The case selected involves water-jug volume-measuring problems. The reader is invited to participate in the solution of a series of such problems.

The Basic Experiment

We ask you, the reader, to participate in an experiment. You are to solve certain problems in which a stipulated volume of water is to be obtained by manipulation of certain (hypothetically) given jugs of stated capacities. Imagine yourself near a source of water such as a kitchen sink or a well. You are given one empty jug which has a capacity of 29 quarts and another with a 3-quart capacity and you are requested to obtain 20 quarts of water. Bear in mind that there are no graduated markings on the containers. All you know about them is that when filled to the top one holds 29 quarts and the other 3 quarts of water. Start by filling the 29-quart jar; then use the empty 3-quart jug three times to remove the excess 9 quarts. Each time empty the contents of the smaller vessel into the sink or well.

Now try this problem: Given an empty jug with a capacity of 21 quarts, another with a capacity of 127 quarts, and a third with a capacity of 3 quarts, you are requested to obtain 100 quarts of water. Allow yourself a maximum of two and one-half minutes to solve this problem and then continue reading.

One way of solving the problem is as follows: First, fill the 127-quart jar, thus introducing an excess of 27 quarts over the desired volume. From this jar, next fill the 21-quart jar once. The excess left in the 127-quart jug will be only 6 quarts. To remove the excess, fill the 3-quart jar twice. The largest container now contains the desired 100 quarts. The solution can be expressed thus: $127 - 21 - 3 - 3 = 100$, or $127 - 3 - 3 - 21 = 100$, or $127 - 3 - 21 - 3 = 100$.

The problem can also be solved by using only the 127-quart and the 3-quart containers. Fill the 127-quart container and remove the excess

27 quarts by filling the 3-quart container nine times; 100 quarts now remain in the largest jar; $127 - 9 \times 3 = 100$.

Now try the eleven problems enumerated below. To obtain the stipulated volume in each instance, use any or all of the jars mentioned in the problem. You will see that the first two problems are those which were just illustrated. If you cannot solve a problem within two and one-half minutes, go on to the next one. You may write your solution verbally, or use mathematical symbols in an equation, or draw arrows to designate the filling and pouring of water.

Problem	Given Containers with These Capacities			Obtain
(1)	....	29	3	20
(2)	21	127	3	100
(3)	14	163	25	99
(4)	18	43	10	5
(5)	9	42	6	21
(6)	20	59	4	31
(7)	23	49	3	20
(8)	15	39	3	18
(9)	28	76	3	25
(10)	18	48	4	22
(11)	14	36	8	6

Please do not read any further until you have attempted the above problems.

Discussion of the Experiment

Did you notice that Problems 2 to 6 are all solvable by one method? If the jars, in the order given, are labeled A, B, C, respectively, then the procedure which solves each of these problems may be characterized as $B - A - 2C$. That is, fill the center jar and from it fill the jar to the left once and the jar to the right twice; the amount of water remaining in the center jar is the required volume. Did you use this method in Problems 2 to 6?* Did you use it in any of the subsequent problems?

If you have not already discovered it, examination of the last five problems will reveal to you that they can be solved by procedures which are somewhat simpler than the $B - A - 2C$ procedure. Still calling the jars A, B, C, we can designate the simpler solution to Problem 7 as $A - C$, to Problem 8 as $A + C$, to Problem 10 as $A + C$, and to Problem 11 as $A - C$. Each of these problems is therefore solvable by addition or subtraction of the end jars and also by the $B - A - 2C$

---

* Two of these five tasks can be solved by methods other than the $B - A - 2C$ method. Problem 5 (9, 42, 6, get 21) can be solved as follows: $6 + 6 + 9 = 21$; and Problem 6 (20, 59, 4, get 31) can be solved as follows: $59 - 7 \times 4 = 31$. Some subjects in the basic experiment gave these solutions (Luchins, 1942, pp. 32-33).

method. Problem 9 cannot be solved by the $B - A - 2C$ method but can be solved by the $A - C$ method.

Did you persist in using the complex procedure, $B - A - 2C$, in the later problems? Did you overlook the simpler alternative in Problems 7, 8, 10, 11 and perhaps even fail Problem 9? If so, your behavior was similar to that exhibited by most of the people who have received these problems. In one investigation (Luchins, 1939; henceforth designated as the basic study), 1,039 subjects received all the problems you did.* It was found that 83 per cent of them used the $B - A - 2C$ procedure in Problems 7 and 8 and 64 per cent of them failed Problem 9. Contrast this with the results made by 970 comparable subjects (control group) who received only the last five problems; less than 1 per cent of them used the $B - A - 2C$ method in Problems 7 and 8, while only 5 per cent failed Problem 9. The differences are of course statistically reliable. The same direction of results (although not always with so very striking a difference between experimental and control groups) has been obtained by the authors through administration of this experiment to many thousands of subjects. The majority of the subjects rigidly adhered to one mode of solution and did not shift to a simpler method even when the method to which they had become habituated was no longer adequate.

Terminology

Differences between the control and experimental groups suggest that it is the experience of working with the first few problems which fosters the utilization or attempted utilization of the $B - A - 2C$ method in subsequent problems. We might refer to this as illustrating the adverse effects of past experience, the negative effects of habit, the deleterious influences of set, the workings of rigidity, etc. It was decided to use the term "Einstellung" and to say that the experience of solving the first few problems developed in the subject an Einstellung. This term is defined by Warren (1934, p. 371) as denoting a certain kind of set, a set which immediately predisposes an individual to one type of conscious or motor act. There were several reasons for this choice. For one thing, it was believed that the influence exerted by the first few problems was highly temporary in nature, that it immediately predisposed the individual to the $B - A - 2C$ method, but that this predisposition wore off very rapidly. (Subsequent experimentation led to the revision of this belief but at the time that our phenomenon was christened, the belief in

---

* In all our experiments, unless otherwise specifically stated, an individual had to solve at least Problems 5 and 6 by the $B - A - 2C$ method in order to have his responses included in the analysis and presentation of results.

its highly temporary nature prevailed.) For another, the term Einstellung had been used by Müller and Schumann (1898), by Werthei-mer (1923), and others to designate an *objective set*, one developed by the sequence of events in the actual experimental situation as distinguished from a set or attitude which is more "subjective" in nature, say, one which the subject brings to the experimental session. Since there was certainly something in the actual problem situation which fostered the set, we preferred to call it an objective set or Einstellung.

The experiment is therefore referred to as an Einstellung situation. Problems 2 to 6 are called the set-inducing or Einstellung or E problems, while Problems 7 to 11 are known as the test problems. Since one purpose in introducing a problem not solvable by the set method was to weaken or extinguish the Einstellung, Problem 9 is called the extinction problem. Problems 7, 8, 10, and 11, solvable by two methods, are called the critical problems. The $B - A - 2C$ method is described as the set or Einstellung or E method and the $A - C$ or $A + C$ procedures are described as the direct or d methods.

Utilization or attempted utilization of the $B - A - 2C$ procedure in the test problems is considered as (possible) evidence of the development of an Einstellung. For a group, the percentage of E solutions of Problems 7 and 8, considered as a unit, and the percentage of failures to solve Problem 9, are taken as indices of Einstellung (E) effects. Conversely, the percentages of direct solutions may serve as inverse indices of E effects. The increase in direct solutions in the last two critical problems, as compared with the first two, may be regarded as an index of the efficacy of the intervening extinction problem in weakening the set, in producing "recovery" from the Einstellung. The subject who fails the ninth problem may be regarded as showing rigid behavior since he adheres to the oft-repeated method (and thereby overlooks a simpler method), even when it is completely inadequate.

A VARIATIONAL PROCEDURE

While other procedures may be used in phenomenon-centered investigation, the one we used may be characterized as a variational procedure. Viewing the specific example of rigid behavior as unbiasedly as possible, we tried to see what factors and conditions were involved in it. Attempts were then made experimentally to manipulate these factors and conditions while observing what happened to rigid behavior. The rationale was that the specific case of rigidity under consideration might better be understood through such experimental variations, that its dynamics might be portrayed in terms of the changes of rigid behavior that were revealed as certain factors and conditions were changed. Clues for experimental variations came mainly from observational sources, from inspection of the original experimental design and the instructions, from keeping one's eyes and ears open during the experimental sessions, listening to subjects' comments, questioning the subjects, and sensing the prevailing social atmosphere during the experiment. Scores of experimental variations were administered to thousands of subjects; the main ones, many hitherto unpublished, are reported herein.

Systematization of the experimental variations was guided by a kind of "extremum principle"—by attempts to maximize or minimize the obtained degree of rigidity. It was hoped that a search for variables that tend to extremize rigidity of behavior in the case under observation, would enhance understanding of this case and of the functional relationship between the behavior and the variables. An "extremum principle" has proved useful in mathematics and the physical sciences as a systematizing principle in formulating and solving problems (Courant and Robbins, 1941). It also possesses potentialities, some virtually untapped, as a systematizing principle for psychological formulations and research.

In our work the "extremum principle" was essentially a guiding principle in the sense that we conducted variations which, on the basis of observational analysis, we thought might work to minimize or maximize E effects. For example, during the basic study it was noted that large E effects were usually yielded by elementary-school classes in which the children appeared to be tense, upset, worried about their "grades on the test," and hurried to get finished. Variations were therefore undertaken to influence these observed conditions in the elementary-school classes (1) by telling certain classes that the test was an important school test and that they must hurry, and by allowing them little time per problem, and (2) by telling other classes that the experiment was not a test and that they could have as much time as they wanted, and by not setting a time limit for solving the problems. Our hunch was that the first instructions would work to maximize and the latter to minimize E effects. It turned out that the speed conditions did maximize E effects whereas the nonspeed conditions did not minimize E effects. But neither the success of one hunch nor the failure of another required a decision to be made concerning the validity of a hypothesis testing the deductive power of any theory. Since the hunches had come from observational analysis, we returned to observational analysis (observing, listening to comments, questioning the children and the teachers) to try to discover why the variations yielded the results they did and to gain hints for new variations.

Directions of Variations

As has been indicated, experimental variations were suggested by observation and analysis of (1) the basic experimental procedure, (2) the quantitative results obtained when the basic experiment was administered to different subjects, (3) subjects' comments and other qualitative reactions, and (4) the social atmosphere prevailing during the experimental session. The experimental variations were then themselves observed and analyzed along similar lines, and, as a result, new experimental variations were developed. In this manner we were led to vary the test population, the task variables (including the problems, the time factor, the instructions), previous and subsequent experiences afforded the subject, the experimenters and their relations to the subject, and certain environmental variables. Below are presented in outline form examples of the kinds of variations worked out.

Populations Tested. The experiment was administered, in individual or group sessions, to males and females ranging from nine-year-old children to seventy-five-year-old adults, from those with no formal education to those who held several graduate degrees, from the feebleminded to those having superior intelligence, and from so-called normal individuals to hospitalized neuropsychiatric patients.

The Problems. Some of the variations in the problems are presented below.

(1) Number of Problems in the Series. We varied the number of set-inducing problems so that they ranged from zero to over 100. We also increased or decreased the number of critical and extinction problems beyond or below the number in the basic experiment.

(2) Order of Problems in the Series. The basic design was altered so that critical problems or extinction problems came before the E problems or were interspersed among them.

(3) Alterations Within the Problem. The order of the three jars in a problem was changed so that the largest jar was not always in the center. In one variation, the end jars were written in ink of one color and the center jar in ink of another color. Changes of this nature were made in all of the problems or only in the E problems or only in the test problems.

(4) Different Kinds of Problems. Some of the E problems in the basic experiment are solvable by a method other than $B - A - 2C$. New E tasks were therefore used each of which was solvable by a variety of procedures. In some experiments, problems were introduced which could not be solved by any method.

In some experiments, we added one or more containers to the containers given in each problem in the basic design. This meant that the subject had to select appropriate jars before he could use the E method.

(5) Alterations in the Relationship Between Set and Nonset Methods. New series of problems were used which involved new set and new nonset procedures. In some cases, both the set and nonset method required the use of all three jars but the set method was somewhat more complex. However, in other experiments the relative complexity of the methods was altered so that the method which solved the *E* problems was much simpler than the nonset method.

(6) Alterations in the Relationship Between the Method and the Goal. The *E* problems in the basic experiment involve a fixed method. New *E* problems were used in which, not the method, but the goal (the required volume of water) was the same for each problem. Still other *E* tasks involved both a fixed method and a fixed goal; here the test problems were incomplete tasks which the subject could complete to conform either to the practiced method or to the fixed goal, so that we could test the relative strength of a method set and a goal set.

(7) Variations in the Nature of the Material. The basic design was concretized by introducing actual containers, scaled to size, and an actual source of fluid. The paradigm of the basic design was also applied to different kinds of material, including mazes, geometric problems, hidden-word puzzles, jig-saw puzzles, and reasoning tasks.

The Time Factor. Let us now turn to some of the variations related to the time factor.

(1) Time per Problem. In the basic experiment about two minutes were allowed per problem. The time allotment was varied from a small fraction of a minute to no time limitation. In some cases one time allotment served for each *E* task and another for each test task.

(2) Time Between Problems. Some experiments varied the time between successive problems or introduced different time intervals between the *E* tasks and the test tasks. Time intervals, ranging from a few seconds to over one month, were introduced before the presentation of the extinction task and/or the last two criticals.

(3) Experiences During Time Intervals. In some cases no attempt was made to control the subject's activity during the introduced time intervals. In other cases, tasks of various kinds were assigned during the time intervals.

(4) Estimation of Time. Before he solved each problem, the subject was asked, in some cases, to estimate the time it would take. After its completion, he was told his time of solution. In other words, the so-called "level of aspiration" with regard to time was compared with the "level of achievement."

The Factor of Instructions. Some of the ways in which the instructions were altered are listed below.

(1) The instructions were altered with the specific intent of ruling out the possible assumption, on the subject's part, that he must use all the given jars, or that he must begin with the center jar or must begin with the largest jar, or that he must subtract.

(2) Subjects were told that they were to try to find as many methods of solving each problem as possible. This instruction was issued prior to the presentation of the problems in their entirety or just prior to the presentation of the first test problem.

(3) Subjects were told that the important matter was to finish all the problems as rapidly as possible.

(4) Subjects were told to take their time and to view each problem as a separate item.

(5) Warnings of various sorts were issued aimed at minimizing E effects; for example, before the first test task was given, subjects were told to write the words "Don't be blind" or were told, "Now you must not use the previous method any more."

(6) The source of fluid, actual or hypothetical, was fixed at a certain amount. The subject was told that the stipulated amount of fluid would suffice to solve all the problems if he did not waste fluid unnecessarily. The stipulated amount was such that it would suffice if the test problems were solved by the direct method but would not suffice if they were solved by the E method. In some experiments the subjects were warned that they would lose half credit or full credit for each problem in which they unnecessarily wasted fluid.

(7) Subjects were told, sometimes during the experiment, to try to generalize a rule or formula of solution.

Previous and Subsequent Experiences. Prior to receiving the usual problems, some subjects were afforded experiences of various kinds. For some, the $B - A - 2C$ method was taught as a general rule of solution. Others received a critical problem (solvable by $B - A - 2C$ and a direct method) before the usual design. Other previous experiences included variable problems, each solvable by a number of methods. Still others were given experience in making water-jar measuring problems. Some were afforded experiences with different kinds of set-creating tasks or with different series of problems.

Subsequent experiences of different kinds were also provided. Problems solvable only by the $B - A - 2C$ method were introduced following the completion of the basic experiment to see whether a subject who had employed the direct method in the test problems would now be able to shift back to the E method, that is, to see whether he had perhaps developed a set for the direct procedure. Some subjects received a battery of tests, one immediately after the other, or with various time intervals between them. They were founded on the basic design but involved different kinds of material. For example, an individual first received the jar problems, then the mazes, and finally various picture series. Other subjects were given the basic experiment (involving the jar problems) more than once, in order to see how they would behave in successive presentations. Still others received the basic design under various conditions of administration, e.g., first as the basic experiment and then as a speed test, or first involving hypothetical jars and then the corresponding concrete jars.

The Experimenters. The experimenter was chosen so that his age was younger, older, or the same as the subject's, so that he was of the same or different sex as the subject, and so that he had considerable or little prestige value. In addition, the experimenter's manner varied so that in some cases he was a friendly, easygoing, apparently warm individual and in other cases a more cold and formal or even autocratic person. In some cases the problems were so presented that each of them was offered by a different person in the room. We wondered whether diverse sources, in place of one source, would influence Einstellung behavior.

Environmental Factors. Different environments or atmospheres were perforce created by the introduction of diverse task variables and different experimenters. In addition, specific attempts were made to study the influence of various kinds of social atmospheres on Einstellung behavior. Thus the experiment was administered as a game at an informal party. At the other extreme, efforts were made to create a tense, stressful atmosphere by presenting the experiment in a school setting as a speed test or as an intelligence test.

Appeal to Theories

After over a decade of experimental variations derived from observational analysis, we turned to theories for suggestions as to what might maximize or minimize E effects. Each of the theories of rigidity described in the earlier chapters was focused upon the selected case. Although these theories differed considerably "in the large," it was found that the differences did not tend to be so great "in the small"—that is, when applied to one specific case. Several of the theories yielded essentially similar suggestions or predictions concerning E effects. For example, most of the psychoanalytic orientations suggested that rigid behavior would tend to be greater under conditions that spell anxiety or danger than under less stressful conditions, and that neurotics would tend to show more rigidity than normals. The theories of Goldstein, Lewin, and Werner gave rise to the prediction that rigid behavior would increase with age and that feeble-minded individuals would tend to show greater rigidity than normals of the same chronological age. It is noteworthy that the theories of rigidity gave rise to fewer experimental variations than had observational analysis and that most of the variations suggested by the theories had previously been suggested by observational analysis. There were some exceptions; for example, the Lewin-Kounin concept of rigidity suggested the study of the relation of E effects to cosatiation indices, and several theories suggested the correlation of E effects with scores on various tests, such as tests of the concrete or abstract attitude.

The question may be raised whether an appeal to theories violates a phenomenon-centered approach. It seems to us that it does not. A phenomenon-centered orientation is not inherently adverse to theories; rather, it holds that naive observation of the phenomenon should precede any appeal to a theory since a theory can blind one to certain aspects of the phenomenon. It will be remembered that we first immersed ourselves in observational analysis before appealing to the theories and even then we did not get involved in theoretical ramifications. Moreover, deliberate use of *different* theories, as in the variational approach, lessens the danger of being blinded to aspects of the phenomenon. It may, in fact, result in viewing the phenomenon from new points of view.

Focusing of various theories upon one case of behavior may be considered as yielding multitheoretical interpretations of the case. Multitheoretical interpretations are not synonymous with an eclectic approach since they do not presuppose synthesis of portions of the various theories into one "eclectic" or combined theory. Multitheoretical interpretations are not common in psychology since it is customary for the investigator to offer one theoretical interpretation; he is, so to speak, usually a theoretical monist, at least with reference to any one study.

Moreover, there is a difference in the role accorded theories. It is not unusual to find a theory treated as an *objective* of science rather than as a *tool* (cf. Marx, 1951a for a discussion of the different outlooks). Our phenomenon-centered approach views theories as primarily tools used in efforts to further understanding of the case under investigation. Hence, there is no need to become sidetracked from the case under investigation in order to defend or attack a theory, to patch weak spots in a theory, or to get involved in theoretical controversies. In short, even throughout the theoretical explorations, the focal point of interest remains the concrete example under consideration. We are interested in making decisions concerning what maximizes or minimizes the phenomena rather than in making decisions concerning the relative deductive power of various theories.

A Note on the Einstellung Test

The basic experiment and variations of it have been used by many investigators (cf. Taylor, 1955) as tests of rigidity. A version which the writers have used as a clinical test of rigidity will be briefly described. It is referred to as the "arithmetical Einstellung test" or "volume-measuring test" to distinguish it from the "basic experiment." The test differs from the basic experiment in that it involves a greater number and variety of test tasks. After the E tasks, four criticals are given; the first two criticals are similar to the criticals in the basic experiment, while the next two are solvable not only by the E method and by the usual direct methods ($A - C$ or $A + C$) but also by simply filling one jar. Ten extinction tasks are then given. (When the test is group administered, four extinction tasks are often used.) After the extinction tasks, four criticals similar to the ones described above are presented. Finally, two problems are given, one solvable by methods not used in any of the preceding tasks and one solvable only by the E method.

The examiner is interested in whether and how the subject varied his mode of solution. Did he vary within the E tasks themselves (some can be solved by methods other than the E method)? Did he first shift from the E method when a solution involving two jars was possible or when a one-jar solution was possible, or when the E method no longer was applicable or only after failing one or more extinction tasks? How many extinction tasks did he fail? If he solved several extinction tasks, did he become habituated to the method used in these tasks; that is, did he substitute one mechanized habit for another? The last question may be answered by analysis of the responses made to the problems following the extinction tasks. The examiner is interested in whether the subject solved criticals that require a method other than that used in the extinction tasks, how many jars he used in the solutions, whether he was able to deal with the problem solvable by methods not used in any of the preceding tasks, and whether he now failed a task solvable only by the $B - A - 2C$ method.

Quick indices of the extent of rigid behavior are furnished by the point of shift to the direct method and by the number of extinction tasks failed. But it is preferable, particularly in using the test as a clinical instrument, to undertake a thorough analysis of behavior during the entire examination.

The paradigm of the arithmetical Einstellung test of rigidity has also been used in devising tests involving mazes, hidden words, word blocks, and series of pictures. Together, they constitute a battery of tests described in detail in manuals (Luchins, 1948, 1950a) distributed by the Veterans Administration.

ORGANIZATION OF EXPERIMENTAL VARIATIONS

Several plans were considered for the exposition of the results of the experiments. One plan was to present the variations in sequence, according to the extent of E effects they had yielded. But this meant grouping together experiments which had little in common except their outcome. Another plan was to arrange the experiments according to what had been varied, say the factor of time or the factor of instructions. The difficulty here was that many experiments varied more than one factor.

It was finally decided to group the experiments under headings pertaining to various concepts and issues relevant to rigidity. Such an arrangement has the advantage of heightening the potential value of the experiments to psychologists who may not be interested in the water-jug-problem E effect per se, since it allows the results of the experiments to be seen in the broader context of various issues that have arisen concerning rigidity. In order to tie together the experiments and the theories presented in earlier chapters, the introduction to a group of experiments generally reminds the reader of the roles the related concept played in various theories. This should not be interpreted to mean that the theories suggested all the described experiments. For example, the chapter on anxiety and rigidity recalls the role anxiety plays in various theories of rigidity, but most of the experiments described therein were derived, not from these theories, but from observational analysis. To take another example: the section on age and intelligence recalls the role that these factors play in various theories of rigidity, but most of the experiments dealt with in the section were conducted in the interest of studying various populations and without recourse to the theories.

In order to enrich the presentation, there are included, not only the experiments conducted by the writers and their students, but also experiments conducted by some of the many other investigators who in the past decade have used Einstellung experiments in their studies of rigidity. Moreover, where it seems relevant to do so, concepts and issues pertinent to rigidity are subjected to critical evaluation on the basis of the experimental findings.

Chapter V

PSYCHOLOGICAL STRESS AND RIGIDITY

P SYCHOANALYSTS, whether traditional or not, accept the dictum that anxiety and danger to the ego intensify behavioral rigidity. Psychologists also assert that rigidity is produced or heightened by tensions due to anxiety, frustrations, shock, and catastrophic situations. Thus, Goldstein (1939, 1943) regards a catastrophic situation as a prerequisite for secondary rigidity and Werner (1946b, p. 43) writes that lack of variability appears as a behavior trait of frustrated individuals. Similarly Maier, who has conducted extensive investigations of abnormal fixations in animals, concludes that "frustration tends to fixate or freeze a sample of behavior" (1949, p. 35). These dicta have permeated psychological and educational theory and practice.

It is widely accepted that frustrating agents and anxiety-provoking situations should be avoided in teaching, child training, psychotherapy, and, more generally, whenever and wherever one wishes to change behavior and minimize rigidity. It is, therefore, of considerable interest, both theoretically and practically, to investigate the influence of frustration and anxiety in the selected case.

SPEED-TEST CONDITIONS AS A SOURCE OF STRESS

We attempted to create an anxiety-provoking social atmosphere in elementary-school classes by presenting the basic experiment (described in the preceding chapter) as a speed test. After the method of solution for the first E problem had been illustrated, the children were told that they were to be timed while working on the remaining problems, all of which had previously been written on the blackboard. They were told to work as quickly as they could since speed of response would be taken into account in determining their scores. As soon as a subject finished, he was instructed to bring his paper to the experimenter so that his time of completion could be recorded. The children were also told that the principal of the school and the teachers would examine the papers, and that report-card grades and grade placement would be influenced by the test scores. While the children were working, the experimenter expressed astonishment that they had not yet finished, claimed that they were very slow, and said that children in lower grades had usually finished in less time.

When this speed-test experiment was administered to seven classes, we observed strained and even tearful faces (Luchins, 1942, p. 55). In the discussion after the experiment, the children spoke of having been worried, upset, and afraid. Some said that all they could think of was subtraction and hurrying. Some hoped never again to get such a test.

The quantitative results indicate marked rigidity. Of ninety-eight children, only two used the direct method in the test problems and only three solved the extinction task. Most classes showed 100 per cent E solution of the criticals and 100 per cent failure to solve the extinction problem. Many children used the E method in this problem, writing $76 - 28 - 3 - 3 = 25$, whereas the method actually yields an answer of 42. Whereas comparable groups that participated in the basic experiment yielded from 52 to 88 per cent E solution of the criticals (average of 70 per cent), the speed-test groups yielded from 93 to 100 per cent (average of 98 per cent). This completely bimodal distribution is again revealed in the responses to the extinction problem: failures in the comparable groups taking the basic test ranged from 39 to 76 per cent (average of 58 per cent), whereas failures to solve this problem under speed-test conditions ranged from 93 to 100 per cent (average of 97 per cent).

The speed-test experiment was also administered to eight college classes. Since direct references to report cards were inappropriate, the students were told that the test was part of an intelligence test and much ado was made over the fact that they were being timed. Time was indicated by a large clock on the wall, by an arrangement of stop watches on the experimenter's desk, and by the recording of minutes on the blackboard. During the experiment the students were repeatedly told that elementary-school children usually had finished in less time.

In contrast to the rather carefree atmosphere existing in college classes during the usual presentation of the basic experiment, there was now a tense atmosphere. Subjects reported that they had felt anxious, under strain, and "nervous." The ninety college students averaged 93 per cent E solution of the criticals as compared with 82 per cent averaged by college classes that participated in the basic experiment. The difference is even more striking for the extinction task, for which the speed-test groups averaged 84 per cent failure as compared with 56 per cent failure for those taking the basic experiment. In the speed test, college students, for the first time, applied the E method to the extinction problem; 14 per cent made this error.

Although there were significantly greater E effects under speed-test conditions, it must be emphasized that speed of solution was not in and of itself an indicant of E effect. Indeed, in some classes the first subject to hand in his paper had direct solutions of every test problem. It was seeing others hand in their papers while they themselves were still not finished, some subjects later admitted, that intensified their fear and nervousness. Not speed alone, but the subject's reaction to the emphasis on speed, increased rigidity.

Further evidence of the deleterious effects of the speed-test atmosphere is the fact that it vitiated prior attempts at preventing rigidity (Luchins, 1942, p. 79). For example, prior to receiving any of the problems, upperclassmen at Brooklyn College were given illustrations of how children had developed a mental set in solving arithmetical problems (variations of the basic problems) and how the children had overlooked direct solutions. The college students were told to keep their eyes open and try to do problems in the most direct way instead of just mechanically repeating a method; they were admonished not to fall into the same trap that the children had fallen into. When the basic experiment was then administered, there were revealed very little E effects; but, when it was administered as a speed test, considerable E effects were revealed. The percentages for the groups given the experiment under nonspeed and speed conditions are set forth in the summary just below. (In the summary, "C" stands for "critical"; "F," for "failure"; and "E," of course for "Einstellung.")

Clarification,
 then basic
 experiment .... 15 col. students C_1C_2: 10% E Ext.: 7% F C_3C_4: 0% E

Clarification, then
 speed test .... 11 col. students C_1C_2: 55% E Ext.: 55% F C_3C_4: 55% E

Subjects taking the speed test reported that they realized that they should have watched out for tricky, easy problems but that they had been unable to do so because of their nervous tension and haste.

The experiment was also administered as a speed test to an elementary-school class that had received the basic experiment three months before (Luchins, 1942, p. 56). Whereas readministration of the experiment after such a time lapse usually resulted in about the same or somewhat less E effects, under speed-test conditions E effects were greater than before.

Basic experiment
 three months
 later .... 35 elem.-sch. students C_1C_2: 60% E Ext.: 40% F C_3C_4: 51% E

Speed test
 three months
 later .... 35 elem.-sch. students C_1C_2: 100% E Ext.: 88% F C_3C_4: 100% E

These findings high-light the role that speed-test conditions of work may play in determining the extent of rigidity.

Maze Tracing as a Stressful Situation

Observations during the basic experiment revealed that elementary-school children who were poor in arithmetic (as shown by their low grades and by their remedial training in arithmetic) tended to be anxious and concerned about the calculations involved in the problems and also experienced some difficulties in carrying out the calculations; these children tended to show very large E effects. (See Luchins, 1942, p. 79 for data regarding this point.) This suggested to us that E effects may be fostered by difficulties involved in the execution of the task, difficulties in using the means to a goal. But there was the possibility that the noted E effects were related to the particular kind of remedial-arithmetic training the subjects had had or to their relatively low arithmetic and general intellectual ability. It seemed advisable to separate arithmetic and intellectual ability from difficulty in the execution of a task. To this end, it was decided to use mirror tracing of the pencil-and-paper mazes (Luchins, 1942, p. 24), which is not arithmetical in nature and involves relatively little intellectual ability. Tracing of a circuitous, twisting path to the goal box constituted the E method.

McGill University students, tested individually, were given the mazes under mirror tracing or normal tracing conditions (Shulman, 1951 and Luchins, 1954). The initial instructions were:

You are required to find a nonobstructed path from the arrow [starting point] to the X [goal box] and trace this path . . . this type of test is usually included in an over-all test of intelligence. I am going to count the number of errors you make, that is, the number of times you go into a wrong path and the number of times you go outside the lines of the figure. And I am going to time you. The smoother and faster you trace, the better score you will achieve.

When a subject went beyond the bounds of the path, he had to return to the starting place.

Tracing of the direct, straight path proved a facile process under normal and mirror tracing. Tracing of the circuitous path was achieved within a few seconds outside of the mirror, but mirror tracers found it difficult to keep within the bounds of the circuitous path, tended to veer from the path at the turning points, and took as long as ten minutes to achieve an accurate tracing. Moreover, mirror tracing (but not normal tracing) was accompanied by overt signs of anxiety and frustration, including fidgeting, sweating, clamping of elbows on the table, groaning and cursing, and comments that the task was annoying and frustrating.

Twenty-two subjects received the mazes in the mirror apparatus and an equal number got them for normal tracing. For mirror tracing, 89 per cent gave E solutions of Criticals 1 and 2 as compared with 71 per cent for normal tracing. Attempts to follow the circuitous route in the extinction maze were made by 68 per cent of the mirror tracers but only by 32 per cent of the others. While following the E route in the extinction maze, some subjects realized that it did not lead to the goal and abandoned it for the direct route, but others followed the E route into the goal box, and thus crossed the line intended as a barrier and failed the task. The 55 per cent failure in the mirror situation was significantly greater than the 18 per cent failure in the nonmirror situation.

The experiment did not end for the subject with the Critical 4 maze. A subject who had received the mazes under mirror tracing conditions, immediately afterwards received the same series under normal tracing conditions, while a subject who had traced them normally now got them in the mirror apparatus. The re-presentations were marked by signs of greater effort and anxiety on the part of the mirror tracers although not so pronounced as in the initial presentation. While groaning over the set-inducing mazes, many of the mirror tracers commented that they wished the easy mazes would come soon or said that they were glad that the short path would soon be unblocked. Subjects apparently realized that they were again receiving the same series and transferred understanding of or insight into the nature of the series which they had gained in the initial presentation. The re-presentation yielded the same results in or out of the mirror; only one subject in each case used the circuitous route in the criticals and no one attempted to use it in the extinction task. These findings suggest that insight into the nature of the series and/or the accompanying expectation of the easier method, sufficed to nullify the influences that might have been exerted on E effects by the greater difficulties and frustrations involved in mirror tracing.

It is of interest to compare college students' responses to the mazes with the responses of neurotics. Hospitalized in Montreal, the neurotics tested had been diagnosed as suffering from anxiety neuroses. In view of the diagnosis and the tension evinced by the patients, it was decided to modify the initial instructions by eliminating references to an intelligence test and to a better score. The patient was told that he was to be timed and that it would count as an error each time he went into an obstructed path or outside the bounds of a path. Neurotics who first received the mazes for mirror tracing showed more symptoms of effort, frustration, and anxiety, than did neurotics who first received the mazes for normal tracing. In line with the thesis that anxiety heightens E effects, the mirror tracers showed somewhat greater E effects than did those who traced without the mirror.

Mirror   .... 18 neurotics C_1C_2: 77% E Ext.: 39% E attempts, 22% F
Nonmirror   .... 18 neurotics C_1C_2: 62% E Ext.: 10% E attempts, 19% F

Signs of anxiety and frustration during mirror tracing were more pronounced for the neurotics than they had been for the college students. This observation, together with the patients' diagnosis and the intimate relationship widely assumed to hold between neurosis and anxiety, led to the expectation of greater E effects on the part of the neurotics. But the findings contradicted this expectation since the college students showed more E solutions, more E attempts, and significantly more failures of the extinction maze.

Mirror .... 22 col. stud. $C_1 C_2$: 89% E Ext.: 68% E attempts, 55% F
Mirror .... 18 neurotics $C_1 C_2$: 77% E Ext.: 39% E attempts, 22% F

One might interpret this finding as possibly related to differences in age and intelligence (the neurotics were a few years older and had somewhat lower I.Q.'s than the college students). Or one might hypothesize that reference to an intelligence test and a better score, made only to the students, sufficed to increase their specific anxiety with reference to the maze situation beyond that experienced by the neurotics. A point in line with this interpretation is the finding that, even when the mazes were first presented for nonmirror tracing, the college students had somewhat greater E solutions and E attempts than the neurotics (but about the same percentage of failures). Speaking against this interpretation is the observation that symptoms of anxiety and frustration, during mirror or nonmirror tracing, were more pronounced for the neurotics than for the students. Another plausible interpretation is that the neurotics' intense anxiety and frustration led to abandonment of the E route more readily than did the milder psychological stress experienced by the students. This implies that the relationship between anxiety and rigidity is not monotonic, but that, under certain conditions, greater anxiety may foster change while somewhat lesser anxiety may still make for adherence to a frustrating procedure.

When the mazes were presented to eighteen psychotics in the same hospital as the neurotics, they showed about the same E effects as the neurotics under comparable tracing conditions, or slightly less, and, hence, considerably less than the students. But in the second presentation of the mazes (under mirror conditions for those who first traced without a mirror; under nonmirror conditions for those who previously traced using a mirror), the neurotics, as well as the psychotics, showed somewhat greater E effects than did the students during the re-presentation. This suggests that the patients may have seen less resemblance between the two presentations, may have learned less from the first series, or may have transferred less adequately any insight developed during the first presentation.

HIDDEN-WORD TEST AS A STRESSFUL SITUATION FOR STUTTERERS

In still another way we studied the influence on E effects of anxiety and difficulties that stemmed from the very act of executing a task. In the administration of the hidden-word Einstellung experiment (Luchins, 1942, p. 25), it was noted incidentally that individuals with speech difficulties tended to show large E effects. It seemed worth while, therefore, to compare the oral performances on the hidden-word Einstellung test of individuals with and without pronounced speech difficulties.

The data was collected by Solomon (1953), who tested thirteen male college students diagnosed as stutterers at the University of Michigan's speech clinic and thirteen male students rated as fluent speakers by speech instructors. Each fluent speaker was paired with one of the stutterers according to age and class level. Tested individually, the subjects received three tests from Luchins' rigidity manual: the maze test under mirror-tracing conditions as a performance task, the arithmetical test as a written task, and the hidden-word test as an oral task. The order of presentation of the tests was varied but was the same for each matched pair (stutterer and fluent speaker). To enhance the anxiety-arousing potential of the hidden-word test, it was always introduced as "the speech test."

No consistent or significant differences prevailed between stutterers and nonstutterers on either the arithmetical or mirror-maze test. But the hidden-word test yielded striking and significant differences. For the fluent speakers, E solution of the first two criticals averaged only 4 per cent, while, for the stutterers, it averaged 58 per cent. Moreover, the fluent speakers required a mean time of 4.0 seconds per critical whereas the stutterers required 6.2 seconds. That the direction of this result cannot be attributed to a general slowness of stutterers on oral tasks, is indicated by the fact that they took somewhat less time than the nonstutterers on the set-inducing tasks. In the extinction tasks and subsequent criticals, stutterers also showed somewhat more failures and more E solutions than nonstutterers.

What may have happened to the stutterers was that, once they discovered a method of finding words, they concentrated on the oral communication of the words obtained. Because of their speech difficulties, the speech execution of the found word—and not the method of obtaining it—became the central aspect of their task. Here, as in the mirror mazes, difficulties of executing a means to a goal led to a focusing on the execution of the means rather than on the goal or on better means of reaching the goal.

Further Studies of Frustration and Threat

Other investigators, employing modified arithmetical Einstellung tests, have sought to arouse anxiety and frustration. Christie (1949) tested thirty college students who gave E solutions to a critical that followed E problems; they then received a task requiring the connection of geometric figures with nonintersecting lines. For half the subjects this task was solvable and they were allowed as much time as they desired; for the others it was unsolvable and they were allowed two minutes. Those who had the unsolvable task took significantly longer to solve a subsequent arithmetical extinction task. Christie also divided thirty junior-high-school students into ten "low frustrates" and twenty "high frustrates" on the basis of the degree to which they appeared to be frustrated by the unsolvable task. The "high frustrates" took significantly longer to solve the subsequent extinction problem and made significantly more attempts to use the set method in attempting to solve it.

Before administering volume-measuring problems, Harris (1951) sought to create anxiety in each of eighteen college students by adopting a formal, aggressive, critical attitude; by saying that the subject's personality and intellectual ability were being evaluated; by interpreting responses to a questionnaire as revealing unconscious neurotic tendencies; and by evaluating the subject's performance on an unsolvable geometric problem as the "worst" he had seen. For eighteen other students he tried to be friendly and informal and gave no questionnaire or unsolvable task. Those tested under anxiety-provoking conditions took significantly longer to solve an arithmetical extinction problem.

Cowen (1950), prior to the presentation of E problems to four groups of twenty-five college students, subjected each group to a preliminary situation. The situations were: (1) a control situation involving no attempt at anxiety, (2) a peripheral frustration situation involving an unsolvable geometric problem, (3) a central threat expected–praise received situation (central to the ego) in which the Levy movement test was introduced as a personality test and the performance praised, and (4) a central threat expected–threat received situation in which the Levy movement test was introduced in the same way but the performance was negatively evaluated. E effects increased from Situation 1 through Situation 4, and the conclusion was drawn that the stronger the threat to the ego, the greater the E effects.

Common to all these studies is the use of an unsolvable task as a frustrating agent.* The underlying assumption apparently was that fail-

---

* It is interesting to note how unacceptable and frustrating the very notion of an unsolvable problem can be to some individuals. One of the writers, while teaching elementary college mathematics, found students who rebelled at the idea of

ure would arouse frustration and frustration would enhance maladaptive perseverative behavior. Actually Christie found that some subjects were not frustrated by the unsolvable task, that individuals differed in the extent to which they were upset by the task, and that some subjects were apparently upset or frustrated by minor errors they made in the solvable task. There does not seem to be a simple relationship between failure and frustration or between solution and nonfrustration. Nor does it seem plausible to us that there is a simple relationship between failure and E effects. In the basic experiment (Luchins, 1942), we know that some subjects failed the extinction task and yet went on to give direct solutions of subsequent criticals. What happened in some cases was that the experience of attempting to solve the extinction task made the subjects realize that the E method was not always applicable and led to a fresh view of the subsequent problems. Now, the extinction task is similar in appearance to the other arithmetical tasks in the basic experiment and can be solved, whereas the interpolated geometric problems in some studies just reviewed differed markedly from the arithmetical tasks and were unsolvable. The question therefore arose: How are E effects influenced by similarity or dissimilarity between the interpolated tasks and the arithmetical tasks, and by solvability or unsolvability of the interpolated tasks?

An experimental attack on this question was made by Cynthia Lewin (1951). In individual administration, she gave New York City elementary-school children five E problems, two criticals, four interpolated tasks, two more criticals, and, finally, an extinction problem. The eighty children who used the E method in all the set-inducing problems and the first two criticals, were divided into four equal groups based on the kind of interpolated tasks received. The group given solvable, dissimilar tasks received solvable hidden-word tasks considered by the experimenter as dissimilar to the arithmetical problems. For the unsolvable-dissimilar group, the first two hidden-word tasks were solvable but the last two unsolvable. The solvable-similar group received solvable potato problems in each of which there were given three (hypothetical) bushels with a stipulated number of whole potatoes in each, and the task was to distribute the potatoes so that there would be an equal number of

---

unsolvable mathematical problems. They felt that with sufficient ingenuity and knowledge any problem can be solved. This refusal or perhaps inability to grasp the concept of a problem which is impossible of solution (as opposed to a problem which has not yet been solved), as well as the attendant refusal or inability to grasp how it is possible to prove mathematically that something is impossible, may account for the perennial attempts by nonmathematicians to prove the possibility of trisecting any angle or of squaring the circle by means of straightedge and compass alone in spite of the fact that both have been proved impossible (Richardson, 1941, c. VIII).

whole potatoes in each bushel; the potato problems were considered by the experimenter as similar to the arithmetical problems. For the unsolvable-similar group, the first two potato problems were solvable but the last two unsolvable.

The studies reviewed earlier in this section could not compare the strength of E effects before and after the unsolvable task. But this could be done in the Lewin study. It was found that percentages of E effects were always less in the criticals after the interpolated tasks than in the prior criticals. This suggests that the interpolated tasks, whether solvable or unsolvable, whether similar or dissimilar to the arithmetical tasks, tended to weaken the set. Moreover, the least E effects in the subsequent criticals occurred for the groups receiving the unsolvable tasks. E solution of all the criticals coupled with failure of the extinction task occurred for 70 per cent of the children in both the solvable-dissimilar group and the solvable-similar group; but it occurred for only 55 per cent of the unsolvable-dissimilar group and for only 35 per cent of the unsolvable-similar group; the difference between the unsolvable-similar group and each of the other groups was significant at the 0.01 level.

Why did less E effects occur after the unsolvable interpolated tasks than after the solvable ones, and why did the least occur after the unsolvable tasks similar to the arithmetical problems? That the same method which worked in the first two interpolated tasks did not work in the last two, might have led some children to question the general applicability of the method. This attitude might then have been transferred, so that the children questioned the general applicability of the E method to all volume-measuring problems. It is plausible that transfer would be greater after potato tasks, which were arithmetical in nature, than after the dissimilar hidden-word tasks. Moreover, the solvable or unsolvable character of a problem could more readily be discovered in the potato tasks than in the hidden-word tasks; a child might be quite confident that a given sum of potatoes could not be divided into three equal piles whereas he might wonder whether there was a hidden word which he had overlooked. Insight into the unsolvability of the potato problems might have fostered careful examination of the subsequent problems; might have aroused suspicion concerning the problems, the experimenter, or the assumption that all the jar problems could be solved or solved in one way; or might conceivably have led to other attitudes conducive to disruption of the Einstellung. (Insight into the unsolvable character of the interpolated geometric problems used in the various investigations alluded to above, depended on a knowledge of mathematical topology, presumably possessed by few or none of the subjects; moreover, one of the reports explicitly notes that a subject who mentioned that the problem was unsolvable was falsely assured that it was solvable.)

Whatever may be the reasons for Cynthia Lewin's results, it is important to note that the children who received unsolvable tasks showed more overt signs of anxiety and frustration than did those who received the solvable tasks. Her findings cast doubt on the generality of the thesis that frustration, as induced by failure to solve a problem, necessarily preserves or strengthens rigidity.

EVALUATION OF CONDITIONS OF WORK

In the experiments described thus far in this chapter, conditions of work did not favor a change from the E method to the direct method. A mirror tracer absorbed in the difficulties of following the circuitous route, or a stutterer concentrating on executing a speech pattern, is focused on only one aspect of the problem situation—a particular method —and is not facing the situation freely to see whether there are better methods of solution. Likewise, a subject who feels anxious—because of a tense social atmosphere, the need for haste, the experimenter's hostile attitude, his failure on a supposedly simple problem, his results on a personality test, etc.—is focused on himself, his inadequacies, or his feeling of uneasiness, rather than on the problem-solving situation. We wondered whether conditions of work could be introduced that would focus the subject on the problems and make him more alert to the need for change. In particular, we wondered whether psychological stresses could be made to enhance the possibility of shift to the direct method, could be made to work against rigidity. Experimental attempts to study these issues will now be described.

Relaxed Conditions of Work

The speed-test experiments emphasized that a test was being given and that a subject might get a poor grade on the test. Subjects in these experiments, as we have seen, seemed to be concerned about how well they did on the test and reported that they were worried, upset, afraid, anxious, under strain, or nervous. If we could get subjects to relax, not to regard the experiment as a test, and not to be anxious about their performances, would E effects disappear?

In attempts to answer this question, we enlisted the services of several students in an undergraduate experimental-psychology class of one of the writers. Each of these students, in a casual and offhand manner, asked a fellow student—while the latter was in his room in the dormitory or in the student lounge or in the study hall—to "please do me a favor and help me check these problems that I have to use in the lab tomorrow." The problems of the basic experiment were then presented one at a time, with the usual two-and-one-half-minute maximum time allotment per problem. After the experiment, each subject was interviewed by the student assistant in an attempt to ascertain the subject's reactions to the experiment. On the basis of the subjects' comments and observations of their behavior during the interview and the experiment itself, we selected only those subjects who apparently had a relaxed, carefree, casual attitude toward the problems, who did not consider that they had taken a test, and who did not seem concerned about how their performance would affect their status. In short, we selected those subjects who did not report that they were, and who did not seem to be, anxious, nervous, upset, under strain, etc., as had subjects under speed-test conditions. The experiment was conducted until twenty subjects met the described criteria. Analysis of the solutions of the problems by these twenty subjects, considered as a group, showed that 70 per cent gave E solutions to Criticals 1 and 2 and 35 per cent failed the extinction task, results which are within the range found in the basic experiment. Those who failed the extinction problem did not regard it as an indication of failure on their part; rather they noted that this problem did not "check" and some behaved as if they were pleased that they had helped their fellow student by discovering that one problem was an error. No subject used the maximum time allotment in any problem.

These results show that E effects, although not as great as under speed-test conditions, were manifested under apparently relaxed, carefree conditions of work. Attitudes of subjects toward the tasks and toward their performances, including their failures to attain solution, were radically different than under speed-test conditions; and, possibly, the processes that brought about E effects also differed under the different conditions. In the present experiment, although subjects were relaxed, they were not relaxed to the point of being indifferent to the problems or uncritical; they were helping to "check" the problems. Variations should also be conducted in which attempts are made to relax subjects to the extent that they become uncritical, indifferent to the tasks, and have a superficial relation to the problems. While such variations remain to be conducted, it is known that subjects in the basic study who seemed to have such attitudes usually showed large E effects.

Nonspeed Conditions

Under speed-test conditions very large E effects were obtained. It is conceivable that the E effects obtained even in the basic experiment were related to the fact that the subjects were timed (two and a half minutes allowed per problem). Perhaps they reacted to the timing with tension and anxiety; perhaps they felt that they had to hurry and, therefore, did not take time out to look at the problems carefully in order to discover a better solution. Speaking against this conjecture is the observation that most subjects in the basic experiment finished each of the problems (with the exception of the extinction task) well within the time allotted and spent the remainder of the time waiting for the next task. Nonetheless, it was decided to relax time limits.

With the timing eliminated, there resulted E effects as great as those in the basic experiment. It was therefore decided explicitly to tell subjects to look for the best possible solution to each problem. Elementary-school children (Luchins, 1942, p. 57) were given this instruction and were also told that the next problem would not be presented until everyone in the class was satisfied with his solution. If a pupil finished before the others, he was told to spend the extra time examining anew the problem on the blackboard and examining his answer in order to make sure that he had the best possible answer. With each problem, the experimenter inquired, "Are you sure you don't want to work on it any longer? Are you satisfied with your answer?" The children took from three to six minutes per problem except in the extinction task. In view of their fidgeting and strained faces while working on the extinction task, we told them after ten minutes that somewhat too much time was being spent on this problem and that we would discard it so that they could all go on to the next problem. Despite the relaxation on timing and the instructions to search for better solutions, E effects were as great as in comparable groups doing the basic experiment.

30 elem.-sch. students .... C_1C_2: 90% E Ext.: 83% F C_3C_4: 95% E

After the experiment, the children were shown the direct methods and asked why they had not used them. Their answers can be summarized in the statement: "How were we supposed to know what you meant by a 'better answer' or by 'being satisfied'? We were satisfied—we had done our best to check the arithmetic and to see that the answer was correct and clearly and neatly written."

Since the set-inducing problems do not have a direct method of solution, subjects may have sought in vain to improve their answers to these problems and may have given up such attempts by the time the test problems came. Other children were therefore given the set-inducing problems just as in the basic experiment but, beginning with the first test problem, and in each subsequent problem, they were told not to hurry and they received the same instructions as in the experiment just described. In addition, on the blackboard the following was printed: "Look for the best way to do the example." Again pupils worked slowly, the extinction problem had to be "discarded" after ten minutes, and E effects were within the range found in the basic experiment.

29 elem.-sch. students .... $C_1 C_2$: 83% E Ext.: 76% F $C_3 C_4$: 83% E

When the procedure was used in a college class, there were somewhat less E effects than usual.

31 college students .... $C_1 C_2$: 61% E Ext.: 35% F $C_3 C_4$: 34% E

Some subjects said that they first really understood the import of the instructions on doing the ninth task while others complained that they failed to see the relevancy of the instructions or the need for extra time in the later (test) problems.

Similar E effects were obtained in another college class when the experiment was conducted as a speed test up to and including the last set-inducing problem, but, for each test problem, the timing was relaxed and students were given the instructions not to hurry, to look for the best solution, etc.

35 college students .... $C_1 C_2$: 60% E Ext.: 34% F $C_3 C_4$: 43% E

From this group, also, some comments bespoke confusion about the meaning of a better solution or being satisfied with a solution and about the reason for the extra time.

The relaxation of time limits did not noticeably reduce emotional tensions below those observed in the basic experiment while the "speed" condition did noticeably increase tensions; this suggests that the relationship between the time factor and psychological stresses is not a simple one. Moreover, some subjects were apparently concerned and anxious about whether or not they had the best answer, and yet they did not know how to interpret a "better answer" or being "satisfied" with one's answer. Apparently the increase in available time and the exhortation to look for better solutions did not suffice to make some subjects discard the E method. It was therefore decided to conduct experiments in which subjects would be explicitly told not to continue the oft-repeated method.

Warnings Against Use of the E Method

In one elementary-school class the procedure of the basic experiment was used up to the last set-inducing problem (Luchins, 1942, p. 49). Then we collected the papers and asked each child to formulate the rule of solution he had used. They were then told, "Try not to use that rule hereafter. I'll give you one minute to make up your mind not to use it any more." New papers were distributed and the test problems were presented at two-and-one-half-minute intervals. With each test problem the experimenter cautioned, "Look for the new ways. Do you see a different method?" After the experiment, the pupils were asked whether the second series of problems was similar or dissimilar to the first series. Those who reported them as dissimilar showed low E effects:

12 elem.-sch. students .... C_1C_2: 17% E Ext.: 8% F C_3C_4: 4% E

But the half of the class that reported them as similiar (e.g., "They are all subtraction examples") gave large E effects:

12 elem.-sch. students .... C_1C_2: 75% E Ext.: 50% F C_3C_4: 75% E

To strengthen the admonition against use of the E method, we had another class formulate the rule of solution with each set-inducing problem and we then wrote the E method on the blackboard, using pictures of jars and arrows. After presentation of the last set-inducing problem, the children were told that they would now be given problems in which they must not use the old (E) method. "DO NOT USE IT ANY MORE" was printed on the blackboard and the experimenter added, "Remember, not the answer, but the way you get the answer counts. If you try to use the old method, you are wrong. Do not use it. There are other and better ways of solving the problems. I want you to find them." The test problems were then presented at two-and-one-half-minute intervals.

When questioned after the experiment about the similarity of the two series of problems, the ten children describing them as dissimilar showed relatively low E effects:

10 elem.-sch. students .... C_1C_2: 15% E Ext.: 10% F C_3C_4: 20% E

The fourteen children who said that the two series were similar or the same, showed large E effects:

14 elem.-sch. students .... C_1C_2: 14% E and 53% F Ext.: 64% F C_3C_4: 49% E

Most of these children failed the first two criticals, that is, they heeded the warning not to use the old method and yet could not see another method; in subsequent problems they tended to ignore the warning. Some of the children claimed that the old method kept "popping up" in their minds and that they could not help using it, while others admitted that they used it because offhand they could see no other solution or because they did not care to start searching for other methods while the old one worked.

When the same procedure was used in a college class of twenty-two students, the fifteen who reported the two series as dissimilar gave no

E effect at all while the seven who saw them as similar showed some E effects.

   7 college students .... C_1C_2: 43% E Ext.: 43% F C_3C_4: 43% E

The college students who used the E method commented: "I saw no difference; I tried the old method and it worked so I used it; it still gave the right answer; I couldn't find a new way."

Thus our attempts to distinguish between the set-inducing and test problems were vitiated by some subjects' attitudes; they grouped all the tasks under one category, refused to look for a new method when the old one worked, or were blinded to any other procedure.

Instructions to Conserve Fluid

Since the E method does lead to the solution of the critical problems, and since the repeated utilization of this method may have made the subject highly efficient in its application, it may be reasoned (both by the subject and by the present reader) that it actually is *not* more efficient to shift to the direct method in these problems. But there is a sense in which the E method is actually less efficient than the direct method for the solution of these problems: the former method wastes more fluid than the direct procedure. Thus, in the first critical the E method involves beginning with 49 quarts of which only 20 are called for by the solution, so that 29 are discarded, while the direct method begins with 23 quarts and therefore wastes only 3 quarts; in the second critical the E method begins with 39 quarts of which 18 are required, so that 21 are wasted, but the direct method uses only the 18 quarts required by the solution; etc. Emphasis on the need for conserving fluid, it was thought, might help to make the subject aware of the relative inefficiency of the E method, might serve as "negative motivation" so far as this method was concerned, and foster the search for new, less wasteful methods. It was therefore decided to conduct variations of the basic experiment which would stress conservation of fluid (Luchins and Luchins, 1950).

Experiment 1. To make the need for conserving fluid more realistic, the fluid was described as milk. The total volume available was stipulated as 539 quarts. This is exactly enough to solve the ten problems if the E method is used in each E problem and the direct method in every test task. If a subject should use the E method in the first two criticals, he would be left with only 17 quarts, insufficient to solve any of the remaining problems by the E method and only enough to solve the last problem by the direct method.

After the introductory remarks and the illustrative problem were presented as in the basic experiment, we said:

> You will receive ten more problems. In each, your task will be to measure the amount of milk asked for by a customer, using as measures any or all of the empty containers he gives to you. There is a large tank from which you may take out the milk but, for sanitary reasons, once you put milk in a certain customer's containers, you cannot pour it back into the tank or use it for anyone else; you will have to throw away any milk you do not actually give to him, once it is in his containers. The tank contains 539 quarts of milk which will satisfy the orders of all ten customers if you are careful to use methods which waste as little milk as possible.
>
> When you finish a problem, figure out how much milk is left in the tank. Write down the amount in the space allowed for the next problem so that you will be able to see whether there is enough milk left with which to solve that problem.

After the first E problem, the experimenter demonstrated how to determine and record the amount of milk remaining in the tank.

This procedure was used in four New York City sixth-year classes of an elementary school. Two similar classes received the same procedure under speed-test conditions. While 24 per cent of those studied under nonspeed conditions consistently recorded the available volume, only 6 per cent did so under speed conditions. Those working under nonspeed conditions later gave various explanations of why they had not consistently kept account of available fluids; a few claimed that they did not have time, some said they forgot the instructions, others that they did not bother to keep the record after the first few problems because it seemed a waste of time as long as they were able to get the correct answer to the problem. Those studied under speed-test conditions who did not keep the record attributed their failure to the fact that they were working against time or said that they were too nervous to remember to compute the amount of available fluid.

The subjects who consistently kept a record of available fluid, showed little E effects under speed or nonspeed conditions.

Speed .... 4 elem.-sch. students C_1C_2:   0% E Ext.:   0% F C_3C_4: 0% E
Nonspeed .... 33 elem.-sch. students C_1C_2: 35% E Ext.: 15% F C_3C_4: 5% E

Those who did not consistently keep the record showed large E effects under nonspeed conditions and maximum effects under speed conditions.

Speed .... 58 elem.-sch. students C_1C_2: 100% E Ext.: 100% F C_3C_4: 100% E
Nonspeed .. 106 elem.-sch. students C_1C_2: 81% E Ext.: 76% F C_3C_4: 79% E

As each of the children who showed complete E effects under speed conditions brought his paper to the experimenter, he was told that he had failed to keep tab of the amount of milk remaining in the tank and that, because of the wasteful methods he had used, he actually had not had enough fluid to do even the ninth problem. He was given another sheet of paper, told to do all the problems again, to keep a record, and to pay particular heed to the last five problems.

On their second chance, sixteen children recovered while forty-two children still used the E method throughout, even in the extinction task where it did not lead to a solution. Thus the fifty-eight children now gave 73 per cent E effect in each test problem. Most of those who had to do their work over later said that they had been disturbed and humiliated by the announcement that they had not solved the problems correctly and must do them again, since it meant that, in spite of all their hurrying, they would now be among the last to finish and might even fail the test. They said that, when they attempted to do the problems over, they could not think clearly; they could think of nothing but their failure and the need for speed. Some of them submitted their second papers within a few minutes, often running to the experimenter's desk in order to save time. Many were clearly under the influence of the "speed atmosphere," the effects of which were seen in strained faces and occasional tears. Yet, no mention had been made of timing when they were told to do the problems again.

In short, our attempts to motivate for the use of direct methods, through emphasis on conservation of fluid, were not very successful under nonspeed conditions and were vitiated by speed-test conditions.

Experiment 2. Since so many children did not keep track of the fluid in the previous experiment, it was decided to use the nonspeed procedure of the previous experiment and also to remind the subjects with each problem to record the amount of available fluid. Each of sixty children in two sixth-grade classes kept a consistent, fairly accurate account of available fluid and yet they showed large E effects: C_1C_2, 80% E; Ext., 73% F.

When the extinction task had been on the blackboard for two and a half minutes, the subjects were told that they should have 64 quarts of milk left in the tank before the solution of this task. If a subject did, he was told to go on to the last two critical problems; if he did not, he was instructed first to do over the last few problems in order to find ways that would waste less milk and only then to go on to the final two critical problems. After this interruption, the sixty children showed very low E effects; it is of interest to compare their second attempts with the second attempts made in the previous experiment under speed-test conditions.

Speed .... 58 elem.-sch. students C_1C_2: 73% E Ext.: 73% F C_3C_4: 73% E
Nonspeed .... 60 elem.-sch. students C_1C_2: 17% E Ext.: 13% F C_3C_4: 13% E

This suggests that under nonspeed conditions the interruption served as a dramatic occurrence which disrupted the set by centering subjects on the lack of fluid and by reminding them that wasteful methods were responsible for their difficulties. But under speed-test conditions the second chance to solve the problems was largely ineffective because it centered subjects on their failure on the test and only intensified their haste and tension.

The question arises as to why those who kept the record in the previous experiment showed little E effects, while keeping the record in the first trial of the present experiment was largely ineffectual. Comments suggest that many of those who kept track of fluid in the first trial did so in a mechanical fashion, only because they were reminded to do so with each problem; they did not relate their computations to their method of solution.

When we noticed that most subjects did not keep a record of available fluid (except in Experiment 2), that many who kept the record did not bother to consult it, and that some merrily continued to use the E method even when aware that their record did not permit its use, we could not help thinking that the children might be reflecting the behavior of those adults in our society who do not budget their finances or who carefully work out a budget and then ignore it, and in either case live beyond their means, or of the charity pledgers who feel it is better to pledge and not pay than not to pledge at all.

It is interesting to speculate whether the general lack of success of this variation is in any way a reflection of our nation's tendency to waste natural resources and foods. Perhaps the procedure would be more successful if it was employed with groups that are less wasteful of resources and, specifically, with children who hunger for milk, youngsters all too plentiful in famine-swept countries.

Experiment 3. In the previous variations, a subject did not know whether or not he had wasted an undue amount of fluid in a given problem. In the present experiment, hitherto unpublished, we did not announce the supply available but, instead, with one group, stipulated with each problem the maximum amount of fluid that could be wasted. In each test problem this was two to four quarts less than that lost by the E procedure but more than enough to cover the amount lost by the direct methods. Following Critical 4, there were given two more criticals solvable by the E method, by $A - C$, and by the filling of one jar (36, 90, 18, get 18 quarts; 32, 80, 16, get 16 quarts), a new extinction task solvable only by the $2A - C$ method (40, 118, 18, get 62 quarts), and a final critical solvable by the E method and by $2A - 3C$ (19, 53, 4, get 26 quarts).

In order to focus more attention on the conservation of fluid, additional instructions were added for a second group of students. They were told that the amount of credit received for a problem would depend on the amount of fluid wasted—the greater the waste, the lower the score—and that, if one solved a problem but exceeded the allowable amount of waste, then he would lose half credit for the problem. As the subject solved each task, he was told how much credit he had lost and what his total score was up to that point. If he did not receive full credit for a problem, he was given the opportunity then and there to do the problem again if he wished to do so.

The connection of credit and mode of solution may make the subject realize that there exists more than one method of solving a problem, some within and some exceeding the allowable wastage. It may make him more concerned and more "ego involved" about not surpassing the permissible wastage. Loss of half credit for the use of the E method in the critical problems may serve to weaken the "reward" or "reinforcement value" associated with this method or may be regarded as a threat of (symbolic) punishment.

In an attempt to heighten the ego involvement still further, we introduced the experiment to a third group of subjects as part of a proposed McGill University entrance test. "The results will give me an indication of whether or not you are possible college material, so try your best." When a subject lost credit on a problem, he was told that others of his age usually received full credit, that he was not doing well, and that if he continued to lose credit his score probably would not meet admission standards. He was also told that he could have another chance then and there to do the problem again.

Thus, the experimental procedures consisted of these steps:

(1) Stipulation of allowable wastage with each problem.

(2) Stipulation that the subject would lose credit on each problem for which the limit was exceeded, plus an opportunity to do the problem again if credit was lost.

(3) Interpretation of the experiment as a college-entrance test.

Tested individually, with the assistance of Herta Hoffman and Ellen Reicher, in a Montreal high school, forty-five students who were known to desire to enter McGill University received one or more of these steps. Step 1 only was used with fifteen students (Group 1); Steps 1 and 2 with fifteen others (Group 2); Steps 1, 2, and 3 with fifteen others (Group 3). The groups were equated for age, I.Q., sex, and educational level. The results, which take into consideration only the first solutions of the problems, are contained in Table I.

TABLE I. E EFFECTS UNDER VARIOUS EXPERIMENTALLY INTRODUCED
LEVELS OF EGO THREAT (HIGH-SCHOOL STUDENTS)

	Subjects	C_1C_2	Ext.$_1$	C_3C_4	C_5C_6	Ext.$_2$	C_7
Group 1	15	100	87	100	80	100	100
Group 2	15	30	0	0	0	7	13
Group 3	15	97	87	80	73	87	93

It is seen that E effects are high for Groups 1 and 3 but low for Group 2. While differences between the results for Groups 1 and 3 are not significant, there are significant differences between the results for Group 2 and each of the other groups.

It will be remembered that subjects in Groups 2 and 3 were allowed to do over a problem for which they had not received full credit. In Group 2, students who had not given the least wasteful method on their first attempt invariably gave it on their second. But in Group 3 little shift to another method was found. Of the fifteen subjects in Group 3 who gave E solutions to Critical 1, only two, on their second attempt, shifted to the direct method; of the fourteen who gave E solutions to Critical 2, only one shifted to a direct method; of the eleven who failed the extinction task, only one found a solution on his second attempt; and, beginning with Critical 3 and for each subsequent task, not one of the subjects who offered an E solution or failed, was able to discover any other method. Thus, if we consider the second attempts, we find no E effects at all for Group 2 but E effects almost as large as on the first trial for Group 3. Comments made by students in Group 3 contained such terms as "anxious," "nervous," and "worried"; they spoke of being discouraged by the continual loss of credit but admitted that they had not been able to see another solution.

The degree of ego involvement or ego threat may be considered to increase from Group 1 through Group 3. The findings suggest that a low degree of ego threat (Group 1) or a high degree (Group 3) may each foster rigid behavior. Note that in our experiments low ego threat was even more conducive to E effects than intense ego threat. A medium level of ego threat (Group 2) was accompanied by the smallest E effects. These results imply that rigidity and ego threat are not necessarily linearly related.

Procedures used with Groups 1 through 3 were also used in a Montreal recreational center with children aged from ten to fourteen years. The experiment was group administered to the twenty children in each group. It was the experimenter's impression that for the present Group 1 the extent of ego involvement was about as low as in the corresponding high-school group, but that the social atmosphere was more relaxed and informal. The degree of ego involvement seemed to be considerably lower for the present Group 2 than for the corresponding high-school group; the children had come to the recreational center for fun and the attitude of the majority was that "it doesn't count anyway." The speed-test procedure used for Group 3 (in which the children were told at the outset that they were to receive problems from a test given to students entering Grade 10, and then were told at intervals that they must hurry and that they were doing worse than younger children) produced considerable tension and even tears, and seemed to be as ego threatening as was the procedure for the high-school Group 3.

The thesis that a tense social atmosphere is more conducive to E effects than a somewhat relaxed atmosphere, together with the thesis that extremes of ego threat are more conducive to E effects than a moderate threat to the ego, leads to the expectation that the present Group 3 should have more E effects than the present Groups 1 and 2, that the present Group 1 should have less E effects than the corresponding high-school group, and that the present Group 2 should have more E effects than the corresponding high-school group. All these expectations are supported by the findings (cf. Tables I and II). What is particularly interesting is that the same instruction about loss of credit was received

TABLE II. E EFFECTS UNDER VARIOUS EXPERIMENTALLY INTRODUCED LEVELS OF EGO THREAT (CHILDREN AGED 10-14, RECREATIONAL CENTER)

	Subjects	C_1C_2	Ext.$_1$	C_3C_4	C_5C_6	Ext.$_2$	C_7
Group 1	20	63	50	55	28	70	65
Group 2	20	75	65	50	30	75	70
Group 3	20	80	80	85	75	100	90

quite differently in the recreational center than in the high school, a fact that illustrates once more that the same experimentally introduced variable may induce different amounts of anxiety and ego threat (depending, for example, on the subject's attitudes and assumptions with regard to this variable), and be associated with strikingly different amounts of E effects.

Comments

Problem-Solving Training

Why were our attempts to center individuals on the problems and to instigate a search for better solutions often unsuccessful? Why were motivations stemming from the problem situation itself (such as limiting the supply of fluid) generally insufficient by themselves to break the Einstellung, but more successful when linked with extrinsic rewards

and punishments (loss of credit) ? The answer, at least in part, may lie
in the kind of problem-solving training given in our schools. The students learn to be interested in a problem, mainly for the sake of extrinsic
rewards, such as grades, rather than for the problem's own sake. School
experiences teach them to categorize and type problems (as is so often
done in arithmetic and algebra), and once they type a problem (or a
situation or a person), it may be the category which becomes the frame
of reference so that the problem (or the situation or the person) is no
longer freely faced.

Anxiety may be aroused in the individual when he is forced to abandon the category into which he has pigeonholed something or someone.
Some of the children said that they were not accustomed to having
problems of a different kind interjected in a series, and some complained
that the test was "tricky" or "not fair"; they were accustomed, they said,
to learning a method and then repeating it, or practicing it, in a series
of problems (isolated drill in the initial learning period).

Moreover, our subjects had little conception of what was meant by a
"better" solution and many of them seemed genuinely surprised when
shown that there were two methods of solving the critical problems.
Perhaps this was because their training, largely confined to one-method
solutions, led them to believe that a problem has one and only one correct method of solution. They had little or no experience with nonsolvable problems or with problems that have multiple, nonunique methods of solution. Moreover, the emphasis in examinations (e.g., objective
tests) is often on the answer and not on the method or process that leads
to the answer, on the end and not on the means to the end. Learning to
pass such tests may make it difficult for students to grasp that some
processes are better than others or that the means to the end may be as
important as the end itself. In life situations, it often makes a considerable difference (say, from the point of view of time saving or of law,
ethics, and morals) whether an individual employs one rather than
another means to an end. What we are suggesting is that the results
of our experiments may be, in part, artifacts of the education of the
subjects. Their training may not have fostered adequate problem solving but may instead have fostered categorization and repetition. This
is an issue to which we shall return again in subsequent chapters.

Investigations of Anxiety

Many investigations introduce a frustrating or anxiety-provoking
agent and assume that frustration or anxiety are necessarily provoked,
or they introduce factors intended to make for a relaxed "anxiety-free"
condition and assume that this has been accomplished. We have seen

that a so-called frustrating agent (e.g., an unsolvable problem) or an attempt to allay anxiety (e.g., relaxation of time limits) may produce diverse subjective reactions in different subjects. There are methodological dangers in the prevalent practice of defining "anxiety," "frustration," "ego threat," etc., in terms of operations performed by the investigator in the experimental situation. These are phenomenally experienced states of being of the subject and should be defined in terms of what the subject feels and does and not in terms of the experimenter's a priori hypotheses. The experimenter should attempt to appraise the subject's reactions to the experimental conditions; fractionization of the subjects according to their reactions may clarify the relationship between psychological stresses and qualitative or quantitative data.

What is needed is research to develop objective methods of determining the characteristic psychological and physiological features of experienced anxiety and frustration. Such research may show that one cannot speak of anxiety, frustration, or ego threat as an absolute, as something which is either present or absent, but must take degree or intensity into account. It may reveal that there are not only different intensities of anxiety but also different kinds of anxiety. It is conceivable that anxiety (or frustration, etc.) exerts different influences, depending on its origin, direction, and the role it plays for the person and his environment. Perhaps it is fallacious to use the unqualified terms of anxiety, frustration, and ego threat as if each represented one state or one drive. Another problem for research is to clarify the similarities and differences between the concepts of anxiety, frustration, and ego threat, which are sometimes used interchangeably and at other times as if they were distinct.

Most investigations of the relationship between E effects and anxiety have used anxiety-provoking agents of only one genotypical character: those whose source or origin was extrinsic to the main problem-solving situation, which focused the subject on aspects of the situation other than the problem at hand, and which afforded him little or no opportunity to learn or understand the reason for his failure or his poor performance. Thus, the source or origin has been an unsolvable task interpolated among problems of an Einstellung test, a hostile attitude of the experimenter, unfavorable interpretations of results on a so-called personality test, a tense social atmosphere, etc. Moreover, the vectors arousing anxiety have been directed at focusing the subject on himself, his inadequacies, his feeling of tension, possible reasons for the experimenter's hostile attitude toward him, etc., but not directed at focusing him on the main problem-solving situation. If he is seriously concerned with these extraproblem aspects, the subject may so reorganize (restructurize, recenter) his cognitive grasp of the situation that these become central while the problems of the Einstellung test become peripheral.

The concept of restructuring or recentering is well illustrated in the incident of the new college coed who, sheet-clad, was waiting in line to have her feet examined by the school physician. When her turn came, she found that her shoe laces would not come untied. Tugging at the laces and at the shoe was of no avail. Embarrassed by the impatience of the doctor, the tittering of the girls behind her, and the slipping sheet, she struggled with the shoe until, after what seemed an interminable period, she finally succeeded in pulling it off. Heaving a sigh of relief, she announced, "Here!" and thumped the shoe down on the stool in front of the physician. The latter reminded her that the clean towel on the stool was intended for her foot and not for the shoe.

What happened here? Because of her struggle with the shoe, because of the accompanying embarrassment, the student recentered her view of the situation so that the shoe and its removal—and not the examination of the foot—became central. Similarly, in some of the investigations concerned with the influences of psychological stress on rigidity, the subject may have become so preoccupied with the extraproblem factors that there resulted a restructuring of the problem-solving situation in which these factors—and not the problems of the Einstellung test—became central. The subject who is focused on these extraproblem demands or on himself and his inadequacies, may well be expected to require a longer period of time than one who attends primarily to the problem at hand to discover there is another method of solution or that the extinction task, apparently similar to other tasks he has solved, actually requires a change in the method of solution. One might liken the experimenter to a prestidigitator. The latter's sleight-of-hand tricks require that he divert the audience's attention; similarly, the experimenter focuses the subject on the extraproblem demands while slipping in a problem requiring a shift in method of solution.

Moreover, in many of the investigations the frustrating agent was arbitrary in nature; for example, the experimenter's hostile attitude when there seemed no reason for hostility, the experimenter's chiding remark that the subject was not working fast enough when he was working as fast as he could, or the false statement that everyone but the subject had solved an unsolvable problem. The subject could learn little or nothing from such arbitrary and no-solution situations. They represented evidence-free situations for one who might seek evidence in terms of which to understand his allegedly poor performance; any possibility of insight into the reason for the poor performance or failure was ruled out in these experiments.

Not only studies of E effect in relation to anxiety, but many other investigations on anxiety and rigidity, have used psychological stresses of a similar genotypical character. Thus, in studies on stereotypy in rats, electric shock may be administered at the choice point in a discrimination box (cf. Hamilton and Krechevsky, 1933). This shock, which certainly is not intrinsically related to the stimuli that are to be discriminated, may become the aspect of the situation on which the animal is focused; that is, the shock and the avoidance of shock may become central in the rat's "view" of the situation. An extensively used frustrating situation with rats is an unsolvable problem in a Lashley type of discrimination apparatus (Maier, 1949). In this no-solution situation, the experimenter arbitrarily distributes successes and failures at random, so that the animal has no way of learning which card or window leads to food and which to punishment; the situation is later changed to one involving a definite pattern of reward and punishment. The abnormal fixations found in some of the animals, hindering learning of the subsequent pattern, may be related to the arbitrary nature of the frustrating agent. If one cares to indulge in anthropomorphic thinking, he may conceive of the rat as generalizing from his experience with the no-solution series that all the tasks are arbitrary and meaningless, that he dare not hope that a definite pattern will consistently be followed, that a rodent just does not stand a chance to win here, so he might as well continue to give the same response (or no response). Seriously, the conclusion drawn from these studies that frustration tends to induce arbitrary fixations may not necessarily be applicable to situations in which frustration arises from less arbitrary situations.

Marquart's experiments (1948) represent the analogue with human beings of fixation experiments on rats. A no-solution series was used in which electric shock attendant on the opening of one of two doors was randomly and arbitrarily distributed; with no warning to the subject, the series was then changed so that one door consistently produced shock while the other did not (position pattern). For some subjects, evidence was found of stereotypy induced by the no-solution series which hindered learning the position pattern. It is interesting to note that at the beginning of the study the subject was falsely informed that there would be a definite pattern running throughout the situation and that the subjects' comments that this seemed not to be the case were ignored by the experimenter. In short, the frustrating situation was arbitrary and the subject was misled with regard to the unsolvable character of part of the situation. Protocols presented by Marquart indicate that the reasoning we facetiously attributed to the rat actually occurred for some of her subjects. One must be careful not to generalize from such findings to situations in which emotional stresses arise in less arbitrary, less blind situations.

Forces arousing psychological tensions, including anxiety or frustration, may differ in origin, direction, role, and function from those used in the afore-mentioned studies. Their source may be the problem itself or the solution or attempted solution of the problem (e.g., as in mirror tracing). One may become frustrated at not making progress in solving a problem or emotionally elated at suddenly getting a new slant on a problem; a problem is an unresolved state of affairs, involving tensions and disequilibrium. The origin may be the ego in the sense that a person brings existing anxieties into the situation. While it may be claimed that anxiety or frustration does not exist except in relation to the ego, it seems important to distinguish psychologically between anxiety stemming from the ego, from a problem, or from an extraproblem demand introduced by others.

Moreover, it may be inaccurate to equate all anxiety and frustration with ego threat. Thus, an individual may be anxious and concerned about a scientific or mathematical problem without necessarily experiencing any ego threat in relation to it. He may be interested in solving the problem for its own sake and not for his ego's sake. There may not be a problem without an "I"; but "I" may see the problem outside of myself and not see my ego as the center of the problem nor use myself as the center of the coordinate system from which to view or evaluate the problem. The point just raised is related to the fundamental issue of how man views the universe and of the conditions under which he is or is not ego-centered; it also challenges the alleged dichotomy between emotions and thinking and the conception of emotions as necessarily interfering with thinking, issues which will be discussed in a later chapter.

Another variable that requires investigation is the relation of behavior to the degree of specificity or generality of anxiety. The same intensity of anxiety may conceivably be of a vague, general nature, a general unrest and disquietude, or it may be of an extremely specific nature focused on a limited area; for example, the neurotics' general anxiety which they bring with them to all or many situations as opposed to specific anxiety associated with mirror tracing.

Also requiring study is the effect on behavior of the point in the person's time-space manifold at which anxiety enters the situation.

Another problem to be considered pertains to the relationship between the frustrating agent and the rigidified aspect of behavior (or of personality). For example, in mirror tracing of the mazes, the procedure that was the source of anxiety was also the one for which rigidity developed; when failure on an interpolated unsolvable problem was the frustrating agent, rigidity developed not for the procedures attempted in that problem but for another procedure.

An important consideration is the role and function of anxiety in the subject's cognitive grasp of the situation. What direction does the anxiety take? Does it focus the individual on himself, on certain responses, on a problem, or on other people? Does he learn anything during the anxiety? What becomes central and what peripheral in his cognitive grasp of the situation, what becomes the figure and what the background? Psychological tensions, whatever their origin, may center the individual on a problem and its most effective solution. Frustration arising from failure to cope with a problem may itself spur one on to new and more effective attempts at solution, particularly if one gains insight into the reason for the failure (e.g., an understanding that the E method does not apply to the extinction task or that the potato tasks are unsolvable); that failure is coupled with understanding does not necessarily rule out a feeling of frustration or anxiety. To avoid a possible one-sided view of the workings of anxiety and frustration, and to obtain a clearer delineation, it may be advisable to experiment with other types of psychological stresses. There is also a great need (at present completely neglected) of investigations in which the same individual is studied in a variety of anxiety-provoking situations in order to see whether or not he has characteristic ways of reacting to anxiety and what those ways are, and how he alters his reactions in different situations.

Anxiety and frustration are often treated as experimentally manipulated or independent variables. What we have suggested is that the experimenter cannot directly manipulate the amount or operation of anxiety, but that the intensity and the functioning of anxiety are themselves dependent on other variables (origin, direction, attitudes, etc.) and in turn induce other processes which influence behavior. It may therefore be more adequate and methodologically more fruitful, to think of anxiety not as an independent variable but as a process of processes or a function of functions. Investigations could then be undertaken of the functions involved in anxiety and the functional relationships connecting them.

Should Anxiety Be Avoided?

In many studies (perhaps because psychological stresses of only one genotypical character were used), it has been concluded that frustration and anxiety produce or intensify rigidity. A widely promulgated dictum, apparently supported by these studies and by various theoretical considerations, is that, to avoid rigidity and to foster desirable changes in behavior, one ought to avoid frustration and anxiety.

But the experimental evidence which we surveyed speaks against this dictum. It suggests that there is no simple linear or even curvilinear relationship between the amount of anxiety and its influence on behavior. As the amount increases there may be quantitative and qualitative changes, even of a discontinuous nature. For example, a rather large amount of frustration associated with a given procedure (say, college students' mirror tracing of the circuitous route) may foster rigid adherence to it, but an increase in the amount of frustration may make further adherence to it so intolerable that one gives it up (as the neurotics tended to). A certain gain or loss in anxiety may have different influences at different points in the anxiety gradient, so that the relationship between the increment in anxiety and the increment in rigidity (or other behavioral change) is not constant.

What our findings do suggest is that, under certain conditions, either low or high anxiety may foster rigidity while a more moderate level may work against it. The finding that low anxiety or low ego threat facilitated rigidity may seem contrary to some theoretical conceptualizations. Yet it seems a rather understandable finding when other considerations are taken into account. An individual who is not anxious or frustrated may have no reason to change his behavior. Change involves disequilibrium, arises from tension; if psychological tension is low, if the person is not disturbed by anxiety, by doubts, why should he change his behavior? Smugness, self-satisfaction, complacency, all betoken satisfaction with the *status quo* and furnish little basis for change. For example, people who were quite conceited about their arithmetical ability, who regarded the arithmetical problems of the basic experiment as child's play, often showed E effects; their extreme self-assurance led to automatic repetition of the E method instead of to a facing up to the requirements of the problems. A stubborn, "pigheaded" individual may be a source of anxiety to others but often he is not anxious or doubtful about his behavior; he is only too sure that he is correct. Some anxiety or doubts about oneself, about one's behavior, or one's interpersonal relationships may be needed for change, contrary to the notion that frustration and anxiety are the enemies of mental health and of adequate interpersonal relations. As Browning said, "doubts irk not the maw-crammed bird." While the starving organism may not be in a position to think clearly or to change his behavior appropriately, a certain level or amount of psychological gnawing—rather than a maw-crammed and frustration-free condition—may be more likely to foster doubting, questioning, and change, may be more likely to provoke the organism to think about his behavior and its adequacy.

The aura of opprobrium associated with frustration, anxiety, and ego threat are unjustified since, under certain conditions, they may operate against rigidity, complacency, and dogmatism. They may sometimes be detrimental to interpersonal relationships and thinking, but under different conditions they may stimulate and foster effective interpersonal relationships and thinking. Kurt Lewin once remarked that experiments show it is as correct to say that frustration leads to increased friendliness and nonaggression as it is to say that it leads to aggression. He noted that "frustration leads to increased as well as to decreased productivity, that it leads to new efforts as well as to passivity" (1951, p. 35). Our conclusion, too, is that, depending on what role frustration plays in a particular psychological situation, it may lead to passivity or to new efforts, to continuation of a set, to rigidity, or to new attacks on problems.

Parenthetically, we note that some of the psychologists, educators, and therapists who plead for the avoidance of frustration, also speak of the importance of developing frustration tolerance. Yet how is one to develop tolerance for frustration if he is spared frustration? The problem, it seems to us, is not to avoid frustration, anxiety, and ego threat, but how to utilize them for positive rather than negative consequences. What is needed is study of the variables which are conducive to one or another consequence and of what can be done to maximize or minimize them.

It seems appropriate to end this chapter by distinguishing between two kinds of psychological tensions. Some tensions are necessary for the life activities of an organism, are essential for its development and growth, for the attainment and maintenance of its equilibrium. These were referred to as tensions with a small t by the late Max Wertheimer in his lectures. When he referred to tensions with a capital T, he meant those tensions whose direction of operation is opposed to that of the organism, tensions which interfere with the adequate functioning of the organism, which may hinder development, and which may even overwhelm and destroy the organism. This distinction may be of value in dealing with anxiety, frustration, and other psychological stresses; anxiety or frustration may create tensions with a small t or tensions with a capital T. It may be more fruitful for research to study conditions under which one or another kind of tension arises and operates, and to seek to create conditions that favor tensions with a small t, rather than to seek to eliminate or reduce tensions in general.

CHAPTER VI

CONCRETENESS OF THINKING AND RIGIDITY

B EHAVIORAL RIGIDITY is often considered to be intimately linked to concreteness of thinking. Goldstein (1943) maintains that behavioral rigidity (secondary rigidity) is a direct consequence of an impairment of the abstract attitude, an impairment that compels the individual to behave concretely. Werner (1946b, p. 47) regards concreteness of thinking as one cause of behavioral rigidity. In the clinic, evidence of concreteness of thinking, as yielded by tests of concept formation, is often interpreted as an indication of rigidity while test signs of behavioral rigidity are in turn interpreted as indicating concrete-mindedness. In general, many psychologists assume a positive relationship between behavioral rigidity and concreteness of thinking, regard concreteness as a prerequisite for rigidity, or use the two concepts interchangeably.

We were interested in determining whether the assumed positive relationship actually holds between concreteness, on the one hand, and E effects, on the other. Some suspicion was cast on the validity of this assumption by data relating E effects to age and intelligence. Lewin regards the tendency to concreteness in thinking as a general feature of the childlike or otherwise undifferentiated person (1935, p. 222). Werner describes concrete thinking as a less differentiated activity than abstract thinking, noting that immature persons tend to think in a concrete manner (1946b, p. 47) and that concreteness is one sign of undifferentiated behavior (1946b, p. 51). Impairment of the abstract attitude is viewed by Goldstein as practically synonymous with an unusually small degree or a lack of differentiation. Differentiation, in turn, is assumed by Lewin, Goldstein, and Werner to increase with age, at least from infancy until maturity. Moreover, the more mentally developed the individual, the more differentiated he is assumed to be. Thus, Werner (1940, p. 44) formulates the fundamental law of development as involving an increase of differentiation and Kounin (1941a) uses the I.Q. as a gauge of the degree of differentiation. In short, concreteness of thinking has been assumed to be negatively related to development and differentiation, and, hence, negatively related to age (at least from infancy until maturity) and to intelligence. Now, if one accepts this assumption as well as the assumption that concreteness and behavioral rigidity are positively related, then it follows that behavioral rigidity should be negatively related to age and to intelligence.

The reasoning involved may become clearer if presented in syllogistic form: Premise 1: Behavioral rigidity is positively related to concreteness of thinking. Premise 2: Concreteness of thinking is negatively related to age and to intelligence. Conclusion: Behavioral rigidity is negatively related to age and to intelligence.

A specific form of this conclusion is that behavioral rigidity as measured by the Einstellung tests should be negatively related to age and to intelligence. We did find a slight negative relationship (not statistically significant) between E effects and I.Q. or mental age; however, the analysis with respect to chronological age failed to support a negative relationship. If the Einstellung tests are measures of behavioral rigidity, this finding casts doubt on the truth of the conclusion validly deduced from the premises. Hence, it casts doubt on the truth of the premises, since in logically valid reasoning true premises can lead only to true conclusions. This means that it may be erroneous to assume that behavioral rigidity as measured by Einstellung tests is positively related to concreteness of thinking.

Opposing directions of trends obtained by analyzing the relationship of E effects to age and to indices of intelligence, testify to the ambiguity of theoretical speculations concerning concreteness of thinking. In any event, it would seem timely to turn from theoretical speculations to actual experimental investigation of the relationship between E effects and concreteness of thinking.

Criteria of Abstract and Concrete Thinking

Pierce (1951) divided 130 subjects into an abstract and a concrete group on the basis of their responses in the arithmetical Einstellung test. The abstract group consisted of those who had solved all the E problems by the E method and who were regarded as having thereby revealed their ability to "abstract out" a common formula of solution. The concrete group consisted of those who had not solved more than two of the E problems by the E method and who were regarded as having thereby revealed inability to "abstract out" the common formula. The abstract group was further subdivided into an abstract-flexible and an abstract-rigid group, the former consisting of those who used the direct method in every test problem and the latter of those who used the E method in the first two criticals and failed the extinction task. In the Einstellung test, as well as in various other tests, the abstract-rigid group tended to show more rigidity than the abstract-flexible group and about as much as the concrete group. Pierce interprets the results as suggesting: (1) that the concrete-abstract continuum is distinct from the rigid-flexible continuum since a group of individuals manifesting ab-

stract behavior can be divided into those who behave rigidly and those
who do not, and (2) that behavorial rigidity resulted from a lack of
understanding for an individual characterized as concrete but from a
rigid personality structure (topological rigidity) for an individual characterized as abstract-rigid.

Pierce's investigation hinges on the assumption that E solutions of
all the E problems reflect abstract ability. To assume that the formula
has been "abstracted out" is tantamount to assuming that E solutions
of the E problems necessarily result from conscious generalization of
one mode of solution. But our investigation of the Einstellung phenomena suggests that an individual who uses the E method in all the E problems does not necessarily do so because of generalization of a rule or
formula. Some subjects are apparently not aware that they are repeatedly employing the same method; they do not seem to have generalized
or "abstracted out" any formula. Moreover, failures to solve the E problems have also been known to arise from a number of different causes,
including misunderstanding of instructions, undue excitement, fear,
confusion, and faulty arithmetical computation. But then why should
failure be regarded as necessarily indicating concreteness in thinking?
In short, we question the validity of utilizing E solutions or lack of
E solutions of the set-inducing problems as a criterion for characterizing individuals as abstract or concrete.

In another study (Rokeach, 1948), the relationship of concreteness
of thinking to rigidity was studied in the following manner. Subjects
were permitted to write their solutions to water-jar volume-measuring
problems in words or arithmetical symbols. The investigator claimed
that the use of arithmetical symbols was more abstract, concise, and
efficient than words. The use of scratch paper, and erasures and computations were also considered to constitute concrete aids in obtaining
the answers. We have elsewhere criticized these criteria of concreteness
(Luchins, 1949). Conciseness and efficiency are not necessarily signs of
abstraction, and arithmetical symbols are not in and of themselves any
more abstract than verbal symbols. Verbal expression rather than
arithmetical expression of a solution does not seem to us to constitute
proof that the underlying thought process is more concrete or more
childlike. Indeed, a child might be able to write $61 - 31 - 4 - 4 = 22$
before he could express the operations involved in words. Nor can we
see that the use of a few more or a few less words in expressing an
answer gives any clues as to the concreteness of thinking involved. And
a subject may conceivably have erased or used scratch paper or written
his answer in a detailed manner because he wanted to check on his
mental calculations or because he wished to reveal his calculations, per-

haps in order to show that he understood the operations involved and was not simply copying the procedure which the experimenter had illustrated. In any event, the employed criteria do not seem to constitute evidence of concreteness of thinking.

It is not a simple matter to find adequate criteria of concrete or abstract thinking. It is a problem which confronted the writers in the investigations described in the remainder of this chapter. To resolve it, use was made of criteria advanced by Goldstein and Scheerer (1941) in their description of the abstract and concrete level and of criteria used in contemporary clinical tests.

GENERALIZATION OF A RULE AND E EFFECTS

The ability to generalize is one of the indicants of the abstract level (Goldstein and Scheerer, 1941). It is therefore relevant to examine the relationship between E effects and generalization of a rule. Before any of the problems of the basic experiment were presented, subjects were told, "While solving the subsequent tasks, try to generalize or discover a method of solution or a rule to solve these problems" (Luchins, 1942, p. 68). Questioning after the experiment revealed that the majority had generalized the E method. In three elementary-school classes of forty, forty, and thirty-three students, thirty-three, thirty-one, and twenty-three claimed to have generalized the E method, and in a college class of twenty-two students, everyone claimed to have done so. The minority, who said that they did not draw any generalization, showed considerable E effect: from 67 to 80 per cent used E solutions for the criticals and from 56 to 71 per cent failed the extinction task. But E effects were even greater for those who said they had generalized a rule. These subjects showed maximum E effects in two of the three elementary-school classes: their E solutions of the criticals ranged from 91 to 100 per cent and their failures of the extinction task from 86 to 100 per cent. On the average, the two groups showed the following responses.

Generalized
a rule .... 109 students C_1C_2: 100% E Ext.: 97% F C_3C_4: 95% E

Did not generalize
a rule .... 26 students C_1C_2: 75% E Ext.: 73% F C_3C_4: 66% F

Apropos of the extinction task, some who generalized the rule wrote, "You made a mistake in this problem" or "The answer is 42, not 25"; others mechanically used the E method and did not indicate that they knew it was inappropriate, but a few wrote, "The rule does not work here."

The findings reveal that E effects within the range found in the basic experiment can result for subjects who apparently did not consciously generalize a rule. But those who "abstracted out" the E method showed even larger E effects. Here generalization was concomitant with greater rigidity. To the extent that ability to generalize a rule is an index of abstract ability, the results suggest that abstraction was concomitant with greater rigidity; the results therefore fail to support the thesis that a negative relationship exists between abstract ability and E effects, or between abstract ability and behavioral rigidity as measured by E effects.

CONCRETIZING THE PROBLEMS

Experimentation with the basic experiment revealed that there were subjects who regarded each of the numbers given in the problems as an essentially abstract symbol rather than as the capacity of a jar. This was even more clearly seen when, at the end of the basic experiment, one of the following problems was added: given a 5-quart jar, a 25-quart jar, and a 10-quart jar, get 0 quarts of water; given a 3-quart jar, a 65-quart jar, and a 29-quart jar, get 3 quarts; given a 4-quart jar, a 67-quart jar and a 17-quart jar, get 4 quarts. For the first-mentioned problem, 50 per cent of a class of college students went through the mechanics of the E method in order to obtain *no* water: $25 - 5 - 10 - 10 = 0$, indicating that this was to them an abstract, arithmetical operation. An ingenious solution was given by 30 per cent of another college class to the second-mentioned problem: $65 - 29 - (11 \times 3) = 3$; in "eleven times three" they repeatedly used the 3-quart jar, but failed to give the obvious solution to the problem—filling this jar once! The last-mentioned problem, which required only the filling of the 4-quart jar, was failed by 62 per cent of a third college class. It seemed that these subjects did not view the numbers as representations of the contents of jars. We therefore wondered what would be the influence on E effects of concretizing the tasks by introducing actual containers and an actual supply of water (Luchins and Luchins, 1950).

The experiment was administered individually in a classroom containing a sink. The sink's faucet served as the source of water and the sink as the receptacle for excess water. Three containers were placed on a table before the subject, in the order in which the jar capacities had been written in each problem, and on each jar, facing the subject, the volume was printed in large numerals. The jars were made from cardboard milk containers of the two-gill, pint, and quart size, cut down to be roughly proportional to the numerals printed on them. The numerals were said to refer to the number of cubic centimeters contained in each jar. Pencil and paper were furnished at the outset "to be used if needed."

Of twenty-six sixth-grade children, the results of four were eliminated from consideration because of their failure to solve the last two

E problems. Of the remaining twenty-two children, all but two calculated the answer to each problem with pencil and paper before manipulating the jars. The two who made no prior written calculations, showed no E effects. The group as a whole gave results which fell within the range of results of comparable subjects in the basic experiment: C_1C_2, 68% E; Ext., 64% F; C_3C_4, 68% E.

When the experiment was administered to thirty college students, they, too, showed E effects although somewhat less than similar groups receiving the basic experiment: C_1C_2, 60% E; Ext., 33% F; C_3C_4, 33% E. Many of the college students made some written calculations before manipulating the jars. Others quickly generalized the E method as a rule of solution and, as soon as three jars were presented, they filled the center one and poured from it, once into the container to the left and twice into the container to the right.

Since some subjects first figured out the solutions on paper, thereby defeating our purpose in using actual jars, it was decided not to provide pencil and paper and expressly to forbid their use. Under these conditions, ten elementary-school students were incapable of solving most of the E problems. College students were capable of solving them; for twenty students the results were: C_1C_2, 55% E; Ext., 50% F; C_3C_4, 30% E. Some mentally calculated the arithmetic involved before manipulating the jars, thus putting the problems on a symbolic level. Others generalized the E method as a rule or formula or claimed that they caught on to the "trick" which worked in these problems.

Concretizing the problems did not eliminate the E effect but, in some cases, did reduce it below the amount found in the basic experiment. Our purpose in introducing the actual jars and fluid was defeated in some cases by written or mental calculations resorted to prior to manipulation of the jars. Generalization of a formula seemed to result in rather strong E effect. It was our impression that those who carefully examined each set of containers, who treated each problem as possessing individual requirements, showed little or no E effects. In short, those who dealt with the problems on the concrete level tended to manifest less E effect than those who dealt with the problems on the "abstract" arithmetical level or who "abstracted out" a formula. The results do not support the positive relationship between concreteness and behavioral rigidity which is often accepted.

E Effects and a Verbal Test of Abstraction

In order to study the relation of E effects to performance in a popular test of verbal abstraction, we gave a group of ninety-one female freshman students of Royal Victoria College of Montreal the arithmetical Einstellung test and, immediately afterwards, the similarities subtest of the Wechsler-Bellevue adult-intelligence scales (Luchins, 1951c). Subjects who used the E method in all the E problems were fractionized into four groups according to the point of shift to the direct method: Group 1 consisted of twenty-five students who showed no E effects; Group 2, of nine who used the E method in the first and/or second critical but who used the direct method in all subsequent problems; Group 3, of fifteen who used the E method in three or four criticals but solved all four extinction tasks; Group 4, of twenty-two who used the E method in four criticals and failed all four extinction tasks.

With failures to solve the extinction tasks taken as evidence of behavioral rigidity, the least rigidity may be attributed to Group 1 and the most rigidity to Group 4. If rigidity, as evidenced by this criterion, is positively related to concreteness of thinking, then, on the basis of the customary interpretation of the similarities subtest, Group 1 should show a larger percentage of abstract responses and a smaller percentage of concrete-functional responses than Group 4; and the percentage of failures to respond for Group 1 should be the same as or smaller than that for Group 4. On the whole, the results show a fairly consistent but unreliable trend in line with these expectations. Results in accord with expectations are found on eight of the twelve items of the similarities test for concrete-functional replies; on nine items for abstract replies; and on eleven items for failures. Differences generally failed to attain statistical significance.

The average percentages of responses that fell into the abstract, concrete-functional, and failure categories were as follows:

Group 1..............
    25 least rigid stud.   Abstract: 63%   Conc.-func.: 25%   Failure: 12%

Group 4..............
    22 most rigid stud.   Abstract: 52%   Conc.-func.: 31%   Failure: 17%

These results fit the thesis that greater behavioral rigidity is accompanied by greater evidence of concreteness and less evidence of abstractness of thinking.

Some investigators (e.g., Rokeach, 1948) accept E solutions of the criticals as a criterion of behavioral rigidity. In terms of this criterion, rigidity may be said to increase from Group 1 through Group 4 since the percentages of E solutions of the criticals increase from group to group. A positive relationship between rigidity and concreteness would then lead to the expectation that, from Group 1 through Group 4, the percentages of concrete-functional responses should consistently increase, abstract responses consistently decrease, and failures remain the same or increase. But the trends of results fail to substantiate these expectations. (See Luchins, 1951c, for details of results.)

In short, the results yielded a rather consistent (but generally un-reliable) trend toward a positive relationship between behavioral rigidity and concreteness of thinking when one criterion of behavioral rigidity was employed but did not yield any consistent trend when another criterion was employed. This illustrates that the particular relationship which is found between rigidity and concreteness may depend on the particular criterion of rigidity employed. It also raises the issue of what constitutes rigid behavior in the Einstellung situation. If rigidity is defined as a lack of shift in behavior when the situation calls for a shift, then it may be said that a change from the E method to the direct method is called for in the extinction tasks but is not demanded in the criticals since these are solvable by the E method. For this reason we have criticized the use of E solutions of the criticals as evidence of rigidity (Luchins, 1949).

RIGIDITY IN TERMS OF SHIFTS IN CONCEPTS

Abstract and concrete thinking refer to conceptual activities; be-havioral rigidity also has been defined in terms of conceptual behavior, and, in particular, in terms of resistance to change of concepts. Thus, Rapaport, Gill, and Schafer refer to rigidity as "the inability to discard an idea once conceived, so that it permeates or obstructs all consequent attempts; . . . a resistance to apperceive the implications of clues for modification or discarding of concepts" (1945, vol. 1, p. 465), while they refer to flexibility as "the ability to modify concepts once developed, upon encountering difficulty or failure; . . . a freedom of shifting from one concept to another" (p. 464).

The relationship between conceptual behavior and E effects is not always clear; solutions to the problems of the Einstellung test need not tell us what is happening on the conceptual level and, in particular, whether or not a shift in concept has occurred. In order to compare rigidity, measured in terms of shift in concepts, with concreteness of thinking, we decided to utilize a test of concept formation both as an index of rigidity and as an index of concreteness.

The similarities subtest of the Wechsler-Bellevue adult-intelligence scales was group administered in the standard manner; immediately upon its completion, the test was readministered and then again read-ministered. The second and third administrations differed from the first only in so far as subjects were told, for each pair of words, to give a new similarity, one which they had not previously given. (There are several possible similarities between the members of each pair, particu-larly in the concrete and functional categories.) All of a subject's re-plies were written on the same sheet of paper so that he could refer to his previous responses.

In addition to scoring as failure an incorrect response or no response, we marked as failure any response which was a repetition of, or tantamount to a repetition of, an answer the subject had previously given to a particular test item.

The subjects were thirty McGill University male seniors. The mean time required per response was less than one minute in the initial administration but over two minutes in the next trial. In the third trial, the students' protests that they did not have enough time to think, led us to write all twelve test items on the blackboard and leave them there for thirty minutes. At the end of the allotted time we told the students that this trial was over and proposed that they now find new similarities. The roar of protest was so great that we abandoned attempts at a fourth trial.

The group's percentages of responses in the abstract, concrete-functional, and failure categories were computed for each trial.

First trial .... Abstract: 65%   Concrete-functional: 23%   Failure: 12%
Second trial .... Abstract: 15%   Concrete-functional: 40%   Failure: 45%
Third trial ...... Abstract: 9%   Concrete-functional: 22%   Failure: 69%

From trial to trial there was a decrease in abstract replies but an increase in failures (including a few responses that were essentially repetitions of previous ones). The decrease in abstract replies from the first to the second trial and from the first to the third trial and the increase in failures from the first to the third trial proved significant at the 0.01 level. A capsule picture of differences between the results of the first and the last trial is contained in the statement that the proportion of concrete replies is about unchanged, while abstract responses and failures have shifted their roles, the abstract category predominating and failures being relatively few in the first trial, while failures predominate and abstract replies are relatively few in the third administration.

Because the subjects were explicitly told that their previous responses should not be repeated, the test called for shifts in concepts. Yet, the time increase from trial to trial, the comments, and the quantitative results, indicate that the group as a whole did not readily shift. Lack of shift, or rigidity, was manifested despite the high percentage (65 per cent) of abstract responses on the initial administration. In other words, an "abstract attitude," as measured by responses to the similarities subtest, did not go hand in hand with nonrigid behavior. The findings therefore do not suggest a negative relationship between rigidity and abstractness, even when both are measured by the same medium.

What the quantitative scores fail to reveal is that individuals who had initially given concrete or functional replies to test items usually gave an abstract response on the second or third trial, while those who had initially given abstract responses sometimes failed to give any other similarity for the test items; one might say that the latter were so blinded by the abstraction which they had deduced on the first administration that they were not aware of concrete and functional similarities. This result is particularly interesting in the light of two assumptions implicit in the interpretation of many tests of conceptualization. One of these assumptions is that an individual who reveals an abstract attitude is capable of noting concrete or functional similarities between items, that the ability to abstract is a higher-order function which presupposes the ability to behave concretely. The second assumption is that an individual who is concrete is incapable of abstract behavior. Both of these assumptions would seem to require re-evaluation in light of the above results.

The experiment also shows that a change in test instructions (to find a new similarity) resulted, for some subjects, in a change in conceptual performance. This implies that the same individual's conceptual behavior may differ under different conditions. We might mention also that, when the similarities subtest was administered under various conditions (e.g., under nonspeed and then under speed conditions), responses of subjects were sometimes radically altered, so that a subject who gave predominantly concrete responses under one condition, gave predominantly abstract responses under another condition.

Also of interest are exploratory experiments with college students in which the similarities subtest was administered only once but in which changes were made in the customary instructions or certain experiences were provided just prior to the administration of the test. For example, it was found that, when the administration was preceded by a lecture-discussion on the laws of logic, particularly as they refer to categorization and abstraction, the group showed relatively more abstract replies in the similarities subtest than did control college groups that received the similarities subtest but not the lecture-discussion. In another experiment the experimenter offered three examples of similarities for the illustrative task ("In what way are an orange and a banana the same?"), which may be done in the standardized method of administration; but, in addition, the experimenter noted that one similarity ("They are both fruit") was characterized as abstract, another ("You can eat them both") as functional, and the third ("They both have skins") as concrete. Moreover, subjects were told that they would receive more credit on the test for abstract similarities than for concrete or functional similarities. These subjects gave relatively more abstract replies than college subjects who received the usual administration. In still other variations, prior to the subtest subjects were given several examples of similarities all of which belonged to one category (e.g., all were concrete or all functional), but no mention was made of the nature of the category or of credit allowed for responses. These subjects tended to show more responses that fell into the illustrated category than did college subjects who received the customary instructions.

E EFFECTS IN BRAIN-DAMAGED INDIVIDUALS

The chief characteristic of brain-damaged individuals has been described by Goldstein as a loss of abstract ability which compels them to behave on the concrete level. If concreteness and behavioral rigidity are positively related, then brain-damaged individuals might be expected to differ from normals both on tests of abstraction and on tests of rigidity. Rabinowitz (1951), testing male World War II Canadian veterans, compared nineteen veterans who had gunshot head wounds (which varied in locus, extent, and severity) with twenty-five veterans hospitalized for various physical disabilities but with no brain damage. At the time of the study, the subjects with brain injuries were engaged in normal civilian pursuits but had been called to the hospital for a routine examination. The group with head wounds and the control group were equated for mean age (thirty-one years) and average educational level (grade nine).

The subjects were tested individually. Abstraction was studied by use of the McGill University analogies test and picture-anomalies test. In line with Goldstein's thesis concerning the relationship between brain damage and abstract ability, the head-wound group made somewhat inferior scores on both tests of abstraction. The mean number of errors on the analogies test was 5.56 for this group, significantly more than the 3.52 figure for the control group. On the anomalies test, the mean number of errors was 10.02 for the head-wound group but only 7.64 for the control group.

Modified forms of the arithmetical and maze Einstellung tests were employed. The head-wound group showed relatively more direct solutions of the criticals but also relatively more failures of the extinction tasks than the control group; differences were small and insignificant. Only the time required to do the test mazes differentiated significantly between the two groups. The mean time in seconds for the critical mazes was 14.95 for the head-wound group but only 9.04 for the control group, and for the extinction mazes it was 15.37 for the former but only 9.16 for the latter. Note that the time required by the head-wound group was within the permissible limit and that the greater time needed by them might have been a resultant of poorer motor coordination. Hence, in the sense of criteria ordinarily used as indices of E effects, we do not find striking differences between the brain-damaged individuals and the controls.

Taken in conjunction with the inferior scores the brain-damaged individuals made on the tests of abstraction, the findings in the Einstellung tests suggest that significant differences in abstract ability need not necessarily be concomitant with significant differences in rigidity.

Einstellung Test and a Nonverbal Test of Abstraction

The similarities subtest of the Wechsler-Bellevue adult-intelligence scales has been recognized as having certain shortcomings as a test of conceptual behavior. For example, Rapaport, Gill, and Schafer say:

> The concept formation required by this subtest is on a purely verbal level; that is, no reference to the specific samples of the objects takes place, and the definitions offered are usually based on the verbal coherence established in everyday experience between the objects and their generic terms ... These verbal coherences become so stereotyped and ingrained in an individual's thinking that profound impairment or even deterioration of active concept formation may leave them untouched. (1945, vol. 1, pp. 394-95.)

Since this weakness is common to all verbal tests of concept formation, it was decided to study the relation of behavior on the Einstellung test to behavior on a nonverbal test of conceptualization. The revision by Rapaport, Gill, and Schafer of the Gelb-Goldstein-Weigl-Scheerer object-sorting test was selected because of the detailed analysis and quantitative scoring methods which are available for it (1945, vol. 1, c. III).

The subjects, seventy-five McGill University students, were tested individually by Lyman (1951). The sorting test was given in one session and the arithmetical Einstellung test in a later session. The sixty-eight subjects (thirty-three females, thirty-five males) who solved all the E problems by the E method were divided into five groups according to the point of shift to the direct method, with Group 1 showing no E effects and Group 5 the most E effects (failure of all four extinction tasks).

The sorting test is divided into two parts. In Part 1, which deals with active concept formation, the subject is asked to pick objects which he thinks belong with a given object and then to say why they belong together. In Part 2, which deals with passive concept formation, the examiner places a group of objects before the subject and asks him why they belong together. The subject's explanations as to why the objects belonged together were characterized, in accordance with the rationale of Rapaport *et al.*, as abstract, concrete, or functional. For each of the five groups there was determined the mean percentage of responses in each of these three categories; the results are presented in Table III.

TABLE III. PERCENTAGES OF RESPONSES IN OBJECT-SORTING TEST

	Subjects	Part 1 Active Concept Formation Abstract Concrete Functional			Part 2 Passive Concept Formation Abstract Concrete Functional		
Group 1........	18	53	19	21	82	1	8
Group 2........	20	57	7	28	75	2	7
Group 3........	11	57	2	29	72	2	8
Group 4........	11	53	3	34	74	2	11
Group 5........	8	53	9	28	76	5	9

The table reveals that abstract replies constitute about one half of each group's responses in Part 1 but about three quarters of each group's responses in Part 2, that functional responses are more frequent in Part 1 than in Part 2, and that concrete responses tend to be less in the second part than in the first. That Part 1 tends to be characterized by relatively less abstract and by relatively more concrete and functional replies than Part 2 has also been reported by Rapaport et al. for their normal subjects (1945, vol. 1, p. 433). (Would the same trends prevail if the two parts had been given in reverse order?) The present results, revealing rather small intergroup differences in each category and large differences between the two parts of the sorting test, suggest that conceptual behavior may depend less on the degree of rigidity and more on the particular testing instrument.

From Group 1 through Group 5, there are no consistent trends in any category, a fact that hints that there is no consistent relationship between conceptual behavior and rigidity when a criterion of the latter is the point of shift to the direct method.

Regarding Group 1 as the least rigid and Group 5 as the most rigid, we find a confused picture for Part 1, since the least rigid group and the most rigid group show the same proportion of abstract replies, while the most rigid group shows relatively more functional, but relatively less concrete, replies than the least rigid group; the difference approaches significance (0.05 level) for concrete replies. The pattern with respect to concrete replies is just the reverse of what should be expected if rigidity and concreteness are positively related. The trend for functional replies, which is in line with expectations, is opposed to the trend for concrete replies. The findings suggest that the conceptual level to be inferred from functional responses is not necessarily similar to that which should be inferred from concrete responses. This raises the problem of the advisability of grouping together concrete and functional replies as is usually done; for example, in the scoring of the similarities subtest of the Wechsler-Bellevue adult-intelligence scales.

Results in Part 2 of the test tend to confirm a positive relationship between rigidity and concreteness since the least rigid group has relatively more abstract responses and relatively fewer concrete and functional responses than the most rigid; significant differences prevail for abstract as well as for concrete responses.

Thus, the findings of the present investigation suggest that the relationship prevailing between behavioral rigidity and concreteness of thinking may vary considerably, depending on (1) the criterion of degree of rigidity; (2) the test of concreteness used and, even, the particular part of the test; and (3) the criterion of the degree of concreteness of thinking; e.g., the categories of responses regarded as indices of concrete or of abstract thinking.

EINSTELLUNG-TYPE SORTING TESTS

Einstellung-type tests were developed to serve as sorting tests so that E effects and conceptual behavior could be studied in the same context. The Einstellung object-sorting test consists of sixteen groups of objects with three objects in each group. One group at a time is put before the subject and he is asked to write why the three objects belong together. The first five groups present E problems since the three objects in each of the groups can be classified according to one principle; that is, they belong to a common category. The next two groups present critical tasks since the three objects in each group can be classified according to two principles: they belong to a common category and they have a common color. There follow five extinction tasks in each of which the three objects cannot readily be grouped according to a common category but in each of which they have the same color. There then come two more criticals (common category, common color) and, finally, two more E problems (common category only). For example, the first group in the test consists of cutlery: a pink fork, a blue spoon, and a silver knife; the second group consists of writing equipment: a grey pen, a red crayon, and white chalk; a critical problem consists of yellow clothing: a blouse, a sock, and a glove; an extinction task consists of three pink rather unrelated objects: a box, a calendar, and a fork. We were interested in ascertaining whether subjects would develop an Einstellung to classify the items according to a common category, and would overlook the color common to the three items in the critical and extinction tasks; that is, whether they would show E effects in the sense of failing to report color as a basis of similarity.

An Einstellung card-sorting test was also developed which paralleled the object-sorting test. Instead of an object, there was now a white card with the name of the object printed on it in the color that corresponded as closely as possible to the color of the object. For example, the first group consisted of three cards with the word FORK printed in pink on one card, the word SPOON printed in blue on another card, and the word KNIFE printed in silver on another card; an extinction task consisted of a card with the word BOX, another with the word CALENDAR, and another with the word FORK, all printed in pink. The sixteen groups of cards were presented to the subject in the same order as the corresponding groups of objects. As in the object-sorting test, the subject's task was to write why the three words put before him belonged together.

A question raised for investigation was whether E effects would differ in the object-sorting and card-sorting tests. Also, what would be the influence on E effects of first receiving the object-sorting test and then the card-sorting test, or vice versa?

The reasons given by subjects for the "belongingness" of three objects or three words were classified as abstract, functional, concrete, or failure. The classification criteria used were the same as those used in the sorting test of Rapaport *et al.* For example, if the subject said for the first task (pink fork, blue spoon, silver knife) that the objects or words pertained to cutlery or eating equipment, his response was classified as abstract; if he said "we eat with them," his response was classified as functional; if he said "they all go on the table," it was classified as concrete; if he did not respond or gave an incorrect answer, it was classified as a failure. Raised for investigation was the question what relationships would prevail between E effects and these conceptual categories and whether the relationships would differ for the object-sorting test and the card-sorting test.

Rita Brownstein Kopin administered the tests individually to forty Montreal college students. Half of them received the object-sorting test and immediately afterwards the card-sorting test, while others received the card-sorting test first.

There seemed to be more awareness of color when actual objects were used than when cards were used. Many individuals later said that they were not aware of the fact that the words were printed in different colors, while a few said that they were more or less aware of a difference in colors, but did not think of using color as a classificatory basis. A common color was reported as the reason for the three items belonging together significantly more frequently for the objects than for the cards. On the first tests, percentages of color responses to the criticals, first extinction task, and five extinction tasks considered as a unit were:

Object sorting............
  20 students C_1C_2: 15%   First ext.: 80%   All ext.: 90% C_3C_4: 62%
Card sorting............
  20 students C_1C_2: 0%   First ext.: 5%   All ext.: 5% C_3C_4: 0%

It is seen that, for the objects, the majority gave color responses to the extinction tasks and subsequent criticals, while few or none did so for the cards. Color responses to the criticals were almost invariably accompanied by reports of a common category as another basis for similarity. For Criticals 1 and 2, 15 per cent saw such multiple bases for similarity, and for Criticals 3 and 4, 55 per cent. Thus, the objects made for awareness of both color and category in the later criticals, while, with the cards, subjects were restricted to the common category and blind to the common color.

For the extinction tasks, subjects who overlooked the common color in which the words were printed came up with such superficial similarities as these: the three words share a common letter of the alphabet or have a common number of letters; all three words pertain to things which are rather elongated in shape or which may be used by children or which are touched by hands. Some invented involved stories of how the words might be related. Some failed completely to give a basis for classification; failures of the extinction tasks averaged only 5 per cent for the objects but 51 per cent for the cards.

It will be remembered that those who first received the objects later received the cards, and vice versa. While prior experience with the cards did not enhance color responses when objects were subsequently given, prior experience with the objects did make for more color responses when cards were subsequently given than when they were given first. Nonetheless, color responses were never as frequent for the cards as for the objects. This was still so in the special test where subjects were first given the cards, then the objects, and finally the cards again. Table IV indicates that E effects (in terms of failures to offer color responses) for cards were greater than for objects and were influenced by prior experience with the objects. The findings suggest that the strength of E effects and of rigidity is dependent on the particular contextual medium in which they are studied and on past experiences.

TABLE IV. E EFFECTS IN EINSTELLUNG-TYPE SORTING TESTS (IN TERMS OF PERCENTAGES OF FAILURES TO REPORT A COMMON COLOR)

	First Test, Objects	Second Test, Cards	First Test, Cards	Second Test, Objects	Third Test, Cards
	(20 subjects)		(20 subjects)		
Criticals 1 and 2............	85	87	100	87	90
Extinction tasks............	10	39	95	36	61
Criticals 3 and 4............	38	79	100	47	87

Past experience, in a broader sense (cf. Koffka, 1935), may help to account for the results. When confronted with actual objects, we are accustomed to perceive and react to their color and other physical properties, and to use color occasionally as a criterion for grouping, separating, or distinguishing objects. But usually, when confronted with words, we react to the abstract symbols they represent, and not to the particular color or colors in which they happen to be written or printed. Past experiences may therefore have fostered greater blinding effects for the words than for the objects.

Whatever may be responsible for the fact, it is apparent that the words are more abstract in nature than the actual, concrete objects for which they stand. Moreover, the reasons given for belongingness fell into an abstract category somewhat more often for the words than for the objects. When responses to the E problems and criticals of the respective first tests are considered (responses to the extinction tasks are not considered here because of the many failures in the card-sorting test), we find that abstract responses constitute 67 per cent of the total responses for the cards but only 55 per cent of the total responses for the objects; that functional responses average 25 per cent for the cards but 38 per cent for the objects, and that concrete responses average about 8 per cent for each test. (Incidentally, this finding also suggests the inadvisability of lumping functional and concrete responses together or of assuming that each is an equivalent index of conceptual functioning.) If abstract responses are regarded as connoting an abstract conceptual level, and functional responses as connoting a more concrete level, then the findings imply that the abstract medium (printed words) tended to promote more abstract and less concrete conceptual behavior than the concrete medium. This indicates that the kind of testing medium employed may be a determinant of conceptual behavior. That the cards provoked greater E effects than the objects, implies that the more abstract medium, which fostered more abstract conceptual behavior, also fostered greater rigidity, while the more concrete medium, which fostered more concrete conceptual behavior, led to less rigidity. This seems to go counter to the notions that abstraction works against rigidity and that concreteness and rigidity are positively related.

In a further analysis of the results, we fractionized subjects according to whether the reasons for belongingness which they gave for the E problems fell predominantly into the abstract category or into other categories. No consistent relationship was found between conceptual categories and strength of E effects. Those who gave abstract reasons were not better able to shift to color responses than those who gave predominantly concrete or functional reasons. Individual differences prevailed in each conceptual category. For example, when the card-sorting test was the second test given, of three subjects who gave abstract responses to every E problem, two failed every extinction task while the third gave color responses to all the extinction tasks and thereby solved all of them. There were also marked differences for the cards as compared with the objects. Thus, considering the respective first tests, we find that the five subjects who gave abstract responses to the last three E problems of the object-sorting test, gave, together, a total of thirty-two color responses in this test or an average of over six color responses each; on the other hand, the eleven subjects who gave abstract responses to the last three E problems of the card-sorting test, contributed a total of only one color solution among them for the whole test, or an average of virtually zero color responses each. In the second tests, the differences were not so marked (perhaps because of the preceding experiences) but went in the same direction; those who gave abstract responses to the last three E problems of the object-sorting test contributed an average of over five color responses each, while the corresponding subjects in the card-sorting test gave an average of only three color responses each. The findings suggest that the relationship which prevails between abstract conceptual behavior and E effects is influenced by individual differences, the nature of the testing medium, and previous experiences; they imply that it may be fruitless to seek to characterize the relationship *in vacuo* as if it were independent of such factors.

A final word is in order about failures to give reasons for belongingness for the extinction tasks. These failures may be interpreted as indicants of rigidity since the subject was blinded to the common color; they may also be interpreted as indicants of concreteness of thinking since the subject did not find the similarity, did not "abstract out" the common property of color. That the cards gave rise to more abstract responses to the E problems than the objects, but also gave rise to more failures in the extinction tasks, suggests that the "abstract-conceptual" level in the E problems changed to a "concrete-conceptual" level in the extinction tasks. In any event, no one conceptual level seemed to be invariantly characteristic of any subject.

A color response, whether it refers to objects or words, may be classified as a concrete response since color is a common, rather unessential property of three items—on "the concrete level of concept formation, 'things' are considered to belong together because of a common unessential property" (Rapaport, Gill, and Schafer, 1945, vol. 1, p. 170). What the results show is that, in the card-sorting test, those who gave abstract responses to all of the other test problems were not necessarily able to give the concrete color response to the extinction tasks and often failed to give any basis of belongingness for these tasks. Thus, again we see that being capable of operating on the abstract level does not necessarily imply an ability to operate on the concrete level, counter to the assumption that abstract ability is a higher-order function which presupposes the ability to behave concretely. Goldstein and Scheerer (1941) maintain that in the normal adult the abstract and concrete levels are fluidly interwoven so that he can shift at will from one to another level except in catastrophic situations. The college students were presumably normal adults and the extinction tasks of the card-sorting test can in no sense be regarded as constituting catastrophic or shock situations for them or situations beyond their intellectual ken—and yet in this test they were usually not able to shift from the abstract level when the situation called for shift.

The findings of this study therefore hint at the need for evaluation of some of the characteristics attributed to abstract and concrete thinking and of the assumed relationship of abstract and concrete thinking to rigidity.

COMMENTS

It has been widely accepted that concreteness of thinking is closely linked with rigidity of behavior. While some of the cited investigations point to a positive relationship between concreteness and rigidity, others fail to do so. The findings as a whole therefore cast doubt on the universality of the theses: (1) that concreteness of thinking necessarily bears a positive relationship to rigidity of behavior; (2) that abstractness necessarily bears a negative relationship to rigidity; (3) that abstract ability presupposes an ability to shift volitionally; (4) that the ability to abstract is a higher-order function which presupposes the ability to behave concretely; and (5) that an individual who exhibits concrete behavior is incapable of abstract behavior. Our findings suggest that the particular relationship which is found to prevail between conceptual behavior and rigidity may be dependent on the particular definitions of rigidity, abstraction, and concreteness which are employed, and on the particular tests and criteria which are used to measure these constructs. Moreover, relationships which prevail between conceptual behavior and rigidity seem to vary for different individuals and for the same individual after various experiences, and do not seem capable of being characterized in an absolute manner.

Experimental findings suggested the need for evaluation of some of the assumptions pertaining to abstract and concrete thinking. We shall now attempt an evaluation.

Function of Individual or Function of Field Conditions

While Goldstein and Scheerer note that there are gradations of abstract and of concrete behavior, in clinical practice it has become customary to deal with abstract ability as an all-or-none affair, rather than to deal with degrees of abstract ability manifested under certain conditions. Abstract ability is treated as an absolute, as a characteristic that an individual either possesses or does not possess. This is well exemplified in the prevalence of such concepts as "abstract-mindedness" and "concrete-mindedness." The cited experimental findings indicate that an individual's conceptual performance may vary with different tests, different kinds of testing material, different instructions, different social atmospheres, and after various experiences. The findings suggest that whether a person manifests so-called abstract or concrete behavior, or whether he manifests one or another degree of abstraction, may not be solely a function of his capacity level but may more accurately be described as a function of field conditions. The findings speak against the advisability of classifying a person as abstract-minded or concrete-minded, since these dichotomous classifications ignore the degree of abstractness and imply that the individual's conceptual behavior is a fixed characteristic which is independent of conditions.

To regard conceptual behavior as a function of field conditions is methodologically and therapeutically more fruitful than to pigeonhole an individual as concrete-minded or abstract-minded. Methodologically, this approach requires study of the conditions under which an individual shows one or another kind or degree of conceptual behavior. Therapeutically, it calls for the creation of those conditions which tend to maximize certain conceptual performances and to minimize others. This is in keeping with the spirit of Goldstein's fundamental approach to conceptual behavior and with his therapeutic orientation.

Is the Young Child Capable Only of Concrete Thinking?

Many psychologists assume that the young child is confined to the concrete level but that as he grows older he gradually acquires the abstract attitude. The difference between the younger normal child and the older one is not simply a quantitative, but is more a qualitative, one; it concerns particularly the development of the abstract attitude (Goldstein, 1943, p. 222). Lewin notes that "the tendency to concreteness and primitiveness appears to be a general feature of the childlike or otherwise undifferentiated person" (1935, p. 223). Let us consider some of the evidence supposedly attesting to the thesis that the young child is confined to the concrete level.

Class Concepts. Among the arguments raised in support of the young child's concreteness is the contention that he lacks abstract concepts. "The child's concepts always have a concrete content" (Werner, 1940, p. 271). The child "does not have at his command any class concept in the adult sense" (Goldstein and Scheerer, 1941, p. 12). While the child may utilize verbal expressions which seem to signify something general or categorical, it is asserted that he actually lacks general concepts. His use of such expressions arises, Goldstein and Scheerer explain, because adults tend to teach him class concepts, words which are suited to different objects of the same class; he may, for example, they say, be taught the word "flower" before he is taught the names of specific flowers. In short, the child may use class words but he necessarily lacks the meaning of the conceptional generality implied in the words.

Yet verbatim records kept of the conversation of nursery-school children and even younger children speak against this contention. Records kept of the present writers' children, and observations of young children in experimental and free situations, suggest that grasping and understanding abstract concepts is not beyond the young child's ability. Our oldest son, at the age of two years and five months, when asked what he meant by the word "children," which he frequently employed, answered, "I is a children, Danny is a children, and all little ones in the whole wide world is children"—surely broad enough to be regarded as a conceptual rather than as a concrete meaning. The same child, at the age of two years and seven months, frequently used the expression "apple money." An apparently concrete term growing out of his awareness that money was used for the purchase of apples, the term was actually employed by him in the sense of a broad class concept. Thus he begged for apple money to buy lollipops with or to put into his piggy-bank, explained that his daddy was away doing work for which he would be paid apple money, and stated that his mother used this apple money to buy milk, bread, meat, toys, etc. Here we have an example of a concrete term being used as a class concept.

An objection may be raised to our illustrations on the grounds that perhaps adults taught the child the conceptual meanings of the terms. Perhaps. But the issue at stake is whether the child is capable of grasping such meanings. Surely one would not object to a general concept when used by an adult on the grounds that its conceptual meaning may have been taught him by others.

Consider another illustration. Utilizing various Gestalt-oriented teaching procedures, Catherine Stern (1949) has enabled preschool children—even those with relatively low I.Q.'s—to discover the abstract concepts of number, addition, multiplication, etc. If these children were truly concrete-minded, then they should not have proved capable of understanding such abstract concepts. In this connection it should be noted that these children's understanding was evinced by their performances; they probably could not have verbalized the concepts. But, as Goldstein and Scheerer (1941, p. 26) and others have pointed out, verbalization is not necessarily characteristic of every abstraction. In view of the child's limited experience in expressing his thoughts, the possibility should be kept in mind that the child may understand a general concept but be unable to verbalize his understanding adequately.

Our implication is not that the child signifies something general, categorical, or universal whenever he uses a class concept. On the other hand, it should not be assumed that he is necessarily echoing a word taught him by an adult without understanding its conceptual generality. Whether or not a child understands an abstract concept must be determined in each case, always with due allowance being made for possible difficulties in verbal expression.

Verbalization in a Symbolic Sense. As further evidence of the child's concreteness, it has been asserted that he does not use verbalization in a representational or symbolic sense (Goldstein and Scheerer, 1941, p. 12). That is, he does not use a word to represent an object or idea but to denote a concrete situational act to which he associates the term. In a similar vein, Guillaume (cited in Werner, 1940, p. 277) states that, when a child uses such personal names as "Papa," "Mama," "Mary," they are not so much nouns as imperatives, linguistic participants in concrete action.

While we are aware of the importance of recognizing that not all nouns as used by children actually represent objects or ideas, we think that there is a danger in going to the other extreme and assuming that young children do not or cannot use verbal expressions in a representational or symbolic sense. When a child asks for a glass of milk, is he necessarily referring to the particular glass of milk? May he not be using the phrase in a representational or symbolic sense?

Egocentrism. Egocentrism is regarded as a characteristic of the concrete approach. Goldstein and Scheerer contend that egocentrism involves an inability to detach the ego from the outer world or from inner experiences while abstract behavior is indispensable "whenever the situation cannot be mastered without the individual's detaching his ego from the situation" (1941, p. 29). The alleged egocentrism of the child has therefore been used as testifying to his concreteness. But examination of some of the evidence supposedly bearing on the egocentric nature of the child, we saw in a previous chapter, reveals a rather contro-

versial situation, indicating that the child is not necessarily more egocentric than the adult, that he does not necessarily experience more difficulty in detaching the ego from the outer world or inner experiences.
Since the child's greater egocentrism is in dispute, it would hardly seem
justifiable to utilize it as indisputably testifying to his concrete attitude.

General Considerations. Consider some of the implications stemming
from the young child's alleged concreteness and compare them with actual observations of children's behavior. A child at play may vary his
roles, within a few minutes, from fireman to policeman to doctor to
butcher to dog to wagon. He may decide that a scatter rug represents a
boat, a train, a ferocious lion, or simply a scatter rug. Does such behavior
warrant being labeled as realistic in nature, as close to immediate reality,
as involving an inability to assume a mental set willfully and consciously,
as stimulus-bound, as being tied to the experienced uniqueness of the
object or situation and unable to shift actively? (All these are criteria
of the concrete level.) Rather, such behavior seems to have all the earmarks of being the very antithesis of concrete behavior. It seems to us
that there is much in the behavior of children which makes it rather incongruous to describe their behavior as concrete. More generally: instances can be cited of the thinking and behavior of children, even very
young children, which seem to negate the generalization that children
are confined to the concrete level.

Is Primitive Man Capable Only of Concrete Thinking?

Let us consider some of the arguments that Werner (1940) presents
to support the thesis that conceptual activity of primitives is on the
concrete level, characterized as a lower level developmentally speaking
than the abstract level of the more civilized adult. Before doing so, we
note that he uses, without explicit definition, such phrases as "primitive mentality," "mentality of the civilized man," "the European mentality," "the European mind," and "the typical European reflection."

Transcendence of Concrete Situations. Primitive man is described
as pinned down to the reality of the thinglike world, whereas "typical
European reflection is universal in nature, abstract; it functions more
or less independently of the immediate, concrete reality, and is governed
by an awareness of general laws" (Werner, 1940, p. 299). Religious
and artistic forms of behavior of primitive man, it seems to us, are not
pinned down to the thinglike world, and do transcend the immediate
concrete situation. On the other hand, there is no conclusive evidence
that "typical European reflection" is necessarily universal and abstract
in nature. Goldstein and Scheerer note that the normal person's be-

havior is prevailingly concrete. Nor is there conclusive evidence that "typical European reflection" is governed by an awareness of general laws, be these the laws of logic or the laws of nature. Even the trained logician and scientist may fail to show much awareness of general laws in his thinking outside of his particular realm of specialization. It is not clear whether Werner is referring to the laws of traditional logic, as formulated by Aristotle, and whether he intends to imply that the "typical European" has learned these laws or is aware of them without any formal learning. Werner himself points out (1940, p. 18) that a kind of logic, although not necessarily Aristotelian logic, may prevail in primitive thinking. There is no a priori basis for assuming that this thinking is governed by more or less awareness of general laws than is "European reflection."

Causal Thinking. Werner claims that primitive thinking about causality is concrete, in the same temporal dimension as the facts it attempts to account for, and not, "as in western scientific thought, behind or beyond empirical phenomena" (p. 305). We raise the problems of what constitutes "western" scientific thought and whether all its explanations of causality are necessarily behind or beyond empirical phenomena. Werner notes, for example, that primitives tend to explain natural phenomena in terms of a myth, a story which tells "how it happened." Controversy is currently being waged as to whether the "scientific explanation" of natural phenomena in terms of evolution—a theory which plays a fundamental role in Werner's approach—is anything more than a myth which seeks to tell "how it happened."

Processes of explanation and of inference in the primitive mentality are described as thoroughly concrete in character while the "civilized man's methods of explanations are representative of a universal lawful mode of thought" (p. 300). Here again is the conception that the causal thinking of the adult in our society is necessarily abstract and universal whereas that of the "primitive mind" (the child, primitive man) is necessarily concrete.

Some Unfounded Generalizations. One wonders about the possible scientific basis for the claim that "primitive reflection always means concrete configuration" (p. 299). Even if all studies of primitive people agreed on this characteristic, one could not jump, with any scientific assurance, to the generalization that it must always be so. Similarly, we question the contention that "the concept of lawful necessity is beyond primitive man's conception" (p. 302). The only valid claim that might conceivably be made would be that, in some studies, selected peoples of a so-called primitive society did not convey to the investigator that they understood the concept of lawful necessity. But such apparent inability might be traceable to difficulties in communication and interpretation and would in no way allow the generalization that the concept is beyond the grasp of all primitive men.

Parenthetically, we note that Werner regards young children as incapable of understanding the concept of lawful necessity, basing his claim on investigations such as those of Piaget (1930), but other investigators, for example, Deutsche (1943), have found that some young children did seem to grasp the concept. The child's "capability" would thus seem to depend on the particular investigation. The analogy for primitives is clear.

Primitive mentality is regarded as not capable of operating on the abstract level while more civilized mentalities, in particular, the European mentality, are regarded as possessing a plurality of mental levels, ranging from the concrete level ("concrete abstraction") to the abstract-conceptual level. It is in this plurality of mental levels, Werner claims, that there "lies the solution of the mystery of how the European mind can understand primitive types of mentality" (p. 39). It is implied that primitive man, since he cannot operate on the abstract level, is incapable of understanding the European mind. But is this a fact? It has never been established that primitive man is incapable of gaining an understanding of "civilized types of mentality" which may be as great as the understanding of "primitive types of mentality" gained by civilized man.

Inherent Concreteness. Werner refers to the "inherent concreteness" of primitive man. But some other psychologists and anthropologists support a contrary view, and maintain that primitive man reasons as he does partly because he lacks the fund of knowledge and the background of the members of a more civilized culture, while possessing other knowledge and background (Klineberg, 1935; Köhler, 1937). Köhler maintains that there is no sharp difference between the mental processes of individuals of a primitive society and those of a more civilized society; the observed differences are due to differences, not in processes of thinking, but in the backgrounds in which the thinking process occurs. We shall deal, in later paragraphs, with Wertheimer's claim that primitive man is capable of abstraction.

Are Pathological States Characterized by Concreteness?

Individuals suffering from various pathological conditions have been described as having lost the capacity to think abstractly. "The conceptual activity of the individual who has regressed to a pathological form of behavior is also concretely determined. The decline of the con-

cept from the abstract to the concrete is a specific pathological symptom"
(Werner, 1940, p. 274). For all acquired cortical damage, such as
from tumors, injuries, intoxications, for schizophrenia, and for mental
changes due to malformation of the brain cortex, such as in feeble-mindedness, "the defect . . . consists first and mainly of an impairment of
the abstract attitude" (Goldstein, 1943, p. 213).

Realistic Approach. The concrete attitude is characterized by Goldstein and Scheerer as realistic with respect to outer-world situations
as well as ideas, thoughts, and feelings; it is said to be close to concrete
reality (1941, p. 2). Werner also characterizes the concrete level as a
realistic one in which the individual is close to and unable to transcend
concrete reality (1940, p. 194). But it seems to us somewhat incongruous to describe an individual suffering from cortical pathology or a
psychosis as operating on the concrete level, if by this one means that
his thinking and behavior are realistic, that his responses are close to
immediate reality. Often the psychotic is divorced from reality, unable to get along in this concrete world, his very illness being a possible
escape from reality. Should he then be labeled as concrete, as realistic
in his approach? More than a matter of terminology is involved here.
The very essence of the concrete attitude, when positively characterized,
is that it is realistic. Contrariwise, the very essence of some pathologies
may be an inability to cope with reality, to adjust "realistically" to the
concrete world. It would therefore seem that, even when an individual's
performances on various tests of abstraction indicate that he has an
impairment of the abstract attitude, it does not follow that he should be
considered to be concrete in the sense that he has a realistic approach.

Inability to Think or Perform Symbolically. There are pathological
individuals who escape into a highly abstract (private) world, who are
concerned with problems of a metaphysical, philosophical, or even
mathematical nature, and whose speech and behavior are replete with
symbols. While these may be symbols other than those used by normals,
or while the interpretations may differ from those given by normals, it
may be said of these individuals that they are concerned with "abstract
thoughts" and that they are thinking and performing symbolically. And
yet the defect in some cortical pathologies and in schizophrenia has
been described as consisting "first and mainly" of an impairment of the
abstract attitude, resulting in the inability "to think or perform symbolically" (Goldstein and Scheerer, 1941, p. 4). It is conceivable that
there may be abstract thinking and performances with symbols which
differ in character from those studied by the various tests of abstraction so that scores on such tests do not necessarily indicate general
inability to think abstractly and symbolically.

Inconsistency of the Assumptions

The assumptions that the young child and the primitive lack the abstract attitude seem to be logically inconsistent with the assumption that the defect in certain pathologies is chiefly an impairment of the abstract attitude. Consider the case of two children of the same chronological age, one of whom has some pathological defect while the other is normal. If both children are young enough, then, according to the assumption accepted by certain psychologists, they will be regarded as necessarily behaving concretely, as both lacking the abstract attitude. But, if the child who is pathological does not have the abstract attitude to begin with, how can his pathology be assumed to consist mainly in an impairment or loss of something he never had? Or consider the case of a primitive adult who is psychotic or has suffered some brain injury. If his defect consists mainly in an impairment of the abstract attitude and confinement to concrete behavior, it will hardly be a defect at all in his society if it is assumed that even the normal primitive adult is pretty much confined to this level. Yet the psychotic or brain-injured primitive individual has been known to be regarded as abnormal in his behavior and thinking when compared with normal primitives. And even a young child suffering from mental deficiency or cortical pathology may manifest behavior which is strikingly different from that of a normal child of the same chronological or mental age. It would seem that the various assumptions are not compatible. To avoid logical inconsistencies, one must reject either one or both of the two assumptions: that the young child and the primitive adult are confined to the concrete level and that the defect in cortical pathologies, schizophrenia, and feeble-mindedness is mainly an impairment of the abstract attitude.

Abstract and Concrete Thinking in Relation to Scientific Thinking

Concrete thinking has been described as "prescientific" thinking and as "low-level" thinking while the abstract mode of thought is regarded as reaching its highest form in scientific thinking (Werner, 1940, p. 17). Is it true that scientific thinking manifests the criteria which have been attributed to the abstract level and does not manifest those attributed to the concrete level?

Conscious Will Essential to Abstract Thinking. The abstract level, Goldstein and Scheerer state, is characterized by the appearance of "the paramount factor of conscious will" (1941, p. 23) so that the presence or absence of conscious will "coincides with the presence or absence of the abstract attitude" (p. 10). The factor of conscious will or conscious volition is said to be essential to abstraction so that so-called involuntary abstraction is not abstraction at all. At times they seem to equate the factors of conscious will and reflective apprehension, as when they note that what at first glance appears to be "involuntary abstraction" turns out to be an entirely concrete procedure, determined by an unreflective apprehension.

Let us turn to some examples of thinking which apparently do not involve the factor of conscious will or reflective apprehension in order to see whether they are actually concrete, "low-level," "prescientific" thinking.

Helmholtz, Poincaré, and other scientists, mathematicians, and inventors claim that often their discoveries came to them *not* while they were consciously and volitionally seeking after them, but during a time when "attention is on something remote from the problem" (Woodworth, 1938, p. 819). Helmholtz states that his "good ideas" were often there in the morning when he awoke. Some creative thinkers even subscribe to the theory of unconscious work or unconscious cerebration. "The part played by unconscious work in mathematical discovery seems to me indisputable," asserts Poincaré (cited in Woodworth, p. 818). Whether or not one subscribes to a theory of unconscious cerebration, one cannot help being impressed by the reports of many scientists, poets, and artists which indicate that often their creative thoughts came to them when they were not consciously and volitionally seeking after them.

Since such intellectual activity apparently lacks the factor of conscious will, it must—if Goldstein and Scheerer's thesis is accepted—be regarded as not true abstract thinking but as functioning on the concrete level. Yet it hardly seems plausible to assign to such creative activity the characteristics which have been attached to concrete thinking; that is, to say that it is low-level, prescientific thinking, less difficult than abstract thinking. While Goldstein and Scheerer have the prerogative of defining the abstract level as necessarily involving conscious will or reflective apprehension, such a definition would seem to exclude many cases of creative, productive thinking.

Conscious Will Versus Sense Experiences. The characterization of the abstract level in terms of conscious will is related to the assumption that activity which stems from and is determined by the self is of a higher level than activity which is essentially determined by sense experiences or by the phenomenal field. A criterion of the concrete level is a tendency to react to the claims, the demands, or the so-called Gestalt or configurational properties of an object or situation. Werner describes as concrete any thinking in which the perceptual configuration and the concept stand together undifferentiated and maintains that "a tendency toward configurational completion" is characteristic of concrete thinking (1940, p. 328). Goldstein and Scheerer state that in the sorting tests "any sorting which involves genuine abstraction is necessarily bound to a conscious and volitional act of reflecting upon the properties of objects with reference to a concept, a class, or category" (1941, p. 24). Conversely, if the individual responds to a "definite organization ... within the purely phenomenal realm of immediate experience," then he is operating on the concrete level (p. 24). For an individual with a concrete attitude, "thinking and acting are directed by the immediate claims which one particular aspect of the object or of the outerworld situation makes," these claims being thrust upon him as "palpable configurations or palpable contexts in the experiential phenomenal realm" (p. 3). In the Gelb-Goldstein-Weigl-Scheerer object-sorting test, the activity of the subject with the concrete attitude is described as "not primarily directed towards an isolated object, but oriented towards the total configuration of the articles" (p. 85). In the concrete approach the individual tends to fit things together "according to how they cohere together sensorially," so that the redness of two or more objects may be experienced as a unitary Gestalt comprising the objects which are members of that "embracing color whole" (p. 84). Underlying this interpretation is the rationale that the subject is not indulging in the higher activity of abstractive isolation, abstracting and isolating the common property of redness; rather, he "surrenders to one immediate unitary color impression, and the two (or more) articles are parts of that sustaining totality as an experiential whole" (p. 84).

Take as another example the interpretation of performances in the Weigl-Goldstein-Scheerer color-form sorting test. The subject with a concrete approach is said to have the attitude of "passive surrender to the organization of his sense impressions" (p. 112). Abnormal concreteness is marked by the tendency to arrange the objects in a definite spatial pattern, where this pattern "is not arbitrary but follows definite structural laws ... may be determined by Gestalt laws, such as balance, symmetry, closure, etc." (p. 115). In contrast, the abstract approach is characterized, among other factors, by the tendency casually to throw the objects into different piles without regard for spatial order within each pile.

In short, in the concrete approach one tends to react to the so-called configurational, Gestalt, or structural demands of an object or situation and to be guided by the Gestalt principles of perception, including the tendency toward configurational completion. Now, it is precisely such a tendency which Wertheimer and other Gestalt psychologists have described as involved in thinking in general, and not only in concrete thinking.* Wertheimer writes that thinking "consists in envisaging, realizing structural features and structural requirements; proceeding in accordance with, and determined by, these requirements... thereby changing the situation in the direction of structural improvements" (1945, p. 190).

Thus, some of the characteristics attributed to concrete thinking are precisely the features which Wertheimer has described as characteristic of thinking, including such highly scientific thinking as that involved in Galileo's discovery which led to the formulation of the principle of inertia and in Einstein's discovery of the relativity theory.

The criterion that concrete thinking involves reactions to phenomenal groupings and organizations, while abstract thinking ignores them and instead involves an organization determined by the self, offers no means of distinguishing between a genius's invention and a maniac's scheme, both of which may sometimes ignore palpably given organizations. Because of his delusions, a paranoid individual may achieve an organization which is very different from the given organization but which is in line with his delusion system. Is he then to be characterized as having an abstract approach? If, on the other hand, he manifests some of the criteria of the concrete attitude (e.g., apparent inability to shift), is he to be characterized as having a concrete approach?

Gestalt theory maintains that phenomenal groupings which arise spontaneously in response to the field are determined by very definite principles and may arise because of "the structural requirements of the given situation" (Wertheimer, 1945, p. 135). But Goldstein and Scheerer maintain that to react on the basis of such phenomenal groupings is to give evidence of the concrete approach; only if the individual is able to ignore such groupings and to achieve a grouping in line with his goal (his specific purpose of abstracting, grouping, generalizing, etc.), they say, may he be regarded as behaving on the abstract level; that is, to impose an organization in line with one's particular task or goal or attitude is a sign of abstract thinking. Consider in this connection Wertheimer's characterization of good thinking. He does not deny that the self is part of the field and that vectors directing thinking may stem from the self and its particular wishes or goals. Nonetheless, he maintains that often thinking advances only when the individual does not seek actively to impose his viewpoint on the situation but looks to see what the situation itself suggests.

---

* Our frequent reference in this chapter to Wertheimer's account of thinking should *not* be interpreted to mean that we regard it as the most accurate account. We are primarily concerned with showing that there exists a conception of thinking which differs from that implied in the constructs of abstract and concrete thinking and with comparing the two conceptions for heuristic purposes.

In a sense a subject may become virtually blind if he looks only at that goal, and is entirely governed by the urge toward *it*. Often he must first forget what he happens to wish before he can become susceptible to what the situation itself requires.... Real thinkers forget about themselves in thinking. The main vectors in genuine thought do not refer to the I with its personal interests; rather, they represent the structural requirements of the given situation. (Wertheimer, 1945, p. 135.)

Since reacting to a definite organization within the phenomenal realm of immediate experience has been interpreted as evidence of operating on the concrete level, and since in abstract thinking the individual is said not to allow himself to be unduly influenced by immediate or sense experiences, but, instead, actively to impose his will on the external situation, it may be inferred that scientific thinking is largely divorced from the phenomenal realm of immediate or sense experience and is created by the free will, the free choice, of the scientist. This view of science finds proponents both among scientists and laymen. There are others, however, who have criticized such a view of science and who offer a very different conception.

Particularly illuminating in this respect, it seems to us, are some remarks made by Einstein in a paper concerned with the method of science. Science is concerned, he states, with the totality of the primary concepts, i.e., "concepts directly connected with sense experiences" (1950, p. 63). The totality of connections between concepts and complexes of sense experience "is the only thing which differentiates the great building which is science from a logical but empty scheme of concepts" (p. 62). An essential aim of science is "a comprehension, as *complete* as possible, of the connection between the sense experiences in their totality" (p. 63); a related aim is to represent primary concepts and relations, those "close to experience," as "theorems, logically deduced and belonging to a basis, as narrow as possible, of fundamental concepts and fundamental relations which themselves can be chosen freely (axioms)" (p. 64). But the liberty of choice of these fundamental concepts and axioms, Einstein states, is of a special kind not at all analogous to the liberty of a writer of fiction. "Rather, it is similar to that of a man engaged in solving a well designed word puzzle. He may, it is true, propose any word as the solution; but there is only *one* word which really solves the puzzle in all its forms" (p. 64). How are these hypothetical, fundamental concepts and axioms to be chosen in order to justify the expectation of success? The most satisfactory solution "is evidently to be found in cases where the new fundamental hypotheses are suggested by *the world of experience itself*" (p. 78, italics ours). Einstein adds that it is essential to make use only of concepts "concerning whose coordination to our experience we feel no doubt" (p. 66, n.).

Here a world-renowned scientist characterizes science as not dictated by the whims or will of the scientist. If science is to be more than a logical but empty scheme of concepts, it cannot ignore the "phenomenal realm of immediate experience" but must select hypotheses suggested by sense experiences and utilize concepts coordinated to these experiences. Werner has characterized the ability to "transcend concrete reality," presumably referring to the immediate experiential realm, as a fundamental indication of mental development (1940, p. 194). If Einstein and others sharing his viewpoint are correct, then this transcendence, even for the scientist, must never be so great that the plumb line of his thinking fails to keep in contact with concrete reality.

There are those who regard mathematics as completely divorced from phenomenal experiences, from physical reality, and as created by the free will of the mathematician. But there are mathematicians who disagree with this viewpoint.

> However, while the theoretical and postulational tendency of Greek mathematics remains one of its important characteristics and has exercised an enormous influence, it cannot be emphasized too strongly that application and connection with physical reality played just as important a part ... A serious threat to the very life of science is implied in the assertion that mathematics is nothing but a system of conclusions drawn from definitions and postulates that must be consistent but otherwise may be created by the free will of the mathematician. If this description were accurate, mathematics could not attract any intelligent person. It would be a game with definitions, rules, and syllogisms, without motive or goal. The notion that the intellect can create meaningful postulational systems at its whim is a deceptive half-truth. Only under the discipline of responsibility to the organic whole, only guided by intrinsic necessity, can the free mind achieve results of scientific value. (Courant and Robbins, 1941, pp. xvi-xvii.)

Of course, it is the privilege of psychologists to define as abstract only that thinking which is determined by the active imposition of an individual's will on the external situation, and to define as concrete thinking any determined by the palpably given phenomenal organization or by sense experiences. To do so, however, serves to exclude from the abstract level and to relegate to the concrete level, many examples of productive thinking and even the entire realm of science and mathematics, at least as characterized by some scientists. Yet it seems incongruous to apply to such examples and characterizations of productive thinking, science, and mathematics, the various appellatives which have been connected with concrete thinking; namely, that it is primitive in nature, prescientific, and on a low level on the developmental or evolutionary scale.

Abstract Thinking Independent of Perception, Imagination, and Emotions. Some psychologists maintain that concrete thinking is linked with perception, imagination, and emotion, while abstract thinking is independent of such processes. Thus Werner describes as a distinctive feature of concrete thinking its operation "in indivisible unity with motor-perceptual and imaginative processes" (1940, p. 52); in contrast, he regards abstract thinking as a nonsensorimotor mode of thinking, rather independent of motor-perceptual and imaginative processes. Apropos of the concept of necessity, Werner writes: "Necessity in its exact meaning as pertaining to abstract and universal laws can be conceived of only when thinking begins to function *per se*, free from any interdependence with respect to perception, emotion, and imagination" (p. 304).

Is there such thinking? Gestalt psychologists assert that there cannot be thinking devoid of perception, emotion, and imagination, that there is no sharp cleavage between so-called cognitive and so-called emotional conative processes. "Generally speaking, it is an artificial and narrow view which conceives of thinking as only an intellectual operation and separates it entirely from questions of human attitude, feeling, and emotion" (Wertheimer, 1945, p. 134). Moreover, imagination, intuition, perception, and even emotions have played constructive roles in scientific and mathematical thinking (cf. Courant and Robbins, 1941; Einstein, 1950; Wertheimer, 1945).

The notion that abstract thinking is separated from emotions and perception may be founded on the notion, not rare in everyday life and in psychological writings, that these processes hinder and blur thinking and that sense experiences cannot be trusted; the highest thinking is therefore regarded as divorced from such "subversive" elements. What this notion overlooks is that such processes need not exert a deleterious influence on reasoning, that the thinking process itself may exert strong emotional forces helping to direct one to the correct solution, and that emotion, imagination, and perception are intimately tied to thinking, particularly to what has been called insightful and productive thinking, and therefore also to scientific thinking.

Levels of Concepts and Abstractions. The most abstract concept has been described as the true class concept which is obtained by abstractive isolation—isolating "common from particular properties" (Goldstein and Scheerer, 1941, p. 3). But not all scientific and mathematical concepts are class concepts. Nor are all scientific concepts obtained by abstractive isolation. Can the concepts of "time" and "space," for example, be regarded as class concepts or as obtained by isolating "common from particular properties"?

The highest degree of abstract behavior has been described as categorical activity (Werner, 1940, p. 243). Now, while classification and categorization undoubtedly play an important role in some sciences, they certainly do not exhaust all of scientific thinking. Indeed, classification and categorization tend not to be involved in some of the fine thinking which has led to scientific discoveries but only to be subsequent to such discoveries. For example, in the reasoning process which led Einstein to the discovery of the relativity theory, as described by Einstein himself or by Wertheimer (1945), there is little use of classification and categorization. Moreover, such operations have little value in the solution of mathematical problems. About the only science in which they seem essential is the "science of library work." Why then should categorical activity be regarded as the highest degree of abstract behavior?

Goldstein and Scheerer state:

> ... there are various degrees of abstract behavior corresponding to the degree of ideational complexity which the performance in question involves. For instance, the highest degree of abstract behavior is required for the conscious and volitional act of forming generalized and hierarchic concepts or of thinking in terms of a principle and its subordinate cases and to verbalize these acts. Another instance of similar abstract behavior is the act of consciously and volitionally directing and controlling every phase of a performance—and of accounting for it verbally. A lower degree of abstraction obtains the anticipatory, ideational act of consciously and volitionally planning or initiating insightful behavior without a distinct awareness or self-accounting of every phase of its further course. (1941, p. 8.)

In the description of their thinking by various scientists (Einstein, Helmholtz, Hadamard, Poincaré, Wertheimer), there is little evidence of the formation of generalized and hierarchic concepts, characterized by Goldstein and Scheerer as requiring the highest degree of abstract behavior. The formation of such concepts often is subsequent to and not involved in the process of scientific discovery; it is strongly akin to classification and categorization which we have already discussed.

Nor does "thinking in terms of a principle and its subordinate cases," regarded as requiring a high level of abstraction, seem an adequate description of scientific thinking. The aim, the outcome, of the thinking may be a new principle but the thinking itself need not be in terms of an established principle. Again, the description may apply to thinking which makes use of scientific laws or principles but is not necessarily commensurate with the thinking leading to the discovery of these principles.

Why does "insightful behavior without a distinct awareness or self-accounting of every phase of its further course" involve a lower level of abstraction than behavior in which every phase of a performance is directed and controlled? In the untrampled virgin forests through which scientific discoverers must often move, it is virtually impossible to be aware of every phase of one's further course. Indeed, if such awareness existed, the problem would be solved before one began. Is a scientist working his way through a relatively unexplored segment of scientific territory, unable to know in advance every turn which his thinking will have to take, operating on a lower level of abstraction than a schoolboy who can account for every step in the solution of a geometric problem? Direction and control of every phase of a performance may be quite all right for a successful stage presentation but they hardly seem the essence of the thinking leading to a scientific discovery.

Whatever may be the personal and philosophical predilections which led Goldstein and Scheerer to set up these levels of abstraction, these levels do not seem applicable to some cases of genuine creativity and productivity in scientific thinking.

Verbalization as an Index of Higher Abstraction. While abstraction need not involve verbalization, "verbalization is an index of a higher level of abstraction" (Goldstein and Scheerer, 1941, p. 26). Yet there is highly abstract, creative thinking which does not involve verbalization. Protocols of their thinking processes by some eminent mathematicians and scientists (cf. Woodworth, 1938) state that the thinking which led them to discoveries often proceeded on the nonverbal level. Einstein writes of the thinking involved in the relativity theory: "These thoughts did not come in any verbal formulation. I very rarely think in words at all. A thought comes, and I may try to express it in words afterwards" (Wertheimer, 1945, p. 184). There is no a priori basis for characterizing his original thought processes as on a lower level of abstraction than his later attempts to verbalize them. Nor is it likely that his thinking, even though it rarely involved words, was on a lower level of abstraction than that of another individual who does tend to think in words.

Abstract Thinking Portrayed by Rules of Logic

While we have not seen it explicitly acknowledged, there seems to be a definite link between abstract thinking and operations of formal logic. These operations include comparison and discrimination, analysis, abstraction, generalization, formation of class concepts, formation of inferences, and syllogisms. Many of these operations are exactly those assumed to be required in abstract thinking. Thus, various tests of abstraction require comparison of various objects, analysis to determine common properties, abstraction ("abstractive isolation") of these properties, generalizations, and class concepts. To be labeled as operating on the abstract level in these tests therefore requires that one be able to perform readily the operations of traditional logic. Conversely, if one experiences difficulties or is apparently unable to perform such operations, then he is labeled as operating on the concrete level. Wertheimer writes:

> Some psychologists [not Wertheimer] would hold that a person is able to think, is intelligent, when he can carry out the operations of traditional logic correctly and easily. The inability to form general concepts, to abstract, to draw conclusions of certain formal types is viewed as a mental deficiency which is determined and measured in experiments. (1945, p. 7.)

Paraphrasing this thought, we may say that the ability to carry out the operations of traditional logic correctly and easily, as required by the various tests of abstraction, is regarded as an indication of a high abstract level of thinking; not to manifest this ability is interpreted as an indication of a lower, more primitive level of thinking or even of a kind of mental deficiency, namely, an impairment of the abstract attitude.

Dichotomization of thinking into abstract and concrete categories perhaps rests on the premise that formal logic actually pictures the reasoning process, the inference being that the ability to carry out the operations of traditional logic (abstract level) portrays higher reasoning while inability to do so (concrete level) portrays a lower kind of reasoning power. But the assumption that formal logic portrays the reasoning process has been challenged. Woodworth (1938) refers to the "old idea that logic teaches the laws of thought." He continues:

> Recent students of logic and of psychology agree that logic, or at least the formal logic which has come down from Aristotle, is not psychology to any great extent... Its principles and rules afford essential checks on the validity of an act of reasoning but they do not picture the actual process of reasoning. (P. 801.)

If formal logic does not always picture the actual reasoning process, then the constructs of concrete and abstract thinking, insofar as they are intimately linked to the operations and principles of formal logic, may also fail to portray actual reasoning.

While he does not deny that operations of formal logic may be involved in thinking, Wertheimer states that one cannot understand thinking by focusing on these operations in isolation. Rather, one must seek to understand the role and function of the operations in the total thought process. He offers the analogy of a man seeking to understand a work of architecture who focuses on the single bricks and on the way in which they are cemented by the mortar. "What he has at the end is not the building at all but a survey of the bricks and of their connections" (1945, p. 182).

Similarly, the constructs of abstract and concrete thinking and the various tests designed to study them are concerned with whether or not the subject can generalize, form class concepts, abstract similarities, etc., but not with the role and function these operations play in the total thinking process. Perhaps because of the emphasis on operations of formal logic, there is a neglect of other operations and factors which may be essential to thinking, including such features as centering, grasping, restructuring. Nor are the constructs of abstract and concrete thinking concerned with the direction or pattern of thinking, and with whether it is productive or nonproductive in nature.

Although scientific thinking may involve operations of formal logic, these operations, when considered in isolation, cannot be used to explain or account for scientific thinking. Dissatisfaction with the manner in which formal logic handles "sensible, productive processes of thinking" was voiced by Wertheimer:

> In comparison with actual, sensible, and productive processes, the topics as well as the customary examples of traditional logic often look dull, insipid, lifeless. To be sure, the treatment is rigorous enough, yet often it seems barren, boring, empty, unproductive. If one tries to describe processes of genuine thinking in terms of formal traditional logic, the result is often unsatisfactory: one has, then a series of correct operations, but the sense of the process and what was vital, forceful, creative in it seems somehow to have evaporated in the formulations. On the other hand it is possible to have a chain of logical operations, each perfectly correct in itself, which does not form a sensible train of thought. (1945, p. 10.)

Apropos of the thinking which led Einstein to the relativity theory, Wertheimer wrote:

> If we were to describe the process [Einstein's thinking] in the way of traditional logic, we would state numerous operations, like making abstractions, stating syllogisms, formulating axioms and general formulas, stating contradictions, ...and so forth...
>
> But what do we get if we follow such a procedure? We get an aggregate, a concatenation of a large number of operations, syllogisms, etc....
>
> In order to get at the real picture, we have to ask: How did the operations arise, how did they enter into the situation, what was their function within the actual process?...
>
> When we proceed with an analysis in the sense of traditional logic, we easily forget that actually all the operations were parts of a unitary and beautifully consistent picture...
>
> Radical structural changes were involved in the process, changes with regard to separateness and inner relatedness, grouping, centering, etc.; thereby deepening, changing the meaning of the items involved, their structural role, place, and function... (1945, pp. 182-87.)

Einstein wrote of his thinking on the relativity theory:

> Such things [as direction] were very strongly present. During all these years there was a feeling of direction... It is, of course, very hard to express that feeling in words; but it was decidedly the case, and clearly to be distinguished from later considerations about the rational form of the solution. Of course, behind such a direction there is always something logical; but I have it in a kind of survey, in a way visually. (Quoted in Wertheimer, 1945, p. 184, n.)

Such operations and concepts as centering, direction of thinking, role, inner relatedness, etc., neglected in studies of abstract-concrete thinking, seemed to play a decisive role in Einstein's thinking, so that operations and concepts involved in the constructs of abstract and concrete thinking do not seem adequate to account for this case of scientific thinking.

Abstract Thinking as Arbitrary, Senseless Abstraction

A distinction has been drawn between arbitrary abstraction and less arbitrary, less structure-blind abstraction (Wertheimer, 1945). The former focuses on elements and ignores structure, role, meaning, direction. The latter groups together items and classes, not on the basis of piecemeal similarity, but on the basis of structural equality and meaningfulness. Operations of traditional logic may be employed in either kind of abstraction. For example, "comparison" and "discrimination" may mean comparing various objects to see if they have a common element or they may refer to a search for "structural equality, which can obtain even when the piecemeal data show no equality at all" (Wertheimer, 1945, p. 204). "Analysis" may mean "that a field or an object is cut into and-summative parts, blind to structure, or it may mean structurally adequate division, and viewing parts in their part-nature" (p. 204). "Abstraction," "generalization," and the "formation of class concepts" may involve the isolation (subtractive isolation) of an element or elements common to various objects or situations, with no reference to the role which the isolated element plays in the objects or situations; or these operations may refer to the role and meaning of the common element and to its relationship with other aspects of the various objects or situations.

The tendency to take into account whole properties and the function, place, and meaning of parts within the whole is often interpreted as evidence of concrete thinking. Conversely, the ability to focus simply on pieces, to isolate parts, to ignore their function and meaning, to ignore the part they play within the whole—this ability is often interpreted as evidence of abstract thinking. More succinctly: the ability to perform rather arbitrary abstractions seems to be accepted as the keynote of the abstract attitude.

Definitions of Abstraction. Consider in this connection Werner's definition of abstraction as a "mental quality by means of which parts of a unit are detached from the whole, and separate qualities ... are experienced in isolation" (1940, p. 234). He claims that the difference between a grouping based upon concrete abstraction and a generalization at the abstract conceptual level is essentially this:

Concrete grouping reveals a certain quality through the configuration of the elements possessing that quality, whereas in a true generalization the quality (e.g., a color) common to all the elements involved is deliberately detached—mentally isolated, as it were—and the elements themselves appear only as visible exemplifications of the common quality. (P. 243.)

Werner refers to the young child's tendency to conceive of a group as a naturalistic situation "in which the single elements are embedded and from which they get their meaning" (p. 227). He regards as on a lower level than categorical abstraction the comprehension of a manifold of objects under one name if that name "somehow preserves the variability and the individual difference of the single objects" (p. 244). The highest kind of abstraction, Werner implies, would ignore variability and individual differences; in other words, true abstraction, as he conceives of it, would focus on the common property, would ignore variability, would ignore the role of the common property and the relationship between it and other properties. Werner's concept of true abstraction, therefore, coincides with Wertheimer's description of highly arbitrary, structure-blind abstraction.

Tests of Abstraction. As an example of rather "structure-blind" thinking in tests of abstraction, consider the interpretation of performances in the Gelb-Goldstein color-sorting test. Only if the subject is able to disregard or to abstract from the given individual shades, and to be oriented as to the common element in the various presented shades is he regarded as operating on the abstract level. In the Goldstein-Scheerer stick test it is assumed that the copying or reproducing of senseless figures requires the abstract attitude. It is presupposed, in the Gelb-Goldstein-Weigl-Scheerer object-sorting test, that the abstract attitude requires isolation and abstraction of the common property of woodness or redness or oblongness and the grouping together of all objects having the common property—a grouping that brings together objects having disparate functions or structures. It is explicitly stated in the manual for the test that, if the subject seems to be reacting to situational context, situational belongingness, or functional belongingness, then he is to be suspected of operating on the concrete level. Abnormal concreteness in reacting to the Weigl-Goldstein-Scheerer color-form sorting test is characterized by a tendency to arrange the objects in a definite pattern which "is not arbitrary" (Goldstein and Scheerer, 1941, p. 115), whereas the abstract approach is marked by a tendency to throw the objects into different piles in any arbitrary, disorderly manner.

It would therefore seem justifiable to conclude that some of the tests of abstract-concrete thinking are based on the thesis that operation on the abstract level requires the ignoring of meanings and functions and calls for the isolation of an element common to various objects and the arbitrary grouping together of objects on the basis of piecemeal similarity. Hence, what is regarded as abstract thinking in some of these tests virtually coincides with arbitrary structure-blind abstraction, as described by Wertheimer.

Situational Testing. The extent to which rather arbitrary thinking permeates the criteria of the abstract level seems to us to be well illustrated in some of the protocols of supposedly concrete behavior evinced by patients with cerebral pathology. To illustrate patients' inability to detach their egos from outer-world or inner experiences, Goldstein and Scheerer refer to patients who will not say that the snow is black, or that the sun is shining if it happens to be a rainy day; they mention a patient who will not drink water unless he is thirsty and another, suffering from paralysis of the right arm, who will not declare, "I can write well with my right hand" (1941, p. 5). As examples of inability to assume an attitude toward the "mere possible" and to think or perform symbolically, they cite (p. 7) the cases of patients who will not use a key if there is no door present, who will drink from a glass containing water but not from an empty glass, who will not demonstrate how to knock at the door if pulled away by the experimenter so that their hand does not reach the door, who will write their name on a piece of paper but not in the air, who will not continue hammering if the nail is removed.

All these examples are interpreted as evidence that the individual cannot operate on the abstract level but is confined to the concrete level. What is not mentioned is that every one of the instances cited calls for essentially arbitrary, "senseless" behavior, incompatible with the given situation. Certainly it would be quite senseless in an ordinary life situation to attempt to drink water from a glass that is empty, to use a key when there is no door present, to continue hammering after the nail is removed, or to assert that the snow is black. Does the fact that the doctor requested such extraordinary behavior automatically make it less senseless? Do these examples actually support the contention that the individual is operating on a lower level of thought than if he indulged in such senseless, arbitrary activity? Does it require a high conceptual level to perform such assignments? The assertion that these examples testify to impairment of the abstract ability seems to us to rest on the following implicit assumptions: (1) the patient is unable to indulge in "senseless" activities; (2) senseless, arbitrary, structure-blind thinking is the prototype or the highest form of abstract activity; (3) therefore, the patient suffers from a general impairment of the abstract ability.

With reference to the apparent inability of the patient to carry through these assignments, we point out that there is quite a difference between refusal to carry through an assignment and inability to execute it. The cited examples may be interpreted to mean that the patients *could not* carry through the requests; but they may also be interpreted to mean that the patients *would not* carry them through. In clinical practice it is not unusual to find a patient who will not participate in certain activities; e.g., answer the examiner's questions or take a certain test. That this cannot be regarded as absolute evidence of inability to participate is attested to by the fact that often the patient can be made to participate if suitable changes are introduced in the atmosphere of the room, if the relation between the patient and the examiner is altered, if the patient's understanding of the task is modified; e.g., if he can be made to realize that participation may help him to recover or if he can be made to play the game. It probably would not be easy to convince a patient that he will be helped by knocking on an absent door or hammering on an absent nail. Nonetheless, it is conceivable that, with proper changes in instructions, the patients might have been willing to execute the seemingly foolish assignments. In any event, the possibility must be kept in mind that their failure to perform may stem from conscious refusal and not from inability.

It may be conjectured that the assignments described by Goldstein and Scheerer call for a kind of playful activity. But the patient may be in no mood to play. His personal troubles and difficulties may not be conducive to such playful activity as drinking from an empty glass or opening an invisible door. Does this imply that he is operating on a lower level or that he cannot abstract? A normal person who is in trouble—say, is suffering from a toothache—may also be in no mood to play or, on the other hand, to carry out a difficult, mathematical problem. The conclusion that refusal to play is evidence of a general impairment of abstract ability may not be more valid for the patient than for the normal person with the toothache.

"Sensible" Abstraction of Primitive People. It is conceivable that an individual who will not (or cannot) indulge in highly arbitrary thinking may nonetheless be capable of less arbitrary abstraction. Wertheimer claimed that this is true of so-called primitive people. In a lecture at the New School for Social Research, he questioned the prevalent notion that primitive men are not able to abstract. He contended that primitive people are able to abstract but that they do not tend to do so in an arbitrary way; they do not put together objects which have common elements or piecemeal similarity but those which seem to be structurally or functionally equivalent, to belong together sensibly. Their apparent

inability to think abstractly has been deduced, he claimed, from the fact that the tests and situations used to test their thinking were limited largely to those which were highly arbitrary, meaningless, and "structure-blind" when viewed from the point of view of the primitive person.

Wertheimer told the story of the singer from a primitive tribe who, on being tested by musicologists of the University of Berlin, proved unable to sing the notes that were played for him. While the musicologists puzzled over this phenomenon, Wertheimer heard the native composing a melody which, upon closer inspection, proved to incorporate the very notes he had heard. When asked why he was now able to sing the notes that he had previously been unable to sing, the native replied that if someone gave him a pot broken into bits he would not attempt to cook in it. To sing the notes in isolation was as senseless for him as trying to cook in a broken pot; to sing them as part of a melody, constituted a sensible task.

Another of Wertheimer's anecdotes concerned the commission sent by the Russian czar to determine the educability of the natives of Turkestan. It was the commission's conclusion that it was hopeless to attempt to educate the natives since they could not think abstractly. For example, they were unable, the commission said, to do the following syllogism: Premise 1: There are camels everywhere in Turkestan. Premise 2: Samarkand is in Turkestan. Conclusion: There are camels in Samarkand. Although agreeing to the premises, the natives would not draw the conclusion, usually pointing out that they had never been to Samarkand.

Wertheimer questioned whether the natives had actually accepted the first premise which implies a rather impossible state of affairs; namely, that Turkestan is completely covered by camels. He further noted that they were able to do other syllogisms—whether the content was concrete or abstract, familiar or unfamiliar—provided that the syllogisms were "sensible" to them.

Another example may be cited from Wertheimer's discussion (1912) of the number concepts of primitive people (in Ellis, 1938). Told that two of their boats and three of the enemy's boats were approaching, some natives would not total the number of boats when asked how many there were altogether. This might be interpreted as evidence that they lack the abstract number concept. What must be borne in mind is that the enemy's boats were not identical with their boats. In our own schools we teach that in addition or subtraction the natures of the objects or the units involved in the computation must be the same. The natives' refusal to give the total number of boats is therefore akin to our refusal to add together three apples and two pears. They refused to abstract

the common property of "being a boat" from the two different groups
of items. But when told that two of their boats and three more of their
boats were approaching, they were perfectly capable of calculating that
there was a total of five boats. In short, Wertheimer stated, they do not
lack the number concept but they will not add together objects which
do not seem to them to be structurally or functionally equivalent.

Wertheimer concluded that primitive people tend not to abstract in
an arbitrary manner but may be capable of doing more sensible abstractions. Anthropologists will not learn about this capability so long
as they confine themselves to tests and situations that involve what constitutes for the primitive highly senseless, structure-blind abstraction.

Is Arbitrary Abstraction Characteristic of High-Level Thinking?
We have seen that the construct of abstract thinking (often regarded as
high-level thinking) has been characterized by some psychologists and
measured in their tests as if a central feature of it is arbitrary, structure-
blind abstraction. We have also seen that the thinking of primitive people (which some psychologists regard as lower-level thinking) may involve sensible abstraction. The question arises : Is arbitrary, structure-
blind abstraction a crucial feature of high-level thinking, of productive
thinking, and is sensible abstraction a mark of a lower level of thinking,
or of poorer thinking? Some psychologists, for example, Wertheimer,
offer a negative answer to such a question.

As a specific point at issue, let us recall that the ability to use the
operations of traditional logic in arbitrary abstraction is sometimes
regarded as a keynote of the abstract attitude. Wertheimer (1945) contends that, while the operations of traditional logic may be involved in
good, productive thinking, they do not tend to be involved in such thinking in arbitrary, structure-blind ways.

As another point at issue, let us recall that conscious will is sometimes
accepted as the paramount factor in abstract thinking ; one who operates
on the abstract level is considered to be capable of active imposition of
his will on the external situation, to be able arbitrarily and volitionally
to change his view of the situation without regard to its structural features. Compare this with Wertheimer's assertion that intelligent thinking does not proceed in this manner.

> ... it is not the ease of arbitrary change as such which characterizes intelligent
> behavior ; nor is it the ability in a given situation to produce one or another or a
> third structural view at will, as some seem to believe. Rather what matters here,
> and what is characteristic of intelligent processes, is the firm transition from a
> less adequate, a less proper structural view to a more sensible one. And in fact
> experiences seem to show that sensible persons, real thinkers ... show little ability
> and even less willingness to engage in *senseless* changes of given situations. (1945,
> p. 126.)

It is incorrect, Wertheimer states, to assume that thinking processes which are "structurally senseless" are the prototype of all thinking or of the best thinking. The scientifically more accurate procedure, he notes, is to study the character of each type of thinking process, that which is sensible and that which is arbitrary. He suggests that the former may be the proper theoretical center and the latter only a special case in the following sense. The study of "structurally sensible" thinking, thinking that takes structural properties into account, may yield laws that pertain to structural properties; the laws could also apply to cases of arbitrary thinking if the degree to which structural properties are taken into account in the laws is assumed to approach zero. But, the study of cases of arbitrary thinking may yield laws that do not at all pertain to structural properties and hence would not be adequate to account for "structurally sensible" thinking.

Concluding Remarks

The terms abstract-mindedness and concrete-mindedness categorize an individual and ignore the possibility that his conceptual behavior may vary under different conditions. Examination of the evidence supposedly supporting the assumptions that the young child, primitive peoples, and individuals suffering from certain pathologies are capable only of concrete thinking, revealed deficiencies in the evidence as well as logical inconsistencies among the assumptions. We noted that scientific thinking, supposedly the highest form of abstract thinking, may possess some of the criteria attributed to concrete thinking, may lack some of the criteria attributed to abstract thinking, and may have features which are neglected by the constructs of abstract or concrete thinking. If one regards scientific thinking as essentially abstract thinking, then he must seriously question the validity of some criteria and tests of abstract thinking. There are instances of thinking in which one does not find all the criteria of either abstract or concrete thinking. One suspects that concrete thinking is not necessarily the only alternative to abstract thinking and that the concepts of abstractness and concreteness cannot account for all conceptual behavior.

We sought to establish that certain criteria of concrete and abstract thinking are rooted in the system of traditional logic, a link which is not usually explicitly recognized. Some of the criteria of the abstract approach were seen to coincide with or to depend upon the ability to perform the operations of traditional logic. This may help to explain why young children in our culture and primitive people are reputed not to show certain criteria of abstract thinking; they have not been trained in formal logic.

There is some doubt as to whether rather arbitrary, structure-blind abstractions represent the only or the best kind of abstraction. Primitive man's refusal or inability to do such abstractions should therefore not be accepted as a lack of abstract ability or as evidence that he is operating on a lower conceptual level. Likewise, the mental patient's refusal or inability to do the highly arbitrary thinking stressed in many current tests and criteria of abstraction, should not be accepted as evidence that he is suffering from a general impairment of the abstract ability or that he has regressed to a lower conceptual level. Ability or inability to do rather arbitrary, structure-blind abstraction under certain conditions may furnish no clue to ability to do the same abstraction under other conditions or to ability to engage in more structurally related abstractions. Thorough exploration of conceptual behavior requires development of tests involving more structurally related, more "sensible" abstractions. Moreover, an attempt should be made to vary situational conditions systematically in order to seek to discover the conditions under which an individual will (or will not) perform abstractions of various degrees of structural relatedness or of various degrees of arbitrariness.

We differentiated among abstractions in terms of the degree to which they are related to structure. Other distinctions can be drawn; for example, in terms of the origin of the abstractions or in terms of the role and function of the abstraction in the subject's cognitive grasp of the situation, in his personality functioning and interpersonal relations. Perhaps what has been said suffices to illustrate that not all abstractions are alike, that abstraction is not homogeneous, and that it is important to distinguish various types of abstractions. If abstraction is not homogeneous, it follows that neither is concreteness. In short, the term concrete (or abstract) does not refer to one well-delineated level of conceptual behavior but includes a multitude of conceptual behaviors.

To appeal to concreteness as a predeterminant of rigidity does not answer the question what brings about rigidity, but involves many questions about concreteness, questions which await adequate formulation and attack. One line of attack is to study the relationships between behavorial rigidity and abstractions, for abstractions which differ in origin, degree of structural relationship, the role and function they play, etc. Experimentation is also needed to ascertain whether, for a given individual, the relationships vary under different conditions. Such research may help to clarify the beclouded problem of how conceptual behavior is related to rigidity.

CHAPTER VII

VARIABILITY AND RIGIDITY

RIGIDITY is defined as a lack of variability in response by Werner (1940) and by others. Underlying current discussions and tests of rigidity there is often the implicit or explicit assumption that variability is the inverse of rigidity. For example, Fisher states that variability "has been implicit in almost all past rigidity measures" (1950, p. i).

Is variability actually the inverse of rigidity? Is the individual who gives the more varied response necessarily less rigid in his behavior? Experimental evidence bearing on such questions is virtually nil, perhaps because acceptance of variability as antithetical to rigidity has been so prevalent that experimental proof seemed superfluous. It is therefore of interest to see what was found in investigations of E effects in relation to variability.

PROBLEMS ENCOUNTERED IN MEASURING VARIABILITY

Variability of response is measured by some psychologists (e.g., Thorndike, 1913) as multiplicity of response, including all overt reactions made by the organism in the problem-solving situation, without any restriction to responses relevant to the particular situation at hand. If the same notion of multiple reaction were employed, an individual in the Einstellung situation who scratched his chin or blew his nose before solving a problem, would be considered more variable than one who gave the correct solution immediately. There seemed something quite amiss in such a conception of variability, quite aside from the impracticality of determining the number of discrete reactions made by each subject. It was decided, in measuring variability, to be restricted to those responses which were pertinent to the problem situation and were in the nature of solutions or attempted solutions. But, even with this restriction, many questions arose. Should superficial variations of the E method be labeled as distinct solutions; for example, should a $B - A - 2C$ method be considered distinct from a $B - 2C - A$ or a $B - C - A - C$ method? Should variability be measured solely in terms of the number of methods used or should the nature of the method used also be taken into account; for example, was the E method to be given the same weight as the direct methods? If a subject used more than one method in solving a problem, should the order in which the methods were used be considered in determining the extent of his variability?

It was decided, somewhat arbitrarily, to adopt the following standards: (1) as already indicated, to include only responses pertinent to the
problem situation, (2) to regard all minor variations of the E method
as essentially the same and to give credit for only one method no matter
how many of these superficial variations were made, (3) aside from
this last restriction, to give equal credit for each method used, and (4)
not to take into account the order in which the methods were used.

Tendency to Alternate; Experiments on Satiation

Investigators studying the behavior of rats in a two-choice situation
have often reported a tendency to alternate responses. There have been
few studies of alternation of behavior in humans. Consider what our
results have to say on this matter.

The critical problems are two-choice situations since each is solvable
by the E method and a direct method. Yet most subjects did not alternate between the E method and the direct methods; with few exceptions, those in the control groups who received the criticals without the
preceding E problems, solved the criticals only by the direct methods;
contrariwise, most of those in the experimental groups solved the criticals only by the E method. In other words, our subjects did not show
the tendency to alternate so often as rats have been observed to do.

The question arises whether a tendency to alternate did not appear
because not enough criticals were given. Perhaps if more criticals were
used, an alternating tendency would be found. Of particular interest in
this connection are experiments in which a subject was given critical
problems until he became "satiated," until he refused to do any more.
A series of 25 criticals solvable by the $A + C$ method (as well as the E
method) was given, one problem at a time, and the series was readministered again and again in the same order until the subject (studied
individually) refused to do more. Ten high-school students who received
these criticals only, almost invariably employed the $A + C$ method
throughout, sometimes for more than 100 criticals. Ten similar students who received these criticals after the usual five set-inducing problems, tended to employ the $B - A - 2C$ method throughout, sometimes
for as many as 150 criticals.

When these criticals were given to each of ten college students, after
the usual five E problems, they solved from 16 to 64 criticals, with a
mean of 35, before they refused to do any more. (That satiation was
apparently reached sooner for them than for the high-school students
may be the consequence, among other factors, of the greater prestige
of the experiment and the experimenter with the younger subjects and
the more frequent recognition by college subjects of the fact that the

problems were being repeated.) Half of the college subjects never shifted from the $B - A - 2C$ procedure but used it in from 17 to 37 criticals.
They gave the problems an increasingly unenthusiastic reception. One
subject claimed that he must stop because he was hungry for "lunch"
(at 10:30 A.M.) ; another suddenly remembered an urgent appointment
although he had stated at the beginning of the session that he was free
for one hour ; another complained that he could not continue because
his arm was sore. They pleaded, "They're coming out of my ears" and
"Have a heart and don't give me any more of these problems." Thus
the repeated use of the $B - A - 2C$ method seemingly created "negative
motivation" or "negative drive" against its subsequent occurrence and
yet no tendency to vary the response was exhibited. The other five college subjects did shift to the $A + C$ procedure and continued using it
until the point of satiation ; two shifted from the $B - A - 2C$ method
after only two problems, two others after about 25 repetitions of this
method, and one after 50 repetitions ; all then continued the $A + C$
procedure for from 14 to 28 trials. Alternation of the two methods,
which might have been expected if responses in a two-choice situation
were regulated by a tendency to alternate, was shown by no subject.

EXPERIMENTAL ATTEMPTS TO ENCOURAGE VARIABILITY

Attempts were made to induce variability by preceding the basic experiment with tasks that allowed for numerous combinations of the jars
(Luchins, 1942, pp. 63-64). Sixth-grade children were told to imagine
that they were grocers measuring out milk, that their three measures
had capacities of 8, 7, and 30 quarts, and that different customers came
into the store asking for various amounts of milk. The administration
of seven such problems requiring different combinations of the same
measures, did not result in any observable tendency to vary when the
basic experiment was then presented. The forty children in the class
showed large E effects: C_1C_2, 80% E; Ext., 65% F; C_3C_4, 75% E.

Another sixth-grade class received, prior to the basic experiment, the
following three problems in each of which the assigned task was to find
as many methods of solution as possible :

	15	5	30	get 20
18	7	5	2	get 9
	16	8	4	get 12

Five minutes were allowed for each of these problems. After the expira-
tion of the time limit for each problem, we demonstrated its various
solutions, among which were combinations of two jars by addition or

subtraction as in the direct methods. Yet, when the basic experiment was given, the thirty-six children in the class showed little tendency to vary and considerable E effects: C_1C_2, 67% E; Ext., 56% F; C_3C_4, 67% E.

Prior experience with tasks in which the subjects were asked to vary their solutions apparently did not induce a tendency to vary in the basic experiment. It was therefore decided to tell subjects to find as many solutions as possible for the problems of the basic experiment (Luchins, 1942, pp. 64-67). When this instruction was issued to two college classes with every problem, and three minutes were allowed per problem, about two-fifths of each class did not find direct methods in the criticals but, to give the appearance of different solutions, gave superficial variations of the E procedure; one-quarter of one class and two-fifths of the other failed the extinction task.

Since it is difficult to find other methods for solving the E problems, these problems were presented to three sixth-grade classes as in the basic experiment, but, for each test problem, we allowed three minutes and asked the subjects to find as many solutions as possible. From one-quarter to one-half of the three classes gave only the E method in the criticals and from about one-quarter to one-half failed the extinction task.

When only the test problems were given to three other sixth-grade classes, and they were told, as each problem was given, to find as many different methods of solution as possible, from one-half to three-quarters of the groups never found the E method.

In order to increase the possibilities for varied solutions, we used new test problems in place of the usual ones, each of which had at least four different methods of solution. A fifth-grade class received these new test problems after the usual E problems and was told, at the beginning of the first critical and with each subsequent task, to find as many solutions as possible. Yet one-third of the group gave only the E method in the criticals and failed the extinction task; they never found any of the other methods.

Variable E Problems

The basic experiment does not allow much variability in solving the E problems since most of them are solvable only by the E method. What would happen if, instead of the usual E problems, we substituted tasks each of which was solvable by the E method as well as by many other methods? Would subjects show a tendency to vary their responses? After solutions to the usual first E task had been illustrated, a college class received the following E tasks:

8	32	4	get 16
9	39	6	get 18
9	30	3	get 15
10	34	4	get 16

Despite the variety of methods which are available, two-thirds of the class used only the E method in each of these problems. How different this is from the variable behavior often reported for rats in the initial learning period. Krechevsky (1937b, 1937c) found that, when there were two routes to the goal, one a fixed route and the other a variable route, normal rats (no brain lesions) chose the variable path, whether it was the longer or the shorter route. But most of our subjects, presumably having no brain lesions, chose the fixed method even when it was the less direct method and did not select the variable methods. Perhaps normal rats are more prone to vary their "hypotheses," to use Krechevsky's terminology (1932), than normal human beings.

The presolution period in Krechevsky's rat experiments involved repeated trials in one test situation. Somewhat analogous are experiments in which human subjects were given the same problem several times in order to discover if they would manifest variability. When (after the usual two illustrative problems had been presented) the first E problem was administered four additional times in succession to groups of children or adults, no tendency to vary the solution was found although a method other than the $B - A - 2C$ procedure is applicable (Luchins, 1942, pp. 70-71). But, since this other method is not a simple one, after the solutions to the first E problem had been illustrated, we gave a college class the following problem: 10, 25, 5, get 5. This was presented four times in place of the last four E tasks in the basic experiment. Here many modes of solution are possible and yet over two-thirds of the group used only the E method (or minor variations) four times in a row. Lifted eyebrows, sighs, and signs of boredom accompanied the successive administration of the same task—but not variability in response.

Further Studies of Variability and E Effects

Apparently our attempts to encourage variability through previous experiences requiring variation in method, through instructions to vary, or through the use of the new E problems each of which allowed various methods of solution, were not very successful. But surely we cannot study the relation of variability to E effects if we cannot get subjects to show variability. New experimentation was therefore undertaken.

Four experiments were designed to study the influence on E effects and on variability of behavior of (a) the repetition of the same E problem as compared with different E problems, (b) the use of an E problem solvable by many methods as compared with one solvable only by the E method, and (c) the number and kind of methods employed by a subject. The two illustrative problems in each case were the same as in the basic experiment, but, after two methods of solving the first E problem had been illustrated, modifications in the basic experiment were introduced. In Experiment 1 four new E problems (following the first illustrative E problem) were formulated so that each was solvable only by the $B - A - 2C$ method. In Experiment 2 the second E problem of the basic experiment was given four times. In Experiment 3 four new E problems were used, each of which was solvable by the $B - A - 2C$ method as well as by other methods (e.g., 8, 32, 4, get 16; 9, 30, 3, get 15). In Experiment 4, the same E problem (10, 25, 5, get 5, which is solvable by many methods) was given four times in succession.

The test problems, used in all the experiments, were the following, in the order listed:

C_1'	16	40	8	get	8
C_2'	14	35	7	get	7
C_3'	26	65	13	get	13
C_4'	12	30	6	get	6
E_6	6	21	4	get	7
New	40	118	18	get	62

The first four are criticals, solvable by many methods, including $B - A - 2C$, $A - C$, $B - 2A$, and C (simply the filling of one jar). The fifth is an E task, solvable only by the $B - A - 2C$ method. The last is a problem solvable by none of the methods which worked in the preceding tasks but by a new method, $2A - C$.

Experiments with High-School Subjects

With the assistance of Laddie Schnaiberg and Louis Tannenbaum, each experiment was administered to a group of thirty Montreal high-school students.

We were interested in how many subjects would show nonvariable behavior, in the sense that they would use the same method (or minor variations of it) throughout the E problems and the criticals (whenever possible). We were also interested in how many subjects would fail the last problem which may be regarded as a crucial indicant of rigidity since it requires a shift to a completely new method. Percentages of subjects who showed nonvariable behavior and who failed the last problem in Experiments 1 through 4, respectively, were as follows:

| Percentage showing nonvariable behavior | 67 | 53 | 37 | 57 |
| Percentage failing last problem | 70 | 70 | 60 | 33 |

It is seen that there is no consistent relationship between lack of variability and rigidity, as measured by failure of the last problem. This finding does not substantiate the thesis that rigidity is the converse of variability.

Subjects in each experiment were then fractionized according to whether they had shown nonvariable or variable behavior in the E tasks and criticals—that is, whether they had used the same method (or minor variations of it) throughout these tasks or whether they had shifted to another method somewhere in these tasks; and the percentages of failure of the last problem were then computed separately for each group (nonvariable and variable). Percentages of failure for those showing nonvariable and variable behavior in Experiments 1 through 4, respectively, were as follows:

| Percentage of failure after nonvariable behavior | 80 | 75 | 46 | 35 |
| Percentage of failure after variable behavior | 40 | 75 | 67 | 31 |

If rigidity and variability were inversely related, those who manifested nonvariable behavior in the E tasks and criticals might be expected to show relatively more rigidity (more failure of the last problem) than those who manifested variability. This expectation is upheld in Experiments 1 and 4, while a contrary trend is revealed in Experiment 3, and the two groups show the same proportion of failures in Experiment 2. The findings therefore do not consistently support an inverse relationship between rigidity and variability.

The question arose as to the influence on behavior of the method to which the subject adhered in the E problems and criticals. In Experiments 1, 2, and 3, the only method common to these tasks was the E method so that a subject who showed nonvariable behavior was perforce limited to the E method. But in Experiment 4 there were other methods common to these tasks, and eleven subjects in this experiment consistently used the simplest possible method, filling the third jar (except in the last two problems). These eleven subjects showed 28 per cent failure of the last problem, which is considerably less than the 80, 75, and 46 per cent failure shown by those who were nonvariable with respect to the E method in Experiments 1, 2, and 3, respectively. Moreover, the eleven subjects who used the simplest procedure whenever it was available, showed 90 per cent E solution of E_6 (the last problem solvable only by the E method) despite the fact that they had not used the E method in any of the eight preceding tasks; this compares favorably with the mean of 94 per cent solution of E_6 made by those in Experiments 1, 2, and 3 who used the E method in all the eight preceding problems. In short, those who were nonvariable with respect to the simplest procedure available, were often able to shift to the E method in E_6 and to a completely new method in the last task, so that they showed very little rigidity. Despite the fact that their behavior in the first four E tasks and the criticals showed as much lack of variability as the behavior of those who adhered to the E method, they showed considerably less rigid behavior. This finding suggests that, in discussing variability or lack of variability, especially in relation to rigidity, it may not suffice to consider the number of methods used; the *kind* of methods must also be taken into account.

How can we explain the greater readiness to shift, when shift was necessary, of those who used only one jar in the preceding tasks? Their behavior is perhaps related to the greater simplicity of the method they adhered to as compared with the more complex E method. A glance at a problem sufficed to reveal whether or not the capacity of one jar equaled the required volume, whereas a subject had to go through the computations involved in the E method in order to see if it led to the required volume. Some subjects failed the last problem because they blindly applied the E method without checking to see if it led to the stipulated volume; no one tried to solve the last problem (or E_6) by filling one jar. Apparently it was easier to be blinded to features of the problem by the E method than by the simplest method. Moreover, the E method was the only procedure common to the first eight tasks in Experiments 1, 2, and 3, whereas there were several common methods in Experiment 4, so that filling of one jar may have represented a matter of choice. Substantiating this supposition are comments made in interviews after the experiment. Subjects who used the E method whenever it was available often admitted that they had not been aware of other methods, whereas subjects who used one jar whenever possible claimed that they saw other solutions but felt they were using the simplest, the fastest, or the best method. Also, those who used one jar were deliberately discarding some containers, and were therefore perhaps more inclined to use the two jars required in the last problem than subjects who had used the E method and perhaps developed the assumption that all the given jars must be used.

Experiments with College Subjects

In order to study further the influence on behavior of having various common methods available, the procedure of Experiment 3 (different problems with various methods) was modified; after the illustrative tasks, four new problems were used, each solvable by many methods, including $B - A - 2C$, $A - C$, and C (e.g., 10, 25, 5, get 5; 8, 20, 4, get 4; 18, 45, 9, get 9). With the assistance of Joseph Zweig, this modified Experiment 3 was administered to college students in Montreal while similar college students participated in Experiments 1, 2, and 4, which were the same as for the high-school students. The numbers of college subjects in Experiments 1 through 4 were 17, 18, 47, and 45, respectively.

Percentages of subjects in each experiment who used the same method (or minor variations of it) throughout the E tasks and criticals (whenever possible) were computed, as were the percentages of failures of the last problem. These percentages in Experiments 1 through 4, respectively, were as follows:

Percentage showing nonvariable behavior	76	44	68	67
Percentage failing last problem	65	50	49	76

Again there is no consistent relationship between lack of variability and rigidity.

Subjects were fractionized according to whether they had shown nonvariable or variable behavior in the E tasks and criticals, and the percentages of failure of the last problem were then computed separately for those showing nonvariable and variable behavior. The percentages in Experiments 1 through 4, respectively, were:

Percentage of failure after nonvariable behavior	67	88	47	80
Percentage of failure after variable behavior	60	20	53	67

If variability were the inverse of rigidity, one might expect that failure of the last problem would be greater in each experiment following nonvariable behavior. This expectation is upheld in Experiments 1, 2, and 4 while the reverse trend prevails in Experiment 3.

In Experiment 4, where a problem with variable solutions was repeatedly presented, seven subjects used the simplest possible method in the E problems and criticals, filling of one jar (whenever possible), while twenty-three subjects displayed nonvariable behavior with reference to the E method or other methods involving subtraction from the center jar. The seven who used the simplest method gave 57 per cent failure of the last problem as compared with 87 per cent failure for the twenty-three who were nonvariable with reference to use of the center jar. Moreover, six of the seven subjects solved E_6, despite the lack of previous practice in the E method. Again nonvariable behavior with respect to the simplest method was followed by less rigidity than nonvariable behavior with respect to other methods. As for the high-school groups, this finding suggests that the relationship between variability and rigidity is not independent of the method of solution employed.

This is even more strongly substantiated in the present Experiment 3, in which there were fourteen subjects who used only one jar whenever possible and sixteen who used the E method throughout the E tasks and criticals. Those who were nonvariable with reference to the simplest method gave only 7 per cent failure of the last problem as compared with 86 per cent failure following nonvariability with reference to the E method. Moreover, of the fourteen subjects who used the simplest available method, thirteen solved E_6. Here again shift in behavior, when shift was required, followed nonvariability with reference to the simplest method, whereas greater rigidity prevailed after an equal extent of nonvariability with reference to the E method.

Comparison of Results with High-School and College Subjects

Nonvariable behavior throughout the E problems and criticals was shown by about one-third to two-thirds of the high-school groups and was even more pronounced for the college students, where it was shown by over two-fifths to three-quarters of the groups. Such nonvariable behavior decreased in frequency from Experiments 1 to 4 to 2 to 3 for the high-school subjects and from Experiments 1 to 3 to 4 to 2 for the college subjects. Comparison reveals that, for both high-school and college subjects, the greatest degree of nonvariable behavior occurred in Experiment 1, in which four problems solvable only by the E method were used, and that the extent of nonvariability was greater in Experiment 4, where the repeated problem had various solutions, than in Experiment 2, where the repeated problem had only one solution. This last result suggests that greater availability of methods does not necessarily make for more variability in response.

Failures of the last problem, used as a criterion of rigidity, decreased monotonically from Experiments 1 through 4 for the high-school subjects and from Experiments 4 to 1 to 2 to 3 for the college subjects. Comparison reveals that, for both the high-school and college groups, rigid behavior decreased monotonically from Experiments 1 through 3; that is, the most rigidity (measured by failure of the last task) occurred when the four E problems were solvable by one method only; the same or somewhat less rigidity was found when an E problem, with only one method available, was repeated; and still less rigidity was found when the four E tasks were each solvable by various methods. This indicates that the kind of problems given may influence the degree of subsequent rigid behavior.

Frequency of failure of the last task, for those who showed nonvariable behavior in the first nine problems, decreased from Experiments 1 through 4 for the high-school subjects and from Experiments 2 to 4 to 1 to 3 for the college subjects. For both high-school and college subjects, there was more rigidity, following nonvariable behavior, in Experiment 1 than in Experiment 3 and more in Experiment 2 than in either Experiments 3 or 4. This indicates that rigidity tended to follow nonvariable behavior more often when the four E tasks had only one solution than when the four E tasks had various solutions, and that rigidity was more likely to follow nonvariable behavior when an E task with one method was repeated than when various solutions were available for the different E tasks or the repeated E task.

Failure of the last task, for those who varied their methods in the first nine problems, decreased in frequency from Experiments 2 to 3 to 1 to 4 for the high-school subjects while precisely the reverse trend prevailed for the college subjects; that is, failures increased, instead of decreased, in this order. This suggests that the relationship between variable behavior and rigid behavior, even in the same experiments, may differ for different subjects. The results illustrate the difficulty of formulating the relationship between variability and rigidity.

In summary, for both the high-school and college subjects, the extent of variable behavior was not consistently related to the extent of rigid behavior; the relationship between nonvariable behavior and rigidity was not opposite in direction to the relationship between variable behavior and rigidity; and the kind of method to which an individual adhered seemed to play an important role in determining the extent of subsequent rigidity.

One implication is that in measuring variability we ought to take into account not only the number of methods but also the kind of methods; for example, an individual who adheres to an inefficient method when more efficient ones are possible, should not be considered just as invariant as one who adheres to the most efficient, the simplest, or the only method possible.

Variability Measured by Current Tests

Our attempts to use Einstellung situations to study both rigidity and variability revealed that a considerable proportion of the subjects (over half in most groups) usually adhered to one method; they seemed to show a preference for nonvariability. It was therefore decided to use other tests for studying variability.

Contemporary tests which may be interpreted as measuring preferences for variability and variety, are the sameness and change scales developed by Murray (1938) involving two questionnaires dealing with some categories of behavior. In the sameness questionnaire, a high degree of preference for sameness is considered to be indicated by preferences for association over a period of years with the same people, for walking on the same streets, for constant views with regard to politics, cigarettes, and the like, for regularity in one's routine, and for situations calling for no change in established behavior. In the change questionnaire, a high degree of preference for change is considered to be indicated by preferences for irregularity in routine, for travel, for novelty of experience, etc.

With the assistance of Leo Shapiro, the sameness and change questionnaires were administered to ninety McGill University students who also received the basic experiment. In the experiment thirty-four solved the extinction problem and fifty-six failed it. If rigidity in the Einstellung situation were concomitant with a lack of variability, then those who failed the extinction task might be expected to show a greater preference for sameness and less preference for change than those who solved the problem. But the results reveal little difference between the two groups. Those who failed the extinction task made a mean score of 41.8 on the sameness scale and a mean score of 39.5 on the change scale; those who solved this task made a mean score of 40.0 on the sameness scale and a mean score of 41.0 on the change scale; none of the intergroup or intragroup differences proved statistically significant at acceptable levels of confidence.

Investigators studying variability in human subjects have sometimes employed the Necker cube or a picture of a reversible staircase, with a greater number of reported reversals in perspective in a given period of time considered an index of greater variability. When twenty-five college students were tested individually with the Necker cube and the arithmetical Einstellung test, a low (statistically not significant) positive correlation was found; that is, there was some trend for greater variability on the Necker cube to be associated with greater E effects— rather out of line with the thesis that variability is the converse of rigidity. Similarly, Horwitz (1951) found, for a normal population of fifty subjects, a correlation of $+0.30$ between reported reversals on the Necker cube and rigidity scores in an arithmetical Einstellung situation, and a correlation of $+0.25$ between such reversals and rigidity scores in a hidden-word Einstellung situation. But, for the same subjects, he found low, statistically not significant, negative correlations between reported oscillations on a reversible-staircase figure and rigidity scores in these Einstellung situations (-0.12 for the arithmetical and -0.20 for the hidden-word situation). These contradictory findings suggest that there may be no neat formula with which one can sum up the relationship between variability, as measured by commonly used tests, and E effects.

RESPONSE VARIABILITY AND PRINCIPLE VARIABILITY

Would the relationship between rigidity and variability differ if variability were measured sheerly in terms of the number of responses given or if it were measured in terms of the number of principles underlying the responses? Ronald Forgus (1951) tested sixty-four college students in Montreal with the arithmetical Einstellung test and with three tests designed to measure variability. The first variability test involved geometric designs, with the assigned task to write everything one saw in the designs. Answers were scored for the total number of responses as well as for the total number of principles used. Thus, if a subject gave seven responses referring to geometric figures, letters of the alphabet, and digits, he received a response score of 7 and a principle score of 3.

The second variability test consisted of a series of numbers which the subject was to group into as many categories of three or more numbers as he could discover; next to each category the subject was to designate the principle on which it was based. Again a response score and a principle score were assigned. For example, a subject who listed ten categories which were correctly designated as based on arithmetic progressions, geometric progressions, prime numbers, and odd numbers, received a response score of 10 and a principle score of 4.

The third variability test involved hidden-object drawings. A response score was based on the total number of responses and another score on the total number of whole objects discovered.

On the basis of their responses to the Einstellung test, subjects were divided into five groups, with Group 1 showing the least E effect and Group 5 the most. The mean response scores and the mean principle scores were computed for every group. On none of the tests did variability, as measured by the response score, consistently decrease or increase from Groups 1 to 5. The mean number of whole objects also did not show any consistent relationship to E effects. But a clear-cut relationship was found between E effects and variability based on the number of principles. From Groups 1 through 5, respectively, the mean number of principles utilized was as follows:

Geometric-design test	7.81	6.61	6.25	5.20	4.28
Arithmetic-grouping test	6.31	5.33	4.63	3.67	2.71

That is, the greater the E effects shown by the group, the fewer the number of distinct principles found. In each test, the difference in mean number of principles proved significant at least at the 0.05 level for two groups separated by one grouping (e.g., Groups 1 and 3, Groups 2 and 4) and at the 0.01 level for two groups separated by two or more groupings.

In short, variability in terms of principles underlying responses proved to be inversely related to E effects, while variability in terms of number of responses did not prove to be consistently related to E effects. Once more we see that the relationship between variability and rigidity may depend on the manner in which variability is measured. Further experimentation is needed in which variability is measured in terms of principles underlying responses.

Variability and E Effects in Rats*

While there have been many investigations of variability in rats' behavior, they have not been concerned with the relationship of variability to rigidity. Our attempts to study E effects and variability in rats required the devising of suitable Einstellung situations. Mazes were decided upon as most appropriate. Rats run on mazes which were roughly analogous to the pencil-and-paper mazes used with human subjects, showed more tendency to vary and alternate responses than humans. Moreover, there seemed to be no consistent relationship between the extent of variability and the extent of rigidity. It was decided, however, to investigate the relationship when other mazes were used.

Experiment 1

In Experiment 1 the maze was of an elevated type, with no side walls, consisting of three equilateral triangles so placed that their bases formed a continuous vertical pathway from the entrance point to the food box. This vertical path was the shortest one from the entrance point to the food box. There were also available longer paths, the lengths being dependent on the number of arms of the equilateral triangles which were traversed.

The subjects were ten male rats, kept in a communal cage, run on the maze after 24-hour food-deprivation periods. After each run the animal was allowed to eat in the food box for approximately fifteen seconds.

Variability was studied in a preliminary free-choice period of ten trials during which the rat was permitted to follow any path. There

---

* Rita Brownstein Kopin, Ronald Forgus, Thomas MacBride, I. H. Scheier, and Robert Shulman assisted in the experiments described in this section. The experiments were conducted at McGill University.

followed a mechanization period of fifty trials in which the rat was forced to follow the longest path; he was not permitted to use the vertical route but had to traverse the arms of the three triangles. This was accomplished by placing around the rat's neck a harness (key ring) to which a long string was attached, and by applying pressure on the string whenever the rat deviated from the longest route. *E* effects were studied in a subsequent test period of ten trials during which no harness was utilized and the rat was allowed to follow any route.

Variability was gauged by the number of different routes followed by the animal in the preliminary free-choice period. *E* effects were gauged by noting how often the rat followed the longest path and how often he followed shorter paths during the test period. There proved to be no consistent relationship between variability and rigidity. For example, complete adherence to the longest route during the test trials was shown by two animals that had manifested little variability in the preliminary period (they had used two or three different paths) as well as by two others that had manifested more variability in the preliminary period (four or five different paths); during the test period the longest route was never used by one rat that had shown little variability in the preliminary period (three different paths) as well as by another that had shown the greatest variability (six different paths); of the rats that used three different routes during the free-choice period, one never followed the longest path in the test trials, another used it in four trials, another in five trials, and still another in nine trials. The hypothesis that variability is the converse of rigidity was therefore not supported by the data.

Experiment 2

The various paths in the maze utilized in Experiment 1 were not of equal length. It is therefore debatable whether the different routes used in the preliminary free-choice period should be given equal weight in determining the variability score. In order to eliminate this difficulty, a new elevated maze was used in the preliminary period which contained four equidistant paths, each leading to food. Ten naive rats were given ten trials per day for fourteen days on this maze. In the mechanization and test phases, the maze used was similar to the one in Experiment 1 except that it contained two rather than three triangles. Mechanization for the longest path, accomplished by means of a harness, consisted of eight trials per day for a period of eleven days. There followed a test period of eight trials each day for nine days, during which the harness was not employed and the rat was permitted to follow any route.

Variability was measured in terms of the number of different routes used during the preliminary phase. Relative ease or difficulty of mechanization, during the trials with the harness, was gauged in terms of the number of trials in which the animal did not hesitate at the choice points or attempt to follow the short vertical route. E effects were measured in terms of the total of the lengths of the paths used by the rat in all the test trials, a greater total length being considered indicative of greater E effects.

If variability were the converse of rigidity, the more variable animal would be expected to show less E effects and, possibly, more resistance to mechanization. But the results suggest the opposite trend, with the more variable rats tending to show less resistance to mechanization and more E effects. Product moment correlations of $+0.60$ were computed between variability and ease of mechanization and of $+0.45$ between variability and E effects. The results indicate that, with variability and rigidity measured as they were in the present experiment, one was not the converse of the other.

COMMENTS

Our experimental findings highlight the importance of the manner in which variability is measured. Variability in terms of number of responses was not consistently related to the measure of rigidity, while the two were negatively related when variability was gauged in terms of the number of principles underlying responses. Moreover, lack of variability proved to have different relations to rigidity, depending on the kind of procedure for which the individual manifested a lack of variability. Further research is needed using other indices of variability and of rigidity. Moreover, there seems to be a need for delineation of what is involved in the concept of variability. Here we shall survey some of the points that might be covered in such a delineation.

Meanings and Measurements of Variability

Many explanations of variability have been offered by psychologists. Variability has been attributed to a tendency toward varied reactions considered as a fundamental principle of behavior (Thorndike, 1913), to an innate tendency toward varying responses (Tolman, 1925), to an innate tendency to alternate (Hunter, 1920), to an ability to vary (Krechevsky, 1937), to a need for variation or a preference for variety (Maier, 1939), to reactive inhibition—the hypothesized tendency of a response to serve as a block to subsequent occurrence of the response (Hull, 1943), to the physiological concept of the refractory phase which follows the use of a given set of muscles, and to other physiological and learning principles.

Considerable controversy has arisen as to which of these constitutes the most adequate explanation of variability of behavior. For example, observations of variability in rats' behavior led Hunter to infer an innate tendency to alternate and led Tolman to infer an innate tendency toward varying responses, while Yoshioka (1929) concluded that the available evidence does not justify such inferences. Hull and his disciples do not consider it necessary to postulate an innate tendency toward variety, or an ability to vary, or a need or preference for variety, but consider that variability can be explained in terms of such principles of learning as reactive inhibition, spontaneous recovery, and reinforcement. Discussing Maier's postulation of a need to vary, Spence wrote: "Such circular reasoning is to be contrasted with the interpretation given above in which variability of behavior is recognized as a behavioral phenomenon to be explained in terms of principles" (1951, p. 717). To cite another example of controversy: From experiments on variability in the behavior of rats, with and without cortical lesions (1937), Krechevsky concludes that rats with cortical lesions have less ability to vary; but Maier interprets the findings as attesting to less need or less preference for variety on the part of the rats with the lesions, contending that the results fit the interpretation that "variability is behavior based upon a need [whereas] Krechevsky thinks of variability as an ability" (Maier, 1939, p. 246).

The definitions of variability and the processes assumed to bring it about, may determine whether or not variability should be considered the converse of rigidity. For example, Krechevsky (1937) equates variability to plasticity, stating that rats with cortical lesions have lost plasticity, whereas Maier (1939) contends that plasticity is best regarded as a process distinct from variability. Since plasticity is often interpreted as the converse of rigidity, Maier implies that the converse of rigidity is distinct from variability. Lack of variability in behavior, he maintains, may result from two different processes, from stereotypy in which an animal becomes a slave to a given mode of behavior, or from a preference for one mode of behavior over another. Only in the case of the first process, he believes, does it seem justifiable to regard variability as the converse of stereotypy or rigidity. To assume that a converse relationship always prevails, he says, is to ignore the possibility that the second process may be operating.

Maier's distinction between two processes that may bring about an overtly similar lack of (or low) variability in behavior, seems to be useful in accounting for some of our findings. It may be remembered that subjects who used the E method throughout the E problems and criticals usually admitted that they saw no other method, whereas subjects who adhered to the simplest method—the filling of one jar—later said that they considered it the best method, preferable to others of which they were more or less aware. It would seem that those who showed lack of variability with respect to the E method usually acted from blind stereotypy, were slaves to a given mode of behavior, while those who showed lack of variability with respect to the simplest method were usually directed by a preference for one mode of behavior over another. The lack of variability shown by the former may have been the consequence of rigidity, whereas the latter's lack of variability may have been the consequence of a preference for a certain method, a preference put aside when the method was no longer appropriate.

Not only is there lack of agreement as to what brings about variability; there is also lack of agreement as to its meanings and indices. A survey of the literature reveals that, among the meanings and indices attached to variability, are the following abilities: to form different hypotheses, to restructure a perceptual situation, to shift perspective, to engage in a number of exploratory acts, to alternate responses, to associate fluently, to react to different clues rather than consistently to select one clue. These are not equivalent meanings or indices. If, for example, an individual is able to readily restructure a perceptual situation, it does not follow that he will be particularly fluent in forming associations. Consequently, differences in conclusions drawn about variability may depend on the particular meaning or index employed.

The differences may be reflected in conclusions drawn about rigidity if one considers it the converse of variability. For example, if fluency of association is used as a measure of variability, then the mental patient engaging in a flight of ideas in response to a stimulus word, may be regarded as highly variable and, hence, as low in rigidity. One might insist that only relevant, meaningful associations should be counted in determining fluency of association. But such a limitation is opposed to certain contemporary measures of fluency; for example, fluency as tested by a nonsense syllable test in which the subject is required to give *meaningless* words or syllables (Cattell and Tiner, 1949).

Contemporary tests of rigidity reflect the diverse conceptions of variability. The conception of variability in terms of fluency of association, with low fluency considered high rigidity, is implied in the use of the nonsense syllable test to measure rigidity. Cattell and Tiner note that psychiatrists and others seeking to design tests "near" to what is clinically perceived as rigidity, have frequently put forward tests that are "practically pure measures" of fluency of association (1949, p. 323). Variability regarded as ability to employ alternative responses or to shift perspective or to restructure perceptual situations is implicit in the same investigators' measurement of rigidity with the Necker cube, the Weigl figures, and hidden-object pictures. Rigidity as the inverse of variability, where the latter refers to the ability to employ alternative responses, is involved in Fisher's measurement of rigidity (1950) in terms of responses to an ink blot, a cartoon, the Vigotsky block test, and the Thematic Apperception Test, with the number of responses considered inversely related to the degree of rigidity. To cite but one more example: Horwitz (1951) includes, in his battery of rigidity tests, three tests which involve the conception of variability as ability to shift perspective in viewing reversible figures, with high variability considered low rigidity.

Since not all the conceptions of variability are equivalent, it follows that neither are the corresponding conceptions of rigidity. But then one must seriously consider (1) whether the various meanings and indices currently employed to measure variability are sufficiently similar in dynamics to warrant inclusion under the one concept of variability, and (2) whether their converses are sufficiently similar to warrant inclusion under the one concept of rigidity. Perhaps ubiquity in the meanings and indices of variability is leading to unnecessary and confusing ubiquity in the meanings and indices of rigidity.

Psychologists disagree, not only on the conception of variability, but even upon an issue as accessible to observation as the influence of practice on variability. Studies have yielded the contradictory conclusions that, with practice, variability increases (Ryans, 1939), decreases (Ehrlich, 1943), or stays the same (Owens, 1942). Hovland (1951, p. 635), noting that there is no obvious reason for the discrepancies among different studies, implies that diverse measures of variability may have been used and he raises the problem of determining the appropriate measure of variability.

It has been recognized (Woodworth, 1938, pp. 173-74) that the extent of variability differs depending upon whether one employs as an index the rate of work per unit of time or the rate of time per unit of work, depending upon whether one employs absolute variability (in terms of deviation from a mean) or relative variability (standard deviation divided by the mean). Woodworth considers that the question which is the best or correct measure of variability does not make much sense.

Past discussions of variability, as well as related discussions of rigidity, have tended to overlook the issue of the degree of compatibility between responses and the problem situation, an issue which seems to be pertinent to all of the cited meanings of variability. In measuring variability, should one take into account the meaningfulness of the response and its degree of compatibility (appropriateness, relevance, fitness, requiredness) to the problem at hand, and on what basis should these be determined? For example, should every hypothesis or exploratory act or association be admissible and be given equal weight in determining the extent of variability? Should every shift of perspective, every interpretation or "restructurization" of a perceptual situation, be included in measuring variability regardless of the extent to which it is supported by the objective evidence? Should variability be adjudged differently in an ambiguous situation which lends itself to various interpretations or structurizations as compared with a situation in which the forces of organization support one structure? Should blind trial-and-error responses be given the same weight, in measuring variability, as responses that solve or fit the problem at hand? Should sensible errors be distinguished from senseless errors (Köhler, 1925; Koffka, 1925)?

Also neglected are the issues of the relation of the various responses to each other and to responses needed in subsequent situations. A very important but neglected issue is that of the origin and direction of variability. Variability may stem from the problem situation itself in the sense that it varies and requires various responses, or it may stem from the subject himself (e.g., from a preference for variety and change, regardless of whether the situation itself calls for change), or it may stem from external forces (e.g., the experimenter may issue instructions to vary regardless of whether it is possible or advisable to vary responses). Research is required to ascertain whether differences in variability (and in rigidity) may depend on its origin and direction. It may be well for such research to suspend the bias, commonly implicit in the literature, that variability is a virtue, that it is "good" to vary. There may be situations where problems can best be solved, or a need met most adequately, by adhering to one solution. For example, adherence to the simplest method of solving the E tasks and criticals may have been no worse (and possibly more adequate) than the use of many different methods of solving these problems. One must take into account whether or not the problem situation calls for change and whether or not the manifested variability is in line with the demands of the situation.

In summary, there are considerable disagreements, controversies, and unsolved problems surrounding the variability concept. Attempts to clarify understanding of rigidity through an appeal to variability may only substitute one mystery for another and may unnecessarily confound the rigidity concept.

*Relation of Variability to Darwin's Concepts of Variation
and Natural Selection*

It may not be out of place to point out that the psychological concept of variability is intimately linked with the biological concept of variation. It has long been recognized by biologists that members of the same species are not identical but show variations in structure and in activities. The phenomenon of variation has been central to theories of evolution. Of particular interest to biologists have been those variations which make for what have been called adjustments or adaptations of the organism to its environment.

> To many biologists the outstanding perplexity in the field of variation is not so much the mere appearance of changes ... as the appearance of the particular kinds of change that eventually lead to that hand-in-glove relationship between organism and environment that we call adaptation. (Guyer, 1941, p. 607.)

Most widely known of the theories that relate variation and adaptation is Darwin's theory of random variation and natural selection. Variations in structure and activity are seen by Darwin as random, blind, arbitrary, not guided by a corrective influence or by any goal or purpose or by any directional tendency to foster organisms fitted to the environment. But it happens, Darwin contends, that through the "power of chance" some variations in structure and activity fit the organism's environment better than others. Individuals who possess variations that happen to be adapted to the environment, the theory continues, tend to survive and to pass the advantageous variations down to their descendants, while those who do not have the advantage of such variations tend to perish; thus, a natural selective process is in operation.

Darwin's concepts of random variation and natural selection have had a striking impact on psychological thought. That a parallel exists between these concepts and trial-and-error learning has been recognized by psychologists. The conception of trial-and-error learning envisions learning or problem solving as involving activities that occur in a random, arbitrary, blind, nonpurposeful manner. (Note how similar this is to the concept of random variation.) But it may happen that some of the activities, by chance, happen to solve the problem at hand and these will tend to be "learned" (to "survive"), while the others will tend to be "extinguished." (Note how similar this notion of learning is to natural selection.) That an advocate of trial-and-error learning, for example, Thorndike, considers that in assessing variability any activity or response should be taken into account, seems to reflect the influence of the notion of random variation. This notion, as well as the idea of natural selection, seems to underlie the dictum, which we have seen is accepted by some psychologists, that the more variable the organism or the species, the greater its adaptability. The underlying assumption here may be that the organism or species which is more variable, in the sense that it engages in more activities or makes more responses or has a greater response repertoire, has a greater chance—sheerly on the basis of probability considerations—of making a response that happens to lead to adaptation than does a less variable organism or species. If rigidity is considered as maladaptability, then a related dictum is that variability is inversely related to rigidity.

In a broader sense, the concept of random variation seems to have influenced those schools of psychological thought that emphasize the random, arbitrary nature of human behavior. But, there are psychologists who do not subscribe to this conception of behavior; for example, Gestalt psychologists, who, in particular, do not regard trial-and-error learning as the prototype of all learning and who deny that the sheer quantity of responses made or merely the magnitude of experiential background determines problem-solving ability or adaptability. This is not the place to discuss the experimental evidence marshaled by psychologists who believe in one or another conception of behavior. What is of importance, it seems to us, is that Darwin's theory is not the only theory of variation or of adaptation. (Cf. Nordenskiöld, 1936; Simpson, 1949; Lillie, 1945; and Schrödinger, 1945.) Moreover, much has been learned in the field of variation since Darwin formulated his theory. "Much less was known of the nature of variations in Darwin's time than at present. . . . It is in understanding more of the nature of variation, indeed, that we have made our chief advance since Darwin's day toward a better understanding of evolution" (Guyer, 1941, p. 592). Since the psychological concept of variability has come from the stream of biological thought concerning variation, it seems appropriate for contemporary psychologists again to dip into this stream in order to see whether some modern conceptions of variation can be used to dispel some of the aridness of contemporary discussions of psychological variability. Moreover, since the notion of chance is involved in the concepts of random variation and natural selection and in some of the psychological thinking they have influenced, it may be advisable for psychologists to see whether the great advances made during the past decade in the mathematical thinking about chance, randomness, and probability, hold any implications for the psychological concept of variability.

Intraspecies and Interspecies Comparison of Variability

A major hypothesis advanced by Werner (1940) pertains to increasing variability (and hence decreasing rigidity) along the ontogenetic and phylogenetic scales. That is, the more mature individual is considered to be more variable than the less advanced member of the same species, and the more advanced species to be more variable than the less advanced species.

This implies that variability is a fixed characteristic of the individual. But, while variability may apply as a descriptive term to certain behavior, it has never been established that there is a general factor of variability which is always characteristic of the individual. It is conceivable that the extent of variability shown by a person may differ in different situations and at different times, perhaps during the span of a day or even of a shorter period of time, or may differ depending on the index that is used. The use of one index of variability may show an adult to be more variable than a child, while the reverse may be shown if another index is employed. Even with the same index, it is conceivable that the relative variability of the adult and child may be reversed; that is, in one situation or at one time, a given child may be better able to restructure a situation (or to form associations, etc.) than a given adult, whereas in another situation he may be less able to do so. It does not seem justifiable, therefore, to compare the relative variability of two individuals, independent of a specific situational context and a stipulated index of variability.

In any event, the experimental findings did not reveal that adult subjects were consistently more variable than children, or that variability was consistently related to age or intelligence. For example, in the experiments involving different kinds of E problems, the college students showed less variability, on the average, than the high-school students—quite contrary to the thesis that variability increases with age.

Comparison of variability becomes even more difficult when different species are involved. For one thing, indices and tests of variability must be found which can appropriately be applied to different species. Keeping these difficulties in mind, we point to a thought-provoking comparison. Many investigators have reported that rats, cats, and other infrahuman species show a tendency toward variability of response and a trend toward alternation of responses. There have been few studies of variability in human beings. Our investigations with human subjects revealed little tendency to vary or to alternate responses; this was true even when the problem at hand had various solutions, even when the subjects were specifically instructed to vary, and even when they had been given previous experience in finding various methods. (Incidentally, the data did not reveal that adult subjects were consistently more variable than younger children.) Moreover, in mazes which were roughly the analogue of our pencil-and-paper mazes, rats showed more tendency to alternate responses in the test problems than did human subjects in the pencil-and-paper mazes. Why these differences in extent of variability?

To begin with, the test situations are of course not comparable for the two species. Aside from this, the answer perhaps lies partly in the faster learning of which the human is capable. Much of the variability reported for infrahumans has presumably occurred in the initial learning or presolution period. Because the human subjects were able to learn more rapidly, the presolution period (during which they might have shown a variety of responses) may have been of negligible extent as compared to that of the rats studied. One demonstration of a procedure may have sufficed for most of the human subjects to learn the procedure, whereas, for the rats, which learn less rapidly and which cannot "abstract" or formulate a method so well or so swiftly, one demonstration (say, being led over all the routes in a maze) may not have sufficed for the learning of any of the routes.

Another possible determinant of the difference in results may have been the difference in certainty of solution. Our human subjects knew, upon obtaining the required volume of fluid or arriving at the goal box, that a solution had been attained, whereas the rat that reached the goal box and nibbled at food, may not have considered the problem (of its hunger) adequately solved. It may have followed another path in the hope of obtaining a more substantial repast. Perhaps, if human subjects were hungry or thirsty, and if the problems given to them involved opportunities to obtain various amounts or kinds of food or drink, they too would have shown greater variability of response or a tendency to alternation. Here is a suggestive problem for future research.

Finally, there are other factors which warrant discussion. Many of the human subjects had participated, during their school training, in isolated drill wherein the same procedure or skill was practiced over and over again. Moreover, all of them had had years of formal schooling during which they had often been asked to find a solution to a problem but rarely required to find various methods of achieving the same end product. Persistence in one response may have been an artifact, to some extent, of their school training. How strange elementary-school children found the request to discover different methods for each problem. Their complaints were numerous: "It's senseless to do the same things many different ways," "It's unfair—it's hard," "I did the best I could do and, after all, my answer was correct," "You teach one thing and expect us to do another," "Why should I bother seeking new methods?" Perhaps the variability of the human subjects would have been greater if they had not been subjected to these school experiences and, conversely, that of the rats less if they had had the "advantages" of such schooling.

What we are trying to suggest is that recognition of possible differences in degree of variability between species does not commit one to the proposition that the cause of the difference lies in the phylogenetic levels; differences in past experiences and in environmental conditions may also be contributing factors. It has been demonstrated (Luchins and Forgus, 1955) that differences in environmental and experiential backgrounds can have striking differential influences on the extent of variability shown by rats. Such influences may not be confined to one species but, when properly interpreted, may help to account for interspecies differences in variability.

This is not intended to rule out the hypothesis that rats or other infrahuman species are more or less variable than the human species. Such a hypothesis has not been established, and its establishment must await the development of tests of variability that allow for adequate interspecies comparisons. If such experimentation should show rats to be more variable than human beings, the findings would contradict the thesis that variability increases with phylogenetic development and the related thesis that rigidity, considered as the converse of variability, decreases with phylogenetic development. But of course, as we noted in the preceding paragraph, one cannot lightly dismiss the possibility that observed differences in variability of behavior may not be so much the consequences of differences in phylogenetic levels as of the specific experiences, training, and background of the subjects.

Relation of Variability to Spencer's Theory of Organic Evolution

We have seen that Werner regards variability as closely related to phylogenetic and ontogenetic development. The fundamental law governing development, according to Werner, is an "increase of differentiation and hierarchic integration" (1940, p. 44). This law is reminiscent of the law of development basal to Spencer's theory of organic evolution, a theory that emphasizes differentiation and also brings in a process of integration or consolidation.

... [Spencer holds] that the development of the individual proceeds from the homogeneous to the heterogeneous; out of the egg, which is uniform throughout, both in structure and composition, is evolved an individual possessing various parts and organs, which are the more differentiated the further the development proceeds. This law Spencer believes holds good for everything ... At a later period Spencer tried also to expand his evolution theory. He sees in it a process of consolidation ... (Nordenskiöld, 1936, pp. 494-95.)

Spencer's views have had considerable influence on social thought, particularly sociology, but have had relatively little acceptance by biologists. His theory of organic evolution—"of the gradual progress of life from simple to more complex forms, from primitive homogeneity to ultimate heterogeneity" (Joad, 1934, p. 295)—has been challenged by many biologists. Biological research does not give much support, some biologists contend, for the view that life proceeds from the simple to the complex, from homogeneity to heterogeneity, from a nondifferentiated state to a differentiated state. For example, "in modern times, the egg is certainly not regarded as non-differentiated; rather, with its numerous hereditary factors and the orientation given it from the very beginning, it is a tremendously complex structure" (Nordenskiöld, 1936, p. 495).

Without getting involved in controversies over (1) the meaning of such terms as simple, complex, differentiated, nondifferentiated, uniform, nonuniform, and the like; (2) whether the egg, for example, is simple, or complex, uniform or nonuniform, differentiated or nondifferentiated; and (3) the merits or demerits of Spencer's views on development and evolution, we want to point out that these views seem to be implicit in some psychologists' conceptions of variability and of the relationship of variability to development. It may be worth while for psychologists to turn also to other theories of and orientations toward development and evolution (as revealed, for example, in recent work in genetics and embryology) in order to see what implications they may hold for variability, for rigidity, for the relationship between variability and rigidity, and for the relationship of each to phylogenetic and ontogenetic development. This would be in keeping with a multitheoretical variational approach.

Concluding Remarks

Experimental evidence does not support the assumptions that rigidity is necessarily the converse of variability or that variability increases with ontogenetic or phylogenetic development. Moreover, we have seen that there is considerable controversy and confusion concerning the meaning, processes, and indices of variability. To regard rigidity as the inverse of variability not only seems unjustified by actual data, but does not contribute to our understanding of rigidity.

CHAPTER VIII

TOPOLOGICAL RIGIDITY AND BEHAVORIAL RIGIDITY

I N DISCUSSING the Lewinian concept of rigidity, we noted that topological rigidity does not necessarily coincide with behavioral rigidity. As Kounin words it, "rigidity of overt behavior cannot be directly coordinated with rigidity of the boundaries of the regions making up a person's structure, i.e., with his dynamic [or topological] rigidity" (1941a, p. 250). Bearing this in mind, we were interested in studying the relationship between topological rigidity and E effects.

From the definition of topological rigidity as "that property of a functional boundary which prevents communication between neighboring regions," Kounin (1941a) derived the following proposition: Other things being equal, the greater the topological rigidity, the less likely is an individual to be in an overlapping situation, a situation in which he is influenced simultaneously by more than one region. If the E problems are considered to correspond to one activity region and the test problems to a neighboring activity region, then it follows that, other things being equal, the greater the individual's topological rigidity, the less likely is he to be influenced by the region corresponding to the E problems while "in" the region corresponding to the test problems, and, hence, the less likely is he to use the E method in solving the test problems; that is, the greater the topological rigidity, the smaller the E effects. To test the cited proposition, Kounin used a "transfer of habit" experiment in which the subject was first required to depress a lever in order to release a marble (Situation 1) and then required to raise this lever in order to release the marble (Situation 2). The proposition was considered as confirmed by the results, which showed that the subjects who were assumed to have greater topological rigidity showed less "transfer of habit," less tendency to use the Situation 1 method while in Situation 2. If an analogy may be drawn between this experiment and the Einstellung experiment, then we may expect subjects with greater topological rigidity to show less tendency to "transfer the habit" used in the E problems (Situation 1) to the test problems (Situation 2); that is, greater topological rigidity should be concomitant with less E effects.

Thus, an inverse relationship between topological rigidity and E effects is suggested by one proposition derived from the definition of topological rigidity as well as by the experiment intended to test that proposition. But a different kind of relationship is suggested by another proposition derived from the same definition and by its corresponding experiment. We are referring to the proposition that, other things being equal, the greater an individual's topological rigidity, the less easily can he perform a task which requires that he restructure a given field. If use of the direct method in a test problem is considered to involve a restructurization of the field in a direction away from the structurization required by the E method, then it follows from the just-cited proposition that, other things being equal, the greater the individual's topological rigidity, the less likely he will be to use the direct method in a test problem and, hence, the more likely to show E effects; that is, topological rigidity may be expected to be positively related to E effects.

To test the above proposition, Kounin used a "classification" experiment, with the results regarded as substantiating it, since subjects who were considered to have greater topological rigidity showed less tendency to change to another classification when the change required restructuring. If the Einstellung experiment may be regarded as analogous to the classification experiment, then we may expect that subjects with greater topological rigidity will have more difficulty in changing to a direct method. In short, one proposition derived from the definition of topological rigidity, as well as its corresponding experiment, suggests a direct relationship between this rigidity and E effects, while a similarly derived proposition and its corresponding experiment suggest an inverse relationship. To see which suggested relationship is confirmed by research, let us turn to investigations correlating E effects and certain indices of topological rigidity.

COSATIATION AND E EFFECTS

Cosatiation scores have been used by Kounin as indices of topological rigidity. A subject was assigned the task of drawing a certain object and, when he became satiated, was assigned the task of drawing another object; a cosatiation score was computed, with a low score indicating that satiation in one drawing activity had little effect upon satiation in a subsequent activity and a higher score indicative of a greater effect. The thesis, which was regarded as substantiated, was that the greater the topological rigidity, the less effect a change of state in one region will have upon the state of neighboring regions and, hence, the smaller the cosatiation score.

Preliminary investigations, which we conducted in 1941, revealed no consistent relationship between E effects and cosatiation scores computed in situations similar to those employed by Kounin. Horwitz (1951) studied cosatiation by assigning subjects the tasks of drawing small strokes in various specified spatial arrangements. The first assignment was a 3-5 arrangement (three strokes close together separated by an interval of space from five strokes close together); after the subject refused to do any more, he was assigned a 4-4 arrangement; upon satiation, he was assigned a 2-6 arrangement and, finally, a 1-7 arrangement. For fifty normal subjects, the cosatiation scores yielded correlations of $+0.20$ with E effects in the arithmetical Einstellung test and -0.12 with E effects in the Einstellung hidden-word test. Thus Horwitz' findings also failed to reveal significant or consistent correlation between cosatiation scores and E effects. Lack of a consistent relationship was also attested to by Horwitz' factorial analysis which yielded seven factors, known as Factors A through G. On Factor F, the highest loadings (0.62 and 0.70) were made by the two cosatiation indices; yet this factor was not loaded significantly by scores on either Einstellung experiment. Indeed, Factor F was not loaded significantly by scores on any of the rigidity tests employed by Horwitz, a fact that led him to conclude that the rigidity measured by the cosatiation scores is "relatively independent of other types of rigidity" (1951, p. 76).

Schwartzman (1952) studied the relationship between cosatiation scores and E effects for eighty Montreal college students. Tested individually, the subjects received the arithmetical Einstellung test as well as a cosatiation test, which consisted of the repeated writing of phrases, followed, upon satiation, by the drawing of geometric figures. Subjects were divided into five groups, with E effects increasing from Group 1 through Group 5. For Groups 1 through 5, respectively, with twenty-four, sixteen, ten, fourteen, and sixteen subjects, mean cosatiation scores were 48.28, 59.38, 63.40, 59.18, and 42.55; again no consistent relationship was found to prevail between E effects and cosatiation indices.

In summary: From the concept of topological rigidity we derived two contradictory relationships, neither of which was substantiated by empirical data. To the extent that a score on the Einstellung test is indicative of a certain degree of behavioral rigidity and a cosatiation score of a certain degree of topological rigidity, the findings suggest a lack of a consistent relationship between behavioral and topological rigidity.

SATIATION AND E EFFECTS

While Lewin and his associates have not used the phenomenon of satiation to measure topological rigidity, their writings suggest that a close relationship may prevail. Feeble-minded children, whom Lewin described as having a greater degree of topological rigidity than normal children, are also described by him as differing from normals in the process of satiation (1935, p. 200). Likewise, Kounin (1941a, p. 259) concluded that there were marked differences in satiation among three groups of subjects, with the group considered to be characterized by the greatest topological rigidity (old feeble-minded subjects) requiring the most time to become satiated in an activity, and the group considered to be characterized by the least topological rigidity (young normal subjects) requiring the least time to become satiated in the same activity.

Assuming that the process of satiation may hint at the extent of topological rigidity, we were interested in comparing satiation scores with E effects. The cosatiation investigations permit such comparisons. In Horwitz' study (1951), each of fifty normal adults engaged in four activities (drawing of strokes in specified spatial arrangements); correlation ratios were computed by him connecting satiation time in each activity with E effects in the arithmetical and hidden-word Einstellung tests. The eight correlation ratios obtained ranged from —0.12 to +0.40 and revealed no consistent trend. Moreover, among the extracted factors was one, identified as Factor C, on which the four highest loadings (0.81 to 0.90) were made by the four satiation scores; but test items corresponding to E effects had low loadings on this factor (0.23 and 0.31), a fact that suggests that there is at best a weak relationship between time of satiation and E effects.

In the investigation by Schwartzman, where the students were divided into five groups depending on the extent of E effects, there was computed for each group the mean satiation time in the two activities (writing phrases and drawing figures). The mean satiation time for Groups 1 through 5, respectively, was 35.8, 43.1, 35.2, 42.4, and 29.5 minutes, revealing neither a consistent trend nor statistically significant intergroup differences.

Satiation in Water-Jug Problems

Thus far we have dealt with satiation in activities which bear little resemblance to the tasks of the Einstellung test. What relationship would there be between E effects and satiation for problems of the Einstellung test? Experimental data, described in chapter VII on variability, showed no consistent relationship between E effects and time of satiation in critical problems. In order to study the matter further, we attempted to satiate subjects for E problems. The experiments were administered with the assistance of Rose Apostolatos, Natalie Kolber, and Sylvia Trossman. A series of twenty-four E problems was administered and, if necessary, readministered again and again, in the same order, until the subject refused to do any more; after this, he was requested to do only a few more problems and was thereupon given the first two criticals and an extinction task. A few subjects remarked that they had previously received some of the problems. Two subjects were so adamant that each problem being given to them now was identical with one which they had previously received, that we discontinued the experiment for them and excluded their responses from the results. Included in the final analysis were the responses from thirty McGill University students. The number of E problems which they solved (always by the E method) before refusing to do any more, ranged from 11 to 203, with a mean of 70. Up to the point of satiation, each of ten subjects solved less than 55 E problems, each of another ten subjects solved from 55 to 75 E problems, and each of the remaining ten subjects completed more than 75 such problems. Consider now the time spent on E problems. The satiation time ranged from seven minutes to eighty minutes, with a mean of 42.3 minutes; the point of satiation occurred within the first half hour for eleven subjects, within the second half hour for ten subjects, and within the third half hour for nine subjects. No simple relationship existed between satiation time and the number of E problems solved; for example, one subject completed 203 E problems in fifty minutes while another completed only 54 E problems in fifty-five minutes.

We were interested in comparing E effects with satiation time and with the number of E problems solved. Of the thirty subjects, only one —who up to the point of satiation completed 58 E tasks in thirty-five minutes—used the direct method in the first critical but he used the E method in the subsequent critical. Hence, 59 of 60 responses to the two criticals involved the E method; this method was used whether time of satiation was seven minutes or eighty minutes and whether the number of problems solved before satiation was only 11 or over 200. The extinction task was failed by twelve subjects, or 40 per cent, within the time allotment of three minutes. Since more frequent repetitions of the E method could conceivably foster a stronger set, we might expect that those who completed more E problems would tend to show more failures of the extinction task. This expectation is supported by the results; the ten subjects who completed less than 55 E problems each, showed 20 per cent failure of the extinction task; the ten who completed from 55 to 75 E problems each showed 30 per cent failure; and the ten who completed more than 75 E problems each showed 70 per cent failure. Hence, the number of E problems solved up to reported satiation, was related to the extent of failures of the extinction task. But time of satiation was not positively related to failures. Instead, a slight negative relationship prevailed between satiation time and failure of the extinction problem; subjects whose satiation times were less than one-half hour showed 46 per cent failure of this problem, subjects whose satiation times ranged from one-half hour to one hour showed 40 per cent failure, while those whose satiation times were more than one hour showed 33 per cent failure.

Extent of satiation may be gauged either by the number of E problems completed or by the time spent on these problems. Dependent upon whether one or the other criterion is selected, either a positive or a negative relationship obtained between extent of satiation and failures of the extinction problem. If the extent of satiation is considered to reflect the degree of topological rigidity, and failures of the extinction task the degree of behavioral rigidity, then it may be said that, dependent upon whether one or the other criterion of satiation is used, either a positive or a negative relationship prevailed between topological and behavioral rigidity. These contradictory relations are reminiscent of the conflicting relations derived from the definition of topological rigidity.

INTERRUPTED TASKS AND E EFFECTS

Lewin appeals to his construct of (topological) rigidity to account for the experimental finding that feeble-minded children showed a greater frequency of resumption of interrupted tasks than normal children. The high frequency of resumption for the feeble-minded, Lewin explains, is a consequence of the fact that a tension system, once built up, stays unchanged without being diffusely discharged because of the relatively pronounced rigidity of the psychical systems. Topological rigidity is also appealed to in order to account for the fact that an activity which was completed after the interrupted task, has relatively low substitute value for the feeble-minded, as shown by their high frequency of later resumption of the interrupted task.

Thus, it would seem from Lewin's writings that high topological rigidity tends to foster resumption of interrupted tasks whether or not there is a substitute activity (except where the substitute task develops out of the original task). We wondered how frequency of resumption of tasks, considered as an index of topological rigidity, relates to E effects. To study this problem, preliminary experimentaton was undertaken with normal high-school students of New York City who, about four months previously, had participated in the basic Einstellung experiment, administered as a group experiment. The experiments involving interrupted tasks were individually administered.

A technique modeled after that used by Rickers-Ovsiankina (1928) was used with twenty-one subjects. An activity was interrupted and, after a while, a situation of relative freedom was created in which the subject was free to resume or not to resume work on the interrupted task. Our subjects showed considerably lower frequency of resumption of interrupted tasks than had been reported by Rickers-Ovsiankina for her German subjects. Our finding is in line with results obtained by one of the writers in an unpublished experiment with normal elementary-school children in New York City, wherein strikingly lower frequency of resumption was revealed than the 79 per cent resumption found by Köpke for normal Berlin children, as reported by Lewin (1935). The New York City children apparently regarded the experiment as a school test, and seemed to carry over to it the attitudes and general normative behavior associated with test situations; for example, the attitude that, when a test is over, one does not usually get a chance to return to problems in it that one did not complete. Possibly cultural factors also influenced the results.

For twenty-three other high-school subjects, an activity was interrupted, a substitute activity was completed, and then the subject was free to return to the interrupted task. We found that few of our subjects resumed the interrupted activity. One does not know whether this is a consequence of the substitute value of the completed activity or of an initially low tendency toward resumption.

A technique modeled after that used by Zeigarnik (1927) was employed with eighteen other high-school subjects. A sequence of tasks was given, some of which the subject was allowed to complete while others were interrupted. The subject was later tested for his recall of the tasks. Zeigarnik found much better recall of the uncompleted tasks, a result interpreted as implying that the tension corresponding to the incompleted tasks was greater than that for the completed tasks (cf. Lewin, 1935, p. 244). We reasoned that, if relatively pronounced topological rigidity tends to prevent dissipation of tension associated with an interrupted task (as Lewin states in explaining the high frequency of resumption by feeble-minded children), then greater topological rigidity should be reflected in better recall of an uncompleted activity.

Our results differed from those reported by Zeigarnik for German children and adolescents, in that we found less striking differences between the recall of completed and uncompleted tasks. For most subjects, memory of a task seemed unrelated to whether it had or had not been completed.

Thus far we have been concerned only with what happened in the interrupted-task experiments. The question remains: How do the results in these experiments compare with those for the same subjects in the water-jar experiment? Specifically, how do E effects relate to indices of topological rigidity? As already indicated, we decided to use as possible indices of greater topological rigidity the greater frequency of resumption of interrupted tasks and the relatively more frequent recall of uncompleted as compared with completed activities. The fact that most of our subjects did not resume the interrupted tasks and did not differentiate in their recall of uncompleted versus completed activities, made it difficult to compare these indices with E effects. However, the results were examined for possible trends. In the experiment with the substitute activity, the few subjects who returned to the interrupted task did not differ in E effects from those who did not resume the first task. In the other two experiments, there was a slight trend (which did not attain statistical significance) for the few subjects who resumed the interrupted task or who showed better recall of the uncompleted tasks, also to show somewhat more E effects; to this limited extent the indices which we associated with greater topological rigidity were positively related to greater behavioral rigidity as reflected in E effects.

Changes in Levels of Aspiration and E Effects

"Once a feeble-minded child has in mind a definite goal," Lewin writes (1935, p. 204), "he often shows a peculiarly rigid fixation on it." The pronounced topological rigidity which is assumed characteristic of the feeble-minded is used by Lewin to account both for this "peculiar rigidity of the will . . . in facing momentary goals" (1935, p. 204) and also for the tendency to accept a substitute goal which the feeble-minded show under certain conditions.

We thought it would be of interest to study, for normal subjects, the relationship between E effects and the "rigidity . . . in facing momentary goals." It seemed particularly appropriate to use a technique developed by Lewin and his associates for the study of behavior in relation to facing goals. We refer to the level-of-aspiration technique. Briefly, it is a procedure in which an individual is requested to make some estimations concerning his future performance in a particular task. The estimation is regarded (sometimes unjustifiably) as representing the goal or level of aspiration, and the performance subsequent to the estimation is considered the achievement, with the difference between the two constituting the discrepancy between aspiration (goal) and achievement. Among the tasks employed in the study of level of aspiration, both in the laboratory and in the clinic, are the cancellation of letters of the alphabet, throwing rings on a stake, and getting a ball into holes of a miniature pinball machine (with no jackpot possible). Because it seemed no less meaningful than other devices commonly employed to study level of aspiration, it was decided to use a pegboard and to ask the subject to estimate, before each of ten trials, how many pegs he could fit into the holes within thirty seconds.

The experiments were conducted in 1948 as part of the project on level of aspiration in one of the author's experimental-psychology classes. Individually administered to each of forty New York City high-school students was the arithmetical Einstellung test followed by the pegboard level-of-aspiration experiment. For each subject there was computed the number of successes (the number of trials in which the performance reached or exceeded the level of aspiration) ; the number of failures ; the discrepancies between aspiration and achievement ; the differences between the estimation and the performance on the last trial ; the number of times that consecutive estimations were identical ; the index of flexibility (the sum of the absolute differences between successive estimates) ; and the index of responsiveness (the number of times the subject raised his level of aspiration upon reaching or exceeding his previous level and lowered it upon failing to meet his estimation). Comparison of each of these indices with the point of breaking the set in the arithmetical Einstellung test (shift score) failed to reveal any statistically significant relationships. However, each of the last three indices—the number of identical consecutive estimations, the index of flexibility, and the index of responsiveness—yielded negative, low correlations (averaging about −0.20) to the point of breaking the set in the Einstellung test. Since each of these three indices pertains to flexibility in changing the level of aspiration, the findings hint at a slight tendency (not statistically reliable) for those who show less flexibility in the Einstellung test (that is, who show more E effects) also to show less flexibility in changing their estimations of performances. If estimations of performances are taken as representative of aspirations or goals, then the findings hint at a slight tendency for those who are more rigid in the Einstellung test also to be more rigid in adhering to aspirations or goals.

Similar results were reported by Horwitz (1951), who correlated the point of breaking the set in the arithmetical Einstellung test with the index of flexibility and the index of responsiveness on a level-of-aspiration test utilizing the Rotter board (Rotter, 1942). By means of a cue stick the subject had to drive a tiny ball bearing along an alley into holes in the board. The target hole was numbered 10 (and counted 10 toward the score) while nine other holes were numbered from 1 to 9 (and counted from 1 to 9 toward the score), the numbers decreasing as the distance from the target hole increased. The subject was instructed to aim for the target hole and to try to get as high a score as possible. After some practice shots, he was asked to tell what score he expected to make in the next series of five shots. A total of ten series of five shots was then given, with an estimation called for before each series.

The correlations were carried out for fifty normal adults and for fifty adult psychiatric patients. Correlations involving the indices of flexibility and responsiveness, respectively, were —0.11 and —0.18 for the normals and —0.12 and —0.16 for the psychiatric group. These results also suggest a statistically unreliable tendency for those who are more rigid in the arithmetical Einstellung test to be more rigid in their goal estimations.

Horwitz (1951) also correlated the indices of flexibility and responsiveness on the Rotter board level-of-aspiration test with the point of breaking the set in the hidden-word Einstellung test. Correlations yielded by the normal and psychiatric populations for the index of flexibility were similar to those he found when using the arithmetical Einstellung test. But the correlations involving the index of responsiveness were very close to zero. Thus, the relationship between rigidity in the hidden-word Einstellung test and in the level-of-aspiration test was found to be even more tenuous than in the previously described investigations.

Use of Einstellung Tests as Level-of-Aspiration Situations

It seemed desirable to use the same situation to study both E effects and rigidity in adhering to goals (or goal estimations). We therefore decided to utilize the Einstellung tests both for studying E effects and as level-of-aspiration situations. This was done with the water-jar Einstellung test by asking the subject to estimate his time of solution prior to each problem. The estimated time was treated (although with misgivings) as the momentary goal or level of aspiration. An experiment done individually with fourteen McGill University students revealed a trend of results similar to those already reported: the least fluctuations in time estimates occurred among those who showed the most rigid adherence to the E method.

The mirror-maze Einstellung test seemed to lend itself even more readily for use as a level-of-aspiration situation. With the assistance of Neysa Rosen and Clair Singerman, then students at McGill University, the experiment was administered individually to twenty Montreal college students. The instructions were to retrace each maze until an errorless tracing was achieved. Before each trial the subject was asked to estimate the time it would take to complete the trial, the number of errors he would make during the trial, and the number of trials he would need to achieve an errorless tracing. As an index of flexibility for each of the estimations (time, errors, trials), there was used the mean of the absolute value of the difference between successive estimations (of time, errors, and trials, respectively) in the mazes prior to the first critical. Each index of flexibility was compared with the point of shifting to the direct pathway. The analysis with reference to estimation of trials showed no consistent trend since most subjects estimated that it would take them one or two trials per maze to achieve an errorless mirror tracing. But the analysis with reference to estimation of time and errors did show a tendency for more E effects to go hand in hand with more rigidity in adhering to an estimation. Thus, the ten subjects who used the direct pathway in a critical prior to the extinction tasks, showed more than twice as much flexibility (as gauged by each of the indices used for time estimation and error estimation) as did the six subjects who failed the first extinction maze. If time and error estimations are interpreted as momentary goals or levels of aspiration, then these preliminary results hint at a tendency for rigidity in adhering to these momentary goals to be positively related to E effects.

To the extent that these exploratory studies measured rigidity in adhering to momentary goals, and to the extent that such rigidity is an indication of topological rigidity, the findings point to a tendency, not altogether consistent, for topological rigidity to be positively related to behavioral rigidity as gauged by E effects.

Methodological Difficulties Involved in the Level-of-Aspiration Technique

Quite aside from the matter of rigidity, the described experiments brought to our attention some of the difficulties attendant on the use and interpretation of the level-of-aspiration technique. Does the "estimation" made prior to each performance refer to the subject's goal, intentions, or aspirations with regard to his performance? Such referents are implied in the term "level-or-aspiration technique." Does the estimation perhaps refer to the subject's appraisal of his ability, to what he believes he probably will score, as opposed to what he hopes to score? Or does the figure named by the subject refer neither to what he hopes to achieve nor to what he expects to achieve? Such seemed to be the case for some of the participants in the described experiments. Upon questioning, a few of them admitted that their estimations were lower than their hoped-for or expected achievement, presumably because of the belief that underestimation of performance not only made them appear more modest in their appraisal of their abilities but also enhanced the value of their subsequent performance (apparently because of greater contrast between expectation and achievement). There were participants who balked at the idea of making an estimation. They protested that they were not clairvoyant. "What! Tell you before I do it!" sums up their astonishment at the unusual request made of them. When they did answer the request, it was often with a figurative shrug of the shoulders at the nonsense, as if neither the assigned task nor the figure they named deserved serious consideration. They seemed not to be at all ego-involved, so that it would be misleading to interpret their estimations as goals or aspirations.

It was clear that there was a great variety of interpretations and attitudes with regard to the instructions and with regard to the assigned task, the "expectation," and the actual performance score. Moreover, while a performance may have been arbitrarily classified as a success or failure by the examiner, depending upon whether or not it met or exceeded the estimation, it may not have been similarly regarded by the subject. In short, the experimenter's designation of an estimation as the subject's "goal" and of a particular performance as a failure or an achievement may not have accorded with the roles that the estimation and the performance played for the subject.

It seems to us that, if a level-of-aspiration procedure is to be more than a formal (possibly misleading) technique, it is essential to supplement it with procedures aimed at gaining information concerning the subject's interpretation of the instructions, the basis on which he makes each estimate, the goals (if any) which he sets for himself, as well as the meaning which he assigns to each estimation, to each corresponding performance, and to the discrepancy between the two.

COMMENTS

Our attempts to relate topological rigidity and E effects have merely scratched the surface of the research needed in this area. In order to stimulate more intensive research we shall propose a number of projects for future work. These projects may also be pertinent to the construct of topological rigidity and its associated experimental techniques.

How do people who do not develop an Einstellung compare with those who do not even recover from the Einstellung, in the behavior they show in *all* of the experiments which have been used to study topological rigidity? The answer to this question calls for having the same people participate in Einstellung situations, in satiation and co-satiation experiments, in resumption-of-interrupted-tasks experiments, in experiments both with and without substitute activities, and in level-of-aspiration experiments. Will it be found that subjects who differ considerably in E effects also show characteristically different patterns of responses in all the topological-rigidity experiments?

Another way of dealing with the problem is to compare subjects who in these experiments consistently show behavior regarded as indicating relatively high (or relatively low) topological rigidity. Thus one group of subjects would consist of those who show low cosatiation effects, who resume interrupted tasks, for whom experimentally introduced substitute activities seem to have low substitute value, and who adhere to their estimations (or other "goals") in level-of-aspiration experiments; another group would consist of those who show the other extreme in the respective experiments. Such subjects (if there are any who are so consistent) presumably differ considerably in their topological rigidity. Do they also differ sharply in E effects?

Ideally, the same subjects should be given more than one experiment in each category (that is, more than one Einstellung situation, several satiation and cosatiation situations, a variety of interrupted-task and level-of-aspiration situations). This should be done in order to yield a broader sampling of their behavior and a picture of how consistent they are in each type of situation. It would also be of interest to include among the subjects those who have been described in the literature as characterized by different degrees of topological rigidity. Thus ideally the subjects should include feeble-minded as well as normal individuals and individuals of various ages.

The project suggested above relates behavior in one situation with behavior in another situation. The *same* situation should be used both to study E effects and to derive possible indicants of topological rigidity. Experiments have been described in this chapter in which this was attempted; for example, the use of water-measuring problems as tasks in a satiation situation and the use of mazes in a "level of aspiration" experiment. In the same way, the Einstellung-type situation can be modified so as to study both E effects and the resumption of interrupted tasks, the substitute value of a substitute activity, or the recall of interrupted tasks. On the other hand, each of the experiments used to study topological rigidity can be modified so that it also involves the possibility of the development of an Einstellung. We think that it is of value to use situations in which E effects and topological rigidity are functionally related in the same experiment, rather than to have to relate them postexperimentally.

In our discussion of some of the techniques used to study topological rigidity, we pointed out the need for clarification of concepts and methods. A step in this direction may be taken by intensive experimentation with each of the techniques. This can be done by focusing on a particular situation which has been used to study topological rigidity and attempting to vary conditions so as to produce extremes in results. For example, we are interested in discovering conditions under which all or most of the individuals who are studied resume an interrupted task or, on the other hand, do not do so; or recall interrupted tasks better than completed tasks or conversely. Similarly, we are interested in the conditions under which most subjects show strong cosatiation effects or, on the other hand, low cosatiation effects, etc. In short, the aim is to create conditions under which extremes in results tend to be obtained. (An example from the Einstellung experiment is furnished by the tendency of "speed-test" conditions to maximize E effects.) Such experimentation may throw light on the concepts and on the crucial variables operating in each case.

This approach can also be used for a particular subject in attempts to bring about changes in his behavior. This is in line with what we call a variational approach to the individual case (about which we shall have more to say in this monograph). For example, changes may be introduced in experimental conditions in attempts to increase or decrease the particular subject's frequency of resumption of interrupted tasks; or to increase or decrease the apparent substitute value for him of a particular substitute task; or to maximize or minimize his ratio of recall of interrupted tasks to recall of completed tasks.

Such experimentation may be valuable in allowing a characterization of the subject's behavioral rigidity in terms of the strength and direction of changes in experimental conditions under which a given change in his behavior is observed. To the extent that responses in various situations (cosatiation, interrupted tasks, etc.) have been used as indicants of topological rigidity, the research may throw light on the constancy of a given person's topological rigidity and its susceptibility to change by environmental factors.

If an individual's topological rigidity is regarded as an inherited, predetermined characteristic largely independent of environmental conditions and subject only to changes with age (as is implied in some of Lewin's writings), then it may seem pointless to conduct research in order to study the consistency of topological rigidity and its susceptibility to change through experimental variations. However, we think that it is scientifically more fruitful not to regard topological rigidity as necessarily a predetermined characteristic or "essence" of the person which operates *in vacuo*.

Research findings may conceivably show remarkable consistency and even constancy in a given individual's indicants of topological rigidity. But to discover this experimentally is quite different from assuming it on a priori grounds. An experimental approach, and in particular the variational approach we have sketched, can point to the constants or invariants as well as to the variables in behavior. It is also possible that research may show that certain environmental conditions do influence topological rigidity or, at least, influence its indicants. An experimental approach to the relationship between topological rigidity and environmental conditions, seems to us to be more in accord with the Galilean mode of thought which Lewin (1935) advocates, than is an approach that assumes at the outset that there is strictly a one-way relationship and that topological rigidity is immune from environmental influences. Moreover, as Goldstein implies, topological rigidity considered as a predetermined characteristic, is a therapeutically futile concept. On the other hand, the kind of research which has just been proposed may suggest ways of modifying an individual's topological rigidity and thus have therapeutic consequences.

Finally, it is hoped that the proposed research may yield information which will serve as a basis for a more operational definition of topological rigidity than is at present available. In speaking of an operational definition of topological rigidity, we are fully aware that topological rigidity is not directly related to observable facts; that it does not refer to the phenomenological realm; that it is a theoretical construct, what some would call a hypothetical construct and others an intervening variable. Nonetheless, observable facts have been used to support the construct, the construct has been used to account for certain behavior, and experimentation has been carried out which purportedly referred to topological rigidity. Hence, it seems important to aim at an operational definition or at operational criteria which will allow one to know whether or not an experiment is relevant to whatever this construct of topological rigidity may be.

CHAPTER IX

INDIVIDUAL DIFFERENCES IN EINSTELLUNG EFFECTS

UNTIL now we have been dealing with theoretical explanations of rigidity in order to see what light they throw on E effects in the basic experiment. We have assumed that E effects are examples of rigid behavior. There are many who agree with this assumption and who even go beyond it and regard E effects as indices of a personality trait of rigidity. A survey of psychological literature in the past decade (cf. Taylor and McNemar, 1955) reveals that the water-jug problems have frequently been used to test rigidity both for experimental and for clinical purposes. It is not uncommon to find E solution of a critical water-jug problem or failure of an extinction water-jug problem interpreted as an index of rigidity in the personality of the problem solver. Moreover, individual differences in E effects have been interpreted as denoting corresponding differences in rigidity of personality. Scores on the water-jug problems have been correlated with various indices of rigidity as well as with scores on various personality tests. We turn now to a review of some of this work.

E Effects in Relation to Age, Intelligence, and Sex

It is not uncommon for psychologists interested in individual differences in a particular phenomenon to study its variation with age, intelligence, and sex. Let us, therefore, examine the relationship between E effects and each of these factors.

Age in Relation to Rigidity

We remind the reader that theories of rigidity generally posit a relationship between rigidity and age. But, while some posit a *decrease* of rigidity with increasing age, others posit an *increase* of rigidity with age.

Werner, in whose theoretical framework age is a central concept, regards rigidity as a negative function of ontogenetic development. He therefore considers the child to be more rigid than the adult and the younger child more rigid than the older one. Lewin's views on this relationship hinge on the factor of the degree of differentiation. The more differentiated individual, because of his greater wealth of subparts, is considered to be capable, other things being equal, of more ways of conceiving a given situation, and, hence, to have a greater

[236]

chance of changing his conceptions, of re-forming the field, when the situation is unsatisfactory. Lewin therefore conceives of a greater degree of differentiation as being associated with greater mobility of behavior (less behavioral rigidity). Since differentiation is assumed to increase with age, as long as the individual does not become senile, it follows that rigidity of behavior should decrease monotonically with an increase in age, barring senility (Lewin, 1935, p. 235). Since Goldstein equates lack of differentiation or little differentiation with impairment of the abstract attitude (1943, p. 224) and since he regards differentiation as tending to increase with age in the normal developmental pattern, it follows that behavioral rigidity (as an aspect of concrete behavior) tends to decrease with an increase in age.

On the other hand, an increase of rigidity with age is implied by many psychoanalysts. Freud implies that the older person has had more opportunities to develop fixations and therefore tends to have less libidinal energy available for change and progress; he states that beyond a certain age there is usually less plasticity than in earlier years (1953, vols. 2 and 3). Some psychoanalysts consider that rigidity is a reaction to threat to the ego, that the ego defense system is more developed in the older individual, and hence that the older individual should be more prone to rigid behavior. Reluctance of some psychoanalysts to undertake treatment of patients past middle age may stem from the assumption that these people are more rigid.

The afore-mentioned relationships are theoretical inferences. Let us turn to an actual case of rigidity to see what empirical data reveal.

Experimentation with hundreds of groups of subjects reveals that most groups, regardless of the age of their members, tend to show rather large Einstellung effects. These findings confirm the conclusion drawn in 1942: "All the reported groups, whether young or old, whether with little education or much, showed large E-Effects. Neither were the E-Effects great only in the groups of old subjects and small in the groups of young subjects, nor the opposite" (Luchins, 1942, p. 18). While striking variation of behavior in the Einstellung situation in different age groups should not be expected, there still remains the question whether some trend can be found and whether such a trend will support a negative or a positive relationship between rigidity and age.

Children's Einstellung Behavior. The children who participated in the original administration of the basic experiment (Luchins, 1939, 1942) were in Grades 4, 5, and 6 in New York City elementary schools and ranged from nine to twelve years in age (computed to nearest birthday). Prior to being given any of the problems, half of the children

were told to write the words "Don't be blind" on their papers after
Problem 6 in order to remind them not to act blindly (see p. 368 for
exact instructions). These children are said to constitute the "D.B.B.
group," while the others, who received the usual instructions, are
known as the "plain group." Subjects in each group were further divided on the basis of sex. Thus, in each of the four age levels (nine, ten,
eleven, and twelve), the subjects were divided into four groups, depending on the nature of the instructions received and the sex of their
members. Attempting to control to some extent the possible influence
of the factor of intelligence (which has been considered an index of
differentiation), we further subdivided each group. One subgroup consisted of those whose I.Q.'s ranged from 90 to 109 and the other of
those whose I.Q.'s were 110 or higher (I.Q.'s were based on the National Intelligence Test). There were thus eight subgroups for each
of the four age levels or a total of thirty-two subgroups. The number
of subjects in the subgroups ranged from seven to twenty with a mean
of fifteen. In order to hold constant the number of repetitions of the
E method prior to the critical problems, we used in the analysis relating
results to age only those subjects who had solved all of the E problems
by the E method. All in all, 483 subjects were involved in the final
statistical analysis, in which we were assisted by Leon Goldberger.

To study the influence of age, we compared only corresponding subgroups; that is, those equivalent with respect to sex, nature of instructions, and I.Q. range. Each subgroup in one age level was compared
with its corresponding subgroup in the three other age levels for the
percentage of E solutions of the first two critical problems, considered
as a unit, and the percentage of failures of the subsequent extinction
problem. Of the forty-eight comparisons made for the critical problems,
a smaller percentage of E solutions was shown by the younger group in
thirty-three cases and by the older group in only eleven cases, while
percentages were equivalent for the two age groups in the remaining
four cases. Failure of the extinction problem, which may be used as
a crucial criterion of behavioral rigidity, was lower for the younger
age group in twenty-seven of the forty-eight comparisons; five of these
differences were significant at the 5 per cent level of confidence while
none of the twenty-one differences which favored the older group attained this degree of statistical significance. The only comparison of
two age levels which revealed a tendency for the younger group to show
more E effects was that between the ten- and eleven-year-olds; the
other five comparisons (nine- and ten-year-olds, nine- and eleven-
year-olds, etc.) showed greater E effects for the older groups. Finally,
when we consider the analysis with respect to age separately for each

of the sex groups, for each of the instruction groups, and for each of the two I.Q. ranges, the majority of the comparisons show more E effects for the older groups, apparently counter to the negative relationship some psychologists have posited between age and rigidity.

Educational level was not controlled in the above analysis. Perhaps the greater E effects shown by older children were related to their longer exposure to schooling that stressed drill and repetition. What is required is a study of the relation of age to rigidity, with the educational factor controlled. Let us turn to such a study.

Adults' Einstellung Behavior. Ross (1952) tested active registrants in the Sales and Clerical Section of the National Employment Service of Montreal with several Einstellung tests (Luchins, 1950). The middle-aged group consisted of thirty-seven women aged from 30 to 45 with a mean of 37.3 years; and the older group, of thirty-three women aged from 50 to 78 with a mean of 60.8 years. The groups were equated for I.Q., occupational classifications, vocational training, and years of formal schooling. Tested individually, each subject received the maze test, the hidden-word test, and the face-bottle pictures in one session, and, one week later, the arithmetical Einstellung test and sailor-goblet pictures (a series in which a picture of a sailor gradually is transformed into the picture of a goblet). Included in the analysis of the results of each test are only those subjects who solved all the E tasks by the E method.

The reader is reminded that the arithmetical Einstellung test differs from the basic experiment in that the former involves a greater number and variety of test tasks (see the section of Chapter IV entitled "A Note on the Einstellung Test," p. 118). Up through and including the first two criticals, the problems are the same in both the arithmetical test and the basic experiment. In the arithmetical test there then follow two more criticals (34, 85, 17, get 17; 26, 65, 13, get 13), which we designate as C_3' and C_4', respectively. The usual extinction task, which is then given, is called Ext.$_1$ since as many as ten extinction problems may be used. Ross, following one of the suggested methods to be used in individual administration of the test, gave extinction problems until the subject solved one (or until all ten were failed), after which she gave the final six problems of the test: four criticals; a problem not solvable by any of the methods used in the preceding tasks but by a new method, $2A - C$; and then another E problem. A somewhat similar procedure was followed in the maze test and the hidden-word test, in which a series of several extinction tasks were given after the first two criticals.

E effects for the middle-aged and the older group in the arithmetical Einstellung test follow:

Middle-aged .. 28 subjects C_1C_2: 57% E $C_3'C_4'$: 36% E $Ext._1$: 29% F
Older .... 26 subjects C_1C_2: 79% E $C_3'C_4'$: 54% E $Ext._1$: 65% F

We see that for both the critical problems and the extinction task the older group had greater E effects. Moreover, the older group required a total of sixty-three extinction tasks while the middle-aged group required a total of only forty-eight such tasks before solving one. Differences in E effects between the two groups were significant at the 0.01 level of confidence for the criticals preceding the extinction task, for failures of the first extinction task, and for the first critical that followed the extinction tasks.

Similar trends prevailed in every test. Consistently the older group showed more persistence in adhering to the E method or to the first percept, failed more extinction tasks, and reported the emerging percept later in the series. For example, in the sailor-goblet series most middle-aged subjects reported the goblet by the sixth card, but most older subjects did not do so until the sixteenth card. Table V presents

TABLE V. INDICES OF BEHAVORIAL RIGIDITY FOR TWO AGE GROUPS*

	NUMBER OF SUBJECTS		PERCENTAGE OF FAILURES	
	Middle-aged	Older	Middle-aged	Older
Arithmetical test	26	28	29	65
Maze test	36	33	6	23
Hidden-word test	34	31	8	18
Face-bottle series	36	32	8	25
Sailor-goblet series	32	28	3	36

* Adapted from Ross (1952).

certain indices of behavioral rigidity for the two groups: failure in the face-bottle series to report a bottle by the fourteenth card, failure in the sailor-goblet series to report a goblet by the sixteenth card, and failure of the first extinction task in each of the remaining tests. We see that the older group consistently showed more behavioral rigidity than the middle-aged group; for each test the difference is significant at or beyond the 0.05 level of confidence. Thus, this study, as does the previous one, reveals an increase in rigidity of behavior with age.

Comparison of E Effects of Children and Adults. How do E effects of children compare with those of young adults and older adults? To answer this question, we selected subjects of disparate ages who had participated in the original administration of the basic experiment and who had solved at least the last two E problems by the E method. The three groups consisted of one hundred and forty children in Grade 5 who averaged 10½ years, a young adult group of seventy-nine college students with a mean age of 21 years, and an older adult group of one hundred and twenty-one adults who averaged 43 years. E solutions of the first two criticals increased with age, being 73, 80, and 88 per cent for the children, the young adults, and the older adults, respectively. But failures of the extinction task were only 56 per cent for the young adults as compared with 68 per cent for the children and 69 per cent for the older group. This suggests a curvilinear relationship between age and behavioral rigidity, with the young adults showing less E effects than the children or older adults. A similar curvilinear relationship was found between age and recovery from E effect since the young adults had only 63 per cent E effect in the last two criticals as compared with 69 per cent for each of the other groups.

Similar results were found by Heglin (1955) with a variation of the arithmetical Einstellung test. Equated for I.Q., there were three groups of fifty subjects each, ranging in age from 14 to 19 (median, 16.05), 20 to 49 (median, 31.75), and 50 to 85 (median, 66.02). E solutions of the criticals prior to the extinction task increased with age. But recovery from E effect (as measured by solutions of an extinction task or by behavior in a subsequent hidden-word Einstellung experiment) was significantly better for the middle group than for the youngest or oldest group.

Summary and Comments. Susceptibility to set (as measured by E solution of the criticals prior to the extinction task) increased with age. Behavioral rigidity (as measured by failure of the extinction task) was less for younger children than older children, less for middle-aged adults (mean age of 37.3 years) than older adults (mean age of 60.8 years), and less for young adults (mean age of 21) than for either children or for older adults (mean age of 43 years). The results do not fit formulations that posit either a monotonically increasing or decreasing relationship between age and rigidity but instead hint at a curvilinear relationship. They suggest the need for critical evaluation of the theoretical considerations which have led some psychologists to posit a negative relationship between age and behavioral rigidity as a central or important dictum of their theories.

To the extent that old adults showed more rigid behavior than younger adults, the findings support certain implications from psychoanalysis. They also support assertions made in everyday speech such as "You can't teach an old dog new tricks" and "Older people are set in their ways."

Still unanswered is the question whether different processes bring about overtly similar behavioral rigidity at different age levels. Another problem concerns the changes that occur in the same person's behavioral rigidity as he ages. The studies reported herein and, as far as we know, all other relevant studies described in the literature, compare the behavioral rigidity of different individuals; what are needed are studies of the behavioral rigidity manifested by the same person at different ages.

Intelligence in Relation to Rigidity

Common to several theories of rigidity is the notion that greater intelligence betokens a higher degree of differentiation. Goldstein relates differentiation and abstract ability. Werner notes that in "a *mentally growing* organism the regions become more differentiated" (1946b, p. 46). Achievement of a person on an intelligence test, writes Lewin, depends "above all on the degree of differentiation of the person" (1936, p. 187). Accept this belief and the belief that behavioral rigidity decreases as differentiation increases (a thesis advanced by these psychologists), and you are led to the conclusion that behavioral rigidity should stand in a negative relationship to intelligence or, at least, to achievement on intelligence tests. Is such a relationship supported by actual data? Some support for the relationship is found in reports in the literature (Heymans and Brugmans, 1913; Stephenson, 1932) which cite low, negative correlations between scores on intelligence tests and scores on tests of perseveration. Let us now turn to studies that relate E effects to scores on intelligence tests.

E Effects and I.Q. In our original investigation, most groups, regardless of the apparent intellectual status of their members, showed quite large E effects. It was therefore not expected that any striking relationship would be found between intelligence and E effects. To study the trends in the original study, we turned to the children for whom I.Q. scores were available (on the National Intelligence Test). But the practice of the schools of placing children in the same grade level into separate classes mainly on the basis of the I.Q. (homogeneous I.Q. groupings) introduced a number of complicating factors (Luchins, 1942, pp. 19-21; Luchins and Luchins, 1948). Methods of teaching and curricula differed for the low-I.Q. groups (below 90) and the higher-I.Q. groups. Some of the teachers believed that drill methods had to be used for dull children whereas appeals to reasoning and problem solving might be used for brighter children. Moreover, during the experimental sessions the social atmosphere in the dull classes was marked by less spontaneity, by stricter discipline, and by more tension and fear than in the brighter classes. Also, we suspected that superficially similar behavior was brought about by different processes in individuals of disparate intelligence; for example, comments suggested that brighter children quickly generalized the E method as the rule of solution while low-I.Q. children, insecure in their arithmetical ability, blindly stuck to the E method once they hit upon it.

In order to reduce some of the complicating factors, we eliminated from the analysis of the E effects–I.Q. relationship the results of those children whose I.Q.'s were below 90. Analysis was undertaken of the results for the 483 children who had solved all the E problems by the E method (and whose data had been analyzed for relationship of E effects to age—see pp. 237-39 above). Holding constant the factors of sex, age, and instructions, we compared high-I.Q. groups (110 or over) with medium-I.Q. groups (90-109). On twelve of sixteen comparisons, the high-I.Q. groups had a smaller percentage of E solutions of the first two criticals, and percentages of failures of the extinction problem were smaller for the high-I.Q. groups in eleven of the sixteen comparisons. When each instruction group and each sex group were considered separately, there was also revealed a tendency for the high-I.Q. groups to have less E effects.

Consider now the children in the plain group who solved at least the last two E problems by the E method. The fifty-two children who showed no E effects (used the direct method in all test problems) had I.Q.'s ranging from 75 to 155, with a median of 104, a Q_1 of 92, and a Q_3 of 128; for the 377 children who showed some E effects, I.Q.'s ranged from 51 to 160, with a median of 101, a Q_1 of 90, and a Q_3 of 112. This suggests a slight negative relationship.

The writers have found small negative correlations (statistically not significant) between E effects in the arithmetical Einstellung test and the intelligence of sixty-five normal adults as measured by the Wechsler-Bellevue test. Similar findings have been reported for a total of about 300 subjects by other investigators who used variants of the arithmetical test and the Wechsler-Bellevue, Stanford-Binet, or A.C.E. tests (Rokeach, 1947; Horwitz, 1951; Brown, 1951); an exception to the negative correlations is a correlation of $+0.25$ between E effects of forty-four subjects and their scores on the Cattell culture-free test of intelligence (Brown, 1951).

Comparison of Feeble-minded and Normal Children. While feeble-minded individuals are said to be more rigid than normals, there is a dearth of experimental evidence to support this statement. Our experience with feeble-minded children was that they could not do the arithmetical problems but were able to deal with the paper-and-pencil mazes. Paquet (1952) individually administered a modified version of the maze Einstellung test to fifty-nine boys in a Montreal institution for the feeble-minded as well as to forty-two boys in a Montreal orphanage. Instructions were given in French, the children's language. The two groups were matched for age, which ranged from 9.5 to 14.5 years. The I.Q.'s (Binet) of the feeble-minded ranged from 51 to 88, and those of the normals from 100 to 134; the mental age of the feeble-minded ranged from 5.3 to 10.8 years, and that of the normals from 9.5 to 18.5 years.

The maze test consisted of an illustrative task in which there were three paths to the goal box (all of which were illustrated), eight set-inducing mazes each solvable by a zigzag path but with the direct path blocked, two criticals in which both the direct and indirect paths could be used, four extinction tasks in which only the direct path could be used, and two final criticals.

Every normal child and all but three of the feeble-minded boys solved the illustrative task by following the direct path. Attempts to use the direct path in the subsequent maze, where it did not lead to the goal, were made by 75 per cent of the feeble-minded but only by 19 per cent of the normal boys. While these attempts were confined to the first E maze among the normal subjects, 46 per cent of the feeble-minded group attempted to follow the direct route in two or more of the E mazes. Indeed, fourteen feeble-minded boys did so in each of the eight E mazes; upon discovering or being told that the short path did not lead to the goal box, they found and traced the zigzag route; but, in the next E maze, they again attempted to use the direct path. That these fourteen subjects all used the direct path in the critical and extinction mazes is, therefore, not evidence of recovery from a set; they never developed a set for the circuitous route. On the contrary, it may be said that they were set for the direct route, attempting to follow it even when it was inappropriate. Such consistently maladaptive behavior in the E mazes was not shown by any of the thousands of normal subjects tested by the present writers.

Selecting from Paquet's data the findings for only those subjects who used the circuitous path on their initial attempt to solve the last four E tasks, we obtained E effects as follows for the respective groups:

Feeble-minded...
  39 subjects C_1: 87% E C_2: 79% E Ext.$_1$: 59% F C_3: 31% E C_4: 44% E
Normals...
  42 subjects C_1: 50% E C_2: 43% E Ext.$_1$: 24% F C_3: 2% E C_4: 0% E

In every test problem the feeble-minded children showed more E effects than the normals, significantly more on each of the criticals and on the first extinction maze. Similar trends were found for each chronological age level. Here we have experimental evidence to substantiate the thesis, derived from theoretical considerations, that feeble-minded individuals are more rigid than normals of the same chronological age.

Summary and Comments. For normal individuals, the correlations between E effects and scores on intelligence tests were usually found to be negative, although rather small in some studies. Comparison of feeble-minded and normal boys revealed that the former showed significantly more rigid behavior on a maze Einstellung test. These trends give some support to the thesis, common to the theories of Goldstein, Werner, and Lewin, that behavioral rigidity decreases with intelligence. The jumping-off point in this thesis is the construct of differentiation, considered either as the number of psychological regions into which the personality is divided or as the distinction which the individual draws between himself and the environment. Differentiation is assumed to increase both with mental age (or intelligence) and with chronological age; behavioral rigidity is assumed to decrease with differentiation; hence, it has been concluded (a) that behavioral rigidity decreases with mental age and (b) that behavioral rigidity decreases with chronological age. The earlier section on age in relation to rigidity did not reveal that children who were chronologically older showed less rigid behavior than younger children; that is, the results did not support conclusion (b). The results set forth in the present section revealed that children with higher mental ages showed less rigid behavior than children with lower mental ages; that is, the present results support conclusion (a). Thus, the results are in line with one conclusion, drawn from certain assumptions about differentiation, but run counter to another conclusion. Perhaps it is fallacious to assume that behavioral rigidity is consistently related to differentiation or perhaps re-evaluation is required of the meanings and indices of differentiation as well as of its assumed positive relationship to chronological age and intelligence. Possibly differentiation is positively related to mental age but not to chronological age.

Investigations are needed to study the processes that underlie E effects and other instances of behavioral rigidity in individuals of different intellectual ability, in order to see whether different processes are involved at diverse intellectual levels. Moreover, investigations are required to ascertain whether different factors are required to minimize or maximize rigidity at different intellectual levels.

Sex in Relation to Rigidity

A survey of the literature reveals that the question whether or not sex is a differential determinant of rigidity has, by and large, been

neglected by theorists. Let us consider whether sex differences tend
to be consistently related to *E* effects.

Sex Differences in Children's E Effects. *E* effects of the 483 elementary-school children who had solved all the *E* problems by the *E*
method, already analyzed from the standpoint of age and intelligence,
were again analyzed to study the factor of sex. In the group were 274
girls and 209 boys. With the factors of age, instructions, and intelligence held constant, we compared the males and females for *E* solutions of the criticals and failures of the extinction task. The boys showed
less *E* effects in thirteen of the sixteen comparisons made for the first
two criticals, in eleven of the sixteen comparisons made for the extinction task, and in thirteen of the sixteen comparisons made for the last
two criticals; that is, the boys tended to manifest less *E* effects than
the girls.

It will be remembered that half of the subjects were told, prior to
receiving any of the problems that, after Problem 6, they were to
write the words "Don't be blind!" on their papers. Subsequent questioning revealed that various interpretations were given to this admonition. Some children took it to mean, "Don't be blind to the rule
which solves the problems." Others interpreted it to mean, "Be clever,
show how quickly you can solve the problems." For some children, the
D.B.B. instruction was simply an additional test item—some words
which one must not forget to write. Apropos of such interpretations,
we were led to write: "They did not take D.B.B. as a challenge to do
some thinking of their own, to drop the habituated method in favor of a
better one, or to see the possibility of solving the problems by the D
method; their interpretation was contrary indeed" (Luchins, 1942,
p. 18). At the time that the questioning took place, our impression was
that such "contrary" interpretations were more often offered by the
girls. The results substantiate this impression. While the male D.B.B.
groups showed a larger percentage of direct solutions than their corresponding plain groups in seven of the eight comparisons made for
the first two criticals and in six of the eight comparisons made for the
extinction problem, the female D.B.B. groups showed a larger percentage of direct solutions than their corresponding plain groups in
only three of the eight comparisons made for the first two criticals and
in only three of the eight comparisons made for the extinction task.

In the higher I.Q. range (110 and over), every D.B.B. female group,
in each of the four age levels, proved to have less direct solutions of each
test problem than did the corresponding plain groups; but in the lower
I.Q. range this was true only for the twelve-year-olds. These results
suggest that girls with higher I.Q.'s may be more prone to interpret

(or rather misinterpret) the D.B.B. instruction in a manner which is conducive to stronger Einstellung.

Sex Differences in Adults' E Effects. College students' responses to the maze Einstellung test (Luchins, 1950a) were analyzed for sex differences; in every test problem forty females showed somewhat more E effects (not significantly more) than forty males. Using a variation of the arithmetical experiment with 194 adults, Guetzkow (1951) found that men and women gave about equal percentages of E solutions to the criticals but that men gave significantly more solutions to the subsequent extinction task. But Heglin (1955), using variants of the arithmetical and hidden-word tests, failed to find any consistent or significant sex differences in his population of 150 females and 150 males.

Comments. Why do some of the described investigations reveal a trend for more rigid behavior on the part of females? We venture an explanation based on observations made in elementary-school classes. The social atmosphere in the classroom and certain pupil-teacher relationships often seemed to foster strong E effects: a rather autocratic atmosphere in which the teacher demanded blind confidence and dependency, in which restraint, pedantry, passivity, and submissiveness were desired traits while free initiative was not encouraged. It is fairly evident how such an atmosphere and how such characteristics can enhance behavioral rigidity. It is also evident that these traits of submissiveness and dependency are often associated with the female of our society. Indeed, such traits go into making up the constellation denoted as "femininity" as opposed to "masculinity" (see, for example, the Terman-Miles masculinity-femininity test). We hypothesize that the greater E effects shown by the females may be associated with their possessing, to a greater degree than males, such traits as dependency, submissiveness, etc., traits that may foster differences between the sexes with regard to attitudes toward and interpretations of the experiment. Differences in interpretation of the "Don't be blind" admonition is a case in point. More generally, we posit that those individuals, regardless of sex, who adhere to the pattern of "femininity" referred to above, would tend to show strong E effects. Comparison of subjects' behavior in Einstellung tests and in the Terman-Miles masculinity-femininity test may yield some clues as to the plausibility of our hypothesis and it is suggested as an avenue for future research.

We have not, it will be noticed, suggested that the difference in behavioral rigidity between the males and females is due to some innate, biological difference. Not infrequently the finding of a sex differential has been interpreted as *ipso facto* evidence that the difference is biologically generated. Even if future experimentation should reveal that females tend to manifest more behavioral rigidity, not only in Einstellung situations but in other tests of rigidity as well, we would hesitate to conclude that there are necessarily biological determinants involved or that rigidity is necessarily a biological sex-linked characteristic. To assume biological determination of results is to overlook the negative instances in which females do not manifest rigid behavior and yet are presumably similar biologically to other females, or the instances in which males show much rigidity.

Also, we should like to administer the tests under various conditions in order to ascertain whether there are conditions which enhance or weaken sex differences in E effects. We should also like to compare males and females with similar and diverse personality structures. Comparative studies to discover whether a similar trend of sex differences prevails among other species, would be of interest. Incidentally, investigations of rats with a maze Einstellung experiment have to date failed to reveal a tendency for the female rat to be more rigid than the male. There is also the problem whether processes that bring about rigidity and whether factors that maximize or minimize rigidity, differ for males and females.

Finally, it should prove of interest to study peoples of different cultures in order to discover whether there are consistent sex differences in rigidity. It would be well to include cultures in which woman's typical role is different than in ours and in which the social milieu does not necessarily foster the traits which have come to be associated with "femininity" in our culture. There are, it seems to us, dangers involved in interpreting sex differences in results as biologically generated without first investigating whether they are culturally generated.

COMPARISON OF E EFFECTS OF PSYCHOTICS, NEUROTICS, AND NORMALS

Another dimension along which individual differences are often studied is that of degree of psychopathology—considered to lie along a gradient ranging from normal to neurotic to psychotic. An intimate link between neuroses and rigidity is postulated by psychoanalysts. Moreover, many psychologists (including Goldstein and Werner) hold that individuals with psychopathological disturbances are characterized by greater rigidity than normal individuals. But, despite these common and prevalent assertions, there is little experimental evidence on the relative rigidity of psychotics, neurotics, and normals derived from studies in which a single objective standard of rigidity is used. It therefore seemed of considerable importance to compare the behavior of psychotics, neurotics, and normals in the same Einstellung tests.

We considered as psychotic or as neurotic an individual who was confined to a mental hospital at the time of testing and who had been diagnosed by hospital personnel as psychotic or neurotic, respectively. The patients used were all Canadian veterans of World War II, aged between twenty-five and forty, and confined to veterans' hospitals in Quebec. Those diagnosed as neurotic were in open wards, those diagnosed as psychotic in closed wards. In each study the neurotic and psychotic groups (and the normal group when one was used) were similar in age and in I.Q. as measured by the Wechsler-Bellevue test. We considered as normal an individual who apparently was free from psychopathological disturbances.

Psychotics and Neurotics

Thirty-nine neurotics and thirty-nine psychotics were tested individually with the arithmetical and maze Einstellung tests (Luchins, 1950). If a patient did not solve an E task in the E manner, the test was discontinued for him; that is, only the results of those who had solved all E tasks in the E manner were considered in the analysis. E effects were as follows in the first extinction task and the preceding criticals of the arithmetical test:

39 neurotics C_1: 100% E C_2: 91% E C_3': 67% E C_4': 49% E   Ext.$_1$: 74% F
39 psychotics C_1: 87% E C_2: 73% E C_3': 27% E C_4': 30% E   Ext.$_1$: 47% F

We see that in each of these test problems the neurotics showed more E effects than the psychotics; the differences proved significant at the 0.05 level in some of the problems.

E effects in the first two criticals and the first extinction problem of the maze test are given below. (See pp. 124-25 for other maze data on neurotics and psychotics.)

39 neurotics .... C_1: 58% E C_2: 33% E   Ext.$_1$: 19% F
39 psychotics .... C_1: 43% E C_2: 24% E   Ext.$_1$: 10% F

Here again the neurotics showed somewhat greater E effects than the psychotics.

These two studies suggest greater rigidity on the part of neurotics; but the study to which we now turn shows that this is not always the trend.

Psychotics, Neurotics, and Nonhospitalized Normals

The arithmetical, hidden-word, and word-block Einstellung tests, in that order, were administered individually to each of thirty-six psychotics and thirty-six neurotics, as well as to twenty normal individuals who were not hospitalized. In each test, only the results of those subjects who had solved the last three E tasks by the E method were included in the analysis. While all normals met this criterion, some of the patients failed to do so and this accounts for the different numbers of subjects appearing in the table summarizing results of the various tests.

Since there are three tests involved here, with different numbers of critical problems and of extinction problems, it was decided to simplify the presentation of results by assigning a special test score to indicate each person's performance on a test. This was a shift score which marked the point in each test at which the subject first employed the direct method in two consecutive test problems. For example, an individual who shifted to the direct method in the first test problem (and employed it also in the next problem) was assigned a score of 1; an individual who shifted to the direct method in the fifth test problem (and employed it also in the next problem) was assigned a score of 5. A higher shift score thus denotes later shift to the direct method and hence more persistence in the E method, which, in turn, may be interpreted as evidence of greater behavioral rigidity.

Mean shift scores in each test for the neurotics, psychotics, and normals are given in Table VI. Differences between neurotics and psychotics are small and inconsistent, and do not corroborate the findings of the study summarized in the preceding subsection. But there are

TABLE VI. E EFFECTS OF NEUROTICS, PSYCHOTICS, AND NORMALS

	NUMBER OF SUBJECTS			SHIFT SCORES		
	Arith. Test	Hidden-Word Test	Word-Block Test	Arith. Test	Hidden-Word Test	Word-Block Test
Neurotics	31	24	34	6.73	2.62	8.28
Psychotics	30	28	32	6.72	2.65	9.18
Normals	20	20	20	3.04	1.80	4.50

striking differences between normals and each of the patient groups. On the average, normals shifted to the direct method (gave up the E method) about four problems earlier in the arithmetical test and in the word-block test, and about one problem earlier in the hidden-word test. Differences between the mean shift scores of the normals and each of the patient groups proved statistically significant at or beyond the 0.01 level in each of the three tests. The findings are in line with the thesis, common to many theories of rigidity, that psychopathological individuals are characterized by greater rigidity than normals. However, some of the studies to be described in the next subsection do not bear out this thesis.

Psychotics, Neurotics, and Hospitalized Normals

Whereas the normal population in the study described in the preceding subsection consisted of individuals who were not hospitalized at the time of testing and who were not all war veterans, the normal population in the studies to be described in the present subsection consisted of Canadian World War II veterans who were in the orthopedic wards of the hospitals which yielded the psychiatric subjects. As far as was known, these normals did not have any psychiatric disorders; they were relatively free from physical pain at the time of testing and were well on the way to recovery from the physical infirmities which had brought about their hospitalization.

Since these normals not only were similar to the psychiatric patients in sex, age, and I.Q. range, but also were veterans and hospitalized at the time of testing, it might be reasoned that they represented a more comparable normal group with respect to the psychiatric patients than did the normals in the experiment reported in the preceding subsection. Whether this was the case, and whether the present normal group or the nonhospitalized one was more adequately representative of "normals" in the general population, are matters on which we are not able to pronounce judgment. They are matters linked to the knotty problems—common to all comparative studies that require that part of the sample population be "normal" and part "abnormal"—of what shall constitute the criterion for each of these categories, of the bases to be used in selecting groups that are comparable except for the differential aspect under investigation, and of how to guarantee that the groups are fairly representative of the general populations.

The investigations described in this subsection constitute part of a project conducted with the cooperation of Dr. George Dufresne, chief psychologist of the Queen Mary Veterans Hospital of Montreal. McGill University students who, while serving as psychological interns, assisted in the collection and tabulation of data, include: Rita Brownstein Kopin, Leo Goldberger, Esther Halprin, Asher Kahn, Lisa Lowie, Sheila Lubin, Joan Notkin, F. Peretz, Melvin Simak, Eva Stearns, Carmen Zuckerman, and James Westcott.

Each subject was tested individually. Where several Einstellung tests were given to the same subject, the testing was usually done in several sessions in order not to tire the patient. For the arithmetical (volume-measuring), maze, and hidden-word Einstellung tests, we adopted the criterion that the results of only those subjects who had solved at least the last three E tasks in the E manner would be included in the analysis.

Maze Test. In one study the maze Einstellung test was given to (hospitalized) psychotics, neurotics, and normals. The results, in terms of percentages of direct solutions (D), were as follows:

40 psychotics .... C_1: 53 C_2: 65 $Ext._1$: 90 C_3: 90 C_4: 80
21 neurotics .... C_1: 42 C_2: 67 $Ext._1$: 81 C_3: 96 C_4: 90
19 normals .... C_1: 79 C_2: 74 $Ext._1$: 100 C_3: 79 C_4: 95

It is seen that, in the first critical and in the first extinction task, the normals had the largest percentage of direct solutions, the psychotics were next, and the neurotics last. In the other criticals, however, this trend did not prevail.

Arithmetical Test. Some of these subjects, as well as additional subjects, received the arithmetical Einstellung test with the following results, again given in terms of the percentages of direct solutions (including both two-jar and one-jar solutions in C_3' and C_4').

43 psychotics .... C_1: 14 C_2: 28 C_3': 70 C_4': 70 $Ext._1$: 56
33 neurotics .... C_1: 0 C_2: 9 C_3': 33 C_4': 51 $Ext._1$: 36
12 normals .... C_1: 8 C_2: 17 C_3': 25 C_4': 25 $Ext._1$: 42

Note that consistently the psychotics had the largest percentage of direct solutions. In the first two critical problems and in the first extinction task, the normals were next and the neurotics were last. Differences between the psychotics' and neurotics' direct solutions of the first four criticals and the first extinction task proved statistically significant at the 0.01, 0.02, 0.001, 0.1, and 0.1 levels of confidence, respectively. Differences between the psychotics' and normals' direct solutions of C_3' and C_4' each proved statistically significant at the 0.001 level. The difference between the neurotics' and normals' direct solutions of C_4' was statistically significant at the 0.1 level. (Differences not specifically enumerated failed to reach the 0.1 level.)

That psychotics gave relatively more direct solutions—showed less E effects—than neurotics corroborates the results of some of the investigations described earlier in this chapter. But that psychotics now gave relatively more direct solutions than the normals is a new result, one which was not found when nonhospitalized normals were used. One wonders whether the results were influenced by the fact that the normals were hospitalized and that the testing took place in the hospital.

Picture-Series Tests Administered Under Different Conditions. For some of the subjects who had received the maze test and/or the arithmetical test, it was possible to continue the testing so that they received, over a period of two days, some or all of the picture series (Luchins, 1950). In these series one percept is gradually transformed, in successive drawings, into another percept. Nineteen of the psychotics and nineteen of the normals received thirteen picture series while nineteen neurotics each received only the first eight of these series.

We delay consideration of the results of these picture-series tests in order to introduce another investigation wherein the thirteen picture series were given to forty other hospitalized neurotics and to forty other hospitalized normals, but under different conditions of administration. Each of these subjects had previously received the maze, the hidden-word, and the arithmetical Einstellung tests, in that order. Also, after each of these tests, the experimenter had pointed to each problem in which the subject had overlooked the direct method and had asked the subject why he had solved the problem as he had; then, if the subject did not discover the direct method, the experimenter showed it to him. Similarly, after each picture series, the experimenter and the subject together looked at the pictures again and the subject was asked why he had not reported an emerging percept earlier in the series. In this and in other chapters, this condition of administration, called Condition 1, is designated as "analysis of responses after each test." In addition to receiving the analysis of responses after each of the picture-series tests and the three preceding tests, half of the subjects (twenty neurotics and twenty normals) were told after each analysis that these tests had been designed to lead people to overlook or to be blinded to changes which they should observe, and each subject was challenged, after each test and picture series, not to let himself become mechanized, blinded, or tricked in the next test or picture series but to face each problem or picture separately. This condition of administration (Condition 2) is designated as "analysis of responses after each test plus challenge not to be blinded in the next test."

Since our primary interest here is in comparing results in the picture series made by different kinds of subjects and under various conditions of administration, we are not concerned now with results in the tests that preceded the picture series. However, some of those results are discussed in the chapter on transfer of training (pp. 380-82).

A shift score was assigned to each subject corresponding to the place in each series of drawings at which he first reported an emerging percept; for example, a subject who first reported seeing a bottle on the fourteenth card of the face-bottle series was assigned a shift score of 14 in this series. A higher score thus represents later shift to a new percept, which may be interpreted as evidence of greater behavioral rigidity. A subject who did not report a particular percept anywhere in the series was given a "shift score" corresponding to the number of the last drawing that contained this particular percept.

Several series involve more than one emerging percept; for example, one series portrays the gradual transformation of the picture of a sailor into that of a goblet (first emerging percept), which in turn is transformed into the picture of a woman (second emerging percept). The thirteen series (given to all groups except the nineteen neurotics) involve a total of nineteen emerging percepts (and hence nineteen different shift scores), while the first eight of these series (given to the group of nineteen neurotics) involve a total of twelve emerging percepts (and hence twelve different shift scores).

TABLE VII. MEAN SHIFT SCORES IN PICTURE SERIES OF HOSPITALIZED
PATIENTS STUDIED UNDER VARIOUS CONDITIONS

Percept No.	Description of Series	Condition 0 No Discussion of Results Between Series			Condition 1 Analysis of Responses After Each Series		Condition 2 Analysis of Responses After Each Series Plus Challenge Not to Be Blinded in Next Series	
		19 Psych.	19 Norm.	19 Neuro.	20 Norm.	20 Neuro.	20 Norm.	20 Neuro.
1	Fisherman-lad................	8.6	9.9	8.8	7.9	9.5	9.0	7.5
2	Rooster-woman..............	11.4	11.4	10.9	11.3	11.2	11.2	11.3
3	Woman in bathtub (1).	14.6	15.3	14.7	14.7	14.6	14.9	14.5
4	Face-bottle (1)...............	14.5	13.5	13.8	13.6	13.6	15.8	14.3
5	Napoleon's tomb...........	7.8	7.1	6.2	6.9	6.8	7.2	7.4
6a	Fruit-flower....................	7.4	6.1	7.1	7.0	7.0	7.6	6.9
6b	Fruit-flower.........	15.9	14.5	15.3	15.1	14.6	14.1	15.2
7a	Fruit-clothes (1)...........	4.4	4.3	4.3	4.4	5.0	4.9	4.4
7b	Fruit-clothes (1)...........	10.3	9.3	9.6	10.2	12.0	10.7	10.4
7c	Fruit-clothes (1)...........	19.5	18.9	19.4	19.6	19.9	19.1	19.2
8a	Sailor-goblet..................	9.5	9.8	9.7	9.2	9.6	10.5	10.4
8b	Sailor-goblet..................	18.4	17.8	17.8	18.2	17.1	17.9	18.0
9a	Fruit-clothes (2)...........	7.2	7.7		7.6	7.3	5.9	6.2
9b	Fruit-clothes (2)...........	15.7	14.7		15.8	15.9	14.3	14.2
9c	Fruit-clothes (2)...........	28.7	28.4		27.3	27.2	26.2	26.3
10a	Face-bottle (2)...............	11.2	11.2		12.0	11.9	12.3	11.5
11	Woman in bathtub (2)..	13.9	12.1		12.3	11.8	11.6	11.3
12	Beauty-old hag..............	10.1	9.7		8.0	8.5	8.6	8.8
13	Horse-face......................	11.8	12.1		13.1	13.1	13.3	13.2

The results, in terms of mean shift scores, are given in Table VII for various groups of subjects under the various conditions of administration, which are referred to in the table as Conditions 0, 1, and 2. Subjects tested under Condition 0 were the psychotics, normals, and neurotics (nineteen of each) with whom there was no discussion of the results of preceding tests or of the picture-series tests themselves. Those tested under Condition 1 were the normals and neurotics (twenty of each) who had analysis of responses after each test and picture series. Those tested under Condition 2 were the normals and neurotics (twenty of each) who, in addition to receiving the analysis of responses after each test or picture series, were challenged not to become blinded or mechanized or tricked in the forthcoming test or picture series.

The number in the first column of the table refers to the number of the emerging percept; e.g., Percept 3 refers to the emerging percept in the third series; Percept 7a, to the first emerging percept in the seventh series; and 7b, to the second emerging percept in this series.

The brief description of each series that is given in the second column usually refers to two percepts in a series (e.g., "rooster-woman" refers to a series in which a picture of a rooster is gradually transformed into a picture of a woman); but, in some cases, for the sake of brevity, only one percept in the series is named (e.g., "woman in bathtub"). Variations of the same series are given in some cases; e.g., "face-bottle (1)" refers to one series and "face-bottle (2)" to a variation of this series.

Consider first the results under Condition 0 (no discussion of performance with subjects). Probably the most striking feature of the findings is the fact that for any given percept there are small differences in mean shift scores among psychotics, normals, and neurotics. The largest difference between shift scores for a given percept is less than two units; and, of the forty-three comparisons that may be made (nineteen comparisons for psychotics and normals, twelve for psychotics and neurotics, and twelve for normals and neurotics), only six comparisons yield differences of more than one unit. Since each unit corresponds to one picture, the results mean that, on the average, the psychotics, neurotics, and normals first reported the emerging percept in the same picture or in the next picture of a series. These results suggest that there were little differences among the three groups of subjects with regard to the extent to which they were attending to and were guided by the pictures themselves. We think that this is a particularly interesting result for the psychotics since they are often characterized as being divorced from reality; here they were about as alert to the reality of the pictures as the neurotics and normals.

While the differences among the three groups studied under Condition 0 are small, we are interested in the relative ranking of the groups. A glance at the results shows that, for the first three emerging percepts, the normals made shift scores that were as high as, or higher than, those made by the psychiatric patients. But for the next nine percepts, the normals made the lowest shift score in five cases and as low a shift score as either of the patient groups in two other cases. While the psychotics had the lowest shift scores for two of the first three percepts, they had the lowest shift score for only one of the next nine percepts and they had lower shift scores than the normals for only two of the last seven percepts. These results hint that under Condition 0 the normals may have learned somewhat more from their experience with the preceding series than did the patients.

Although differences among the three groups studied under Condition 0 are small, let us examine the direction of the differences. The psychotics showed slightly higher mean shift scores than the normals for twelve out of nineteen percepts and the same mean shift scores as the normals for only two percepts. The psychotics showed slightly higher mean shift scores than the neurotics for nine out of twelve percepts. The neurotics and normals each made somewhat higher mean scores than the other in five cases and equal scores in two cases. If the magnitude of the differences is taken into account, then, on the whole, the psychotics tended to have the highest shift scores (a higher shift score being interpreted as a sign of greater behavioral rigidity), while there was very little difference between the neurotics and normals.

Let us turn now to results obtained under Condition 1 (analysis of responses). Here, only normals and neurotics were studied. Again differences are small, never as large as two units and smaller than one unit for sixteen of the nineteen percepts. The neurotics showed somewhat lower mean shift scores than the normals for nine of the nineteen percepts and the same scores as the normals for three percepts. But, if the magnitude of the differences is taken into account, then the neurotics on the whole tended to have higher shift scores than the normals.

Under Condition 2 (analysis plus challenge), differences between mean shift scores for any given percept also are small, never as large as two units and greater than one unit for only three of the nineteen percepts. On eleven of the nineteen percepts, the normals made higher mean shift scores than the neurotics, and the magnitude of the differences revealed higher scores, on the whole, for normals. Thus, while under Condition 1 the normals showed signs of somewhat less behavioral rigidity than the neurotics, the reverse was true under Condition 2.

The results suggest that differences in the nature of the conditions under which the picture series are administered may exert greater differential effects than differences in the kinds of subjects studied. For example, comparison of the normals under Conditions 0, 1, and 2 reveals differences, for some percepts, as large or larger than two units, a larger difference than was found between normals and psychiatric patients studied under the same conditions of administration. Similarly, comparison of neurotics under Conditions 0, 1, and 2 reveals some differences as large or larger than two units. (See pp. 380-82 for a discussion of a similar finding in the arithmetical test given under Conditions 1 and 2.) It would seem that the degree of behavioral rigidity evidenced may depend more upon the conditions under which individuals are studied than upon their psychopathological status.

It should be noted that mean shift scores, while allowing a convenient comparison of group results, by no means reveal all the quantitative results. Mean shift scores, for instance, fail to reveal the extent to which an individual "improved" (in the sense of noticing the emerging percepts earlier) from series to series. Even a particular individual's shift scores do not indicate all the nuances of his responses, e.g., how long he held on to an old percept although reporting a new one too; how many responses he gave and what kind of responses they were; how many responses he gave that referred to parts of objects and how many to whole objects; how much time he took to respond. In this connection it should be noted that, under Conditions 1 and 2, where the time of response was recorded, it was found that the neurotics generally took more time per test problem and more time before responding to a picture than the normals.

Qualitative results should also be mentioned. Records of qualitative data were kept particularly well for subjects studied under Conditions 1 and 2. Consider, for example, some of the observations that were noted with respect to those studied under Condition 1. Here, neurotics, on the whole, appeared more tense, anxious, and insecure than the normals. They appealed more often to the experimenter to let them know if they were doing "all right" or were giving the "right answers." They apparently were more concerned than the normals about failure of a problem, showed overt signs of distress, and commented on their stupidity or inability to think clearly. Some of the neurotics seemed to be upset by an ambiguous picture, reported after considerable hesitation that they saw nothing, or gave answers suggestive of personal projections. When they were aware of two percepts in a picture (or two methods of solution), they sometimes hesitated about making a decision and wondered which was the "right" answer. This may help to account for the fact that the average time per test problem and per picture was greater, on the average, for neurotics than normals. More often than normals, neurotics inquired about whether they had done well on the tests and wanted to know what the tests had disclosed about their personalities and their illness. When they were shown the direct methods and asked why they had not used them or when they were asked why they had not reported a percept in an earlier picture, normals usually reacted with surprise and humor; neurotics, with chagrin and shame. Explanations of their behavior offered by normals were usually related to specific factors in the test situation; neurotics' answers were more often ego-involved, reflected greater lack of self-confidence, and related their behavior in the tests to personal failings, to a general inability to cope with life, or to other factors not specific to the test situation. Typical comments from normals were the following: "The same method worked over and over again and became a habit"; "I was so used to looking at it in one way that I didn't see anything else." Comments obtained from neurotics included the following: "I have a thick head"; "I'm dumb"; "I didn't stop to think"; "I didn't feel well"; "I was too nervous to see it before"; "I'm not able to concentrate well"; "My reflexes are slow after the treatments [subshock insulin therapy]"; "I'm not good at anything."

Observations suggest that there was less difference between neurotics' and normals' qualitative data under Condition 2 than under Condition 1. For example, when asked why they had not used direct methods or had not reported a percept earlier, the normals' reactions under Condition 2 were closer to the chagrin and shame usually shown by neurotics (under either Condition 1 or 2) than to the surprise and humor usually shown by normals under Condition 1. It seemed that the challenge not to be blinded, issued under Condition 2, made some of the normals quite anxious about their behavior; some of them interpreted the discussion of their results to mean that they had been blinded, that they had failed to meet the challenge. Indeed, some of the normals under Condition 2 showed more overt anxiety than the neurotics studied under this condition. Perhaps this may help to explain the fact that under Condition 2 the normals showed higher mean shift scores on the picture series than the neurotics.

It is noteworthy that both hospitalized normals and hospitalized neurotics tended to show more E effects in various Einstellung tests (for example, the arithmetical test) under Condition 2 than under Condition 1. Thus, in the hospital setting, the challenge not to be blinded seemed to foster E effects. Yet, when some of the Einstellung tests (but not the picture series) were administered in a nonhospital setting to college students, those studied under Condition 2 showed less E effects. See pp. 378-83 of the chapter on transfer of training for these results and for a discussion of the apparent greater anxiety which the challenge not to be blinded aroused in the hospital setting as compared with the nonhospital setting. One wonders what the results of the college students would have been if the tests had been administered to them in a hospital setting. One wonders also what their results would have been on the picture series had they received them. More information is needed about responses of nonhospitalized normals to the picture series. More generally, there is a need for further investigations using the picture series and the other Einstellung tests under Conditions 0, 1, and 2 with both hospitalized and nonhospitalized individuals.

Summary and Comments

The first study described in this section showed hospitalized psychotics manifesting less E effects than hospitalized neurotics in the arithmetical and maze Einstellung tests. The second study, involving three Einstellung tests, did not reveal significant or consistent differences between psychotics or neurotics, but did reveal that each of these groups showed more E effects than normals (not hospitalized). This finding may be interpreted as supporting the thesis, common to psychoanalysis and several rigidity theories, that psychopathological individuals are characterized by greater rigidity than normals. This thesis was also supported by some but not all of the investigations in which the normal and abnormal subjects were hospitalized war veterans. One investigation, using the maze Einstellung test, showed that percentages of direct solutions of the first critical and the first extinction task were highest for the hospitalized normals, with the psychotics next and the neurotics last. But on the arithmetical Einstellung test psychotics had a larger percentage of direct solutions of each of the first four criticals and the first extinction task than either hospitalized normals or neurotics—a result that goes counter to the cited thesis. Other investigations, in which the picture series were administered under various conditions, showed very small, statistically not significant, differences between psychiatric patients and hospitalized normals. Somewhat higher mean shift scores on the picture series (which may be regarded as a sign of greater behavioral rigidity) were made by the psychotics than by either the neurotics or the hospitalized normals under one condition of administration. While neurotics showed higher shift scores than normals under one condition of administration, the reverse was the case under another condition. It is noteworthy that larger differences in mean shift scores were found when performance of hospitalized normals or of neurotics was compared under different conditions of administration than when performance of the two groups of subjects was compared under the same condition. The condition of administration under which normals made higher mean shift scores than neurotics seemed to arouse considerable anxiety on the part of the normals, so that they seemed as anxious or even more anxious than some of the neurotics.

A Proposal for the Utilization of the Einstellung Tests

It was noted above that the shift score, or knowledge of the point at which the subject shifted to the direct method or to a new percept, does not reveal all the nuances of a subject's reactions to an Einstellung test. It is proposed that, in future utilization of these tests, the investigator (whether he is using the test for experimental or clinical purposes) should aim, during the administration of the tests and in the analysis of results, to obtain information on the following:

(1) The point of shift to the nonset solution or to an emergent percept in each Einstellung test.

(2) The pattern of responses in each test, in the E tasks as well as the test tasks.

(3) The attitudes and assumptions of the subject toward each test.

(4) The nature of the process underlying the E effects.

(5) The influence of certain experimental variations on the subject's behavior.

(6) The kinds of experimental variations which tend to maximize or minimize E effects for the subject.

(7) General changes in the subject's behavior from test to test. Data on the six points just enumerated would, in a thorough analysis, also be compared from test to test to obtain a "vertical" or "pattern" analysis for the subject.

(8) The subject's reactions when he is informed of his results on the various tests and is shown methods and percepts which he overlooked.

When data pertaining to these points are available for sufficiently large numbers of subjects, it should prove of value to examine them for possible relationships and trends. Do certain attitudes and assumptions toward the test tend to be associated with certain shift points or patterns of responses? What kinds of subjects have shown certain patterns of responses? How does the same experimental variation affect different subjects?

Here it seems to us is a possibly fruitful approach to the study of various "individual differences" in relation to behavior on the Einstellung tests (or on other tests). For example, do normals tend to differ from psychiatric patients in their shift scores, in their attitudes toward the test, in the nature of the process underlying development of an Einstellung, in the relationship between the nature of their attitudes toward the test and their shift score, in the relationship between the nature of the underlying process and their shift score, in their reactions to various experimental variations, in the kind of factors which must be introduced to minimize or maximize E effects, in changes of behavior from test to test, in their reactions when shown the nonset methods and the overlooked percepts and when informed of their results? To gather data that compares normals with psychiatric patients in the indicated manner may prove more illuminating (although admittedly less precise and compact) than simply to stipulate certain scores on the Einstellung tests as the "norms" for this or that group.

It is also hoped that future experimentation will compare the person's behavior in Einstellung tests with his rigid behavior in the hospital or in various life situations. One point of interest would be to see whether methods that increase or decrease E effects in the tests also do so in hospital and various life situations. In the actual clinical testing of the patient, we recommend that, after some standard test has been employed (not necessarily an Einstellung test), systematic variations of it be introduced in attempts to produce changes in the patient's response (cf. Luchins, 1950). This is in line with our conception of a clinical test as more than a static instrument whose function is to assign a score to the patient or to place him in a certain category. The patient's amenability or resistance to change in various clinical testing situations and the apparent influence of certain methods introduced to change his test response, could then be compared with his amenability or resistance to change in the Einstellung situations and with the apparent influence of variations introduced therein.

If two groups of individuals (say, normals and psychiatric patients or, more generally, Groups X and Y) do show characteristically different behavior trends in the detailed analysis of their responses to a battery of Einstellung tests, then an additional phase might be included in an ideal testing program. This phase would be concerned with the determination of how conditions should be altered in order to obtain behavior from Group X which was previously found to be characteristic of Group Y, and vice versa. That is, the endeavor would be to find the "transformation conditions" under which the characteristic behavior of one group is "transformed" into that of another group.

We wish to emphasize that the program described above is not limited to the study of differences between psychiatric patients and normals. It is applicable, we believe, to detailed analysis and comparison of behavior in the Einstellung tests of males and females, various chronological age groups, various mental age groups, different I.Q. groups, etc. If one group is found to show certain behavioral trends and patterns which differ from those of another group, it might be in order to seek to discover the "transformation conditions" referred to above.

This, in short, seems to us to represent the ideal utilization of the Einstellung tests for the study of an individual or a group, for comparisons of individuals or groups, and for the determination of relevant individual differences and group differences.

E EFFECTS IN RELATION TO SCORES ON PERSONALITY AND ATTITUDE
TESTS

We continue the study of individual differences in E effects by comparing scores in Einstellung tests with various indices on certain personality and attitude tests.

Relation to Rorschach Indices

Responses to the Rorschach test, the key diagnostic instrument of
contemporary clinical psychology, have been interpreted by clinicians
as reflecting on the rigidity of the respondent. A small total number
of responses is said to denote rigidity of perceptual-organizing processes since such rigidity makes it difficult to look at the ink blot from
different points of view, to shift the degree of articulation or the figure-
ground relationship (Rapaport and Schafer, 1945, p. 120). A high
percentage of responses based on the form of the blot is interpreted as
an indication of rigidity (Bochner and Halpern, 1945, p. 35; Rapaport
and Schafer, 1945, p. 194). An absence of color responses is treated
as denoting a "rigid suppression of affects" (Rapaport and Schafer,
1945, p. 243), and few color or movement responses are treated as
indicants of a coarcted individual, one who is emotionally constricted,
lacks spontaneity, and manifests rigidity. It has also been suggested
by some clinicians that the greater the time required to respond to the
Rorschach cards, the greater the rigidity.

The Rorschach test and the arithmetical and hidden-word Einstellung tests were administered individually to each of twenty-three presumably normal adults. For each Einstellung test, the subjects were
divided into two groups, those who recovered from the Einstellung
(used the direct method in test problems) before the first extinction
problem was presented and those who recovered only after this extinction problem was presented. For brevity of exposition, we refer to the
former as the "less-rigid group" and to the latter as the "more-rigid
group." The means and the standard deviations of various Rorschach
response categories were computed for the less-rigid and the more-rigid
group in each Einstellung test. The study was done with the assistance
of Alastair Burnett, then a student at McGill University.

If rigidity scores on the Einstellung tests are related to the indices
of rigidity on the Rorschach test, then we should expect the more-rigid
group to show a smaller total number of responses, a higher percentage
of form responses, fewer color responses and movement responses, and
a greater average time of response (in seconds) than the less-rigid
group. These expectations are upheld. Table VIII shows the mean

Rorschach indices for the more-rigid and less-rigid groups on the arithmetical test.

TABLE VIII. COMPARISON OF RESPONSES ON THE RORSCHACH TEST OF A MORE-RIGID GROUP AND A LESS-RIGID GROUP ON THE ARITHMETICAL EINSTELLUNG TEST

	Total Number of Rorschach Responses	Percentage of Form Responses	Number of Color and Movement Responses	Mean Time of Response (in Seconds)
More-rigid group	25	38.7	5.6	64.1
Less-rigid group	43	34.7	12.2	41.6

The difference between the mean total numbers of responses for the two groups (25 and 43) is significant at the 0.01 level; the difference between the corresponding standard deviations (7.5 for the more-rigid and 21.2 for the less-rigid group) is significant at the 0.02 level. For the other indicated Rorschach indices, the differences are not significant at acceptable levels. Nonetheless, it is of interest that the direction of results in every case was in line with expectations derived from the thesis that the more-rigid group, as judged by E effects, also tends to be more rigid as judged by Rorschach indices. A similar trend was found when Rorschach indices were compared for the more-rigid group and the less-rigid group in the hidden-word Einstellung test.

The Rorschach test was also administered to each of twenty hospitalized neurotics and twenty hospitalized psychotics who were tested individually with the hidden-word, arithmetical, and word-block Einstellung tests. The mean shift score on each of these Einstellung tests was correlated by Leon Goldberger with the total number of responses and the percentage of form responses in the Rorschach test. Correlations between mean shift scores and percentages of form responses were small, inconsistent, and statistically insignificant. Correlations between mean shift scores and the total number of Rorschach responses were consistently in line with the expectation that the greater the E effect, the fewer the Rorschach responses; that is, each correlation was negative. In the case of the neurotics' responses, the correlation (−0.6231) between the mean shift score on the arithmetical test and the total number of Rorschach responses proved significant at the 0.01 level, while the correlation for psychotics was not significant at acceptable levels.

In short, for at least one of the Rorschach indices of rigidity, the results for normals, neurotics, and psychotics showed rigidity in the Rorschach test (usually interpreted as rigidity of perceptual-organizing processes) to be positively related to rigidity in Einstellung tests, although not all the correlations were statistically significant.

Relation to Scores on Security Scales

Psychoanalytic writings on rigidity may be interpreted to mean that the more-secure individual is less anxious and, hence, less rigid than the less-secure individual. To test this hypothesis, Ainsworth (1950) gave subjects the arithmetical Einstellung test as well as a scale of insecurity based upon the concepts of Professor Blatz of the University of Toronto. A statistically significant positive relationship was found between E effects and degree of insecurity, thus confirming the hypothesis.

Similar trends were found by Meer and Gebhard (1950). Out of 120 subjects, they selected the fourteen who scored on each extreme of the distribution of scores on the Maslow security-insecurity scale. None of the fourteen subjects in the "secure" group failed an extinction problem in a variation of the arithmetical Einstellung test, whereas five of the fourteen in the "insecure" group failed this problem. The results are thus again suggestive of a positive relationship between E effects and insecurity.

How should these positive relationships be interpreted? Do they mean that a person who tends to be insecure also tends to be rigid? Since a person generally feels more secure in some situations than in others, will his level of rigidity also vary correspondingly in these situations? The possibility should not be overlooked that some of the individuals who were tested may have felt insecure both in responding to questions on the insecurity scale and in taking the Einstellung test, perhaps because of their reactions to the testing atmosphere. Hence, the obtained positive relationships between E effects and insecurity may be artifacts of the testing conditions rather than resultants of an invariant relationship between insecurity and rigidity.

It should be noted that, while insecurity may have fostered E effects in some cases, it is not plausible to attribute all E effects to insecurity (either insecurity basal to the individual's personality or insecurity induced by the test situation). As a matter of fact, there is experimental evidence which suggests that a feeling of security, being very confident, perhaps overconfident, may sometimes also foster rigid behavior (Luchins, 1942, p. 30).

Relation to Index of Maladjustment

Various theories of rigidity suggest that the maladjusted individual tends to be more rigid than the better-adjusted individual. Maladjustment may be described as a lack of adequate shift or adjustment when the situation calls for such shift or adjustment—which in turn could be a description of rigidity. To study the relation between maladjustment and rigidity, Horwitz (1951) administered to fifty normal adults the Cornell index of personality adjustment as well as the arithmetical and hidden-word Einstellung tests, with a high score on the index reflecting maladjustment and a high score on the Einstellung test reflecting high E effects. He found correlations of $+0.46$ between scores on the Cornell index and scores on the arithmetical test and of $+0.24$ between scores on the Cornell index and scores on the hidden-word test. Moreover, in carrying out a factor analysis, Horwitz found that the only scores which had positive loadings on the first extracted factor were those pertaining to high rigidity scores on the Einstellung tests and to high maladjustment scores on the Cornell index. These findings suggest a positive relationship between E effects and maladjustment.

Relation to Indices of Frustration Tolerance

Psychoanalytic writings on rigidity may be interpreted as suggesting that an individual who is not able to withstand frustrations tends to be more rigid than one who is better able to do so. Frustration tolerance has been defined as "an individual's capacity to withstand frustration ... without resorting to inadequate modes of response" (Rosenzweig, 1944, p. 385). In seeking to formulate a criterion of adequacy, Rosenzweig notes: "Responses which tend to bind the subject to his past unduly or interfere with reactions in later situations because of such binding are less adequate than those which leave the individual free to meet new situations as they arise" (p. 384). But this might just as well have been a description of responses which represent *rigid* behavior. The concept of frustration tolerance would therefore seem to be directly related to the concept of rigidity. Indeed, Rosenzweig links low frustration tolerance with incapacity to think abstractly and describes a "catastrophic situation" (which plays a prominent role in Goldstein's writings on rigidity) as a situation that extends beyond the individual's frustration tolerance.

Frustration tolerance has been invoked in explaining E effects, with greater E effects regarded as related to a lower threshold for tolerating frustration. But hitherto there has been no experimental evidence available on the relationship between E effects and frustration tolerance. We therefore conducted a study comparing scores on the arithmetical Einstellung test with scores on the Rosenzweig picture-frustration test (Rosenzweig, 1944, 1945, and 1950).

The picture-frustration test consists of twenty-four cartoonlike drawings in each of which the person to the left is saying something of presumably frustrating significance to the person on the right. The subject is asked to imagine the answer of the person on the right (the frustrated character), and to write the first reply that comes into his mind. The answers are written in blank caption boxes that are provided for each drawing.

Scoring is based on the direction of the aggression expressed in the reply: extrapunitiveness, in which aggression is directed against the environment; intrapunitiveness, in which aggression is directed inward toward the self (the figure on the right is assumed to be identified with the subject), and impunitiveness, in which aggression is evaded or glossed over. A group conformity rating is obtained by comparing the subjects' scores with "popular" scores on the various items made by groups used in the standardization of the test. Trends in responses reflect changes in the mode of response with continuing frustration; a tendency to adhere to any one type of reaction to frustration despite the changes in the frustrating situation, has been considered indicative of inadequate responses and of low frustration tolerance (Clarke, 1951, p. 314).

The arithmetical Einstellung test and the picture-frustration test were administered, with the assistance of Leo Shapiro, then a student at McGill University, to small groups of Montreal college students, totaling eighty-three in all. Fifty-three failed the first extinction problem in the arithmetical test (more-rigid group) while thirty solved this problem (less-rigid group). Responses made by the two groups in the picture-frustration test were analyzed in terms of the mean number of extrapunitive, intrapunitive, and impunitive replies, the percentage of group conformity (conf.), and the mean number of trends.

More-rigid group...
    Extrapun.: 11.8   Intrapun.: 6.4   Impun.: 5.8   Conf.: 63.8   Trends: 1.9
Less-rigid group...
    Extrapun.: 12.3   Intrapun.: 6.2   Impun.: 5.5   Conf.: 65.0   Trends: 2.0

In each response category the two groups show similar results, differences being small and statistically insignificant. The findings suggest that the level of rigidity in the Einstellung test need not be positively related to the threshold for frustration tolerance in the picture-frustration test; a person who makes inadequate responses to a problem in the Einstellung test does not necessarily make inadequate responses to the frustrating situations involved in the picture-frustration test. The findings therefore hint that differences in E effect may not be accounted for adequately in terms of differences in frustration tolerance (at least as measured by the utilized scoring categories of the picture-frustration test). But the findings do not mean that the concept of rigidity is unrelated to the concept of frustration tolerance.

There is a need for further studies in which the picture-frustration test is administered individually so as to permit inclusion of a later phase in which the subject reads his answers and replies to questions, and, in so doing, possibly gives further clues to the experimenter, by the inflection of his voice or through his replies to questioning, as to the character of his replies to the cards. We should also like to see studies in which an individual's reactions to various frustrations that arise in the course of his daily living are compared with his responses in the picture-frustration test and in various tests of rigidity.

Relation to Scores on Ethnocentrism Scales

Rokeach (1948) initiated research on the relationship between E effects and ethnocentrism. He found that subjects who scored above the medium of the group on the California ethnocentrism scale (high scorers) averaged more E solutions of an arithmetical critical task that followed a series of E tasks, than did subjects who scored below the medium (low scorers). The results were interpreted to mean that the ethnocentric or prejudiced person is more rigid than the less-ethnocentric or unprejudiced person.

Thirty subjects comparable to those in Rokeach's study (college students not members of a minority group), were given the California ethnocentrism scale and the basic experiment with the assistance of Leo Shapiro. The sixteen high-ethnocentrism scorers (above the medium) solved an average of 2.67 critical problems by the E method, whereas the fourteen low-ethnocentrism scorers averaged 2.06 E solutions. The difference, which is less than one problem, did not prove significant at acceptable levels of confidence. But, when the two groups were compared for solution of the extinction problem, the difference was significant at the 0.05 level, with ten high-ethnocentrism scorers failing the problem and only four low-ethnocentrism scorers failing it; that is, there was 63 per cent failure of the extinction task among those who scored high in ethnocentrism but only 29 per cent failure among those who scored low.

Subsequent studies relating E effects and ethnocentrism scores have not yielded consistent results. The relationship has been found to vary with the criteria used to measure E effects and ethnocentrism, as well as with the particular instructions used and the social atmosphere of the testing session. For example, the correlation of $+0.40$ which Brown (1951) found between E effects and ethnocentrism scores under a tense test atmosphere proved significantly greater, at the 0.01 level, than the correlation he obtained in a more relaxed atmosphere.

Where positive relationships have been found between E effects and ethnocentrism scores, they have often been interpreted to mean that "prejudiced" individuals are generally more rigid than "unprejudiced" individuals. Such a conclusion is subject to criticism on several grounds (cf. the evaluation given in Luchins, 1949). For one thing, the relationship is usually so slight that knowledge of a person's score in the ethnocentrism scale would not allow prediction, with a degree of accuracy above chance, of his behavior on the Einstellung test, or vice versa. Moreover, it is not known whether the subject would remain a high- (or low-) ethnocentrism scorer if another method of division into groups were employed, or if another population were used, or if another test of ethnocentrism were used. Nor is it known whether an individual who shows high E effects in one test is necessarily rigid in other tests or other situations; that is, whether he is generally rigid.

Also, since prejudice is not an absolute which one either possesses or lacks, it may be erroneous to speak of the prejudiced person and the unprejudiced person (or, for that matter, of the rigid person and the nonrigid person); there is a question of degree and of qualifying conditional factors. Finally, it is dubious that an ethnocentrism scale necessarily tests actual prejudices. There may be discrepancies between actual prejudices and responses to the scale, possibly because of the nature and interpretation of the questions, differences between actual beliefs and overt expression of them, attempts to conceal one's prejudices, etc. Commenting on the California ethnocentrism scale, which they were instrumental in developing, Levinson and Sanford (1944) note that the scale does not measure whether a person is prejudiced; rather, a score on the scale is said to represent the strength of a subject's explicit tendency to accept or reject a given statement, with a low score representing opposition to the statement and a high score acquiescence. In view of this, the following is one interpretation that may be given of a positive relationship between ethnocentrism scores and E effects. It may be that subjects who acquiesced in the suggestion that all the problems are solvable by the E method (a suggestion perhaps brought about by similarity in appearance between the E tasks and test tasks, by the homogeneity of the series) showed here the same tendency toward acquiescence or gullibility revealed in their reactions to the statements in the ethnocentrism scale.

However valid and reliable ethnocentrism scales or other attitude questionnaires may be, they should not serve as substitutes for the study of prejudices in which the criteria are based on behavior and attitudes as revealed in the actual social scene. A preliminary attempt to utilize socially valid criteria of prejudice was involved in a study we conducted at McGill University. Members of a class in social psychology, who belonged to the majority group, were asked to name from their campus contacts students whose remarks and actions around the campus suggested that they were either anti-Catholic, anti-Negro, or anti-Semitic, and students whose remarks and actions around the campus suggested that they were extremely tolerant or liberal. Twenty of the students named in each category were then tested individually with all the Einstellung tests of the manual (Luchins, 1948). The results for the various tests not only failed to reveal any statistically significant differences between the two groups but also failed to reveal any consistent trends.

Further investigations are required to compare the performances in tests of rigidity of individuals whose behavior in the social scene bespeaks strong prejudice and of those whose behavior betokens tolerance toward minority groups. There is also a need to study separately the relationship between rigidity and prejudices of various kinds. For example, the relationship between rigidity and anti-Negro attitudes and behavior may conceivably differ from the relationship between rigidity and anti-Semitic attitudes and behavior. Moreover, it should prove of interest to investigate the relationship between E effects (or rigidity in other tests) and the ease with which an individual gives up or modifies his prejudices when facts are presented to him about the social issue that is at stake.

Data available at present do not permit any decisive conclusion to be drawn concerning the relationship between ethnocentrism and rigidity or between various kinds of prejudice and rigidity.

Relation to Dogmatism of Religious Beliefs

Investigation of the relationship between E effects and dogmatism was suggested by Professor Charles Wrigley, then at McGill University. Following his suggestion, the arithmetical Einstellung test and the Thouless scale for the measurement of dogmatism or certainty of religious beliefs (1935-36) were administered individually to fifty-eight adults with the assistance of Hillel Becker and Eli Schwartz, then students at McGill University. Scores on the Thouless scale may be interpreted as indicating the strength of dogmatic or rigid adherence to certain beliefs. If this kind of rigid adherence goes hand in hand with rigid adherence to the E method, then we should expect a positive relationship between scores on the dogmatism scale and scores on the Einstellung test; but the findings point to a slight negative relationship. Thus, the subjects who showed no E solutions to either of the first two criticals made an average score of 101 on the dogmatism scale, whereas those subjects who failed all four extinction tasks had an average dogmatism score of 85; that is, the least-rigid group in the arithmetical Einstellung test showed more dogmatism than the most-rigid group. As a further check on the results, the product-moment correlations between E scores and dogmatism scores were computed. For subjects who solved the extinction tasks, the correlation was -0.22, suggesting a slight negative relationship between E effects and dogmatism scores. For subjects who failed one or more of the extinction tasks, the correlation was -0.16, again suggestive of a negative relationship.

Relation to Sameness and Change of Behavior

In their daily activities some individuals show a greater tendency toward stereotypy than do others. Observations of behavior over a period of time, including time-study samples and detailed diaries of behavior, would probably be the best means of studying this tendency toward rigidity in life activities. But, if one must be restricted to tests, then the sameness and change scales developed by Murray (1938) seem appropriate. The scales and an experiment referred to in relation to variability (p. 206) are described here in more detail.

The sameness scale is concerned with the tendency toward, and the preference for, fixation and repetition of behavior. A strong degree of fixation and repetitiveness is considered to be indicated by the individual's overtly described preferences for a few chosen pathways and haunts and by his tendency to walk on the same street, to associate over a period of years with the same people, to maintain constant views with regard to his brand of politics or cigarettes or other tastes, to dislike novelty, to feel uneasy in situations calling for a change in established behavior, to dote on regularity in his routine (e.g., rising always at the same time and adhering to a prescribed order of behavior during the day), etc. The change scale deals with the same categories of behavior, with a high degree of change considered to be denoted by irregularity in one's daily routine, a preference for travel and novelty, etc.

These scales and the basic experiment were administered to ninety McGill University students with the assistance of Leo Shapiro. Subjects were divided into two groups: the less-rigid group consisted of thirty-four subjects who solved the extinction problem and the more-rigid group of fifty-six subjects who failed this problem. If rigidity in the basic experiment is positively related to rigidity in daily activities as measured by the sameness and change scales, then the less-rigid group should be expected to show a greater tendency toward and preference for change, and a lesser tendency toward and preference for sameness, than the more-rigid group. The results do not support such an expectation.

Less-rigid group .... 34 students   Sameness: 40.0 ± 8.7   Change: 41.0 ± 9.4
More-rigid group .. 56 students   Sameness: 41.8 ± 8.8   Change: 39.5 ± 8.6

Differences between the two groups' mean scores and between their standard deviations proved to be small and statistically not significant at acceptable levels. In short, rigidity in the basic experiment did not turn out to be positively related to rigidity as measured by the sameness and change scales.

Relation to Improvement in Reading Rate

The question may be raised whether an individual's shift scores on Einstellung tests are related to the amounts of shift or change that he shows in the direction of improvement in certain learning and therapeutic situations. A study that is pertinent to this question was done with the assistance of J. A. Sproule (then a student of one of the writers) who was teaching a remedial-reading course in Sir George Williams College in Montreal. Enrolled in this course were fourteen students, mostly business executives, who were tested for their rate of reading at the beginning and again at the end of the course. Every student showed some improvement; that is, the reading rate of each student increased. At the beginning of the course the students received, in group administration, the maze, hidden-word, arithmetical, and word-block Einstellung tests, in that order. (These Einstellung tests were not readministered at the conclusion of the course. Had they been, one wonders whether those who showed more change in reading rate would also have shown more change in performances on the Einstellung tests.) For each Einstellung test, a shift score was assigned to a subject according to the point in the test at which he first used the direct method in two consecutive problems, with a smaller shift score denoting smaller E effects.

For each Einstellung test the results of only those subjects were used who had solved all the E tasks in the E manner. Rank correlations were computed between the improvement (increase) in reading rate and shift scores on each Einstellung test. The highest increase in reading rate was assigned a rank of 1, the next highest a rank of 2, and so on; in each test the smallest shift score was assigned a rank of 1, the next smallest a rank of 2, and so on. Rank correlations were +0.33, +0.54, +0.69, and −0.97 for the word-block, arithmetical, hidden-word, and maze Einstellung tests, respectively; the correlations involved the scores of twelve, fourteen, twelve, and thirteen subjects, respectively. A positive correlation indicates some tendency for those who changed more in reading rate also to have shifted earlier on an Einstellung test. Note that positive correlations were involved in the tests that required the subject to read (he had to read the arithmetical and verbal symbols in the arithmetical test and the letters and words in the hidden-word test and word-block test), whereas a negative correlation—in absolute value the largest correlation—was obtained for the maze test, which required no reading. Thus, each of the Einstellung tests that required the subject to read revealed that subjects who showed smaller E effects tended to show more improvement in reading rate.

The criterion of solving all the E tasks by the E method was met in at least three Einstellung tests by twelve of the fourteen subjects. Seven subjects met this criterion in all four tests. For each of these seven subjects, the average of his shift scores in the four tests was correlated with his increase in reading rate; the resultant rank order was $+0.79$, signifying a tendency for those who improved more in reading rate to shift earlier in the Einstellung tests; that is, to show less E effects.

We believe that the relationship of shift scores on Einstellung tests to improvement in reading rate warrants further study. It should also prove of interest to study the relationship of such shift scores to the improvement that an individual shows after participating in other remedial-teaching programs (e.g., remedial training in arithmetic or in speech) and after participating in various therapeutic programs. In connection with therapeutic programs, we mention that we were interested in studying the relationship of shift scores to the extent and rate of recovery shown by the hospitalized neurotics and psychotics who received some of the Einstellung tests. The major difficulty here was to develop an adequate definition and measure of "recovery" or "results of therapy." Preliminary attempts were made to gauge the relative extent to which the patient had improved during a specified period of time (or after a specific program of therapy) through utilization of the patient's progress reports, length of his stay in the hospital, number of relapses and readmissions, and other data in his chart and case file. But critical evaluation of these criteria suggested that they were not entirely adequate as gauges of the extent and rate of recovery. It appears to us that a possible measure of recovery may be developed based on measurement of specific knowledge and skills which the patient acquires during the course of therapy, just as the effectiveness of the education process in the school is measured by subject-matter achievement as shown in tests. For examples of some specific skills that may be measured, see Luchins, 1950b and 1951a.

E Effects in Relation to Perceptual Rigidity

The past decade has witnessed a vigorous attempt to relate perception to the perceiver's personality (Bruner and Postman, 1948; Fren-

kel-Brunswik, 1949 and 1951; Klein, 1951; Witkin *et al.*, 1954). Not
merely to study individual differences in perception, as do the differential psychologists, but to seek for the uniqueness or the individuality of
the perceiver, is a prime objective of this "New Look" research in perception. Its shibboleths are: no perception without a perceiver; no
Gestalt without a Gestalter; every act of perception expresses the personality structure and dynamics of the perceiver. It has been claimed
that, among other traits, rigidity of personality has been detected in
the individual's perceptual activities. To the Einstellung phenomenon
there have been applied some of the concepts developed by this person-
ality-through-perception approach (cf. Frenkel-Brunswik, 1949). Let
us turn now to some of the work relating E effects to various perceptual concepts.

E Effects and Closure

The concept of closure was introduced by Wertheimer in his paper
on the principles of perceptual organization (1923). Closure was considered as only one of several Gestalt principles of organization, all
assumed to be operating in the direction of *Prägnanz*, a word used by
Wertheimer to denote a tendency for organization to be as "good" (as
clear, as stable) as is possible under prevailing conditions. Specifically,
the principle of closure refers to the tendency towards greater perceptual stability possessed by closed areas as compared with enclosed ones,
and hence to the tendency for closed areas to be more readily attained
and maintained in perception. But, in actual use, the concept of closure
has been given other and broader interpretations.

Dramatic proof of the law of closure was considered by the early
Gestalt psychologists to be furnished by Fuchs's demonstration (Fuchs,
1921) that patients suffering from hemianopic vision (blindness in
one half of the visual field) reported seeing *all* of such objects as circles
and spheres when these were presented in such a manner that half of
them actually lay in the part of the visual field to which the patient was
blinded. These patients also reported seeing a whole circle when, in
fact, only half of a circle was presented, with the omitted portion of the
circumference lying in the part of the visual field to which the patient
was blind; that is, the patients apparently "completed" or "closed" the
configuration. Less dramatic but more common evidence is furnished
by the tendency to perceive a complete geometric figure (a circle or
triangle) when such a figure with a small gap is presented (provided
that the gap is sufficiently small).

In a factorial study of perception involving a battery of sixty tests,
Thurstone (1944) isolated factors that he interpreted as closure factors.

One was identified as the "speed and strength of closure," which was considered to represent the speed with which closure is attained as well as the strength with which a configuration is maintained despite distractions. Another factor was identified as "flexibility of closure," which refers to flexibility in the manipulation of several configurations; here the subject is presented with perceptual material which is immediately perceived as a unified configuration and in which he is asked to perceive a different configuration, the perception of which requires that he first destroy the immediately perceived unity. Flexibility of closure operates against "what the Gestalt psychologists have called *Gestaltbindung* which seems to refer to the rigidity of the perceived unity in a presentation" (Thurstone, 1944, p. 20).

E Effects and Flexibility of Closure. Perception of the embedded or hidden figures in the Gottschaldt figures (Gottschaldt, 1926) was regarded by Thurstone (1944) as an excellent example of the operation of flexibility of closure. The Gottschaldt-figures test and the arithmetical Einstellung test were included in a battery of rigidity tests given to Montreal college students (Oliver, 1950). Oliver found a correlation of $+0.245$ between scores on these two tests, suggesting a slight tendency for those who had higher E effects to show less flexibility of closure. He kindly lent us the original data so that we might analyze them further with reference to the Einstellung test. The subjects were categorized into distinct groups depending on their responses to the test problems: eighteen who showed no E effect; twelve who used the E method in only the first two criticals and thereafter used the direct methods; eighteen who failed only the first extinction task; eight who failed only two extinction tasks; ten who failed three extinction tasks; and eighteen who failed all four extinction tasks. Scores in the Gottschaldt-figures test for these groups were 15.4, 17.0, 13.5, 15.1, 13.5, and 12.4, respectively; no consistent trend is apparent. Comparisons were also made of the thirty least-rigid subjects who failed none of the extinction problems and of the eighteen most-rigid subjects who failed all four extinction problems; the Gottschaldt-figures scores were 16.0 for the former and 12.4 for the latter, with the difference significant at the 0.01 level. Thus, the least-rigid group in the Einstellung test saw significantly more embedded figures than the most-rigid group. The findings might be interpreted to mean that, while there was no completely consistent relationship between scores on the two tests, the most rigid in the Einstellung test tended to show the most *Gestaltbindung* (or rigidity of perceived unity) in the Gottschaldt-figures test; or, to put it in other words, the most flexible in the Einstellung test showed the most flexibility of closure in the Gottschaldt-figures test.

E Effects and Speed of Closure. As already noted, an illustration of the operation of the principle of closure is that in which an objectively incomplete circle (a gap in the circumference) is perceived as complete if the gap is sufficiently small (Koffka, 1935). We utilized this illustration in a preliminary experimental attack on the relationship between *E* effects and speed of closure.

An apparatus was designed in which cards could be moved in a groove on a wooden base. Attached to the base was a ruler graded in millimeters. Two stimulus cards were used, each 15 cm. by 10 cm., on each of which was drawn, in black India ink, a semicircle 8 cm. in diameter and 1 mm. in thickness. The two cards could be so placed together that the figure of a complete circle would result. The subject, seated three feet away from the apparatus and at eye level with the center of the stimulus cards, first was shown the two cards side by side so that they formed the figure of a circle. Then the cards were separated and slid along the groove until they were at opposite ends of the apparatus. In the instructions to the subject, he was told that the cards would first be shown together and then would be drawn apart and that his task would be to report the point at which he no longer saw a circle (descending series). Later, he was told, the cards would be placed apart and gradually drawn closer together and his task would be to report when he first perceived a complete circle (ascending series). "Your task is to determine at which point the figure loses the quality of oneness and acquires the quality of twoness . . . [and] to determine when the two figures acquire the quality of oneness."

Each of the ascending and descending series was presented five times. The distance in millimeters between the two cards at the instant that the subject first reported seeing a circle (ascending order) or just before he reported no longer seeing a circle (descending order) was recorded. The mean of these ten distances was recorded as the subject's mean "threshold for closure." Subjects used were thirty Montreal boys and girls between the ages of fourteen and eighteen, who were tested with the assistance of Joan Notkin and Rhoda Finkle, then students at McGill University.

Included in the battery of tests given individually to these subjects was the arithmetical Einstellung test. The subjects were divided into two groups: those who solved all four extinction tasks (less rigid) and those who failed at least one of them (more rigid). It was found that the less-rigid group had a mean threshold for closure of 13.22 mm. while the more-rigid group had a mean threshold of 20.82 mm., with the difference significant at the 0.01 level; that is, the more-rigid group tended to see a circle when the cards were further apart. If the distance between the cards is considered as a gauge of the speed of closure, then it may be said that the more-rigid subjects tended to have greater speed of closure. We would prefer not to attribute "premature closure" to them, although the term has been employed in the literature, since it generally implies that closure occurred when stimulus conditions did not warrant closure; we did not determine whether or not a distance of 20.82 mm. between cards could be regarded as "objectively" allowing a circle to be perceived.

An analysis was also carried through in which the differential criterion for dividing certain subjects into two groups was their method of solution of the criticals. Among those subjects who solved all the extinction tasks, a division was made into these two categories: those who used the direct method in the first two critical problems and those who used the E method here. Comparison of the mean threshold for closure for the two categories did not reveal a statistically significant difference. Hence, once again, as a criterion of rigidity, use of behavior in the criticals told a different story than use of behavior in the extinction problems. We mention this because of the use of the former criterion by some psychologists.

It is conceivable that, in the investigation just described, the factor of Einstellung was operative, not only in the arithmetical test, but also in the test of closure; that is, the factor of Einstellung may have influenced the perception of the presented figures. It is noteworthy that, in the laws of perceptual organization, Wertheimer included (in addition to closure and other factors) the factor of Einstellung, which he also called the factor of "objective set" in order to emphasize that it referred to a set developed by the sequence of events, by what is objectively given, as distinguished from a set which is more "subjective" in nature. In his paper on the laws of perceptual organization, Wertheimer warned: "In view of its great strength this Factor [of Einstellung or objective set] must in all cases be considered with much care" (Wertheimer, 1923, p. 320; Ellis, 1938, p. 80). As an example of the operation in perception of this factor, Wertheimer noted that, when a sequence of rows of dots is presented, the perception of any particular row may depend on the nature of the sequence; in particular, the initial arrangement of dots may tend to maintain itself in subsequent rows. Similarly, in the closure test just described, a sequence of figures was presented and the perception of any particular figure may have been influenced by the sequence of which it was a part. Since the complete circle was given first, this figure may have tended to maintain itself in subsequent figures (somewhat as the E method tended to persist in subsequent problems). The gradual nature of the increase or decrease in the size of the gap between the semicircles may have helped to foster the operation of an Einstellung.

In order to weaken the operation of the factor of Einstellung in the investigation of closure, a preliminary experiment was conducted in which the extent of the gap did not consistently increase or decrease. A series of twenty-five cards was prepared, each containing a drawing of an incomplete circle, with gaps ranging from a fine hairline to a semicircle. The cards were shuffled several times so that they were in random order. Tested individually, each of sixteen Montreal college women received the series in the same random order five times. Each card was shown for ten seconds and the subject requested to state whether or not she saw the figure drawn on it as a circle. Responses were compared for subjects who solved all four extinction problems of the arithmetical Einstellung test (less rigid) and for subjects who failed at least one of these problems (more rigid). The more-rigid group reported circles more often and for greater gaps, on the average, than did the less-rigid group, with differences significant at the 0.05 level; that is, the more-rigid group tended to show greater speed of closure. Analysis utilizing the method of solution of the critical problems as the distinguishing criterion of rigidity, did not yield any significant differences in closure thresholds.

Comparison of Closure Thresholds in Various Perceptual Situations. Current interest in the utilization of closure for the purpose of gaining insight into personality structure and functioning, seems to rest on the implicit assumption that the closure threshold which an individual manifests in one perceptual situation is an indicant of the kind of closure which he generally manifests. Thus, an individual who showed relatively high speed of closure in one experiment is sometimes described as having exhibited "premature closure," and the conclusion is also drawn, by some investigators, that such "premature closure" not only tends to prevail in his perceptual activities but also is characteristic of his conative-emotional behavior. Yet there is a dearth of experimental evidence on the invariance, for a given individual, of his closure thresholds in perceptual activities and even less evidence on how closure functions (or even on how its operation can be detected) in other activities.

A preliminary attack was undertaken on the relationship among closure thresholds in various perceptual activities, by testing individually the same sixteen college women who served in the experiment just described. We were interested in ascertaining the number of clues a subject needed for closure (in the sense of completion of a figure) to occur for "boxlike" figures that had a three-dimensional appearance. A set of twenty-two cards (Series A) was devised on which, beginning with some scattered dash marks, the picture of a cube gradually developed. Another series of seventeen cards (Series B) began with a diagram of a cross which gradually evolved into a picture of a parallelepiped. Half of the subjects first received Series A five times in ascending order (depicting the gradual emergence of the cube) and then five times in descending order (depicting the cube's gradual disappearance); they were then given Series B in the same way. For the other half, five ascending and then five descending trials on Series B preceded similar presentations of Series A. Each subject also received a picture-series test from the Luchins' manual on rigidity (1950). The test given—fruit-clothes (2)—consists of twenty-eight cards on which drawings depict the gradual alteration of various fruits into a female torso, then into a tree, and, finally, into articles of clothing. Half of the subjects received the picture series beginning with the drawing of the fruits, while the other half received the series in reversed order, beginning with the drawing of the articles of clothing. All subjects received the arithmetical Einstellung test.

We are aware that factors other than closure may have influenced perception in the administration of Series A and Series B; various principles of organization, including the factor of objective set or Einstellung (Wertheimer, 1923, p. 319; Ellis, 1938, p. 79), may have affected perception of the cube and parallelepiped. What interests us is that closure presumably was one of the processes that influenced the perception of these figures. Closure may also be regarded as one of the processes that influenced the reported perception of an emergent percept in the picture series. Thus, while we are accustomed to interpreting behavior in the picture series in terms of Einstellung, we recognize that the process of closure may also have been operative; in particular, a subject's threshold or speed of closure for a particular percept may have influenced when he first reported it.

A gauge of the subject's threshold or speed of closure for a cube, a parallelepiped, or one of the emergent percepts in the picture series, was considered to be given by the number of clues needed before perception of the object or percept was reported, as reflected by the number of cards in the series that were presented prior to report of the object or percept. Specifically, for each ascending trial of Series A, a subject was given a "closure score" that was equal to the number of cards in Series A that had been presented before she first reported the appearance of the cube; for each descending trial of Series A, she was given a "closure score" equal to the number of cards that had been presented before she first reported the disappearance of the cube, that is, before she no longer saw a cube. The subject's "initial closure score" for the cube was the average of her closure scores for the first ascending trial and the first descending trial. The subject's "average closure score" for the cube was the average of her closure scores on the ten trials involving Series A. A similar procedure was followed with regard to initial and average closure scores for the parallelepiped in Series B. Since the picture series was presented only once to each subject, only the subject's "initial closure score" was computed for each emergent percept; regardless of the order in which the series was presented, this score was equal to the number of pictures that had been presented before the subject reported a particular percept. (Incidentally, each of the sixteen subjects, who it may be remembered were Montreal college women, did report all of the emergent percepts.)

Before comparing closure scores in the various perceptual situations, let us consider the relationships between E effects in the arithmetical Einstellung test and closure scores. Subjects were divided into two groups: those who failed any of the extinction problems of the arithmetical Einstellung test (more-rigid group) and those who solved them (less-rigid group). An initial closure score for the cube (the parallelepiped) was obtained for the more-rigid and less-rigid groups by taking the mean of the initial closure scores of the members of each group. Similarly, an average closure score for the cube (the parallelepiped) was obtained for each of the two groups by taking the mean of the average closure scores of its members. Comparisons failed to reveal any statistically significant differences between the more-rigid and less-rigid groups with reference to initial closure scores or average closure scores for the cube and parallelepiped; nor was any consistent direction of results apparent.

To allow for study of the relation of E effects in the arithmetical test to closure scores for the picture series, subjects who received the series in one order and those who received them in the reverse order were divided into more-rigid and less-rigid groups. Initial closure scores for the various emergent percepts, computed for each group (more-rigid and less-rigid), were the means of the initial closure scores of the members of the group. Comparisons (carried out separately for the two orders of presentation of the series) did not reveal any statistically significant or consistent relationships between E effects and initial closure scores for the various percepts. In short, rigidity in the arithmetical test, as measured herein, did not prove to be significantly or consistently related to closure, as measured herein.

In order to compare closure thresholds in various perceptual situations, the college women's initial closure scores for the cube and parallelepiped were correlated and the same subjects' average closure scores for these two figures were also correlated. The correlations yielded a rather inconsistent picture. When Series A (cube) was followed by Series B (parallelepiped), a correlation of −0.01 was obtained between initial closure scores in the two series. Similarly, when Series A followed Series B, a correlation of −0.06 was found. These values suggested that there was practically zero correlation between the number of clues the subject needed for initial perception of a cube and the number needed for initial perception of a parallelepiped. When average closure scores were considered, a correlation of only −0.10 was found when Series B followed Series A, whereas a statistically significant correlation of +0.67 was found when Series A was last. Hence, the numbers of clues a subject required for reported perception of tridimensional figures seemed to be unrelated when the parallelepiped followed the cube, but a trend toward a positive relationship was revealed when the cube was last. Why this should be so is a matter for speculation. Perhaps perception of a cube led to an expectation of further cubes or other symmetrical solids which hindered subsequent perception of the parallelepiped, whereas perception of the parallelepiped did not lead to an expectation which hindered perception of the cube. In any event, what is of immediate concern to us here is the suggestion that the clues needed for reported perception of a tridimensional figure may be decidedly influenced by the particular sequence in which clues are presented, by the order and nature of the preceding experiences. These results speak against the thesis that a particular individual has a constant threshold of closure for a given figure.

It will be remembered that half of the subjects were shown the picture series starting with the clearly drawn picture of fruit. Here the emerging percepts were woman, tree, and clothes, in that order. Correlations of these subjects' initial closure scores for the different percepts yielded correlation ratios between woman-tree, tree-clothes, and woman-clothes of 0.39, 0.23, and 0.62. When the picture series was presented in reverse order, the emerging percepts were tree, woman, and fruit, in that order. Between tree-woman, woman-fruit, and tree-fruit, correlations of initial closure scores were 0.65, 0.33, and 0.17. Thus, while all correlations are positive, they are too small to allow the conclusion to be drawn that an individual who was early (or late) in seeing one emerging percept would likewise be early (or late) in seeing another emerging percept. If the reported perception of an emerging percept is considered to be influenced by a process of closure, then it may be said that the same individual did not show similar speeds or thresholds of closure for all the percepts.

In short, comparison of initial closure scores in the picture-series test and of initial and average closure scores in Series A and Series B usually did not yield significant correlations or consistent trends. To the extent, then, that the process of closure plays a role in each of these situations, it would seem that an individual does not always manifest similar speeds or thresholds of closure.

Comments on the Concept of Closure. Analysis of the utilization of the concept of closure left us with the impression that a multiplicity of meanings is associated with the concept. To begin with, "closure" is used, even in Gestalt psychological writings, to denote (1) a *process*, (2) a *resultant* or terminating phase or consummation of the process, and, finally, (3) a *principle* underlying the process; for example, the term "closure" has been applied to the process of "completing" an incomplete circle, and to the perceived "completed" circle itself, and finally to the principle or Gestalt law which is basal to this process. Moreover, despite Wertheimer's denial that closure is necessarily the dominant factor in organization, some current writings imply that a tendency toward closure is necessarily the main, even the sole, factor in a sensory or cognitive organization. Indeed, closure is sometimes used as if it were synonymous with *organization* or with *Prägnanz*. Closure has also been used as if it were synonymous with *insight* or with any *restructurization* of the field. It has been used to denote the act of extracting meaning from the environment and the act of deducing conclusions. In addition, the term is sometimes employed as if it were equivalent to the terms *Gestalt* and *good Gestalt*.

Some example of the diversity of the meanings which may be attached to the term, even by the same writers, can be obtained by scanning through a text such as Allport and Postman's (1947) on the psychology of rumor. They speak of "closure" as the achievement of a "better Gestalt" or as the achievement of a "simpler, more significant configuration" (p. 56), or as a "form of sharpening" (p. 97), or as "the subject's urge to make his experiences as complete, coherent and meaningful as possible" (p. 97). Noting that "we continually seek to extract meaning from our environment" (p. 37), they speak of the "pursuit of a 'good closure'" as the search for "a plausible reason for a confused situation" (p. 37); they also refer to a "good closure" as an experience, writing: "We experience a good closure when we find satisfying explanations and when our view of a situation is clear and stable" (p. 37, n.).

It would probably be futile to get involved here in any discussion of whether it is proper for a psychological concept to have so many meanings. Certainly the ambiguity does not add to the clarity of writings pertaining to closure. Perhaps it may add to the meaningfulness and usefulness of the concept of closure if the term is used only when evidence is available that a process of closure (in the sense originally used by Wertheimer) is operative. In particular, attempts to account for rigidity in terms of closure (or vice versa) or to relate rigidity to closure, will generate less confusion if the term closure is explicitly defined and if the evidence supporting a process of closure is clearly presented. Personally, we advocate a moratorium on the use of this term despite the current popularity of Gestalt terminology.

E Effects and Other Gestalt Perceptual Concepts

Prägnanzstufen. In his paper on perceptual organization (1923), Wertheimer refers to the concept of *Prägnanzstufen*, literally, steps or stages of *Prägnanz*. The term *Prägnanzstufen* may be interpreted to mean *"regions* of figural stability," (Ellis, 1938, p. 79, n.) or principal or major stages in organization. Discussing the case where one side of an angle is held in a constant, horizontal position and the other passes through an arc from 30 to 150 degrees, Wertheimer remarked that each degree is not of equal value psychologically. Instead, he said, there are three principal stages or *Prägnanzstufen*: acute angle, right angle, and obtuse angle. An example given is an angle of 93 degrees, which, he said, will usually be viewed as a more or less adequate right angle. "Stages intermediate between the major ones have the character of indefiniteness about them and are readily seen in the sense of one *or* the other adjacent Prägnanzstufen" (Ellis, 1938, p. 79).

The Einstellung picture series may be considered as composed of various *Prägnanzstufen*, represented by clear-cut pictures of the various percepts, with the transitional cards representing stages intermediate between *Prägnanzstufen*. But it was decided to devise a new series more clearly representing the concept of *Prägnanzstufen*. To this end, we turned to Wertheimer's illustrations of the angles. On a series of twenty-two cards, angles were drawn depicting various stages in the sweep of the terminal arm of an angle while the initial arm was held in a constant, horizontal position. The cards depicted angles of 1, 2, 29, 30, 31, 59, 60, 61, 88, 89, 90, 91, 92, 119, 120, 121, 149, 150, 151, 178, 179, and 180 degrees.

Random order prevailed when the cards were handed to the subject, who was asked to arrange them in any way he liked. We were interested in seeing whether he would arrange the angles in consecutive order, as a series with increasing or decreasing numbers of degrees, or whether he would group them around distinct *Prägnanzstufen*. Would he perhaps use 180 degrees as one pivotal point, with angles of 1, 2, 178, and 179 degrees described as belonging with it, as constituting more or less adequate straight angles? Would he also perhaps use as similar pivotal points angles of 150, 120, 90, 60, and 30 degrees, or would he perhaps use only the three groupings of acute, right, and obtuse?

It has been suggested that rigidity may be related to one's use of *Prägnanzstufen*. For example, it has been suggested that rigid persons may show a tendency to adhere to clear-cut configurations and "to discard entirely differences which others would be able to integrate into a continuum of gradual steps" (Frenkel-Brunswik, 1951, p. 128). This would seem to imply that, in our present experiment, greater rigidity should be associated with a tendency to use various *Prägnanzstufen* as pivotal points in arranging the angles than with a tendency to arrange the angles consecutively in an increasing or decreasing series. A test of this implication was attempted by comparing subjects' performances on the arithmetical Einstellung test with their arrangement of the angles. The experiment was done with the assistance of Joan Notkin and Rhoda Finkle, then students at McGill University.

The cards with the angles drawn on them were presented, in random order, to the sixteen female college students who served as subjects in the experiment designed to compare closure thresholds in various perceptual situations. It was found that thirteen arranged the angles in consecutive order, on the first trial. Three subjects used various *Prägnanzstufen* as pivotal points. Thus, one subject arranged the cards in four piles, using 30, 60, 90, and 180 degrees as her organizing points; she disregarded not only small differences between angles but also the quadrant in which the terminal arm of the angle lay. For example, she grouped together angles of 59, 60, 61, 119, 120, and 121 degrees and described them as 60-degree angles; similarly, she grouped together angles of 29, 30, 31, 149, 150, and 151 degrees and described them as 30-degree angles. When these three subjects were asked if they could make some other arrangement, two claimed that they could not and the third made another arrangement which still did not involve consecutive order. Scores made by these three subjects on the arithmetical Einstellung test showed that only one of them had failed an extinction problem and hence belonged to the more-rigid group, while the other two belonged to the less-rigid group. The thirteen subjects who arranged the angles in consecutive order consisted of nine subjects in the more-rigid group and four in the less-rigid group. Hence, the data obtained from this exploratory study do not support the hypothesis that greater rigidity is associated with a tendency to focus on *Prägnanzstufen* and to discard differences rather than to integrate differences into a continuum of gradual steps. Further research on this hypothesis is very much in order.

Part-Whole Relationship. A little-known paper on the part-whole relationship (Wertheimer, 1933) suggested to us an interesting test on perception as related to rigidity. The paper describes the successive addition of dots in the following manner. First come dots in the points of the plane designated in the diagram (see Fig. 1) by Digit 1; next dots are added at the points designated by Digit 2; then, in successive steps, dots are added at the points designated by Digits 3, 4, 5, and 6.

```
              • 6
           • 6   • 6
        • 2   • 5   • 3
     • 1   • 1   • 5   • 4
  • 2   • 1         • 4   • 4
     • 1   • 1   • 3   • 4
        • 2   • 5   • 6
           • 6   • 6
              • 3
```

F ɪɢ. 1. Compact presentation of the part-whole series of dots (after Wertheimer, 1933).

When only dots numbered 1 in the diagram are presented, the pattern is usually reported as the corners and mid-point of a square or, simply, as a square. As the dots corresponding to Digits 2, 3, 4, and 5 are added, the figure seems lopsided, asymmetrical, and incomplete and it is sometimes described as a square plus extraneous dots. But, with the addition of the last dots, there suddenly emerges a new figure, a complete pattern of a diamond (of dots) within a diamond. There is apprehended "a consistent clear whole in a new orientation, in a strong reorganization and recentering, all fitting the structural requirements" (translated from Wertheimer, 1933, p. 356).

We thought that it would be of interest to study reactions to the additions of the dots. Therefore six cards were prepared, the first card containing the dots designated by Digit 1, the second containing these dots as well as those designated by Digit 2, the third containing all these dots as well as those designated by Digit 3, and so on (see Fig. 2). The subject was shown each of the cards, in order, and told to report what he saw. One point was assigned to each card on which the stimulus pattern was reported as constituting a unit, that is, on which the subject apparently succeeded in seeing all of the dots as belonging to one "whole." This allowed a possible score range of from zero to six.

When the cards were presented to twenty Montreal high-school subjects, the obtained scores included every number from zero to six. The number of subjects who made scores of zero through six, respec-

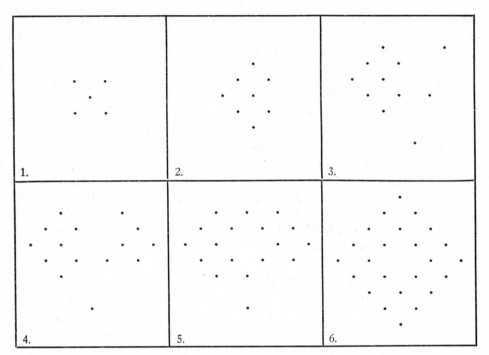

FIG. 2. Successive stages in the part-whole series of dots.

tively, were 3, 4, 4, 3, 2, 2, 2; that is, 3 of the twenty subjects never reported seeing a whole pattern, not even on the last card, 4 subjects reported seeing a unit only once, 4 reported a whole pattern twice (on the first and last cards), and so on, with 2 subjects being able, according to their reports, to so view each card that the dots on it were organized into a unit.

To see whether there was any consistent relationship between these scores and scores on the arithmetical Einstellung test, the average score in the part-whole series was computed for those subjects who solved all four extinction problems (less-rigid group) and for those who failed one or more of these problems (more-rigid group). The latter reported a whole pattern on three cards, on the average, as compared with two cards for the less-rigid group; the difference is not statistically significant. Thus, the results suggest that the more-rigid group had a slightly stronger tendency to organize parts into Gestalten than the less-rigid group.

We should like to see further studies conducted relating behavior in the part-whole dot sequence to behavior in various tests of rigidity. Aside from its possible usefulness in this respect, the part-whole dot sequence and other illustrations in Wertheimer's 1933 paper seem to us to constitute potentially fruitful means of exploring individual differences in the tendency to organize parts into Gestalten, a tendency which probably brings into play many of the Gestalt factors (closure, proximity, similarity, etc.) and which may perhaps be described, not too inaccurately, as a *Prägnanz* tendency. In short, we may have here one means of hewing a path in the virgin territory of individual differences in a *Prägnanz* tendency. In particular, further study is needed of the specific percepts, the specific constellations or "wholes" or units, that subjects report for a given dot sequence. Analysis of the kinds and variety of reported percepts may not only throw light on individual differences in a *Prägnanz* tendency, but may also help to reveal the extent to which the reported percepts are determined by subjective factors, on the one hand, and by organizational features of the given dot sequence, on the other hand.

E Effects and Intolerance of Ambiguity

The term "rigidity" has been used to denote intolerance of ambiguity, considered both as a perceptual and an emotional personality variable (Frenkel-Brunswik, 1949). Inability to tolerate ambiguity is considered to lead to a tendency rigidly to avoid ambiguity of any sort, a tendency which is reflected in clinging to the familiar, in rigidly adhering to rules, norms, and stereotyped patterns. Intolerance of ambiguity has been invoked to account for E solutions of the arithmetical critical problems (Frenkel-Brunswik, 1949, p. 130). We were therefore interested in investigating the relationship between E effects and reactions to various ambiguous perceptual situations.

In one experiment, seventy-eight college students received three drawings of a rather ambiguous nature. For each of these drawings (selected from transitional cards in the picture-series Einstellung tests), the subject was asked to describe everything he saw. It was assumed that the person who could not readily tolerate perceptual ambiguity would "reject" such drawings, would find himself blocked by the uncertainties in the perceptual situation (Frenkel-Brunswik, 1949, p. 128), and would tend to report few percepts. The person who could more readily tolerate ambiguity would be more prone to view the drawings and to attend to the various organizations to which the drawings lend themselves, and hence would tend to report more percepts.

All these subjects had participated in the basic experiment. If greater rigidity is linked with greater intolerance of ambiguity, we should expect that the fifty subjects who failed the extinction problem would tend to report less percepts in the drawings than the twenty-eight who solved this problem. While the results are in line with this expectation, they show little difference in the number of percepts reported by the two groups. Those who failed the extinction task reported a mean of 4.0 percepts while those who solved it reported a mean of 4.5 percepts; the difference is not statistically significant. Hence, these findings do not give much support to the thesis that more-rigid behavior is concomitant with greater intolerance of perceptual ambiguity.

Relevant here are the experiments discussed in the chapter on variability in which ambiguous pictures were used. There, no relation was found between the number of responses per picture and E effects. But analysis of the data in terms of the number of *principles* used by a subject yielded positive correlations between principles and E effects; that is, the more-rigid group used fewer principles as a basis for responding than the less-rigid group.

In another experiment, conducted with the assistance of Joan Notkin, then a student at McGill University, six drawings were shown to twenty high-school subjects each of whom was asked to select the drawing that he preferred most and the one that he preferred least. Three of the drawings were very clear-cut in nature, each containing one definite percept, while the three others, chosen from the transitional cards in the picture-series Einstellung tests, were ambiguous in nature. It was reasoned that an individual who finds it difficult to tolerate ambiguity and hence seeks to avoid ambiguity, would tend to select his preferred drawing from the clear-cut ones and his least preferred from the ambiguous ones.

Subjects were divided into two groups on the basis of their performance in the arithmetical Einstellung test. The less-rigid group consisted of thirteen subjects who solved all four extinction problems by the direct method, the more-rigid group of seven who failed at least one of the extinction tasks. If rigidity and intolerance of ambiguity are closely associated, then the more-rigid group might have been expected to choose preferred cards from the clear-cut drawings and to reject the ambiguous drawings. But an analysis showed no significant differences between the choices of the two groups nor even any distinguishing trend of choices. A further analysis was made in terms of the critical problems (*ambiguous* problems in the sense that they are solvable by two methods) by comparing the preferences of those subjects who solved the criticals by the E method with the preferences of those who solved them by the direct method. No significant trends or differences were found.

In short, the obtained data failed to support a positive relationship between evidence of greater rigidity in the Einstellung tests and criteria of greater intolerance of perceptual ambiguity. The results therefore cast doubt on the advisability of appealing to the concept of intolerance of ambiguity in accounting for rigidity in general and for rigidity in the Einstellung situation in particular. The problem also arises as to whether intolerance of ambiguity is, as some psychologists imply, a basic personality characteristic operating in more or less invariant fashion in all kinds of emotional and perceptual situations. The possibility should be investigated that the degree of tolerance or intolerance of ambiguity manifested by a particular individual may vary from one situation to another.

E Effects and Autokinetic Effects

The name "autokinetic effect" has been given to the phenomenon of apparent movement which often occurs when an individual fixates a small dot of light in a dark room. Variations of the standard autokinetic-effect experiments have been conducted (Luchins, 1954) in which the degree of illumination of the background of the dot of light was gradually increased from darkness to brightness and then decreased back again to darkness. We were interested in the influence of the background illumination on the autokinetic phenomenon and, among other problems, in ascertaining the illumination intensity of the background at which the subject would cease to report movement of the dot but instead would report the dot to be steady, immobile.

With the assistance of Melvyn Schwartzben, then a McGill University student, ten high-school students were tested individually in the described autokinetic-effect situation and in the Einstellung situation. A rank correlation of $+0.42$ was found between the amount of illumination at which the autokinetic phenomenon ceased (the dot of light became stabilized) and the point of shift to the direct method in the arithmetical Einstellung situation. This indicates a slight (statistically not significant) tendency for the subjects who persisted longer in using the E method in the arithmetical test to persist longer in seeing the autokinetic movement as the brightness of the background was increased. It might be conjectured that those who continued to report the autokinetic phenomenon for a greater range of background illumination were manifesting greater "perceptual rigidity." But whether the degree of perceptual rigidity manifested in this situation is consistently characteristic of the person and whether it tends to be consistently related to performances in the Einstellung tests, are matters which require further investigation.

E Effects and "Perceptual Lag"

The use of ansekonic lenses, developed by Adelbert Ames and utilized in some of his perceptual demonstrations (1949), results in distortions in the appearance of perceptual objects. In a personal communication, Professor Albert H. Hastorf of Dartmouth College reports that a rank correlation of +0.30, significant at the 5 per cent level, was found between the time fifty subjects took to report a change in the appearance of objects after donning ansekonic lenses (delay time) and the time they took to solve the extinction problem in the basic Einstellung experiment. This result suggests that there may be a relationship between rigidity as measured by the time required to solve the extinction problem (a measure used by some investigators; for example, Christie, 1949) and "perceptual lag," as measured by the time it takes to note (or, at least, to report) changes induced by the wearing of ansekonic lenses.

It was decided to use the lenses on subjects who had participated in some of our closure tests. Seated facing a table on which were a number of objects, the subject was told to fixate on a certain point. When fixating on this point, he was able to see the entire table and the objects on it. He was then asked to close his eyes. Ansekonic lenses were placed on his eyes and he was told that, when signaled to do so, he was to open his eyes, to look at the same fixation point, and to report what he saw. Every subject reported a change in what he saw now as compared with what he saw without the lenses. Note was made of the number of seconds which elapsed between the time the subject opened his eyes and the time he first reported such a change. For the thirteen college students who had solved all four extinction problems in the arithmetical Einstellung test (less-rigid group), the mean time which elapsed was 46.4 seconds, while for the seven college students who failed one of the extinction problems (more-rigid group), the mean time which elapsed was 79.3 seconds. Although the difference is not statistically significant, the direction is in line with that reported by Hastorf, since here too rigidity on the Einstellung test tended to be positively associated with "perceptual lag" in noting changes induced by wearing ansekonic lenses. Incidentally, division of the subjects on the basis of their solutions to the critical problems, yielded no differences between the two groups in "perceptual lag."

Not only the ansekonic lenses but most of the ingenious devices developed by Ames can provide a multitude of suggestive clues to psychologists concerned with the role of perceptual factors in behavioral rigidity.

COMMENTS ON TESTS CORRELATED TO EINSTELLUNG TESTS AND ON THEIR UNDERLYING CONCEPTS

It seems to us that some tests to which Einstellung tests have been correlated are based on concepts which are ambiguous and in need of clarification. Recall, for example, the discussions of the concepts of closure and frustration tolerance. Furthermore, the validity and reliability of some of the tests employed are questionable. When we know little about what a test is testing, when the concepts on which it is based are poorly defined or not clearly delineated, then to correlate such a test with the Einstellung test may be to correlate one mystery with another mystery.

Some investigators have attempted to account for rigidity in an Einstellung test (or for rigidity in general) by invoking such concepts as premature closure, low frustration tolerance, inability to tolerate ambiguity, high ethnocentrism, etc., despite the fact that these concepts are unclear, that the validity and reliability of many of the tests measuring them are doubtful, and that the correlations between scores on those tests and scores on the Einstellung tests are generally low; conversely, there have been attempts to account for these constructs by appealing to the concept of rigidity.

It seems to us that these interpretations are based on the assumption that the dynamics underlying performances in one test situation can be used to account for performances in another test that is correlated to it. Such an assumption is suspect on several grounds. To begin with, it is questionable that the concepts appealed to are actually tapped by a given test or that they adequately describe performances in the test. The constructs usually depend heavily on a particular theoretical position. Even if an invoked concept is adequate to account for the main trend of results, it need not have been operative in a particular case. But, even if it is granted that an invoked concept (e.g., frustration tolerance) does adequately account for a particular individual's performance in a given test, it does not follow that the same concept is appropriate to account for his performance in a correlated test (e.g., the Einstellung test). Moreover, a statistically significant positive correlation between the results of Test A and Test B does not constitute evidence that similar dynamics of behavior were basal to the performances of a given person in the two tests or even basal to the average trends of results. Positive correlations may be produced by a variety of causes and not necessarily by similarity or isomorphism in behavioral dynamics; the conclusion that the underlying dynamics are similar is not justified by the statistical nature of a correlation.

Finally, attempts to account for rigidity in terms of insecurity, ethnocentrism, intolerance of ambiguity, frustration tolerance, premature closure, etc., often imply that the latter constructs (and rigidity also) represent characteristics of the individual that remain rather invariant from one situation to another, that are sufficiently stable to serve as pegs on which to hang explanations. But it is a moot issue that the degree of rigidity or of ethnocentrism or of intolerance of ambiguity, etc. is necessarily a rather invariant characteristic of the person.

By thus emphasizing the limitations of studies relating Einstellung tests and other tests, we do not intend to depreciate their possible value. Such studies may have the merits of *suggesting* factors and conditions which influence behavioral rigidity; but the roles played by these factors and conditions should be investigated by introducing them systematically into situations designed to study behavioral rigidity. Relating Phenomenon A to Phenomenon B through correlations or other statistical formulas is not an adequate substitute for experimental interrelation of the phenomena.

As a concrete illustration, suppose that a positive, statistically significant correlation has been found between scores on a test designed to measure frustration tolerance and scores on the arithmetical Einstellung test. It would be necessary to go beyond the concern with averages and average trends of which the correlation is a reflection. Consider the subjects as individuals. How did those who made extreme scores, very high or very low, on the test designed to measure frustration tolerance, fare on other tests of frustration tolerance? How did they fare on the Einstellung test? Not only final scores should be compared, but also the nature of the performances. Were there any characteristic differences between the subjects who made very high scores and those who made very low scores on the frustration-tolerance test with regard to the reported (or observed) approach to the Einstellung test, the relation to the experimenter, attitudes and assumptions concerning the problems, methods of attack on the problems, etc.? Ideally, each subject should be studied intensively as the conditions of the arithmetical test are changed. What are the reactions as factors are introduced into the Einstellung situation in an attempt to induce frustration? For each subject experiments should be aimed at increasing and decreasing the subject's strength of Einstellung and at weakening or strengthening his recovery from the set. Will it be found that those who scored high in the frustration-tolerance test need the introduction of conditions to bring about or to approach maximum or minimum E effects that are different from the conditions needed by those who scored low in this test? Clues as to the influence of the factor of frustration tolerance on behavior in the Einstellung situation may be derived from comparisons of the different conditions—and not simply deduced, on theoretical grounds, from a correlation between the scores on the two tests.

We are making an appeal for a variational approach to an individual, for experimental study of a given individual's performances under various conditions. We are further suggesting that a test (or group of tests) which allows for relation of performances therein to performances in the Einstellung situations should be studied in order to see if it offers suggestions as to the kinds of conditions and factors which influence behavioral rigidity, and, hence, the kinds of factors and conditions which should be systematically varied experimentally. Experimental manipulations may be guided by statistical correlations but should not be replaced by them. In short, a statistically significant correlation should not be treated as a red light for research to stop, but as a green light for research to continue in order to reveal more about the indicated relationship.

E Effects and Generalized Rigidity

A statistically significant relationship between E effects and rigidity scores on another test has been interpreted by some investigators as evidence that rigidity is a general factor which is invariantly characteristic of a given individual. For example, a correlation of 0.42 between E effects in an arithmetical critical problem and rigidity scores in a verbal-maze test was interpreted to mean that rigidity is a general factor (Cowen, Wiener, and Hess, 1953). We saw that in one study those who scored above the medium on an ethnocentrism scale averaged significantly more E solutions of an arithmetical critical problem than those who scored below the medium; this finding was regarded by Rokeach (1948) as supporting the hypothesis that rigidity is a general factor of the individual operative in all situations, be they social or nonsocial. Elsewhere (Luchins, 1949) we criticized the assumptions that the Einstellung test constitutes a nonsocial situation and that ethnocentrism scores represent rigidity in a social situation, noting that ethnocentrism scores need not necessarily reflect rigidity. But, even if it is granted that two tests actually measure rigidity, does the finding of a positive relationship between scores constitute evidence that rigidity is a general factor? There is a wide gap between such a finding and the thesis that rigidity is consistent or invariant for an individual in *all* situations; he who presumes to cross this lacuna does so at the risk of jumping to unwarranted conclusions since a positive correlation between scores in two rigidity tests does not imply that positive relationships will necessarily hold among scores in all rigidity tests and reveals little about how consistent rigidity is for any given individual. Even if positive correlations were found among scores on many rigidity tests, one could not validly conclude that rigidity is necessarily a general factor. But the use of more tests would at least furnish firmer grounds for tentative hypotheses concerning the extent of consistency of rigidity. Let us therefore turn to some studies that have used cluster analysis or factor analysis on a battery of tests in order to study the degree of consistency of rigidity, and its relation to other factors.

Rigidity Factors for Psychotics and Neurotics

Various tests were administered, in individual testing sessions, to each of sixty hospitalized Canadian male veterans of World War II, half of whom were diagnosed by the psychiatric staff as psychotic and the others as neurotic. A matrix of intercorrelations was computed for each population by Leon Goldberger, who assisted in the testing. The matrices were subjected to cluster analysis by Professor Leona Tyler of the University of Oregon.

The intercorrelation matrix of psychotics' scores yielded the following clusters:

Cluster 1: Wechsler-Bellevue (W-B) test
Similarities subtest of W-B test
Block-design subtest of W-B test
Object-assembly subtest of W-B test
Rorschach test, percentage of form responses

Cluster 2: Rorschach test, total number of responses
Rorschach test, human and animal responses
Digit-symbol subtest of W-B test

Cluster 3: Einstellung arithmetical test
Einstellung word-block test
Einstellung maze tracing with mirror
Einstellung maze tracing without mirror

The first cluster is predominantly composed of scores on the Wechsler-Bellevue test and its subtests and may be designated, for convenience of exposition, as representing mainly a factor of low intelligence or low abstract ability. Since Cluster 2 is loaded by some Rorschach indices of rigidity, as well as by responses to the digit-symbol subtest, which are sometimes interpreted by clinicians as indices of rigidity, this cluster may be designated as representing primarily clinical indicants of rigidity or, if you wish, "clinical rigidity." Five Einstellung tests were administered, with half of each population receiving the mazes for mirror tracing and the others for nonmirror tracing. Scores on the hidden-word test did not fall into any cluster while the other four Einstellung scores all lay in Cluster 3; this cluster may be designated as representing Einstellung indicants of rigidity or the "Einstellung type of rigidity."

The results may be related to Kurt Goldstein's distinction between primary and secondary rigidity: that primary rigidity refers to rigidity

of the Einstellung mechanism while secondary rigidity refers to concreteness of thinking manifested as rigidity of behavior in those situations that require a more abstract level than the level to which the individual is more or less confined. In terms of this distinction, Cluster 1,
since it is predominantly composed of scores that refer to low abstract
ability, may be designated as representing secondary rigidity and
Cluster 3, since it is composed entirely of scores on the Einstelling tests,
may be designated as representing primary rigidity.

Analysis of the matrix of neurotics' scores revealed the following
clusters:

Cluster 1: Wechsler-Bellevue (W-B) test
Similarities subtest of W-B test
Block-design subtest of W-B test
Digit-symbol subtest of W-B test
Rorschach test, percentage of form responses
Einstellung maze tracing without mirror

Cluster 2: Rorschach test, total number of responses
Rorschach test, human and animal responses
Einstellung arithmetical test
Einstellung word-block test
Einstellung maze tracing with mirror

Cluster 3: Einstellung hidden-word test
Object-assembly subtest of W-B test

The clusters are less clear-cut, more difficult to identify than those
for the psychotics. For example, every cluster contains some Einstellung tests, unlike what occurred for the psychotics.

While the findings are preliminary, they suggest that the relationship prevailing among various factors of rigidity may vary for different
populations. To see whether or not such a finding is corroborated, let us
turn to another study of rigidity that used two different populations.

Rigidity Factors for a Normal and a Psychiatric Group

Horwitz (1951) tested fifty patients hospitalized in the psychiatric
wards of the Bronx Veterans Hospital (twenty neurotics and thirty
psychotics), all apparently in good contact with reality at the time of
testing. He also tested fifty normal adults, surgical postoperative cases
in the same hospital who had no history of psychopathology.

Factorial analysis of the normal subjects' data showed a tendency
for rigidity indices of a particular kind to load one factor and rigidity
indices of another kind to load a different factor. Thus, the first factor
extracted was loaded most heavily by scores on the two Einstellung tests
included in the battery (arithmetical and hidden word); the second

factor was loaded by scores on perceptual and motor tests of rigidity; the third factor was loaded most heavily by high-satiation scores; another factor was loaded most heavily by cosatiation indices; still another factor was loaded most heavily by indices of rigid adherence to a "level of aspiration."

Analysis of the psychiatric group's data yielded a different picture. The first factor extracted seemed to be broader and more encompassing than any found for the normal group. It was loaded by many of the indices, including high rigidity in the Einstellung tests, in the motor perseveration tests, and in the reversible-figures tests, as well as by low scores on the Wechsler-Bellevue test, low education, and low speed of writing. While each of the remaining factors was loaded by some rigidity indices, unlike what had occurred for the normals, there was now little tendency for indices of one particular kind to load the same factor. So impressed was Horwitz by the difference in factorial composition of the two groups that he concluded that the same tests do not tap the same kind of rigidity for both groups.

This study corroborates the finding yielded by our investigation of psychotics and neurotics; namely, different kinds of subjects may differ considerably with reference to the extent and pattern of interrelatedness of various indices of rigidity. Such findings cast suspicion on conclusions concerning the purported degree of consistency or generality of rigidity which are worded as if they were universal truths, holding for all populations.

Interfering Effects That Are Experimentally or Culturally Induced

In some publications on rigidity a distinction is drawn between the interfering influences of a culturally induced behavior pattern and the interfering influences of an experimentally induced behavior pattern, where the former refers to a pattern of long standing, an old-established habit, and the latter to a relatively new behavior pattern, one organized just prior to or within the context of the experimental (or test) situation.

In a factorial study of rigidity (Oliver, 1950; Oliver and Ferguson, 1951), the following tests were utilized: five tests regarded, on a priori grounds, as measuring interfering effects of *culturally* induced behavior patterns, the arithmetical Einstellung test regarded as measuring interfering effects of *experimentally* induced behavior patterns, the Gottschaldt-figures test, and three subtests of the American Council on Education (A.C.E.) examination. The tests were administered to McGill University students. Three factors were extracted. On Factor A close to zero loadings were made by each of the five tests constructed to measure culturally induced interfering effects and significant loadings by each of the five other tests (a loading greater than +0.25 was considered significant). Factor B was loaded significantly by three of the tests constructed to measure culturally induced interfering effects and by one other test (the same-opposite test of the A.C.E. examination). Factor C was loaded significantly by three of the tests purporting to measure culturally induced interfering effects and by two tests of the A.C.E. examination. No interpretation was offered of Factors A and C, while Factor B was interpreted as "a factor which can be unambiguously identified as a rigidity or habit-interference factor" (Oliver and Ferguson, 1951, p. 57). Since the arithmetical Einstellung test (regarded as measuring interfering effects of experimentally induced behavior patterns) had a zero loading on Factor B (interpreted as pertaining to interfering effects of culturally induced behavior patterns), the investigators concluded that the study furnished no evidence that any relationship exists between the interfering effects of culturally induced and experimentally induced behavior patterns.

Oliver made the data available to us for further analysis. Subjects were divided into six groups representing increasing E effects in the arithmetical Einstellung test. Group 1 consisted of those who showed no E effects, Group 2 of those who showed E effects only in the first two criticals, Group 3 of those who failed one extinction task, and so on until we come to Group 6, consisting of those who failed all four extinction tasks. There were 18, 12, 18, 8, 10, and 18 subjects in Groups 1 through 6, respectively. For each of these Einstellung groups there was computed the mean score on each of the nine other tests in the battery. Comparisons of the mean scores of successive Einstellung groups on each of the nine tests yielded 45 t-ratios, none of which proved significant at acceptable levels. However, there was some tendency for mean scores on each test to decrease as E effects increased. Analysis of trends (using the standard error of the proportion) revealed that this tendency was statistically significant at the 0.01 level for five tests. Four of these had loaded Factor A significantly, the same factor loaded significantly by the Einstellung test; only one of the five differentiating tests had been constructed to measure culturally induced interfering effects. Analysis of trends, using tau coefficient, showed that on four tests the tendency for mean scores to decrease as E effects increased was significant at the 0.01 level; again only one of these tests had been constructed to measure culturally induced interfering effects.

Offhand, these findings might seem to support the distinction between interfering effects of culturally induced and experimentally induced behavior patterns and to strengthen the thesis proffered by some psychologists (e.g., Cattell) that there is a factor of rigidity pertaining to interfering effects of culturally induced or well-established habits (disposition rigidity) and a possibly distinct factor of rigidity pertaining to experimentally induced interfering effects. Yet more careful analysis reveals that in this study the distinction between experimentally induced and culturally induced rigidity is not a clear-cut one. For example, the same-opposite test, which showed a statistically significant tendency with reference to E effects and which had significant loadings on Factor A, also had significant loadings on Factor B, identified as the factor pertaining to culturally induced rigidity. Moreover, in explaining their interpretation of this factor, Oliver and Ferguson (1951) state that reanalysis of the same-opposite test justifies relating it to interfering effects of culturally induced behavior patterns. Yet this same test was related to the Einstellung test which they regarded as measuring interfering effects of experimentally induced behavior patterns. As another illustration, consider the Gottschaldt-figures test which had a significant loading on Factor A and a zero loading on Factor B, identified as the factor pertaining to culturally induced rigidity. Moreover, there was a tendency for mean scores on the Gottschaldt-figures test to decrease as E effects increased; analysis of trends revealed that this tendency was significant at the 0.01 level. Such findings suggest that the Gottschaldt-figures test does not measure the interfering effects of culturally induced or old-established habits but is more closely related to interfering effects of experimentally induced patterns. But this seems to be at variance with the nature of the Gottschaldt-figures test; it does not seem plausible that failure to find the embedded Figure A (which is first shown to the subject) in the more complex Figure B is due to experimentally induced interfering effects. It seems at least as plausible that well-established patterns of perception and past experiences (not just those in the testing session) were contributing factors.

In short, the distinction between culturally induced and experimentally induced interfering effects does not seem to us to be clearly delineated. Nor does the available evidence support the thesis that distinct factors or varieties of rigidity are involved. More careful analysis is needed of the concepts themselves, of tests used to measure interfering effects of one or another kind, and of the relationship between a given individual's behavior when showing the interfering influences of a long-established behavioral pattern and his behavior when showing the interfering influences of a recently established behavioral pattern.

Moreover, so far as the operation or influences of rigidity are con-

cerned, little light may be thrown by such classifications as "experimentally induced" and "culturally induced," which are essentially
genetic in nature; they do not tell how rigidity functions or the extent
to which it interferes with shift to more adequate behavior.

Investigation by Cattell and Tiner

A factorial study of rigidity tests by Cattell and Tiner (1949) included the Einstellung hidden-word test. This test, as scored, made a
higher loading than any other test in the battery on a factor identified as
"ideational inertia" or "ideational rigidity" and described as "inability
to break with perceptual habits and habits of thinking" (p. 339). There
may seem nothing remarkable about an Einstellung test making a high
loading on this factor since E effects presumably involve persistence in
perceptual habits and habits of thinking. But what is remarkable is that
not E effects, but the obverse of E effects (as measured by the number
of direct solutions), loaded this factor; the interpretation that was offered was that *the more direct solutions an individual gave to the test
problems, the more ideational rigidity he was manifesting.* In the hidden-word test the assigned task is to find a word of four or more letters
in each group of letters; an alternation scheme, using every other letter,
yielded the name of an animal in the E tasks and criticals but did not
yield a word in the extinction task; each of the test problems also contained within it a nonanimal word made up of consecutive letters. In
scoring this test, we have always considered that an Einstellung developed for the alternation scheme and/or for animal words and have,
therefore, scored animal words as E solutions and as evidence of E
effects. Cattell and Tiner, however, gave a diametrically opposed interpretation, considering that the more animal words offered, the smaller
the rigidity and, conversely, the more direct solutions offered (words
made up of consecutive letters), the greater the rigidity.

They do not state why they introduced so different an interpretation. Deviation from our interpretation of responses seems particularly
surprising in view of their claim that their factorial analysis dealt with
"measures chosen with catholicity from past researches on rigidity"
(p. 339).

We suspect that the interpretation may be traced to their interest
in the interfering effects of well-established habits (or culturally induced habits) on new behavioral patterns. Presumably, to them, the
well-established habit was that of forming words from consecutive
letters and the new activity that of using the alternation scheme. Accordingly, animal names were considered responses arising from the
new activity while direct solutions were considered to reflect interfering

influences of the well-established habit on the acquisition of a new activity and, hence, rigidity. Note that such phrases as "well-established habit," "new activity," and "interfering influences" may also be applied to our customary interpretation; the alternation scheme may be denoted the well-established habit, well-established through its repeated employment in the E tasks, while the direct solutions may be said to call for a new activity in the test problems, an activity not feasible in the E tasks, and use of the alternation scheme may be considered an indicant of the interfering influences of a well-established habit on the acquisition of a new habit. Thus, we see that, depending on the meanings attached to such phrases as "well-established habit," "new activity," and "interfering influences," two completely contrary interpretations may be given to the same responses. This illustrates how difficult it is to offer noncontextual definitions of these phrases and how important it is to specify their meanings in any given context.

Actually the crux of the difference in interpretation does not lie in how well-established a habit is, or how old it is, or whether it is experimentally induced or culturally induced; the crux of the difference is that E effects involve a habitual mode of activity which *blinds one to direct methods* and such blinding effects were not considered in the interpretation offered by Cattell and Tiner. Instead, the use of direct methods (evidence of not having developed an Einstellung) was taken as an indicant of rigidity.

We note again that the Einstellung hidden-word test, as interpreted in the Cattell and Tiner investigation, made a higher loading than any other test on a factor subsequently interpreted as ideational inertia. The proffered interpretation of this test presumably played a role in determining that the extracted factor should be designated as ideational inertia. But it is conceivable that, had test responses been scored as we customarily score them (rather than inversely with reference to the gradient of rigidity), a different interpretation might well have been offered for this factor. This illustrates that the factors derived in a factorial study may be artifacts of the manner in which responses are scored and classified; hence, the factors may not correspond to the actual factors that determined test behavior and test responses, since the actual factors certainly are independent of later interpretations of responses. We are implying, in particular, that factors of rigidity isolated in factorial studies may be artifacts of interpretation on the part of the experimenter and need not necessarily reflect actual rigidity factors in the behavior or personality of the subjects.

Before leaving the Cattell and Tiner study, we note that Cattell has often designated disposition rigidity as pertinent to the interfering effects of well-established habits on new activities. Some investigations utilizing arithmetical Einstellung problems are cited by Cattell and Tiner as studies concerned with disposition rigidity, while ability to surmount the set involved in these investigations is said to be the inverse of disposition rigidity. But ability to surmount the experimentally induced set, as reflected in direct solutions to the hidden-word test, was taken by Cattell and Tiner as evidence of high ideational inertia. Is ideational inertia then to be interpreted as the inverse of disposition rigidity? And is it feasible that one rigidity factor should be inversely related to another when both are aspects of rigidity?

Adding to the confusion is the fact that the description given of ideational inertia makes it seem very similar to, even identical with, disposition rigidity. Cattell and Tiner state that "ideational inertia" is manifested in inability to break with perceptual habits and habits of thinking and suggest that it may turn out to be primarily a rigidity of well-established or old-established habits; but "disposition rigidity" is described as "essentially a rigidity of old established habits in the presence of new demands" (1949, p. 339). To judge from these descriptions, one cannot distinguish between ideational inertia and disposition rigidity. Yet they were found to be factorially distinct and possibly even inversely related.

We have presented this detailed account in order to emphasize the difficulties involved in ascertaining (1) the relationship among what factorially appear to be distinct varieties of rigidity and (2) the relationship of the factorially extracted factors to actual factors of rigidity. Such difficulties leave room for the possibility that rigidity is perhaps not of such diverse varieties as present factorial studies indicate or, at least, that the particular varieties of rigidity described in factorial studies may not all have counterparts in actual varieties of rigidity of behavior manifested in daily life.

Comments on E Effects and Generalized Rigidity

Consider now what has been learned concerning the question of the generality or specificity of rigidity. It has been seen that some psychologists who found positive correlations between E effects and scores on other tests have concluded that rigidity is a general factor of the individual, operating as a functional unity. But other investigators utilizing Einstellung tests have promulgated a variety of rigidity factors. Some factorial studies have found that Einstellung tests loaded the same factor as did tests of intelligence, whereas other studies have found that Einstellung tests loaded a factor distinct from that loaded by intelligence tests; some investigators have found that all the Einstellung tests included in the battery loaded the same factor, whereas others have found that different Einstellung tests weighed diverse factors; some studies have found that the Einstellung tests loaded the same factor as other tests of rigidity, whereas some have found that Einstellung tests separated from other tests of rigidity in the factorial analysis.

The equivocal nature of the findings concerning Einstellung tests may be partly a consequence of (1) innovations which different investigators have introduced in the instructions, design, and interpretation of Einstellung tests, (2) doubtful validity and reliability of some of the tests included in the batteries, (3) differences in the populations studied, and (4) differences in the test batteries employed.

It may not be out of place to mention again that no two factorial studies of rigidity have utilized the same battery of tests. Moreover, it is not uncommon for an investigator undertaking a factorial study to introduce innovations in existing tests and to devise new tests of rigidity. It is not established that the innovations improve the test or that the devised tests are better, more valid, or more reliable measures of rigidity than the existing ones. One wonders whether some of the energy used to conceive of innovations and to construct new tests used only in one investigation, would not be better invested in finding out more about the validity and reliability of current tests of rigidity and in developing standardized tests of rigidity that have high predictive value. After these tasks are well along the way, a grand factor analysis of rigidity tests may prove of value.

The limitations of existing correlation and factorial studies of rigidity, and the conflicting nature of the findings, do not allow any decisive conclusions to be drawn concerning the extent of consistency, generality, or specificity of rigidity. Our evaluation of the existing evidence suggests that there is some trend toward consistency in rigidity but not sufficient to allow rigidity to be classified as a general factor, operating as a functional unity in every individual. It also seems to us that rigidity may not be as specific in nature and that there may not be as many distinct varieties of rigidity as some investigators have implied. Recall the discussion of the difficulties involved in distinguishing between ideational inertia and disposition rigidity despite the application of the terms to factorially distinct factors; recall also that it is not known if extracted factors that are interpreted as varieties of rigidity, correspond to actual traits of behavioral rigidity. A possibility which warrants serious consideration stems from Shevach's suggestion (1936b) that perseveration operates as a functional unity in some individuals but not in others. It may be that individuals differ in the degree of consistency that characterizes the rigidity they show at different times and in different situations. Such differences may help to account for some of the conflicting results reported in the literature on the specificity or generality of rigidity.

It seems that individual differences in consistency of rigidity cannot be revealed through analysis of group trends but require study of the individual case. One possible procedure is to administer several rigidity tests to the same individual and to study the pattern of the psychograph composed of test scores. The difficulty here is that we lack a common denominator in terms of which we can translate scores on different tests so that they are comparable. Moreover, the use of several rigidity tests administered to the same individual may involve group trends to the extent that interpretations of the individual's scores on a test are based on group norms; that is, a group may be used as the base line with which to compare the individual's performance. Another possible approach is to use the individual himself as a base line of reference. This is done in what we have called the variational approach to the individual case. Such an approach observes the individual in one rigidity situation (or one test of rigidity) and then studies his behavior as conditions in the situation (or in the test) are varied by the experimenter. The individuality of the person is not violated; his behavior in a given situation is compared with *his* behavior in a modified situation. The rigidity of the individual may be characterized in terms of the changes in conditions required to produce a given change in behavior or in terms of the functional relationship connecting transformations of conditions and transformations in his behavior. A variational approach to the individual case may throw light on the degree of consistency of rigidity in a given individual and on the specificity or generality of rigidity. (See Luchins, 1952 and 1957b, for elaboration of this point.)

CHAPTER X

LEARNING AND RIGIDITY

O UR ATTEMPTS to focus theories of rigidity onto the example of rigid behavior have led to no decisive answer. Perhaps we did not have to turn to these theories. What occurs in the Einstellung situation can perhaps be treated more adequately as a case of learned behavior. The literature of learning may conceivably furnish clues to E effects and even to all or many instances of rigid behavior.

A simple explanation of E effects as learned behavior is not available in the literature. For example, Tresselt (1951) concludes that E effects in the arithmetical Einstellung situation can be described in conditioning terminology as corresponding to the acquisition phase of the conditioning process. Kendler *et al.* (1952), using the same terminology, concludes that these E effects correspond to the extinction phase of the conditioning process. That two psychologists can draw such diverse conclusions indicates that E effects defy one ready explanation. Let us therefore focus various theories of learning (cf. Hilgard, 1948) onto our example of rigid behavior to see how each might account for it.

Explanations Stemming from Association Theories

Habit formation, often used as synonymous with association, has traditionally been studied in a situation involving repetition of a response to a repeated stimulus or stimulus pattern. In the basic experiment, the same stimulus was not repeated but, to simplify the exposition, let us assume momentarily that it was; this simplifying assumption will shortly be removed. Let us also assume that repeated use (or attempted use) of the E method corresponds to repetition of a response.

Association by Contiguity

Several principles of association have been formulated at one time or another, including association by similarity, association by contrast, and association by contiguity. While there has been considerable debate over the relative importance of these principles (see Humphry, 1951, c. 1), contiguity seems to have won out and is now generally regarded as the most important (or the only) law of association. Promulgation of a principle of contiguity is to be found in the writings of Thomas Hobbes (1651), David Hume (1748), David Hartley (1749), James Mill (1829), William James (1890), and, to skip to more recent years, the principle is included in the learning theories of Guthrie (1935) (whose theory is known as contiguous conditioning), Robinson (1932), and others. While there are variations in the specific formulations of the principle as enunciated by these and other philosophers and psychologists, the thesis of contiguity can be described as follows: If A has occurred in the spatial or temporal neighborhood of B, then a bond will be established between A and B so that, if subsequently A (or B) occurs, it will tend to reinstate the other.

There are involved here two ideas: the first being an association or connection between A and B due to their simultaneity or proximity; and the second being the effect of this connection as seen in the reproduction of one item of the bond when the other occurs. Classical association theory has used the term "association" indiscriminately for both, assuming that the first necessarily implies the second; that is, that contiguous association automatically leads to reproduction of associated items. This reproductive tendency, as it has been called, not only was accepted by classical associationists but was regarded by them as adequate to account for mental events.

The first serious challenge to the adequacy of the reproductive tendency was made by members of the so-called Würzburg school, notably Watt (1905), Messer (1906), and Ach (1905). Employing different instructions (e.g., "find a part" or "name an example"), Watt found differences in reaction time and in imagery with the same stimuli, a fact which led him to conclude that there is a dichotomous grouping of the factors in thinking: (1) a stimulus with a number of reproductive tendencies attached to it and (2) the particular task or *Aufgabe*, which may operate largely on the unconscious level, and which acts to facilitate certain reproductive tendencies attached to the stimulus and to inhibit others. Ach introduced the notion of "determining tendencies" to account for the influence of the task. One might summarize the viewpoint of the Würzburg school by noting that it accepted the principle of an associative reproductive tendency but supplemented it with the principle that the task exerts a directive force to foster some and to inhibit other reproductive tendencies that belong to the stimulus; they considered a summative combination of the two principles to be adequate to account for mental events.

From the point of view of classical association theory, what occurred in the basic experiment may be described as follows. (We remind the reader that we are here pretending, as a simplifying assumption, that the same problem was repeatedly presented.) Use of the E method in the first problem established an association between the problem and the method, so that when the problem was subsequently presented the method was reproduced. Adherents of the Würzburg school would modify this account by adding the working of a task or directive tendency.

More Recent Associationistic Theories of Learning

Let us turn to more recent associationistic theories of learning. Thorndike (1913) regarded contiguity as the cause of the formation of an association or connection. He also invoked the law of exercise which refers to the strengthening of connections with practice or use and to their weakening when practice is discontinued, where strengthening is defined in terms of an increase in probability that the same response will be made when the situation recurs. Thorndike's greatest departure from classical association theory lies in his introduction of a law of effect, the strengthening of a connection as a consequence of its being accompanied by or followed by "a satisfying state of affairs." With respect to the basic experiment, one following Thorndike's theory would say that a connection was established in the first problem between the problem and the E method, and that the connection was strengthened by exercise (repetition of the method in subsequent presentations of the problem) and by effect (the response led to the required goal, to reward), so that the probability was high that the response would be made when the problem was again presented.

But Watson (1914) would account for the E effects by evoking his principles of frequency and recency without appealing to a principle of effect. He believed that learning could be explained according to what the animal had most often done in the situation, with the most recent act favored in recall. Because the successful act was both most frequent and most recent, its recurrence could be explained without appealing to any principle of effect. Since the E method was the most frequent and recent method of dealing with the presented tasks, subjects tended to use it in subsequent similar tasks.

Not only the principle of effect but also that of frequency is eliminated from the list by Guthrie's theory of contiguous association. Guthrie reduces all association to the one principle of contiguity. He maintains that a "stimulus pattern gains its full associative strength on the occasion of its first pairing with a response" (1942, p. 30) and that a "combination of stimuli which has accompanied a movement will on its recurrence tend to be followed by that movement" (1935, p. 26). He does appeal to a principle of recency; "principle of postremity" is what Voeks (1950) prefers to call it in her formalization of Guthrie's theory in view of the many meanings that have been associated with the concept of recency. This principle may be stated as follows: ". . . the last response before termination of any stimulus-pattern will be the only one whose learned association with those stimuli is preserved, and hence it will be the response elicited by them upon their next presentation" (Voeks, 1950, pp. 346-47). What is fundamental to the Einstellung phenomenon, then, from Guthrie's point of view is not that the *E* method was *repeatedly* used in the *E* problems but that it was applied in the response made to the last problem which preceded the test tasks; the *E* method was what the subject used in the last similar stimulus situation. It is interesting to note that Guthrie has stressed the element of repetitiveness and stereotypy in behavior. The cats in the Guthrie and Horton experiment (1946) repeated in a stereotyped manner the last movement, the movement made at the time of their release from the box. This is explained by Guthrie's principle that the last act or movement in a particular stimulus situation tends to be made again when the situation recurs. That much stereotypy should be shown by subjects in our Einstellung experiment would be quite in agreement with Guthrie's idea that stereotypy is the prototype of learning.

Hull's theory of learning—one of the most elegant and formalized approaches to learning—hinges on a reinforcement hypothesis which Hull notes "is distinctly related to that of Thorndike's 'law of effect' " (1943, p. 80). Hull maintains that learning can occur only under conditions of reinforcement, where reinforcement may be either primary or secondary—involving either direct or indirect need reduction, respectively. An association or habit is considered to be strengthened if a contiguous stimulus-response connection occurs in conjunction with primary or secondary reinforcement. The maximum strength of the habit is not regarded as reached on the first trial (as promulgated by Guthrie); instead, habit strength is considered to increase monotonically with each reinforcement. Hull does not accept an automatic associative reproductive tendency but instead postulates that readiness to respond to a stimulus with an associated response requires a directing force in the form of a drive. The potentiality to respond to a stimulus (reaction potential) depends both on the strength of the habits associated with the stimulus and on the nature and strength of the drives active at the time. The actual response is also influenced by resistances or "inhibitions" associated with the habit that work against its reoccurrence.

The repeated solution of the *E* task by the *E* method may be described, in terms of Hull's theory, as involving a summation of increments in the strength of the *E* habit as it was repeated under reinforcing conditions (success in solving the problems may be considered as a reinforcement pertaining to the need or drive for success). That the same response was made in subsequent presentations of the problem may be accounted for on the ground that habit strength and drive sufficed to overcome resistances or "inhibitions" associated with the E habit.

E effects would be accounted for by the theories of Carr (1931) and Robinson (1932) through an appeal to the law of contiguity stated in this way: The fact that two psychological processes occur together in time or in immediate succession increases the probability that an associative connection between them will develop—that one process will become the associative instigator of the other (Robinson, 1932, p. 72).

And so one could go on, seeking to account for the E effects in the words of one associationist or another.

Associationistic Explanations of E Effects Without Simplifying Assumption

It will be recalled that we have pretended that the same problem was repeatedly presented in the foundation experiment. Actually, similar-appearing problems were utilized; whether it would therefore be proper to describe the experiment as consisting of repetitions of the "same stimulus pattern" would depend on how this term is defined. If it refers to a particular class or type of problem (a three-jar-volume-measuring problem), then such a description is appropriate; but, if it refers to identity of all components, then it is inappropriate. But, even if the tasks are considered to represent different stimulus patterns, there are principles of association theory which can apparently account for the use of the E method both in the later E problems and in the test problems. At the turn of the century Müller and Pilzecker (1900) formulated a law of substitution: If an association has been formed between a and b, then b may be reproduced not only by a but also by any a' similar to a, the degree of similarity between a and a' determining the strength of the reproductive tendency aroused by a'. In terms of this principle, it may be said that, since an association has been formed between the first (or first few) problems (a) and the E method (b), any of the subsequent problems (a') is able to reproduce this method because of its similarity to a.

A principle akin to that of substitution has been adopted by many learning theorists. Thorndike includes it in his principle of assimilation which is to the effect that an individual responds to a new situation (or to an element of this situation) as he has to a similar situation (or element) in the past. Conditioning theories such as Hull's or Guthrie's utilize it in the concept of generalization and stimulus equivalence: the more similar one stimulus, B, is to another, A, the greater is the probability that B will succeed in arousing the response which has been conditioned to A. Robinson adopts a principle of assimilation which does not mention similarity: "Whenever an associative connection is so established that an activity, A, becomes capable of instigating an activity, B, activities other than A also undergo an increase or decrease in their capacity to instigate B" (Robinson, 1932, p. 86). Robinson rejects the law of similarity, Hilgard notes, since "similarity refers to a logical relationship, whereas psychological similarity has to be defined circularly, according to things reacted to *as* similar. Reacting to things *as* similar is exactly what the law of assimilaton is about" (Hilgard, 1948, p. 150).

While Robinson's principle of assimilation does not reveal what activities other than A vary in their capacity to instigate B and while he does not state the conditions which affect the variation, it should be realized that those writers who adopt a principle of similarity also do not make explicit the kind and degree of similarity that must exist in order for generalization to occur.

The concept of transfer may also be appealed to in seeking to account for *E* effects. Under the identical-element (or identical-component) theory of transfer, as advocated by Thorndike and others, the degree of transfer is dependent on the extent to which identical elements are present in the original and the new learning situations, where identity may pertain to either content or procedure. In the case of the Einstellung experiment, transfer would be facilitated by identity in content (e.g., three containers), pattern, and procedure. Since transfer of the *E* method to the test problems was disadvantageous in the sense that it blinded one to the direct solution, it might be described as positive transfer with negative effects. Such an interpretation of the basic experiment was offered some years ago (Luchins, 1939).

The concept of retroactive inhibition has also been invoked to account for *E* effects (Luchins, 1939). Consider that, in life situations prior to the experimental session, the subject had formed the associations necessary for the direct method (e.g., $23 - 3 = 20$) so that, if he had received the test problems first, he would have solved them by the direct method. This is indeed the trend of results in the control group. Since the *E* problems were interpolated between these life experiences and the test tasks, the use of the *E* method in the test problems may be explained as a consequence of "inhibition" of the direct method due to similarity between the *E* tasks and test tasks.

Associationistic Explanations of Lack of Einstellung and Recovery from Einstellung

Thus far we have been concerned with *E* solutions of the test problems. How can associationists account for the fact that some subjects gave direct solutions to some or all of the test problems? It might be said that in the past, prior to the experimental session, these subjects had experienced the combinations necessary for the direct solution (e.g., $23 - 3 = 20$) and so frequently had they made the association involving the direct method that it aroused a greater reproductive tendency than did the association involving the E method; that is, frequency triumphed over recency. Another explanation might refer to a lack of sufficient similarity between the test tasks and the E tasks, insufficient stimulus equivalence to bring about assimilation or generalization. An appeal might be made to Hull's concept of the habit-family hierarchy, which has been defined as: "A number of habitual alternative behavior sequences having in common the initial stimulus situation and the final reinforcing state of affairs, the alternative sequences having a preferential order which constitutes them a hierarchy" (Hilgard and Marquis, 1940, p. 345). The hierarchy may be regarded as consisting of various routes between a starting point and a goal, with some routes more favored than others. Discussing the concept, Hilgard (1948, p. 94) notes that the shorter routes tend to be more strongly reinforced (and more strongly conditioned to the "fractional anticipatory goal reaction") and hence tend to be favored while the less favored routes are chosen only when the more favored are blocked. The E and direct methods may be regarded as belonging to one habit-family hierarchy with the E method being used when the more favored direct method is blocked (as it is in the E tasks) and the direct method being used in the test problems when there is no blockage. The habit-family concept thus seems to provide a neat means of accounting for direct solutions of the test tasks; but it is inadequate to account for E solutions.

In cases where the direct method was used in the problems following the extinction task, an explanation might be given in terms of disuse (Thorndike) or in terms of extinction and nonreinforcement in conditioning terminology. According to Hull, extinction of the conditioned response is due to nonreinforced repetitions but, according to Guthrie, extinction occurs through the learning of an incompatible response. Hull's thesis would mean that unsuccessful application of the E method in the extinction task favored the decay of the E response whereas Guthrie's thesis would imply that this occurred only if the subject learned the direct method. In other words, failure of the extinction task (nonreinforced repetition of the conditioned response) would suffice to induce weakening of the E method as a conditioned response, as far as Hull is concerned, whereas Guthrie would require not simply failure of this task but the learning of another method, as indicated by direct solution of the extinction task. Here we seem to have a possibility of concretely comparing the consequences of the two theories. Do the results show that failure of the extinction task is as effective in producing recovery from the Einstellung as is direct solution of the extinction task? We shall shortly present experiments bearing on this matter.

TOLMAN'S CONCEPTS OF LEARNING FOCUSED ON THE BASIC EXPERIMENT

Rejecting a stimulus-response theory of learning, Tolman (1932) introduced the concept of expectancy or, as he prefers to call it, "sign-gestalt-expectancy." What is learned is not a stimulus-response connection but certain signs to a goal (significate), certain means-end relations (sign-significate relations), leading to the development of an expectancy that given behavior will result in a goal object. Principles of frequency and recency are accepted in the following form: ". . . the more frequently and more recently the actual sequence of sign, means-end-relation and significate have been presented, the stronger, other things being equal, this resulting sign-gestalt will tend to be" (Tolman, 1932, p. 386). Repetition thus plays the role of increasing the strength of an expectancy, the probability that it will be realized. From this point of view, solution of the first E task (or first few E tasks) may be said to have established an expectancy that the applied method (the means-end relation, e.g., $B - A - 2C =$ the volume of water) will lead to the goal, while repetition of this method in successive tasks increases the strength of this expectancy or the probability of its realization.

While Tolman once considered all learning to fall into the "sign-gestalt-expectancy" category, he has since suggested that this may be only one of several kinds of learning (1949a). Connections or relations that get learned are considered to be of at least six types: cathexes, equivalence beliefs, field expectancies, field-cognition modes, drive discrimination, motor patterns. Cathexes refer to connections of final goal objects (positive goal object or negative disturbance object) to basic drives, and the learning of cathexes refers to the acquisition by the organism of positive dispositions for certain types of objects and of negative dispositions against others. Application of the concept of cathexes to the Einstellung situation would seem somewhat farfetched, unless of course one was willing to consider the drive for successful solution of the problem as a "basic drive," whatever that much-abused phrase may actually mean. Also, it would require circumlocution to apply to E effects the concept of drive discrimination, which refers to the organism's learning to discriminate between drives. But the four other "types of learning" seem to lend themselves more readily to interpretations of the experiment.

Field Expectancies

Field expectancies are the "sign-gestalt-expectancies" renamed in the interest of brevity. The term "sign-gestalt-expectancies" was shortened to "expectancies" by Hilgard and Marquis (1940)—"mercifully" shortened, according to Allport (1946). Viewing such a contraction as "too disgustingly short," Tolman compromised to the extent of mercilessly rechristening these entities "field expectancies" (1949a, p. 146). As possible synonyms for "field expectancy," Tolman (1949a) suggests "cognitive map" and "cognitive structure."

How aptly the concept of field expectancies fits our experimental situation may be deduced from the following quotations from Tolman:

> It is my contention that when an organism is repeatedly presented on successive occasions with an environmental set-up ... he also tends to acquire a "set" such that, upon the apprehension of the first group of stimuli in the field, he becomes prepared for the further "to come" groups of stimuli and also for some of the interconnections or field relationships between such groups of stimuli. (1949a, p. 145.)

> [Field expectancies are] ... those sets which get built up in an organism relative to a specific environmental field. (1949a, p. 150.)

In the Einstellung experiment the organism may have acquired such a "set" or field expectancy, so that as soon as the first stimulus (say, the first jar) was given he became prepared for the subsequent stimuli (including the remaining jars) and for some of the interconnections $(B - A - 2C)$ between them.

The conditions and laws of learning of field expectancies are considered by Tolman to deviate radically from those accepted in stimulus-response reinforcement theories. The form and range of any expectancy is considered to be a function not only of repetition but of the "interacting processes of perception, memory, and inference" (1949a, p. 145). While Tolman admits that motivational conditions must be assumed to play a role in the building up of field expectancies, he does not regard field expectancies as involving the stamping in of stimulus-response habits by reinforcement (1949a, p. 151). As for the deacquisition or unlearning of field expectancies, it is Tolman's hunch that this occurs only when the environment is so changed that the previous expectancy is no longer suitable; "de-acquisition of one field expectancy results from the learning of another conflicting expectancy" (p. 152). For the Einstellung situation this would mean that the expectancy for the E method is *not* deacquired in the critical tasks, where this method is still suitable, but only in the extinction task, where it is no longer suitable, and then only on the condition that a conflicting expectancy (the more direct method of solution) is learned. This is more similar to Guthrie's views than to Hull's. True forgetting, defined as weakening with the mere passage of time, is said to take place for all field expectancies; this suggests that in the foundation experiment the expectancy for the E method should decrease with time. This suggestion has been tested by studying E effects after varying lengths of time had elapsed; the results will be described later.

Equivalence Beliefs

By a "positive equivalence belief" Tolman means "the attachment of a type of sub-goal to a type of final goal such that this sub-goal comes (for the period during which the given equivalence belief holds) to be sought for as if it were the final goal" (1949a, p. 148). The individual accepts what was originally a mere means to a goal as equivalent to a goal, experiencing some degree of drive reduction in connection with this means. Such an "equivalence belief" may have been established in our experiment. The subject may have come to equate what was originally a means to a goal (the $B - A - 2C$ method) with the goal itself, so that the means came to be sought for as if it were the final goal.

Tolman continues:

> As long as an equivalence belief is not misleading in the sense that the sub-goal is usually actually followed by the true goal, the belief probably serves some physiological economy. But when an equivalence belief persists, even though now the sub-goal practically never leads to the true goal, such an equivalence belief would seem bad. (1949a, p. 149.)

Application to the Einstellung situation is rather apparent and needs no elaboration.

Little is known, Tolman says, about the laws for either the deacquisition or the forgetting of equivalence beliefs but available experimentation suggests that such beliefs are not merely forgotten (do not weaken with mere passage of time) but have to be unlearned. If what occurs in the Einstellung situation is appropriately described as the development of an equivalence belief, we should expect that E effects would not lessen with the passage of time.

Field-Cognition Modes

This term is applied to the modes of functioning of perception, memory, and inference. Under this category Tolman is attempting to summarize "all those principles as to the structure of environmental fields which are relevant to all environmental fields, and which (whether innate or learned) are carried around by the individual and applied to each new field with which he is presented" (1949a, p. 153). In the course of the usual learning experiment, Tolman asserts, the subject may acquire not only a specific field expectancy but also new field-cognition modes which he may utilize later. Perhaps during the Einstellung experiment the subject acquired some new field-cognition modes, "new modes or ways of perceiving, remembering and inferring" (Tolman, 1949a, p. 145), which he applied to the later problems.

As an alternative name for field-cognition modes, Tolman suggests "field lore—that is, perceptual, memorial and inferential lores" (p. 152). He adds that much of these lores seem to be innate and, as an example of a field lore which seems to be "innately strong," he cites the following: "...if a certain sequence of events has occurred on one occasion, this same sequence of events is likely to occur on subsequent occasions" (p. 152). Such a principle may possibly have operated in the Einstellung situation, the subject reasoning that, since a certain sequence of events occurred previously (e.g., volume-measuring problems solved by a $B - A - 2C$ procedure), it was likely to occur again.

Motor Patterns

The concept of motor patterns (or sensory-motor skills) is regarded by Tolman as similar to Guthrie's concept of movements. In line with Guthrie's views (1940), Tolman suggests that motor patterns get conditioned on a single trial, the last movement tending to be conditioned to whatever stimuli are present, since this movement removes the individual from these stimuli so that no subsequent movements have a chance to occur and to displace it. "A motor pattern thus gets learned without reinforcement....once a movement sequence gets learned in one situation, it is ready, I believe, to be tried out in other situations" (Tolman, 1949a, p. 154).

Applied to the Einstellung situation, the concept of motor patterns implies that what occurred therein was the conditioning of a movement sequence in the first E problem and its subsequent utilization in the following problems. Unlearning of this movement, in accordance with Guthrie's beliefs, which Tolman is willing to accept, would require not only "nonreinforcements" but the learning of a conflicting movement (e.g., one corresponding to the direct method of solution).

Koffka's Trace Theory Focused on the Basic Experiment

Koffka (1935) considers that excitations create chemical deposits of various concentrations in the brain. Upon cessation of the excitation these deposits do not automatically disappear but remain for some time as traces, remnants of the process distribution in the brain. It is assumed that "the trace retained the dynamics of the process in a latent form" (p. 594). In contrast with the associationistic concept of a trace as a number of separate items merely joined or coupled together by some bond, Koffka conceives of traces as "organized products of organized processes" (p. 564), governed by and changing in accordance with the Gestalt laws of organization. A number of studies, among them investigations of successive reproductions of figures (Wulf, 1922; Gibson, 1929; Allport, 1930; Perkins, 1932), have not yet satisfactorily settled the issue whether the changes that traces undergo in time are in accordance with Gestalt laws of organization or associationistic theories.

Interaction Between Trace and Present Excitation

In order for previous experiences to influence present processes, it is necessary that the traces of these previous experiences interact with present excitations. Koffka hypothesizes that the process will communicate with those trace systems which tend to foster the stability of the process. Similarity in pattern or whole character between process and trace is said to be one of the ways by which greater stability of a process can be reached (p. 600).

A process should, *ceteris paribus*, communicate with a trace system which possessed the same whole character. This must be a trace which had been produced by a process of the same whole character, because we assumed that the trace retained the dynamic character of the process in the form of tensions or stresses. (P. 463.)

Recency is also a factor since, *"ceteris paribus* a similar trace will have a better chance to be chosen by a present process when it is recent . . . than when it is old" (p. 599). Forces starting within the ego system (attitudes, voluntary sets, intentions) are recognized as "powerful factors in bringing about communication between a process and a trace" (p. 583).

Suppose that conditions for communication are fulfilled and that a present process contacts a trace. What is the trace's influence on the process? Koffka hypothesizes that the trace exerts an influence on the process in the direction of making the trace as stable as possible. Thus there is a two-way striving for stability, with the process selecting that trace system which will further the stability of the process, while the trace exerts an influence on the process to maintain or increase the trace's stability. In general, the trace exerts an influence on the process in the direction of making it similar to the process which originally produced the trace, since this similarity will foster the trace's stability.

Koffka holds that under certain conditions repetition of a process may be "a very powerful factor in stabilizing traces" (p. 545). Repetition does not involve the strengthening of one trace but a gain in the stability of the trace system. With repetition "the trace system becomes more and more fixed, [and] ... acquires a greater and greater influence on future processes. It is ... at least a plausible hypothesis to assume that the extension of the trace system is one of the factors which determine its efficacy, an extension which is steadily increased with each new repetition" (p. 546). (If one substitutes "habit strength" for "extension," then the foregoing quote from Koffka finds a parallel in Hull's formulation of the increase of habit strength with each reinforced repetition.)

Learning is defined by Koffka as consisting in the creation of trace systems, in consolidating them, and in making them more and more available both in repeated and in new situations (p. 544). Learning is also defined as any influence exerted by a trace on a later performance (p. 546).

Application to the Einstellung Situation

What occurred in the basic experiment may be described in accordance with Koffka's conceptions of learning. Utilization of the E method in the first problem may be said to have left a trace in the subject's brain. Similarity in pattern between subsequent excitations and this trace made for communication between excitation and trace. Influence of the trace was in the direction of making the present process similar to the process that originally produced the trace, i.e., the process corresponding to the E method. Repetition of the E method made for extension of the trace system, for its consolidation, and for its availability in subsequent situations.

The same stimulus situation is *not* repeatedly presented in the basic experiment. It will be remembered that it was on this account that we adopted a simplifying assumption in applying associationistic theories. But such an assumption proves unnecessary in connection with Koffka's trace theory since Koffka is concerned with repetition of a process and not with repetition of a stimulus. Repetition is said to affect learning directly only qua repetition of the process (p. 537). Moreover, Koffka deals specifically with the case where the same process occurs repeatedly in different contexts and states that in such a case the process may gain stability by the role it plays in the trace system corresponding to each of these contexts.

Why do subjects tend to use the E method rather than the direct method in the test problems? We can find an answer in these words of

Koffka's: "... repetition of activity A will create an aggregated trace system of such a kind that activity A will become more stable and regular and thereby exclude variation into a very different activity B" (p. 537).

Koffka's trace theory of learning does not seem to account for direct solutions of test problems as readily as for E solutions. One might explain direct solutions on the ground that the present process did not communicate with the trace corresponding to the E method or that it communicated with the trace corresponding to the direct method. The critical problem might be considered as an ambiguous situation allowing two organizations or structurizations, toward the E or the direct method, while in the extinction task forces of organization point to the direct solution. But why does one organization win over the other in the critical or why in the extinction task do forces of organization sometimes succumb to the influence of the E trace? Perhaps Koffka would answer by pointing out that account must be taken of the extension or strength of the traces corresponding to the E and to the direct method as well as of the subject's attitudes, of those ego forces which he describes as important factors in determining communication between present process and trace.

WHEELER'S ORGANISMIC THEORY FOCUSED ON THE BASIC EXPERIMENT

The organismic approach to learning (Wheeler, 1929; Wheeler and Perkins, 1932) represents an out-and-out attack on associationistic theories. Since man is a part of nature, his behavior is considered to follow laws that apply to nature generally; since man is a system of energy, his behavior is considered to follow the laws of energy which hold in the natural sciences. Accordingly, laws of nature are presented, described as organismic laws "because they imply the organic or unified character of objects in nature" (Wheeler and Perkins, 1932, p. 18).

One of these laws is the law of least action, "nature's universal law of economy or parsimony" (Wheeler, 1940, p. 40). With action defined as units of energy multiplied by units of time, this law states that for given conditions action is always at a minimum; movement occurs from one position to another over the shortest route in time (e.g., a stream of water follows the steepest downward slope possible under the circumstances). One set of movements is said to be forsaken for another if the latter provides a shorter route to the goal, one which involves less expenditure of time and energy. At first blush, the findings of the basic experiment seem to run counter to the law of least action since most subjects did not forsake the E method. One could try to reconcile our results with this law by assuming that it was less wasteful of time and energy to continue with the E method than to switch to the other solution; an Einstellung can be interpreted in terms of economy of the organism's energy (Immergluck, 1952). Later we present experimental data bearing on the relationship between E effects and the law of least action.

Wheeler and Perkins' statement that inevitably the organism takes the shortest route to the goal which it is able to perceive under the existing conditions also serves as a means of reconciliation. Under the existing conditions, it might be said, our subjects could not perceive the direct method; the repeated stimulation may have served to establish conditions which prevented such perception. "Stereotyped reactions ... mean that the perceived relationships are restricted in their scope" (p. 117).

Another organismic law is that of maximum work which states that in an energy system a maximum amount of energy will be spent in retaining the *status quo* against forces that would alter the pre-existing balance of potentials (Wheeler and Perkins, 1932, p. 33). "An idea, any whole, will retain its *status quo* until something alters it. This is but a special case of ... Newton's first law of motion" (p. 464). Continued use of the E method may be interpreted in terms of the law of maximum work which is essentially a principle of inertia.

Also, stemming from the law of maximum work is the idea that those responses will be made which best relieve the organism's tension. That some of the rats in an experiment by Kuo (1922) continued to choose the long path for a considerable time, is accounted for "in light of certain conditions in these animals ... which meant that the long path relieved the most tension or relieved the tension so adequately that the short path was never discovered as a shorter path to the goal" (Wheeler and Perkins, 1932, p. 273). A similar explanation might be proposed for our findings.

Of relevance to the basic experiment is the theory of transfer developed by Wheeler and Perkins. They note that, "strictly speaking, *there is no transfer*. Indeed, the essential fact about that behavior designated as transfer *is a duplication of response in the first and subsequent performances*" (1932, p. 321). Transfer occurs only "when the two tasks are so similar that the learner can apprehend them in the same whole" (p. 321), can perceive them as "undifferentiated members of the same spatial and temporal pattern" (p. 325). It may be said that a subject transferred the E method to the later tasks because he perceived these and the E tasks as belonging to the same configuration.

It is interesting to note that, while the organismic theory is considered a Gestalt theory of learning, it rejects a trace hypothesis: "... *a given experience is not represented by a brain-pattern except when the stimulus-situation is keeping the pattern set up. The instant the stimulus is removed the brain-pattern disappears*" (Wheeler and Perkins, 1932, p. 387). Discussing a case of behavior occurring again—an illustration for which Koffka (1935, p. 459) offers a very different interpretation, in line with his Gestalt trace theory—Wheeler and Perkins state that the original response was made to the total situation, and was configurational in character, and there "was enough of this situation left to produce the response a second time" (p. 397). Applied to the Einstellung situation, this interpretation would mean that, to explain repetition of the E method, one need not invoke traces but need only note that the test problems contained "enough" of the previous "total situation" to produce the E response again. Unfortunately, just what "enough" means in this context is rather difficult to specify. Also, it raises the question why what is "enough" for one person should not be "enough" to produce the response again in another person. But perhaps Wheeler would answer such questions, as well as the broader problem why direct solutions were given when they were, by appealing to the organismic laws as they fit the particular field conditions of each case.

Of particular relevance to E effects are the views of Wheeler and Perkins on the role of repetition in learning. They reject the thesis that repetition of response is essential to learning. They claim that this thesis is based on the idea that a synapse in the nervous system functions more easily the more it is used, and insist that this implies a faulty conception; the synapse is a switch and a current of electricity traverses a switch as easily the first time as the millionth. The nerve impulse depends upon differentials of potentials in a field of "fluid" energy and the nerve routes followed by the impulse are paths of least action whose functioning at any one time is determined by the surrounding field. If there is a high potential behind a certain synapse and a low potential in front, then a nerve current will pass through and it will pass through as easily the first time as thereafter. *"Forces in nature, anywhere, do not require experience in order to function perfectly"* (p. 350). For example, the apple need not repeat the act of falling before its performance will be perfect. Moreover, responses are not made because they occurred more or less frequently in the past. "Since all learning is insightful, responses are not selected through their frequency of occurrence. In fact, frequency of occurrence has nothing to do with their 'survival' " (p. 108).

While repetition of response is not a condition of learning, Wheeler and Perkins say, repetition of a stimulus pattern may be a cause of learning if the stimulus pattern is properly presented. The stimulus pattern is said to give rise to certain differentials of potential in brain energy. The repeated presentation of a stimulus pattern helps to maintain this energy distribution and thereby to favor a particular nerve route corresponding to a particular response. Thus repetition of response is not a cause of but a consequence of learning.

As applied to the Einstellung situation, Wheeler and Perkins' position implies that the occurrence of the E method in the later problems is not a function of its past frequency of occurrence. Rather, the repeated presentation of a similar stimulus pattern helps to maintain certain conditions in the brain which favor nerve routes corresponding to the E method.

Skinner's Behaviorism Focused on the Basic Experiment

The business of a science of behavior, Skinner (1950) maintains, is to evaluate probability of response and to explore the conditions that determine the probability. Learning, he notes, may be defined as "a change in probability of response" (1950, p. 199). The conditions under which learning comes about, he emphasizes, must be specified. Reinforcement is one condition, for reinforcement of a response is considered always to increase the probability of this response. Skinner subscribes to the law of effect, which "is no theory . . . [but] simply specifies a procedure for altering the probability of a chosen response" (1950, p. 200).

Skinner's major deviation from traditional stimulus-response theories lies in his rejection of the dictum that every response presupposes a stimulus. While he recognizes that some responses are elicited by specific stimuli, he maintains that there are many which are not correlated to known stimuli. The former he refers to as elicited responses and the latter as emitted responses. For example, a reflex such as pupillary constriction to light is an elicited response, whereas such activities as eating a meal or composing a poem, which do not appear to be correlated to known stimuli, are emitted responses. The pupillary constriction may also be referred to as a respondent, and eating a meal or composing a poem as an operant, in line with the distinction Skinner draws between respondent and operant behavior.

Thus, respondent behavior refers to the elicitation of a response by a definite, recognizable stimulus. Operant behavior refers to that large segment of behavior in which the relation of stimulus to response is not that of invariable elicitation or in which no correlated stimulus can be detected upon occasions when the response is observed to occur. It may happen that operant behavior becomes related to stimulus but then the stimulus acts as an "occasion" for the response but does not by itself elicit or "cause" the response.

Corresponding to the two types of behavior, Skinner envisions two kinds of conditioning. One of these is Type S (or Pavlovian) conditioning which influences the strength of respondent behavior, where strength is measured by the magnitude of the response or the latency period between the stimulus and the response. The other type is Type R conditioning which influences the strength of operant behavior, where strength refers to frequency of occurrence. In Type S conditioning the reinforcing agent is associated with the stimulus so that the unconditioned stimulus (e.g., food) is presented simultaneously with the conditioned stimulus (e.g., a tone). But, in Type R conditioning, reinforcement is correlated with the response; the response must appear before it can be reinforced. Reinforcements determine the total number of responses which will be made, if enough time is given for them to be made. This number is referred to as the "reflex reserve," a reserve built up by reinforcement and exhausted by extinctions, a reserve which is emptied according to the rate of responding. The momentary rate of responding, which is called the "reflex strength," depends on the reflex reserve, a larger reserve making for a higher rate, but may also be altered by changes in the condition of the organism.

It should be noted that Skinner (1950, p. 203) has questioned the usefulness of the concept of reflex reserve, which he introduced in his early work (1938), as well as the usefulness of the view that extinction is a process of exhaustion (e.g., exhaustion of the reflex reserve). The concept of reflex strength seems also to have been discarded. Instead, he usually refers to the number of responses made during the extinction period (that is, during the period when the given response is not reinforced) as a measure of resistance to extinction. The rate at which the response that had been reinforced is made during the extinction period, although it is not called the reflex strength, remains the focus of attention. The rate or frequency of response (not only during extinction) is regarded by Skinner as a most appropriate variable or datum for the study of learning—perhaps the "only appropriate datum" (1950, p. 198) for a science of behavior.

While a psychologist who is concerned with movement contends that "action and posture are the most important data available for prediction of the immediate action to follow" (Guthrie, 1952, p. 240), Skinner is so little concerned with posture, action, or movement that he studies an animal in an opaque box. The concern is not with how the animal operates the lever nor even with prediction of the next lever pressing, but simply with the frequency of lever pressing in a given interval of time, a frequency which is automatically recorded day and night by a device in the box.

Skinner notes that "frequency of response is a valuable datum just because it provides a substantial basis for the concept of probability of action—a concept toward which a science of behavior seems to have been groping for many decades" (1953b, p. 77). He objects to giving probability of action the physical status of a *thing*. Attempts to embody probability of action in the organism, in its neurological or psychic states or events, are said to underlie the use of such terminology as readiness or tendencies to behave, preparatory sets, dispositions and predispositions, habits and instincts, attitudes, opinions, wishes, and even personality itself. If an individual's frequency of response over an appreciable length of time is studied, then we can dispense with the "superfluous trappings to be found in traditional definitions of terms like habit, attitude, wish, and so on" (p. 77), which are nothing but inferences from observed frequencies of behavior.

In place of the one-trial learning advocated by Guthrie, Skinner suggests that there may be one-reinforcement learning of a single operant; that is, if a single operant could be isolated (but it is difficult to do so), it would reach its maximum probability of being used again after a single reinforcement. A given act of behavior generally involves several operants and hence may require more than one trial to attain maximum probability.

Skinner has been particularly interested in the effects on behavior of schedules of reinforcement; e.g., during the "reinforcement period" the experimenter reinforces responses intermittently, say, every third response or every response made at ten-minute intervals. By making use of proper arrangements of reinforcements and other experimental techniques, e.g., successive approximations, and ingenious devices, Skinner and his students have been able to control animal and human subjects (as in animal training, in training and drilling children in arithmetic, and in regulating responses of psychotic patients with the use of certain "vending machines"). It could be said that what Skinner is doing, engineeringwise, is to arrange reinforcing agents of the organism's environment so that certain responses become highly probable (Skinner, 1953a).

With reference to the basic experiment, Skinner would undoubtedly object to the use of such terms as habit, set, or Einstellung. One might conceivably regard the experiment as involving respondent behavior, at least for those subjects for whom the three-jar-volume-measuring problems invariably elicited the E response; Type S conditioning might be said to be involved, with the strength of the respondent behavior (or reflex) measured by the latency period between the presentation of the problem and the occurrence of the E response. Or one might describe the experiment as involving operant behavior in which the E method is correlated with reinforcement (successful solution). A class of stimuli, the volume-measuring problems, acquires a relation to this operant and does not automatically "cause" or elicit the E method but serves as an occasion for emission of this response. The E problems are reinforcing situations which build up the reflex reserve of the response made to these problems through Type R conditioning and thereby increase the probability of occurrence of this response in the test problems. Problems which cannot be solved by the E method constitute extinction tasks which diminish the reflex reserve. The subject will keep on responding with the E method, if other conditions are appropriate, until the reflex reserve is exhausted. The strength of respondent behavior can be roughly gauged from the number of E solutions to the test problems. Somewhat more analogous to Skinner's conditions would be the presentation of many test problems which the subject can solve (or not solve) at his own rate, with frequency of E solutions serving as an index of the reflex reserve created by reinforcements and momentary rate of responding serving as an index of the reflex strength. (An interpretation of these conditions and of the conditions in the basic experiment can also be given, in line with Skinner's view, that does not use such terms as "reflex reserve" and "reflex strength.")

The closest we come to conditions that permit the study of the rate of responding during extinction are our experiments on satiation in the test problems, presented in the chapter, "Topological Rigidity and Behavioral Rigidity." The use of intermittent reinforcements in the presentation of the E tasks suggests various experimental variations. We shall later turn to an experiment in which, instead of giving successive E tasks, E tasks are alternated with extinction tasks, so that not every attempt at an E response is reinforced.

MAIER'S CONCEPTS FOCUSED ON THE BASIC EXPERIMENT

While Guthrie is impressed by the stereotypy which animals display in learning situations, Maier (1939) is impressed by their variability, so much so that he posits a need to vary and a preference for variety. Maier recognizes that, as learning occurs, variability usually decreases and the animal adheres to one specific pattern of behavior. But the animal is said to be able readily to change his behavior if new alternatives become available and the learned pattern no longer leads to reward. "Learned behavior is subject to change when it ceases to be adequate for obtaining a goal" (Maier, 1949, p. 18).

Maier's studies of the behavior of rats under conditions of frustration (1949) provide ample evidence that stereotyped behavior may not be abandoned when new alternatives are available but may be continued for hundreds of trials even though consistently punished. He refers to such behavior, considered the experimental analogue of compulsions, as abnormal fixation produced by frustration, where a fixation is characterized as an end in itself rather than as a means to an end. Fixations are considered distinct from learned responses in many respects: fixations are repeated over and over without any variation whatsoever; they possess a greater resistance to change than habits; they tend not to be modified in the face of persistent punishment; they are specific to the particular situation and do not transfer; etc.

Maier (1949) notes that, while his experiments show that frustration leads to fixation, they do not fully explain why one particular response rather than another becomes fixated. The relevant evidence suggests the following:

It seems that the response fixated is one that is highly available to the animal. Position responses are simple and highly available. In one study where alleys were used it was found that runs into forward-going alleys were more likely to be fixated than runs into alleys that required a turn. It was also found that the fixated response was likely to be one that the animal was expressing during the period of [frustration] ... These facts point to the principle of *availability* as a factor in determining the particular response that is fixated. (Maier, 1949, p. 82.)

Maier postulates two distinct mechanisms or processes underlying behavior, the process of frustration, which underlies fixations, and the process of motivation or goal orientation, which underlies learning. While fixations are usually developed in situations designed to produce frustration (e.g., the no-solution situation where no one pattern or position consistently leads to reward in the Lashley jumping apparatus), a few animals did not develop fixations in a frustration situation, while a few did develop them in an ordinary learning situation (defined as one in which response consistently leads to reward, at least for a series of trials). The criterion for a fixation in this case was the failure to learn a new response in the same jumping apparatus. To account for these results, Maier assumes that the frustration situation must have failed to frustrate a few hardy animals while having to learn a new response frustrated a few with a sufficiently low threshold for frustration.

How does this apply to the basic experiment? Our experiment has the earmarks of an "ordinary learning situation" since one response consistently leads to reward, at least in the E problems. Yet most subjects did not readily change their behavior when new alternatives became available (in the critical problems) and some did not change even when the E method no longer led to the goal (in the extinction task). But Maier contends that learned behavior is subject to change when it ceases to be adequate for obtaining a goal. He uses failure to learn a new response in 200 trials as evidence of fixation in his rats. How many trials must elapse in which the direct method is not learned in order that a human being may be regarded as having a fixation in the Einstellung situation, has not been established. We know from the experiments on satiation that some subjects did not find the direct method even after twenty successive extinction problems and that some persisted in using the E method in 150 criticals even though thoroughly "satiated" with this response. It may be conjectured that, for those individuals, and possibly for some in the basic experiment, the E response was not a habit but a fixation, of an available response, produced by frustration. Counter to this conjecture runs the evidence that the behavior did not have all the other earmarks of a fixation, e.g., it was not highly specific to one situation but was used even when the jar numbers were changed; although the behavior may not have met the goal stipulated in the extinction problem, it was seemingly motivated by the goal of attaining successful solutions and hence was goal oriented. But, if persistent use of the E method is characterized not as a fixation but only as a strong habit, then it must be granted, apparently counter to Maier's conception of learning, that learned responses need not be changed even after repeated failures.

Parenthetically, we note that Guthrie (1952) seeks to account for behavior shown by Maier's rats under conditions of frustration in terms of learning theory. The fixated response, the available response, is considered the organism's response to frustration, by which he is taken out of a state that had included tension and restless action. Maier's principle of availability is considered a special case of the principle of association by contiguity. The rats are said to have persisted in the fixated response because the necessary associative cues were still present; they continued to give the response last made to these cues. That Maier finds it necessary to regard frustrated behavior which is resistant to change as not learned, is described as a consequence of the assumption on his part that learning must lead to adjustment; from this assumption it follows that a learned response will be changed when it is no longer adequate, when it no longer leads to reward. Guthrie does not require learning to lead to adjustment or reward or to be regulated by goals. While Maier's definition of learning rules out fixations from the proper territory of learning, to Guthrie a fixation is learning. In fact, he regards fixation or stereotypy as the prototype of learning. Hence, Guthrie would regard fixations for the *E* method as learned behavior.

Another concept of Maier's may be pertinent to the Einstellung situation. His studies of problem solving in humans and in rats (1930, 1937, 1938) led him to stress the importance of direction in reasoning. A direction is "a predisposition on the part of the organism [which] ... cannot easily be imposed from without ... an active organizing process [which] ... is specific for the problem at hand" (1949, p. 230). While the proper direction in thinking is necessary to achieve effective solution, a faulty direction may hinder solution. Maier's concept of direction as something imposed upon the situation by the organism differs from the more traditional Gestalt conception of forces of direction stemming from the problem-solving situation itself.

> The characteristic of direction in thinking is that when a line of thinking has been adopted it tends to persist. In all problem solving, individuals vary their procedures, but the variation is primarily confined to a particular point of view.... Not only will [the individual] ... tend to think along a particular line and persist, but he will also tend to be blind to and will even actively resist suggestions that do not conform to his direction of thinking. (Maier, 1949, pp. 229-30.)

What occurred in the basic experiment for most individuals may be interpreted as the development of a direction, in this case imposed by the early problems, which persisted even when it was no longer the best line of attack and which blinded the subjects to a solution not in conformance with this direction. In his studies of reasoning in human adults, Maier was able to increase the number of correct solutions substantially by issuing several instructions, among them these hints, "Do not be a creature of habit and stay in a rut ... Keep your mind open for new combinations, and do not waste your time on unsuccessful attempts" (1933, p. 152). This finding is interpreted as indicating that reasoning is in part the overcoming of habitual responses formed during the process of working on the problems. The instructions are essentially what we hoped would be conveyed to our subjects by the phrase, "Don't be blind," given in some experimental variations. It would be of interest to see the influence on *E* effects of introducing the precise words cited from Maier.

In brief, Maier offers us three distinct alternatives in terms of which to describe the Einstellung phenomenon: a strong habit which is a learned response, a fixation resulting from frustration, a direction in a reasoning situation. Our evidence points to the applicability of the first and third alternatives.

HILGARD'S CONCEPTS FOCUSED ON THE BASIC EXPERIMENT

After reviewing the major learning theories, and concluding that there is as yet no generally satisfactory theory, Hilgard (1948) offers some suggestions which may lead to the development of a more complete theory of learning. Of particular interest to us is his concept of the provisional try. He rejects the notion that the initial adjustment to a learning situation is the running off of previously acquired sensori-motor habits in random, trial-and-error fashion or according to some other conditioning principles. Instead, the initial adjustment is interpreted as a genuine attempt at discovering the route to the goal. While past experience is used, it is employed in a manner which is appropriate to the present. A provisional try, similar to the notion of "hypothesis" behavior described by Krech and Tolman, is a "provisional behavior route . . . kept in suspension until its consequences change its provisional status; if it is confirmed it is an appropriate path of action to be followed under like circumstances, if it is not confirmed it is inappropriate" (pp. 336-37). To explain the so-called backward action of effect, Hilgard assumes that the organism has some memorial representation of his provisional attempt at solution.

One objection to a theory of the provisional try is that behavior is often more stereotyped and less reasonable than such a theory would suggest. "A theory which assumes that behavior is regulated reasonably on the basis of available information is put to it to account for the persistence of habits in situations in which they are no longer adaptive" (p. 339). Hilgard believes that one kind of stereotypy results from overlearning, defined as the facilitation of response with repetition after the essential learning has been mastered. The oft-repeated activity may attain some measure of goal character and blind the learner to new possibilities.

Another source of stereotypy is the insoluble problem as in Maier's experiment where there is no predictable pattern of success or failure. Because the environment is unresponsive to the learner's genuine attempts to predict the occurrence of reward on the basis of "correct" behavior, the learner adopts a fixed response, which represents the giving up of such attempts. It is a way of coping with an unreasonable situation, one which is cognitively too difficult for the animal. When the situation is changed so that there is a definite pattern of reward and punishment, the animal may still display the fixated behavior. As an alternative to Maier's belief that the fixations represent compulsions, Hilgard suggests that "the situation is misinterpreted in the light of the learner's experience, and the sense of alternative has been lost" (p. 341). The kind of stereotypy which Guthrie and Horton (1946) report in their experiments with cats is also accounted for by Hilgard in terms of cognitive difficulty. That a cat that happened to back into the post, which opens the door, may repeat in stereotyped manner what he last did when the door opened instead of moving directly to the post may be due to the cat's failure to cognize clearly the relationship between pole and door. Another source of fixated behavior, excessive punishment at the time of choice, is also explained in terms of interference with orderly cognitive processes.

Stereotyped and fixated behavior are therefore regarded as consistent with the theory of the provisional try if two assumptions are accepted: after sufficient overlearning, the learner no longer tries but prefers the oft-repeated activity "unless something dramatic again arouses his searching behavior"; situations which are cognitively too difficult result in stereotypy (p. 342).

The main trend of results in the basic experiment might be accounted for in terms of overlearning, the extinction problem constituting (for some subjects) the dramatic event which awakened their searching behavior. Less plausible would be an explanation in terms of cognitive difficulty. But for some subjects the E problems may have been very complex, requiring as they do the "*Umweg*" procedure of starting with too much fluid and then discarding some of it, and this complexity may have fostered stereotypy. By the time the test problems were given, "the sense of alternative" may have been lost so far as such volume-measuring problems were concerned. The finding of the direct method in the test problems could be attributed to genuine trying to solve each task reasonably, on the basis of available information.

EVALUATION OF SURVEY

Controversies among psychologists advancing various learning theories have been considered due in part to the concern of those involved with diverse aspects of the learning situation and with different typical experiments. Here we have attempted to focus many learning theories on one experimental situation. This was done with the dual objective of increasing our understanding of E effects and of revealing the essential differences and similarities among the various theories. Have these objectives been achieved?

We have seen that many constructs and principles may be appealed to in accounting for E effects in the basic experiment. They include association by similarity, association by contiguity, stimulus-response bonds, a spontaneous or automatic tendency to reproduce behavior, reproduction resulting from an *Aufgabe* or an intention to repeat behavior, the principle of substitution, the principle of assimilation, stimulus generalization, stimulus equivalence, transfer of training, retroactive inhibition, law of exercise or frequency of response, frequency of stimulation, recency of response, the principle of effect or reward, reinforcement deriving from need reduction, extension of a trace system through reinforcement, increase of reflex reserve through reinforcement, operant behavior and Type R conditioning, respondent behavior and Type S conditioning, law of maximum work, law of minimum effort, cognitive map, equivalence belief, field-cognition modes, motor pattern, fixation through frustration, learning of a strong habit, persistence of direction, stereotypy considered as the prototype of learning, stereotypy where variability is considered to be the prototype of learning, stereotypy resulting from overlearning or from cognitive difficulty of the problem or from the fact that the learner has lost the sense of alternative, and so on and so on.

It is hardly likely that *all* these constructs are essential to an understanding of the basic experiment. Indeed, no learning theorist would offer all of them; he would advocate some, specifically reject others, and possibly be indifferent to the remainder.

So far as an understanding of what actually occurs in the foundation experiment is concerned, the diversity of concepts can only becloud and not illuminate, until we have some means of deciding which are the most adequate and valid and which are similar and which dissimilar. With respect to an understanding of the essential similarities and differences between the learning theories reviewed, we must confess that we have gained very little. Perhaps it is because we lack the knowledge of how to translate the terminology of one theory into the terminology of another. There seems to us to be a genuine need for attempts to relate the diverse terminologies of learning theories perhaps through a threefold enterprise: (1) to list the various constructs employed in a theory, (2) to define those which constitute the defined terms and to indicate which are undefined,* (3) to relate the defined and undefined terms to the constructs used in other major learning theories. Serious endeavors to carry through the threefold enterprise for the major learning theories may help to dissipate some of the current con-

---

* There must be undefined terms if circular definitions are to be avoided. By circular definitions are meant those in which one word A is defined in terms of B and B is defined ultimately in terms of A, perhaps through intervening steps in which, for example, B is defined in terms of C and then C is defined in terms of A. Of course, a dictionary uses circular definitions, and so must any theory or other system of thought that proposes to define all the terms it uses. Hence, if the trap of circular definitions is to be avoided, certain terms must be taken without definition; all other terms may be defined ultimately in terms of the undefined terms. (See Richardson, 1941, p. 23, for a discussion of this point as well as of the related point that a theory or any other system of thought must have some unproved statements.)

troversy. We are not suggesting that *all* the differences between the major points of view rest on semantic usage, but, until the semantic confusion is clarified, it will be difficult to separate verbal from non-verbal distinctions.

Hilgard laments that, while the study of learning has been a most active field of investigation in experimental psychology since Ebbinghaus' classical work in 1885, a field which has attracted many distinguished psychologists, nonetheless there "are no laws of learning which can be taught with confidence [and even] . . . the most obvious facts of improvement with practice and the regulation of learning under reward and punishment are matters of theoretical dispute" (1948, p. 326). How much has the multiplicity of constructs—and the failure to relate them—contributed to this indecisive state of affairs? Imagine what would happen if some physicists concerned with the study of gases used constructs other than pressure, temperature, and volume, and did not trouble to relate their constructs to these three. There might well result "theoretical dispute" over the "facts" concerning the behavior of gases and there might be no laws on the behavior of gases. The analogue in psychology is unfortunately only too apparent.

To repeat, we are not suggesting that differences between learning theories are solely semantic in nature, but only that essential differences and similarities may be hidden behind the diversity of terminology. If a common universe of discourse can be achieved, it will help to reveal nonsemantic differences between the theories. Moreover, translation of current concepts into a common terminology may reveal that some concepts are appropriate to certain aspects of the learning situation but not to other aspects. (Hilgard has suggested that, while each major theorist believes his concepts to be appropriate to all of learning, the concepts may be suitable only for particular aspects of the learning situation.) If various current concepts prove to be synonymous, there will probably be reasons why one is preferred by a particular psychologist. It would be well if psychologists would denote the reasons for their preference for a specific terminology, so that we may know whether a predilection is akin to the Englishman's who insisted that what he was holding really looked like an *apple* and not, as the Frenchman near him insisted, like a *pomme*, or whether more intrinsic reasons underlie a selection.

A common universe of discourse would facilitate comparison of various theories with reference to their undefined terms, their defined terms, their axioms or premises, and their derived theorems. It should prove of interest to compare the axiomatic foundations of various theories in order to see what axioms they have in common and in what axioms they differ. Conceivably, theories which differ considerably with respect to theorems may differ only in a few axioms or only in one axiom; an example is furnished by mathematics wherein three plane geometries—Euclidean, hyperbolic, elliptic—that differ in many theorems, differ only with respect to one axiom (the axiom of parallel lines) while having in common all the other axioms. Research might then be centered on obtaining experimental evidence pertaining to the diverse axioms or to theorems derived from the diverse axioms. Experimental evidence may prove to favor one axiom over a contradictory one belonging to another theory. Or research may indicate that the differing axioms (or related theorems) are "experimentally equivalent" in the sense that, with existing methods and instruments of measurement, a crucial decision cannot be made among the diverse axioms but that (for the time being) they are equally acceptable so far as psychological reality is concerned; for example, the three plane geometries have been found to be "experimentally equivalent" (Courant and Robbins, 1941, p. 223) for measurements on our earth, so that all three are equally applicable, within the limits of error, given existing methods of measuring. In short, a common universe of discourse would high-light essential differences and similarities between the theorems and allow research to be devoted to making crucial decisions (or to demonstrating why such decisions cannot be made) rather than dissipated over controversies which are perhaps superficial, not essential, or only semantic in nature.

Common terminology may reveal that there are essentially different theories of learning that apply to the same aspect of the learning situation and research may prove these theories to be "experimentally equivalent" under existing conditions. Conceivably this may trouble some psychologists who hope to find one answer to the problem of learning. That so many apparently different theories of learning have already been proposed, has been interpreted as an indication that the problem "What is learning?" is an unsolvable problem (Kendler, 1952). And yet the possibility should also be considered that this problem may have more than one solution (just as there are mathematical problems with nonunique solutions) so that the different theories may conceivably constitute different answers to the same problem. Likewise, the problem "What is rigidity?" may be a problem with no solution, with one solution, or with various solutions as represented by different theories. Involved are the methodological issues of the nature of a solution and the nature of a problem—whether it is solvable, unsolvable, or just unsolved but not proved unsolvable; whether it has no solution, only one solution, or more than one solution.

The preceding discussion is not intended to imply that the focusing of various theories onto a common situation, as advocated in a variational approach, is valueless unless a common universe of discourse has first been achieved. Focusing of theories of learning onto the Einstellung situation, although hampered by diversities in terminology, did prove of value. For one thing, it suggested certain factors to be manipulated and certain experimental variations (e.g., those to be described in Chapter XII, "Association as a Force for Spontaneous Reproduction"). For another, it suggested various foci along which to organize the data obtained in other variations as well as certain issues in learning theory to which the obtained data could be applied. While most of the experimental variations which will be described in subsequent chapters were not conducted in order to obtain evidence concerning controversial issues in learning theory—the primary objective was the procurement of information concerning the Einstellung situation—it nonetheless proved stimulating to see how the obtained data relate to these controversial issues and what the issues suggest concerning the Einstellung situation. Let us now turn to the experiments pertinent to learning variables.

CHAPTER XI

THE INFLUENCE OF RECENCY AND FREQUENCY

THE ROLE OF RECENCY

A PRINCIPLE of recency is accepted in many learning theories and is afforded a prominent position in some; e.g., Guthrie's. Such a principle might account for E effects on the ground that the E method was the most recent act performed by the subject and was therefore repeated in a subsequent similar task and then, because of recency, in the next task, etc. Recency may therefore account for some or all of the E effects found in the basic experiment and variations of it. But a tendency to repeat the most recent act cannot explain the behavior of those subjects who did not show E effects. And recency cannot be invoked to account for the results obtained in certain experimental variations.

For example, in place of the usual E tasks, ten Montreal college students were given six tasks each solvable by only one method; the methods were $A - C$, $A + C$, $B - A - 2C$, $A - C$, $A + C$, $B - A - 2C$. Then they received Criticals 1, 2, 3, and 4. The $B - A - 2C$ procedure was used by every subject in the task just prior to the criticals; yet, despite its recent use, the method was employed in only 10 per cent of the solutions of the criticals, while direct methods were used in 90 per cent of the solutions. Recency therefore cannot explain these results.

Further evidence is furnished by the "alternation" experiment done with 124 sixth-grade children. They received problems in the following order: E_1, E_3, an extinction task solvable only by $A - C$, E_4, an extinction task solvable only by $A + C$, E_5, C_1, and C_2. The E procedure was used in 92 per cent of the solutions of each E task, including the one just before C_1C_2. But, despite its recent use, the procedure was used in only 16 per cent of the solutions of C_1C_2, 84 per cent of the solutions being by the direct method (Luchins, 1942, p. 41).

The results obtained in these variations not only show the inadequacy of the recency principle but also speak against frequency as the determinant of responses. In the experiment with college students, prior to the criticals the $B - A - 2C$ procedure was repeated just as many times as the $A + C$ or $A - C$ procedures and yet the latter were used far more frequently in the criticals. In the experiment with sixth-grade children, prior to the criticals the $B - A - 2C$ method was used four times and the $A + C$ and $A - C$ procedures only once each, and yet the latter predominated in solutions to the criticals. In short, these findings cannot readily be attributed to either recency or frequency, or to recency together with frequency.

Experiments in which we attempted to separate the E tasks from the test tasks by time intervals or by various instructions (Luchins, 1942, pp. 45-53) are also relevant to the relationship between recency and E effects. Despite the time interval, large E effects were shown in the test problems by those who reported that they regarded the second series of problems as a continuation of the first or who said that they recognized the similarity of the later problems to the earlier ones. Instructions devised to separate the test and E tasks produced little or no E effects among those who considered the test tasks as distinct from the E tasks, while large E effects prevailed among those who regarded them as similar, as belonging to the same series. Here we see that E effects may occur even though the test tasks do not follow immediately after the E tasks but are separated by a time interval ranging from a few minutes to a few weeks, and, on the other hand, that E effects may not even occur, even though the E method was the most recent act performed by the subject. What seemed to be important was not the recency of the E method, or that the test tasks immediately followed the E tasks, but the subject's attitude; that is, whether or not he viewed the tasks as belonging together, as members of a homogeneous series.

The Role of Frequency of Repetition

Confusion has been introduced into discussions of the role of frequency of repetition in learning because of a failure to distinguish explicitly between repetition of response and repetition of stimulus. It seems to us that clarification would be enhanced if, in discussions of frequency in repetition, it were stated explicitly whether reference is to repetition of the stimulus accompanied by repetition of a response; repetition of the stimulus without repetition of a response; repetition of a response without repetition of a stimulus.

One may question whether a response can be the same if the stimulus is not. But then one may go further and question the very notions of *same* response and of *same* stimulus. Is any stimulus ever precisely the same as any other stimulus, any response ever precisely the same as any other response? What kind and degree of similarity must prevail in order that two stimuli (or two responses) may be considered as the "same" for experimental purposes? From whose point of view shall the stimuli and the responses be viewed in order to ascertain the prevailing degree of similarity?

In the present context, where we are concerned with the relationship of frequency of E responses to E effects, these questions play a central role. Since the various E problems are not identical, whether or not they may be regarded as constituting a repetition of the same stimulus or even of the same stimulus pattern, depends on the particular answers which are given to these questions. If, for example, a subject does not recognize any similar pattern among the various problems while the experimenter does, shall the problems be regarded as of the same pattern? Likewise, if the subject is not aware that he is repeating the $B - A - 2C$ procedure in each of these problems, shall he be described as having made the same response to each? Whether one or another answer is given will determine which notion of repetition is invoked.

We shall assume that all responses to the E tasks which entail the $B - A - 2C$ (or $B - C - A - C$, $B - C - C - A$) procedure are the "same" kind of response. But, before studying the influence of the frequency of occurrence of this response on behavior in the subsequent test problems, we wish to remind the reader of the diversity of opinion which has been expressed concerning the role of frequency.

Frequency of response is recognized as an effective factor in learning in Thorndike's early formulation of the principle of exercise, Watson's principle of frequency, Hull's thesis that habit strength increases step by step with each reinforcement up to a theoretical maximum, Tolman's belief that one of the factors influencing the strength of the resulting "sign-gestalt" is the frequency with which the actual sequence of sign, means-end relation, and significate have been presented, Skinner's thesis that the reflex reserve increases with reinforcements, and Koffka's contention that the trace system becomes more and more fixed with repetition and that the extension of the trace system increases with each repetition. But frequency of response is explicitly rejected as a necessary factor in learning in Guthrie's thesis that each individual habit is learned at full strength in a single occurrence and in Wheeler's statement that frequency of occurrence has nothing to do with selection or survival of response. While Wheeler does not regard repetition of response as a cause of learning, he does note that repetition of a stimulus pattern may be a condition of learning if the stimulus pattern is properly presented. Koffka distinguishes between repetition of accomplishment (the end result) and repetition of a process that led to the accomplishment. Repetition of the same accomplishment, he notes, may have very different effects if somewhere along the line a particular process A occurs for the first time; prior to this occurrence, repetition can have no effect for A, whereas afterwards it can.

Since repetitions have thus a different function before and after a critical occasion [the first time a particular process occurs], the mere counting of repetitions [of accomplishment] *per se* does not seem to be valuable for a better understanding of the learning process unless the experimenter knows beforehand that the process in the development of which he is interested occurred at the first repetition. (Koffka, 1935, p. 538.)

One might summarize the various opinions by noting that they run the gamut from the view that repetition of response is both a necessary and sufficient condition (the earlier law of exercise of Thorndike, Watson's principle of frequency) to Wheeler's view that it is neither necessary nor sufficient, from the view that it is necessary but not sufficient (Hovland, 1951) to the opinion of Guthrie that it may be sufficient but is not necessary.

Which point of view is supported by the experimental evidence pertaining to the influence on E effects of frequency of response in E tasks?

Relationship Between Number of E Tasks Solved and E Effects

While five E tasks were presented in the basic experiment, not all five were solved by each elementary-school subject. In reporting the responses we used the data of only those subjects who solved at least the last two E tasks. But the data of all the elementary-school subjects were still available and gave us the possibility of seeing how E effects varied with the number of E problems solved.

For each grade level (the fourth, fifth, and sixth) of each of three public elementary schools, we computed the percentage of direct solutions of the first two test problems as well as the percentage of direct solutions of the extinction task, for each of the following groups:

(1) The control group, those children who received none of the E tasks.

(2) Those who solved none of the E problems (hereinafter called the "did-no-E group").

(3) Those who failed to solve at least the last two E problems ("did-no-E_4E_5 group").

(4) Those who did solve at least the last two E problems ("did-E_4E_5 group").

(5) Those who solved all the E problems ("did-all-E group").

None of the E tasks was solved by the control group or by the did-no-E group. But the children in the latter group may have been manifesting a general inability to deal with the problems so that it is not unreasonable to expect that they would show a larger percentage of failures of the test problems than the control group. Moreover, since the did-no-E group represents children who had seen the E method demonstrated and who may have been attempting to apply it, it is conceivable that some of them would finally succeed in the test problems and would therefore show more E solutions and fewer direct solutions than the control group.

If E effects vary directly with the number of E problems solved, we should expect to find that the percentages of direct solutions would decrease from group to group when, for each grade level of each school, the groups are arranged in this order: control, did no E, did no E_4E_5, did E_4E_5, did all E. The findings (Luchins, 1942, p. 16) substantiate this expectation. In general, with but few exceptions, the percentages of direct solutions decrease as we go from a group in which fewer of the E tasks were solved to one in which more of these tasks were solved.

Of particular interest are the differences between the did-no-E group and the did-all-E group. On the average, the did-all-E group had 55 and 52 per cent more E effects in C_1C_2 and in the extinction task, respectively, than did the did-no-E group. Thus, although these two groups received the same number of E tasks, they differed sharply with respect to E effects.

These results are pertinent to a theoretical issue that concerns interpretations of the law of frequency or exercise (cf. Koffka, 1935, p. 538). For example, Tolman distinguishes between two meanings of the law of exercise.

The Law of Exercise [holds that what] ... is meant by exercise is frequent and recent repetition of the whole stimulus situation, irrespective of whether in the given trial the animal chooses a correct or incorrect path. Exercise in this sense means the frequency and recency with which the whole problem, as a problem, is met and responded to. (1932, p. 346.)

In the second meaning of the Law of Exercise ... what is meant by frequent and recent exercise seems to be frequent and recent "differential" exercise upon the correct path at the expense of the incorrect paths. (P. 347.)

The first meaning of the law of exercise, wherein frequency refers essentially to frequency of presentation of a stimulus pattern, suggests that in the E tasks the same frequency of exercise was had by all subjects in the experimental groups or, at least, by all who responded to the five E tasks, irrespective of whether or not they correctly applied the E method or any other method. If it is assumed that all (or most) of the subjects in the did-no-E group responded, with the E or any other method, correctly or incorrectly, to all (or most of) the E problems, then, according to the first meaning of the law of exercise, these subjects would be said to have (about) the same frequency of exercise as the did-all-E group. Hence, if frequency is positively related to E effects, we should expect that the did-no-E and did-all-E groups would have about the same strength of E effects. But we have seen that the did-all-E group had strikingly more E effects than the did-no-E group. This finding seems to fit in better with the second meaning of the law of exercise wherein frequency is interpreted to refer to frequency of a correct response (in this case, the E method in the E tasks). The fact that E effects increased, on the whole, from a group that solved fewer of the E tasks to a group that solved more, also seems to support the second meaning of the law of exercise at the expense of the first. This, of course, rests on the assumption that frequency is positively related to E effects.

We just made the assumption that all or most subjects responded, correctly or incorrectly, to the E tasks. Such an assumption could be avoided if we had experiments in which various numbers of E tasks were presented, so that, for example, we could compare the E effects of subjects who received and solved five E tasks by the E method with the E effects of subjects who received and solved two E tasks by this method. Results of such experiments might also allow for a more clear-cut decision with regard to the relationship between E effects and the frequency of repetition of stimulus patterns corresponding to the E tasks. Moreover, there seems to be a need, on other grounds, for experiments which vary the number of E tasks presented. It is quite a different matter, it seems to us, for a subject to receive five E problems, but to solve only two of them, than for a subject to receive only two E problems and solve them both. The former subject may have been attempting to practice the E method in some of the E tasks and have failed, perhaps because of computational errors. There is also the influence on the subject of his possible awareness of having failed some of the E tasks. For these reasons, it was decided to study the relationship between E effects and frequency by presenting various numbers of E tasks. Let us turn now to these experiments.

Relationship Between Number of E Tasks Presented and E Effects

Experiments were conducted in which the number of E tasks was varied above or below five (the number in the basic experiment) in order to discover whether there would be a concomitant increase or decrease in E effects. In other respects the procedure was that of the basic experiment, including the illustration of the E method in the first E task.

Only the first two E tasks were presented prior to the test problems to two elementary-school classes, two college classes, and one adult-education class (Luchins, 1942, p. 39). But, their percentages of E solutions of the first two test problems, ranging from 64 to 80 per cent, were as high as the percentages of comparable groups taking the basic experiment. Failures of the extinction task (52 and 61 per cent) were as frequent as usual in the elementary-school classes, but in the adult group the failures (37 per cent) were less than for adults taking the basic experiment, while in the college groups there were virtually no failures (0 and 6 per cent) and hence far less than for college students in the basic experiment. E solutions of the last two criticals were 31 per cent for one college group and ranged from 60 to 63 per cent for the remaining groups. Thus, in some groups, particularly those composed of children, the use of two E tasks resulted in considerable E effects.

When only the first E problem was given prior to the test problems (Luchins, 1942, p. 40), an elementary-school group showed about as large E effects as similar groups in the basic experiment: C_1C_2, 64% E; Ext., 44% F; C_3C_4, 59% E. Discussion after the experiment revealed that most of those who used the E method did so because it was the method illustrated by the experimenter or because they believed that they had to practice in all the problems the method which worked in the first.

When the number of E tasks was increased to ten (Luchins, 1942, p. 38), three elementary-school classes showed almost complete E effects. Each class gave 100 per cent E solution of the first two criticals; 97, 100, and 100 per cent failure of the extinction task, and the same percentages of E solutions of the last two criticals. Doubling the number of set-inducing tasks thus seemed to be an effective method of maximizing E effects.

But individual experiments conducted with college students did not yield such clear-cut results (Luchins, 1942, p. 39). Preliminary experimentation, involving the presentation of 10, 15, 20, 25, or 30 set-inducing tasks, showed no simple relationship between number of problems presented and E effects. Individual attitudes—for example, regarding the experiment as a speed test and rapidly applying the practiced procedure, becoming bored and using this method in each case without even examining the problem, becoming bored and looking for new methods—seemed to influence the results.

Also relevant here are experiments by Tresselt and Leeds (1951) and by Vineberg (1951). Vineberg gave three groups, each composed of forty subjects, three, six, or nine arithmetical E problems. He reported an increase in the percentage of E solutions of a subsequent critical problem as the number of E tasks increased. All differences were statistically significant except those between the results following six and nine E tasks, a fact that led the investigator to conclude that the

E effect is a negatively accelerated function of training trials with the plateau reached after six to eight training trials. Tresselt and Leeds used seven groups, ten subjects in each, which received 2, 4, 6, 8, 10, 12, and 14 E problems. An almost linear relationship was found between percentages of E solutions of a subsequent critical and the number of E tasks up to six E tasks, but beyond that number E effects had a tendency to level off. It was hypothesized by these investigators that, when there are more than six E problems, other variables, including attitudinal factors, become active and interfere with or foster E effects.

Also pertinent are the experiments on satiation, already described in a previous chapter, in which we found no consistent relationship between strength of E effects and number of E problems presented. It was found that the number of E tasks presented seemed to have a greater effect on solutions of extinction tasks than on solutions of critical tasks.

Other Experiments Relating Frequency and E Effects

In the experiments to be surveyed now, a distinction will not be drawn between the number of E tasks presented and the number of E tasks solved, since all or most subjects solved (by the E method) all of the E tasks that were presented.

E Effects and Many E Tasks. In the experiment on satiation in the E tasks (see Chapter VIII), a series of twenty-four E problems was administered, and, if necessary, readministered again and again, in the same order, until the subject refused to do any more; then he was requested to do only a few more problems and was thereupon given the first two criticals and an extinction task. The number of E problems which thirty McGill University students solved (always by the E method) before refusing to do any more, ranged from 11 to 203, with a mean of 70. Of the 60 responses that the subjects gave to the first two criticals, 59 involved the E method. (One subject—who had completed 58 E tasks—used the direct method in the first critical but the E method in the second.) Hence, the E method was used in the criticals whether the number of prior E tasks solved was only 11 or over 200. The number of E tasks solved proved to be more consistently related to the extent of failures of the extinction task. Ten subjects, who completed less than 55 E problems each, showed 20 per cent failure of the extinction task; another ten subjects, who completed from 55 to 75 E problems each, showed 30 per cent failure; and another ten, who completed over 75 E problems each, showed 70 per cent failure. These results show that the relationship between frequency and E effects depends on whether E effects are measured in terms of E solutions of the criticals or in terms of failure of the extinction task. More generally, the results suggest that the relationship between frequency and habit strength may depend on how the strength of the habit is measured.

Relationship Between Frequency and E Effects When the E Method Is Regarded as the Rule of Solution. Observations made in the basic experiment reveal that some subjects showed E effects because they assumed that the E method was the rule to be used in solving the problems of the experiment. It was therefore decided to introduce this factor explicitly in experimental variations (Luchins, 1942, pp. 67-70).

Before any problems were given, four New York City classes (one college and three elementary-school classes) were told, "While solving the subsequent tasks, try to generalize or discover a method of solution or a rule to solve these problems." Fractionization of the results on the basis of the subject's answer to the question whether or not he had generalized a method and what the method was, revealed that those who had generalized the E method (all the college students had) showed almost complete E effects, while the others showed less, although within the range found in the basic experiment. While the results in each class are not of interest in this context, it may be worth while to list the results, with the elementary-school subjects considered as one group.

22 college subjects who said they had
   generalized E method .... C_1C_2: 100% E Ext.: 86% F C_3C_4: 91% E
87 pupils who said they had generalized
   E method .... C_1C_2: 100% E Ext.: 98% F C_3C_4: 99% E
26 pupils who said they had not generalized
   or found a rule .... C_1C_2: 75% E Ext.: 65% F C_3C_4: 73% E

These results suggest that the assumption that the E method is the rule of solution increases the probability of the appearance of E effects. We wondered whether, if the E method were described as the rule of solution by the experimenter, fewer E tasks would be needed to attain high E effects. For example, would one E task plus the rule yield E effects as large as those which resulted from five E tasks in the basic experiment? Let us turn to experimental attacks on this question.

Each of three New York City sixth-grade classes received the usual experiment through and including E_1 (the illustrated E task). Then, with the aid of the experimenter, the class formulated this rule: Fill the middle jar, and from it pour out once into the jar to the left and twice into the jar to the right. This was written on the blackboard and left there for the duration of the experiment. Subjects were told that it was the rule which solved the new type of problem that they were learning that day. Instead of more E problems, the test problems were then presented. Thus, these classes had only one E task plus a rule;

and, yet, their E effects were as large as those shown by elementary-school groups in the basic experiment.

45 subjects ...... C_1C_2: 87% E Ext.: 73% F C_3C_4: 87% E
37 subjects ...... C_1C_2: 96% E Ext.: 78% F C_3C_4: 93% E
41 subjects ...... C_1C_2: 100% E Ext.: 85% F C_3C_4: 100% E

In another variation, a New York City sixth-grade class of forty subjects received the basic experiment through and including E_1 (whose solutions were illustrated as usual) ; then C_1 was given and followed by E_4. After E_4 had been on the blackboard for the usual two and one-half minutes, the E solution for it was illustrated as in E_1; in addition, subjects were told, "This is the rule for this type of problem." After this, C_3, C_4, the extinction task, C_1, and C_2 were presented, in that order, at intervals of two and one-half minutes. This experiment allows comparison of the influence on the same class of one E problem but with no rule explicitly formulated, with the influence of one E problem plus a rule; it also allows comparison of solutions of the same critical (C_1) before and after the rule is offered.

After the first E problem, only five of the forty subjects solved C_1 by the E procedure; following E_4 plus the rule, these five subjects showed complete E effects, all solving the criticals by the E method and failing the extinction task. The remaining thirty-five subjects, who had no E solutions of C_1 at first, gave 60 per cent E solutions of it when it followed the rule, and showed large E effects in the other test problems. After the rule was presented, the class, as a whole, showed E effects as large as shown by elementary-school groups in the basic experiment.

Before rule ...... E_1: 97% E, 3% F C_1: 13% E E_4: 62% E, 38% F
After rule .... C_3: 80% E C_4: 73% E Ext.: 65% F C_1: 65% E C_2: 75% E

The results of the present and the previously described experiments show that the influence of one E task or two E tasks may be quite different depending on whether or not the E method is presented as the rule of solution. It would seem that one E task (or two E tasks) plus the formulation of the E method as a rule can be equivalent, in the strength of E effects yielded, to mechanization resulting from repetition of the E method in a series of successive E tasks.

The findings suggest that attitudes toward the E method and the problems may influence the relationship between frequency and E effects. The findings raise the question: For different attitudes toward the E method and toward the problems, does the relationship between E effects and frequency differ? It has been suggested that diverse processes may underlie E effects so that, for example, in some but not all cases generalization may produce E effects. Hence, a related question: For diverse processes that underlie or produce E effects, does the relationship between frequency of E tasks and E effects differ? For example, subjects who generalize the E method as a rule may need fewer E tasks to attain a certain strength of E effects than subjects who do not. To study adequately the questions that were raised calls for further experimental variations as well as for the development of better techniques than are presently available for ascertaining subjects' attitudes toward the tasks and toward the E method and for determining the processes that produce E effects in a given subject.

We want to remind the reader that in the experiment last described, there was only 13 per cent E solution of C_1 the first time it occurred (when only E_1 preceded it). Far more E effects were obtained when another elementary-school class received the usual test problems after E_1; as reported earlier in this chapter, this class showed 64 per cent E solutions of C_1C_2. While not many experiments have been conducted with only one E task given prior to the test problems, it is our impression that there is a wider range of E effects under this condition than in the basic experiment where five E tasks precede the criticals and that attitudinal factors are very important.

> The situation is much more labile; attitudinal factors play a very large role. One may with such a set-up, one E before the criticals, obtain no E responses at all in the later problems or E responses in each of them. In the simplest case, the one result or the other will be obtained depending on whether the subject or group of subjects believes or does not believe that the problems subsequent to the one E problem are intended for application of the method used there. (Luchins, 1942, p. 69, n.)

It is interesting to speculate whether there is a certain range of E tasks—perhaps from four to six—which tends to yield a narrower range of E effects and wherein attitudinal factors are less important than when fewer or more E tasks are presented.

Repetition of One E Task Five Times. Formulations of principles of exercise or frequency generally imply a repetition of the "same" stimulus situation and/or of the "same" response. Since the same problem was not repeated in the basic experiment, we turn to variations (Luchins, 1942, pp. 70-71) in which the same E problem, E_1, was presented five times in lieu of the usual five E problems. Subjects were elementary-school and college students in New York City.

Two sixth-grade classes were told that the problem was being repeated "so that you will learn the solution well." They used the E method repeatedly in E_1 without any overt protest. Their E effects were as large as shown by elementary-school groups in the basic experiment.

36 subjects .... C_1C_2: 75% E Ext.: 64% F C_3C_4: 75% E
41 subjects .... C_1C_2: 89% E Ext.: 68% F C_3C_4: 78% E

In another variation thirty-six children in a fifth-grade class were not told why E_1 was being presented five times but, with each presentation of this problem, they were told, "Now please do it again." This time there were a few children whose faces and comments registered surprise at the repetition. In this class also E effects were large: C_1C_2: 75% E; Ext.: 72% F; C_3C_4: 71% E.

Another fifth-grade class received E_1 five times without any remarks or explanation by the experimenter which would indicate that he was aware that the same problem was being repeated. With the first presentation of E_1, the subjects were told that they must not call out and that they should do each example given to them. When E_1 was introduced each time as the "next example," astonishment and chagrin were reflected on some faces. Some children wrote, "Why are you repeating it?" (Such signs of surprise were more marked and more frequent than in the just-described variation.) When C_1 was presented there were gasps of joy and the problem was apparently attacked with zeal. Yet E effects were as large as shown by elementary-school groups in the basic experiment: C_1C_2: 75% E; Ext.: 63% F; C_3C_4: 65% E.

After the experiment the children were asked to write why they thought the same example had been given five times. Three children gave no answer. Most children answered that they thought this was done to help them learn or understand or memorize the method of solution; to see that they did not forget it; to prepare them for the problem or the solution or the method in a test; to teach them a rule or method that would help them in future problems. Some said that they thought it was repeated because it was hard and not done by some children; because they were supposed to do it faster than before; or because they were supposed to be patient and do it again without making a fuss. Thus, we see that, when subjects were given no explanation for the repetition, they were puzzled by the repetition and concocted a variety of explanations.

The last-described procedure (in which subjects were told on the first presentation of E_1 not to call out and in which, in lieu of the other E tasks, E_1 was repeatedly introduced as the "next example") was also used in a college class of twenty-nine subjects. Signs of astonishment and chagrin were more noticeable than in any of the elementary-school groups. Moreover, the college students' facial expressions, bodily gestures, and written comments bespoke boredom and even annoyance at the repetition. While some E effects were found, failures of the extinction task and E solutions of C_3C_4 were particularly low;

results were: C_1C_2: 52% E; Ext.: 17% F; C_3C_4: 28% E. These results, which reveal less E effects than shown by college groups in the basic experiment, suggest that in some cases repetition of one E task five times may yield different E effects than result from the use of five different E tasks.

After the experiment, college students were asked to write why they thought the same problem was repeated and what their reactions had been to the repetition. Some wrote that the repetition had seemed pointless when it occurred but that, in retrospect, they believed that it was done to make them fall into a rut. A few subjects said that it was done to see if they would vary their methods or guess at a rule. Some wrote that they had sought reasons for the repetition, had been bored by it, had become tired of giving the same answer, had hoped that a different problem would be given, had waited for something to change, or had been on their guard for a trap.

On the whole, college students' comments concerning the repetition of one problem were rather different than those made by the elementary-school children. While the comments given by the children implied that they thought the problem was being repeated so that they could learn it better, this was not true of most college subjects' comments. Such a difference is understandable both because the children were more accustomed to repetition of a problem or of problems of one type, as in isolated drill in teaching arithmetical skills, and because the problem presumably constituted a more difficult task for the children than for the college students so that some practice may have seemed justified to them.

Comparison of E Effects After the Same Frequency of (Repeated or Nonrepeated) Variable or Nonvariable Problems. We think it worth while to consider here briefly four experiments which were discussed, from another point of view, in Chapter VII, "Variability and Rigidity." We summarize the experiments by noting that, prior to a series of new test problems, four problems—let us call them practice problems —were presented in each experiment. For practice problems, Experiment 1 had four different nonvariable problems (that is, only the E method could be used in each); Experiment 2 had a nonvariable problem (E_2) presented four times; Experiment 3 had four different variable problems (that is, each could be solved by the E method as well as by other methods); and Experiment 4 had a variable problem (10, 25, 5, get 5) presented four times. The six test problems, used in all four experiments, consisted of four new criticals (C_1' through C_4'), each solvable by many methods, including $B - A - 2C$, $A - C$, $B - 2A$, and C, the filling of one jar; a new E problem, E_6, solvable by the

$B - A - 2C$ method; and a final problem, solvable by none of these methods but by a new method, $2A - C$. Subjects were 120 Montreal high-school students with thirty in each experiment. Their results in the test problems are contained in Table IX.

TABLE IX. RESULTS IN TEST PROBLEMS FOLLOWING THE SAME
FREQUENCY OF (REPEATED OR NONREPEATED) VARIABLE
OR NONVARIABLE PROBLEMS (THIRTY SUBJECTS
IN EACH EXPERIMENT)

Experiment Type of Practice Problem	% E C_1'	% E C_2'	% E C_3'	% E C_4'	% E E_6	% Solution, % E Final Problem $(2A-C)$
1............Four nonvariable problems	76	76	70	70	90	30
2............One nonvariable problem four times	83	76	66	63	96	30
3............Four variable problems	57	50	50	40	87	40
4............One variable problem four times	10	13	13	13	90	67

Compare the results in Experiments 3 and 4, where the practice problems allowed several methods, with those in Experiments 1 and 2, where the practice problems were nonvariable in nature. It is seen that, following the nonvariable practice problems, where the E method had to be used, about two-thirds to three-quarters of the subjects continued to use the E method. It is interesting that most subjects in Experiment 2 complained of boredom when the one nonvariable problem was repeated and yet did not shift to a new method when the criticals were given; apparently the use of the $B - A - 2C$ method with different jars was sufficient novelty. Following the variable practice problems (where most subjects did not use the E method), only about one half of the subjects in Experiment 3 and only about a tenth of the subjects in Experiment 4 used the E method in the criticals; the others solved the criticals by simpler methods. Despite the less frequent use of the E method by the subjects in Experiments 3 and 4, their percentages of E solutions of E_6—where the E method was the only one available—compares favorably with those shown by the subjects in Experiments 1 and 2. Moreover, the last problem, which required a shift to a new method, $2A - C$, was solved more often after the variable practice problems (Experiments 3 and 4) than after the nonvariable ones (Experiments 1 and 2). If a shift to the $2A - C$ method is considered as an indication of less rigidity or less blinding effects or of better (more efficient) learning of a new method, then it may be said that the least rigidity or the least blinding effects or the best learning occurred in Experiment 4. This was the experiment where the one variable problem, presented four times, permitted among other solutions a one-jar solution, a solution favored by many subjects. The four variable problems used in Experiment 3 did not permit a one-jar solution; one wonders what results would have been obtained if four other variable problems had been used that did permit such a solution.

The results described so far suggest that not only the frequency of stimulus situations given for practice, but also their nature—in particular, whether they permit a choice of solutions or only one solution, and the kinds of solutions they permit—may be determinants of the influence of the practice.

In Experiment 4, where the variable practice problem was presented four times, eleven subjects gave the one-jar solution every time this problem was presented and also used the one-jar solution in each critical; thus, they used the one-jar method eight times prior to the last two problems. Six subjects in this experiment used the two-jar solution, $A - C$, in each presentation of the practice problem and in every critical. Although the E method could be used throughout the practice and critical problems, no subject used it in Experiment 4 whereas some did in the other experiments, where it was the only method common to these problems. Table X compares the results in the last two problems of subjects who had eight prior usages of the E method (Experiments 1, 2, and 3), of the one-jar method (Experiment 4), or of the two-jar method (Experiment 4).

TABLE X. RESULTS IN TEST PROBLEMS FOLLOWING
EIGHT USAGES OF ONE METHOD

Exper-iment	Type of Practice Problem	Sub-jects	Method Used Eight Times	% E E_8	% Solution, Final Problem $(2A - C)$
1	Four nonvariable problems	20	$B - A - 2C$	90	20
2	One nonvariable problem four times	16	$B - A - 2C$	100	25
3	Four variable problems	11	$B - A - 2C$	100	54
4	One variable problem four times	6	$A - C$	83	50
4	One variable problem four times	11	C	90	72

Consider those subjects in Experiments 1, 2, and 3 who had the same frequency of repetition of the E method (eight times). The subjects in Experiment 3, all of whom solved E_6, had more than twice as high a proportion of solutions of the final problem as those in Experiments 1 and 2. In Experiment 3 the practice problems allowed several methods of solution so that the repeated use of the E method in them may have represented a choice. But in Experiments 1 and 2 there was no choice in the practice problems; the E method was "forced" on the subject if he wanted to solve these problems. The results suggest that —with the method kept constant and with the same frequency of repetition—less rigidity or less blinding effects or better learning of a new method was fostered by the use of choice situations in the initial practice period.

Those subjects in Experiment 4 who used the two-jar solution, $A - C$, eight times had 50 per cent solution of the final problem while those who used the one-jar method eight times had 72 per cent solution of it. This suggests that the kind of choice which is made in prior variable problems may itself influence subsequent learning of a new method (or blinding effects or rigidity).

It would seem that learning may be influenced not only by repetition of a method but by the context in which the repetitions are made—whether or not they are choice situations—as well as by the kind of choice that is made of a method to be repeated.

Comments

What may be concluded about the relationship between frequency of E response or frequency of presentation of E problems and extent of E effects? To begin with, it should be noted that the relationships have been studied only for groups and not for the same individual after varying numbers of E tasks or E responses. Moreover, the particular relationship between frequency and strength of E effects depends in part on how each is measured and on the particular subjects studied. It was found that, with the number of E tasks held constant, as in the basic experiment, the extent of E effects did vary with the number of E responses, as revealed through comparison of the results for the did-no-E, did-no-E_4E_5, did-E_4E_5, did-all-E groups (Luchins, 1942, p. 16). This suggests that repetition of E responses may be more significantly related to strength of Einstellung than repetition of stimulus patterns corresponding to E problems. Certainly the extent of E effects did not seem to be independent of the frequency of E responses; yet such independence might be inferred from Guthrie's or from Wheeler's views. But neither did E effects increase with each repetition of the E response as might be inferred from learning theories that invoke principles of exercise, frequency, incremental gain in habit strength, increase in extent of trace systems with repetition of process, etc.

Experimental variations suggested that the relationship between frequency and E effects may differ for different prevailing attitudes toward the tasks and toward the repetition of the problems and/or the response. For example, when the E method was presented as a rule, one E task yielded E effects as large as were obtained in the basic experiment with five E tasks. To cite another example: children who apparently interpreted the repeated presentation of a problem to mean that they were supposed to "learn" the method well showed larger E effects than college students who did not give this interpretation. Results hint that the relationship between frequency and E effects may possibly differ when different processes produce E effects. Our findings show the importance to the relationship between frequency and learning of the context in which repetition or practice occurs—whether, for example, in a context that permits several methods of solution or only one method. Although it was not explicitly pointed out in this chapter, we note here that the broader context in which repetition occurs may also be important; for example, under speed conditions two E problems were found to produce E effects as strong as were produced by five E problems in the basic experiment.

In general, whether one E task or many E tasks were presented, and whether the E response was made only a few times or many times, there were some subjects who showed E effects in subsequent test problems and others who did not. Situational and attitudinal factors helped to determine whether an individual developed a strong set with a few E tasks or resisted the development of a set even after many such tasks. Knowledge of the frequency of occurrence of stimulus pattern or response was not sufficient information on which to predict behavior in the test problems. Thus, none of the generalizations which learning theorists have drawn about frequency of response or frequency of stimulus proved completely adequate to account for results obtained in the Einstellung situations. Particularly neglected in these generalizations are individual differences, including differences in attitude towards the tasks and their repetition. The very important issue of how the repetition is viewed by the particular learner, of its role and function in the particular learning situation, has not been adequately taken into account in generalizations relating learning and frequency; nor has the related problem of what kind and degree of similarity must prevail between responses (or two stimuli) in order that they may be considered "repeated" or "identical," and from whose point of view the similarity ought to be adjudged.

Moreover, the relationship between present response and past frequency of a similar response, has tended to be treated as if frequency were the independent numerical variable and present response the dependent variable; that is, as if the relationship may be expressed symbolically as $r = g(f)$ where r represents present response, f past frequency of the response, and $g(f)$ a function of the frequency. (Cf. Luchins and Luchins, 1954b, for discussion of such terms as "dependent variable," "independent variable," and "function," as used in psychology and in mathematics.) Our experimental findings suggest that this may not be an adequate formulation, that the frequency may not (or at least may not always) be the independent variable on which the response depends. Rather, present response may be determined by attitudes, interpretations, cognitive grasp of a situation, and on other processes which themselves may be functions of frequency of repetition (as well as functions of other variables). Hence, present response may be more adequately characterized as a function of functions of frequency; e.g., $r = g(p_1(f), p_2(f), \ldots)$ where r represents present response, g a certain functional relationship, $p_1(f)$ a particular function of the frequency, $p_2(f)$ another function of the frequency, and so on. In short, the relationship between present response and past frequency may not be that of a function of an independent variable but may be closer to that of a function of functions of a numerical variable (a functional in mathematical terminology). The distinction is not a trivial one since, mathematically speaking, other procedures are often needed in dealing with functionals than are used in dealing with functions of a finite number of independent numerical variables. Implications that can be derived from mathematics for the treatment of functionals in psychology are beyond the scope of this monograph.

CHAPTER XII

ASSOCIATION AS A FORCE FOR SPONTANEOUS REPRODUCTION

WHETHER or not an association can serve as a force toward spontaneous reproduction of a response is a controversial issue. Before considering whether or not such spontaneous reproduction occurs in the Einstellung situation, let us turn to the controversy itself. Classical association theorists maintained that an association could produce a mental event, i.e., that the energy or motor for thinking could come from the bond between one item and another. Such a conception was seriously disputed by Kurt Lewin (1926). Modifying the technique of paired associations employed by Ach (1910), Lewin found that Item A (one nonsense syllable) of an associative bond tended to reinstate Item B (another syllable) only when the subject had the intention or set to reproduce. Lewin concluded that the association between A and B does not suffice to ensure reproduction of B (or A) when the other item is given. More generally, he asserted that the couplings created by habit "never supply as such the motor of a mental event . . . in all cases certain mental *energies*, originating as a rule in a pressure of will or needs, i.e., mental systems *under stress*, are the necessary conditions of mental events" (1926, p. 311). Analogously, the energy for the movement of a train, Lewin pointed out, comes not from the couplings connecting the cars but from the power of the locomotive. He concluded that automatic or spontaneous reproduction —reproduction without the intention to reproduce—is not possible; the motor must be a mental act, intention, or set to reproduce.

So striking in its implications was this rejection by Lewin of an automatic tendency to reproduction, that it has come to be regarded as an essential feature of the Gestalt theory of thinking. However, all Gestalt psychologists do not share Lewin's views in this respect; e.g., Koffka agrees with Lewin that the definition of an association as a motor does not make sense and that the attitude or set of the subject may be an important determinant of whether or not reproduction occurs, but he claims that automatic or spontaneous reproduction "should be perfectly possible" (Koffka, 1935, p. 572). From the principle that the trace's influence on the process will be such as to maintain or increase the trace's stability, Koffka derives the auxiliary principle that, when a process communicates with a part of a trace system, the whole trace system exerts a force on the process in the direction of making it as complete as it was when it created this trace system (1935,

p. 567). He therefore hypothesizes that, when one of the parts of a trace system is in communication with a process (actually it is a part process in the sense that it is a revival of part of a larger process that gave rise to the trace system), then the trace system may be subjected to new tension or stress which can be relieved by the continuation of the process until there is re-established "the whole process that gave rise to the whole trace" (p. 568). Koffka notes that not all traces are so constituted that asymmetrical communication gives rise to stress. He notes that traces resulting from rote learning are particularly apt to become endowed with tension through communication with part processes, perhaps because they form more or less isolated, self-sufficient systems whereas most other traces "must be connected with innumerable other trace systems" (p. 588). In short, Koffka implies that communication between part of a process and a trace system, by producing tension in the trace, is apt to create a force toward spontaneous reproduction of the whole process, but that this does not mean that such spontaneous reproduction must inevitably occur. Koffka suggests that such spontaneous reproduction did not occur in Lewin's experiment because the revival of the part process did not communicate with the trace system which had resulted from the whole process. In terms of association theory, this means that, when an AB bond has been established, recurrence of A need not carry with it a tendency to rearouse B because the recurrence of A does not necessarily communicate with the AB trace. Thus, instead of bearing on the effect of a trace upon a process, Lewin's results are seen as bearing on the effect produced by a process on the trace system. The fact that reproduction did occur when the subject had appropriate attitudes, is interpreted by Koffka as signifying that these attitudes brought about communication between the A process and the AB trace. This is in line with Koffka's thesis, to which we have referred, that forces stemming from an ego system can be powerful factors in producing communication between process and trace.

Finally, Koffka deals with the relationship between his thesis of possible spontaneous reproduction and the energy principle emphasized by Lewin. For every mental event, Lewin insists, the question must be raised as to the origin of the effective energies, since, in order for a process to occur, energy capable of doing work must be set free. This energy aspect, Koffka claims, is satisfied by the trace theory of spontaneous reproduction; when the whole trace system is put under new tension, because of the fact that only one of its parts is in communication with a process, the energy put into the trace system by the tension goes to work to continue the process or perhaps liberates other energy stored in the brain field that continues the process.

Application of the Association Theory
to the Einstellung Situation

Classical association theory implies that an individual repeats the E method whenever there occurs a problem to which he has associated this method and that this reproduction is automatic, so that it occurs even if he has no intention to reproduce the E response. Lewin would presumably object to such an interpretation and insist that reproduction of the E method presupposes an appropriate intention or attitude on the subject's part. While Koffka presumably would not deny the importance of attitudes in creating an Einstellung, he would conceive of spontaneous reproduction as possible in certain cases.

It is not a simple matter to decide which interpretation is most adequate. For a subject who did not reproduce the E method, it is difficult to determine whether he failed to establish an association between this method and the problems or whether the particular problem at hand failed to rearouse the E response even though such an association had been established; only the latter case would contradict the doctrine of spontaneous reproduction. In the case of a subject who did utilize the E method in the criticals, it is difficult to determine whether or not there was in operation an intention to reproduce. Questioning of subjects after the experiment elicited responses from some indicating that they had not been aware of any intention to reproduce one method or even aware that they were repeatedly using one procedure; but it is conceivable that such an intention existed without awareness on the subject's part or that replies to questioning were not accurate.

In order to gain information more relevant to the issue of association as a force for reproduction, experimental variations were undertaken in which, prior to the administration of the volume-measuring problems, associations were established that involved elements of the direct solutions or of E solutions to the criticals.

Prior to receiving any of the volume-measuring problems, Montreal high-school students, tested individually, were assigned the task of learning a "code." Although it was not introduced as preparation for the later tests, the code involved elements of direct solutions to the usual critical problems for some subjects (Group D), and elements of E solutions to these problems for other subjects (Group E). The subjects received four pairs of cards corresponding to the four criticals, each pair consisting of a "stimulus card" and a "response card." It will be remembered that the first critical can be solved by $23 - 3 = 20$ or by $49 - 23 - 3 - 3 = 20$. The first stimulus card for subjects in each group contained the number 20; for subjects in Group D the first response card contained the numbers 23, 3, in that order, while for subjects in Group E it contained the numbers 49, 23, 3, 3, in that order. The Group D subjects were told to learn "to reply 23, 3 when you see 20," and the Group E subjects "to reply 49, 23, 3, 3 when you see 20." Similarly, the second task in the association-learning period required a subject in Group D "to reply 15, 3 when you see 18," and a subject in Group E "to reply 39, 15, 3, 3 when you see 18," etc.

In order to increase the number of elements of the solutions involved in the associations, other subjects, who also received four pairs of cards, were required to learn not only the numbers involved in the direct or E solutions to the criticals but also the connecting mathematical symbols. Subjects in Group $D\pm$ were "to reply $23 - 3$ when you see 20, $15 + 3$ when you see 18, $18 + 4$ when you see 22, $14 - 8$ when you see 6." Subjects in Group $E\pm$ were "to reply $49 - 23 - 3 - 3$ when you see 20, $39 - 15 - 3 - 3$ when you see 18, etc."

For each subject the four stimulus cards were presented, one at a time, and the corresponding response card was shown only if the subject did not give the correct response. The cards were presented until the subject met the criterion of correct responses to all stimulus cards in five successive trials. About one minute after this criterion was met, the subject received some of the problems of the basic experiment. These experiments were conducted with the assistance of L. Friedman, Beatrice Galler, S. Martin, and Barbara Rosen.

Of the forty-four subjects in Group D, twenty-four received the basic experiment with only the extinction task omitted, while the remainder received the two illustrative problems followed by the four criticals (four E tasks were omitted). Of the thirty-eight subjects in Group E, eighteen received the basic experiment with only the extinction task lacking, while for the others four E tasks also were omitted. If an association serves as a force for automatic reproduction of the response whenever the stimulus appears, then the volume stipulated in a critical problem should have aroused the corresponding learned association and thereby fostered direct solutions for those in Group D and E solutions for those in Group E. This leads to an expectation of more E solutions of the criticals for Group E than Group D. But the findings do not support such an expectation.

Criticals following E tasks .... Group D: 78% E   Group E: 70% E

Criticals following illustrative tasks .... Group D: 10% E   Group E: 5% E

The results clearly show that, regardless of which associations (E elements or D elements) were learned, E responses to the criticals predominated after the E tasks while such responses were infrequent when four E tasks were omitted. This implies that the sequence of problems (or the structure of the problem-solving series) determined responses far more than did associations established prior to the giving of the problems.

Consider now responses made by Groups $D\pm$ and $E\pm$. There were twenty subjects in each of these groups; half of the subjects in each group received the basic experiment with the extinction problem omitted while the others received the four criticals immediately after the illustrative tasks. If an association serves as a force for spontaneous reproduction, then the volume stipulated in a critical should have aroused the corresponding association and thereby fostered direct solutions for those in Group $D\pm$ and E solutions for those in Group $E\pm$. Thus Group $E\pm$ would be expected to have substantially more E solutions of the criticals than Group $D\pm$. But the results do not uphold this expectation.

Criticals following E tasks .... Group $D\pm$: 71% E Group $E\pm$: 61% E

Criticals following illustrative tasks .. Group $D\pm$: 3% E Group $E\pm$: 6% E

Once more we see that, regardless of which associations were established, E responses to the criticals predominated when these tasks were preceded by the E tasks while such responses were infrequent when four E tasks were omitted. Despite the fact that subjects learned associations involving both numbers and related arithmetical symbols, differential associations apparently did not promote differential responses. The fact that the results yielded by Groups $D\pm$ and $E\pm$ do not differ significantly from the results yielded by Groups D and E, respectively, implies that a greater number of common elements between the learned association and a solution to a critical, did not favor reproduction of the associated response. (We shall return to this point in the next chapter on transfer of training.)

Note that Group E had less E solutions of the criticals than Group D both when these problems followed the E tasks and when they followed the illustrative tasks and that Group $E\pm$ had less E solutions of the criticals than Group $D\pm$ when these problems followed the E tasks. Thus, three of the four comparisons show that the subjects who learned associations involving E elements actually gave proportionately fewer E responses in the criticals than subjects who learned associations involving D elements—quite contrary to expectations derived from the doctrine of spontaneous reproduction.

It should also be noted that there was no consistent relationship between the kind of solution a subject gave to the critical problems, and the number of times the series of paired cards had to be presented in the association-learning period before he met the criterion. For example, of two subjects in Group D who gave direct solutions to all the critical problems, one had twelve presentations prior to the first re-

sponse that helped to meet the criterion, the maximum number of presentations required by any subject in this group, while another had
only two presentations.

COMMENTS

How can we account for the findings? A clue may lie in answers that
subjects gave to one of the questions asked at the end of the experiment.
Pointing to the critical problems, the experimenter asked, "Did you
remember or recognize the numbers you memorized when you worked
on these problems?" Only about one-fifth of the 122 subjects claimed
complete or partial recognition. It is important to note that, when the
code numbers were recognized in a volume-measuring problem, the
method of solution generally (but not always) utilized the code numbers. However, four-fifths of the subjects claimed not to have recognized or remembered the numbers while working on the problems.
Such claims predominated in every group, whether the associations had
involved elements of the E or of the direct method, and whether they
had involved numbers only or numbers together with arithmetical
symbols.

Recognition was not related to the number of times the series of
paired cards had been presented in the association-learning period.
For example, in Group D, a subject with two presentations claimed
that the numbers in the problems had looked vaguely familiar but that
he had not realized just where he had seen them and had been too busy
solving the problems to think about them, a subject who had had eleven
presentations claimed not to have recognized the numbers at all, a subject with twelve presentations claimed complete recognition; of two
subjects in Group E, each of whom had had eight presentations, one
claimed that he had not recognized the numbers while the other claimed
that he had.

It is noteworthy that claims of nonrecognition predominated even
when the criticals followed immediately after presentation of the illustrative problems, despite the fact that less than one minute usually
elapsed between the end of the association-learning period and the
presentation of illustrative problems and the criticals. If the claims are
correct (and there seems to be little reason to doubt them), then it
hardly seems plausible to attribute the failure of recognition to sheer
forgetting brought about by lapse of time. But to what can the lack of
recognition be attributed? We think that the answer lies in the combination of dual factors: task and context.

The same numbers occurred in two contexts: once in the context of
the code session where one number was the stimulus and the other

numbers the response and, later, in the context of the volume-measuring problems where these numbers represented the volume of fluid to be obtained and the capacity of the containers, respectively. Lack of recognition of the fact that the same numbers were presented twice may be traced to differences in the two contexts in which the numbers occurred and to differences in their roles and functions in these two contexts.

Most subjects apparently regarded the volume-measuring problems as constituting tasks which were separate and distinct from the code learning. "I didn't see any connection between the code learning and the solving of the water problems," summarizes their viewpoint. As far as they were concerned, testing for their memory of the code responses was over and done with when they had met the criterion for success, and the illustrative problems introduced a new task. Here we may be seeing the influence of a task or *Aufgabe* on recognition of associated items and hence on the spontaneous reproduction of such items. Our findings would seem to be in line with Lewin's thesis that an intention or "set" other than an intention to reproduce may not favor the arousal or reproduction of an association. A familiar analogy may be found in the case of the unmailed letter and the letter box. Until the letter is mailed, the sight of a letter box may create a "tension toward completion"; once it is mailed, the sight of a letter box does not create any tensions. So it was in our study. Once the criterion for the code learning had been met, the sight of a "20" or any of the other stimuli used in the association-learning period no longer created tensions, no longer served as a vector pointing toward the learned response.

Differences in both contexts and tasks (as viewed by the subject) seem to have contributed to nonrecognition, in the problem-solving context, of numbers involved in the associations. Experimental investigations remain to be undertaken to study the influence on recognition, of various degrees of difference in tasks alone or in contexts alone or in both tasks and contexts. For example, one might attempt to lessen differences in the contexts by referring to the numbers presented in the association-learning period as capacities of jars, or by designating the volumes required in the criticals by showing again the stimulus cards used in the association period, or one might attempt to lessen differences in the tasks by telling subjects during the association period that they will need the code later on or by referring to the code just before presentation of the first volume-measuring problem or just before presentation of the first critical or even every critical.

That differences in contexts or differences in tasks (*Aufgaben*) should interfere with the spontaneous reproduction of one associated item when the other associated item appears, is not in accord with the traditional doctrine of spontaneous reproduction. This doctrine holds that, if an association has been established between X and Y, and if X appears, then it should automatically lead to the recall of Y. The context in which X occurs is not taken into account; the association between X and Y is assumed to be formed and to operate independently of the context in which X and Y occur. A strict "elementaristic" account of the formation and operation of an association must be embarrassed by evidence that the nature of the task and the nature of the context are factors determining the formation and the future of the association. Such factors have been stressed in Gestalt-oriented interpretations of associations (or traces) as constituting products of organization (Köhler, 1941; Koffka, 1935).

Our findings are related to Lewin's variation of Ach's experiments. It may be remembered that, in discussing Lewin's investigations, Koffka comments that what happened therein may be described as the failure of X to arouse an XY trace (or association or bond) rather than the failure of the XY trace, once aroused, to reinstate Y. A similar interpretation may be given to our findings. We have not demonstrated that the association, say between "20" and "23, 3," fails to arouse "23, 3" when the whole associative bond is aroused. Rather, we found that—probably because of differences in contexts and tasks—the fact that the elements (23, 3, 20) were given, did not suffice to arouse the previously formed association.

Discussions of the thesis of spontaneous reproduction have been entangled by a failure of some of the participants in the discussions to realize that the traditional doctrine of spontaneous reproduction actually involves two premises: (1) if an association has been formed between X and Y, then, when one of these items occurs, the whole bond between X and Y will be aroused; (2) if this bond between X and Y is aroused, then there will be a tendency for the missing item to be reproduced or reinstated.

Our findings contradict the first premise. Indeed, when it is written in the form given above, the untenability of this first premise seems obvious. Since there may be a multitude of bonds all involving one of the items, say X, but not necessarily the other item Y, by what strange coincidence does the particular bond XY get rearoused just by the appearance of X?

As for the second premise, our findings are not conclusive but the few cases relevant to it seem to support this premise. When recognition of the numbers occurred—so that the association or trace or bond involving these numbers had a chance to be aroused—then the results generally were in line with what would be predicted if the association served as a force for reproduction.

In brief, contrary to the classical association theory, the findings indicate that spontaneous reproduction need not occur. Whether it *may* occur—as Koffka claims—is an issue which is still open.

CHAPTER XIII

TRANSFER OF TRAINING

A major problem in the psychology of learning pertains to the application or transfer to subsequent situations of what has been
learned. This is usually discussed under the rubric of transfer of learning or transfer of training. Elsewhere (Luchins, 1939) the results of
the basic experiment were interpreted in terms of transfer concepts.
Here we shall discuss experimental variations which seem to be pertinent to transfer-of-training issues.

THE THEORY OF IDENTICAL ELEMENTS
AND THE DOCTRINE OF A SPONTANEOUS REPRODUCTIVE TENDENCY

The "identical element" theory of transfer, expounded by Thorndike and others (see Woodworth, 1938), holds that transfer from one
situation to another depends on the presence of identical elements—
elements which are the same in the two situations—with the amount of
transfer considered to be roughly proportional to the number of these
identical elements.

> The question now arises as to where identities occur in the sequence of events
> from stimulus to response.... Most champions of the theory [of identical elements]
> stress identities in the stimulus fields. To react to identities in the midst of diversi-
> ties, they say, is the crux of transfer ... According to the theory, identities in the
> stimulus fields should *of themselves* arouse the habits to which they are bound.
> (Allport, 1937, pp. 270-71.)

Allport has offered a thoroughgoing critique of the identical-element
theory of transfer. We could not hope to improve on it. What we wish
to stress here is the relationship between this theory and the doctrine
of an automatic reproductive tendency. This theory of transfer holds
that identities in the stimulus field should by themselves arouse the
habits to which they are bound; note how closely this is linked to the
doctrine that stimuli arouse the associations to which they are attached.
The experimental findings reported in the previous chapter suggest that
the fact that an element in one situation is identical with an element in
another situation does not suffice, in the second situation, to arouse an
association or habit that was linked with the element in the first situation; for example, the number 20 which occurred in the context of a critical problem did not suffice to arouse the association which had been
attached to the number 20 in the preceding associative-learning situation. Our findings also suggest that it is necessary to distinguish identity

as viewed by the experimenter from identity as viewed by the subject; whether or not a subject regards two elements as identical may depend on their contexts and on various attitudinal factors, including attitudes toward the tasks in which the elements occur. Our findings therefore imply that differences in contextual embeddedness and in nature of the tasks, may influence explicit recognition of similarity (or identity) of elements and may also influence the degree of transfer from one situation to another.

EXPERIMENT ON IDENTICAL ELEMENTS

One might attempt to account for E effects on the ground that transfer to the test tasks of what was learned in the E tasks, was facilitated by the identical elements which these tasks shared. As examples of identical elements shared by these tasks, one might cite (depending in part on how the terms "identical" and "element" are defined) similarities in the nature of the problems (all volume-measuring problems), the parallel wording of the problems, and the fact that three jars were mentioned in each. There is another identity: when the problems were presented in written form, all the numbers were written in the same color (of ink, pencil, or chalk). Alteration of this superficial similarity was undertaken in a number of experimental variations.

In one series of experiments, the capacity of the center jar was written in red ink (in all the problems or in the E tasks only or in the test tasks only), whereas all other components of the problems were written in blue ink. In other variations, the capacities of the end jars were written in red ink (in all problems or in the E tasks only or in the test tasks only) while all other components of the problems were written in blue ink. With the assistance of Ruth Rohrlick and Edith Constantine, the experiments were administered individually to Montreal high-school and college students, with each problem written on a separate index card. The results are summarized in Table XI in terms of the percentages of E solutions of the criticals and the percentages of failures of the extinction task.

More identical elements were shared by the E tasks and test tasks when the center jar was red in all problems, than when it was red only in the former or only in the latter tasks. If transfer depended solely on the number of identical elements, then a greater amount of transfer from the E tasks to the test tasks (and hence more E effects) should have occurred when the center jar was red throughout. Yet, looking at the results of Experiments 1, 2, and 3, we find the reverse of this prediction: less E effects resulted when the center jar was red throughout than when it was red only in the E tasks or only in the test tasks. Moreover, if transfer depended solely on the number of identical elements, E effects should presumably have been the same regardless of whether the center jar was red only in the E tasks or only in the test tasks, since the number of elements common to the two types of tasks was the same in either variation; yet the table reveals that E effects differed somewhat for these variations.

TABLE XI. E EFFECTS WHEN THE PROBLEMS WERE WRITTEN IN
RED AND BLUE INK

Experiment	Description	Kind of Subjects	No. of Subjects	C_1C_2 %E	Ext. %F	C_3C_4 %E
1	Red center jar, all tasks	College	16	66	13	6
2	Red center jar, E tasks only	College	16	84	25	25
3	Red center jar, test tasks only	College	16	84	38	38
4	Red end jars, all tasks	College	15	53	40	40
5	Red end jars, E tasks only	College	15	73	67	60
6	Red end jars, test tasks only	College	15	87	47	37
7	Red end jars, E tasks only	High sch.	20	55	20	33
8	Red end jars, test tasks only	High sch.	20	73	50	53

With reference to the red end jars, the identical-element theory of transfer leads to the expectations that (1) more E effects should have occurred when the end jars were red throughout than when they were red in only some of the tasks, since more identical elements were present in the former instance, and (2) E effects should have been the same whether the end jars were red only in the E tasks or only in the test tasks, since the number of identical elements remained invariant. Yet the results of Experiments 4, 5, and 6 do not substantiate these expectations.

Moreover, since the number of identical elements was the same whether the center jar was red or the end jars were red (in all problems, in the E tasks only, or in the test problems only, respectively), E effects should have been about equal for Experiments 1 and 4, for Experiments 2 and 5, and for Experiments 3 and 6; yet these variations differed in the amounts of E effects they yielded.

Finally, when the experiments involving red end jars in the E tasks only or in the test tasks only were administered to high-school students, the relative direction of results was about the reverse of that obtained with college students; for the high-school subjects red end jars in the test tasks consistently yielded more E effects than red end jars in the E tasks, while for the college subjects the latter variation yielded more E effects than the former in the extinction task and in Criticals 3 and 4.

Thus, despite the equality of the number of identical elements in these variations, different strengths of E effects (or different amounts of transfer) occurred for different kinds of subjects.

Answers to questions at the close of each experimental session, and comments during the session, revealed a multitude of reactions to the "identical" elements. Thus, a few subjects apparently never noticed that inks of two different colors were used in writing the problems, and their lack of observation was somewhat more frequent when the two colors were used in every problem. Even among those who did notice the two colors, reactions varied considerably. We found that, in Experiment 3, where the center jar was red beginning in the test tasks, subjects' responses to the question, "Why do you think the center jar was red in some problems?" included the following: "I don't know"; "To make me notice it because it was the one to start with"; "Because it was the biggest number"; "Because you did not need to use it." In Experiment 4, where the end jars were red in all problems, subjects' answers to the question why they thought those jars were red, included the following: "I can't think of any reason for it"; "I noticed it but didn't even think of it"; "I thought you ran out of ink of one color and therefore used two colors"; "To test my powers of observation by seeing if I'd notice them"; "To make you see that the problems can be worked out an easier way by using only those two"; "Because you had to subtract them from the middle jar"; "They were the smallest numbers"; "Because only the center was blue, I felt that it should be used." Here we see that reactions in the same variation ranged from failure to think about the different colors to inability to think of a reason for them, and from interpretations likely to work against E effects to interpretations likely to promote E effects. The comments indicate that what are regarded as identical elements (or as different elements) by the experimenter, may not be recognized as such by the subjects, and that subjects' reactions to the same elements may vary considerably. Hence, we raise the problems: What is identity? And from whose point of view must "identity" be evaluated?

As has been indicated, the experimental evidence speaks against an explanation of E effects in terms of the identical-element theory of transfer. E effects seemed to be influenced by the subjects' attitudes toward the E tests and test tasks, and no consistent relationship prevailed between such attitudes and the number of identical elements shared by these tasks. Hence, while it may be theoretically feasible to interpret E effects in terms of transfer, and to regard the strength of E effects as an index of the amount of transfer, the experimental findings do not support the contention that the amount of transfer is (even roughly) proportional to the number of identical elements.

Of course, this does not obviate the possibility that transfer from one situation to another requires a certain kind or certain amount of "identity" between the two situations; but perhaps this "identity" cannot be measured sheerly in terms of the quantity of common elements. One may also have to take into account the nature of these elements as well as the number and nature of various common relationships and aspects that cannot adequately be described as elements. It is known that, when a melody is transposed (played in another key), even though all the notes are changed, the melody may still be recognized (by many listeners) as the "same" melody that it was before the transposition; and, yet, when the melody's keynote (tonic, basal note) is the only note changed, the melody may be altered quite beyond recognition. Conceivably, there is something akin to the melody's keynote that makes the E tasks sufficiently "identical" to the test tasks (at least for some subjects) to facilitate transfer from the former to the latter tasks; changing this keynote in, say, the test tasks, may drastically reduce transfer (at least for these subjects), while changing other "elements" or other aspects or relationships may have less striking influences on transfer. Experimentation is needed to discover what can be varied between the E tasks and test tasks, and what must remain invariant or "identical" between these tasks, in order that subjects of various kinds may manifest E effects.

In short, the results imply that the number of elements that are common to two situations may not be the crux of the determinant of the amount of transfer from one situation to the other. The possibility remains that there are some components which must remain "identical" if E effects are to occur; but then it may be necessary to speak specifically of these components and of the roles they play in fostering E effects, and not simply to talk about the number of identical elements, as is done in connection with the traditional identical-element theory of transfer.

TRANSFER OF GENERALIZATION

The theory of identical elements is not the only explanation of transfer. Often pitted against this theory (but sometimes viewed as compatible with it; cf. Woodworth, 1938) is the theory of transfer through generalization, in which a subject is said to transfer to the test series a method or a principle generalized or assumed during the training series (Judd, 1908; McGeoch and Irion, 1952, pp. 328-30). In terms of transfer of generalization, Einstellung effects may be explained as the transfer of a method or a principle (e.g., the $B - A - 2C$ method or a principle of subtraction) from the E tasks to the test tasks. Comments by subjects in the basic experiment suggest that E effects resulted in some instances from transfer of generalization. Thus, when questioned after the experiment, some subjects said they had discovered and used the rule that worked in all the problems (or all but one of the problems). Further evidence of the transfer of generalization is furnished by some experimental variations (Luchins, 1942, pp. 40, 67-69). While some of these variations were described in Chapter XI in connection with the role of frequency, it is appropriate to review them here.

A sixth-grade class of twenty-nine pupils received the test tasks immediately after presentation of the first E task. Yet they showed considerable E effects: C_1C_2, 64% E; Ext., 44% F; C_3C_4, 59% E. After the experiment, many of the children said that they thought they had to use throughout the method, rule, or formula that worked in E_1. (It may be that the teacher of this class often utilized isolated drill, particularly in arithmetic.)

We wondered what would happen to E effects if the E method was explicitly formulated as the rule or principle that solved the problems. Three sixth-grade elementary-school classes, with the aid of the experimenter, formulated this rule after the first E problem was presented: "Fill the middle jar, and from it pour out once into the jar to the left and twice into the jar to the right." This rule was written on the blackboard and left there for the duration of the experiment. The test problems were then given. Although only one E task had been given, E effects were as large as in the basic experiment: C_1C_2, from 87 to 100% E; Ext., from 73 to 85% F; C_3C_4, from 87 to 100% E. E effects were greater than in the experiment described in the preceding paragraph wherein only one E task was presented but no rule of solution was explicitly formulated; this suggests that transfer of the rule enhanced E effects.

In six other Grade 6 classes (totaling 232 subjects), after presentation of the first E problem, the rule of solution was formulated and written (and left) on the blackboard; but then the remaining E tasks were also presented, followed by the test tasks. E effects were very high: C_1C_2, from 96 to 100% E; Ext., from 97 to 100% F; C_3C_4, from 92 to 100% E. Three of the classes showed the maximum E effects possible (100%) in every test problem. Five E tasks, together with the rule, therefore, made for even stronger E effects than did one E task accompanied by the rule.

It is of interest that the procedure used in this experiment (formulation of the rule) was modeled after the lesson plan followed in some elementary schools in presenting a new type of arithmetical problem. It is very likely that some of the E effects found in the basic experiment are attributable to the influence of a similar general teaching procedure. Comments made by some of the subjects in the basic experiment revealed that they regarded it as a teaching situation and took it for granted that they were to practice the same method in all the problems. Further evidence is furnished by the fact that an elementary school wherein such a teaching procedure was not used, showed somewhat less E effects than the schools that used this procedure (Luchins, 1942, p. 13, p. 21). Thus, some cases of E effects in the basic experiment would seem to be attributable to transfer of a rule or principle, which in turn was perhaps prompted by the transfer to the experiment of an attitude developed by certain teaching procedures.

What would be the influence on E effects if the experimenter did not help the class to formulate a rule of solution, but instead asked the class to discover one. A college class and three elementary-school classes were told, before any problems were given, "While solving the subsequent tasks, try to generalize or discover a method of solution or a rule to solve these problems." The basic experiment was then presented and the results were fractionized according to whether or not subjects said they had generalized a method (or a rule). One hundred and nine subjects said that they had generalized the E method and twenty-six claimed not to have generalized any method or rule. E effects were very large for those who claimed to have drawn a generalization: C_1C_2, 100% E; Ext., from 86 to 100% F; C_3C_4, from 91 to 100% E. While E effects were not so large for those who claimed no generalization of a method or rule, they were still well within the range found in the basic experiment: C_1C_2, from 67 to 80% E; Ext., from 56 to 71% F; C_3C_4, from 67 to 80% E.

It would therefore seem that E effects can be brought about by transfer of a generalization or principle, but that they can also occur when no apparent generalization has taken place which could be transferred. Hence, transfer of principle or generalization may quite adequately account for some cases of E effects but apparently not for all.

Transfer Effect: Positive or Negative

The phrase "positive transfer effect" is often used to denote the transfer of a response to a situation wherein it is appropriate, the phrase "negative transfer effect" to denote the transfer of a response to a situation in which it is inappropriate. If some cases of E effects in the basic experiment are attributed to transfer (and the particular theory of transfer is immaterial here), then it is clear that negative transfer effects were involved, at least in the extinction task. A long-accepted generalization is that "the transfer effect is positive when an old response can be transferred to a new stimulus, but negative when a new response is required to an old stimulus" (Wylie, 1919). But this generalization does not seem quite adequate to account for E effects. Whether the test tasks should be described as "new stimuli" or as "old stimuli" depends on how these terms are defined. One might consider them as old stimuli on the ground that, like the E tasks, they are three-jar volume-measuring problems, or as new stimuli on the ground that they involve different numbers than those in the E tasks. But, if a critical task is designated as an old stimulus (or as a new stimulus), then the same designation may be applied to the extinction task. Suppose the test tasks are designated as new stimuli; then E responses to the criticals meet the criterion for positive transfer effects while failure of the extinction task does not fit the conditions mentioned in the generalization for either positive or negative transfer effects. On the other hand, if the test tasks are designated as old stimuli, failure of the extinction task meets the criterion for negative transfer effects, but E solutions of the criticals do not fit the conditions stipulated for either positive or negative transfer effects. It would seem that transfer can occur under conditions not covered by the generalization, and that the same response may or may not meet the criterion of positive (or negative) transfer effects, depending on the characterization of the stimulus. There is a need for sharper delineation of such terms as "new stimulus," "old stimulus," "positive transfer effect," and "negative transfer effect," as well as for further exposition of the conditions under which one or another effect occurs.

Whatever name may be given to it, the kind of "transfer" that occurred in the Einstellung situation frequently had detrimental influences on problem solving. The particular theory of transfer appealed to is immaterial here; the point is that apparently one can be blinded by a generalization, by an associative force, etc. Yet blinding effects of transfer are certainly not the goal of educators who are concerned with the results of transfer of educational experience. They are interested in providing school experiences that will transfer with beneficial influences, that will prepare the student to handle subsequent experiences more adequately. Analogously, we ask: What kind of experiences do we have to give an individual so that he will not become mechanized in the Einstellung situation; so that he will not transfer (whether consciously or unconsciously; whether the transfer is due to a generalization or to the force of an association) when such transfer does not meet the requirements of the problem; so that he will be free from the bondage of the generalization or the stimulus-response bond when either one interferes with productive problem solving? Experiments bearing on this problem will now be considered.

EXPERIENCES DESIGNED TO PREVENT E EFFECTS

Use of Problems Designed to Develop an Attitude of Variability

Before the basic experiment, subjects were provided with experiences intended to develop in them an attitude of variability or flexibility in dealing with volume-measuring problems (Luchins, 1942, pp. 63-64). In one experiment, forty Grade 6 pupils were told to imagine that they had 8-, 7-, and 30-quart jars and were then asked to indicate in writing how they would obtain 15, 1, 21, 24, 23, 22, and 29 quarts. Three minutes were allowed for each of these seven problems and then the basic experiment was presented. Considerable E effects resulted: C_1C_2, 80% E; Ext., 65% F; C_3C_4, 75% E. The initial problems might conceivably have developed an attitude of variability (since the jars could be used in various combinations and not all of the given jars had to be used in a problem) and, if transferred to the basic experiment, such an attitude might well have worked against E effects. The results suggest that either the appropriate attitude did not develop adequately or did not transfer sufficiently.

Another Grade 6 class of thirty-six subjects received, prior to the basic experiment, three problems, each involving three or four given jars, with five minutes allotted to each problem. The assigned task in each of these three initial problems was to discover as many methods as possible for obtaining the designated volume. After each problem, the experimenter illustrated the many methods by which the problem could be solved, some of which involved the manipulation of only two jars (by addition or subtraction). When the basic experiment was then given, considerable E effects resulted: C_1C_2, 67% E; Ext., 56% F; C_3C_4, 67% E. The initial problems might conceivably have developed an attitude of variability in dealing with the problems of the basic experiment since many methods were illustrated for each, including direct methods. But once again the results suggest that such an attitude did not develop or did not transfer in sufficient strength.

Comments made by the children in this experiment and the one described in the preceding paragraph revealed that many of them felt happy and more at ease when they came to the problems which could be solved by one method. Apparently the experience with the initial problems did not suffice to overcome a tendency to adhere to one procedure.

Use of Prior Warnings Against E Effects

"Don't Be Blind" Warning. If we first warn subjects about the possibility of becoming blinded, will this warning transfer to the Einstellung situation and operate against E effects? In the original experimentation

(Luchins, 1939, 1942), half the subjects in each group were given such a warning while the others were not warned. Before the experiment began, the students in each class were told that it would be necessary to send some of them into the hallway. Those remaining in the classroom were told that they were to be given a hint which would help them in the experiment and that they were not to tell the others about this hint. The "hint" was:

"In this experiment you are going to solve some problems. When you finish the sixth problem [the last E problem], write the words, 'Don't be blind,' on your papers. This is to make you aware of the fact that you must be cautious; you must watch out and see that you do not act foolishly while solving the subsequent problems. Remember, it is to remind you to be awake, to look so that you will not act like a blind person who can't see what he is doing."

After the "hint," the students in the hallway were asked to return to the classroom, and the basic experiment was then administered to the class.

Those who received the warning were said to constitute the "D.B.B. groups," while the others, who received the basic experiment without the warning, were said to constitute the "plain groups." With few exceptions, subjects in the D.B.B. groups remembered to write the designated words after the sixth problem (that is, after the last E task). Did the warning transfer to their solution of the test problems? Consider firstly the results yielded by the adult (including college) subjects:

Plain groups .... 501 adults C_1C_2: 81% E Ext.: 62% F C_3C_4: 67% E
D.B.B. groups .... 498 adults C_1C_2: 62% E Ext.: 44% F C_3C_4: 45% E

Here the D.B.B. groups had about 20 per cent less E effects, on the average, than those who were not warned. Yet the E effects that the D.B.B. groups showed are within the range found in some plain groups. Thus, while the warning was somewhat effective with the adults, it certainly did not prevent E effects.

The D.B.B. warning had virtually no beneficial effects for the elementary-school groups.

Plain groups .... 420 children C_1C_2: 70% E Ext.: 64% F C_3C_4: 73% E
D.B.B. groups .... 391 children C_1C_2: 69% E Ext.: 61% F C_3C_4: 72% E

These average results obscure the finding that, in a number of elementary-school classes, the D.B.B. groups had more E effects than the corresponding plain groups. An explanation for this finding, as well as for the general ineffectiveness of the warning to the elementary-school groups, is contained in the comments children made when, after the experiment, they were asked to write the meaning of the words, "Don't be blind." They interpreted these words to mean, "Don't be blind to the method which worked before and which also works here" or "Don't be blind to the rule that solves these problems" or "Don't bother trying to find a new method in each problem." Some said that they thought the experimenter wanted to find out if they would remember to write the words but, other than that, they attached no significance to them. While such comments were also made by adults, they occurred with less frequency. Some of the adults (usually those who showed no E effects), but few of the children, interpreted "Don't be blind" to mean that they must be on guard lest they fall into a rut.

We see that the "Don't be blind" warning did not prevent E effects for most subjects. In some cases it even enhanced such effects. The warning apparently did not transfer at all in some cases (e.g., when it was regarded as a memory item devoid of meaning), had "negative transfer effects" in some elementary-school groups, and had some beneficial effects among the adult groups. The important factor was the interpretation given to the warning.

More Specific Warnings. It was decided to offer a warning before the experiment was conducted that would not be likely to be incorrectly interpreted (Luchins, 1942, pp. 77-80). In Experiment 1, children were told to obtain 10 quarts, using 4-, 28-, and 6-quart jars. Their answer was $4 + 6 = 10$. They were then told that the day before other children had solved the problem in this manner: $28 - 6 - 4 - 4 - 4 = 10$. These other children, it was explained, had first solved problems similar to this one, "Given 5, 57, 20, get 22," by using this method: $57 - 20 - 5 - 5 - 5 = 22$, "and they used this same method in the example I just gave you." The class was shown the similarity. The experimenter continued with words to this effect:

"Yesterday's children called themselves stupid, dumb, and blind when I showed them the more direct method. They said that they had stopped thinking, that they had not bothered to examine each problem but had merely repeated what they had done before.

"What is the moral of this experience? In solving a problem, you must examine it first, not just repeat, like a machine, what you did before. Face each problem, see what has to be done, and do it in the most direct way. Of course, after examining a problem carefully, you may see no other alternative but to repeat what you did before. In such cases you'll have to repeat. However, if you are awake, looking at the problem, and thinking, you will find problems which can be solved in a more direct way.

"Now I am going to see how well you can keep your eyes open and do problems in the most direct way instead of just mechanically repeating what you did before. Look at each problem to see what needs to be done and can be done directly. Don't be blind or stupid; don't fall into the same trap that yesterday's children fell into."

After the introduction set forth above, the basic experiment was presented to two Grade 5 classes. E effects were less than those usually found in the basic experiment but, despite the introduction, there were considerable E solutions and failures of the test problems.

Grade 5 .... 56 students C_1C_2: 38% E Ext.: 25% F C_3C_4: 36% E

In another variation (Experiment 2), a Grade 6 class was given the same introduction and, in addition, was given the "Don't be blind" warning described in the preceding subsection. E effects were quite low, particularly in the extinction task.

Grade 6 .... 32 students C_1C_2: 22% E Ext.: 9% F C_3C_4: 22% E

It is of interest that every pupil who showed E effects in Experiment 2 had been taking remedial arithmetic (although not all who had remedial training showed E effects). The teacher of the class said that, in this remedial training, the children were drilled on one kind of problem until they could pass the test on it, then were drilled on another kind until they could pass the test on that, etc. She complained that these children could solve only problems that they had just practiced and that they failed at something even a little bit new.

To study further the effects of the remedial teaching, in Experiment 3 we used the procedure of Experiment 2 with another sixth-grade class most of whose members had had such remedial training the preceding term. The class was in the same school as the class in Experiment 2 and had a similar I.Q. range and average. Yet E effects were considerably greater than in Experiment 2 or even Experiment 1.

Grade 6 .... 23 students C_1C_2: 52% E Ext.: 39% F C_3C_4: 46% E

Nine children used the E method in every test task, even in the extinction task; all nine had had remedial teaching. Every child who had had remedial training gave some E solutions while, of the eight who had not, only two gave any E solutions.

Whether the greater E effects shown by those who had had remedial training reflects the transfer to the experiment of attitudes developed by the remedial work or whether it is due to their inaptitude for arithmetic or to other factors, is not known. But the results strongly suggest that pre-experimental experiences may greatly influence the results of experimental attempts to reduce E effects.

Experiment 4 used college upperclassmen, with about half the subjects receiving the procedure of Experiment 1 (introduction) and the others the procedure of Experiments 2 and 3 (introduction plus the "Don't be blind" warning described in the preceding subsection). There were less E effects for the group receiving the introduction than for college groups given the basic experiment (without introduction or warning), and no E effects for the group receiving both the introduction and the D.B.B. warning.

Introduction .... 15 col. students C_1C_2: 10% E Ext.: 7% F C_3C_4: 0% E
Intro., plus
    D.B.B. .... 12 col. students C_1C_2: 0% E Ext.: 0% F C_3C_4: 0% E

What would happen if the procedure of the preceding experiment was used but, just before the problems were presented, the class was told, "You will be given thirty seconds per problem. The goal is to solve as many problems as possible." When this was done with a college class, with thirty seconds allowed per problem (as compared with two and one-half minutes per problem in the basic experiment), the class showed somewhat less E effects than did comparable groups in the basic experiment, but far more than the two groups in Experiment 4.

Introduction .... 11 students C_1C_2: 55% E Ext.: 55% F C_3C_4: 55% E
Intro., plus
    D.B.B. .... 11 students C_1C_2: 27% E Ext.: 18% F C_3C_4: 18% E

It is interesting to note that eight subjects in the "introduction" group and four in the "introduction plus D.B.B." group failed to solve the last two E tasks (their results are not included above), whereas these problems were almost invariably solved by college subjects in the basic experiment. Some subjects reported that because of the introduction they realized that they should watch out for tricky problems but were unable to do so because of their haste and tension. Apparently the speed conditions induced by the time limitation nullified some of the potential influence of the introduction and D.B.B. warning.

The introduction used in the experiments described above (without the D.B.B. warning), was used with another college class, but ten, instead of five, E problems were given. E effects were much greater than those in Experiment 4 and approximated those of the basic experiment.

Introduction .... 21 students C_1C_2: 69% E Ext.: 55% F C_3C_4: 59% E

Subjects said that they soon tired of examining each problem, and that after a while they thought the introduction was a jest and that problems having simpler methods would never be given. Here the potential influence of the introduction was weakened by the increased number of E tasks.

Thus, while the introduction with its specific warning against overlooking direct methods, was generally effective in weakening E effects, the extent to which it was transferred to the Einstellung situation depended both on conditions prevailing in this situation (time limitation, greater number of E tasks) and on pre-experimental experiences (such as the remedial-arithmetic training).

Prior Experiences with the Problems of the Basic Experiment

In the preceding section, it was the experimenter who in his instructions offered the subjects an understanding of the ambiguous nature of the test problems. Is it possible to offer the subjects experiences from which they may derive this understanding for themselves? It was thought that giving some of the test problems of the basic experiment before administration of the experiment might help subjects to achieve this understanding.

Criticals 1 and 2 and the usual extinction task were given, followed immediately by all the problems of the basic experiment (Luchins, 1942, p. 76). All subjects gave direct solutions of the three preliminary problems. Yet, when these same problems were presented minutes later as part of the basic experiment, E effects were large, particularly for elementary and high-school groups.

Elementary school ...... 43 students C_1C_2: 66% E Ext.: 65% F C_3C_4: 65% E
High school .... 50 students C_1C_2: 74% E Ext.: 54% F C_3C_4: 53% E
College .... 91 students C_1C_2: 75% E Ext.: 45% F C_3C_4: 29% E

The experience of finding direct solutions to the three preliminary problems might have been expected to exert transfer effects when these same problems were later encountered. But we see that having solved some of the test problems in the direct manner did not necessarily lead to an understanding of the nature of these problems and did not prevent many subjects from later showing E effects in these very problems. What the findings clearly reveal is that the response does not depend on the stimulus only but also on the context in which the stimulus appears; a problem, when viewed as part of a unitary, homogenous series, may elicit a response quite different from that elicited when it is faced individually.

What would happen to E effects if the subjects had prior experience with all the problems; i.e., if the entire experiment were repeated? In a class of college upperclassmen, the experiment was presented again immediately after its first administration (Luchins, 1942, pp. 74-75). E effects were somewhat lower the second time but within the range found when college groups received the basic experiment only once.

First time .... 21 col. students C_1C_2: 86% E Ext.: 62% F C_3C_4: 64% E
Second time .... 21 col. students C_1C_2: 62% E Ext.: 57% F C_3C_4: 59% E

Direct solutions in the readministration were offered mainly by those who had given direct solutions to Criticals 3 and 4 during the first administration. One subject showed complete E effects in the first administration but no E effects in the second; he reported suspecting a reason for the repetition of the experiment and looking carefully at each problem to see what he could now do that he had not done before. But most subjects said that they saw no sense in giving such easy problems twice, while some said that they thought the experimenter was interested in ascertaining whether they could solve the problems faster the second time. With few exceptions, subjects repeated in the second administration the same procedures that they had used in the first.

When the basic experiment was administered and then immediately readministered to a Grade 5 class, subjects worked more rapidly during the second administration but showed about the same E effects, except for an *increase* in failures of the extinction problem.

First time .... 27 students C_1C_2: 87% E Ext.: 66% F C_3C_4: 83% E
Second time .... 27 students C_1C_2: 89% E Ext.: 74% F C_3C_4: 83% E

Most children thought that the problems were being repeated because the teacher had been dissatisfied with their work or their rate of speed during the first administration. A few did not recognize that the same problems were being repeated but thought that they were getting additional practice on similar (but not identical) problems.

To other Grade 5 children the experiment was administered and then readministered two months later. About the same E effects were yielded.

First time .... 45 students C_1C_2: 85% E Ext.: 87% F C_3C_4: 86% E
Second time .... 45 students C_1C_2: 82% E Ext.: 80% F C_3C_4: 82% E

In both variations, repetition of the experiment did not have much influence on E effects. Subjects who were blind to the direct method the first time were generally just as blind the second time.

Prior Experience in Other Einstellung Situations

It may be remembered that a battery of rigidity tests has been devised (Luchins, 1948) in which the Einstellung paradigm is used with different kinds of materials, such as mazes, hidden words, and picture series of various kinds. Part or all of this battery has been administered to many subjects. It is of interest to ascertain if subjects, in earlier tests, learned to overcome sets and transferred this learning so that they showed less E effects in later tests.

Pertinent to this issue are the experiments reported in an earlier chapter, in which the mazes were first presented in the mirror apparatus and then for nonmirror tracing or vice versa. Serving as subjects were normal individuals as well as hospitalized neurotics. The normals showed significantly less E effects on the second administration (e.g., mirror tracing) than in the first administration (e.g., nonmirror tracing), but not the neurotics. Apparently the normals were better able to develop an understanding of the Einstellung situation or were better able to transfer this "insight" than the neurotics. Perhaps the greater anxiety of the neurotics played a role. Whatever may have produced the difference in results, it would seem clear that the condition of the individual who is being tested is a determinant of the extent of transfer from one Einstellung situation to another.

When the mazes were readministered to normals (the first administration under mirror-tracing and the second under nonmirror-tracing conditions or vice versa, or both administrations under the same conditions), the decrease in E effects was greater than when the basic experiment was readministered to normals. Why is this? The answer, at least in part, may lie in the fact that, when the subject attempted to use the circuitous route in the extinction maze, he came to a barrier. If he crossed the barrier, the experimenter told him that he had not solved the problem. But the subject was often aware of the barrier and generally realized (even in those variations in which the experimenter did not comment on failures) that the circuitous path did not lead to the goal box in this maze, although the circuitous path had led to the goal in all the previous mazes. More vividly than in the basic experiment, then, the extinction task in the maze experiment revealed to the subject the inadequacy of the oft-repeated procedure. In the volume-measuring extinction task, the subject might reason that perhaps he had made a computational error in applying the E method, but in the mazes it was quite evident that a route either did or did not lead into the goal box. Moreover, the direct method in the mazes—a short, vertical path to the goal box—was more direct and more likely to impinge on the subject's consciousness (at least after he discovered that the circuitous path did not lead to the goal box) than was the direct method involving manipulation of two jars. In short, the maze situation seemed to offer normals a better opportunity than the basic experiment to see the folly to which repetition had led and to discover a more direct approach.

Turning now to the battery of Einstellung rigidity tests, we note that, when the maze test was given (the nonmirror version was used), it apparently decreased E effects in subsequent tests somewhat more than did any other of the tests. Of course, when the maze test was given near the end of the battery, it had less chance to exert beneficial influences than when it was administered toward the beginning. Thus, it may be said that the extent of transfer depends not only on the kind of subject who is being tested (normal, neurotic), but also on the kind of Einstellung tests included and on the order in which the tests are administered.

When the maze test was not included in the battery, little reduction in E effects was found from test to test. For example, subjects received in succession eight different series of pictures. In each series there was a percept which emerged gradually but of which the subject was not aware for some time because he clung to an old percept. If the subjects had learned from their experiences, they should have recognized the emerging percepts earlier in successive series. Yet subjects who received, say, the face-bottle series after other picture series, generally did not report the emerging bottle percept significantly earlier than those who received the face-bottle series first; and in both cases the bottle percept was reported in a later card than it was by the control subjects who did not receive the pictures of the face (the set-inducing pictures).

It would seem that, with the exception of the mazes, prior experiences with Einstellung situations generally did not suffice to reduce E effects. If we think of the prior Einstellung series as potential opportunities to learn to overcome a tendency toward being set or toward being rigid, then many of our subjects showed little such learning from series to series. They did not manifest what Harlow has called "learning to learn."

The behavior of the human being is not to be understood in terms of the results of single learning situations but rather in terms of the changes which are affected through multiple, though comparable, learning problems.... The learning of primary importance to the primates, at least, is ... *learning how to learn efficiently* in the situations the animal frequently encounters. (Harlow, 1949, p. 51.)

If we think of efficient learning in successive Einstellung series as representing ability to overcome sets (as measured by decreasing E effects), then many of our subjects did not "learn how to learn" from series to series. In this respect, they differ considerably from Harlow's monkeys whose behavior was characterized by "learning to learn" from series to series and from problem to problem. The monkeys gave increasingly better performances on series of object-quality discrimination problems, with the improvement even carrying over to left-right position discrimination problems. Just why our subjects did not learn as well from series to series as did the monkeys constitutes a complex problem. Perhaps part of the answer is that the series we used were Einstellung series and the development of an Einstellung often did not allow the subject to gain any insight into the nature of the series and the nature of the problems. When opportunities to do so were en-

hanced (as in the maze experiment for normal subjects), more "learning to learn" did occur. Let us turn now to variations in which we
attempted experimentally to increase opportunities for the subject to
understand the nature of the series and/or of the problems.

Prior Administration of the Basic Experiment Followed by Explanation

After the basic experiment was completed in five classes from Grades
4 through 6 (Luchins, 1942, p. 75, p. 81), the papers were collected,
new papers distributed, and Criticals 1 and 2 and the extinction task
presented one at a time. Then the children were told a story of a maze
experiment to develop an Einstellung in rats. When asked to predict
the rats' behavior, most of them predicted that the rats would take the
habituated path because of habit. When told that the rats did not develop
an Einstellung, they commented on the rats' cleverness. The children
were then asked to examine their own solutions of Criticals 1 and 2
and the extinction problem. During the discussion of their solutions,
there were soon cries of "How silly I was" and "The rats are more
clever than us." They were then asked to turn their papers over and to
solve Criticals 3 and 4 and a new extinction task. It is of particular
interest to consider the responses made by those subjects (forty-seven
out of the total of ninety-two) who had shown complete E effects in
the basic experiment.

First time .... 47 students C_1C_2: 100% E Ext.: 100% F C_3C_4: 100% E
Second time ...... 47 students C_1C_2: 87% E Ext.: 85% F

After discus-
sion .... 47 students C_3C_4: 12% E New Ext.: 2% F

Note how sharp is the decrease in E effects after the discussion as compared with the slight decrease when the test problems were readministered without the intervening discussion. Apparently the story of the
rats and the discussion of their solutions developed an understanding
in the children which almost nullified E effects.

After college classes finished the basic experiment and papers had
been collected, the students were briefly informed of the purposes of the
test and of the fact that the test problems could be solved by direct
methods (Luchins, 1942, pp. 81-82). When the basic experiment was
then readministered to one class, there were no E effects at all.

First time .... 17 students C_1C_2: 71% E Ext.: 53% F C_3C_4: 56% E
After explanation .... 17 students C_1C_2: 0% E Ext.: 0% F C_3C_4: 0% E

After the explanation, another class received a series of problems
that followed the paradigm of the basic experiment. The problems were
solvable by the same methods (E and direct), but the jar capacities

and stipulated volumes to be obtained differed from those in the basic experiment. E effects virtually disappeared.

First time .... 16 students C_1C_2: 75% E Ext.: 63% F C_3C_4: 56% E
After explanation .. 16 students $C_1'C_2'$: 6% E Ext.': 0% F $C_3'C_4'$: 0% E

Here we see that the insight developed by the explanation transferred even when different numbers were involved.

After the explanation, another college class received a series of problems modeled after those in the basic experiment but in which the E method was $A + B - 4C$ and the more direct method $B - A - 2C$, and the instruction given was that all three jars must be used as measures. E effects decreased considerably, despite the introduction of new numbers and new methods.

First time .... 10 students C_1C_2: 75% E Ext.: 60% F C_3C_4: 65% E
After explanation .. 10 students $C_1'C_2'$: 35% E Ext.': 0% F $C_3'C_4'$: 0% E

In another college class, two months elapsed after the explanation before the basic experiment was readministered, and yet E effects decreased sharply.

First time .... 12 students C_1C_2: 75% E Ext.: 67% F C_3C_4: 58% E
After explanation .. 12 students C_1C_2: 4% E Ext.: 0% F C_3C_4: 0% E

It would seem that the explanation developed an insight which persisted over a period of time and which generalized to somewhat different jar problems. However, some other experiments (Luchins, 1942, p. 83) suggest that the influence of the explanation may be partially nullified under certain conditions. For example, when the explanation after the basic experiment was followed by administration of this experiment under speed-test conditions, considerable E effects resulted. Subjects said that the stress on time gave them so little chance to think that, without realizing it, they again developed an Einstellung. Moreover, when the explanation after the basic experiment was followed by an experiment involving eight E tasks, some subjects showed E effects in the test problems; they said that they expected a direct method to work sooner and, when it did not, they stopped looking for the "trick" problems or thought that they would never be given. Thus, it is possible to produce habituation in an informed subject, to twice burn a person who has been told what produced his previous burns. Nonetheless, the E effects obtained here were not nearly as great as when an explanation did not intervene between the basic experiment and the speed-test experiment or between the basic experiment and the experiment with eight E tasks.

It may be concluded that our attempts to decrease E effects through

an explanation after the subject had already participated in the experiment, were more effective, transferred to a wider range, and prevailed
over a longer period of time, than did our attempts to prevent E effects
by discussion or instructions before the subject participated in the experiment. Apparently the discussion was more meaningful after the
subject had just experienced an Einstellung situation.

Administration of Various Einstellung Tests
Under Different Conditions

A number of the tests from Luchins' rigidity manual (1948, 1950a)
have been administered under diverse conditions in an effort to ascertain how the conditions under which the tests are given affect performance.

Experiment 1. In Experiment 1, conducted with the assistance of Eva
Stearns, the (nonmirror) maze test, five picture-series tests, and the
volume-measuring test were administered, in this order, under three
conditions. Under Condition 0 there was no discussion between tests.
Under Condition 1 (analysis of responses), after the maze test, and
again after the volume-measuring test, the experimenter pointed to the
mazes or to the volume-measuring problems in which the subject had
overlooked a direct method and asked the subject why he had solved
these problems as he had, and, if the subject did not then discover the
direct method, the experimenter indicated it to him; after each picture
series the experimenter and the subject went over the cards together
and the subject was asked why he had not reported the emerging percept earlier in the series. Condition 2 (analysis of responses plus challenge) included the "analysis" of Condition 1, and, in addition, at the
outset the subject was told that these tests were designed to obscure or
hide changes in order to trick a person into overlooking these changes,
and after each test he was urged not to let himself become mechanized,
blinded, or tricked in the next test but to face each problem (or picture)
individually. The term "challenge" includes both the statement of the
purpose of the tests, given at the outset, and the instructions not to
be blinded, etc., given after each test. Thirty Montreal college students
were tested individually, with ten studied under each condition.

Let us consider their responses to the last, the volume-measuring
test. In the E tasks those studied under Conditions 1 and 2 gave more
than twice as many non-E solutions as did those studied under Condition 0, so that, even in the E tasks, we see the influence of the analysis
and challenge between tests.* The influence was naturally even more ap-

---

* The next-to-last E task (9, 42, 6, get 21) can be solved in this non-E manner:
$6 + 6 + 9 = 21$; and the last E task (20, 59, 4, get 31) can be solved in this
non-E manner: $59 - 7 \times 4 = 31$.

parent in the critical problems. Direct solutions were offered to the first
critical problem by 10, 30, and 50 per cent of those studied under Conditions 0, 1, and 2, respectively. In the third critical task—the first that
could be solved by filling only one jar—this very simple procedure was
used by 60, 80, and 100 per cent of those studied under Conditions 0, 1,
and 2, respectively. (Every subject solved the extinction tasks, a result
which may have been due in part to experience in the preceding tests.)
Thus, as judged by direct solutions to the criticals, transfer with positive
effects was enhanced when the subject's responses were briefly analyzed
after each test and still further enhanced when he was informed of the
purpose of the test and challenged not to become mechanized.

Experiment 2. Experiment 2, which was conducted with the assistance of Joan Mortimer-Maddox and Rei Nishio, was concerned with
pitting speed conditions against analysis of responses. Three picture
series, the maze test, the hidden-word test, and the volume-measuring
test used in Experiment 1, were presented in that order, to four groups
of McGill University women students. The tests were administered in
a college dormitory to ten subjects at a time, with four subjects seated
around one table, four others around another table, and two others at
a smaller table. Group 1 was studied under Condition 1 of Experiment
1 (analysis of responses), with the experimenter directing attention
after each test to the direct method or the emerging percept and asking
each subject to indicate (in writing, rather than verbally, as in Experiment 1, which was conducted individually) why she solved the test
problems as she had and why she did not report an emerging percept
earlier in the series. Group 1S (analysis of responses and speed test)
received the same analysis between tests as Group 1, but was tested
under speed conditions. The experimenter mentioned the alleged time
that other college students required for each test and urged the subjects
to try to beat that time; frequently, they were reminded that they were
working too slowly and that the tests must all be completed before lunch
was served in the dormitory; competition among the three tables was
introduced by urging subjects to try to be "the first table finished."

Let us compare responses to the last, the volume-measuring test,
made by Groups 1 and 1S. In the E tasks there were twice as many
non-E solutions under nonspeed conditions as under speed conditions,
a fact that shows a greater tendency toward mechanization when speed
factors are introduced. The same trend prevailed in the test problems.
Whereas 70 per cent of Group 1 solved the first two criticals by the
direct method, only 35 per cent did so under speed conditions. While the
simple method of filling one jar (Critical 3) was used by 60 per cent of
those in Group 1, only 30 per cent used it under speed conditions. The
extinction tasks were solved by 95 per cent of those in Group 1 but

by only 80 per cent of those in Group 1S. In short, the analysis of responses was considerably less effective in reducing mechanization when the tests were given under speed conditions. Yet even Group 1S gave more direct solutions than college students who received these same tests without the intervening analysis of responses and under nonspeed conditions.

The same tests were also administered to two other similar groups. Group 2 received, after each test, the same analysis of responses as had Group 1, together with the challenge (Condition 2 of Experiment 1). Group 2S received the analysis plus the challenge, but was tested under the speed conditions used for Group 1S. Again, fewer direct solutions were obtained under speed conditions but the difference was not so marked as between Groups 1 and 1S. That the challenge was effective is seen in the fact that the groups receiving it gave more direct solutions than the corresponding groups that did not receive it.

This experiment indicates that factors working for transfer with positive effects (analysis of responses and challenge) may be partially vitiated by speed-test conditions of work.

Experiment 3. Experiment 3 was conducted in Queen Mary Veterans Hospital, Montreal, with the cooperation of Dr. George Dufresne, chief psychologist, and the assistance of Asher Kahn, Elizabeth Lowie, Eva Stearns, and Carmen Zuckerman. The maze test, hidden-word test, and the volume-measuring test, in that order, were individually administered to forty patients in the hospital diagnosed as neurotic, all of them veterans of World War II. Half of the patients were tested under Condition 1 of Experiment 1 (analysis of responses between tests) and the other half under Condition 2 of that experiment (analysis of responses between tests plus the challenge). For the last test, the volume-measuring test, the results proved to be very different from those in Experiments 1 and 2. Whereas in those experiments Condition 1 and 2 had yielded considerable non-E solutions even in the E tasks, now there were virtually no non-E solutions in these tasks. While in the two previous experiments those who received the challenge gave more direct solutions to the test problems than those who did not receive it, the opposite trend prevailed in the present experiment. Whereas 50 per cent offered direct solutions to the first two criticals under Condition 1 (analysis of responses), only 28 per cent did so under Condition 2; whereas 60 per cent used the very simple method in the next two criticals under Condition 1, only 38 per cent did so under Condition 2; and, whereas no one failed an extinction task under Condition 1, 50 per cent failed the first extinction task under Condition 2. Apparently the challenge not to become mechanized had an effect opposite to that intended. Also, signs of tension and anxiety appeared to increase as the challenge was given; for instance, facial and finger muscles tightened and subjects' comments were more laden with references to personal failures and shortcomings than under Condition 1.

Are we witnessing here a reaction to the challenge that is peculiar to neurotics? Or did the setting in which the challenge was given—in a military hospital, to patients—contribute to the role it played? To study this question, the same tests, in the same order, were administered to "normal" veterans in this hospital who came from nonpsychiatric wards (mainly from the orthopedic wards) and who were apparently free from psychopathology. Twenty subjects were studied under each condition. Yet the trend of results was similar to that obtained with the neurotics and again contrary to the trends obtained in Experiments 1 and 2 with college students. Again non-E solutions were rare in the E tasks. And again those studied under Condition 2 (analysis plus challenge) showed fewer direct solutions than those studied under Condition 1 (analysis of responses only). Whereas 50 per cent offered direct solutions to the first two criticals under Condition 1, only 18 per cent did so under Condition 2; whereas the very simple solution was used 55 per cent of the time in the next two criticals under Condition 1, it was used only 28 per cent of the time when the challenge was given; and, whereas 35 per cent failed the first extinction task under Condition 1, 50 per cent did so under Condition 2.

It is of interest that the difference between the results obtained under Conditions 1 and 2 (for either neurotics or hospitalized normals) was generally greater than the difference between the results obtained for neurotics and normals under the same conditions of administration. This suggests that effects of different conditions of work may outweigh individual differences between normals and neurotics.

How can one account for the fact that the effect of the challenge on hospitalized patients was diametrically opposite to its effect on college subjects? The differences do not seem to be due solely to factors of age, educational level, or I.Q. There was not much difference in the ages of the patients and the college students, and the patients, particularly the neurotics, included many with high I.Q.'s who had finished high school and had attended or even completed college. Moreover, the patients studied under Condition 1 were roughly equated with those studied under Condition 2 with respect to age, I.Q., and educational level, so that these factors per se would not seem responsible for differences in results under the two conditions.

It seems to us that the trends of results can best be understood in terms of the subject's attitude toward the challenge. The college students were participating in experiments conducted by fellow students. The patients were army veterans being examined in the hospital by a white-jacketed staff member, who, as far as the patients knew, was a psychologist or a doctor. The tests were part of what happened to them in the hospital and, to some degree at least, might partially determine their status in the hospital, their diagnoses, or their pensions. The patients, as a whole, took the tests more seriously than the college students. They were more concerned about what their behavior revealed to the examiner and they seemed to regard the outcome of the tests as having more consequences for them than did the college students. The challenge seemed to heighten anxiety for the patients, both normals and neurotics. Comments suggest that some of the patients interpreted the challenge to mean that they had not done well on the previous test and must do better on the next test in order to pass it or in order to do what the examiner wanted; some tried so hard to do better, while being concerned about what would happen if they did become mechanized, that they became anxious, tense—and mechanized. Their behavior is reminiscent of that of subjects who were "overmotivated" in the experiment on degrees of motivation (p. 140) and of the elementary-school children who misinterpreted "Don't be blind" or other instructions (pp. 132-33; p. 369). In short, it might be said that for the patients in the hospital the challenge served to arouse or strengthen a test atmosphere and test tensions, whereas it did not do so (or at least not to the same extent) for the college students.

Whatever may be the true explanation of the findings, it seems clear that the same instructions that have worked for positive transfer effects (in the sense of decreasing E effects) may work for negative effects in a different setting, the difference in result depending on the subject's attitude toward the instructions.

Demonstration of Structure of Basic-Experiment Problems and Experience in Creating Problems

We have already described attempts to give subjects some understanding of the structure of the series of problems in the basic experiment. The present subsection deals with attempts to give subjects some understanding of the structure of an E task and the structure of a test task, as well as to offer them experiences in creating such problems, and it summarizes the results of these attempts in terms of E effects. The procedures were conducted in junior-high-school classes in Oregon, with the cooperation of Letha Potampa, a teacher of remedial arithmetic. The classroom teachers served as experimenters.

The procedures included a demonstration period, a problem-creating period, and tests designed to measure the effects of the demonstrations and problem-creating experiences. In one demonstration period the subjects in two groups were given the problem, "Given containers holding 56, 90, and 12 quarts, get 10 quarts of water," and the E method of solution was shown. Then they were given the problem, "19, 42, 4, get 15," and both the $B - A - 2C$ and the $A - C$ methods of solution were shown. The experimenter then gave the following demonstration of how a $B - A - 2C$ problem is made. First, one decides beforehand that the problem will be to obtain a certain amount of water, say, 10 quarts. Next he arbitrarily decides that the left-end jar (the A jar) will hold any amount, say 56 quarts, and that the right-end jar (the C jar) also will hold any amount, say 12 quarts. Since the amount desired, 10 quarts, is to remain in the center jar, this jar must hold at least 10 quarts; since the A jar will be filled once from the center jar, the center jar must hold an additional 56 quarts; and, since the C jar will be filled twice from the center jar, the center jar must hold, in addition, 2 times 12 quarts or 24 quarts more. Thus, the center jar must contain $10 + 56 + 24 = 90$ quarts.

The experimenter then noted that the second problem had nonunique modes of solution, both $B - A - 2C$ and $A - C$, and he demonstrated how this problem is made. The essential difference between the construction of this problem and that of the first one, which is solvable only by the $B - A - 2C$ method, is that here one cannot arbitrarily name any capacity for both end jars. As before, one decides that a certain amount of water is to be obtained, say 15 quarts. Then a capacity is selected for the A jar, but only one that is greater than 15 quarts; for example, one may decide that it will hold exactly 19 quarts. Since the problem is to be solvable by the $A - C$ method, the C jar will have to hold exactly 4 quarts ($19 - 4 = 15$). Once the capacities of the end jars are determined, the procedure in determining the capacity of the center jar is precisely that of the previous problem; that is, the center jar must have a capacity of $15 + 19 + 2 \times 4 = 42$ quarts. The problem is thus solvable by both the $A - C$ and $B - A - 2C$ methods. Using further illustrations if necessary, the experimenter continued the demonstration until the group seemed to understand the structure of a problem solvable by the $B - A - 2C$ method as well as the structure of a problem solvable by both the $B - A - 2C$ and $A - C$ methods and how to go about making such problems.

Two other groups received a slightly different demonstration. They got the same E task but the second problem was "10, 41, 7, get 17," which is solvable by the $B - A - 2C$ and $A + C$ methods. The demonstration of how this problem was created was the same as that given in the preceding paragraph except that, once the desired volume was stipulated, capacities were assigned to the end jars whose total would equal this volume (instead of assigning capacities whose difference would equal this volume).

The demonstration (of the $B - A - 2C$ method and either the $A + C$ or $A - C$ method) was followed by a period during which each subject was asked to make four problems. The instructions for the problem making, which were varied for four different groups, are detailed below. Following the problem making, the problems of the basic experiment were administered.

Group 1 received the demonstration involving a problem solvable by the E method and one solvable by both the E method and the $A - C$ method. Then there was erased from the blackboard everything pertaining to the problem with the nonunique solutions, while the material pertaining to the E problem was left on the board. Subjects were then asked to devise a problem that would yield 5 quarts of water by means of the $B - A - 2C$ method *only*. After two minutes they were asked to devise a problem that would yield 3 quarts, again by means of the $B - A - 2C$ method only. Two minutes later all writing was erased from the blackboard, and they were asked to make a problem to yield 2 quarts by the $B - A - 2C$ method only. The final task was to create a problem to yield 7 quarts by the $B - A - 2C$ method only. Three minutes were allowed for each of the last two tasks. Then the basic experiment was presented, introduced with the remark, "Now let us solve rather than create problems."

The same problems were demonstrated to Group 2 as to Group 1; and, except for the instructions with respect to the last two problem-making tasks, the procedure detailed in the preceding paragraph for Group 1 was followed for Group 2. The third task was, "Make a problem in which one has to measure a certain amount of water by means of jars." The fourth task was, "Make another such problem." Thus, the volume to be obtained and the method of solution were not specified in the last two tasks.

Group 3 received the demonstration involving the $B - A - 2C$ and $A + C$ methods. Writing on the blackboard pertaining to the problem with one mode of solution was erased at the beginning of the problem-making period, while that pertaining to the problem with the nonunique solutions remained on the blackboard until completion of the second problem-creating task. The four tasks, given one at a time, were to create problems that would yield 5, 3, 2, and 7 quarts respectively, and that would be solvable by both the $B - A - 2C$ and the $A + C$ methods.

The procedure for Group 4 differed from that for Group 3 only with respect to the last three problem-creating tasks. The second task was, "Make a problem in which one has to obtain 3 quarts of water." The third and fourth tasks were identical with the corresponding tasks given to Group 2; that is, the volume to be obtained and the method of solution were not specified.

With few exceptions, subjects performed correctly the tasks assigned during the problem-creating period. In order to keep the number of repetitions of the E method constant, in the discussion below we consider the results of only those subjects who in the basic experiment solved all five E tasks by the E method. Because the demonstration involved the $A - C$ method for some groups and the $A + C$ method for others, we list separately responses to each test problem. (Criticals 1 and 4, it will be remembered, are solvable by the $A - C$ method, and Criticals 2 and 3 by the $A + C$ method.) Percentages of direct solutions to each test problem of the basic experiment were as follows:

Group 1 .... 16 students C_1:19 C_2:44 Ext.:25 C_3:44 C_4:25
Group 2 .... 24 students C_1: 0 C_2: 0 Ext.:37 C_3:17 C_4: 8
Group 3 .... 18 students C_1:22 C_2:38 Ext.:50 C_3:39 C_4:39
Group 4 .... 19 students C_1:53 C_2:63 Ext.:83 C_3:69 C_4:64

In every test problem Group 4 has considerably more direct solutions than any of the other groups. Group 4, it may be remembered, received the demonstration involving the $B - A - 2C$ and $A + C$ procedures, was asked to create a problem solvable by both these methods, and then was asked to create three problems in one of which only the volume was specified and in the other two of which neither the volume nor the method of solution was specified. Note that the $A - C$ procedure was not taught to Group 4 and yet they used this procedure more frequently, in the two test problems to which it was applicable (Criticals 1 and 4), than did Groups 1 and 2 who had been shown how to construct a problem solvable by $A - C$. Indeed, Group 4 had about 50 per cent or more direct solutions to each test problem than did Group 2.

It is also of interest to compare the results for Groups 3 and 4 since both received the same demonstration; Group 3 created four problems each solvable by both the $B - A - 2C$ and $A + C$ methods, while the problem-making tasks given to Group 4 were not nearly so specific. That Group 4 had more direct solutions to every test task than Group 3 suggests (a) that the problem-creating experience in which the subject took an active part exerted more influence on subsequent behavior than did the demonstration period in which the subject was a more passive spectator, and (b) that the experience of creating four problems with nonunique solutions exerted less transfer effect, in the sense of fostering direct solutions in the basic experiment, than did the experience of creating one problem with a nonunique solution and three other problems in which the subject was allowed greater freedom of decision.

That Group 3 had more experience with the $A + C$ method than Group 4, and yet used this method less frequently in the basic experiment than Group 4, indicates that frequency of past experience with a method was not the significant determinant of the results.

E effects for Groups 1, 2, and 3 (C_1C_2, from 61 to 96% E; Ext., from 50 to 75% F; C_3C_4, from 57 to 87% E) were within the range found in the basic experiment, while E effects for Group 4 (C_1C_2, 34% E; Ext., 17% F; C_3C_4, 34% E) fell below this range. Using failure of the extinction task as the crucial criterion of E effects, we find the least E effects in Group 4 and the most (75% F) in Group 1. The latter group created four problems solvable by the $B - A - 2C$ method only; it would seem that this (repetitive) experience helped to foster E effects.

Procedures used for Groups 1 through 4 were also employed in another Oregon junior high school, again with the cooperation of Letha Potampa. But here, after the basic experiment was administered, four more problems were presented which will be described shortly. Percentages of direct solutions to the test problems of the basic experiment were as follows for subjects who had solved all five E tasks of the basic experiment by the E method:

Group 1 .... 16 students	C_1: 6	C_2: 6	Ext.: 44	C_3: 12	C_4: 12
Group 2 .... 29 students	C_1: 2	C_2: 20	Ext.: 60	C_3: 30	C_4: 30
Group 3 .... 16 students	C_1: 0	C_2: 6	Ext.: 44	C_3: 6	C_4: 6
Group 4 .... 28 students	C_1: 28	C_2: 21	Ext.: 68	C_3: 39	C_4: 39

Again Group 4 showed more direct solutions of each test problem than any of the other groups despite the fact that the $A - C$ method was not demonstrated to it. For Groups 1 through 4, respectively, 50, 3, 19, and 7 per cent failed to solve Critical 3, and 56, 3, 19, and 7 per cent failed to solve Critical 4. Apparently their experience with the extinction task so upset those in Group 1 (who had been asked to create four problems solvable only by the $B - A - 2C$ method) that half or more of them were not able to solve the subsequent problems, even by the E method.

While the present results and the results found in the other junior high school share the common feature that Group 4 showed less E effects in the usual test problems than Groups 1, 2, and 3, there are several rather striking differences between the two sets of results. For one thing, failures to solve Criticals 3 and 4 were more frequent for the present junior-high groups. Moreover, differences among the present four groups did not tend to be as large as were the intergroup differences in the other school. Also, the relationships among the results of the present groups differed from the previously found relationships. For example, in the present junior high school, Group 2 gave higher percentages of direct solutions of most test problems than either Group 1 or Group 3 and almost as high as Group 4; in contrast, in the other junior high school, Group 2 gave the smallest percentages of direct solutions of most test problems. Furthermore, the present Groups 1, 3, and 4 showed a lower percentage of direct solutions of each critical problem than the corresponding groups in the other school, whereas the present Group 2 had a higher percentage of direct solutions in every test problem than Group 2 in the other school. We do not know the reasons for these differences in results. Different schools and subjects were involved; different teachers served as experimenters; there may have been differences in the social atmosphere of the experimental sessions and in the subjects' attitudes and assumptions concerning the tasks—all of which possibly may have exerted differential influences on responses. Perhaps further experimentation with the procedures used for Groups 1 through 4 may yield some clues to the possible reasons for the differences between results in the two schools and may enhance our understanding of the relative efficacy of these procedures in decreasing E effects.†

Immediately after the basic experiment had been administered to the present junior-high-school groups, the following four problems were presented at intervals of two and one-half minutes: Criticals 5 and 6, each solvable by a direct (D) method as well as by filling only one jar ($D!$ method), an extinction task solvable by none of the methods mentioned thus far (40, 118, 18, get 62), and a new E task. The results for Criticals 5 and 6 follow:

---

† In addition to further experimentation with the procedures used for Groups 1 through 4, there seems to us to be a need for variations in the procedures in order to fill in some "gaps" in the experimental design. The following seem to constitute some of the variations in the procedures that are needed to fill in the more apparent "gaps."

(1) Introduce a change in the procedures used for Groups 1 and 2 by demonstrating the $A + C$ rather than the $A - C$ method, but otherwise leave the procedures unaltered.

(2) Introduce a change in the procedures used for Groups 3 and 4 by substituting the $A - C$ method wherever the $A + C$ method occurred in the demonstration period and in the problem-creating period.

(3) Vary the procedure used for Group 2 by substituting for its second task the second task that was used for Group 4; similarly, vary the procedure used for Group 4 by substituting for its second task the second task used for Group 2.

(4) Introduce changes in the procedure used for Groups 3 and 4 by demonstrating $B - A - 2C$ and one direct method (e.g., $A - C$) but requesting that the problems created be solvable by another direct method (e.g., $A + C$).

(5) Vary the jar capacities and the stipulated volumes that are mentioned during the demonstration period or change the demonstration in other ways; vary the volumes to be obtained that are mentioned in some problem-creating periods or vary the instructions used in these periods in other ways.

Group 1 .... C_5: 19% D   0% D!   56% F C_6: 12% D   6% D!   63% F
Group 2 .... C_5: 27% D   10% D!   3% F C_6: 30% D   13% D!   3% F
Group 3 .... C_5: 0% D   19% D!   37% F C_6: 6% D   19% D!   44% F
Group 4 .... C_5: 22% D   19% D!   6% F C_6: 25% D   21% D!   7% F

Note that the most direct method $(D!)$ was used in Group 4 more often than, or as often as, in the other groups and that Group 4 had few failures compared with the large percentages of failures in Groups 1 and 3. Note, too, that it was Group 2 that had the highest percentage of D solutions and the smallest percentage of failures of both Criticals 5 and 6.

Now consider the percentages of failures in the last extinction task and the final E task.

Group 1 .... $Ext._2$: 94 E task: 81
Group 2 .... $Ext._2$: 97 E task: 3
Group 3 .... $Ext._2$: 88 E task: 68
Group 4 .... $Ext._2$: 10 E task: 10

Note that only 10 per cent of Group 4 failed the problem requiring a different method of solution, a problem failed by most subjects in the other groups. Moreover, for the last task, 90 per cent of Group 4 applied the E method, which was the only method that solved this task, while less than one-fifth of Group 1 succeeded in solving this problem, despite the prior experience they had had of creating four problems each solvable by the E method. In this final task, it was Group 2 that showed the smallest percentage of failures.

In both schools the least E effects usually were found in Group 4. This was the group that created one problem with nonunique modes of solution and then was allowed more varied experiences in formulating the other three problems; that is, it was given the most freedom in deciding what kind of problems to create. We may conclude that, through affording certain prior experiences, we can, to some extent, minimize people's tendency to rely on or to repeat habits and, contrariwise, help them to face problems more realistically. The extent of transfer with positive effects clearly did not depend on the frequency of experience with a given direct method but did seem to depend, at least in part, on not being limited to a certain kind of problem in the problem-creating session. The relatively large E effects shown by Groups 1 and 3 in both schools suggest that deleterious effects on subsequent behavior may result if one is limited to one kind of problem in this creative period (whether it be solvable by one method or more than one method); that is, repetition in the initial learning period ought to be avoided, even in a creative activity, if subsequent E effects are to be avoided.

A Note on the Differential Effects of Rats' Environments

A study by Luchins and Forgus (1955) indicated that rats that had been reared in a richer, freer environment, showed less E effects in an Einstellung test of the maze type than did rats reared in a more impoverished, less free environment. While caution is needed in drawing a parallel for other species, the results do suggest (a) that different previous experiences, in the broadest sense of the term, may exert differential influences on behavior, and (b) that an environment that is rich in opportunities for exploration and for "decision making" may foster more transfer with positive effects—in the sense of less E effects, less blinding effects—than a more restricted and more restricting environment. (Cf. results with children in Luchins, 1942, pp. 21-22.) More generally, the results hint that different kinds of experience may create different kinds of experienced organisms.

CHAPTER XIV

THE WORKING OF EXTINCTION

VIEWS CONCERNING EXTINCTION

T HERE are two points of view concerning the extinction of a response. One holds that extinction represents the weakening or decay of a habit brought about by unreinforced repetitions; the other, that extinction occurs through the learning of an incompatible response and not merely through unreinforced repetitions. As representative of the former, we cite Hull's thesis (1943, p. 260) that experimental extinction is a function of unreinforced reactions. Representative of the second is Guthrie's contention (1935, p. 83) that a response becomes detached from its former cue when this cue becomes conditioned to new behavior which inhibits the original response (inhibitory conditioning) or, as Guthrie words it on a later page of the same text: "Established habits disappear only when new habits displace them" (p. 135). As another representative of the second viewpoint, consider Tolman's thesis that the deacquisition of one field expectancy results from the learning of a conflicting expectancy (1949a, p. 153).

Which description of extinction is applicable in our experiments? Since the basic experiment includes an extinction problem (one not solvable by the E method and hence offering an opportunity for an unreinforced reaction), we may be able to determine whether the habit of using the E procedure is weakened by failure of the extinction task or only by the learning of an incompatible response, of a more direct method of solution.

In the basic experiment, the adult (including college) subjects, the elementary-school subjects, and the total of these two kinds of subjects, gave the following percentages of direct solutions:

Adult .... 501 subjects	C_1C_2: 18	Ext.: 38	C_3C_4: 33
Elem. school .... 420 subjects	C_1C_2: 25	Ext.: 36	C_3C_4: 27
Total .... 921 subjects	C_1C_2: 21	Ext.: 37	C_3C_4: 30

Virtually all of the subjects who solved Critical 1 and/or Critical 2 by a direct method also solved the extinction task. Note that the frequency of solution of the extinction task was about the same for the adult subjects as for the elementary-school subjects but that relatively more of the adults had not solved the previous criticals by a direct method. For 20 per cent of the adults, for 11 per cent of the children, and for 16 per cent of the total number of subjects, the extinction prob-

lem was the first test problem that they solved in a direct manner.
Note also that the children showed relatively fewer direct solutions
of the last two criticals than the adults, although the reverse was the
case for the first two criticals. While most subjects who solved the
extinction task also solved the subsequent criticals by a direct method,
about 5 per cent of the adults, 9 per cent of the children, and 7 per
cent of the total subjects solved the extinction problem and yet did not
offer direct solutions subsequently. Practically all of the direct solutions of Criticals 3 and 4 came from subjects who had solved the extinction task, although there were a few subjects who failed this task and
yet gave a direct solution to Critical 3 and/or Critical 4. On the whole,
failure of the extinction task did not suffice to disrupt the employment
of the E method in the subsequent criticals. It would seem offhand that
these results could be interpreted to mean that an unreinforced reaction
(failure of the extinction task) usually did not make for extinction of
the E response whereas learning of an incompatible response (solution of the extinction task) usually did make for extinction. But it
seems to us that this is not an entirely adequate formulation of what
actually occurred.

To begin with, what constitutes an "unreinforced reaction"? Some
subjects apparently believed that they had solved the extinction task
through use of the E method. Indeed, 26 per cent of the elementary-
school pupils in the basic study gave $76 - 28 - 3 - 3 = 25$ as their solution (whereas the subtractions actually yield 42), seemingly without
being aware that they had made an error. Should their responses be
classed as reinforced or unreinforced repetitions of the E method?
Moreover, 34 per cent of the elementary-school subjects wrote that the
experimenter had made an error: "You made a mistake. This problem doesn't come out" or "You gave the wrong jars." Do their attempts
to use the E method constitute reinforced or unreinforced reactions?
Or should they be classified as partially reinforced reactions? Some children wrote $76 - 28 - 3 - 3 = 42$, either not aware that they had introduced a change in the volume of fluid to be obtained or confidently believing that the experimenter had erred in setting the goal. There were
subjects, both children and adults, who reported after the experiment
that, while they were aware that they had failed one problem (the extinction task), they did not attribute the failure to inapplicability of the
E method. They thought that they might have made an error in calcu-
lation and that, if they had had sufficient time, they would have been
able to apply the E procedure to the task. These and the other subjects
just referred to all viewed the extinction task from the frame of reference of the E procedure and failed to recognize the incompatibility
between this procedure and the task. It would therefore hardly seem

adequate to classify their responses as unreinforced responses. In brief, our subjects' responses reveal that there may be difficulties attendant upon the categorization of certain reactions as reinforcements or non-reinforcements of a particular response. But then perhaps such reactions should not be interpreted as testifying for or against the thesis that nonreinforcement of a response fosters its extinction.

Consider now the matter of *incompatible* responses or *conflicting* responses. The extinction task is solvable by the $A - C$ procedure. But the critical immediately following it is not solvable by the $A - C$ method. It is solvable either by the $B - A - 2C$ procedure or by $A + C$. Assuming that, because it solved the extinction task, the $A - C$ response had become "conditioned" to the cue situation (say, the three-jar-volume-measuring task), to use Guthrian terminology, or had been accepted as a field expectancy, to use Tolmanian terminology, what would be the fate of such a conditioned response or expectancy in the subsequent critical? Attempts to apply the $A - C$ method here would prove futile. Some subjects attempted to use it and then reverted to the $B - A - 2C$ procedure. Some of these used the $B - A - 2C$ method in the last critical also while others solved the last critical by the $A - C$ method, which is applicable in this problem. What seems significant to us is that most subjects who solved the extinction task (including most subjects for whom this task was the first test problem in which they used a direct method) used the $A + C$ method in the subsequent critical and the $A - C$ method in the final critical.

Had the experience in the extinction problem served to condition the cues to the $A - C$ response or to develop an expectancy for the $A - C$ response, there would be little reason to expect the relatively frequent $A + C$ solution of the subsequent critical. Individually conducted experiments revealed that solution of the extinction problem was followed usually by rapid, almost instantaneous, $A + C$ solution of the subsequent critical. Such a result cannot be accounted for on the grounds that the $A - C$ procedure replaced the $B - A - 2C$ method as a habit or expectancy. Rather, what seems to have happened, to judge by the subjects' remarks, is that the experience in the extinction task jolted the subjects, awakened them from their complacency, made them suspicious of the method they had been using and of their attitudes toward or assumptions about the problems (e.g., that they were all solved by one method or that all jars were used in a solution). They became aware of the possibility of being blinded by one method and looked at each subsequent problem to see what method of solution it suggested, rather than viewing it from the frame of reference of the oft-repeated procedure. The $A - C$ procedure, as such, did not replace the oft-repeated method as a habit or expectancy. But it did serve to cast doubt on the

E method, to develop what one might call a "negative expectancy." It is not accurate to describe extinction as occurring through the learning of a specific incompatible response or behavior or expectancy, unless one wishes to include under these phrases a general suspicion of the oft-repeated method or of repeating what one has done before.

It will be remembered that there were a few subjects who failed the extinction task and yet solved the subsequent criticals in a direct manner. Their comments after the experiment revealed that their inability to apply the *E* method to the extinction task led to gradual doubt concerning the general applicability of the oft-repeated method. This change in attitude did not make for direct solution within the time allotted for the extinction task, sometimes because it came into full fruition only toward the end of this time interval when a survey of their many attempts to apply the oft-used method had finally led to a loss of faith in the method or in their assumption that one must begin with the center jar or must use all the jars.

But why did such loss of faith in the repeated procedure or in various related assumptions not accompany every failure of the extinction task and why was it more frequent when the extinction task was solved? To answer the first part of the question, we remind the reader of the solutions and assumptions already reported, such as uncritical application of the *E* procedure to the extinction task or the assumptions that the fault lay in the experimenter, in the given jars or goal, in the unsolvability of the problem, in the subject's calculations, in insufficient time—in short, the attitude that the fault lay anywhere but in the *E* procedure. We conjecture that the actual discovery that the $A - C$ method worked in the extinction task furnished concrete proof that the problem was solvable and that the previous attempts at solution via the *E* method were futile, not because of the subject's miscalculations, etc., but because of the inapplicability of the *E* method. Failure of the *E* method to solve the problem (and many subjects' papers revealed one or more attempts via this method prior to an $A - C$ solution) served to cast doubt on the method in some cases but not in all; or we might say that for only a few subjects was the doubt aroused by failure sufficiently intense to cause a casting aside of the method. Discovery of the $A - C$ method was usually sufficient to arouse so much doubt that the *E* method was questioned and found at fault. Indeed, some subjects began to wonder whether the *E* method had not fooled or blinded them in the past and, in individual experiments, they sometimes requested permission (which was not granted) to return to previous problems.

In "reinforcement" terminology, we might say that failure of the *E* method to solve the extinction task within the time allowed did not generally make for sufficient nonreinforcement of this method whereas the discovery of the $A - C$ procedure served as strong additional non-reinforcement.

What about the subjects, relatively few in number, who solved the extinction problem and yet used the E method in the two subsequent criticals? Questioning of these subjects revealed that some of them recognized that the E method would not solve the extinction problem but still held on to the method, perhaps because it had worked so often in the past. (A similar attitude was found among those who failed the extinction problem and recognized that the failure was due to the in-applicability of the E procedure.) But there were others who had not thought only, or even specifically, in terms of the E method. Rather, they had an idea, very definite in some cases, somewhat vague in others, that these constituted subtraction problems—that the answer could be (per-haps should be) obtained by subtracting the contents of one jar from those of a larger jar.* Viewing the tasks as solvable by subtraction in-volves a supposition which is *not* weakened by the experience in the extinction task. But, in the subsequent critical, an attitude that sub-traction must be used cannot yield the $A + C$ method of solution. Sub-traction as an expectancy or frame of reference is not destroyed by an $A - C$ solution of the extinction task but is completely compatible with it. Hence, when the oft-repeated method is viewed as simply a subtraction procedure, the extinction problem need not constitute a nonreinforcing experience nor the method of solving it an incompatible response.

We have gone into so detailed an account of the subjects' attitudes toward the problems in order to reveal that they are determinants of (1) whether a reaction should be classified as a reinforcement, nonre-inforcement, or partial reinforcement of a particular response (or re-lated attitude); (2) whether various responses or expectancies are compatible or incompatible; (3) whether extinction is produced by the replacement of one response or expectancy by another, or whether the learning of the latter serves as additional nonreinforcement of the old response or expectancy.

It would seem that each of the constructs of reinforcement, nonre-inforcement, and incompatible responses does not constitute an inde-pendent variable but may itself be a function of variables (e.g., a func-tion of the subject's attitudes toward and interpretations of the prob-lems and his attempts at solution). Hence, if extinction is to be con-sidered as a function of nonreinforcement and/or the learning of an incompatible response, it may be more appropriate to regard extinction

---

* Use of an $A + C$ rather than an $A - C$ extinction task in several elementary-school classes yielded more recovery, suggesting that the subtraction hypothesis may have been quite prevalent in the basic experiment.

as a function of functions (or as a functional) rather than as a function of a finite number of independent variables.

Use of Several Extinction Problems

We turn now to experiments in which several extinction tasks were used in attempts to ascertain their apparent influence on the solution of subsequent criticals.

Individual experiments were conducted in which the usual E tasks were followed by a critical problem. If it was solved in the E manner, an extinction task was presented and then another critical. If this also was solved in the E manner, increasing numbers of extinction tasks were interspersed between the criticals. Some subjects failed to utilize the direct method in the criticals even after being given a total of ten extinction tasks and, in a very few cases, even after they had solved all or most of the extinction problems. Again we found in operation the attitudinal factors which were just discussed in relation to the basic experiment.

In some group experiments, three extinction tasks were given between the first two and the last two criticals (Luchins, 1942, pp. 42-45). For some groups the extinction problems were all of an $A - C$ character, for others of an $A + C$ character, while for still others both $A - C$ and $A + C$ extinction tasks were used, in this order: $A + C$, $A - C$, $A + C$. These experiments were administered to three college and three elementary-school groups. As a last problem each of these groups received a problem solvable by filling one jar or by the E method (C_5 problem: 3, 64, 29, get 3). Results, in terms of percentages of direct solutions, are presented in Table XII.

TABLE XII. PERCENTAGES OF DIRECT SOLUTIONS IN EXPERIMENTS USING THREE EXTINCTION TASKS

Nature of Extinction Tasks	Group	Sub-jects	C_1C_2	Ext.$_1$	Ext.$_2$	Ext.$_3$	C_3C_4	C_5
$A - C$	College	28	43	64	79	79	70	61
$A - C$	Elem. sch.	33	9	24	24	24	14	15
$A + C$	College	28	16	67	74	74	72	70
$A + C$	Elem. sch.	31	16	42	45	62	52	46
$A - C$ and $A + C$	College	25	20	28	60	56	68	68
$A - C$ and $A + C$	Elem. sch.	15	27	13	33	13	60	20

Examination of Table XII shows that the college groups consistently had more solutions of the extinction tasks and more recovery from the E effect than did the corresponding elementary-school groups (where recovery is measured by comparing the percentage of E solutions of the last two criticals with the percentage of the first two). Comments of the children revealed that many of them thought that they had been practicing one procedure, rule, or method, and that these were subtraction problems. But these comments were less frequent when three $A + C$ extinction tasks had been given; such comments were made by twenty-three of thirty-three pupils who received the three $A - C$ extinction problems but only by eight of the thirty-one pupils who received the $A + C$ extinction tasks. And these latter eight gave no direct solution of any extinction task or critical. Considering the groups as a whole, we find that the use of three $A + C$ extinction tasks produced more recovery than the use of $A - C$ or mixed extinction problems, perhaps because the $A + C$ procedure helped to dispel the opinion that these were all (or mainly) subtraction examples.

The one-jar solution of the last problem, C_5 (which was also solvable by the E method), was offered more frequently by the college students than by the children and was offered more frequently after the three extinction tasks of an $A + C$ character than after the extinction tasks of an $A - C$ character or after the mixed extinction tasks.

In order to study the relation between direct solutions of the subsequent criticals and solution of the extinction tasks, we fractionized the responses to take account of direct solution (D) or failure (F) of each of the three extinction problems. This yielded various categories: FFF, FFD, FDD, DDD, FDF, and DFF. The results indicate that there was the most recovery when all the extinction tasks were solved and the least recovery when none of them were solved. However, there were classes in which one-third of the subjects who had solved all the extinction problems used the E method in one or more of the subsequent test problems. And there were a few subjects who, although they had failed to solve any of the extinction tasks, solved the subsequent test problems in the direct way. Thus, though on the whole there was a correspondence between solution of the extinction problems and direct solutions of the subsequent critical problems, the two did not always go hand in hand.

Alternation of E Tasks and Extinction Tasks

What will be the influence on E effects if E tasks are alternated with extinction tasks (solvable by the $A + C$ or $A - C$ but not by the E method)? After the usual presentation had been used up through and including E_1, the following tasks were given: E_3, an $A - C$ problem, E_4, an $A + C$ problem, E_5, C_1, C_2, and then the usual extinction task. When this variation was administered to four Grade 6 classes, E solutions of Criticals 1 and 2 ranged from 10 to 21 per cent and failures of the usual extinction task from 6 to 19 per cent (Luchins, 1942, p. 41). This was well below the range of E effects found in the basic experiment and considerably less than the E effects found after elementary-school groups had been given three extinction tasks following the E tasks and Criticals 1 and 2 (cf. Table XII). As a last problem the four classes were given

10, 96, 4, get 58, which is not solvable by the E method but is solvable by $B - 2C - 3A$ and by $5A + 2C$. There was 61 to 94 per cent solution of this problem in the four classes; yet, when this same problem had been given to three Grade 6 classes at the conclusion of the basic experiment, not even one subject had solved it.

These results are of interest for several reasons. From the point of view of educational practices, the procedure of alternating problems solvable by three methods was *not* in line with the "rule" of pedagogy that one thing should be taught at a time, a "rule" that is reflected in the common use of isolated drill in the initial learning period. Yet most of our subjects not only learned all the methods and learned to apply each when necessary, but were also able to deal adequately with a problem requiring a different method. After the use of isolated drill (as in the basic experiment), this problem had not been solved. Here we see further evidence of deleterious influences on problem solving exerted through repetition as opposed to the apparent beneficial influences of a less repetitive type of learning.

The results also warrant discussion in terms of intermittent reinforcement. If successful application of the E procedure is termed a reinforcement of this method, then alternation of E tasks and extinction tasks necessarily made for intermittent (or occasional) reinforcement of the E method prior to Criticals 1 and 2, rather than the successive reinforcement that prevailed in the basic experiment. The role played by intermittent reinforcement—in conditioning a response—has been examined in a number of studies. The bulk of the evidence from these studies suggests that intermittent reinforcement may produce conditioning which is no weaker than conditioning produced by successive reinforcement. Indeed it may be more resistant to extinction. Yet our findings seem to constitute contrary evidence since, after intermittent reinforcement, the E effect was more rapidly extinguished. It had not become more resistant to extinction. It is not difficult to see why our results differ from those usually obtained in experiments on intermittent reinforcement. The tasks alternated between the E tasks were solvable so that, in the terminology of reinforcement, they not only served as "nonreinforcements" of the E response but also served as "reinforcements" of $A + C$ or $A - C$ responses. Direct solutions of Criticals 1 and 2 and the subsequent extinction task may therefore be interpreted as evidence of less reinforcement of the E method and stronger reinforcement of direct methods. It is noteworthy that this apparently stronger reinforcement of $A + C$ and $A - C$ occurred despite the fact that each of these methods was used only once prior to Criticals 1 and 2 while the E method was used four times prior to these problems; that is, while the E response was reinforced four times as often as $A + C$ or

$A - C$, the latter was used from about four to nine times as often as the E response in Criticals 1 and 2. Here we see that the frequency of response or of reinforcement need not be directly related to the probability of occurrence of the response nor inversely related to the probability of extinction of the response. The results further suggest that it is worth while to analyze studies on intermittent reinforcement in order to study the role played by the "nonreinforcing" experiences both in strengthening or extinguishing the so-called conditioned response as well as in strengthening other responses. In other words, what positive functions do the nonreinforcements or extinctions have in addition to (or in place of) weakening the response that is being intermittently reinforced?

Finally, alternation of E tasks and extinction tasks may be said to involve distributed or spaced practice in the E method as compared with the massed practice provided by the basic experiment. The findings are therefore of interest in terms of the relative efficacy in learning of massed-versus-distributed practice. We postpone discussion of this subject until later (see Chapter XV).

RESISTANCE TO EXTINCTION

Resistance to extinction has been used as a measure of the strength of conditioning (Brogden, 1951, p. 583). Analogously, we use a group's percentage of failure of the extinction task in the basic experiment as a measure of its strength of Einstellung and the number of extinction tasks an individual fails in an Einstellung test as a measure of his strength of Einstellung.

Studies on conditioning suggest that among factors related to resistance to extinction are (1) the number of trials needed for conditioning, (2) the number of reinforcements, (3) motivational factors, and (4) the schedule of reinforcement. Some of the experiments on E effects are pertinent to these relationships.

(1) Preliminary experiments show that rats that needed more trials for mechanization tended to need more trials for extinction.

(2) Experiments on frequency (Chapter XI) show that, after a larger number of E tasks, the E effect tended to be more resistant to extinction, but that results were influenced by attitudinal and social factors; e.g., two E tasks were as effective under speed conditions or when subjects were told to generalize a rule as five E tasks in the basic experiment. Experiential background was also a factor; thus, the E effect was more resistant to extinction for rats raised in a restricted environment than for rats raised in a freer environment (Luchins and Forgus, 1955).

(3) Resistance to extinction of the E effect was influenced by moti-

vational factors (Chapter V) and proved to be positively related to food deprivation in rats during mechanization (in a study done with the assistance of Rita Brownstein Kopin).

(4) The E effect was more resistant to extinction after successive than after intermittent reinforcement (p. 397).

Conclusion

In conclusion, we have seen that neither failure of the extinction tasks nor solution of them proved to be a necessary or a sufficient condition for extinction of the E habit. Subjects' attitudes toward the problems were important determinants of the influence of the extinction problems. Whether they failed or solved these problems, some subjects were awakened by the experience, were led to reconsider their attitude toward all the problems, or were led to re-evaluate the general applicability of the procedure they had been using.

There tended to be the most recovery when the extinction tasks were solved and the least when they were not solved. But neither the thesis that extinction is produced by unreinforced repetitions nor the thesis that extinction occurs through the learning of an incompatible response can account adequately for all the results.

Moreover, the terms involved in these theses are not as clear in meaning (in the context of the basic experiment) as they may seem to be at first glance; nor are the theses as distinct as learning theorists tend to imply. What constitutes a reinforced response, an unreinforced response, an incompatible response? Not every attempt to apply the E method to the extinction task may be construed as an unreinforced reaction. Moreover, depending on the particular frame of reference from which the problems are viewed, the method of solving the extinction problem may be compatible or incompatible with this reference frame.

The particular spacing of the extinctions or "nonreinforcements" also played a role. Less E effects resulted when extinction tasks were alternated with E tasks than when the same number of extinction tasks were given after these E tasks. This raises the problem of the roles played by the number and the spacing of extinction tasks in so-called intermittent reinforcement.

We surveyed some experiments bearing on resistance to extinction of the E effect. Further experimentation is needed, particularly since resistance to extinction has been related to rigidity of behavior, abnormal fixations, and the Freudian concept of the repetition compulsion (cf. Mowrer, 1948).

CHAPTER XV

THE FACTOR OF TIME

WHAT IS THE DURATION OF THE EINSTELLUNG?

A N Einstellung has been defined as "the set which immediately pre-disposes an organism to one type of motor or conscious act" (Warren, 1934, p. 371). It is the immediate predisposition, the temporary influence on behavior, the momentary nature of the set which is generally considered to be characteristic of an Einstellung. When we first began experimentation with the volume-measuring problems, it seemed to us that the set which subjects were developing was a very temporary sort of thing, similar to the temporary motor adjustment which Müller and Schumann (1898) found in their weight-lifting experiment and which they referred to as an Einstellung. Hence, we designated the phenomenon we were observing as an Einstellung.* But how suitable is this name? How temporary in nature is the set developed in our experimental situation?

It is known that in some cases the set was temporary, almost momentary, in nature. Thus, there were some subjects whose papers showed that they first solved Critical 1 by the E method, but immediately shifted to the direct method and gave a direct solution of this critical within the allotted time (in each of the subsequent test problems they used a direct method). Such behavior was shown by about 2 per cent of the subjects in the basic experiment. (In the analysis of results they were credited with a direct solution, and not an E solution, of Critical 1.) Some of these subjects crossed out their E solution to Critical 1 as if to indicate that they preferred the direct solution. Also, comments written by some of these subjects on their papers and remarks they made after the experiment indicated that they regarded themselves as having been momentarily "carried away" by the E method or having been on the verge of "falling into a rut." For these cases, at least, the Einstellung would seem to have been of a highly temporary nature, in line with the cited definition of an Einstellung. Some other subjects in the basic experiment used or attempted to use the E method and then shifted to a direct method in Critical 2 or in the extinction task or in Criticals 3 or 4. But there were other subjects who did not recover from the set in any test problem. This led to the question: How long can the set last? It was decided to investigate this question by pre-

---

* For another reason for this choice of name, see Chapter IX, pp. 276-77.

senting test problems at various times after the E tasks had been given (Luchins, 1942, pp. 45-47).

In an elementary-school class of thirty-five subjects, we administered only the E tasks of the basic experiment, then collected the papers and left the room. After one hour, during which the class had had a geography lesson, we re-entered the room, distributed new papers, and presented the remaining problems. Now, if the set developed by the E problems was one which *immediately* predisposed the subjects to the use of the E method, and if this predisposition had been dissipated during the one-hour interval, then we should expect to find results similar to those for control groups that had not received the E tasks. But the results obtained were not similar to those for control groups; they were within the range found in the basic study: C_1C_2, 70% E; Ext., 60% F; C_3C_4, 57% E. Thus, for three-fifths of the subjects, predisposition for the use of the E method was sufficiently intense even after one hour to blind them to the solution of the extinction task.

Of course we did not know how much E effect the subjects would have shown if they had been tested immediately after the E tasks had been given. It was decided therefore to give some of the test problems immediately after the E tasks and then to retest after various time intervals. Three elementary-school classes were given the usual experiment through Critical 2. A day later to one class, a week later to a second, and a month later to a third, we gave just Criticals 3 and 4. To simplify the presentation, we considered only those subjects who had shown E solutions in both Criticals 1 and 2. These subjects (21, 28, and 22 students) showed 70, 55, and 27 per cent E solution of Criticals 3 and 4 after a lapse of a day, a week, and a month, respectively, as compared with 100 per cent for Criticals 1 and 2. There was thus a falling off of E effects with time but even after one month some effect still prevailed.

One may suspect that, in the interim between the initial test and the retest, some subjects may have learned of the direct methods from their classmates and that this may have contributed to the decrease in E effects. But, as far as we know, this did not occur. To begin with, very few children had used the direct methods in the initial test. Moreover, when at the end of the retest session subjects were asked such questions as this, "Were any of you clever enough to learn another way of doing these problems since I was here?" no subject gave an affirmative answer.

In four other elementary-school classes to which we had administered the basic experiment, the class teachers presented Criticals 1 and 2 and the extinction task on both the third and eighth day after administration of the initial experiment. Again we simplify the presentation of results by considering only those subjects (22, 17, 17, and 16 students) who in the initial experiment had shown complete E effects. After three days, the percentages of E solutions of Criticals 1 and 2 were 73, 82, 97, and 100 (compared with 100 per cent initially), while after eight days the corresponding percentages were 36, 47, 29, and 56. Failures of the extinction task (compared with 100 per cent initially) were 48, 71, 88, and 44 per cent after three days and 36, 18, 18, and 25 per cent after eight days. Again E effects decreased with time but did not vanish even after eight days.

It would seem that for some subjects the set which was developed was not a momentary set. It is probably significant that, in response to questioning after the last session, many of those who adhered to the E method reported that they regarded the problems which they had just received as constituting a continuation of the initial experiment or a memory test of what they had done the first time and prided themselves on not forgetting.

Experimental variations were conducted in attempts to weaken the attitude that the problems given after a time interval constituted a continuation of the initial experiment (Luchins, 1942, pp. 47-49). To two sixth-grade classes the usual experiment was administered through E_5. Then, after telling the subjects that this was the "end of the experiment" (a statement not made in the previously described time-interval experiments), we collected their papers and left the room. After one-half hour we returned to one class, which in the interim had had a history lesson, and after one hour we returned to the other class, which in the interim had had one-half hour of work of their own choice followed by one-half hour of drill in the addition of fractions. On re-entering each classroom, we told the children that "a new experiment" was about to begin (a statement not made in the time-interval experiments reported above) and then presented the test problems in the usual manner. E effects were much lower than those usually obtained in the basic experiment and were somewhat lower than in the previously described time-interval experiments.

Half-hour interval .... 26 subjects C_1C_2: 29% E Ext.: 15% F C_3C_4: 15% E
One-hour interval ...... 29 subjects C_1C_2: 48% E Ext.: 7% F C_3C_4: 26% E

Note that in the criticals the class that had the one-hour interval showed more E effects than the class with only a half-hour interval. One wonders whether the greater E effects shown by the group with the one-hour interval may have been due in part to the drill they had just had in the addition of fractions; perhaps they carried over to the experiment their attitudes toward arithmetic.

When questioned after the experiment, those who had used the E method after the time intervals said that: they thought they had to subtract or had to use all three jars; they thought the experimenter wanted to see how well they remembered the old method; they wanted to show how well they remembered the old method; since the old method worked in the first problem, they used it in the others and did not bother to look for new ways. One subject said that he saw a direct method, but thought that it was too easy and that it might be wrong to use it.

A change was introduced in the described procedure by a rearrangement of the order of the test problems so that the extinction task was the first problem presented in the second session. This change was made so that subjects would be less prone to regard the second series of problems as similar to the first series because, at the outset, their attempts to use the E method would fail. Thus, in this experimental variation several factors were combined in order to help the subjects view the E problems as distinct from the test problems: a time interval between the E and the test problems, a remark at the end of the first session that this was the end of the experiment and a remark at the start of the second session that a new experiment was about to begin, and, finally, the test problems were rearranged so that the extinction task came first (followed by Criticals 1, 2, 3, and 4). This experimental variation was used in two sixth-grade classes, the time interval in one case being a half hour and in the other case two hours. To allow comparison, another sixth-grade class was given the experiment with the test problems in the rearranged order but without a time interval and without the additional remarks. It was found that the classes with the time intervals and the remarks had much less E effects than the class with no time interval and no remarks.

			Ext.	C_1C_2	C_3C_4
No time interval	20 subjects		68% F	80% E	80% E
Half-hour interval ..	22 subjects		27% F	16% E	22% E
Two-hour interval ..	21 subjects		10% F	10% E	17% E

Note that the class with the two-hour interval had the least E effects. Although the present half-hour-interval group had been given the extinction task first, it showed a higher percentage of failures of this task and a higher percentage of E solutions of C_3C_4 than did the previous half-hour-interval group.

Questioning after the experiment of those who had used the E method after the time interval produced comments similar to some of the comments obtained in the previous experiment. Some subjects said that they tried to remember the method that they had used before and finally did remember. In this connection note that, both after the half-hour and two-hour intervals, E solutions were more frequent for C_3C_4 than for C_1C_2.

Thus, when a time interval was combined with additional factors
(remarks that one experiment had ended and a new one was beginning
or these remarks plus rearrangement of the test problems), E effects
were less than when only a time interval was used and much less than
in the basic experiment. But the additional factors did not work in an
accumulative fashion; that is, the group that had the half-hour interval,
the remarks, and the rearrangement of the test problems, did not show
less E effects than the group that had only the first two of these factors.
Moreover, in every group there were subjects who showed E effects
after the time interval, in some cases apparently because they persisted
in viewing the E and test problems as belonging to one series despite
the factors that had been introduced in attempts to get them to separate
these two sets of problems.

FLUCTUATIONS OF E EFFECTS WITH TIME

In the experiments just described E effects decreased in time. Is it
permissible to generalize that E effects always dissipate in time? There
is evidence that E effects need not decrease after a time interval and
that, when a decrease does occur, it may not be proportional to the
amount of time that has elapsed. For example, in each of the time-interval experiments there were some subjects who had shown complete E
effects initially and who still showed complete E effects after the time
interval. Moreover, we found that a class that had a half-hour interval
between the E problems and the test problems showed less E effects in
the criticals than another that had an hour interval (p. 402). Also, in
individually conducted experiments some persons showed more E
solutions or failures after time intervals than they had when the test
problems immediately followed the E problems. In the main, however,
the trends we obtained point to a weakening of E effects with time.
Precisely the opposite trend has been reported by Tresselt and Leeds
(1951). Comparison between our findings and theirs is difficult because: (1) their subjects, who were tested individually, received varying numbers of E tasks, ranging from two to fourteen; (2) comparisons
were made by them of the E effects shown by different groups, one
of which received two criticals immediately after the E tasks, while
the others received the criticals one day, three days, or seven days after
the E tasks; (3) it is not known what percentages of E effects the
groups would have shown if they had all been tested immediately, which
leaves the possibility that the same trend of results might have prevailed even then (all results are within the range of responses made
by experimental groups in the basic study) and that the small differences found between groups may not be due to time intervals; (4) for all

their subjects the E method was explicitly formulated in terms of the $B - A - 2C$ formula; (5) the nature of the curve they obtained (a "reminiscence curve") suggests that shortly after seven days a downward slope sets in so that the increase in direct solutions which we found after eight days and after a month might also have been obtained in the study by Tresselt and Leeds if greater time intervals had been employed.

Tresselt and Leeds seek to account for the reminiscence-type curve by positing that perhaps with the passing of time the specific sensory material faded while the attitude orientation which was acting as an anchoring or referential point became more available. One might also account for an increase in E effect with time by appealing to a consolidation of the memory trace corresponding to the E method. Or one might give an explanation in terms of the dissipation with time of reactive inhibition, as Hull (1943, p. 295) does in accounting for reminiscence effects.

RELATION TO FORGETTING

Some of the children who employed the E method in the test problems presented after the time interval, reported afterwards that they were proud that they had not forgotten the method they had used before. This raises the question whether those who employed the direct method after the time interval *had forgotten* the E method. Does an increase in direct solutions after a lapse of time represent simply a forgetting of the E method?

The evidence that is available suggests that in many cases awareness of the direct method did not presuppose a forgetting of the E method. The fact that E solutions of the criticals and direct solutions of the extinction task were sometimes made by the same subject would seem to indicate that here the E method had not been forgotten. Moreover, some subjects first gave an E solution and then crossed it out and gave the direct method. Also, while solving a test problem, some subjects wrote that they remembered or were aware of the applicability of the method they had used before, but that they saw a shorter or better method now. Finally, we refer to results obtained with the volume-measuring test from the manual of rigidity tests (Luchins, 1950a) wherein an E task was given after all the test problems; most of those who used the direct methods in the test problems solved this E problem. In brief, that the E method was not used in the test problems should not be interpreted to mean that this method had necessarily been forgotten.

The nature of forgetting is of prime interest to learning theorists. Different kinds of learning have been assumed to be characterized by different "laws of forgetting." Tolman writes that true forgetting, weakening with the mere passage of time, occurs for all field expectancies but not for equivalence beliefs. Measured in terms of forgetting, does the E effect behave more like a field expectancy or more like an equivalence belief? The answer cannot be given until it is decided how "forgetting" should be defined and measured. Should forgetting be designated as weakening of the Einstellung, manifested by disuse of the E method, or should it be designated as actual failure to remember the E procedure as manifested, say, by failure of an E problem? We suspect that, even after a suitable definition of forgetting is decided upon, no neat generalization can be drawn concerning the E effect in relation to forgetting. Studies completed to date show different trends for different individuals and even for the same individual studied under different conditions. Probably no one generalization will prove to be valid for the relation of the E effect with time, since overtly similar E effects may be resultants of different processes which have characteristically different behavior in time.

It is hypothesized that E effects brought about by a sheer repetitive tendency are likely to show a sharp, precipitous drop if a sufficiently large time interval is introduced before the test problems, while E effects brought about by conscious assumptions or generalizations tend to persist, increase, or decline in time depending on the attitudes which the subject has toward the new test problems in relation to the original problems and what he considers to be his task; e.g., whether he regards the problems presented after the time interval as a continuation or memory test of the initial experiment, whether he tries to remember and repeat the method he employed initially, and whether he succeeds in remembering this method. In short, we hypothesize that the carry-over from repetition alone tends to dissipate rapidly if a period of no practice intervenes, whereas E effects that depend on various assumptions and generalizations concerning the problems will show a greater variety of behavior with the passing of time. Before experimentation can be undertaken to test these hypotheses, there must first be devised a method of determining accurately which phenomenon is involved in a particular case of E effect.

MASSED AND DISTRIBUTED PRACTICE

When rest intervals between trials are very short, no more than a few seconds in duration, practice is said to be massed or unspaced, whereas, when rest intervals are longer than this, practice is considered to be distributed or spaced. Many of our experiments may be discussed with reference to the use of massed or distributed practice. For example, the practice may be said to have been massed when the basic experiment was individually administered (Luchins, 1939) since the next problem was presented as soon as one was completed. In the group administration, however, the practice may be regarded as having been massed only for those subjects who required the total amount of time allotted to each problem or only a few seconds short of this amount, whereas the others, who had rest intervals while waiting for the next problem to be presented, may be said to have had spaced practice. Speed experiments (Luchins, 1942, pp. 53-57) may be considered to have involved massed practice for all subjects since they went rapidly from one problem to the next. On the other hand, the nonspeed experiments (Luchins, 1942, pp. 57-58) may be regarded as having involved spaced practice for many subjects since there were no fixed time allotments, subjects were told not to hurry, and (with the exception of the extinction task for which ten minutes was allowed) one problem was not presented until the entire class had finished the previous task, so that many subjects had rest intervals while waiting for the next problem. But in these experiments the nature of the practice was incidental to other factors. We turn now to experiments that were primarily concerned with comparing the influence on E effects of massed and distributed practice.

In one study, twenty-four graduate students at the New School for Social Research in New York City were tested individually with paper-and-pencil mazes, the experiment following the paradigm of the basic experiment. Half of the subjects were told to see how quickly they could do all the mazes and were given one maze immediately after the other. They showed considerable E effects, with all of them using the circuitous path (E method) in Criticals 1 and 2 and more than two-thirds of them following this path even in the extinction maze. Each of the other twelve subjects received the mazes over a period of several hours, with the experimenter chatting informally with the subjects between mazes; the periods between mazes were not uniform but ranged in duration from about five minutes to fifteen minutes. None of these subjects showed any E effects. These results suggest that massed practice may make for more E effects than distributed practice. However, it is recognized that factors other than the difference in the nature of the practice may possibly have contributed to the results; for example, the greater tension apparently experienced by those studied under massed practice (itself probably a function of the instructions to do the mazes quickly and of the rapid, massed presentation of the mazes) may have enhanced E effects.

Another experiment on the influence of massed and distributed practice utilized mazes under mirror-tracing conditions. Thirty Montreal children, from eight to nine years of age, were tested individually (with

the assistance of M. Rotstein) with a series of mazes from the manual
of Einstellung tests (Luchins, 1950a). The first was an illustrative
maze; then there were eight set-inducing mazes, two criticals, four
extinction mazes, and, finally, two more criticals. In an attempt to
reduce the tension which we have often found to be a concomitant of the
maze mirror tracing, the children were told at the outset that the mazes
were puzzles and that this was not a test. Moreover, no mention was
made of speed or of a need to do the mazes quickly. Half of the children
had massed practice; as soon as a child indicated that he had completed
a maze, this maze was removed and the next one was presented. The
others had spaced practice; after a child indicated that he had completed a maze, he was given a paragraph of simple reading matter and
allowed one minute to read it. Different paragraphs, unrelated in their
contents, were given between the mazes. In the first extinction maze
(but never in the subsequent extinction mazes) there were some subjects who indicated that they had completed the maze, whereas they had
actually followed the zigzag path, apparently heedless of the line intended as a barrier. In such cases the experimenter did not point out
the subjects' error to them but proceeded just as if the task had been
completed correctly.

It is noteworthy that every one of the thirty children first followed
the direct path in the illustrative maze (that is, the path straight up-
ward from the starting point to the goal). They were then asked to
see if they could find other paths, so that eventually each child mirror
traced all three paths that led to the goal in this maze (the direct
path, a circuitous, zigzag side path on one side, and a shorter path
on the other side). The time spent on the illustrative maze ranged
from seven to fifteen minutes with an average of ten minutes.

Despite the attempts to reduce tension, the children, under both
conditions of practice, showed signs of considerable tension, particularly in the early set-inducing mazes. There was fidgeting, sighing,
and, in the case of one child, even crying, as they wrestled with the
perplexities of mirror tracing the circuitous path. Many children expressed the hope that each set-inducing maze would be the last or
bemoaned the fact that the only path to the goal was so "crooked"
and so difficult to trace. Yet, in the first two criticals most children
persisted in following the "crooked" path (E method) and did not
shift to the direct, straight path. E effects in these first criticals were
somewhat less pronounced for those who had distributed (spaced)
practice than for those who had massed practice.

Massed practice .... 15 subjects C_1: 93% E C_2: 87% E
Spaced practice .... 15 subjects C_1: 80% E C_2: 80% E

When questioned after the experiment, most children said that they had not realized that the direct path led to the goal in Criticals 1 and 2.

The first extinction maze was failed by four children under each condition of practice; that is, 27 per cent of those who had massed practice and 27 per cent of those who had distributed practice followed the E path in this maze. The three subsequent extinction mazes were solved by every child. Awareness of the direct path carried over to Criticals 3 and 4 where about nine-tenths of the subjects traced this path, often also tracing the E path. Most children who traced both paths said that they did so in order to show that they realized both paths led to the goal or because they weren't sure which path the experimenter wanted or which was the "right" answer. Listed below are the percentages of subjects who offered only an E solution or only a direct (D) solution or both solutions (D + E), as well as the total percentages of E solutions (the percentages of E only plus the percentages of D + E) and the total percentages of direct solutions (the percentages of D only plus the percentages of D + E).

Massed
    practice C_3: 13% E only 27% D only 60% D + E 73% total E 87% total D
Spaced
    practice C_3: 13% E only 34% D only 53% D + E 66% total E 87% total D
Massed
    practice C_4: 13% E only 14% D only 73% D + E 86% total E 87% total D
Spaced
    practice C_4: 7% E only 33% D only 60% D + E 67% total E 93% total D

Note that under spaced practice the frequencies of E solutions only and of total E solutions were as low as or lower than under massed practice while the frequencies of direct solutions and of total direct solutions under spaced practice were as large as or larger than under massed practice. Thus, while E effects in Criticals 3 and 4 were low under either condition of practice, they seemed to be somewhat lower under distributed practice. Recall that it was also distributed practice that yielded lower E effects in Criticals 1 and 2.

It may be in order to refer briefly to children's reactions to the reading material interspersed between the mazes. Many children made comments which suggested that they regarded the readings as secondary, as less important than the mazes. Perhaps this was because they were not questioned about the readings. Extreme lack of interest in the interpolated paragraphs was shown by one youngster who asked if he might do the mazes without the readings. At the other extreme was a youngster who seemed to be deeply absorbed in the readings and seemed to show little interest in the mazes.

Finally, we turn to the time required for the mazes. The time was recorded for each maze through and including Critical 2. The total time, in minutes, spent by the fifteen children studied under each condition, was as follows for the illustrative maze and the eight set-inducing mazes, respectively.

Massed practice 160	94	54	$52\frac{3}{4}$	29	$20\frac{1}{4}$	$17\frac{1}{2}$	15	$13\frac{1}{4}$
Spaced practice 138	64	$46\frac{1}{2}$	32	22	$20\frac{1}{2}$	$16\frac{1}{4}$	$15\frac{1}{2}$	$14\frac{3}{4}$
Difference 22	30	$7\frac{1}{2}$	$20\frac{3}{4}$	7	$-\frac{1}{4}$	$1\frac{1}{4}$	$-\frac{1}{2}$	$-1\frac{1}{2}$

Negative numbers indicate that the total time for a particular maze was greater under spaced practice. Note that the total time required for the illustrative maze was less under spaced than under massed practice. This difference certainly cannot be attributed to the conditions of practice since no spacing had been introduced when the illustrative maze was given; that is, the children had not yet been given any paragraphs to read. It would seem that, by chance, those selected for the spaced practice were somewhat faster in the illustrative maze. One wonders to what extent the time differences in the first four set-inducing mazes, which consistently favor spaced practice, were due to the conditions of practice. Perhaps the interval of one minute between mazes, devoted to reading, gave subjects a chance to recover somewhat from the fatigue and tension associated with the mirror tracing. On three of the last four set-inducing mazes, a smaller total time was required by those who had massed practice, quite unlike what happened in the earlier mazes. One wonders whether these results were influenced by the apparent decrease in strain and emotional tension in the later set-inducing tasks or by the smaller time required for these mazes, which in turn probably made for less fatigue than in the earlier tasks. Perhaps there was less need for rest periods during which to recover from fatigue and strain, when the later set-inducing mazes were solved than was the case for the earlier ones. That the time factor favored distributed practice in the early set-inducing mazes but massed practice in most of the later set-inducing mazes raises the question whether distributed practice is more efficient than massed practice in the early stages of acquiring or learning a skill but less efficient than it in later stages where, for example, one practices at becoming more proficient in executing the skill.

The mean time spent on the set-inducing mazes was computed for all fifteen children studied under each condition of practice and was computed separately for those who gave E solutions to both Criticals 1 and 2 and for those who gave a direct solution to at least one of these criticals. The mean times, in minutes, per set-inducing maze, were as follows:

	Massed Practice	Spaced Practice
All subjects	2.4	1.9
Subjects who gave E solutions to C_1C_2	2.4	2.0
Subjects who gave D solutions to C_1 or C_2	2.5	1.6

We see that the mean time per set-inducing maze was lower under spaced practice. This shows that the relative time advantage enjoyed in the early set-inducing mazes by those who had spaced practice outweighed the relative disadvantage in the later set-inducing mazes. A result which is of some interest, but which is difficult to account for, is that, under spaced but not under massed practice, the mean time per set-inducing maze was less for those who gave a direct solution to Criticals 1 or 2 than for the other subjects.

Totals for the time, in minutes, spent on Criticals 1 and 2 by the fifteen subjects studied under each practice condition were as follows:

	Massed Practice	Spaced Practice
Critical 1	9¾	11½
Critical 2	9¼	10½

The mean time spent on these criticals, considered as a unit, was computed for all the subjects studied under each practice condition and separately for those who gave E solutions to both of these criticals and for those who gave a direct solution to at least one of these criticals. The mean times, in minutes, were as follows:

	Massed Practice	Spaced Practice
All subjects	0.6	0.7
Subjects who gave E solutions to C_1C_2	0.7	0.8
Subjects who gave D solutions to C_1 or C_2	0.3	0.4

Results with respect to both the total time and the mean time show that the time factor, which favored massed practice in the later set-inducing mazes, continued to favor this form of practice in Criticals 1 and 2. It should be noted that under each condition of practice it required only about half as much time, on the average, to trace the direct path as it took to trace the E path.

(Unfortunately, a record was not kept of the number of times the subject stopped and started the tracing of a path or of the number of errors made per maze, for example, the number of times the subject went outside the boundary line or the number of reversals in direction. It would have been of interest to have studied the differential influences, if any, of the conditions of practice on stops and starts and on errors and also the influences on the general smoothness of the tracing. If such factors and other performance factors are studied in future research, there may result a better comprehension of the influence of practice conditions on the total learning situation.)

It is of some interest to discuss the results obtained in the present experiment with reference to a thesis that some psychologists regard as one of the best-established generalizations in the field of learning; namely, the thesis that some form of spaced or distributed practice yields faster learning than does massed practice—the economy and efficiency of distributed practice (McGeoch, 1942, p. 119). For the sake of discussion, we momentarily accept the rather questionable assumption that all differences in results between those who had spaced and those who had massed practice were due solely to the difference in the nature of the practice. The finding that those who had spaced practice took less time to solve the early mazes and less time, on the average, to solve the set-inducing mazes, may be interpreted as supporting the cited generalization. But the finding that those who had massed practice took less time than those who had distributed practice in most of the later set-inducing mazes and less time in Criticals 1 and 2, would seem to run counter to the generalization. The present experiment (and, similarly, the previously described experiment studying non-mirror tracing of mazes under two conditions of practice) suggests that massed practice tends to yield more E effects. Is this finding consistent with the cited generalization? Before attempting to answer this question, we turn to a related finding by other investigators which they interpreted as seemingly inconsistent with the generalization.

In a study of the comparative influence of massed and distributed practice on the development of a mental set (Kendler *et al.*, 1952), a variation of the arithmetical technique was utilized. Actual containers, each labeled as having a capacity of a certain number of cubic inches, and a storage receptacle containing beans, were furnished in every problem. The problems were phrased in terms of beans; thus, the first illustrative problem became: Given an empty 29-cu.-in. container and an empty 3-cu.-in. container, as well as a large supply of beans, obtain 20 cu. in. of beans. After seven E problems, solvable by the $B - A - 2C$ formula, one critical problem was given, solvable also by $A - C$. Not more than five minutes was allowed for working on any one problem. The 100 college subjects to whom the experiment was administered individually were divided into two groups, a "massed" group that received each E problem immediately after completion of the preceding E problem and a "distributed" group that had a three-minute time interval between the completion of one and the beginning of the next E task (an interval devoted to the rating of humorous cartoons). It was found that the massed group had a larger percentage of E solutions than the distributed group, with the difference significant at the 2 per cent level. The results, which are interpreted as suggesting that mental sets are learned to a stronger degree under massed conditions, "appear at first glance to be inconsistent with the generalization that some form of positive distribution yields faster learning than massed practice" (Kendler *et al.*, 1952, p. 23). To integrate their results with those already reported within the area of distribution of practice, they note that in conditioning situations distributed practice has proved superior to massed practice for the acquisition of a new response tendency or the strengthening of a weak response tendency, but inferior to it for the extinction of a response tendency (that is, extinction usually occurred more rapidly under massed trials), and they then offer the novel conjecture that the learning of a mental set does not mainly reflect the acquisition or strengthening portion of the learning process but "mainly reflects that portion of the learning process in which distributed practice is 'inferior' to massed practice, viz., experimental extinction" (p. 24).

This extinction hypothesis of mental set, as it is called, assumes in the case of the Einstellung phenomenon that the responses necessary for the E solution (e.g., filling the larger jar first) are among the dominant response tendencies within the response repertoire of the individual and that learning of the mental set involves weakening or extinction of tendencies to fill either of the end jars first. Considering the results of our control-group subjects, who with few exceptions responded to the problems in the direct manner, we wonder whether the filling of the largest jar is actually a dominant response tendency. It may be remembered that prior memorization of the number combinations involved in the E problems (Chapter XII) failed to make filling of this jar a dominant response tendency when only test problems were given. The facts about behavior in the Einstellung situation would therefore not seem to support this extinction hypothesis of mental set.

Another problem is whether the only reconciliation with what is known concerning distribution of practice is to assume that the learning of a mental set corresponds to the experimental-extinction phase of the conditioning situation. Even in the so-called acquisition phase, distributed practice does not always make either for faster learning or for better retention; so the so-called generalization is by no means without exception (McGeoch, 1942; Hovland, 1951). Hovland (1951, p. 636) concludes that, while most investigators of the subject favor some form of distributed practice, "there are enough studies favoring massed practice to indicate that there are certain factors that favor massing of practice and others that favor distribution." In particular, he notes that massing has been found to be favored when a period of time is required to "get set" or to "warm up" (p. 638). But such "getting set" is presumably what occurs in the development of a mental set so that the reported superiority of massed conditions for the development of an Einstellung is consistent with certain other results that have been reported in the area of distribution of practice.

It should be noted that the problem of the influence of distribution of practice originated in the desire to discover conditions that make for more efficient, more economical learning. We therefore ask whether it is massed or distributed practice that makes for (1) faster learning of a mental set, (2) faster learning of the set method, or (3) more efficient solutions of subsequent problems. The results obtained by Kendler *et al.* were interpreted by them as indicating that massed learning makes for faster learning of a mental set—point (1) above—but were not applied to points (2) and (3). As far as we know, there is no conclusive evidence that one or another distribution of practice consistently makes for faster learning or faster application or better retention of the E method. As we noted when discussing E effects in relation to forgetting, use of direct methods in the criticals did not constitute evidence that the subject had not learned the E method or that he had forgotten it or that he could not apply it when it was needed for solution. Results in the mirror-tracing experiment were rather inconclusive since in the early set-inducing mazes there was generally more rapid tracing of the E path under distributed practice than under massed practice but in the later mazes the reverse tended to be the case. Further research is required to determine whether it is after massed or after distributed practice that there occurs more rapid or more frequent application of the E method in problems where it is required for solution or where it is the most efficient method of solution. Neither this issue nor that of the relative influence of massed and distributed practice on the rate of learning and extent of retention of the E method has as yet been adequately studied. Nor do we know whether the influence of various practice conditions is the same for volume-measuring problems as for mazes or for mirror-tracing mazes or for other kinds of Einstellung situations.

Let us turn now to point (3). For the volume-measuring problems, we found that direct solutions of the critical problems took less time, on the average, than E solutions of these problems. A similar trend prevailed in the study by Kendler *et al.*, with the difference between the time scores of those who solved the critical problem directly and those who solved it by the E method significant beyond the 0.01 level of confidence. To the extent that distributed practice yielded more direct solutions in these experiments, these results may be interpreted as consistent with the generalization concerning the (usual) superiority of distributed practice, provided that the learning under consideration is the learning of the direct method. Or, if the learning under consideration is that of more efficient solutions of problems, and if a shorter solution is considered more efficient, then these results may be regarded as consistent with the generalization. But it is not always an easy matter to decide upon a criterion for efficiency or superiority or speed of learning. Thus, most experiments dealing with the Einstellung phenomenon under different conditions of practice have revealed that, when an extinction task was given, there were more solutions of this task under distributed practice than under massed practice; but the mirror-maze experiment done with children showed no difference in solutions of the extinction task under the two conditions of practice, although there were somewhat more direct solutions of the criticals under spaced practice than under massed practice. Hence, the results of this mirror-maze experiment would point to different conclusions concerning the relative superiority of the two conditions of practice depending on whether the criterion was use of a direct method in the criticals or in the extinction tasks. Even in the criticals, different conclusions could be drawn depending on whether the criterion of an efficient solution was use of a direct method or the time of solution, since under spaced practice there were somewhat more direct solutions of the first two criticals than under massed practice but the average time of solution of these criticals was slightly less under massed practice.

There is one conclusion concerning the distribution of practice which does seem to be contradicted by experiments on the Einstellung effect. Ericksen (1942) concluded from an overview of various studies that distributed practice tends to produce a fixation of response whereas massed practice makes for greater variability of behavior. The reverse trend, however, is suggested by studies dealing with the Einstellung phenomenon. Besides the study by Kendler and his associates, there is a study by Vineberg (1951) in which it was found that the mental set after massed practice was somewhat stronger (although not significantly so) than after distributed practice. Our speed and nonspeed experiments, in which rapid (massed) presentation of the problems yielded more E effects than less hurried (less massed) distribution, may also be interpreted as supporting evidence. Our experiments in which E tasks and extinction tasks were alternated, so that there was distributed practice in the E method, consistently yielded weaker mental sets than the basic experiment where practice was more massed. Moreover, experiments with the mazes showed more E effects under massed practice than under spaced practice, a result true for every test problem in the maze experiment with graduate students and true for criticals in the mirror-maze experiment with children. Thus, Einstellung experiments point to more fixation of response and less variability of behavior with massed practice than with distributed practice.

Let us now return to the question raised in the discussion of results in the mirror-maze experiment: Is the finding of somewhat greater E effects with massed practice consistent with the generalization concerning the (usual) superiority of distributed practice in learning? This finding and, similarly, the finding in other Einstellung experiments that stronger mental sets follow massed practice may be interpreted to mean that under massed practice the learning of mental sets was "superior" to what it was under distributed practice; and hence it may be regarded as *inconsistent* with the cited generalization. On the other hand, these very results, since they imply more direct solutions of test problems under distributed practice, may be interpreted to mean that under distributed practice there was "superior" learning of the direct methods, and hence the results may be regarded as *consistent* with the cited generalization. More generally, whether the results in the mirror-maze experiment and in the other experiments, including that of Kendler and his associates, are considered to be consistent or inconsistent with the cited generalization, may depend on what learning is under consideration and on what criteria are used to measure superiority or efficiency of learning.

In interpreting results found under massed and spaced practice, one must be cautious about attributing differences in results solely to differences in the nature of distribution of practice. Comments and other overt behavior of the subjects in the speed and nonspeed experiments suggest that it was not solely the difference between massed or distributed practice, but also the difference between a speed-test atmosphere and a somewhat less tense, more leisurely atmosphere that affected responses. Also, experiments in which E tasks and extinction tasks were alternated differed from those in which E tasks were massed, not solely with respect to the spacing factor, but also with respect to the nature of the tasks that intervened between the E tasks; that is, the extinction tasks not only served as "spacing" or intervening activities between the E problems, but also served to give subjects some understanding of another method of attack for such problems. Even where the character of the intervening activity is ostensibly different from that of the main activity, one may influence the other. For example, in the study by Kendler *et al.*, the task assigned during the time intervals between E problems was the rating of cartoons. It is conceivable that the critical attitude which such a task required may have carried over to the arithmetical problems, and thus have interfered with the uncritical carry-over of the E method or with the uncritical acceptance of various suppositions concerning the nature of the arithmetical tasks. In such cases, development of a strong mental set might well be hampered by distributed practice but it would hardly seem justified to attribute the interference solely to the degree of spacing between trials.

The very introduction of an intervening activity (and one usually is employed in studies of distributed practice to lessen the likelihood of unauthorized practice between trials) sometimes may interfere with the development of a strong mental set, regardless of the particular nature of the interspersed task. For one thing, it may disrupt or prevent a view of the problems as constituting a homogeneous, unitary sequence (Luchins, 1942, p. 29). For another, the interspersed tasks may make the situation less conducive to the formation and perpetuation of various assumptions concerning the tasks. Finally, the alternation of the set activity with another activity may decrease the power of the former to create a mental set. Again, an appeal to the spacing of trials or to the time interval per se would miss the point.

Many attempts at explaining the relative influence of massed and distributed learning have been concerned with the time intervals. It has been hypothesized that during these intervals there is a chance for fatigue or other inhibitory reactions associated with the response to dissipate (Miller and Mowrer's and Hull's explanations of the economy of distributed learning) or a chance for memory traces to become consolidated (Koffka's explanation of the superiority of distributed learning). But what the subject actually does during an interval, as well as his response to the absence or presence of an interval, may, we contend, influence the results, possibly sufficiently to account for all or part of the discrepancy between the results of the two methods of spacing.

In short, what takes place in experiments involving different distribution of practice may be functions of various factors (such as subjects' attitudes) some of which are themselves functions of the nature of the distribution of practice as well as of other variables. Hence, the difference in results under diverse practice conditions may not be solely a function of differences in the distribution of practice but perhaps may be more adequately characterized as a function of functions or a functional.

CHAPTER XVI

COMPLEXITY OF METHODS

IN the basic experiment, repetition of a rather complex method of
solution blinded many individuals to a simpler method. Would the
reverse also be the case; that is, would repetition of a simple procedure
blind individuals to a more complex procedure? More generally, what
influence is exerted on E effects by the degrees of complexity of the set
method and of the nonset method?

Theoretical speculation allows a diversity of predictions. If the
strength of a set is dependent primarily on the number of repetitions of
the method (or the number of rewarded repetitions), then, with the
number of repetitions (or reinforcements) held constant, one can predict equal strength of set for a complex method and for a simpler
method. The same prediction would follow if the strength of the set
and its blinding effect depended only on the number of "identical elements," those common to both the set and nonset methods. But one can
predict the development of a stronger set for simpler methods on
the grounds that (1) the same number of repetitions will make for
greater strength of association (greater habit strength or more overlearning) of a direct method, which involves fewer subhabits, than of a
more complex procedure, which presumably involves more subhabits;
(2) it is more difficult to discover a complex procedure than a simpler
procedure in the test tasks; (3) the direct method is supported by a
tendency toward least effort or least action or less work. On the other
hand, greater strength of set for the complex procedure can be predicted if it is assumed that the set-inducing tasks solvable by a complex
method are cognitively more difficult than those solvable by direct
methods and that situations which are cognitively very difficult tend to
foster rigidity or stereotypy (Goldstein and Scheerer, 1941; Hilgard,
1948, p. 342). But let us now suspend speculation and turn to some
experimental evidence.

Some of the data presented in Chapter VII may be pertinent here.
In studying the relationship between variability and rigidity, we used in
the set-inducing period tasks solvable by various methods. Here some
subjects used the most direct method—simply filling one jar—eight
successive times; yet they showed less blinding effects than subjects
who had had eight successive repetitions of the $B - A - 2C$ method.
For example, when a problem was given which was solvable by a
method not previously used by any of the subjects, it was failed by only

28 per cent of those who had practiced the simplest possible method but, in some groups, by as many as 80 per cent of those who had practiced only the $B - A - 2C$ method. This suggests that repetition of the simpler method had less blinding effects than repetition of the complex method. However, the results are complicated by the fact that those who used the most direct method often *chose* this procedure, their comments suggesting that they saw other solutions but felt that they were choosing the simplest, fastest, or best method; in contradistinction, many of those who used the $B - A - 2C$ procedure were not aware of other available methods in the set-inducing tasks. In order to eliminate this choice factor, we planned experiments in which the set-inducing tasks would be solvable by only one method.

EFFECTS OF REPETITIONS OF COMPLEX AND SIMPLE METHODS

The experiments, conducted with the assistance of Saul Martin and Martin J. Rabin, were administered to four groups of ten subjects each, mostly college girls attending McGill University. After the illustrative problems, Group 1 received six tasks each solvable only by $B - A - 2C$; Group 2, six tasks each solvable only by $A - C$; Group 3, six tasks solvable only by $A + C$; Group 4, three problems solvable only by $A - C$ alternated with three problems solvable only by $A + C$. Every group then got the usual Criticals 1, 2, 3, and 4. The last task was an extinction task, one not solvable by any of the methods practiced in the six set-inducing tasks; the usual extinction problem (28, 76, 3, get 25) was given to Group 1 while the remaining groups received the problem, 28, 76, 3, get 42, solvable by $B - A - 2C$.

Mean percentages of $B - A - 2C$ solutions to the four critical problems were 50, 15, 5, and 0 for Groups 1 through 4, respectively. Group 1, which had six repetitions of the $B - A - 2C$ method, subsequently used this method much more frequently in the criticals than did any of the other groups. Of the groups that had had practice in $A - C$ and/or $A + C$, from 85 to 100 per cent offered direct solutions to the criticals.

Should this strong tendency to use direct methods in the criticals, after practice in one or more direct methods, be interpreted as evidence of a set or Einstellung for direct methods? To begin with, it is doubtful that the tendency to use direct methods in the criticals should be attributed solely (or even mainly) to the prior experience in the set-inducing tasks; control subjects in the basic study, who received only the test problems, also showed a marked tendency to use direct methods. However, if E effects are interpreted literally as continued use of a practiced method, then a direct solution to a critical in Groups 2, 3, and 4 would have to be taken as evidence of E effect. But, if E effects are interpreted to involve deleterious effects, being blinded to a better or more direct method, then it would not be justifiable to regard a direct solution of a critical as an index of E effect. Also, subjects who practiced only the $A - C$ procedure (or only the $A + C$ procedure) in the set-inducing tasks were often able to discover and use the other direct method when it was needed in a critical, so that they did not adhere to the practiced method when it was inappropriate and they were not blinded to another direct method when it was required for solution.

The crucial criterion of E effects was the fate of the extinction task which could not be solved by the method (or methods) that a group had practiced. Failures of the extinction task were 50, 20, 40, and 20 per cent in Groups 1 through 4, respectively. We see that half of the subjects in Group 1 were unable to discover the $A - C$ solution after repeating $B - A - 2C$, whereas more subjects were able to discover the $B - A - 2C$ procedure after repeating one or more direct methods. Thus, repetition of a complex procedure apparently exerted more blinding effects than repetition of simpler procedures.

Varying the Relation Between Set and Nonset Methods

Experiments were undertaken to study the influence on E effects of set methods which were more complex or less complex than $B - A - 2C$ and of nonset methods which were more or less complex than $A - C$ or $A + C$. The experiments were administered to groups of Montreal high-school students. In each case the paradigm was that of the basic experiment but other set and nonset methods were involved. For Group 1 the set method was $A + B - 4C$ and the nonset method was $B - A - C$; that is, each set-inducing task was solvable only by $A + B - 4C$, the criticals by both methods, and the extinction task only by $B - A - C$; e.g., Critical 1 was 9, 84, 6, get 69 which was solvable by $A + B - 4C = 9 + 84 - 24 = 69$ and by $B - A - C = 84 - 9 - 6 = 69$.

Group 2 was given a related series of problems in which the roles of these methods were reversed. Now the method which solved each of the set-inducing problems was $B - A - C$ while the methods which solved each of the criticals were $A + B - 4C$ and $B - A - C$. The critical problems were identical for Groups 1 and 2 while the extinction problems differed only in the volume to be obtained. The extinction task for Group 2 was solvable by $A + B - 4C$.

For Group 3, another series was employed in which the set method was $B - A - C$ and the nonset method was simply the filling of the first jar, designated symbolically as A. For example, the first critical problem, 2, 12, 8, get 2, was solvable by $B - A - C = 12 - 2 - 8 = 2$, or simply by filling the 2-quart jar. The extinction task was solvable by the A method.

A related series was used for Group 4 in which the roles of these methods were reversed so that the set method was A and the nonset method was $B - A - C$. The critical problems were identical with those given to Group 3, while the jar quantities, but not the goal, were identical in the extinction problems. The extinction task was solvable by $B - A - C$.

In order to keep the number of repetitions of the set method constant, we used in the analysis of results the responses of only those subjects who had succeeded in solving the last four set-inducing problems by the set method. Of the twenty-four subjects in Group 1, thirteen did not meet this criterion. Casualties were fewer in the remaining groups: one out of twenty-two in Group 2, none of the twenty-three in Group 3, and three of the thirty-two in Group 4. The three subjects who failed in Group 4 were apparently baffled by the simplicity of a method which necessitated the filling of only one of the three given jars.

A tabular presentation of results may be helpful here. Table XIII re-

TABLE XIII. EFFECTS OF VARYING THE RELATION BETWEEN SET
AND NONSET METHODS

	Group 1 (11 subjects)	Group 2 (21 subjects)	Group 3 (23 subjects)	Group 4 (29 subjects)
Set method..............................	$A + B - 4C$	$B - A - C$	$B - A - C$	A
Nonset method.........................	$B - A - C$	$A + B - 4C$	A	$B - A - C$
Percentage of set solutions of Criticals 1 and 2..........	45	100	47	100
Percentage of failures of extinction task....................	36	100	9	28
Percentage of set solutions of Criticals 3 and 4............	22	100	39	95

veals that striking differences in results were obtained by reversing the roles of the direct and indirect methods; by holding the set method constant but varying the nonset methods; by holding the nonset method constant but varying the set methods.

Reversal of the set and nonset procedures yielded very different results in the *same* critical problems. When the set and nonset procedures both required three jars, the group set for the *more direct* method (Group 2) never shifted from this method. But, when the group was set for the *less direct* method (Group 1), more than half shifted to the direct procedure in Criticals 1 and 2 and more than three quarters did so in Criticals 3 and 4. Differences between the groups' responses are statistically significant at the 0.01 level. A practically identical trend of results, similarly statistically significant, was obtained when the methods which were reversed differed in the number of jars required.

Reversal of the set and nonset methods also had differential influences on solution of the extinction task. The difference was particularly striking when three-jar methods were involved. In contrast to the complete failure of Group 2 to find the $A + B - 4C$ procedure, only 36 per cent of Group 1 failed to find the $B - A - C$ procedure needed to solve their extinction task; the difference is significant at the 0.01 level.

In the experiments described in the preceding section, groups set for a direct method ($A - C$ or $A + C$ or both) had somewhat less failure of an extinction task than a group set for a more complex method ($B - A - 2C$). But, in the present experiments, the opposite trend prevails. Here a set for a simpler method seemed to have a more blinding effect or interfering effect on the discovery of a complex method than was the case when the roles of the two methods were reversed. Perhaps the present results are partly attributable to the greater number of repetitions of the set method when it was the more direct procedure. In the latter case, it was invariably used in the first two criticals, making for seven repetitions of the method prior to the extinction problem, as compared to five repetitions for some of the subjects who were set for a more complex method. An even more influential factor may have been the relative complexity of the methods which solved the extinction problem. Subjects in the experiments described in the preceding section were mainly college students for whom discovery of the $B - A - 2C$ procedure presumably was not too much of a challenge. But the present study used high-school students, some of whom might have found it difficult to discover the complex method of solving an extinction problem within the two minutes allotted, perhaps even if they had not had the preceding set-inducing problems. The method which solved the extinction problem had not been illustrated and they had had practice only in a much simpler method. It was quite a jump from practice of the A procedure, which did not require subtraction, to discovery of the $B - A - C$ procedure. It was also a considerable jump from practice of the $B - A - C$ method to discovery of the $A + B - 4C$ procedure, which requires "addition" of two jars and "multiplication" of one jar. On the other hand, those who had practiced the more complex method were better prepared to find the simpler procedure needed in their extinction problem. The results therefore emphasize the importance of the relative complexity of the set and nonset methods and of the subject's cognitive ability to discover the methods.

In light of the stress placed on identical elements in some accounts of transfer of training, it is relevant to note that reversal of the set and nonset methods left unaltered the "identical elements" shared by these methods—and yet yielded vivid differences in E effects.

Holding constant the set method $(B - A - C$, Groups 2 and 3) we find that responses to the test problems differed significantly when one or another *nonset* method was required. Particularly striking is the complete failure of the extinction task by those in Group 2, where the $A + B - 4C$ method had to be found, in contrast to only 9 per cent failure by those in Group 3, where the A method had to be found. The same presentation of the same set-inducing problems here yielded very different E effects, depending on the nature of the test problems and of the nonset method. Clearly, the experimenter's knowledge of the set-inducing experience is not sufficient grounds for prediction of subsequent E effect unless he relates it to the kind of test situation to be used.

Holding constant the nonset method $(B - A - C$, Groups 1 and 4), we see that seven repetitions of the A method were not as blinding in their influence on solution of the extinction problem as only five repetitions (for about half of the subjects) of the more complex $A + B - 4C$ procedure. Because of the larger number of repetitions of the A method by those in Group 4 and because of the fewer subhabits involved in the A method, it might be predicted by some learning theorists that the subjects in Group 4 would have the stronger set. And so it had, if set solutions of the critical problems are used as the criterion. But the reverse is true if failures of the extinction task are used as the criterion. Here we see that the relative strength of two sets depends on what is used as an index of the strength of set.

What conclusions may be drawn about the influence on E effects of the relative degree of complexity of the set and nonset methods? Some of the experimental evidence suggests that less blinding effects are exerted by repetition of a simple method than by repetition of a complex method; but the series of experiments just described imply that this is too simple a formulation and suggest that there may be complicating factors, such as a subject's cognitive ability to discover the nonset method even if he had not had the preceding set-inducing experiences. It is tentatively hypothesized that, if this ability is not in issue, then repetition of a simple procedure tends to exert less blinding effects than the same number of repetitions of a more complex procedure; further research on this point is required.

A NOTE ON THE RELATION BETWEEN STRENGTH AND EFFECT OF SET

The experimental findings suggest that the observed E effect may depend not only on the nature of the set-inducing trials but also on the kind of test situation employed, and, in particular, on the relative complexity of the set and nonset method and on the individual's ability to discover the nonset procedure. After the subject has had the set-inducing problems and has presumably developed an Einstellung of a certain strength, the actual *E* effect he shows will depend on the kind of test problems used. Hence, it is necessary to distinguish between *strength* of Einstellung and the observed *effect* of Einstellung. In a more general sense, it is necessary to distinguish between habit strength, considered as a characteristic of the habit, and the observed influences of the habit, as reflected in performances in the test problems.

Habit strength has often been considered to depend on the number of reinforcements, on temporal factors such as the spacing between trials, on the interval between the reinforcing trials and the test trials, on the number of subhabits involved in the habit, etc. Our findings suggest that the nature of the testing situation may influence the observed strength of the habit. The question therefore arises whether habit strength should be treated as a characteristic of the habit or only defined operationally in terms of its observed influence relative to a certain test situation. Whatever answer may be given to this question, it would seem erroneous to equate one measure of the strength of a set with the habit strength itself, a procedure often followed in studies of learning.

Sometimes test problems are used, particularly in conditioning experiments, in which no alternative solution is available; either the organism can or cannot use the habituated procedure or either the habituated procedure does or does not lead to reward or reinforcement. But the use of such situations does not negate the distinction we have drawn between habit strength and the observed workings of habit. It is possible to construct various test situations, each characterized by admissibility or inadmissibility of the habit, or by attainment or nonattainment of a goal when the habit is applied; utilization of one rather than another test situation may make for different working of the habit. Say, the learner may be more aware of the inadmissibility of the habituated procedure or less influenced by the "nonreinforcing" nature of an extinction task when one rather than another test situation is employed. Hence, even in standard conditioning experiments, the observed "strength" of the set must be considered as relative to the particular testing instruments and criteria employed.

In a broader sense, our results suggest that, to understand or to predict a given case of learning (such as the learning of the method needed to solve the extinction problem), it is misleading to concentrate solely or mainly on past experience or solely or mainly on the present learning situation. One must take into account the temporal system of which the past and present are parts. Methods are needed in which past experiences and the present situation will not be studied in isolation, but in their relevant systemic relations to one another.

Finally, we raise the problem of the meaning of such terms as "simple" or "complex." We have implicitly characterized these terms on the basis of the number of arithmetical operations or steps involved in a method, with the method that involved more steps considered more complex. But there are other ways of characterizing complexity. In particular, a method may be described as simple if it is cognitively clear to a subject while a method may be described as less simple or more complex if it is cognitively less clear to a subject. Admittedly, in the context of the water-jug problems it is difficult to distinguish between a characterization based on number of arithmetical operations and a characterization based on cognitive clarity. However, there are contexts wherein the distinction is clearer. For example, to a mathematical problem and, specifically, to a geometric problem, there may be offered a proof which involves few steps but is cognitively unclear, difficult to understand, and an alternative proof which is more detailed, involves more steps, but is cognitively clearer, easier to understand (cf. Wertheimer, 1945, ch. 1). Future research might seek to discover how E effects are influenced if the set method is simpler than the nonset method, or vice versa, where the simpler method is cognitively clearer, easier to grasp, although it does not necessarily involve fewer steps. Cognitive clarity may depend on the particular subjects involved (for example, two proofs to a geometric problem might differ in cognitive clarity for most members of a geometry class but be equally obscure to young children who have never studied geometry and equally clear to mathematicians). However, cognitive clarity may also depend strongly on the structural features of the method and, in particular, on what Wertheimer (1945) has called the structural fittingness or appropriateness or sensibleness of the method for the problem. Hence, future research might seek to explore how E effects are influenced if the set method is structurally more appropriate than the nonset method or vice versa, and, an extreme case, if the set method is structurally sensible, completely fits the structural requirements of the problem, while the nonset method is structurally senseless or arbitrary, quite blind to the requirements of the problem, or vice versa.

Chapter XVII

COMPARISON OF SETS FOR A METHOD
WITH SETS FOR A GOAL

IN the basic experiment the volume required in a problem may be characterized as the goal or the end of the problem, and the procedure which reaches this goal may be characterized as the method or means to the end. The Einstellung developed in this experiment may then be characterized as a "method set" or a "means-end set." The question arose: If set-inducing tasks were used in which the volume to be obtained was the same in every task, would subjects develop a set for a goal and how would the effects of this "goal set" compare with the effects of the usual "method set"?

DESCRIPTION OF EXPERIMENT

Four series of set-inducing problems were devised in which the method and/or the stipulated goal, or neither of these, remained invariant. Each series contained nine set-inducing problems, with three jars given in each problem. In one series, the method $(B - A - 2C)$ and the goal (get 7 quarts of water) remained fixed while the capacities of the three given containers were changed. The first problem was 62, 95, 13, obtain 7; the second, 21, 64, 18, obtain 7; the third 16, 35, 6, obtain 7; etc. This was designated the fixed method–fixed goal $(FM–FG)$ series.

Another series of set-inducing problems was devised in which the method $(B - A - 2C)$ remained the same but not the goal. The required quantities of water for the nine problems were 7, 3, 9, 7, 11, 23, 17, 41, and 6 quarts. This was designated the fixed method–varied goal $(FM–VG)$ series.

In still another series, the volume of 7 quarts was stipulated in each of the set-inducing problems but the methods were varied. The nine problems, in the order given, were solvable by $B - A - 2C, B - A - C,$ $A - C, B - A - 2C, A + C, B - A - 2C, A - C, B - A - 2C,$ and $A - C$. This was called the varied method–fixed goal $(VM–FG)$ series.

In the fourth series of nine problems, both the method and the goal were varied $(VM–VG$ series). As in the $VM–FG$ series, the $B - A - 2C$ procedure was interspersed four times among the $A - C, A + C,$ and $B - A - C$ procedures. And, as in the $FM–VG$ series, the required volume of 7 quarts was twice stipulated among the nine goals.

Each of these four series of problems was given to a group of Montreal high-school students after it had been given the usual illustrative problems of the basic experiment. Following the last set-inducing problem, each group received a critical problem solvable by both the $B - A - 2C$ and the $A - C$ methods; for the two groups which had received problems with a fixed goal of 7 quarts, the stipulated goal was also 7 quarts in this critical problem.

After the critical, all groups received the same series of "incomplete" problems, incomplete in the sense that it was up to the subject to stipulate the volume to be obtained and to solve the problem. The incomplete problems were: 30, 67, 15, get .... quarts; 32, 83, 22, get .... quarts; 22, 59, 15, get .... quarts; 20, 60, 13, get .... quarts. It will be seen that, in the first three, the $B - A - 2C$ procedure leads to 7 quarts while, in the fourth incomplete problem, use of the $B - A - 2C$ procedure does not lead to 7 quarts but to 14 quarts. The first three incomplete problems may be described as "incomplete criticals" since they are compatible with both the fixed goal and the fixed method, while the last problem may be described as a kind of "incomplete extinction problem" since it is not simultaneously compatible with both the fixed method and the fixed goal. This experiment was administered with the assistance of Leonard Simcoe.

RESULTS

The results are presented in Table XIV. The percentage of $B - A - 2C$ solutions are listed as $\%\,E$; the combined percentages of solutions involving the $A - C$ and $A + C$ methods are listed as $\%\,D$; and all other correct solutions are listed as $\%\,O$ (other). The percentage of failures of a problem may be obtained by adding a group's percentages of $E, D,$ and O solutions and then subtracting the total from 100 per cent. For the incomplete problems, there is also presented, as $\%\,G$, the percentage of each group that chose 7 as a goal.

TABLE XIV. EFFECTS OF SETS FOR A METHOD COMPARED WITH
EFFECTS OF SETS FOR A GOAL

Group	Subjects	First Critical Problem			Three Incomplete Critical Problems				Final Incomplete Extinction Problem			
		%E	%D	%O	%E	%D	%O	%G	%E	%D	%O	%G
FM–FG......	28	82	4	0	69	3	17	76	14	0	72	68
FM–VG......	29	83	10	7	60	0	36	60	48	0	46	21
VM–FG......	24	0	100	0	25	24	46	35	4	21	62	50
VM–VG.....	30	0	100	0	19	15	59	24	7	7	69	10

Consider the responses to the first critical, for which the goal was stipulated by the experimenter, and which could be solved by the $B - A - 2C$ or $A - C$ procedures. We cannot study in this problem the relative influence of a fixed or a varied goal, but, rather, that of a fixed or a varied method. The results are clear-cut. When four repetitions of the $B - A - 2C$ procedure had been interspersed among other methods in the set-inducing period, not one subject showed an E solution of the critical problem but, instead, every subject gave a direct solution. But, when the $B - A - 2C$ procedure had been the fixed method in the nine set-inducing problems, over four-fifths of the group used it again in the critical, while few gave direct solutions. This result suggests, as do some other findings, that interspersing other methods between repetitions of the $B - A - 2C$ procedure may be effective in minimizing E effects.

Consider now the responses to the three incomplete criticals, where the E method was compatible with a choice of 7 as the goal. Here we might expect that the largest % G (or the largest % E) would occur in this order: (1) when both method and goal were fixed, (2) when either method or goal alone was fixed, and (3) when neither was invariant. The results substantiate such an expectation. Reading the columns (% G and % E) upwards, we see that the percentages selecting 7 as the goal and also the percentages using the $B - A - 2C$ method increase as we go from the group in which neither method nor goal was fixed, to the group in which the goal alone was fixed, and then to the group in which the method alone was fixed, and, finally, to the group in which both were fixed.

A set for the $B - A - 2C$ procedure inevitably led to the goal of 7 (barring arithmetical errors), whereas the reverse was not the case. Having selected 7 as the goal, the subject could employ methods other than $B - A - 2C$ to attain this goal. The table reveals that the percentages choosing the goal of 7 were never less, and were greater for three of the four groups, than the percentages using the E method. This result would seem to testify to the greater influence of a goal set as compared with a method set.

But such a conclusion cannot be drawn if we deal with intergroup comparisons. When the method was fixed in the set-inducing period, regardless of whether the goal was fixed or varied, at least 60 per cent used the $B - A - 2C$ procedure and chose 7 as the goal. But, when the method was varied, irrespective of whether or not the goal was fixed, no more than 35 per cent chose this goal. A striking contrast is obtained by comparing FM-VG and VM-FG groups. For the latter the goal was fixed in the set-inducing period and yet only 35 per cent chose this goal. For the former the goal was varied and yet 60 per cent chose this goal or, rather, used the $B - A - 2C$ method which here led to the goal. Therefore, it would seem that invariance of the method was a more influential factor in the solution of the incomplete criticals than invariance of the goal.

We are, therefore, led to this rather paradoxical state of affairs: *intragroup* comparisons of the % *G* and % *E* reveal the former to be higher and suggest that goal set was stronger than the method set in the solution of the incomplete criticals; but *intergroup* comparisons show % *E* as well as % *G* to be higher when the method was fixed rather than varied, suggesting that the method set was stronger in the solution of the incomplete criticals.

We shall return to this apparent paradox. Now let us consider responses to the incomplete extinction problem where the method set was antagonistic in its operation to the goal set. Faced with the alternative of using an oft-repeated method or goal, each of which had been subject to the same number of repetitions, 68 per cent of those in the *FM–FG* group chose 7 as the goal, thereby abandoning the practiced method. Only 14 per cent of this group adhered to the *E* method in contrast to its 69 per cent *E* solution of the three preceding incomplete criticals and its 82 per cent *E* solution of the first critical. But, in the *FM–VG* group, which had repeatedly practiced using the *E* method in connection with various goals during the set-inducing period, about half of the group still used this method in the incomplete extinction task.

The fact that most of the *FM–FG* group abandoned the fixed method but adhered to the fixed goal would seem to suggest that the goal set was here a more powerful force in solution than the method set, although both had had an equal number of reinforcements in the set-inducing period.

The table reveals that, when only the method or only the goal was invariant in the set-inducing period, about half of the group chose that fixed factor in the incomplete extinction task; that is, about half in the *FM–VG* group used the *E* method while exactly half in the *VM–FG* group chose the fixed goal. Hence, nine repetitions in the set-inducing period of the goal alone or the method alone was about equally effective in its influence on solution of the extinction task. But nine repetitions in the set-inducing period of *both* goal and method showed just about as little influence in this problem, so far as method was concerned, as nine repetitions in which both goal and method had been varied.

COMMENTS

Whether the goal set should be considered to have exerted a stronger influence than the method set depends on the particular problem in which the effect is observed (incomplete criticals or extinction task) as well as on the particular kind of comparison made (e.g., intragroup or intergroup comparisons in the incomplete criticals). One of the conclusions drawn in the chapter on complexity of the set method was

that the observed effect of the habit may depend on the testing instrument. Here we see that the relative effects of two sets also depend on
the particular problem in which the influences are observed and even
on the mode of comparison. Hence, one must be very cautious about
drawing inferences concerning the *strength* of a habit or the *relative
strength* of two or more habits from observations of their apparent influences. If the *FM–FG* group, for example, had developed a "strong"
method set, the operation of this set was certainly far different in the
extinction task from its operation in the critical tasks. Thorough analysis of the relationship between two habits would seem to call for study
of their effects in test situations in which the two work in harmony, in
which the two are antagonistic, and in which only one or the other
works.

The findings suggest that the number of repetitions is not an appropriate index of the relative influence of two sets. Given the same number
of repetitions of the method and the goal in the set-inducing period, the
FM–FG group tended to abandon the method but to adhere to the goal
when the two were incompatible in the incomplete extinction task.
This finding might be accounted for by various learning theories. An
appeal might be made to a principle of recency since 7 was the goal
selected in the preceding problem (an incomplete critical) by most subjects in the *FM–FG* group. For example, in line with Guthrie's principle of recency, one might say that writing 7 was the last thing done in
such a situation and therefore the movement of writing 7 occurred in the
subsequent similar situation. Hull's goal-gradient hypothesis might be
interpreted to mean that the response made at the goal (in this case the
goal response may be said to be the response of 7) gets the most reinforcement; this hypothesis, together with Hull's concept of a habit-
family hierarchy, can account for the apparently greater influence of the
goal set. Tolman's emphasis on the roles of purposes, ends, and goals,
and on the relationship between means and ends in learning, might also
be mentioned in this context. Gestalt psychologists have stressed the
role of the goal in the total situation, the relationship between the goal
and the solution to the goal, and the fact that the goal may blind one to
the solution. Particular apropos are Köhler's investigations (1925) of
problem solving by apes in which he showed that concentration on the
goal might make the organism unable to use a solution that requires a
detour or *Umweg*. Reference might also be made to Duncker's pene-
trating analysis of the role of the goal in problem solving (Duncker,
1945; Reid, 1951).

The fact that the fixed goal predominated for the *FM–FG* group is
particularly interesting in the light of the answers given to the experimenter's questions at the end of the session. Most subjects in this group,

and, indeed, most subjects in all groups, claimed that they first tried a *method* (usually the $B - A - 2C$ method in the *FM* groups) in the incomplete problems and only then thought of a goal. If this were so, it would mean that the $B - A - 2C$ method was tried and used in the incomplete criticals because it led to 7, while it was tried and abandoned in the extinction problem because it did not lead here to the fixed goal. Shall the fact that the *method* was tried first (analysis of scratchwork also suggests that this occurred in many cases) be used as evidence of the greater influence of the method set? Or does its subsequent abandonment when it failed to lead to the fixed goal mean that the method was used as a temporary expedient, as a provisional try at attaining the fixed goal? If so, then the initial attempt to apply the method might be interpreted as support for the goal set. This high-lights some of the difficulties involved in comparing the relative influence of two sets.

Incidentally, even some of those in the *FG* groups who chose goals other than 7 showed the influence of this number on their selections. Their predominant choices involved 7 as a numeral (27, 37) or were multiples of 7. Such an influence of the goal set was evident even in the case of some who wrote, when the groups were later asked to describe the aim of the experiment, that they believed its aim was to make one fall into a rut for the number 7 and that they personally refused to fall into the rut.

The present experimental variation is a preliminary attack on what seem to us to constitute some extremely important issues. Much research remains to be done to study the roles of the goal and of a goal set when methods leading to the goal are fixed or varied. What is the influence of the kinds of methods and of the *order* of varied methods? What are the roles of the method and of the method set when the goal remains the same or is varied? While "incomplete" problems with the required volume omitted or with one or more jars omitted may prove of value in assessing such influences, other procedures need also to be devised which are appropriate to the particular habits under investigation, procedures which will allow for the study of the operation of the habits when they are compatible and when they are incompatible. Serious consideration also should be given to the nature of the criteria for evaluating the relative effect and the relative strength of two or more sets in a given context.

Related to the present discussion are the concepts of task, *Aufgabe*, and intention. An individual may accept the securement of 7 quarts of fluid as his task or *Aufgabe* in the problem. He may view the problems, including the incomplete problems, with the intention of obtaining 7 quarts. Or he may accept as his task or as his goal the use of the $B - A - 2C$ method or of a subtraction process. In other words, what may to the experimenter constitute a means to an end, may to the subject actually be the end in itself. Early in our experimentation it became evident that some subjects were accepting ends or goals which worked for E effects. Some thought that their task was to repeat what the experimenter showed them, to use all three jars, to give a speedy response, to repeat the $B - A - 2C$ procedure, to use a subtraction process, etc. Such goals often vitiated the experimental attempts to decrease E effects.

To return to the present variation: we have called $B - A - 2C$ the method or means and the required volume, 7, the goal or the end; but a given subject may have had a goal other than 7, may have accepted repetition of the $B - A - 2C$ method or some other method as his goal. In short, a distinction has to be drawn between the means and the goal as viewed by the experimenter, and the means and the goal as viewed by a particular subject. In using such terms as method set and goal set, one should specify whether the terms are to be understood in line with the experimenter's or the subject's grasp of the situation. Procedures are needed ("incomplete problems" may be found useful) which will help the experimenter to gain some understanding of the subject's actual goal, intention, or *Aufgabe,* and of the role it plays in the learning situation.

The experiments described in this chapter suggest many variations for future research. For example, two individuals, one of whom has received set-inducing problems with only the method fixed whereas the other subject has received set-inducing problems with only the goal fixed, might be asked to work together on the test problems. What would be their reactions if one subject solved the incomplete extinction task in accordance with the method set while the other solved it in accordance with the goal set? It would be of interest to compare their reactions with the resolution of conflicts described in the section on conflict in social problem solving (pp. 558-66).

Chapter XVIII

THE ROLE OF EFFORT

A DHERENTS of the principle of parsimony of effort consider that behavior is governed by a tendency to select that course of action which involves the least expenditure of effort or work on the part of the organism. If behavior in the basic experiment is regulated by such a principle of parsimony of effort, then it might be expected that the direct methods would have been used whenever available rather than the more complex, apparently more effortful, *E* method. The results of course reveal a contrary trend. It is questionable, however, whether these results actually constitute a contradiction to a principle of least effort. It is conceivable that it was more effortful for some subjects to shift to another method than to continue using the *E* method after they had become proficient in its use (Luchins, 1939). It has been conjectured by Immergluck (1952), who used the Einstellung situation as his reference case, that mental sets constitute an example of minimal effort, of the economizing of the organism's energy. Use of the *E* method in the test problems may therefore represent an example of the operation of a law of parsimony of effort rather than a contradiction to it. Particularly since the difference in effort expenditure required by the direct and the *E* methods is so small, the path of least action or least effort may have been continued use of the *E* method, once a set was developed, rather than a shift to the direct method.

But what would happen if the differential in effort between the direct and complex methods were increased to the extent that, even if a set were developed, the least effortful procedure would involve a shift to the direct method? Such a question was purely hypothetical until a means could be found to increase the effort differential between the two methods. Before discussing attempts to do this, we note that learning theorists who accept a principle of parsimony of effort have drawn implications from this principle for human behavior. But much of the relevant research has been conducted with rats. Solomon remarked, in his 1948 review of research pertaining to the influence of the effort or work factor in learning, that this research has largely been confined to the animal laboratory and/or has not dealt directly with the effort variable per se but has instead varied the time interval between responses (as in massed-versus-distributed-learning experiments), and thereby presumably varied the effort per unit of time. It is therefore of interest to attempt to manipulate the effort factor itself with human subjects.

Mirror Tracing of Mazes

Of the various kinds of tasks employed in studying the Einstellung phenomenon, those involving mazes seemed to lend themselves particularly well to manipulation of the effort variable. To increase the difference in effort between the practiced procedure and the more direct procedure, the mazes were presented in a mirror-tracing apparatus. A shield over the paper containing the diagram of the maze made it necessary for the subject to use the mirror image as a guide while he was tracing a path. An experiment (Luchins and Luchins, 1954a) in which tracing of the mazes was compared under mirror and nonmirror (normal) conditions indicated that mirror tracing of the practiced path apparently was more effortful and also more psychologically stressful than normal tracing of this path and than either mirror or normal tracing of the direct path. Thus, this experiment confounded psychological stress and effort. The experiment has already been described briefly in Chapter V in relation to psychological stress. Since it is of interest to examine the results in the light of what has been written about the effort factor, we shall now describe the experiment and present the results in greater detail than in Chapter V.

The paradigm of the basic experiment is used with paper-and-pencil mazes. In each maze three paths lead out from the choice point: a short, direct connection to the goal box which is located above the choice point; a circuitous, zigzag path, with numerous twists and turns, which juts out to the left or to the right of the choice point; finally, a blind-alley pathway which ends up well above the goal box. The first maze is an illustrative task wherein both the short, direct path and the circuitous path lead to the goal box. The short, direct path is blocked at the goal box (that is, a line is drawn before the goal box) in the next five mazes, the set-inducing tasks, but is unblocked in the last five mazes. The critical mazes can be solved by tracing either the direct or the circuitous path, while in the ninth maze, the extinction maze, the goal box can be reached only by way of the direct path.

Forty-four freshman students at McGill University were tested individually by Lola Constant, Robert Shulman, and Barbara Turk. The subjects were assigned at random to Group 1 and Group 2, with the latter consisting of eleven men and eleven women and the former of twelve men and ten women. The subjects in Group 1 first received the series of mazes in the mirror-tracing apparatus; immediately afterwards they received the same series but without the mirror-tracing apparatus. For Group 2 the order of presentation was reversed, so that the mazes were first received for nonmirror tracing and then for mirror tracing. In each case the re-presentation was introduced with the remark that the second part of the experiment was now to be given. In the initial instructions, issued before any mazes were presented, the subject was told that he was to find a nonobstructed path from the starting place to the goal and to trace this path with a pencil. Included in the initial instructions were these remarks:

Now, this type of test is usually included in an over-all test of intelligence. I am going to count the number of errors you make, that is, the number of times you go into a wrong path, and the number of times you go outside the lines of the figure. And I am going to time you. The smoother and faster you trace, the better score you will achieve.

As soon as the subject indicated that he had completed a maze, that maze was removed and he was given the next one. Although the circuitous pathway (E method) was blocked in the extinction task, some subjects followed this pathway into the goal box, apparently oblivious to the line drawn as a barrier. In such cases the experimenter pointed to the barrier, reminded the subject that he had erred in crossing it, and then presented the next maze.

We noted that the primary purpose in using the mirror-tracing apparatus was to increase the differential in effort between the E method and the direct method. That it succeeded in so doing is attested to by the time of solution and other data. In the first presentation, under normal tracing conditions subjects readily solved each E maze within a few seconds, whereas mirror-tracing subjects found it difficult to keep within the bounds of the pathway, tended to veer from the path at the turning points, and in some cases took as long as ten minutes to achieve an accurate tracing. The time required to trace the indirect route decreased in successive set-inducing mazes but it was always significantly more than in the nonmirror situation. On the other hand, both in the mirror and outside of it, tracing of the direct route was a rapid, facile process. Thus, the mirror image seemed to have had little influence on the effort required to trace the direct path but it increased the effort involved in tracing the indirect pathway, with a consequent increase in the effort differential.

Even in the re-presentation of the mazes, tracing of the circuitous route seemed to be more difficult under mirror tracing than under normal tracing. Thus, subjects in Group 2, for whom the mirror-tracing apparatus was introduced in the re-presentation, often commented on the difficulties they were now experiencing in tracing the pathway. Conversely, subjects in Group 1 often noted that they found it easier to trace the circuitous route when the mirror-tracing apparatus was removed.

Mirror tracing, particularly in the initial presentation, was characterized by overt signs of effort and stress, including sweating, fidgeting,

clamping of the elbows on the table, and occasional groaning and cursing. Subjects asked, while tracing the circuitous route, "When is this
going to be over with?" and said "I hope that I don't have to do any
more." Such comments were rarely encountered in the nonmirror
situation.

Every subject succeeded, in more or less time, in correctly tracing
the circuitous pathway in each set-inducing maze. Table XV summarizes the results in the test problems in terms of the percentages of subjects who utilized the indirect path in the critical problems and the percentages of subjects who attempted to trace the circuitous pathway in
the ninth problem, where it did not lead to the goal.

TABLE XV.* PERCENTAGES OF INDIRECT RESPONSES TO THE TEST MAZES
(TWENTY-TWO SUBJECTS IN EACH GROUP)

	Initial Presentation		Re-Presentation	
	Group 1 (Mirror)	Group 2 (Nonmirror)	Group 1 (Nonmirror)	Group 2 (Mirror)
Task 7	91	86	5	5
Task 8	86	56	5	5
Task 9	68	32	0	0
Task 10	18	5	5	5
Task 11	14	5	5	5

* Adapted from Luchins and Luchins, 1954a, p. 19.

The table shows that, in the initial presentation of the mazes, the
mirror situation yielded more E effects in every test problem than did
the nonmirror situation. Differences significant at better than the 5 per
cent level of confidence were found in Tasks 8 and 9 (chi-square values
of 3.93 and 4.45, respectively). On the initial presentation, attempts to
follow the circuitous pathway in the extinction (ninth) maze were
made by fifteen subjects in the mirror situation (68 per cent) and by
seven subjects in the nonmirror situation (32 per cent). While tracing
this pathway, some of these subjects became aware of the fact that it
did not lead to the goal, abandoned it, and shifted to the direct path.
But other subjects continued following the circuitous path into the
goal box, and thereby crossed the line intended as a barrier and failed
the task. What the table does not reveal is that, on the initial presentation, failure of the extinction maze was shown by twelve subjects in the
mirror situation (55 per cent) as compared with only four subjects in
the nonmirror situation (18 per cent), with the difference significant
at better than the 5 per cent level of confidence.

On the re-presentation of the mazes, the mirror situation yielded
precisely the same percentages of indirect responses as did the nonmirror situation. No subject now attempted to utilize the indirect procedure in the extinction maze; there was 100 per cent direct solution

of this task. One subject in each group (in each case a female) used the circuitous route in each critical. All other subjects traced the direct route in the criticals.

(It may not be out of place to refer here to some preliminary attempts to obtain physiological measures of effort or energy expended during the tracing of the mazes. In an exploratory study done with five Montreal college students, not those whose results were given above, electromyographic recordings and pneumographic recordings taken during both mirror and nonmirror tracing of the mazes suggested that greater effort or energy per unit of time was expended during mirror tracing.)

Relation of Findings to Principle of Parsimony

The results of the initial presentation of the mazes are especially interesting since a principle of parsimony of effort has often been interpreted as a determinant of the choice of means in a given situation. In the case of a maze, this principle has usually been interpreted as fostering choice of the shorter path; but our findings show a contrary trend. It is true that in successive mazes subjects gradually economized on the effort and time involved in tracing the E route. But, since the time and effort were never as little as the time and effort required to trace the direct pathway, it would seem that economy of effort was mainly limited to the pursuit of one activity rather than including a choice of means or activities, some less effortful than others.

Tolman (1932) postulates a law of least effort described as a selective preference for short or easy means activities as against long or difficult ones. Wheeler postulates a law of least action, characterized as "nature's universal law of economy or parsimony" and stated in the following terms: "When action is defined as units of energy multiplied by units of time, movement occurs from one position to the other, over the shortest possible path" (Wheeler, 1940, p. 40). The circuitous path in our maze-tracing experiments was both longer and more difficult than the direct path and its use involved, particularly under mirror tracing, the greatest expenditure of energy per unit of time as well as the greatest amount of time; the direct path constituted the shortest possible path, the easy and short means activity. The results therefore do not seem to conform to a law of least effort or least action since most subjects, under both mirror and normal tracing conditions, traced the longer, more difficult path in the initial presentation of the first two test problems, and this occurred even more frequently for those working under mirror-tracing conditions.

Wheeler might seek to reconcile this discrepancy by conjecturing that the subject selects the shortest path which he can see under given conditions and that experience in the E tasks blinded him to the direct path. But such a conjecture is tantamount to a modification of his law of least action. Our results speak against an unqualified principle of least effort or least action. Our findings suggest that, whatever may be the factors or forces underlying our subjects' behavior—whether they be described as set, Einstellung, unconscious habituation, conscious assumptions or generalizations, fixation of response, transfer of training, "preference" for indirect route, etc.—they are apparently among the factors which can modify any assumed tendency toward parsimony of effort or action.

Relation of Findings to Hull's Law of Less Work

Hull does not postulate a principle of parsimony of effort, as do some other learning theorists, but derives his law of less work as a corollary from his postulates on work inhibition or reactive inhibition (1943, p. 294). His construct of reactive inhibition takes as its point of departure the Mowrer-Miller-Jones "fatigue hypothesis" (Mowrer and Jones, 1943; Miller and Dollard, 1941). According to this hypothesis, whenever any reaction is evoked in an organism, there is left a condition or state which acts as a primary negative drive or negative motivation in that it has the innate capacity to produce *cessation* of the activity which produced the state. Hull refers to this condition or state, as well as to the negative drive it produces, as reactive inhibition. He assumes that an increment of reactive inhibition is generated by every repetition of the response, whether reinforced or not, that the increments accumulate except as they spontaneously dissipate with the passage of time, and that their effect is to weaken the reaction potential. He also assumes that the intensity of reactive inhibition is proportional to the effort involved in the response.

Since greater effort or work is assumed to produce more reactive inhibition, the effective reaction potential will be greater for a behavior sequence requiring less work, other things being equal. Thus, Hull is led to formulate his law of less work:

> If two or more behavior sequences, each involving a different amount of energy consumption or work (W), have been equally well reinforced an equal number of times, the organism will gradually learn to choose the less laborious behavior sequence leading to the attainment of the reinforcing state of affairs. (1943, p. 294.)

Note that Hull does not accept any innate preference for the shorter or easier or less laborious behavior sequence but instead talks of the organism gradually learning to choose this sequence, of a gradual acquisition of the preference for the behavior sequence involving less energy expenditure or work. Hence, Hull's viewpoint as applied to the Einstellung situation does not demand that the subject inevitably show a preference for the direct method. Such a preference would have to be gradually learned.

It may seem that we do not meet Hull's prerequisites for comparison of behavior sequences which differ in effort, that is, equality in the number and strength of reinforcements. Prior to the test problems, the E method was repeatedly practiced and reinforced in the illustrative task and the E mazes, while the direct method was practiced and reinforced only in the illustrative maze. In stimulus-response terminology it may be said that the two behavior sequences were *not* equally well reinforced an equal number of times. To have introduced such equality would have necessitated considerable revision in the procedure utilized to study the Einstellung phenomenon. In any event, the number of reinforcements of the E method in relation to the direct method was the same under both mirror and nonmirror conditions and would not be a determinant of differences in results under mirror and nonmirror tracing. What is the central issue here, is that the two behavior sequences which we are actually interested in comparing are (1) the E method under mirror-tracing conditions and (2) the E method under nonmirror-tracing conditions. And these two behavior sequences had precisely the same number of reinforcements in the mazes prior to the test problems.

The strength of reinforcement is another matter. Since there was a greater temporal delay between the starting point and the goal under mirror-tracing conditions, it could be predicted from Hull's theory that less habit strength for the E method was developed under mirror conditions. Moreover, since tracing of the circuitous path was more effortful when the mirror image served as a guide, it follows, from the assumption that reactive inhibition is proportional to the energy expenditure, that more reactive inhibition developed under mirror conditions. Hence, it follows that there was less effective reaction potential for the E method under mirror tracing than under nonmirror tracing.

When all these considerations are taken into account, Hull's theory points to the prediction that the rate of acquisition of a preference for the less laborious behavior sequence (now referring to the direct method) should be greater under mirror-tracing conditions. This prediction is not substantiated by our findings.

Relation of Findings to Effort, Extinction, and Variability

From Hull's postulates on reactive inhibition and from the Mowrer-Miller-Jones fatigue hypothesis, there have been deduced various relationships involving the effort variable, among them the following: (1) the greater the effort involved in a response, the faster is the extinction of the response; (2) the greater the effort, the greater is the variability

or oscillation of behavior in a two-choice situation (Hull, 1943; Mowrer
and Jones, 1943; Solomon, 1948).

If one accepts these deduced relationships between effort and extinction and between effort and variability, and if one grants that tracing of
the circuitous pathway while using the mirror image as a guide constitutes a more effortful task than tracing it in the nonmirror situation, then
it follows: that the response of tracing the E route should be extinguished more rapidly in the mirror situation; that the tendency to vary
responses in the two-choice situations (the critical problems) should be
greater in the mirror situation than in the presumably less effortful nonmirror situation. But neither expectation is supported by the results. In
the initial presentation, mirror tracing yielded more adherence to the E
route in every test problem and hence less tendency toward extinction
of this response—the very reverse of the expectation. Moreover, neither
the mirror nor the nonmirror situation revealed a tendency to alternate
between the direct and indirect procedures, the tendency to repeat one
response being more marked in the mirror situation. Our findings thus
fail to substantiate the relationships between effort and extinction and
between effort and variability deduced from the reactive inhibition and
the fatigue theories.

Analysis of the results in the re-presentation of the mazes is of course
complicated by the previous experience with the mazes. To judge from
the subjects' comments, this previous experience developed some understanding of the nature of the series of maze problems as well as an expectation that the direct route would be eventually available. Although
mirror tracing of the circuitous pathway was apparently more effortful
than nonmirror tracing (even in the re-presentation), quantitative results were identical in the mirror and nonmirror situation for the re-
presentation; also extinction and variability did not vary with effort.
Whatever may be the relationships between effort and extinction and
between effort and variability, our findings suggest that these relationships may be modified by such factors as understanding and expectation
—factors which are ignored in the reactive-inhibition and the fatigue
theories of response.

The relationship between effort and variability, as deduced from
Hull's postulates on reactive inhibition, has come to be regarded as a
crucial test of Hull's theory. Discussing this relationship, Solomon
writes:

It is a deduction which has not been tested experimentally ... Actually the
demonstration of the relationship between effortfulness of task and avoidance of
repetition of responses would be very significant. The effects of *time interval variations* were predicted fairly well by the conceptualizations of [other theorists]. In
this case, Hull's theories add little. But the role of the *effort variable* is not a salient

feature of the other theories. If it could be demonstrated that work or effort alters the tendency to avoid repeating responses in a two-choice situation, we would be faced with the necessity of depending on those theories which consider response-produced stimuli, or reactive inhibition, not those which speak of "demands," "negative adaption," or retention of an impression about "where I went on the last trial." . . . Therefore, the effort or work variable becomes crucial in testing the alternative hypotheses. (1948, pp. 25-26.)

The present investigation fails to support the deduction that greater work increases the tendency to avoid repeating responses in a two-choice situation. An experiment by Mowrer and Jones (1943), designed to test this deduction and administered to rats, also failed to support it. The negative findings of these studies speak against those theories which consider response-produced stimuli or reactive inhibition. (But whether the findings support those theories which speak of demands or negative adaptation is another matter.) Since the construct of reactive inhibition is central in Hull's theory of learning, and since the deduction concerning effort and variability follows directly from his postulates on reactive inhibition, the fact that these experiments do not substantiate this deduction suggests a need for careful evaluation of this construct, of the postulates pertaining to it, and of those parts of Hull's theory which rest on the construct and its postulates.

Some Methodological Deficiencies

There are several weaknesses in the present study insofar as it relates to the effort variable. We have already referred to the confounding of emotional stress and effort. The time factor was also involved since tracing of the E route required more time as well as more effort than tracing of the direct route, the time differential and the effort differential both being greater in the mirror situation. Time and effort are inter-related in all studies which utilize a long-versus-short-route situation. This confounding has thus far been unraveled, Solomon notes (1948), only by introducing an additional task into the maze situation.

Moreover, as we observed in discussing the relation of the results to Hull's law of less work, prior to the test mazes practice had been provided in tracing of the E route but not in tracing of the direct route. In defense of our experimental procedure, it may be argued that their daily-life experiences had probably provided subjects with more "practice" in tracing or forming a continuous-line segment than a zigzag, broken-line curve, as well as with more "reinforcements" in using a short, straight path to a goal. In any event, practice in the direct method prior to the test problems was, insofar as the experimental situation was concerned, equally deficient in the initial presentation of both the mirror and the nonmirror situation so that comparisons between the two situations would seem to be permissible.

Tracing of Maze Paths with Light and Heavy Weights

A methodological deficiency in the investigation considered in the preceding section was the heightening of both effort and emotional stress. The experiment to be considered in the present section represents an attempt to separate these factors through varying the weight which the subject carried as he traced the maze paths. Since work is customarily defined as the product of force and length of movement, the use of different weights allows a literal interpretation of the work performed by the subject as he traverses either the shorter or longer maze path. In the previous experiment, under mirror conditions, tracing of the circuitous path was not only more energy-consuming than tracing of the direct path but also more difficult and frustrating. It was reasoned (and sustained by the results) that, when a heavy weight was used, tracing of the circuitous path would involve more expenditure of energy than tracing of the direct path but would not involve greater frustration or other emotional stress.

Mazes similar to those of the previous investigation were employed but were traced onto heavy linoleum, and grooves were formed to represent the routes. After the illustrative problem solvable by three routes, there were given eight set-inducing mazes, two criticals, an extinction maze, and two more criticals. Normal (nonmirror) tracing was used throughout. A stylus was supplied for tracing of the paths. Under "light weight" conditions, a metal cup was screwed on to the top of the stylus. Under "heavy weight" conditions, prior to the presentation of any of the mazes, buckshot was deposited, bit by bit, into this cup until the subject claimed that the stylus felt "uncomfortably heavy" in his hand; he was then given the series of mazes. The amount of buckshot employed varied from subject to subject since it was based on a subjective evaluation of heaviness.

(It may not be out of place to mention that this experiment was a simplification of a preliminary study in which the stylus was attached to a string, which in turn was attached to a modified Mosso ergograph in order to allow measurement of the tension on the string produced by different weights.)

Fifty Montreal high-school students were tested individually by Deitcher (1953). The students were divided into two equal groups. Group 1 first traced the mazes under "heavy weight" conditions and immediately afterwards under "light weight" conditions while for Group 2 the order was reversed so that "light weight" tracing came first.

Results

Under neither light- nor heavy-weight conditions were there found any of the overt signs of frustration, tension, or other emotional stress which had been observed under mirror tracing of the mazes. The present procedure seemed therefore to have succeeded in rather effectively eliminating the factor of emotional stress while introducing a differential in effort.

The mean time required to trace the circuitous path in the E problems was consistently and significantly higher under heavy-weight conditions than under light-weight conditions. But, under a given condition, time spent in the E tasks did not differ significantly for those who shifted to the direct method in the first critical and for those who solved it by the E method. In the initial presentation of the mazes under heavy-weight conditions, the average time per E maze was 8.80 seconds for those who solved the first critical by the E method and 9.05 seconds for those who solved it by the direct method; the corresponding figures for light-weight conditions were 6.28 and 5.85 seconds. While the present experiment confounds the time and effort factors, it therefore seems fairly safe to say that the time factor per se did not contribute importantly to the results.

What about the effort factor? With work defined as force multiplied by distance, or action defined as units of energy multiplied by units of time (Wheeler's definition), use of the direct method, since it represents less distance and less time, clearly involves less work and less action, particularly under heavy-weight conditions. If the subjects' responses were governed by an unqualified principle of parsimony of effort, the direct path should have been employed when it was available, especially when the buckshot was used.

But 50 per cent of those in Group 1 (heavy) and 52 per cent in Group 2 (light) adhered to the E method in the initial presentation of the first test problem. Percentages of E solutions gradually decreased in successive test problems, with substantially the same E effects under heavy- and light-weight conditions. The re-presentation of the mazes revealed less E effects, the results being similar under both conditions. The results therefore do not suggest the operation of an unqualified principle of parsimony of effort. Differences in effort (work or action) did not, in and of themselves, seem to have been differential determinants of responses to the test problems.

Comments on the Results

In the present experiment it would seem that neither differences in time nor in effort influenced the results to any great extent. In the previous experiment there were significantly more E solutions of the test problems under mirror-tracing conditions. That significant differences failed to be found in the present study suggests that the differences in results under mirror and nonmirror conditions may have been largely an artifact of the differences in emotional stress.

Much of what was said in the previous section is appropriate to the present investigation. The results do not favor the postulation of an innate preference for less effortful means in a given task. They hint that factors such as those involved in an Einstellung may modify the operation of any assumed tendency toward parsimony of effort. Again we failed to find the positive relationship between effort and extinction or between effort and variability deduced from the fatigue and reactive-inhibition theories.

That there was an increase in direct solutions in successive test problems would seem to support Hull's notion that the preference for the shorter, easier way is gradually acquired in any particular learning situation, that the preference is not an innate characteristic but is itself an outcome of conditions and laws of learning. Further research remains to be conducted to investigate what happens (1) if an extinction problem is not given; (2) if the effort factor is varied from problem to problem (say, by adding to or subtracting from the weight on the stylus); (3) if massed or spaced distribution is used to test Hull's corollaries concerning the relation between effort and manner of distribution (1943, p. 287, p. 289).

Investigation of the Effort Factor with the Use of Form Boards

The use of form boards or jigsaw puzzles seems to lend itself to study of the effort variable. A preliminary investigation has been done involving a series of ten tasks in each of which the subject was asked to cover rectangular boards of varying lengths, in the shortest possible time, with cardboard forms. We were interested in discovering whether a rather effortful and time-consuming method of covering the area, which was the only one available for the first six boards, would be carried over to subsequent boards where a less effortful, less time-consuming method was also available.

From the first through the tenth task, the rectangular boards, one inch in width, were of the following lengths: 4, 6, 7, 10, 12, 15, 11, 8, 10, and 13 inches. In each task the subject had the same collection of small pieces of cardboard, each one inch in width, and each from one-half to one inch in length. These cardboard pieces included squares, triangles, and other geometric shapes. In each task the area of the rectangular board could be covered by properly putting together some or all of these small pieces of cardboard. In addition, in each task the subject received a rectangular strip of cardboard, one inch in width and considerably longer than any of the other cardboard pieces. The cardboard strip was a fraction of an inch too short to fit the board in the first six tasks and in the ninth task, so that in these tasks the subject had to use the small pieces of cardboard. But the strip precisely fitted the board in the seventh, eighth, and tenth tasks. Would the subjects continue to use the small pieces in these tasks?

The experiment was administered, with the assistance of Leiba L. Aronoff and Kathleen Z. Markus, to twenty Montreal subjects, five of whom were children ranging in age from 10 to 16 years of age, while the remainder were adults. Each subject was told, at the onset of the experiment, that he was to be timed while working on the tasks (as he was) and that he was to finish each task in the shortest possible time.

The first point of interest is that, despite the fact that the long rectangular strip did not fit in any of the first six tasks, most subjects tried to use it in each task. As soon as the board was placed before them, they selected the long strip and put it on the board and only then used the small pieces in those cases where the long strip did not fit. In the various tasks from 75 to 95 per cent of the subjects tried the long strip. Attempts to use the long strip, far from decreasing in subsequent tasks, increased so that an average of 78 per cent of the subjects tried it in the first three tasks, 83 per cent in the next three tasks, and 85 per cent in the last four tasks. In short, subjects did not become set to use the small pieces despite the fact that they had to use them in the first six tasks.

When asked why they had consistently tried the long strip, most subjects said that they did so since it took only a second to try it and since its use would save a good deal of time whenever it fitted exactly. When the few subjects who had not consistently tried the long strip were questioned, they usually said that they discontinued their attempts to use it because it had not fitted in previous tasks.

Spontaneously, or in response to questioning after the experiment, most subjects (including all the children) said that they had enjoyed using the small pieces of cardboard, that it was fun to use them or challenging to work with them or that they liked arranging them in artistic designs. Only two subjects gave contrary comments, saying that they found it tedious or annoying to work with the small pieces. Thus, 90 per cent of the subjects apparently enjoyed the more effortful, more time-consuming procedure.

Comments

Since this experiment confounded the time and effort factors, we do not know whether subjects tried to use the long strip because it was less effortful to use it than the small cardboard pieces or because it took less time or for some other reason. Subjects' comments did not specifically mention the effort factor. Instead, they said that they had tried the long strip because it took only a second to try it whereas it took considerably more time to use the small pieces. One wonders whether subjects tended to try the long strip because they were timed and had been instructed that their job was to finish each task in the shortest possible time. An experimental variation in which this instruction is not given and there is no timing remains to be conducted. Another factor that may have contributed to the results is the fact that the long strip was strikingly different in appearance than the other cardboard pieces, having a different shape and being at least four times as long and even fifteen or more times as long; moreover, the collection of small pieces remained constant from task to task while the long strip was changed in every task; these factors may have helped to make the long strip more outstanding to the subject. Experimental variations remain to be conducted in which there is less difference in length and shape between the rectangular strip and the other pieces or in which the longest strip remains constant throughout while the other pieces are varied.

Most subjects did not comment on the effort involved in working with the small pieces but on the fun or the challenge they derived from working with them. The comments point to individual differences in reactions to effortful tasks and indicate that a procedure that may be tedious and effortful to one person may be enjoyable to another who may not even think of the effort involved in it.

CONCLUSIONS

The upshot of our investigations would seem to be that there is a decided need for experimentation to re-examine the role of the effort factor in learning. Such experimentation is not easy to devise or execute, particularly if one is to avoid the mixing of the effort factor with the factors of time and of emotional tension. To assume that the whole answer lies in an unqualified principle of least effort, to assume that the answer is independent of the particular task and subjects, and, in particular, to assume that what has been learned from experimentation on the effort variable in the animal laboratory may be directly applied to human learning—all may represent serious errors of judgment.

Also there seems to be involved a problem regarding the definition of effort. To define effort merely in terms of energy spent per unit of time may be to overlook the possibility that the individual's subjective feeling about effort need not be proportional to the energy he expends. A subject may regard Task A as more effortful than Task B despite the fact that the total expenditure of energy or the energy per unit of time is the same for both tasks or perhaps is even greater for Task B.

Two subjects engaged in the same kind of task (or the same subject who performs the same kind of task at various times), perhaps even spending the same energy per unit of time or the same total amount of energy, may have very different feelings about the effortfulness of the task. There is a need to investigate, in a given task, the subjective or phenomenal meaning of effort and its determinants, and also to develop methods of measuring subjective effortfulness. (Of course, there is also a need to investigate further the physiological meaning and basis of effort and its determinants and also to develop better methods of measuring physiological effortfulness.) Similarly, there is a need for investigation of the subjective or phenomenal meaning of work and of its determinants. In short, we need to know more about what effort and work mean in an individual's phenomenal world.

We have seen that there are experimental findings which seemingly run counter to a principle of least effort or a law of less work. Many activities of daily life also are not in accord with the assumption that behavior is governed by a tendency toward minimal effort or less work. Does such a tendency govern the frenzied activity of the business world or of the social whirl? Does such a tendency jibe with the energy spent on golf, tennis, bowling, and other recreational, athletic, and "leisure time" activities? Does such a tendency regulate the painting of a picture, the composition of a musical score, the writing of a novel, or other creative activities? Can such a tendency account for the so-called exploratory or investigative drive or "curiosity" that is characteristic of the child and of the scientist (and that has often been observed in animals both in the laboratory and in their natural habitats), that leads men to pose problems and to solve them, to climb mountains, and to explore the sea and underground caves? A case might be made for the proposition that men and animals prefer to expend energy and even like to work. Of course, one might assume that behavior is governed by a tendency toward minimal effort or less work and then seek to account for apparently contrary findings and observations by positing that various factors may interfere with or operate against this tendency under certain conditions. But perhaps there is some justification for the assumption that behavior is governed by a tendency toward maximal effort or most work and that various factors may interfere with or operate against this tendency under certain conditions.*

Basal to the formulation of the principle of least effort there seems to us to be a certain implicit conception of the nature of man (and of other living organisms): Man is viewed as an energy-conserving organism

---

* Will research directed by the hypothesis of maximal effort yield a different conception of work and different underlying variables than research directed by the hypothesis of minimal effort?

whose ideal state, or the state for which he strives, is a "state of equilibrium" characterized by quiescence, by little or no activity. But such a
conception or model of the nature of man not only fails to be in line
with the observational evidence presented in the previous paragraph
but also does not accord with modern knowledge of physiology and
neurology, knowledge which suggests that high activity rather than
low activity is characteristic of living organisms (cf. Hebb, 1949, and
Hebb and Thompson, 1954).

In short, there appear to be many reasons for careful re-evaluation of
the assumption that behavior is governed by a tendency toward least
effort.

Chapter XIX

WHAT IS LEARNED IN
THE EINSTELLUNG SITUATION

THUS far we have been concerned largely with the problem of *how* learning occurred in the Einstellung situation. There is also the problem of *what* is learned in the Einstellung situation. Here phenomenological observations suggest a number of possibilities. Subjects' comments and observations of their behavior suggest that some subjects consciously generalized a rule or formula, such as $B - A - 2C$; some learned to use the E method because it had been demonstrated by the experimenter in the first E task; some learned to start with the center jar, which was also the largest jar. Various assumptions also seem to have been "learned." Thus, some subjects assumed that the problems were of one type or were all solvable by one procedure; some assumed that all three jars were to be used; some assumed that the problems represented practice in subtraction.

We wondered whether any one of these by itself could serve as *the* explanation of E effects. Learning to subtract, or to assume that the problems are subtraction examples, could account for failure to use the $A + C$ procedure but could not account for failure to use the $A - C$ procedure that solved the extinction task and some of the criticals; hence, a tendency to subtract did not suffice to explain all cases of E effects. Questioning of subjects after the experiment suggested that some of them were not aware that they were repeating a method demonstrated by the experimenter or that they had made any assumptions about the nature of the problems or their solutions. Nonetheless, experimentation was undertaken to see what would happen if the E method were not illustrated; if factors were introduced to lessen the likelihood that the problems would be viewed as of one type or as probably all solvable by one procedure; if factors were introduced to weaken a tendency to use all jars or to begin with the largest (center) jar; or if the problems were changed so that a tendency to use all jars or to begin with the largest (center) jar would not foster E effects.

Influence on What Is Learned of Various Attitudes Toward the Experimenter and of Various School Experiences

That the experimenter illustrated the E method in the first E task may have suggested to some subjects that this method should be or could be used in subsequent problems. The subjects may have learned to take the experimenter's demonstration as the cue for their responses. True, the experimenter illustrated another method of solving this problem and also showed a method of solving the previous illustrative problem, but neither of these two demonstrated methods worked in all of the subsequent E problems, whereas the E method did. Perhaps the prestige which the experimenter had for some subjects enhanced the possibility that a method he demonstrated would be followed by them. The underlying process may have involved what is sometimes called "prestige suggestion." Attitudes of confidence and trust in the experimenter may also have enhanced E effects, particularly if the subject assumed that the experimenter was interested in or wanted E solutions.

Since it appears in the E tasks that the experimenter is interested in and wants E performances, and since the experimenter is a friendly looking chap, apparently without any tricky intentions, there is no need for being wary or suspicious. The subject does not suspect that the experimenter will deceive him by giving problems that look like the others but have a different and better method of solution. ... There is a kind of confidence, of innocent reliance, which leads to E responses because the subject does not at all expect that he will be tricked. (Luchins, 1942, p. 30.)

Such attitudes of innocent, almost blind, reliance on the experimenter were particularly marked in some of the elementary-school classes. We suspect that they involved a transference to the experimenter of attitudes toward their teachers. In this connection it should be noted that most children and some adults considered the experimenter a teacher and the experiment a school activity.

In some classes, the relationship of child to teacher seemed to be that of follower to master. In fact, some of the teachers proudly informed us that their children were "very good," saying that they "always did exactly as told." Such a relationship may focus the child on guessing "what teacher wants," instead of examining freely the task at hand to see what solution it requires.

Thus, believing that the experimenter wanted him to use the E method, he may have tried to use it throughout. Problem Nine [the extinction task] may not have helped but merely confused him since he could not do what he thought the teacher wanted. ... In some classes we observed an absolute confidence in the teacher in these regards. Teachers do not fool or trick you; they always tell you what you should do, and for your own good it's best to do it. Whatever the teacher says (or seems to say) is the correct thing. Do as she did, and everything will be all right. There is no reason for free initiative. (Luchins, 1942, pp. 91-92.)

When the direct method was demonstrated at the end of the session, some subjects protested: "It's a trick. I never expected to be tricked. I did what you told me to do"; "I tried to do everything you showed"; "You taught us wrong"; "You did not teach us that [the direct] method"; "You should have shown the other way, too, if you wanted us to use it." Their comments suggested that they were not accustomed to being shown or taught one method and then expected to seek for or to use other methods.

It is noteworthy that most of the elementary schools in which the experiment was conducted used isolated drill in the initial learning period. After introducing a new method or rule or formula, the teacher using isolated drill gives a series of tasks in which the students apply (practice) the just-taught method, rule, or formula. Some of the subjects may have regarded the experiment as an isolated drill lesson and sought to practice a method which they thought they were being taught.

Because of their school training, some subjects, both children and adults, viewed arithmetic as involving the use of fixed habits and skills; they regarded arithmetical (and other mathematical) problems as belonging to certain types and the problem solver's task as that of recognizing the type and then remembering the rule, formula, or "trick" which works for this particular type of problem. Transferring such an attitude to the experiment, a subject may have sought to "type" the problems and to find a rule or trick which would solve the type found. If such a subject received the "Don't be blind" warning, he may have interpreted it along these lines: "Don't be blind to the method which solves the problems" or "Don't be blind to the fact that all are of the same type." If he regarded the E method as the rule and realized that the extinction problem was not solved by the E method, he may have thought that he had made a computational error or that the experimenter had erred in stating the problem.

Experimental variations were undertaken in attempts to weaken the operation of attitudes of confidence in or reliance on the experimenter, to weaken the possibility of "prestige suggestion," and to rule out certain factors favoring the assumption that the demonstrated method should be used or that the problems were of one type or all solvable by one method.

Studies Using Other Experimenters and Nonschool Settings

We attempted to vary the experimenter-subject relationship and the setting in which the experiment was performed. For example, the experiment was administered by a twelve-year-old child to a college class; by high-school boys, none of them leaders in scholastic or extra-curricula activities, to other high-school boys, both in the school and outside of it; by teachers to other teachers; by the writers and others as a parlor game at social gatherings; by a well-known political conservative to members of a liberal political organization; by a well-known political radical to members of conservative political and religious organizations.

These variations yielded E effects within the range found in the basic study. Yet it was not likely that the subjects in all these variations had confidence and trust in the experimenter or regarded him as a prestigeful individual. Nor was it as likely, as in the basic experiment, that the experiment would be viewed as a school activity and the experimenter as a teacher. While further experimentation is needed to vary the experimenter-subject relationship and the setting in which the experiment takes place, these preliminary variations imply that such factors as trust in the experimenter, the prestige of the experimenter, and "prestige suggestion" cannot account for all cases of E effects and that E effects may occur even when the experimenter is not a teacher or the experiment a school activity.

Experiment in Which No Method Was Demonstrated

In a variation of the basic experiment (Luchins, 1942, p. 84), no method of solution was shown for any problem; instead, three minutes were allowed for the first illustrative problem (29, 3, get 3) and four minutes for the second illustrative problem (E_1), while the remaining problems were presented at the usual two-and-a-half-minute intervals. When this variation was administered to a college class of twenty-two students, another college class of seventeen students, a high-school class of twenty-nine students, and a fifth-year elementary-school class of twenty-seven pupils, responses of 10, 1, 9 and 17 subjects, respectively, had to be discarded because the last two E problems were not solved, a result probably due to lack of illustration. But the remaining subjects showed E effects within the range found in the basic experiment: C_1C_2, from 83 to 95 per cent E, with a mean of 89 per cent; Ext., from 38 to 80 per cent F, with a mean of 50 per cent; C_3C_4, from 25 to 90 per cent E, with a mean of 59 per cent. These results imply that the experimenter's illustration of the E method in the first E problem cannot itself account for all cases of E effects.

Experiments in Which No Method Was Demonstrated and Problems Apparently Came from Diverse Sources

Some subjects assumed that they were being given problems of one type, all solvable by the same method. This assumption may have been fostered by school experiences in which, after a procedure had been demonstrated by the teacher or in a textbook, a series of problems solvable by this procedure was given. It is therefore of some interest to see what happened when no procedure was demonstrated *and* when the problems did not apparently come from the same source, so that subjects had little reason to expect them to be of one type or all solvable by one procedure (Luchins, 1942, p. 84).

Students in an adult-education class were asked to solve the first illustrative problem. They were then requested to try, during the forthcoming Christmas holiday, to formulate volume-measuring problems in which three jars were given as measures. At the first class meeting following the holiday, the instructor collected the problems they had formulated and, selecting ten sheets of paper at random, pretended to read a problem from each. Actually, he presented the usual E tasks and test tasks in the usual manner, except that no method was demonstrated. Four minutes were allowed for the first E task but the usual two and a half minutes each for the other problems. Yet, the seventeen adults showed E effects as large as those for similar groups taking the basic experiment: C_1C_2, 76% E; Ext., 59% F; C_3C_4, 65% E.

A variation of this procedure was used in a New York City college psychology class of forty-two students. As in the afore-mentioned adult class, the students were asked, after seeing the first illustrative problem, to create one water-jar measuring problem each. But, instead of collecting the papers, the instructor now called on the students to describe the problems they had created. As a student described his problem, the instructor wrote it on the blackboard, asked the students to work the problem, and allotted them time to do so before calling on another student to give his problem. In this manner, ten students were selected in an apparently random manner. But, actually, prearrangements had been made with these ten students so that the problems they gave were precisely the usual E and test problems. The order in which the students were selected was such that the usual order of the problems was maintained. Time allotments per problem were the same as in the adult class. E effects within the range found in college groups were shown by the thirty-two students who were not involved in the prearrangements.

We see that considerable E effects resulted when no method was illustrated and when the problems apparently came from random sources. In the basic experiment, some E effects presumably might have resulted because the experimenter illustrated the E method and therefore subjects assumed that they must use it, or because subjects assumed that similar-appearing problems all coming from the same individual must be solved by the same method. Such assumptions imply the working of attitudes which may be traced to life experiences and, in particular, to school experiences. In any event, results in the two experiments just described suggest that the operation of such assumptions and attitudes cannot account for all cases of E effects.

Comment on a Probability Expectation

As a possible hypothesis to account for certain cases of E effect in the basic experiment, it was suggested that some subjects may have reasoned along these lines:

> It is very improbable that merely by chance all these problems (the E tasks) are solvable by the same method. There must be some reason for the sameness of the method of solution. This is not a chance distribution of problems, but rather, problems of one type, all solvable by the same method. Therefore, the method I used before will be proper for the subsequent problems too. (Luchins, 1942, pp. 28-29.)

Experimental variations in which the problems apparently come from diversified sources would seem to rule out a reasonable basis for the assumption that the problems probably are of one type. The matter is not settled so simply, however. Perhaps the uniformity of appearance of the E problems and the sameness of the method which solved them testified against their apparently random, chance distribution and led to a probability expectation that subsequent problems would be of the same type. This may have been accomplished in various ways (cf. Luchins, 1942, p. 85). For example, impressed by the uniformity of the appearance and mode of solution of the E tasks, the subject, not thinking for the moment about the supposedly diversified sources of the problems, may have induced that the problems were of one type (or belonged to the same class) and that the E method solved them. Or the subject, puzzled by the uniformity of the problems, may have reasoned along these lines: "These problems are of one type. Why this is so I do not know. Perhaps there is some reason for it of which I am unaware. It is improbable that through a random selection of problems the same problem should occur each time Nevertheless, the problems have been of one type; it is probable that the same type will occur again."

The kind of probability expectation involved in this hypothetical case of reasoning is quite different from the probability expectation that operates in connection with a roulette wheel and similar games of chance. If red should reappear five times in succession on the roulette wheel, the gambler might well stake his next bet on black, reasoning that black will probably appear after all the reds. Why is it that in our case a contrary inference might be drawn by the subject? Perhaps the answer is that one assumes that the roulette wheel, if the game is not "loaded," is a "random" machine. In the described experiments a subject may have thought that there were certain rules governing the uniformity of events (problems) even if these were not concretely realized by him; or he may have suspected that our problems were "loaded," that prearrangements had been made; or, perhaps absorbed in working the problems, he did not even think about the apparent diversified sources of the problems.

There is, of course, also the possibility that a subject did not even think of the problems as being of one type and yet showed E effects; the underlying Einstellung process may not have involved conscious awareness that the problems were similar or that the same method was being repeatedly applied. The Einstellung may have involved, not cognitive, but sheerly mechanical repetitive tendencies.

It would have been helpful to have questioned every subject after the experiment about his impressions of the problems, of their succession, and of the methods that solved them. This remains to be done in replications of the experiments.

EXPERIMENTS WHEREIN SUBJECTS WERE TOLD THAT PROBLEMS WERE NOT OF ONE TYPE OR THAT ONE METHOD SHOULD NOT BE USED

Variations were conducted (Luchins, 1942, pp. 49-53) in which subjects were explicitly instructed that the problems were not of one type or were not solvable by one method. Here we summarize the procedures and results of six variations. It should be kept in mind that, in each of the six experiments, the methods of solving E_1 were illustrated in the usual manner.

Procedures

Experiment 1. After solution of the first problem (29, 3, get 20) had been illustrated, the class was told, "You will receive two series of problems, the first group solvable by one procedure and the second by other procedures. Here is Series 1." Then they were given E_1 through E_5 in the usual manner. After E_5 they were told, "Now comes Series 2 to which other methods apply." The test problems were then presented in the usual manner.

Experiment 2. The new instructions were postponed so that the procedure of the basic experiment was used through E_5. After E_5, we said, "Now you will be given a new set of problems solvable by methods other than the one you've been using up to now." The papers were then collected and new papers were distributed on which the test problems were worked.

Experiment 3. After the first illustrative problem, the subjects were told that they were to receive two groups of problems, the first group solvable in one way, and the second group in "entirely different, easier, and better ways." They were warned: "The problems of both groups will look alike, but, if you keep your eyes open, you'll see that different methods can be used in the second group." After E_5, the papers were collected and new papers distributed. The subjects were again reminded, "We have finished the first set. Now come the examples that have different solutions."

Experiment 4. The procedure of Experiment 2 was followed except that the instructions after E_5 were made more pointed. After collecting the papers on which the E tasks had been solved, we told subjects to formulate in their minds the method they had used. Then we said, "Try not to use the method hereafter. I'll give you one minute to make up your mind not to use it any more." New papers were then distributed and with each test problem the subjects were reminded, "Look for the new ways. Do you see a different method? Write after your answer whether or not you have found it."

Experiment 5. After the first illustrative problem, subjects were given the instructions used at this point in Experiment 1. In addition, with each E task, we said, "Remember, in this group the examples can all be solved by one method. Just think of the method you used before. It will work here too." After E_5, the subjects were asked to formulate in writing the rule or method which they had used. Then: "Now turn over your papers. On this side of the page you are going to do the second group of problems. These also involve the measuring of water, but in these there are other and better ways of getting the water. Let us see if you can find them." With each critical problem we reminded them, "Look for the better way to solve the problem. Write whether or not you have found it." After the extinction task had been on the blackboard for one and a half minutes, we said, "I told you that there is a new and better way to do these problems, but some of you did not believe me. Because you did not look for a new way, you are now having trouble."

Experiment 6. The procedure of Experiment 5 was used through the E tasks. After subjects had been given some time to formulate in writing the rule they had used in the E tasks, we drew jars and arrows on the blackboard to depict the E method. "DO NOT USE IT ANY MORE" was printed on the blackboard under the depicted method after the class had been told that they were to be given a new set of problems solvable in other and better ways and in which they must not use the old method. They were further cautioned, "Remember, not the answer, but the way you get the answer counts. If you try to use the old method, you are wrong. Do not use it. There are other and better ways of solving the problems. I want you to find them." The test problems were then presented in the usual manner.

Experiment 1 was administered to two college classes; Experiment 6, to a college class and a sixth-grade class; and each of the remaining experiments, to a sixth-grade class.

At the conclusion of each experiment, the subjects were asked to write on their papers answers to questions of this sort: Was there a difference between the problems of the first and second series? If so, how did they differ? Did you use different methods for the two series? What were your methods? If you did not change your method of solution in the second series, why did you not change?

Results

Despite the various instructions that had been issued in attempts to get subjects to view the series of E tasks as distinct from the series of test tasks, some subjects in every experiment apparently did not regard them as distinct. Responding to the questions at the end of the session, they wrote: "All the problems are the same"; "They are all subtraction examples"; "I see no difference. The old method still works"; or words to this effect. Percentages of subjects reporting that the two series were different were higher in the college classes (where they ranged from 60 to 89 per cent) than in the elementary-school classes (where they ranged from 0 to 52 per cent).

E effects were computed for those members of each class who reported that the two series were different and also for those who reported that they were alike. Table XVI shows that those who reported the two series to be different showed strikingly less E effects than the ones who found them alike.

TABLE XVI. RESULTS OF EXPERIMENTAL ATTEMPTS TO GET SUBJECTS TO DISTINGUISH E TASKS AND TEST TASKS*

Exp.	Kind of Subjects	No.	Percentage Reporting Two Series to Be		E Effects of Those Reporting Two Series to Be Different (in Percentages)			E Effects of Those Reporting Two Series to Be Alike (in Percentages)		
			Different	Alike	C_1C_2	Ext.	C_3C_4	C_1C_2	Ext.	C_3C_4
1...............	Coll.	20	60	40	38	16	8	100	75	75
1...............	Coll.	27	89	11	13	0	8	100	67	67
6...............	Coll.	22	68	32	0	0	0	43	43	43
2...............	Elem.	20	0	100	..	..	..	80	60	80
3...............	Elem.	20	10	90	0	0	0	92	56	80
4...............	Elem.	24	50	50	17	8	4	75	50	75
5...............	Elem.	25	52	48	12	8	8	100	67	71
6...............	Elem.	24	42	58	15	10	20	14†	64	49

* Adapted from Luchins, 1942, pp. 49-53.
† This group showed 53 per cent failure and only 33 per cent direct solution of C_1C_2.

A word is in order concerning results for the elementary class that participated in Experiment 6. Confronted with the warning "DO NOT USE IT ANY MORE" written on the blackboard under the demonstration of the E method, and with the warning that it was wrong to use the old method, those subjects who reported that the two series were not different apparently were reluctant to use the E method in Criticals 1 and 2 (and only 14 per cent of them did), while over half of them (53 per cent) failed Criticals 1 and 2.

When asked why they had persisted in using the E method in the test tasks, subjects who showed E effects said that they used it because they could see no other method, because they tried the old method and it worked, or because they did not want to search for new methods while the old one sufficed. A few said that the E method or a subtraction process "popped up" in their minds and they "could not help using it."

Comments

Did the subjects develop an Einstellung and show E effects because they regarded the series of test tasks as similar to the series of E tasks, or did they so regard the two series because they developed an Einstellung and showed E effects? We do not know the answer to this question, at least not in all cases. But it is of interest that, even among those who reported the series of E problems as distinct from the series of test problems, there were some who showed E effects—a result which may imply that the assumption that the problems belong to one class is not essential to E effects.

Comments show that the subjects' attitudes sometimes vitiated the additional instructions. Some wanted to use one method throughout and saw no need to give up a method as long as it worked. "Why search for new ways when the old way works?" is a comment that typifies this attitude. Perhaps they were reluctant to give up the safety of the known for the dangers of the unknown, to substitute a possibly more difficult task (finding a new method of solution) for an easy task (repeating a method or process).

That the elementary-school subjects more frequently than the college subjects reported the two series to be alike or "the same" and showed higher E effects perhaps is traceable to the apparent greater difficulty which the problems and the finding of a new solution may have presented to the children. "Thus, it may be that because the children had difficulty in finding a new method, they thought of their previous solution and went back to it; but it may also be that because of the repetition of the E method they had difficulty in discovering a new solution" (Luchins, 1942, pp. 52-53).

In the terminology of suggestion, it could be said that various kinds of suggestions are involved in the present experimental variations. By demonstrating the E method the experimenter may suggest its use. The new additional instructions in the experiments under consideration suggest that the E tasks be viewed as distinct from the test tasks and that the old method not be used (where the instructions are not more explicit). Why was the former "suggestion" more readily accepted by some subjects than the latter? A possible reason may be found in the nature of the suggestions. Demonstration of the E method points to a line of action (positive suggestion). The additional instructions in the present variations prohibit a line of action (negative suggestion); they tell a subject not to view the two series as the same or not to use the old method but do not offer an alternate course of action. Another factor may be that in the beginning of the experiment a subject needed a method with which to deal with the problems; the E method structured his mind and became the frame of reference from which to view the problems. This same frame of reference was still adequate in the criticals so that the subject felt no need to change despite the experimenter's remarks. In brief, the subject may have been less open to suggestion once he had the E method.

The relationship of the instructions to the "objective evidence" may also have played a role. The "objective evidence" belies the additional instructions since the test problems look like the E problems and the old method still works when the second (test) series starts. Indeed, the additional instructions may seem unreasonable to the subject in the light of the evidence (at least until the extinction problem is reached). Subjects who regarded the E and test series as one may be said to have been affected more strongly by the apparent unitary and homogeneous nature of the whole problem series than by the experimentally introduced attempts at distinguishing between the problems.

One can also speak of the "ideomotor suggestion" that stems from the problem sequence and from the repeated use of the E method. This ideomotor suggestion may be regarded as reinforcing the suggestion stemming from the demonstration of the E method.

The writers are not at all sure what is gained by invoking such concepts as prestige suggestion and ideomotor suggestion. Thus, to say that E effects are results of suggestion, still leaves the question of what suggestion is and how it operates.

Parenthetically, we mention that, while suggestion may be used as a possible explanation of Einstellung, the concept of Einstellung may in turn be used to account for ideomotor suggestion. In cases usually subsumed under ideomotor suggestion, an individual makes an old response to (new) stimuli; for example, a person given six bottles of cologne to smell followed by a bottle of distilled water may smell an odor in the seventh bottle. Because of the nature of previous experiences, there is set up a tendency in the subject to respond to certain stimuli in a manner "suggested" or directed by the previous experiences. But to describe such a tendency, concepts of set or of Einstellung may be invoked.

Experimental Attempts to Control the Tendency to Begin with the Largest Jar

Some subjects in the basic experiment commented that the problems, or most of the problems, could be solved by beginning with the largest jar. Variations (Luchins, 1942, pp. 62-63) were therefore conducted in an attempt to weaken a tendency to begin with the largest jar. "You do not have to use the largest jar if you do not want to," an elementary-school class was told with each problem (E and test). But, despite this comment, the group gave large E effects: C_1C_2, 75% E; Ext., 66% F; C_3C_4, 75% E. Remarks made after the experiment indicated that the comment had been rather meaningless and confusing to most of the children or that they ignored it; a few insisted that they had to use the largest jar to attain a solution.

The situation was quite different when the same procedure was followed for a college group. Now fourteen of the thirty-two subjects showed some non-E solutions even in the E tasks; e.g., they gave $9 + 6 + 6 = 21$ in response to E_4. These fourteen subjects showed very little E effects: C_1C_2, only 11% E; Ext., no failures; C_3C_4, only 7% E. E effects for the remaining eighteen subjects, who solved all of the E problems by the E method, were as follows: C_1C_2, 47% E; Ext., 6% F; C_3C_4, 16% E. As a whole, the class had substantially less E effects than college classes taking the basic experiment.

For other groups, the comment "You do not have to use the largest jar if you do not want to" was delayed until the first test problem and then given with each subsequent problem. Two college classes and an elementary-school group showed significantly less E effect than was found for groups taking the basic experiment: C_1C_2, from 25 to 29 per cent E; Ext., from 0 to 10 per cent F; C_3C_4, from 18 to 23 per cent E.

Many of the elementary-school children reported that, when the comment was first made, they suddenly became aware of another method of solution. College students stated that the comment made them expect that a different kind of problem would follow, made a new method become obvious, or caused them to view the problems in a new light so that the largest jar no longer played any role, or made them suspicious so that they stopped and looked twice before writing their answers.

The effectiveness of this comment does not of course imply that the main factor in the basic experiment was the belief that the largest jar must be used. Indeed, even in the present variation, the efficacy of the comment may not have been so much that it dispelled this belief, as that it instigated a search for new methods even in cases where this belief was not held. Nonetheless, the findings do suggest that at least some cases of E effect may have resulted from the tendency (conscious or not) to begin with the largest jar.

EXPERIMENTAL ATTEMPTS TO CONTROL THE TENDENCY TO BEGIN WITH THE CENTER JAR

Observations of subjects in the basic experiment revealed that some of them tended to begin with the center jar (which was also the largest jar). There were some subjects who, even before the experimenter announced the capacities of the jars, drew diagrams of the three jars with arrows designating pouring from the center jar. It might be said that subjects had learned a certain series of movements or a certain positional set. (An appeal might be made to Guthrie's emphasis on movements as the most important data for prediction of subsequent behavior as well as to Tolman's recognition of motions as one of six "kinds of learning.") At any rate, experimental modifications were made in an attempt to prevent the development of a tendency to begin with the center jar or to prevent such tendency from promoting E effects.

In one experiment (Luchins, 1942, pp. 59-60), the order of the jars in the E problems, but not in the test problems, was changed so that the largest jar became an end jar rather than the center jar. If the customary order of the jars is designated as ABC, with B representing the largest jar, then the new order can be expressed as E_1, BAC; E_2, BCA; E_3, ACB; E_4, BAC; E_5, ACB. The largest jar was placed on both the left and right ends in order to reduce any tendency toward positional set. If E effects are due solely or mainly to the learning and carry-over of a particular sequence of movements, then solution of these altered problems should have led to little or no E solutions of the usual test problems. But, when these tasks were presented to two college classes, one high-school class, and two elementary-school classes, E effects were within the range found in the basic study: C_1C_2, from 74 to 92 per cent E; Ext., from 42 to 85 per cent F; C_3C_4, from 30 to 92 per cent E.

In another variation (Luchins, 1942, p. 60), the order of the jars in the E tasks was the same as in the basic experiment but the order in the test tasks was changed from ABC to the following: C_1, ACB; C_2, BAC; Ext., ACB; C_3, BAC; C_4, ACB. Development in the E problems of a tendency to start with the middle jar did not now favor E solutions if the tendency carried over to these altered test problems. Yet, when these altered problems were presented to one college class and two elementary-school classes, results were similar to those found in the basic study: C_1C_2, from 75 to 100 per cent E; Ext., from 65 to 89 per cent F; C_3C_4, from 50 to 100 per cent E.

While these results do not eliminate the possibility that a tendency to start with the center jar is responsible for some E effect, they suggest that it would be misleading to regard it as accountable for all or most E effect.

There is a feature of the last variation which should not be overlooked. Rearrangement of the order of the jars in the test problems made the two jars required for the direct solutions adjacent to one another. This proximity might have been expected to facilitate direct solution, in accordance with the emphasis placed on contiguity or proximity in both associationistic and Gestalt theories of learning. And yet direct solutions were not more frequent than in the basic experiment where such proximity was absent.

Experimental Attempts to Control the Assumption That All Three Jars Must Be Used

It was stated in the instructions given preceding the basic experiment that subjects were to solve the problems by using all or any of the given jars, and the fact that there was a choice in the number was further illustrated in the demonstration of the two methods of solving E_1 ($B - A - 2C$ and $B - 9C$). Nonetheless, some subjects may have misinterpreted or forgotten these initial instructions. (They may have transferred to the experiment the rule taught to them in arithmetic that all the givens must be used in the solution of problems.) Indeed, when after the experiment the direct methods were shown, a few did claim that they did not use them because they thought (or it was understood) that all three jars had to be used in a solution. Variations (Luchins, 1942, p. 61) were therefore conducted in an attempt to prevent the development of an assumption that all three jars had to be used or to exclude its support of the E method at the expense of the direct method.

In one series of experiments, three college groups and three elementary-school groups were asked with each of the usual problems: "Using one, two, or three of these jars, how would you obtain the required volume of water?" Although subjects' remarks clearly revealed that they understood that they might use two of the given jars, E effects were as large as in the basic study: C_1C_2, from 75 to 100 per cent E; Ext., from 45 to 87 per cent F; C_3C_4, only 19 per cent E for one college group but from 38 to 100 per cent E for the other groups.

Reiteration of the phrase "Using one, two, or three of these jars" with each E problem where three jars were required, may conceivably have made it a trite phrase by the time the test problems came. A college class and four elementary-school classes were therefore given the phrase only with each of the test problems. Yet E effects in some groups were within the range found in the basic study: C_1C_2, from 64 to 100 per cent E; Ext., from 37 to 96 per cent F; C_3C_4, from 25 to 100 per cent E.

Another variation utilized a new series of problems in which the E method was $A + B - 4C$ and the direct method was $B - A - C$. Since both methods require three jars, an assumption about the number of jars to be used would be equally conducive to E or direct solutions. To keep this assumption rather constant, subjects were told at the outset that they must use all three jars as measures. When the new problems were presented to three college and one elementary-school class, E effects were as large as in the basic study: C_1C_2, from 75 to 100 per cent E; Ext., from 50 to 100 per cent F; C_3C_4, from 30 to 100 per cent E.

Thus, while the supposition that three given containers must be employed may have been responsible for some E solutions, it cannot suffice as an explanation of all cases of E effect.

Experiments in Which the Problems Contained Superfluous Jars

The tendency to use all three jars (or to begin with the center jar) may be weakened by adding additional jars to each problem. Inclusion of additional jars would require that the subject first survey the given jars, for, even if he were set to use the E method, he would first have to select the three containers to be used, and, in the course of surveying the jars, he might become aware of other solutions. In all the experiments involving superfluous jars, solutions to the first two problems were illustrated as in the basic experiment.

Variations Wherein Each Problem Had Four Jars

Preliminary experimentation revealed that E effects within the range of those in the basic study, were obtained when a fourth jar was added as the first jar in each problem or as the last jar in each problem; that is, when the fourth jar preceded or followed the usual three jars. It was therefore decided to "randomize" the placement of the additional jar, and its capacity was made less than that of the largest jar in the problem. For example, instead of "21, 127, 3, get 100," subjects now received "21, 127, 89, 3, get 100."

When this four-jar variation was administered to four sixth-grade classes (Luchins and Luchins, 1950), significantly more failure of the

E tasks was obtained than in the basic study. Of 148 subjects, 65 per cent failed to solve the last two E tasks in contrast with the average of 12 per cent failure for similar groups in the basic experiment. Twenty-four children (16 per cent) solved one or both of the two problems by another procedure, usually a cumbersome variation of the E method. The remaining twenty-eight subjects, who used the E method in both of these problems, showed significantly less E effects than similar groups in the basic study: C_1C_2, 28% E; Ext., 9% F; C_3C_4, 10% E. The 148 subjects as a whole gave from 4 to 11 per cent E solutions and from 80 to 90 per cent D solutions of the test problems, about the reverse of the results for similar groups in the basic study. Thus, the use of a super-fluous container yielded an increase in direct solutions, offset by an increase in failures and in inefficient solutions of the E tasks.

The four-jar modification was also administered to 125 high-school students in three classes in the High School of Science in New York City. Thirty-five students (28 per cent) failed to solve at least one of the last two E tasks, in contrast to their almost universal solution by high-school groups receiving the basic experiment. Another nineteen solved these problems by methods other than the E method, usually cumbersome variations of this procedure. The seventy-one subjects who did solve these two E problems by the E procedure showed 46, 19, and 16 per cent E effect in C_1C_2, Ext., and C_3C_4, respectively, signif-icantly less than the 74, 49, 61 per cent made by a group of forty-two students from the same school in the basic experiment. The 125 subjects as a whole yielded from 11 to 28 per cent E solutions and from 59 to 74 per cent direct solutions of the test problems, about the reverse of results made by high-school groups in the basic study. Again, the intro-duction of a superfluous container resulted in more direct solutions but also in more failures and inefficient solutions of the E tasks.

In order to promote more solutions of the E tasks in the four-jar variations, the series of four-jar E tasks was repeatedly administered, with the assistance of Diana Kingsmill, up to a maximum of four ad-ministrations, until all were solved or this maximum attained, before the test problems were given. Of twenty-five Montreal high-school girls, tested individually, none solved all five E problems on the first pre-sentation, two girls solved all of them on the second presentation, five girls solved all of them on the third presentation, while the remaining eighteen did not solve all the E problems even on the fourth presenta-tion. On the average, they had twice the number of presentations that were had by fifteen girls in the same school who received the usual three-jar E problems until they solved all of them, up to four presentations if necessary. Failures of the last two E problems, on their final administration, averaged 24 per cent for those receiving the four-jar problems but only 3 per cent for those receiving the usual problems. Those who solved the last two E tasks of the four-jar variation by the E method, showed little E effect: 19 per cent E solution of the criticals and no failure of the extinction task. The four-jar variation, as a whole, yielded 80 per cent direct solutions of the criticals and 88 per cent direct solution of the extinction task, as compared with only 37 and 40 per cent in the three-jar basic experiment (that is, 60 per cent failed the extinction task in the latter experiment). Thus, once more the superfluous jar made for failures of the E tasks but for more direct solutions and less failures of the test tasks.

To decrease failures and cumbersome solutions, the four-jar experiment was given to college students. Moreover, since college students generally solve all five of the usual E problems by the E method, we decided to obtain five successive E solutions of the E tasks in the four-jar variation. This was done by administering the experiment individually (with the assistance of Joyce Avery) and by repeating the series of E tasks until the criterion of five successive E solutions was met. Only then was the first critical presented. When this procedure was tried with ten McGill University students, it was found that, to meet the criterion of five successive E solutions, they needed from five to ten presentations of the E tasks, with an average of seven presentations, as compared with one presentation for ten comparable subjects who received the usual three-jar problems. The former showed 30, 20, 10 per cent E effects in C_1C_2, Ext., and C_3C_4, respectively, markedly less than the 80, 60, 55 per cent made by the latter. Thus, notwithstanding the greater number of times that E solutions had been used in the E problems, this variation sharply lowered the E effects.

In the four-jar variations considered up to this point, the additional jar was never the largest jar in the problem. Some subjects showed a tendency to begin with the largest jar, depending on a "hit and hope" method to obtain the required volume; this resulted frequently in the use of cumbersome variations of the E method. We therefore devised a new experiment in which the additional jar was the largest jar in some problems; e.g., instead of the usual extinction task, "28, 76, 3, get 25," the subject now received "28, 76, 80, 3, get 25." The position of the superfluous jar was varied, and the new E tasks were given only once, followed by the new test tasks. Of twenty-two Montreal children, about thirteen years of age, tested with the assistance of Robert Saul, 59 per cent failed to solve the last two E problems. Those who did solve them showed less E effects than comparable subjects taking the basic experiment, averaging 72 per cent direct solutions of the criticals and 88 per cent direct solution of the extinction task. It might be noted that in this variation many subjects attempted to begin with the largest jar or the next-to-the-largest jar.

Variations Wherein Each Problem Had from Four to Eight Jars

Thus far only one additional jar was used in each problem. What would happen if more superfluous jars were used? Variations were devised in which from one to five jars were added to the problems of the basic experiment, so that some problems contained as many as eight jars while others contained only four jars. The capacities of the superfluous jars varied so that they were the largest jars or the smallest jars in some problems while they fell within the extremes in other problems. In one experiment (adjacent order), the three usual jars were adjacent to each other, while the additional jars were placed before and/or after them. In another experiment (interspersed order), the additional jars were interspersed among the three usual jars. In a third experiment, only the usual three jars were used.

After the fourth critical, there followed two new critical problems each of which could be solved by the E method, $A - C$, and C (filling one jar); a new task (Ext.$_2$) solvable only by $2A - C$; and finally a new E task, E_6. These tasks were included in each of the three experiments. For example, in the usual three-jar experiment, the first problem after the fourth critical was 36, 90, 18, get 18; in the adjacent-order experiment, it was 17, 36, 90, 18, 23, 43, get 18; and in the interspersed-order experiment, it was 36, 23, 17, 90, 18, 43, get 18.

The three experiments were conducted with the assistance of S. Sheldon Merling. Twenty Montreal high-school students were used in each experiment. Results are summarized in Table XVII.

TABLE XVII. RESULTS OF THREE-JAR AND SUPERFLUOUS-JAR EXPERIMENTS

Experiment	% F E_1-E_5	% E C_1C_2	% F Ext.$_1$	% E C_3C_4	% E C_5C_6	% F Ext.$_2$	% F E_6
Three jars	4	78	35	38	35	60	5
Adjacent order	27	0	5	0	0	25	35
Interspersed order	37	8	0	3	0	45	30

The table reveals that failures of the E tasks increase as we go from the three-jar problems to the adjacent-order problems and then to the interspersed-order problems. It is not unexpected that the superfluous-jar variations should have led to less E solutions of the criticals. What the table does not show are the percentages of direct solutions to the test problems, which were as follows in the three-jar, adjacent-order, and interspersed-order experiments, respectively:

C_1C_2	23	90	75
Ext.$_1$	60	85	85
C_3C_4	63	95	90
C_5C_6	67	100	100

We see that the superfluous-jar variations consistently yielded more direct solutions than the three-jar experiment. It is of interest that the most direct solution available in C_5C_6, the filling of one jar, was used about twice as frequently in the experiments with superfluous jars as in the three-jar experiment. On the whole, there were no consistent differences in the results of the test problems in the adjacent-order and interspersed-order experiments.

Average time in seconds, per problem, in the three-jar, adjacent-order, and interspersed-order experiments, respectively, was as follows:

E_1-E_5	30	150	150
Criticals	20	20	20
Ext.$_1$	90	20	20
Ext.$_2$	150	150	150
E_6	40	150	150

Those who received three jars per problem required less time to solve the E tasks than those who received additional jars. That the average time in the criticals was the same in the three experiments, implies that application of an oft-repeated method in the criticals was as time-consuming as searching for and finding a new (more direct) method. Moreover, those who received superfluous jars averaged less time on the first extinction task than those who received three jars. While the second extinction task took the maximum time allotment in each experiment (two and a half minutes), we have seen that experiments with superfluous jars yielded more solutions of it.

In short, these experiments corroborate the same trends found when only one superfluous jar was used in each problem; namely, the use of additional jars fostered more failures of the E tasks but also less E effects, with subjects more prone to use direct solutions when they were available.

Comments

The additional jar or jars made the problems look more complicated and actually increased their complexity by increasing the number of possible numerical combinations of the containers. The basic experiment contained problems that were less complex both in appearance and in structure, since to use the E procedure in them required use of all of the three given containers. In order to employ the E method in the superfluous-jar variations, the subject had to discard certain containers. In selecting the jar to be filled initially, and in selecting the jars into which to pour, he might choose the superfluous containers, and err. Nothing in the statement of a problem told how many and which jars should be employed in the solution.

Moreover, to be given problems in which it was necessary to discard some of the "givens" or hypotheses, as one had to in the superfluous-jar experiments, was an unusual assignment for our subjects. They had been taught to use all the hypotheses given in a problem; some of the high-school students had learned in their geometry classes to check off each hypothesis as they used it and, if any hypotheses were left unchecked, they knew that they had not proceeded correctly. While in natural problem-solving situations the selection of facts and hypotheses from the many available ones (decision making) is an important aspect of the problem-solving process, it appeared to be a highly artificial procedure to many of our subjects because it was contrary to their school training.

An attempt to teach selection of hypotheses underlies the use in certain algebra curricula of problems which have insufficient or superfluous hypotheses. But even the limited value which can arise from the isolated use of such problems in one school subject is almost completely negated by the nature of these problems and by the manner in which they are presented. They are often taught as optionals, which are squeezed in near the close of the semester if time permits; and the problems are generally introduced as possessing one too many or one too few hypotheses, with the one in question often so evidently conspicuous because of its presence or absence that little analysis is required to detect it. Also, these problems are sometimes based on familiar "type exercises," in which the students previously have much practice, so that anything lacking or superfluous is immediately evident to them, and they can quickly proceed to apply the procedure which they have learned to thrust upon this "type." Apropos of this, we mention that our preliminary experiments indicated that, when the additional containers were very outstanding, either because of their size or position, E effects were large and that, when the basic experiment was followed by the four-jar variation, those who showed large E effects in the former tended to do so even in the variation.

To be effective, problems which aim at conveying the importance of discovering, selecting, evaluating, and discarding facts and hypotheses in their solution, should be introduced in all school subjects and should not be treated as curiosities which must be heralded with a special introduction but should be freely intermingled with other, more routine problems. If they involve insufficient or additional hypotheses, these should not be patterned as to number or kind. To be sure, as our experiments indicate, the inclusion of such problems may make learning slower and somewhat less efficient than drill procedures, but it may also tend to produce less mechanical behavior and more productive thinking. Basically, the issue revolves on whether our schools wish to develop mechanical efficiency and a formula-applying attitude, conducive to associating a particular method with a particular situation, or whether they wish to develop individuals who are capable of facing and coping with new and changing problem situations. A fundamental issue is involved here: Shall we teach children by drill or repetition which yields E effects or shall we involve them in decision-making activities? More will be said about this later on.

CONCLUSIONS CONCERNING WHAT IS LEARNED IN THE EINSTELLUNG SITUATION

At the beginning of this chapter, we raised the problem what is learned in the Einstellung situation. Clearly those who found D solutions to the test problems seem to have "learned" something different than those who showed E effects. But even all those who showed E effects did not seem to have "learned" the same thing. Some learned the E method itself, some learned to use all three jars, some learned to begin with a certain jar, etc. Results of experimental variations suggest that some of the tendencies noted may account for more cases of E effect than others. For example, the tendency to begin with the largest jar seemed to be a more potent factor than the tendency to begin with the middle jar, so that E effects decreased more when the first tendency was obviated. But none of the tendencies by itself seemed adequate to account for all or most cases of E effect. Different subjects learned different things and even the same subject may have learned more than one thing in an experiment. Hence, the problem, "What is learned in the Einstellung situation?" seems to be a problem with more than one solution. Here, again, as in the case of focusing learning theories onto the basic experiment, we are confronted with a problem that seemingly has nonunique, multiple solutions.

It is of importance to develop methods of ascertaining just what a particular individual "learned" in the Einstellung experiment. It may be helpful to question the subject or to conduct further experiments with him. A method that has shown some promise in preliminary investigations (in which we were assisted by Joseph Zweig of Sir George Williams College, Montreal) is to use a "completion test" after the Einstellung experiment. In the "completion test" the subject is asked to devise and solve volume-measuring problems and is given incomplete

problems, with the goal and/or the capacity of one or more jars un-
stipulated; the assigned task is to complete the problems and solve
them. The manner in which the subject creates and completes problems,
may hint at what he "learned" in the Einstellung situation.

CHAPTER XX

RETROSPECT

O UR JOURNEY has led through a myriad of theoretical and experimental paths and bypaths. It seems timely to pause here and, without a pretense at a thorough summary, point in retrospect to some landmarks or high lights of the journey, with particular reference to various concepts and issues that were encountered. The order of the subdivisions in the present chapter follows the order of preceding chapters.

PSYCHOANALYTIC APPROACHES TO RIGIDITY

That contemporary clinical and experimental workers on rigidity frequently utilize psychoanalytic concepts is not surprising since most psychoanalysts have been concerned with the kind of maladaptive repetitive behavior that may be described as rigid behavior. We attempted to outline the basic tenets of each of several psychoanalytic theories while high-lighting aspects germane to rigidity. It was shown that Sigmund Freud's observations of the frequency with which rigid, repetitive behavior occurs led him to alter radically his formulation of psychoanalytic theory. Displacing the pleasure principle in his new formulation, and considered as more powerful than the pleasure principle, was the principle of the repetition compulsion: an inherent compulsion to repeat former psychic experiences, regarded as possessed by everyone, although in differing degrees. Carrying to its ultimate conclusion the tendency to return to a former state evinced in the repetition compulsion, Freud made a further drastic change in his formulation by introducing the death instinct: the tendency of all living matter to return to its original inorganic state. Rigid, repetitive behavior, regarded as arising from the repetition compulsion propelled by the death instinct, was considered by Freud as essentially destructive behavior.

The repetition compulsion was regarded as particularly strong in the neurotic, who has, said Freud, given himself up to this compulsion to the point where he is wrecked by his rigidity. The neurotic is tied to his childhood past; his neurotic symptoms, formed for the purpose of escaping anxiety, are but repetitions or disguised repetitions of his infantile sexual experiences. Ego defenses, part of the normal adjustment process, tend to become rigidified in the neurotic so that, while a normal person can give up a particular ego defense when it is no longer adequate, the neurotic rigidly adheres to his ego defenses to the point where

[471]

maintaining and repeating them may become sources of anxiety. Herein lies the crux of what Mowrer has called the neurotic paradox : the paradox of behavior which, although self-defeating, is perpetuated.

Concepts of rigidity and repetition also play a role in Freud's views on development and on character. Characteristic stages of development (oral, anal, phallic, etc.) are regarded as repetitions of outstanding events in the development of the human race and of society. Character types are regarded as corresponding to stages of development. When part or all of the libido becomes fixated at a certain stage, a person maintains throughout life characteristics related to this stage. More generally, Freud sees an individual's character as essentially a repetition or disguised repetition of the individual's past and of mankind's past.

Repetition compulsion and the death instinct are among the most controversial of psychoanalytic concepts, with one or the other concept rejected or doubted by various psychoanalysts. We surveyed the views on these concepts, and other ideas pertinent to rigidity, found in the writings of Franz Alexander, Wilhelm Reich, Carl Jung, Alfred Adler, Karen Horney, Erich Fromm, and Harry S. Sullivan. While they do not necessarily agree with Freud's explanation of rigid, repetitive behavior, they do corroborate his observations as to the occurrence and frequency of such behavior. In particular, they raise doubts about whether rigid, repetitive behavior is (1) due to a repetition compulsion, (2) related to destructiveness, and (3) attributable to a death instinct. While there are diverse opinions among psychoanalysts concerning the nature and origin of character types, there is general agreement that character structure involves habitual attitudes. Moreover, while psychoanalysts differ concerning the mechanisms that produce ego defenses, they generally agree that an individual does develop ego defenses, that the character or personality structure is itself a kind of defense system, that the individual tends to maintain ego defenses, and that ego defenses tend to become rigidified in the neurotic. Finally, there is complete accord that a major task of therapy is to combat rigidity, to release the personality from its rigidity.

Three Theories of Rigidity

Next we surveyed three theories of rigidity : Kurt Goldstein's, Heinz Werner's, and Kurt Lewin's. Goldstein's theory, which is based on a neuropathological approach, distinguishes between primary rigidity and secondary rigidity. Primary rigidity, defined as an inability to change from one set or Einstellung to another, is attributed to a defect in the "Einstellung mechanism" and is observed especially in patients with subcortical lesions. While primary rigidity is regarded as in-

dependent of higher mental processes, secondary rigidity is considered
as secondary to (as a consequence of) a defect in the higher mental
processes. This defect—which is regarded by Goldstein as occurring
in all acquired cortical damage, in cortical malformation accompanying feeble-mindedness, and in schizophrenia—is characterized as an
impairment of the abstract attitude, an impairment that compels the
individual to behave concretely. While primary rigidity affects all performances that involve the "Einstellung mechanism," secondary rigidity is manifested only when the individual is faced by a catastrophic
situation, a situation in which the environment's demands for abstract
behavior exceed the individual's capacity for such behavior. Even
normals may manifest secondary rigidity in catastrophic situations.
The rigidity manifested by normals, according to Goldstein, differs not
in quality but only in frequency of occurrence from that shown by
schizophrenics and individuals with cortical defects, since catastrophic
situations occur less frequently for normals.

Werner's views on rigidity stem from a comparative-developmental
approach. Rigidity, which he defines as a lack of variability in response
or as a lack of adaptability in behavior, is regarded as a negative function of ontogenetic development as well as of phylogenetic development.
It follows that more rigid behavior should be exhibited by the young
child than by the more mature individual, by so-called primitive man
than by so-called civilized man, who is regarded as higher on the developmental scale, and by lower species than by those higher on the evolutionary scale. Increasing development is considered to be characterized by increasing differentiation between the organism and the
outer world and, concomitantly, the greater rigidity considered characteristic of the less well-developed individual is attributed to his being
less differentiated from the outer world. In particular, the young child
is regarded as having an ego which is less differentiated from the outer
world than that of the mature individual and hence as being more
egocentric in his thinking and behavior. Rigidity, according to Werner,
is also particularly characteristic of subnormal and abnormal individuals and is associated with brain injury and with underdevelopment
and disease of the brain.

Lewin's construct of topological rigidity is one of a series of interrelated constructs postulated in his "topological" psychology. The
person is said to be structured and differentiated into different regions;
topological rigidity refers to that property of the functional boundary
between neighboring regions which hinders communication between
them. Topological rigidity is regarded as favoring the formation of
strong Gestalten; it is regarded as hindering the formation of weak

Gestalten and the reorganization of Gestalten. More generally, topological rigidity is considered to underlie various kinds of behavior, some of which may be classified as behavioral rigidity, some of which have no apparent relation to behavioral rigidity, and some of which appear to be the antithesis of behavioral rigidity. Topological rigidity, Lewin hypothesizes, is small in the infant and young child but tends to increase with age, or, as Kounin words it, topological rigidity is a positive monotonous function of chronological age. In normal development there is assumed to be an increasing differentiation of the person (more psychical regions) from infancy until maturity. Assuming that more differentiation tends to foster less behavioral rigidity, Lewin posits that behavioral rigidity should decrease from infancy to maturity. The feeble-minded child is considered as being less differentiated than the normal child of the same chronological age. A major difference between a feeble-minded and a normal younger child both of whom have the same degree of differentiation is that the feeble-minded is considered to be characterized by greater topological rigidity.

Besides describing Goldstein's, Werner's, and Lewin's theories of rigidity, we subjected each theory and its experimental and conceptual foundations to critical evaluation. Included was a survey and evaluation of experiments conducted by Kounin to test hypotheses he derived from the construct of topological rigidity. We also compared the three theories and considered possible bases for underlying controversies over the nature of rigidity in which proponents of these theories have been interlocked.

We saw that considerable semantic confusion surrounds the term "rigidity." Two distinct referents for the term are (1) a characteristic of behavior designated as behavioral rigidity or, simply, rigidity, and (2) a characteristic of the boundaries of personality regions in Kurt Lewin's "topological psychology." Failure to keep the distinction clearly in mind has contributed to some vitriolic controversies. Part of the fuel for these controversies has undoubtedly been supplied by Lewin himself, who incorporated the term "rigidity" into the terminology of his topological psychology without being sufficiently explicit about how the special meaning he gave to it relates to its other connotations. Moreover, he used the term both without qualification and with a multiplicity of modifiers. He employed the terms "psychic rigidity," "dynamic rigidity," "structural rigidity," and "functional rigidity" as if they were all equivalent to "topological rigidity," but with no indication of why they all pertained to the same concept.

But those who have employed the term "rigidity" in a "nontopological," non-Lewinian sense, have also given it many meanings. It has

been used to refer to a characteristic of behavior; to a process underlying behavior; to a characteristic of a person or of personality; to a
factor in the person, either a specific or a general factor. It has been
used in an all-or-none sense, as an attribute of behavior which a person
either possesses or lacks, as well as in a quantitative sense, as if it were
measurable along a gradient. Some psychologists infer from "rigid"
behavior that the behavior is necessarily brought about by a process or
factor of rigidity or that the person who shows such behavior is a rigid
person. Some of the confusion surrounding the concept of rigidity may
be attributed to its rather indiscriminate application to behavior, processes, factors, people—sometimes by the same writer, even in the same
paragraph. It was suggested that confusion may be lessened if those
who use the concept are careful to define it and to adhere to their definitions or to indicate explicitly when and why they are deviating from
them.

Factor-Analytic Approaches to Rigidity

Factor analysis constitutes one of the oldest, and yet one of the most
prevalent contemporary, orientations to rigidity. It was factor analysis
that led Charles Spearman in 1927 to propose an answer to the question
what brings about rigidity of behavior. He proposed that there is a p
factor, the perseveration or mental-inertia factor, that is possessed by
all human beings but in various amounts. In any one individual, he said,
the p factor operates as a functional unity, pervading all behavior processes. Every cognitive activity was regarded by him as having a perseverative tendency. We reviewed the historical background of Spearman's proposal and the critiques which have been leveled against it on
experimental or conceptual grounds.

Some psychologists contend that disposition rigidity, referring to
the perseveration of a habituated activity, and not Spearman's p factor,
is a basic rigidity factor possessed by all individuals but in differing
amounts and operating as a functional unity in any one individual. We
subjected this contention to critical evaluation. It was seen that conflicting definitions have been offered of disposition rigidity, even by
the same writers, and that its relation to Spearman's p factor is not
clear. We objected to the claims that an individual characterized by
"high" disposition rigidity differs from an individual characterized by
"low" disposition rigidity with respect to speed of learning or creativity
or with respect to temperament, character, or personality characteristics. Not only do the claims seem to lack sufficient evidence, but to
speak of an individual as characterized by "high" or "low" disposition
rigidity assumes that disposition rigidity is constant for a given indi-

vidual and operates as a functional unity, an assumption that has not yet been substantiated. There also proved to be insufficient evidence for the claims that disposition rigidity is genetically determined and that it differs for various races.

Factor-analytic studies have yielded over thirty rigidity factors. The relation among the factors is not at all clear, in some cases not even among factors "identified" in the same study. In general, one does not know whether factors with similar names are actually similar or whether different names are semantic façades hiding essential similarities. It is ironic that one of the outcomes of the factorial approach to rigidity has been to propose a greater multiplicity of rigidity factors than has been proposed by any nonfactorial approach, ironic since one of the chief aims of factor analysis has been described as the attainment of scientific parsimony or economy of description. To see why this aim failed of accomplishment in the domain of rigidity, we turned to a critical evaluation of factor analysis. We examined and took issue with some of the assumptions underlying factor analysis; for example, that the variables under analysis are capable of representation as linear functions of a finite number of numerical variables, that the test scores depend on the same factors for all individuals taking the test, or that the contribution of a particular factor to the score is proportionately the same for all individuals taking the test (that is, that the factor coefficients are the same for all individuals). It was noted that factor analysis cannot compensate for poor validity or poor reliability of tests and is not a substitute for experimentation. While one of the chief claims of enthusiasts of factor analysis is that it constitutes an objective means of dealing with psychological phenomena as opposed to older, subjective methods, we showed that, when it comes to interpretation of factors—which has been characterized as the most important aspect of a factorial study—objectivity was sometimes thrown overboard. The interpretation offered of factors is particularly important since some psychologists attribute psychological meaningfulness to the factors (although others do not) and even assume that they correspond to dimensions of personality or to primary abilities.

It was noted that a factorial method involves the application of a coordinate system or reference system to a set of data and that the extracted factors are dependent on the particular coordinate system (that is, on the particular factorial method used) just as the specific form that the equation of a given curve assumes is dependent on the coordinate system employed. In particular, the number of extracted factors may differ when different factorial methods are applied to the same set of data, just as the equation of a circle with center at the origin

involves a different number of terms in polar coordinates than in Cartesian coordinates. We suggested that, if the dependence of the factorial
solution on the particular reference system employed were more generally recognized, there might be fewer claims that the number of
extracted factors is necessarily equivalent to the number of factors that
underlie the data under analysis, as well as fewer claims that the extracted factors necessarily correspond to fundamental factors in the
data, or that the extracted factors are necessarily psychologically meaningful.

The Selected Case of Rigid Behavior

We turned to a phenomenon-centered approach, selecting a specific
case of behavior, which, as the reader well knows by now, involves
water-jug volume-measuring problems and E effects. While other procedures may be used in phenomenon-centered investigations, we used
one that may be characterized as a variational approach. Viewing the
basic experiment as unbiasedly as possible, we tried to see what factors
and conditions were involved in it and then attempted to manipulate
these factors and conditions in variations of the experiment while observing what happened to the E effects. The rationale was that the
specific case might be better understood through such experimental
variations, that its dynamics might be portrayed in terms of changes
of rigid behavior as certain factors and conditions were changed. Clues
for experimental variations came mainly from observations and analysis
of (1) the basic experimental procedure, (2) the quantitative results
obtained when the basic experiment was administered to different subjects, (3) subjects' comments and their answers to questions as well
as other qualitative reactions, and (4) the social atmosphere prevailing
during the experimental sessions. The observation and analysis of
experimental variations led to new experimental variations. An "extremum principle" served as a guiding, systematizing principle in the
sense that we conducted variations which, on the basis of hunches
derived from observational analysis, we thought might work to maximize or minimize E effects. Since the hunches came from observational
analysis, we returned to observational analysis to try to discover why
the variations yielded the results they did.

After conducting experimental variations derived from observational analysis for over a decade, we turned to various theories for suggestions with regard to what might maximize or minimize E effects. It
seems to us that an appeal to theories does not violate a phenomenon-
centered approach. Appeal to a theory is preceded by naive observation
of the phenomenon. The deliberate resort to different theories lessens

the danger of being blinded to aspects of the phenomenon and may yield multitheoretical interpretations of it. Multitheoretical interpretations, which are not equivalent to an eclectic approach for they do not presuppose a synthesis of portions of various theories, are not common in psychology where it is customary for the investigator to be a theoretical monist, at least with reference to any one study. In the phenomenon-centered variational approach, theories are viewed primarily as tools rather than as objectives of science. Hence, there is no need to become sidetracked from the case under investigation in order to defend, attack, or patch a theory; throughout the theoretical explorations the focal point of interest is the concrete case under consideration.

PSYCHOLOGICAL STRESS AND RIGIDITY

Psychoanalysis accepts the dictum that anxiety or danger to the ego intensifies behavioral rigidity; likewise, many psychological theories contend that rigidity is produced or heightened by psychological stresses stemming from anxiety, frustration, shock, or a catastrophic situation. In line with the thesis that anxiety intensifies rigidity, there resulted considerably more E effects than in the basic experiment when the experiment was presented as a speed test under anxiety-provoking conditions. Moreover, speed-test conditions rendered ineffectual our prior attempts at preventing rigidity and increased E effects for a group to which the basic experiment had been administered three months earlier. Also supporting the cited thesis were studies that compared the results of mirror and nonmirror tracing in the maze Einstellung test as well as a study that compared the performance in various Einstellung tests of stutterers and fluent speakers. Mirror tracing of the E path, which apparently was more frustrating than nonmirror tracing, generally yielded more E effects. Similarly, the hidden-word Einstellung test, presented as an oral test and introduced as a "speech test," presumably was more anxiety-provoking for stutterers than for fluent speakers and yielded significantly more E effects for the former; the arithmetical and mirror-maze tests, which presumably did not involve more stress for stutterers than for fluent speakers, did not differentiate between the two groups.

While administration of the basic experiment as a speed test noticeably heightened psychological stress, relaxation of the time limits did not noticeably reduce stress below the level observed in the basic experiment. This finding suggests that there is no simple relationship between the time factor and psychological stress. E effects as large as in the basic experiment were found when time limits were relaxed. This was true even when subjects were told to spend time in searching for the best possible solution to each problem.

While it was generally difficult to reduce psychological stress below the level observed in the basic experiment, a reduction seemed to have been accomplished when a college student informally presented the usual problems to fellow students with this request: "Please do me a favor and help me check these problems that I have to use in the lab tomorrow." Although the students seemed to be (and later reported that they were) relaxed and not anxious when they worked on the problems, yet they showed E effects within the range found in the basic experiment. This finding shows that E effects may be manifested under apparently relaxed conditions of work, where psychological stress presumably is rather low, and suggests that considerable psychological stress is not a prerequisite for rigidity.

Experiments were conducted to test the thesis that rigidity is heightened by psychological stresses stemming from frustration. Results cast doubt on the assumption, underlying the use of an unsolvable task as a frustrating agent, that failure of a problem necessarily induces frustration. The data also cast doubt on the validity of the thesis that frustration, when it is induced by failure of a problem, necessarily preserves or strengthens rigidity of behavior. The results further suggest that ego threat and rigid behavior are not linearly related; that is, the thesis that the greater the threat to the ego, the greater the behavioral rigidity, was not always borne out. We saw that the same experimentally introduced variable may induce different degrees of ego threat (depending, for example, on the subject's attitudes and assumptions with reference to this variable) and may be concomitant with strikingly different amounts of E effects. The findings also suggest that, under certain conditions, either high or low psychological stress may foster rigid behavior while a moderate degree of stress may work against it. That a low degree of stress should foster rigidity may seem to be a surprising finding in view of the widely accepted notion that stress, tension, anxiety, frustration, or ego threat should be kept low or avoided to prevent rigid behavior; yet it is a finding which seems quite understandable when one realizes that, if an individual is not sufficiently disturbed by stress, he will have little cause to change his behavior. We suggested that efforts to avoid frustration, anxiety, and ego threat in child rearing, education, and therapy, may not always be wise since, under certain conditions, psychological stresses may operate against rigidity, complacency, and dogmatism and may foster effective thinking and interpersonal relations.

Certain methodological and research problems were raised. We noted that there are methodological dangers in the common practice of defining anxiety, frustration, and ego threat in terms of variables introduced by the investigator or in terms of operations performed by the investigator. These terms refer to phenomenally experienced states of being of the subject and should be defined in terms of what the subject feels and does rather than in terms of the experimenter's a priori hypotheses. Research is needed to develop objective methods of determining the characteristic psychological and physiological features of experienced psychological stresses of various kinds. Semantic research is required to delineate differences and similarities among the concepts of anxiety, frustration, and ego threat, which are used by some (but not all) investigators as if they were synonyms. Most of the experimentation in this area, whether with subhumans or humans, has dealt with frustrations that were extrinsic in origin to the main problem-solving situation and that were arbitrary in nature in the sense that they allowed no possibility of insight (e.g., an interpolated nonsolvable problem). It was suggested that a more adequate picture of psychological stresses will be obtained if researchers seek to vary (1) the origin and source of the psychological stress, (2) its relation to the main problem-solving situation, (3) the kind and the intensity of the psychological stress, (4) the direction it takes and the role it plays for the person and his environment. Finally, it was suggested that behavior under various psychological stresses may be studied more adequately if behavior is regarded as a function of functions rather than as a function of a finite number of independent variables.

Concreteness of Thinking and Rigidity

Experimental findings showed that the relationship prevailing between behavioral rigidity and concreteness of thinking may vary considerably, depending on (1) the criterion of behavioral rigidity, (2) the criterion of concreteness of thinking, (3) the test of rigidity used and the test of concreteness used, (4) the order in which tests are administered, and (5) the particular subject studied. The findings suggested that it is rather fruitless to seek to characterize the relationship between rigidity and conceptual behavior *in vacuo* as if the relationship were independent of individual differences, the nature of the testing medium and criteria, and previous experiences of various kinds. In our studies no one conceptual level seemed to be invariantly characteristic of any given subject. It was suggested that to regard conceptual behavior as a function of field conditions is methodologically and therapeutically more fruitful than to pigeonhole an individual as concrete-minded or as abstract-minded.

The findings as a whole cast doubt on the universality of the theses that (1) concreteness of thinking is positively related to rigidity; (2)

abstractness of thinking is negatively related to rigidity; (3) abstract ability presupposes an ability to shift voluntarily; (4) ability to abstract is a higher order function than concrete behavior and presupposes ability to behave concretely; (5) an individual who exhibits concreteness of thinking when he is not under extreme psychological stress necessarily lacks abstract ability.

We subjected to critical evaluation the concepts of abstract and concrete thinking as well as the dicta that the young child, primitive man, and certain pathological states are characterized by concreteness. Evidence supposedly supporting these dicta was found to be inconclusive and the dicta themselves were shown to be logically inconsistent. Scientific thinking, supposedly the highest form of abstract thinking, was shown to meet some of the criteria of concreteness, to lack some of the features attributed to abstraction, and to possess features not comprehended in the constructs of either abstract or concrete thinking. We suggested that concrete thinking is not the only alternative to abstract thinking and that, together, the concepts of abstractness and concreteness cannot account for all conceptual behavior.

An intimate link was shown to exist between the criteria of formal logic and those of abstract thinking. This fact may help to explain why young children and primitive people may give the impression that they cannot think abstractly: they have not been trained in formal logic.

In many tests of conceptual behavior, it is interpreted as a sign of concrete-mindedness to react to the so-called configurational, Gestalt, or structural demands of an object or situation and to be guided by the Gestalt principles of perception, including the tendency toward configurational completion. We questioned the validity of such an interpretation.

We also distinguished between arbitrary, structure-blind abstractions and abstractions that are more structurally related. An individual who is unable or unwilling to do rather arbitrary, structure-blind abstractions under certain conditions, may be willing and able to do them under other conditions or he may be capable of doing more structurally related abstractions. Thorough exploration of conceptual behavior requires the development of tests that involve structurally related, "sensible" abstractions rather than only the highly arbitrary abstractions stressed in many current clinical tests and criteria of conceptualization. It may also prove fruitful to vary situational conditions in an attempt to discover the conditions under which a given individual does (or does not) manifest abstractions of various degrees of structural relatedness.

To appeal at present to concreteness as a predeterminant of rigidity, does not answer the question what brings about rigidity, but instead

involves many questions about concreteness and conceptualization—
questions that await adequate formulation and attack.

VARIABILITY AND RIGIDITY

Experimental evidence was found not to support the assumption
that rigidity is the converse of variability. The relationship between
variable and rigid behavior, even in the same experiment, was found
to differ for different subjects, a fact that suggests that there may be
no neat formula with which one can sum up the relationship. When
several methods were available in each of the set-inducing or practice
problems, those subjects who were "nonvariable" with respect to the
simplest possible method showed less rigid behavior in the test problems than those who were nonvariable with respect to a more complex
method; that is, those who had repeatedly used the simplest possible
method available in the practice problems were more prone to shift
from the repeated method when it no longer led to solution than were
those who had adhered to a more complex method in the practice
problems. Moreover, while a consistent relationship was not found
between rigid behavior in the test problems and the number of responses made in the practice problems (which may appear to be an
index of variability), an inverse relationship was found between rigid
behavior and the number of principles underlying responses. The findings suggest that, in discussing variability, particularly in relation to
rigidity, it does not suffice to consider the number of responses; the
kinds of responses must also be taken into account, as well as the generality of the responses and their compatibility with the situation to
which they are applied.

We pointed to the difficulties involved in comparing the variability
of two individuals, independent of a stipulated index of variability and
a specific situational context. These difficulties increase when different
species are compared. Hence, one must be very cautious about accepting the doctrine, promulgated by Werner and other psychologists, that
variability increases with ontogenetic and phylogenetic development.
Apparently contrary to this doctrine is the finding that rats showed
more variability than humans in Einstellung-type maze situations. We
noted that differences in degree of variability between species may not
be due solely to differences in phylogenetic levels, since experiments
suggest that differences in past experiences and in environmental conditions may be contributing factors.

The literature was shown to contain many diverse, even contradictory, conceptions concerning the meaning and measurement of
variability. There is disagreement even on so apparently empirical an

issue as the influence of practice on variability. In view of the beclouded nature of the concept of variability, to regard rigidity as the converse of variability not only seems unjustified by actual data but does not seem to further our understanding of rigidity.

It was noted that the psychological concept of variability is intimately linked with the biological concept of variation and, in particular, with Darwin's concept of random variation. Much has been learned about biological variation since Darwin formulated his views, so that it may be worth while for psychologists to consider whether modern conceptions of biological variation hold any implications for the psychological concept of variability (and perhaps for the concept of rigidity). Moreover, since the concept of random variation involves the concepts of randomness, chance, and probability, contemporary mathematical thinking about these concepts should be examined with regard to their implications for the concept of variability. It was also noted that some psychologists' views on variability and, in particular, on the relationship between variability and development, appear to be influenced by the law of development postulated by Spencer in his theory of organic evolution. It may be worth while to examine other biological views on development and evolution in order to see what implications they hold for variability, for rigidity, and for the relation of each to development. To seek for clues in various biological and mathematical theories and concepts is in keeping with a multitheoretical approach.

Topological Rigidity and Behavioral Rigidity

From one definition of topological rigidity as "that property of a functional boundary which prevents communication between neighboring regions," Kounin (1941a) derived various propositions which he tested experimentally. One proposition and the results of the corresponding experiment suggested an inverse relationship between topological rigidity and E effects, while another proposition and the results of the corresponding experiment suggested a direct relationship. As possible indicants of topological rigidity, we used cosatiation scores and satiation scores (in situations commonly employed to study satiation as well as in Einstellung situations). No consistent or significant relationship was found between these possible indicants of topological rigidity and E effects. The relationship was found to vary with the particular criterion employed for topological rigidity and for E effects. For example, in a study on satiation in E tasks, the extent of satiation could be gauged either by the number of E tasks completed or by the time spent on these tasks. Dependent upon whether one or another criterion was selected, either a direct or inverse relationship prevailed between extent of satiation and failures of the extinction task, a finding which might be interpreted to mean that, dependent upon whether one or another criterion of satiation was used, either a direct or inverse relationship prevailed between topological and behavioral rigidity.

Lewin's writings on feeble-mindedness imply that high topological rigidity tends to foster resumption of interrupted tasks, whether or not there is a substitute activity (except where the substitute activity develops out of the original task). We studied E effects in relation to resumption of interrupted tasks, using no substitute task in one experiment and a substitute activity (which did not develop out of the original task) in another experiment. We also studied E effects in relation to recall of interrupted, uncompleted tasks as compared with recall of uninterrupted, completed tasks, on the assumption that, if relatively pronounced topological rigidity tends to prevent dissipation of tension associated with an interrupted task, as Lewin notes, then the greater the topological rigidity, the better should be the recall of an interrupted, uncompleted task. Our subjects, normal high-school students in New York City, showed strikingly less resumption of interrupted tasks (whether or not there was a substitute activity) and less differences between the recall of completed and uncompleted tasks than have been reported for German subjects. In the experiment with a substitute activity, the few subjects who returned to the interrupted task did not differ in E effects from the remaining subjects. In the remaining experiments, there was a slight trend for indices associated with topological rigidity to be positively related to behavioral rigidity as gauged by E effects.

High topological rigidity is appealed to by Lewin to account for the rigidity shown by the feeble-minded child in facing momentary goals. To study rigidity in facing momentary goals in normal subjects, it seemed appropriate to utilize the level-of-aspiration technique developed by Lewin and his associates. In level-of-aspiration studies, an individual is requested to make some estimations concerning his future performance in a particular task, with the estimation regarded as representing the goal or level of aspiration and the subsequent performance considered the achievement. However, in our discussion of the level-of-aspiration technique, it was noted that the estimations made by the subject may not coincide with his actual goals or aspirations with regard to his performance; it was also pointed out that a performance (achievement) may be classified as a success or failure by the experimenter, depending upon whether it met or fell below the estimation, whereas it may not be similarly viewed by the subject. We used standard situations employed in level-of-aspiration studies as well as the arithmetical and mirror-maze Einstellung situations to study adherence to estimations. If estimations are regarded as momentary goals, then, to the extent that the studies were measuring rigidity in adhering to momentary goals, and to the extent that such rigidity is an indication of topological rigidity, the findings point to a slight tendency for topological rigidity to be positively related to behavioral rigidity as gauged by E effects.

Proposals were made for future research relating topological rigidity and E effects. It was suggested that the same subjects participate in various Einstellung experiments as well as in various experiments (preferably all the experiments) that have been used to study topological rigidity. These should include subjects who have been described in the literature as characterized by different degrees of topological rigidity; for example, feeble-minded and normal individuals as well as individuals of various ages. In the belief that it would be of value to include situations in which E effects and topological rigidity are functionally related, rather than only postexperimentally related, it was proposed that Einstellung-type situations be modified so as to allow study of both E effects and possible indicants of topological rigidity (as we have done for satiation and level of aspiration and as remains to be done for resumption and recall of interrupted tasks and other such indicants) and, moreover, that experiments used to study topological rigidity be modified so as to involve the possibility of the development of an Einstellung.

We raised the questions: Will it be found that subjects who differ considerably in E effects also show characteristically different patterns of responses in all the topological-rigidity experiments? If there are subjects who show a consistent pattern of responses in the topological-rigidity experiments, will they also be consistent in the Einstellung situations, and will those who consistently show relatively high topological rigidity differ strikingly in E effects from those who consistently show relatively low topological rigidity?

It was also proposed that a variational approach be adopted in the study of topological rigidity and, in particular, that attempts be made to extremize the topological rigidity shown by a given person. It may turn out that topological rigidity or its indicants do not seem to be susceptible to change through experimental variations and that a given individual's indicants of topological rigidity show constancy and consistency. But to discover this experimentally is quite different than to assume, as is implied in some of Lewin's writings, that an individual's topological rigidity is a predetermined characteristic, subject to changes with age, but largely independent of environmental conditions. An

experimental approach to the relationship between topological rigidity
and environmental conditions seems to be in accord with the Galilean
mode of thought that Lewin advocates. Moreover, topological rigidity,
considered as a predetermined characteristic, is a therapeutically futile
concept, whereas the proposed research may suggest ways of modifying
an individual's topological rigidity which in turn may have therapeutic
consequences. Finally, the hope was expressed that the proposed research may yield information to serve as a basis for a more operational
definition of topological rigidity than is presently available.

Individual Differences in Einstellung Effects

We surveyed investigations dealing with individual differences in *E*
effects as well as those dealing with the relation of *E* effects to certain
indices and concepts of rigidity and to certain personality and perceptual
factors.

E Effects in Relation to Age, Intelligence, and Sex

Age. Susceptibility to set (as measured by *E* solutions of the critical
problems given prior to the extinction task) tended to increase with age.
Rigidity, as measured by failure of the extinction task, tended to be less
for younger children than for older children, less for middle-aged adults
than for older adults, and less for young adults in their twenties than
for either children or older adults. The results do not fit formulations
that posit either a monotonically increasing or decreasing relation between age and rigidity but instead hint at a curvilinear relationship.
The findings suggest the need for critical evaluation of those considerations which have led some psychologists (e.g., Goldstein, Werner) to
posit a negative relationship between age and behavioral rigidity as a
central or important dictum of their theories of rigidity. What happens
to the *same* person's rigidity as he ages, remains an uninvestigated
problem.

Intelligence. Small negative correlations between *E* effects and I.Q.
usually were found for normal subjects. Comparison of *E* effects of
normal and feeble-minded boys on a maze Einstellung test showed the
latter to be significantly more rigid, a finding which supports the thesis
(common to the theories of Goldstein, Werner, and Lewin) that behavioral rigidity decreases with intelligence. We suspect that *E* effects
and other indicants of behavioral rigidity may be brought about by
different processes in individuals of sharply diverse intellectual ability.

Sex. Some studies of sex differences in *E* effects have not yielded
any consistent or significant differences, whereas other studies have

shown some tendency for female subjects to manifest more E effects than males. It was conjectured that the greater E effects shown by the females may be related to their possessing, to a greater degree than the males, such traits as dependency and submissiveness—traits, often associated with "feminity" in our culture, which can enhance behavioral rigidity. We noted that it is fallacious to interpret a sex differential as necessarily biologically generated, and suggested that one should investigate whether the differential is culturally generated.

Comparison of E Effects of Psychotics, Neurotics, and Normals

Common to psychoanalysis and many theories of rigidity is the thesis that individuals with psychopathological disturbances are more rigid than normals. Since there has been little experimentation pertinent to this thesis in which the same standard of rigidity was employed for normal and psychiatric patients, it was of interest to compare their relative status on Einstellung tests. Psychiatric subjects were Canadian male veterans of World War II hospitalized in a Montreal hospital at the time of testing; normals were similar to them with respect to sex, age, and I.Q. range and mean. When three Einstellung tests were administered to the psychiatric patients (some of whom were diagnosed as psychotic and the others as neurotic) as well as to normals (who were neither war veterans nor hospitalized), the results on each test substantiated the thesis that psychopathology is characterized by greater than normal rigidity; that is, on each test the psychiatric patients showed more E effects than normals. But results were not so clear-cut in other experiments in which the normals, apparently free from psychopathological disturbances, were also Canadian war veterans and were in the same hospital as the abnormals at the time of testing (in the orthopedic wards). The cited thesis tended to be corroborated in most of the test problems of the maze Einstellung test, but a different trend was found for the arithmetical Einstellung test. Here the psychotics had the largest percentages of direct solutions on each of the first four criticals and the first extinction task, with hospitalized normals next and neurotics last; that is, psychotics apparently manifested less behavioral rigidity than normals. We raised the question whether the hospitalized or nonhospitalized normals constituted a more representative group of normals with which to compare the hospitalized psychiatric patients. The influence that the hospital setting may have had on results was also considered.

In other investigations various picture series were administered to hospitalized normals and psychiatric patients under various conditions: Condition 0, no analysis of results between picture series; Condition 1, analysis of results between series; Condition 2, analysis of results between series plus the challenge not to become blinded in the next series. Condition 0 was used with psychotics, neurotics, and normals; Conditions 1 and 2 only with neurotics and normals. Slightly higher mean shift scores (which may be considered a sign of somewhat greater behavioral rigidity) were made by the psychiatric patients under Conditions 0 and 1 but by the hospitalized normals under Condition 2. Condition 2 seemed to arouse considerable anxiety on the part of the normals so that they seemed as anxious or even more anxious than some of the neurotics. On the whole, for any given condition, differences in the results shown by psychiatric patients and hospitalized normals were small and statistically insignificant. It was particularly interesting that psychotics, who are sometimes characterized as divorced from reality, seemed to be about as alert to the reality of the pictures, that is, as alert to the emerging percepts, as were the normals. Differences in mean shift scores were greater when different conditions of administration were compared for the same group of subjects than when two groups were compared under any one condition. It was noted that, while Condition 2 yielded somewhat more behavioral rigidity than Condition 1 for hospitalized normals, the reverse was true for college students who were tested in a nonhospital setting. This again hinted at the possible influence of the setting in which the testing occurs and the status of the subject with regard to the setting.

Results were inconclusive with regard to the relative E effects of psychotics and neurotics. Where there were differences between the two, it was more often the neurotics who showed greater E effects. It was conjectured that the greater rigidity shown by neurotics may be partly a consequence of the greater anxiety they apparently experienced in most test situations.

As a possibly fruitful approach to the study of various "individual differences" in relation to behavior on an Einstellung test, it was proposed that the investigator (whether he is using such a test for experimental or clinical purposes) should aim to obtain information with regard to the following:

(1) The point of shift to the nonset solution.

(2) The pattern of responses.

(3) The subject's attitudes and assumptions toward a test.

(4) The nature of the process underlying each particular case of E effects.

(5) The influence of certain experimental variations on the subject's behavior.

(6) The kinds of experimental variations in which the particular individual shows his largest (smallest) E effects.

(7) Where more than one Einstellung test is used, the changes in the individual's behavior from test to test.

(8) The individual's reactions when he is informed of his results on the various tests and is shown methods and percepts that he overlooked.

We raised the question whether such a detailed analysis of responses to a battery of Einstellung tests would show characteristically different behavior trends for different groups of subjects (for example, normals compared with psychiatric patients, males compared with females, various chronological-age groups, various mental-age groups). If two groups of individuals, Groups X and Y, do show characteristically different behavior trends, then an additional phase is suggested. This phase would be concerned with ascertaining how conditions should be altered in order to obtain behavior from Group X that was previously characteristic of Group Y, and vice versa; that is, with ascertaining "transformation conditions," the conditions under which the behavior of one group is "transformed" into the characteristic behavior of another group. "Transformation conditions" could also be sought for any two individuals.

E Effects in Relation to Scores on Personality and Attitude Tests

Responses to the Rorschach test have been interpreted by clinicians as reflecting on the rigidity of the respondent. Rigidity has been regarded as denoted by each of four Rorschach indices: a small total number of responses, a high percentage of form responses, few color and movement responses, and a high average time of response. Administration of the Rorschach test and the arithmetical and hidden-word Einstellung tests to normal adults, showed that the more-rigid groups on each of these Einstellung tests also tended to be more rigid as judged by each of these four Rorschach indices. Correlations between E effects and two of these Rorschach indices were computed from data obtained when the Rorschach test and the arithmetical, hidden-word, and word-block Einstellung tests were administered to hospitalized neurotics and psychotics; while correlations between E effects and form responses to the Rorschach cards were small and inconsistent, correlations between E effects and the total number of Rorschach responses were consistently negative, that is, greater E effects went hand in hand with greater rigidity as gauged by the total number of Rorschach responses.

Positive relationships have been found between E effects and degree of insecurity as measured by various scales of insecurity. In discussing how these relationships should be interpreted, we noted that a person may feel more secure in some situations than in others and raised the question whether the level of rigidity varies correspondingly in these situations. It was conjectured that some subjects, perhaps because of their reactions to the testing atmosphere, may have felt insecure both when tested for E effects and when tested for insecurity, so that the positive relationships may have been artifacts of testing conditions rather than resultants of an invariant relationship between insecurity and rigidity. A similar interpretation is in order for the positive correlations which have been found between E effects and scores indicative of maladjustment on the Cornell index of personality adjustment.

The concept of frustration tolerance has been used to account for E effects. A study using college students did not reveal any consistent relationship between E effects and various scores of frustration tolerance on Rosenzweig's picture-frustration test. The findings, which do not mean that the concepts of rigidity and frustration tolerance are unrelated, hint that differences in E effects may not be adequately accounted for by an appeal to differences in frustration tolerance.

Studies of the relationship between E effects and scores on ethnocentrism scales have not yielded consistent results. The relationship has been found to vary with the criteria used to measure E effects and ethnocentrism, with the instructions employed, and with the social atmosphere of the testing session. We discussed various ways of interpreting relationships between E effects and ethnocentrism scores and pointed to the need for the study of prejudices based on behavior and attitudes revealed in the actual social scene.

A small negative relationship was found for adults between E effects and scores on the Thouless scale for the measurement of dogmatism of religious beliefs. The finding may be interpreted to mean that rigid adherence to the E method need not go hand in hand with rigid adherence to certain beliefs as tested by the Thouless scale.

No consistent relationship was found for college students between E effects and scores on Murray's sameness and change scales, a fact that suggests that tendencies toward or preferences for change or sameness as measured by Murray's scales need not be positively related to tendencies toward or preferences for change or sameness as measured by the basic experiment.

Students, mostly business executives, enrolled in a remedial-reading course received four Einstellung tests at the beginning of the course. Rank correlations were computed between shift scores on each Einstellung test and the improvement in reading rate (the increase in reading rate at the end of the course compared with the rate at the beginning). Positive rank correlations, which indicate some tendency for those who improved more in reading rate also to have shifted earlier on an Einstellung test, were found for each of the Einstellung tests that required the subject to read (hidden-word, arithmetical, and word-block tests, with correlations of $+0.69$, $+0.54$, and $+0.33$, respectively), whereas a large negative correlation (-0.97) was found for the maze test which required no reading. Of the fourteen students in the class, seven had solved all the E tasks by the E method on each test. When for each of these subjects the average of his shift scores in the four Einstellung tests was correlated with his increase in reading rate, the resultant rank order was $+0.79$, indicating that those who shifted earlier on the Einstellung tests tended to improve more in reading rate. It was suggested that there is a need to study further the relationship of shift scores on Einstellung tests to improvement in reading rate and also to study the relationship of such shift scores to improvement in other remedial-teaching programs and in various therapeutic and rehabilitation programs.

E Effects in Relation to Perceptual Rigidity

Perception of the embedded figures in the Gottschaldt figures has been used to study flexibility of closure (*Gestaltbindung*, rigidity of perceived unity). It was found that the least-rigid group in the arithmetical Einstellung test saw significantly more embedded figures than the most-rigid group; that is, those who were least (most) rigid in the Einstellung test tended to show the least (most) *Gestaltbindung* in the Gottschaldt-figures test.

Speed of closure was studied by means of gradually decreasing (or increasing) the size of a gap in the circumference of a circle, and noting the size of the gap when the subject began (ceased) to report a circle; this was presumably when "closure" occurred for him (if the reported circle represented a perceived circle). The more-rigid group in the arithmetical Einstellung test reported a circle for significantly larger gaps than did the less-rigid group; if the size of the gap is considered an indicant of the speed of closure, then it may be said that the more-rigid subjects tended to have greater speed of closure. This method of investigating closure may have inadvertently introduced the factor of Einstellung (objective set) through the gradual increase or decrease in the size of the gap. A new experiment, using other subjects, was therefore conducted in which the extent of the gap was randomized and did not consistently increase or decrease. Here the more-rigid group in the arithmetical Einstellung test reported circles more often and for greater gaps, on the average, than did the less-rigid group; that is, again the more-rigid group tended to show greater speed of closure.

Contemporary interest in the utilization of closure for studying personality seems to rest on the assumption that the speed of closure is rather invariant for a given individual. There has been no experimental evidence to support this assumption. Our attempts to study the same subjects' speeds of closure in various perceptual situations, suggested that an individual does not always manifest similar speeds or thresholds of closure. We pointed to the diversity of meanings which have been attached to the term closure, a diversity which invites semantic confusion, and advocated a moratorium on the use of the term.

E effects were also studied in relation to other Gestalt perceptual concepts. The concept of *Prägnanzstufen*, steps or stages of *Prägnanz*, can perhaps be best translated as "regions of figural stability." It has been hypothesized by some psychologists that rigidity is associated with a tendency to focus on *Prägnanzstufen* and to discard certain differences rather than to integrate the differences into a continuum of gradual steps. This hypothesis was not supported by a preliminary study in which no clearly defined relationship was found between E effects on the arithmetical Einstellung test and the tendency to group angles around distinct *Prägnanzstufen* rather than to arrange them so they constituted a continuum.

Wertheimer's paper on the part-whole relationship (1933) describes the successive additions of dots to form a final pattern of dots (a diamond within a diamond). We presented six cards on which appeared the accumulating dots to subjects who also received the arithmetical Einstellung test. The group which manifested more-rigid behavior on the latter test reported the dots on the cards as belonging to one "whole" somewhat more often than did those who showed less-rigid behavior. We suggested that the dot sequence and other examples offered in Wertheimer's 1933 paper might provide fruitful means of exploring individual differences in perception.

The phrase "intolerance of ambiguity," considered both as a perceptual and an emotional personality variable, has been used both as a synonym for, and an explanation of, rigidity. In particular, it has been used to account for E solutions of the arithmetical critical problems. Data obtained from various studies did not support a positive relationship between E effects (either in a critical or in an extinction task) and criteria of intolerance of ambiguity. The findings cast some doubt on the advisability of equating rigidity and intolerance of ambiguity or of using the latter to account for rigidity in general or for E effects in particular. The possibility was raised that intolerance of ambiguity is not necessarily an invariant characteristic of a given individual but that the degree of tolerance or intolerance of ambiguity which he manifests may vary from one situation to another.

A preliminary investigation showed that subjects who persisted longer in the E method in the arithmetical Einstellung test, tended to persist longer in reporting autokinetic movement (apparent movement of a fixed light source) despite the increasing luminosity of the surroundings. This finding might be interpreted to mean that those who were more rigid in the Einstellung situation tended to show greater "perceptual rigidity" in the autokinetic-effect experiment.

Ansekonic lenses, developed by Ames (1949), produce distortions in the appearance of perceptual objects. Rigidity in an arithmetical Einstellung situation (as measured by failure of an extinction task or by the time required to solve such a task) proved to be positively related to "perceptual lag" as measured by the time that elapsed between the subject's donning of ansekonic lenses and his report of a change in the appearance of objects. The ingenious devices developed by Ames were described as potentially useful to psychologists interested in the role of various perceptual factors in behavioral rigidity.

E Effects and Generalized Rigidity

The results of batteries of tests, including Einstellung tests, have been subjected by several investigators to factor analysis or to cluster analysis. In one of our studies, a battery of tests (including Einstellung tests, the Rorschach test, and the Wechsler-Bellevue test) was administered to hospitalized patients, half of whom were diagnosed as psychotic and the others as neurotic. Cluster analysis yielded clusters for the neurotics that were less clear-cut and more difficult to identify than the clusters for the psychotics. This suggests that different populations may differ considerably with reference to the extent and pattern of interrelatedness of various indices of rigidity. A similar finding was reported by Horwitz (1951), who used factor analysis on the data of a population of hospitalized psychiatric adults (psychotics and neurotics) and of another population of hospitalized postoperative normal adults. So striking was the difference in factorial composition that Horwitz concluded that the same tests did not tap the same kind of rigidity for his two populations. Such findings cast doubt on conclusions or generalizations concerning rigidity which are worded as if they held for all populations.

A distinction has been drawn between the interfering effects of culturally induced or well-established behavior patterns, on the one hand, and the interfering effects of experimentally induced behavior patterns, on the other. We noted that the distinction is not clear-cut; that, depending on the meanings attached to such phrases as "well-established habits," "new activity," and "interfering influences," two contrary interpretations may be given to the same response; and that the available evidence does not substantiate the thesis that culturally induced rigidity is factorially distinct from experimentally induced rigidity.

Most of the tests to which Einstellung tests have been correlated were of doubtful validity or reliability and involved rather ambiguous concepts. Nonetheless, finding positive (usually low) correlations, some investigators have invoked one or more of these concepts to account for rigidity in an Einstellung test (or for rigidity in general) or, conversely, have invoked rigidity to account for one or more of these concepts. The underlying assumption seems to be that, if a particular concept is adequate to account for a performance on one test, it is necessarily adequate to account for a performance on a correlated test. We questioned the validity of this assumption since a positive correlation does not imply similarity in behavioral dynamics. It was also suggested that the finding of a statistically significant correlation between two variables should not call a halt to research but should be regarded as a signal light for continued research into the nature of the relationship between variables.

The diversity of findings of factorial studies which included variations of the Einstellung tests, was tentatively attributed to innovations which different investigators have introduced in Einstellung tests; to the questionable validity and reliability of some of the tests included in the battery; to differences in the studied populations; and to differences in the test batteries employed. It was noted that no two factorial studies of rigidity have utilized the same battery of tests. We wondered if some of the energy spent in introducing innovations in existing tests and in devising new tests, would not be better spent in finding out more about the validity and reliability of current tests and in developing standardized tests of rigidity. After this, a grand factor analysis, with several investigators utilizing the same battery, may prove of value.

Existing evidence does not permit any decisive conclusions to be drawn concerning the extent of consistency, generality, or specificity of rigidity. Some of the factors identified as distinct varieties of rigidity may not have distinct counterparts in actual rigidity factors. There seems to be some trend toward consistency but not enough to allow rigidity to be classified as a general factor operating as a functional unity in every individual. There is the possibility that individuals differ in the degree of consistency or functional unity that characterizes the rigidity that they show at different times and under different conditions. Individual differences cannot be garnered from group trends but require study of the individual case. We advocated a variational approach to the individual case in which the individual himself will serve as a base line for comparisons and in which his behavior in a given situation (or test) will be compared with his behavior as conditions in the situation (or test) are modified. Such an approach may yield new knowledge concerning the nature, varieties, and consistency of rigidity.

Learning and Rigidity

It was suggested that what occurs in the Einstellung situation may be understood as a case of learned behavior and that the literature on learning and, in particular, learning theories may furnish clues to E effects and to other instances of rigid behavior. Focused on the selected case were many learning theories, including the views expressed by Thorndike, Watson, Guthrie, Hull, Carr, Robinson, Tolman, Koffka, Wheeler and Perkins, Skinner, Maier, and Hilgard. While the focusing of various learning theories on this one case had certain advantages (for example, in suggesting some experimental variations and in suggesting means of organizing data), it did little to achieve our dual objectives; namely, to increase our understanding of E effects and to reveal differences and similarities among the theories. It was found that a multiplicity of constructs could be appealed to in accounting for E effects, but we did not know in general how to translate the constructs of one theory into those of another theory. The discord of jargons did not allow essential differences between constructs to be distinguished from verbal differences. It was suggested that attempts be made, at least for each of the major learning theories, to delineate the undefined and defined terms and to relate these to corresponding terms of the other theories. If this could be done, or better yet, if a common universe of discourse could be achieved, then the following comparisons would be facilitated:

(1) Comparison of the constructs of various theories in order to reveal semantic and nonsemantic differences and similarities.

(2) Comparison of the concepts of various theories in order to see whether some concepts (or some theories) are appropriate to certain aspects of the learning situation but not to others.

(3) Comparison of the axiomatic foundations of various theories as well as comparison of theorems derived from the axioms.

Theories which differ considerably with respect to theorems may be found to differ with respect to only a few axioms or only one axiom. (An example is found in mathematics wherein three plane geometries, one Euclidean and two non-Euclidean, that differ considerably in many theorems, differ with respect to only one axiom, the axiom concerning parallel lines.) Research may then focus on obtaining experimental evidence pertinent to the particular axioms that differ for two or more theories or pertinent to theorems that depend on these particular axioms. Research may yield evidence that conclusively favors one axiom over another (or one theorem over another). Or research may indicate that the different axioms (or theorems) are experimentally equivalent in the sense that a crucial decision cannot be made, given existing methods and instruments of measurement. In short, semantic clarification may cause research to be centered on crucial decisions (or on demonstrating why such decisions cannot be made) rather than allowing it to be dissipated on controversies which are perhaps superficial or only semantic in nature.

Research may even reveal that different theories of learning (or different theories of rigidity or, specifically, different theories of E effects) are experimentally equivalent. (For example, the three plane geometries have all proved to be experimentally equivalent with reference to applicability to measurements on our planet.) It was noted that, if theories of learning (or of rigidity) prove to be experimentally equivalent, this may prove disturbing to psychologists who expect to find one answer to the problem "what is learning?" (or "what is rigidity?"). That so many theories of learning (and of rigidity) have been proposed to date does not necessarily mean that either of these problems is unsolvable. It is conceivable that either of these problems has more than one solution (just as there are mathematical problems with nonunique solutions). Different theories may possibly (but not necessarily) constitute different answers to the problems. Involved here are the methodological issues of the nature of a solution and the nature of a problem and, in particular, the issue whether a problem is unsolvable, unsolved but not unsolvable, solvable and having only one solution, or solvable and having more than one solution.

THE INFLUENCE OF RECENCY AND FREQUENCY

The Role of Recency

A principle of recency is assumed in many learning theories, and in some theories, such as Guthrie's, it is given a central position. E effects might be explained, in terms of this principle, as a tendency to repeat the most recent act performed in a similar situation. But recency cannot account for the behavior of those subjects who did not show E effects in the basic experiment. Nor can it explain the finding that, when E tasks were alternated with problems solvable by more direct methods, 90 per cent or more of the subjects solved test tasks by direct methods rather than by the E method despite the fact that the latter was the most recent method utilized just before the test tasks. Experiments in which an attempt was made, by the use of instructions or time intervals, to demarcate E tasks from test tasks suggested that whether or not E effects were produced did not depend on how recently the E method had been used before the test tasks were presented, but on the subject's attitudes towards the tasks; E effects did not tend to be shown by those who regarded the test tasks as distinct from the E tasks, whereas they did tend to be shown by those who considered the test tasks as similar to the E tasks.

The Role of Frequency of Repetition

The term "repetition" has been used to refer to repetition of the stimulus without repetition of the response, to repetition of the response without repetition of the stimulus, and to repetition of both stimulus and response. Moreover, diverse views have been expressed concerning the role played by repetition of response in learning, including the views that repetition of response is both a necessary and sufficient condition for learning (Thorndike, Watson), that it is neither necessary nor sufficient (Wheeler), that it is necessary but not sufficient (Hovland), and that it is sufficient but not necessary (Guthrie). While some investigators use the term repetition only when the *same* response (and/or stimulus) is repeated, others apply it to the occurrence of *similar* responses (and/or stimuli). We questioned whether any two responses (or two stimuli) are ever precisely the "same," and we noted that, while two stimuli (or two responses) may be regarded as the same or similar by the investigator, they may not be so regarded by the subject, or vice versa. This raised the problem of the kind and degree of similarity that must prevail in order that two responses (or two stimuli) may be considered as the "same" or "similar" for experimental purposes and the further problem from whose point of view the "sameness" or "similarity" should be adjudged.

In the discussion of frequency, it was noted that there are two different meanings of the law of exercise. The first interprets frequency to mean frequency of presentation of a stimulus pattern, while the second interprets it to mean frequency of a particular response. According to the first meaning, all subjects who received five E problems (whether or not they correctly solved them) had the same frequency of exercise; according to the second meaning, a subject who received five E problems and solved all of them by the E method had more frequency of exercise than a subject who failed to use the E method in some of these problems. Supporting the second meaning at the expense of the first is the finding that subjects in the basic experiment who solved all five E problems had considerably more E effects than those who failed some of these problems.

The relation between E effects and frequency was also studied by presenting various groups with different numbers of E tasks. The results did not reveal any simple relationship between E effects and the number of set-inducing problems received or solved. The extent of E effects was not independent of the frequency of E responses in the set-inducing problems, apparently contrary to expectations derived from certain learning theories (Guthrie, Wheeler). But neither did the extent of E effects increase with each repetition, apparently contrary to expectations derived from learning theories that invoke principles of exercise (Thorndike), frequency (Watson), incremental gain in habit strength (Hull), or increase in extent of trace systems (Koffka). Knowledge of the number of E problems received by an individual and of the number of E responses made by him was not sufficient to allow accurate prediction of his behavior in the test problems. Individual differences, including attitudinal factors, and social-field conditions seemed to be determinants of whether an individual developed a strong set with a few E tasks or resisted the development of a set even after many E tasks. It was found, for example, that two E tasks yielded E effects as large as did the usual five when a modified experiment was administered under speed conditions or when the subjects were told to generalize a rule. None of the principles that learning theorists have promulgated about frequency, repetition, or reinforcement, could by itself explain the obtained results, perhaps because none of the principles takes into sufficient account the influence of individual differences, including attitudinal factors, and of social-field conditions.

Experiments in which many E tasks were given (until the subject became satiated and refused to do any more, after which test tasks were given) indicated that the relationship between frequency and E effects depended on whether E effects were measured in terms of E solutions of criticals or in terms of failure of the extinction problem. More generally, the results suggested that the relationship between frequency and habit strength was dependent on how the strength of the habit was measured.

When arithmetical test problems were preceded by practice problems of various kinds, some of which permitted more than one kind of solution, the results showed that the relationship between frequency and *E* effects was influenced by the nature of the practice problems and, in particular, by whether they permitted only one solution or more than one solution. The relationship was also found to be influenced by the particular choice of solution the subject made; for example, subjects who repeatedly used the simplest available method in the practice problems showed less *E* effects than those who repeatedly used a less simple method in these same practice problems.

In short, the results suggested that the relationship between frequency and *E* effects may depend on (1) the attitudes toward the *E* method and the repetition, (2) the social atmosphere or the broad context in which the repetitions occur, (3) the nature of the practice problems and the particular choice of solution in these problems where a choice is possible, and (4) the particular process that brings about a given case of *E* effects.

Association as a Force for Spontaneous Reproduction

Discussions of spontaneous reproduction in conceptual behavior have been confounded by the failure of some of the participants to realize that the traditional doctrine of spontaneous reproduction actually involves two premises: (1) if an association has been formed between two items, X and Y, then, when one of these items occurs, the whole bond between X and Y will be aroused; and (2) if one of the items occurs and if the bond between X and Y is aroused, then there will be a tendency for the other item to be reproduced or reinstated. The first premise was demonstrated as untenable on both logical and experimental grounds. The second premise was not confirmed by experimental data pertaining to *E* effects. Indeed, three out of four comparisons showed that subjects who had learned associations involving elements of the *E* solutions to the critical problems actually gave proportionately fewer *E* responses in the criticals than did subjects who had learned associations involving elements of the direct solutions to these problems—quite contrary to expectations derived from the doctrine of spontaneous reproduction. In short, contrary to classical association theory, the findings indicate that spontaneous reproduction need not occur; whether it may occur is an open issue.

Transfer of Training

In our experimental attempts to evaluate the doctrine of transfer of training based on identical elements, we were confronted by the questions: What is an element? What are identical elements? And, who will judge whether elements are identical? Comments by subjects indicated that what may be regarded as identical elements (or as different elements) by the experimenter may not be so regarded by every subject. The experimental evidence speaks against an explanation of E effects in terms of the identical-element theory of transfer since the amount of transfer from the E tasks to the test tasks did not prove to be proportional to the number of identical elements shared by the two sets of tasks (with identity judged by the experimenter). The findings also implied that the nature of the task and the particular context in which elements occur may influence explicit recognition of similarity or identity of elements and may also influence the degree of transfer from one situation to another. The possibility remains that, if E effects are to occur, then there must be a certain kind or amount of "identity" between the E tasks and test tasks; but this "identity" cannot be measured in terms of the number of identical elements.

Transfer of principles or generalizations seemed adequate to account for some but not *all* cases of E effects.

Wylie's long-accepted generalization that the transfer effect is positive when an old response can be transferred to a new stimulus, but negative when a new response is required for an old stimulus, was not upheld by the results; the terms "new stimulus," "old stimulus," "new response," etc., were found to be in need of clarification.

Studies in which an Einstellung test was twice presented to the same subjects or in which a battery of Einstellung tests was administered showed that our subjects generally did not "learn how to learn" (in the sense of learning to avoid the development of an Einstellung), perhaps because the Einstellung did not allow them to develop insight into the nature of the problems. When opportunities to develop such insight were enhanced, more "learning to learn" occurred. Challenges not to become blinded were reacted to very differently when a battery of Einstellung tests was administered in a hospital to patients (both neurotics and those apparently free from psychopathology) than when the battery was administered in a nonhospital setting to college students, a fact illustrating that the instructions that work for positive transfer in one setting may work for negative transfer in another setting, with the difference depending on how the instructions are interpreted by the subjects.

Just prior to presentation of the basic experiment, subjects were given volume-measuring problems each of which was solvable by various methods in attempts to develop an attitude of variability or flexibility in dealing with such problems. Results suggested that in most cases the desired attitude either did not develop or did not transfer sufficiently to the basic experiment. The warning "Don't be blind" issued before the basic experiment apparently did not transfer at all in some cases, had "negative" transfer effects (that is, apparently enhanced E effects) for some elementary-school groups, and had "positive" transfer effects (that is, apparently decreased E effects) for the older groups; the important factor seemed to be the interpretation given to the warning. When prior warnings against the development of an Einstellung were very specific in nature, so that they were not likely to be misinterpreted, they generally made for less E effects than were usually obtained in the basic experiment. However, it was found that the effectiveness of such specific warnings, as well as of attempts at giving subjects an understanding of the ambiguous nature of the test problems, was weakened by giving more E tasks or by introducing a speed factor into the experiment.

When Criticals 1 and 2 and the usual extinction task were given just before the basic experiment, every one of 184 subjects offered direct solutions to each of these three problems. Yet many of these subjects showed E effects in these same problems when minutes later they were presented as part of the basic experiment; almost three-quarters of the subjects gave E solutions to Criticals 1 and 2 and over half of the subjects failed the same extinction task they had previously solved. Clearly for these subjects the direct solution did not transfer. The results suggest that transfer of a response does not depend solely on the stimulus or on the recency of the response to the stimulus but depends also on the context in which the stimulus appears. A problem, when viewed as part of a unitary series, may elicit quite a different response than that elicited when it is faced individually.

Prior to presentation of the basic experiment, a demonstration session followed immediately by a problem-creating session was conducted for students in two junior high schools. During the demonstration period, the experimenter demonstrated how to construct a volume-measuring problem with three jars which was solvable by the $B - A - 2C$ procedure; he also showed how to construct a critical problem, with some groups being shown how to construct one solvable by both $A + C$ and $B - A - 2C$ and other groups being shown how to construct one solvable by both $A - C$ and $B - A - 2C$. During the problem-creating period, subjects were asked to construct and to solve four water-jug problems; the particular instructions varied for different groups. Results in the basic experiment, which immediately followed the problem-creating period, seemed to be influenced more by the nature of the experiences in the problem-creating periods (during which the subject was an active participant) than by the nature of the experiences in the demonstration period (during which the subject tended to be a passive spectator). In each of the two schools, the least E effects in every test problem of the basic experiment were shown by the group that had had the most freedom of decision during the problem-creating period with reference to the kind of problems to be created. This group used the $A + C$ method more frequently in the basic experiment than did the groups that had been told to construct problems solvable by this method. Moreover, this group used the $A - C$ method more frequently in the test problems to which it applied, despite the fact that this method had not been demonstrated to it, than did groups to whom this method had been demonstrated. These results show that frequency of experience with a particular direct method, during the demonstration or problem-creating period, was not as significant a determinant of the results as was freedom of decision during the problem-creating period. That in most groups E effects were within the range found in the basic experiment indicates that demonstration of a direct method and demonstration of the structure of problems with two solutions, even when coupled with opportunities to construct and solve problems with nonunique solutions that are solvable by the demonstrated direct method, do not guarantee that this direct method will be used in subsequent criticals.

In one of the schools, immediately after presentation of the basic experiment there were presented two criticals, solvable by the filling of one jar in addition to the $B - A - 2C$ and $A - C$ methods, a new extinction task solvable by none of the methods used to date, and a new E task. The group that had the most freedom of decision in creating problems showed as many or more one-jar solutions of the criticals than the other groups, far less failure of the new extinction task (only 10 per cent failure as compared with about 90 per cent or more for each of the other groups), and relatively little failure of the new E task (only 10 per cent of this group failed the new E task as compared with 81 per cent of a group that, during the problem-creating period, had created and solved four problems each solvable only by the E method).

The results suggest that, if subsequent E effects are to be avoided, one should not be limited to a particular kind of problem (whether it be solvable by one method or more than one method) in a problem-creating period; that is, repetition ought to be avoided in a creative activity. The results further suggest that problem-creating experiences that allow freedom of decision may be a means of combating rigidity in problem solving.

The Working of Extinction

The findings concerning the extinction task were brought to bear on the issue whether habits are extinguished by disuse or, on the other hand, by the learning of a new incompatible habit. Failure of one or more extinction tasks usually did not suffice to bring about direct solutions of subsequent criticals; that is, disuse of the E method in the extinction task (or tasks) usually did not extinguish the habit. On the other hand, solution of one extinction task usually did suffice to bring about direct solutions of subsequent criticals. But this latter finding cannot be explained solely on the ground that a new habit was learned which was incompatible with the old one, since subjects who solved an extinction task by the $A - C$ method were usually able to solve the subsequent critical by the $A + C$ method and were also able to use the E method again when a problem was given for which it was the only solution. What happened, to judge by comments and results in experimental variations, was that the experience of solving an extinction task revealed to many subjects the dangers of mechanical repetition and led them to examine subsequent problems carefully. Thus, we see that the nature of the so-called nonreinforcing experience, and the subject's reactions to it, are factors which should be included in accounts of learning, problem solving, and resistance to extinction.

Such terms as "reinforcement," "nonreinforcement," "compatible response," and "incompatible response," proved to lack clarity of meaning in the context of the basic experiment. For example, some subjects apparently believed that they had solved the extinction task by the E method; others did not attribute their failure to solve the extinction task to inapplicability of the E procedure but instead attributed the failure to insufficient time, to a mistake in calculations, to an error on the experimenter's part, or to the unsolvability of the problem, etc. Should such experiences be considered reinforcements or nonreinforcements of the E method? Whether the method of solving the extinction task should be considered as compatible or noncompatible with the previously reinforced method, would seem to depend on the frame of reference from which the problems are viewed; for example, viewing the tasks as solvable by a subtractive process involves a supposition which is not weakened by or incompatible with the experience of solving the extinction task. It would seem that each of the constructs of reinforcement, nonreinforcement, compatible response, and incompatible response, is not a single variable but may itself be a function of variables (e.g., a function of the subject's attitudes toward and interpretations of the problems and his attempts at solution). Hence, if extinction is considered to be a function of nonreinforcement and/or the learning of an incompatible response, it may be more appropriate to regard extinction as a function of functions, or functional, than as a function of a finite number of independent variables.

When extinction tasks were alternated with E tasks, E effects were less than when the same number of extinction tasks given in succession followed the same number of E tasks given successively. This raises the problem of the roles played by intermittent reinforcement and by other factors in resistance to extinction.

The Factor of Time

One of the reasons for the choice of the term "Einstellung" was that we thought, when we first started working with the selected case, that the set which was developed was temporary, almost momentary, in nature. For some subjects in the basic experiment, the set seemed to have been of a highly temporary nature (for example, they started to use the E method in Critical 1 but then shifted to a direct method in this problem), but for others the set was less temporary (for example, they did not recover from the set in any test problem). This led to the question: How long can the set last?

This question was investigated by presenting test problems at various time intervals after the basic experiment (or only the E problems) had been presented. While E effects for a group generally decreased after a time interval, the decrease was not proportional to the amount of time that had elapsed; for example, the decrease was less for one group after an hour interval than it was for another group after a half-hour interval. Moreover, in each of the time-interval experiments, some subjects who had shown complete E effects initially still showed E effects after the time interval, even when the interval was one of several weeks. Apparently contributing to these persistent E effects was the attitude that the problems given after a time interval constituted a continuation of the initial experiment. In attempts to weaken this attitude, changes in the conditions of administration were introduced in the time-interval experiments. Some groups were told, after the last E problem had been given, that the experiment was concluded, and, just before the test problems were presented after a time interval, they were told that a new experiment was about to begin. Still other groups, in addition to receiving these remarks, were given the test problems in a new order so that the extinction task was the first problem presented in the second session. The change in the order of the test problems was to prevent the subjects from regarding the second series of problems as similar to the first series; that is, the E method would not work in the first test problem given (the extinction task). Decreases in E effects under these changes in the conditions of administration were greater than when only a time interval was used, and the E effects obtained were much lower than in the basic experiment. The additional changes in the conditions of administration, however, did not work in an accumulative fashion; thus, a group that had a half-hour time interval, the remarks, and the rearrangement of the test problems, did not show less E effects than another group that had only the half-hour interval and the remarks. Moreover, in every group there were subjects who showed some E effects, apparently because they viewed the E and test problems as belonging to one series, despite the attempts made to get them to differentiate between the two series of problems.

Some of the subjects who showed E effects after a time interval said that they remembered and applied the method they had used in the initial session. The question, therefore, was raised whether those who did not use the E method after a time interval had perhaps forgotten this method. This in turn led to the problem of how forgetting of the E method should be defined and measured. For example, should a subject be considered to have forgotten the E method if he did not apply it to any test problem after a time interval or should he be considered to have forgotten it if he failed an E problem after a time interval?

The term "massed practice" refers to a learning situation in which tasks of one kind are given without a break, whereas the terms "distributed practice" and "spaced practice" refer to a learning situation in which tasks of one kind are always separated by a time interval (usually of more than a few seconds and devoted to a rest period or to another kind of task). Some of the experiments (for example, the basic experiment and the speed-test experiment) were discussed in relation to the use of massed or distributed practice and other experiments were described that were more directly concerned with the influence on E effects of the particular distribution of trials. Results of these experiments were also discussed with reference to what is regarded by some psychologists as one of the best-established generalizations in the field of learning, namely, the thesis that spaced or distributed practice makes for faster, more economical, more efficient learning. Whether results obtained in Einstellung experiments are interpreted as compatible or incompatible with this thesis (even under the questionable assumption that differences in results are due solely to differences in the nature of the practice) depends on what learning one is concerned with and how one defines such terms as "faster learning," "more efficient learning," "more economical learning," and "superior learning." In particular, the interpretation depends on whether one is interested in the learning of a mental set, or in the learning of the practiced method, or in the learning of more efficient solutions. Thus, if the learning under consideration is that of a mental set (with a stronger set representing "superior" learning), then the finding that massed practice generally yielded more E effects than distributed practice might be interpreted as inconsistent with the thesis concerning the superiority of distributed practice. But, if the learning under consideration is that of the E method, then the results are inconclusive since it was not shown that the E method was learned better under one rather than another condition of practice. Moreover, if the learning under consideration is that of more efficient solutions of problems, and if the direct method is considered more efficient than the E method, then the finding that massed practice yielded more E effects and hence less direct solutions than distributed practice may be interpreted as consistent with the generalization. Whether results are interpreted as compatible or incompatible with the thesis that distributed practice makes for superior learning depends also on the particular criterion of efficiency or superiority of learning; for example, the results of a mirror-maze experiment done with children pointed to different conclusions concerning the relative superiority of distributed and massed practice, depending on whether the criterion was use of a direct method in the criticals or its use in the extinction tasks. Results of this experiment suggested that distributed practice may be more efficient than massed practice in the early stages of acquiring or learning a skill but perhaps less efficient in later stages where, for example, one practices at becoming more proficient in executing the skill. For future research, we raised the problem whether influences of various practice conditions on solutions of certain kinds of tasks (for example, mirror mazes) also hold for solutions of other kinds of tasks (for example, volume-measuring problems) as well as the problem what practice conditions yield the most retention of the E method or the most frequent or most rapid application of this method.

The finding that E effects were greater under massed practice has been interpreted by Kendler and his associates as inconsistent with the thesis concerning the superiority of distributed practice. Noting that, in conditioning situations, distributed practice has proved superior to massed practice for the acquisition of a new response tendency but inferior to it for the extinction of a response tendency, they conjectured that the learning of a mental set corresponds, not to the acquisition phase, but to the extinction phase of conditioning—the extinction hypothesis of mental set. (Interestingly enough, other investigators studying Einstellung situations have concluded that the learning of a mental set corresponds to the acquisition phase of conditioning.) We examined the extinction hypothesis of mental set and found it incompatible with what is known about the Einstellung phenomenon.

Surveying the literature, Ericksen concluded that distributed practice tends to produce a fixation of response whereas massed practice makes for greater variability of behavior. Yet the reverse trend is suggested by most studies involving E effects.

We pointed out that research on massed and distributed practice has tended to neglect the possible influence of nonspacing factors; in particular, inadequate attention has been paid to subjects' attitudes toward the spacing and the influence of the particular intervening tasks employed in distributed practice.

Complexity of Methods

Different theories of learning suggest diverse hypotheses with regard to the influence on E effects of the relative degree of complexity of the set method and of the nonset method. Several experiments, in each of which the same test problems were used, yielded data suggesting that more blinding effects are exerted by repetitions of a complex method than by repetitions of a simpler method in the set-inducing problems. But other experiments revealed complicating factors, such as a subject's cognitive ability to discover the nonset method without assistance, even if he had not had the preceding set-inducing experiences. It was tentatively hypothesized that, if this ability is not at stake, then repetitions of a simple procedure tend to exert less blinding effects than repetitions of a more complex procedure.

Reversal of the roles of the set and nonset methods yielded striking differences in E effects. Since the reversal left unaltered the "identical elements" shared by the set method and the nonset method, the finding is particularly interesting in view of the stress placed on identical elements in some accounts of transfer of training.

Several experiments in each of which the same set-inducing problems were used, yielded very different E effects, depending on the kind of test problems given, the nature of the nonset method, and the criterion of effect of set. If habit strength is considered to depend on the number of repetitions or reinforcements, then presumably, after the last set-inducing task, a habit of a certain strength has developed. The concept of habit strength has been used as if it were a characteristic of the habit and also as if it were synonymous with, or at least concomitant with, the influence of the habit. Our findings suggest that it may be misleading to equate the observed influence of set with habit strength, considered as a characteristic of the habit, as is often done in studies of learning, since we found that the observed influence of the habit varied with the kind of test problems used, the nature of the nonset method, and the criterion of effect of set. The findings suggest that habit strength should not be treated as a characteristic of the habit but should be defined operationally in terms of its observed influence relative to certain test situations.

Comparison of Sets for a Method with Sets for a Goal

Set-inducing problems were devised in which both the method and the goal (the stipulated volume) remained invariant. When test problems were then given which were incomplete criticals, most subjects completed them by making the volume to be obtained the same as in the set-inducing problems. Moreover, they applied to them the oft-repeated method. In other words, they completed the incomplete criticals by adhering to both the practiced method and the practiced goal. E effects were very high. Lower E effects were shown in these same test problems by subjects who had received set-inducing problems in which only the method or only the goal was invariant. In short, it was found that, when a set for a method was compatible with a set for a goal, the observed combined influence of these two sets was greater than the influence of either one of the sets.

An incomplete extinction task, given as a last problem, could be completed in accordance with the practiced method or the practiced goal but not both. This problem, in which a set for a method was not compatible with a set for a goal, could presumably serve to test the relative strength of a method set and a goal set. The findings suggest that the relative strength of these two sets could not be adequately gauged by the number of repetitions, since subjects who had the same number of repetitions of the method as of the goal in the set-inducing problems, tended to abandon the method but adhered to the goal when the two were incompatible. Most subjects claimed that they first tried a method and only then thought of a goal. Scratchwork verifies that the oft-repeated method was often tried and then abandoned, presumably because it did not lead to the fixed goal. Such findings led us to raise this question: Should the fact that the fixed method was tried first be considered evidence of the greater influence of the method set, or should the subsequent abandonment of the method in favor of the goal set be taken as evidence of the greater influence of the goal set? This illustrates some of the difficulties involved in comparing the relative influence of two sets. It was also found that whether the goal set was to be considered as having exerted a stronger influence than the method set depended on the particular problem in which the effect was observed (incomplete criticals or incomplete extinction task) as well as on the particular kind of comparison made for a problem (intergroup or intragroup comparisons). Thus, we see that the relative influence of two sets may vary for different problems and for different kinds of comparisons, so that caution is needed in drawing inferences

about the relative strength of two or more sets (or habits) from observations of their apparent influence. Analysis of the relationship
between two habits indicated the need for study of their influence in
test situations in which both or only one or the other works.

A distinction was drawn between the means and the goal as viewed
by the experimenter, and the means and the goal as viewed by a particular subject. It was suggested that procedures are needed to help
the experimenter discover the subject's actual goal (or *Aufgabe*) and
the role it plays in the learning situation, and that, in using such terms
as method set and goal set, one ought to specify whether the terms are
to be understood in line with the experimenter's or the subject's conception of what constitutes the method and the goal.

The Role of Effort

Experimentation on the role of effort has largely been confined to
subhuman species. Yet many psychologists regard behavior, both human and subhuman, as governed by a tendency to select that course of
action which involves the least expenditure of effort on the part of
the organism. This has been described as the law of least effort, of
least action, of parsimony of effort, of minimal effort, etc. The tendency to use the E method rather than the apparently less-effortful
direct methods might seem offhand to contradict a principle of least
effort. But such a tendency can be reconciled with a least-effort principle on the ground that it is more effortful for some subjects to shift
to another method than to continue using the E method once they have
become proficient in its use.

Experiments were undertaken in which the differential in effort between the E method and the direct method was heightened so that a
shift to the direct method would clearly result in a saving in effort.
Tracing of mazes, with the mirror image serving as a guide, succeeded
in heightening the differential, since tracing of the circuitous E route
was lengthy and difficult while tracing of the straight, direct route was
rapid and easy. If subjects' behavior were governed by a principle of
least effort, then a shift to the direct method in the test problems would
be expected, particularly under mirror-tracing conditions. Yet adherence to the E method in the test problems was even greater in the
case of mirror tracing than in the case of normal (nonmirror) tracing.
These findings speak against an unqualified principle of least effort
and suggest that, if a tendency toward least effort is operative, it may
be modified by factors and processes that produce E effects. The re-
presentation of the mazes (under mirror-tracing conditions for those
who had previously received them for normal tracing, and vice versa),

showed similar findings for mirror and normal tracing, despite the difference in effort, and suggested that, if a tendency toward least effort is operative, it can be modified by factors not taken into account in the usual formulations of the principle of least effort, e.g., an expectation for a particular method.

The mirror-maze experiment not only heightened the differential in effort between the E method and direct method but apparently also heightened the differential in emotional stress, since mirror tracing of the E route seemed to be accompanied by greater emotional stress and frustration. Attempts to unravel the factors of effort and emotional stress led to a new experiment in which weights were affixed to the stylus used in tracing the mazes (nonmirror tracing). This experiment apparently succeeded in heightening the effort differential without introducing changes in emotional stress. If a principle of least effort were operative, subjects would be expected to show more shift to the direct route when carrying heavier weights, but the results did not substantiate this expectation.

The results of our experiments on effort were discussed in relation to Hull's law of less work, which states that the organism gradually learns to choose, in a two-choice situation, that behavior sequence which involves less energy or less work. Hull does not posit an innate tendency for less effort but deduces the law of less work from his postulates on reactive inhibition. From these postulates and related notions, there have also been deduced the theses that (1) the greater the work involved in a response, the faster the extinction of the response and (2) the greater the work involved in a response, the greater the variability or alternation of behavior in a two-choice situation. Our findings do not support either Hull's law of less work or the latter two deductions. The findings suggest a need for re-evaluation of those portions of Hull's theory pertaining to reactive inhibition and less work.

We pointed to a need for eliminating some of the methodological defects that have characterized all studies on effort, including our own, and for further experimentation, particularly with human beings, on the role of effort.

What Is Learned in the Einstellung Situation

Those who found direct solutions to the test problems clearly seem to have learned something different from that learned by those who did not. But even all who showed E effects did not seem to have "learned" the same thing. Some learned the E method itself, some learned to use all three jars, some learned to begin with the largest jar or with the center jar (which happened also to be the largest jar), etc. Various assumptions also seem to have been learned. Thus, some subjects assumed that they had to use the E method because it had been demonstrated by the experimenter; some assumed that the experimenter was a trustworthy person who would not fool them by showing one method and expecting another; some assumed that the problems were of one type or that one method was supposed to be used throughout. Such assumptions seemed to be aroused or strengthened by administration of the basic experiment in schools. The school setting apparently led subjects to view the experiment as a school activity and to view the experimenter as a teacher or other prestigeful figure, which in turn led to assumptions that contributed to E effects. Experimental variations described below were conducted in order to see whether any one thing that was learned in the Einstellung situation could serve as *the* explanation of E effects. Specifically, experimentation was undertaken to ascertain whether certain assumptions that were learned and factors that fostered these assumptions were essential to E effects.

(1) Variations in which the experimenter-subject relationship and the setting of the experiment were varied (for example, by giving the experiment as a game at a social gathering, by having a twelve-year-old child administer it to a college class, or by having a known member of one political party administer it to members of an opposing political organization) show that considerable E effects may occur even when the subjects are not likely to assume that the experimenter is a teacher or the experiment a school activity. Since it was not as likely in these variations as it was in most administrations of the basic experiment that the subjects had confidence and trust in the experimenter, or that the experimenter was regarded as a prestigeful figure, the results suggest that, while such factors as trust, prestige, and "prestige suggestion" may have enhanced E effects in the usual administration of the basic experiment, they cannot account for every case of E effects.

(2) In an experimental variation in which no method was illustrated, considerable E effects resulted. This suggests that the experimenter's illustration of the E method in the first E task cannot explain all cases of E effects.

(3) In a variation in which no method was demonstrated and the problems apparently came from diverse sources (that is, the various problems apparently came from different individuals), considerable E effects were obtained. This suggests that, while some E effects in the basic experiment may have resulted because subjects assumed that similar-appearing problems, all coming from the same individual, must be solvable by the same method or must be solvable by the method

demonstrated by the experimenter, the operation of such assumptions does not suffice to account for all cases of E effects.

(4) In a variation in which subjects were explicitly told that the E problems and the test problems were not of one type, that two distinct series were involved, and even that one method should not be used throughout the problems, some subjects (the majority in elementary-school classes, the minority in college classes) nonetheless reported that they viewed the problems as being of one type. These subjects showed considerable E effects, but we do not know whether this was caused by or was itself the cause of their regarding the problems as being of one type. Among those who reported that they regarded the E problems as distinct from the test problems, E effects were lower but still existed. The results suggest that the assumption that the problems belong to one class probably enhances but is not essential to E effects.

(5) In another variation, in an attempt to control the tendency to begin with the center jar, we rearranged the order of the jars in all or some of the problems. Large E effects resulted (even when the two jars required for the direct solution were adjacent). This suggests that, while the assumption that it is necessary to start with the center jar may account for some cases of E effects, it clearly is not essential to E effects.

(6) When college subjects, in another variation, were instructed with each problem that they did not have to use the largest jar, E effects were below the level found in the basic experiment (but this instruction was not effective for an elementary-school group). When this instruction was given only with each test problem, both college and elementary-school groups showed lower E effects than in the basic study. That E effects decreased more when the tendency to begin with the largest jar was obviated than when the tendency to begin with the center jar was obviated, suggests that the former tendency may be a more influential or more prevalent determinant of E effects than the latter tendency, despite the fact that the largest jar and the center jar are one and the same in the basic experiment.

(7) Variations were conducted in which subjects were reminded, with each problem or with each test problem, that they might use one, two, or three jars. In another variation, problems were used in which three jars were required both by the set method and by the somewhat simpler nonset method. That considerable E effects were found in all these variations implies that the assumption that all the jars must be used cannot account for every case where nonset methods fail to be used in test problems.

(8) The assumption that one must use all three jars or must begin with the center jar may be weakened by adding additional jars to each problem. Preliminary experimentation showed that E effects within the range found in the basic study were obtained when a fourth (superfluous) jar was added as the first or the last jar in each problem. Variations were therefore conducted in which the position of the added jar was varied from problem to problem. Variations were also conducted in which the number of added jars in a problem was varied from one to five, so that some problems contained as many as eight jars while others contained only four jars. In one experiment, the three usual jars were adjacent to one another with the additional jars placed before or after them, while in another experiment the additional jars were interspersed among the three usual jars. All these variations yielded significantly more failures of the E tasks but also significantly less E effects than the basic experiment. In particular, lower E effects were shown by those who solved all five E tasks of these variations in the E manner (sometimes only after several presentations of the E tasks) than by those who solved all five E tasks of the basic experiment in the E manner. That there were more failures of the E tasks that involved added superfluous jars than of the usual E tasks is understandable since the additional jars increased the complexity of the problems. Moreover, while in natural problem-solving situations the selection of facts and hypotheses from the many available ones is an important decision-making aspect of the problem-solving process, it appeared quite unnatural and unusual to many of our subjects, perhaps because they were accustomed to receiving problems in school in which every hypothesis or "given" is supposed to be used.

It was suggested that problems involving additional (or insufficient) hypotheses, which are not patterned as to number or kind, should be used in all school subjects and should be freely intermingled with other, more routine problems. Our results suggest that inclusion of such problems may make learning slower and somewhat less efficient than drill procedures, but it may also make for less mechanized behavior and more productive problem solving.

Results of these experimental variations, as well as observations made during the basic experiment, suggest that the problem, "What is learned in the Einstellung situation?" is a problem with multiple solutions.

Chapter XXI

SURVEY OF FINDINGS AND CONCLUSIONS CONCERNING EINSTELLUNG EFFECTS

THE variations of the basic Einstellung experiment presented in the earlier chapters have been organized around certain theories, concepts, and issues relating to rigidity and to learning. But most of the variations did not stem from, and were not conducted primarily in the interest of, theories, concepts, and issues. Rather, most of the variations were suggested by observational analysis of what occurred in the basic experiment and in certain variations of it. Our primary interest in conducting the variations was to add to knowledge and understanding of the Einstellung phenomenon. It is therefore timely to survey the findings of the experimental variations in order to see what conclusions may be drawn about this phenomenon. Since the experimentation was partially systematized by attempts to maximize or minimize E effects or, at least, to increase and decrease E effects beyond the upper and lower bounds found in the basic study, we shall organize some of the findings in terms of the variations that yielded (or came close to yielding) extremes in E effects.

Some Conclusions Concerning E Effects

Diverse Processes May Underlie E Effects

Qualitative as well as quantitative findings suggest that different processes gave rise to overtly similar E effects. Of those subjects who showed E effects, some were aware that they were repeating one method while others were unaware that they were doing so; some generalized a formula or rule of solution whereas others failed to draw a generalization; some became set for the $B - A - 2C$ formula while others became set to subtract or to use all three jars or to begin with the largest jar or to begin with the center jar; some were uncertain of themselves and of their ability to do the problems and grasped at the E method as a means of dealing with what was to them a difficult, complex situation; some were very confident about their ability to deal with the problems and, without carefully examining the problems which they regarded as child's play, they applied the E method to them. For some who showed E effects, the underlying process seemed to be essentially an involuntary or unconscious, inertialike process; for others the process was founded on conscious assumptions or generalizations of various sorts; and for still others the process apparently began with conscious assumptions but then turned into the inertialike process (or vice versa). (See Luchins, 1942, pp. 28-30 and 87-89, for detailed descriptions of processes that may underlie E effects.)

Duration of E Effects May Vary

The duration of E effects showed considerable variations; some individuals no longer showed the effect minutes after the initial testing while others showed the effect several weeks later. There is a need to study the same individual over a considerable span of time in order to see whether E effects tend to increase or decrease with time, whether a plateau is reached after a certain period, or whether, for example, E effects disappear and then reappear at a later time. As a tentative hypothesis, we suggest that what happens to E effects in time may depend on the particular process that gave rise to the E effects.

E Effects May Differ in Meaning in Different Problems

It is recognized that E effects may differ in meaning in various test problems. Failure to offer direct solutions to the first two critical problems may serve, at least in some cases, as evidence of the development of a set. Failure to offer the direct solution to the extinction task may indicate that the individual was unaware of the direct method (was blinded to a method) or that he was aware of the direct method but thought that it should not be used, possibly because he assumed that all three jars must be employed in a solution (because he was blinded by an assumption). Failure to offer direct solutions to the last two critical problems may indicate a lack of recovery from the set even after the intervening experience with the extinction task. Still finer distinctions are feasible. For example, some subjects solved the $A - C$ criticals by the direct method and yet used the $B - A - 2C$ procedure in the $A + C$ criticals, perhaps because they had developed a set to subtract or because they thought it was not permissible to add the contents. In short, E effects do not mean the same thing, psychologically speaking, for all test problems.

In this connection, it is interesting to recall that investigators who have used Einstellung situations to study rigidity have differed in the criteria adopted to indicate rigid behavior. We suggest a thorough analysis of the pattern of behavior throughout the Einstellung test when it is employed to study rigidity. We have indicated that, if rigidity is defined as failure to shift when shift is required, then failure of an extinction task is the criterion of rigid behavior. Some investigators have used the time taken to solve an extinction task as the index of rigidity. Other investigators, some of whom have given no extinction tasks and in some cases only one critical problem, have used E solutions to a critical problem as the criterion of rigidity. Moreover, some of the investigators who employed this latter criterion defined rigidity as a lack of shift in behavior when shift is called for; yet it may be argued that a shift from the E method to the direct method is not called for in a critical problem since the E method does solve a critical (whereas it does not solve an extinction task). That is, the criterion of rigidity they used was actually not compatible with the definition of rigidity they accepted. The stress we are placing on the criterion of rigidity used in Einstellung situations involves more than academic quibbling; it was found that in many of the experimental variations different trends of results, supporting diverse conclusions, were obtained, depending on whether one or another criterion was employed.

Same Individual May Show Different Amounts of E Effects and Different Underlying Processes

It was found that administration of the experiment to the same individual under speed and nonspeed conditions, or before and after the arousal of various attitudes, often yielded E effects of different intensities, and, in some cases, the E effects seemed to result from different processes. To understand such findings, attitudinal factors and (social) field conditions must be taken into account. This is not to say that E effects are independent of personality factors or of individual differences of various kinds. The findings do imply, however, that E effects shown by an individual cannot be accounted for by appealing to some invariant factor in him. In particular, the E effects one shows cannot be understood solely in terms of a factor of rigidity which he possesses if this factor is regarded as invariant in its operation. Yet some investigators have interpreted E effects as evidence of a general factor of rigidity inherently characteristic of the person. Our findings do not support such a conclusion. Rather, our findings suggest that not only the intensity or amount of rigidity, but also the process that brings about rigidity, may differ at different times for the same individual.

SURVEY OF VARIATIONS THAT TENDED TO EXTREMIZE E EFFECTS*

Observational Analysis as a Source of Extremizing Variations

It is noteworthy that every variation which maximized or minimized

---

* With few exceptions, from 60 to 85 per cent of the subjects in the elementary-school groups in the basic experiment gave E solutions to Criticals 1 and 2 and from 55 to 85 per cent failed the extinction task. With few exceptions, from 70 to 85 per cent of the subjects in the college groups in the basic experiment gave E solutions to Criticals 1 and 2 and from 50 to 70 per cent failed the extinction task.

E effects was conducted before 1940 and was derived from observational analysis rather than from an appeal to theories. Appeals to different theories of learning and rigidity have produced some interesting suggestions for experimentation, but none of the experiments based on the suggestions has actually extremized E effects.

Maximizing Variations

Maximum or complete E effects may be considered to have been shown by a group when each of its members used the E method in every critical problem and failed to solve the extinction task. Complete E effects were shown by some of the groups given the speed experiments in which attempts were made to create a stressful "speed test" atmosphere. Four of the seven elementary-school groups in the speed-test study showed maximum E effects, whereas only two of the ten college groups did so, although seven of the college groups had 100 per cent E solution of every critical. These findings supported our impression, garnered from observations, that the speed-test atmosphere was more pronounced in the elementary-school classes than in the college classes. This may have been a consequence of the children's greater susceptibility to the experimental conditions intended to heighten emotional tension as well as of the fact that certain attempts that were made to heighten tension among the children could not be used with the college students; for example, remarks linking performance on the "test" to report-card grades and remarks that the principal and teachers were interested in this test and would examine their papers, were made to the children, but not to the college students, since they did not seem to be appropriate on the college level. Of the various variations that were conducted in attempts to maximize E effects, the speed-test variation was one of the most effective and certainly the most dramatic.

When ten E tasks were used instead of the usual five in the basic experiment, two of three elementary-school groups showed maximum E effects. When the same test was given to adults, E effects were somewhat less pronounced.

In one elementary school, the children in six Grade 6 classes, with the aid of the experimenter, formulated the E method as a rule of solution after presentation of the first E task, and they were told that this was the rule which would solve the new type of problem they were to learn on that particular day. This procedure was modeled after the lesson plan (isolated drill) usually employed in this elementary school in presenting a new type of problem. Of the six classes, three showed maximum E effects and the other three very high E effects.

When three elementary-school classes (Grades 5 or 6) were told before the experiment to try to generalize or discover a method of solution or a rule to solve the problems, those children who later claimed to have generalized a rule showed maximum E effects in two classes and high E effects in the third class. E effects were somewhat lower in a college class given the same preliminary instruction and still lower for those few children who later said that they had not generalized a procedure or rule.

When a new series of problems was used that followed the paradigm of the basic experiment but in which the E method was $A + B - 4C$ and the direct method was $B - A - C$ (Luchins, 1942, pp. 61, 94), maximum E effects were shown by a Grade 6 group but much lower E effects by college groups.

Where the roles of the just-mentioned methods were reversed so that the method that solved the E tasks was $B - A - C$ while that needed to solve the extinction task was $A + B - 4C$, a high-school class showed maximum E effects.

We turn now to the relatively few variations that minimized E effects.

Minimizing Variations

Minimum or zero E effects may be considered to have been shown by a group when each of its members solved every critical and the extinction task by a direct method. Attempts at clarification in which, prior to giving the experiment, we tried to help subjects grasp the idea that they might develop an Einstellung were generally not successful in minimizing E effects (Luchins, 1942, pp. 77-80). The only exception occurred in a college group wherein the attempt at clarification was combined with a warning "Don't be blind." Before any other instructions were given, the twelve subjects in this group were told: "After the sixth problem write the words 'Don't be blind' on your paper. This is to remind you to watch out, to be careful, or you will make a foolish error." These subjects are said to constitute the "D.B.B. group" and the remaining fifteen students in the college class the "plain group." All twenty-seven students in the class, before they received the basic experiment, were told a story about children who had developed an Einstellung for a cumbersome method of solving water-jug problems $(B - C - 3A)$ and who had called themselves stupid and blind when shown the direct method $(A + C)$. The D.B.B. group showed no E effects while the plain group showed very low E effects $(C_1 C_2, 10\% E;$ Ext., $7\% F; C_3 C_4, 0\% E)$.

Since the story involved a habituated method quite similar to the E method of the basic experiment and a direct method identical with a direct method of the basic experiment $(A + C$ solved Criticals 2 and 3 of the basic experiment), the surprising factor is not that the procedure (clarification plus D.B.B. warning) eliminated E effects in this college D.B.B. group but that it did not do so in elementary-school groups. Perhaps the remedial-arithmetic training taken by some children in these classes operated against the attempt at clarification. In any event, of the many warnings and attempted clarifications given before the experiment, this procedure was the only one that succeeded in eliminating E effects even in one group.

Attempts at clarification, when made *after* subjects had participated in the basic experiment (Luchins, 1942, pp. 80-83), were more successful in producing minimum or close-to-minimum E effects, particularly in college groups. For example, after the basic experiment was administered to a college class, there was a discussion of the experiment during which the experimenter described the direct methods and made subjects aware that some of them had probably developed an Einstellung that had caused them to overlook the direct methods; when the experiment was then readministered, no one showed E effects. (Repetition of the basic experiment without the intervening discussion usually yielded considerable E effects although less than in the original administration.) In other college classes, wherein half of each class served as a D.D.B. group, the experiment conducted immediately after the discussion involved new numbers or even involved new methods (E method: $A + B - 4C$; direct method: $B - A - C$). Here the D.B.B. groups showed no E effects while the plain groups (those not given the "Don't be blind" warning) gave some E solutions of the first two criticals but used the direct method thereafter. Even after two months had elapsed between the discussion that followed the basic experiment and the second presentation of the basic experiment, or between the discussion and the administration of the experiment involving a new E method and a new direct method, college D.B.B. groups showed no E effects.

In general, attempts to decrease E effects through clarification were more effective, transferred to a wider range of problems, and prevailed over a longer period, when the explanations were offered after, rather than before, the subject had participated in an Einstellung experiment. Apparently the explanations were more meaningful after the subject had had an experience in which he could develop an Einstellung.

Comparison of Maximizing and Minimizing Variations

We found it far more difficult to minimize E effects than to maximize them. It is of interest that varying the experiment in one direction might maximize E effects while varying it in an apparently opposing direction did not minimize them. For example, attempts to increase emotional tension and haste through speed-test conditions, maximized E effects in several classes; but attempts to decrease emotional tension and haste through nonspeed (no-timing) conditions did not minimize E effects in even one group, but instead yielded E effects within or above the range found in the basic experiment. Elementary-school groups, tested under no-timing conditions, yielded an average of 90 per cent E in Criticals 1 and 2, 87 per cent F in the extinction task, and 98 per cent E in Criticals 3 and 4. The use of ten E tasks yielded maximum E effects in several elementary-school groups, but the use of only one E task did not minimize E effects in even one such group (although it reduced the effects considerably for adult groups).

Further indications of the greater power of maximizing factors were furnished by those experiments in which maximizing factors were pitted against minimizing factors. For example, the basic experiment was administered to college groups and then discussed (clarification); when an experiment involving eight E tasks was given immediately after the discussion, instead of showing zero E effects, the groups showed effects approximating those found in the basic experiment. In other college groups the basic experiment was administered, discussed, and then readministered as a speed test; large E effects were found in the speed test. Some subjects later said that, because of the discussion, they tried to avoid becoming habituated to the $B - A - 2C$ method but that the stress on time gave them so little chance to think that, without realizing it, they developed an Einstellung. Here we see maximizing factors triumphing over minimizing factors.

The relatively greater ease with which E effects could be maximized might be accounted for on the ground that, in the range of results obtained in the basic experiment, the upper level of the range was closer to complete E effects than was the lower level to minimum E effects. Hence, less modification of the basic experiment would be needed in order to obtain complete E effects. Whatever may be the true explanation of the findings, it is apparent from the results of the variations that it was a simpler matter to induce every member of a group to exhibit mechanized, rigid behavior than to prevent every member from showing such behavior.

These findings might be interpreted to mean that to repeat blindly, to persevere in a habituated mode of response, is a basic characteristic of human behavior. Such an interpretation would accord with the doctrines advanced by some philosophers and psychologists, ranging from David Hume's principle of mental inertia to Guthrie's principle of stereotypy in behavior. But such a conclusion overlooks the negative instances—those individuals who did not develop an Einstellung, who faced each problem in order to discover the most adequate mode of solution. Another interpretation—which seems to be more in accordance with the findings—is that blind, repetitive activity is not the result of a fundamental tendency in human behavior but is created by special factors and conditions in the situation; that is, E effects cannot be understood solely by appealing to a basic tendency in human behavior but only by studying characteristics of situations in which E effects of various intensities occur. We shall return to a consideration of these characteristics.

Variations That Strongly Influenced Failures of the Extinction Task

Since we have regarded failure of the extinction task as a more crucial index of E effects and behavioral rigidity than E solution of a critical problem, it might interest the reader to see which variations extremized, or came close to extremizing, failures of the extinction task. We are concerned here not only with the variations, already described, that in certain groups tended to extremize E effects in both the criticals and extinction task, but also with those variations that in some groups tended to extremize only failures of the extinction task.

The use of ten E tasks in three Grade 6 classes with 112 subjects, gave from 97 to 100 per cent failure of the extinction task (average of 99 per cent). When the experiment was patterned after an isolated-drill lesson, with the E method presented as the rule to be practiced, six Grade 6 classes, with 232 subjects, showed from 97 to 100 per cent failure of the extinction task (average of 99 per cent). When three elementary-school classes were told, prior to the experiment, to try to generalize a method or rule, the eighty-seven children who later said that they had succeeded in generalizing a rule showed from 94 to 100 per cent failure of the extinction problem (average of 98 per cent); a college group averaged 86 per cent failure. Under speed-test conditions, seven elementary-school classes, with 196 children, showed from 93 to 100 per cent failure (average of 98 per cent), while ten college classes showed from 60 to 100 per cent failure (average of 87 per cent). Where a new series of problems was used that followed the paradigm of the basic experiment but in which the E method was $A + B - 4C$ and the direct method was $B - A - C$, a Grade 6 group showed complete failure of the extinction task, while college groups showed only from 50 to 78 per cent failure (average of 60 per cent). When the roles of these methods were reversed so that the method which solved the E tasks was $B - A - C$ while that needed to solve the extinction task was $A + B - 4C$, a high-school class showed maximum failure of the extinction task.

It may be recalled that minimum E effects were obtained only in some variations that involved attempts at clarification. When attempts at

clarification were made *before* the basic experiment was administered
to four elementary-school classes and one college class, with two of the
elementary-school classes and about half of the college class constituting
"Don't be blind" groups, only the college D.B.B. group gave no failures
of the extinction task. When the attempt at clarification was made *after*
the basic experiment and the experiment was then repeated, a college
class of twenty-nine subjects showed no E effects and hence no failures
of the extinction task. In other college classes, where half of each class
served as a D.B.B. group, the attempts at clarification after the basic
experiment were followed by an experiment that used the paradigm of
the basic experiment but in which the problems involved new methods
and/or new numbers; here, not only did the D.B.B. groups show no E
effects, but the "plain groups" (those that did not receive the "Don't be
blind" warning) showed no failures of the extinction problem (although
they showed some E solutions of criticals). Even when two months had
elapsed between the discussion that followed the basic experiment and
the readministration of this experiment, or between the discussion and
the administration of the experiment involving a new E and a new direct
method, both college D.B.B. groups and plain groups showed no failures of the extinction problem. Minimum failures of the extinction task
were also obtained in college classes that received only one E task or
that were told with each problem of the basic experiment that they did
not necessarily have to use the largest jar.

When the comment about the largest jar was given with each test
problem but not with the E problems, relatively little failure of the extinction task (10 per cent or less) was obtained in elementary-school as
well as in college classes; subjects' comments suggest that the remark
helped to separate the test tasks from the E tasks. Other experimental
attempts to separate the test tasks from the E tasks included: (1) the
statement with the first critical that a new series was about to begin;
(2) the experimenter's statement, made just before the giving of the
first critical, that a new method or a better method should be used thereafter or that the old method (E procedure) should not be used; and (3)
the use of time intervals between the E tasks and the test tasks. Questioning after the experiment showed that, despite these attempts at separating E tasks and test tasks, some subjects still regarded the two kinds
of tasks as similar or even identical; these subjects showed considerable
E effects while the remaining subjects showed little E effects, averaging
less than 10 per cent failure of the extinction task. In short, these experimental variations worked in a minimizing direction only when they
were successful in destroying the apparent unitary, homogeneous nature of the series of problems.

Less than 10 per cent failure of the extinction task was obtained for high-school students in a variation where the allowable wastage of fluid was stipulated with each problem, where credit was lost whenever a method was used (such as the E method) that wasted more than the stipulated amount, and, moreover, where the subject was given the opportunity to do the problem again if he so desired.

Another variation that yielded less than 10 per cent failure of the extinction task was the experiment, administered to a high-school class, in which the E method was $B - A - C$ and the direct method, which solved the extinction task, was simply the filling of the A jar.

In nearly every group that participated in the basic study, 50 per cent or more of the subjects failed the extinction task. A variation that gave less than 20 per cent failure of the extinction task might therefore be regarded as having quite successfully lowered failures. Failures of less than 20 per cent (but not less than 10 per cent) were attained when (1) superfluous jars were added to the statement of each problem; (2) E tasks were not presented in succession, but were alternated with extinction-type tasks; (3) prior to administration of the basic experiment, subjects were given the opportunity to create water-jug problems in which they were free to decide the volumes to be found and/or the methods to be used; and (4) in the E tasks only, the end jars were written in red ink and the center jars in blue ink.

The Broader Applicability of Variations That Maximized or Minimized E Effects

Research has revealed that variations which most successfully maximized (or minimized) E effects in the volume-measuring problems, were similarly successful when the paradigm of the basic experiment was used with other kinds of tasks, including mazes, hidden words, geometric problems, sorting tasks, and pictures. Moreover, these same variations were found to work in an extremizing direction in situations that did not follow precisely the paradigm of the basic experiment. For example, a study by one of the present writers of the formation of impressions of personality was concerned with so-called "primacy effects," the tendency to form an impression of a person mainly in terms of the earlier information received about him. When several of the variations used in studying the Einstellung phenomenon were utilized in the work on impressions of personality in attempts to extremize primacy effects, it was found (cf. Luchins, 1957a) that not only did those variations which tended to maximize (or minimize) E effects operate in the same manner for primacy effects, but even the relative status of the variations remained the same; that is, a variation that yielded more (or less)

E effects than another, also yielded more (or less) primacy effects than this other one. Preliminary research in other areas suggests that the extremizing variations may have still broader applicability.

E Effects Fostered by Conditions That Hindered Genuine Problem Solving

Examination of the basic experiment and of the variations that succeeded in (or came close to) extremizing E effects, suggests that E effects tended to be fostered by conditions that hindered attempts at genuine problem solving. We use the phrase "genuine problem solving" to refer to processes that include examination of a problem and decision making with reference to a solution for the problem. Genuine problem solving stands in counterdistinction to uncritical application of a method to a problem since the former invokes decision-making processes while the latter merely represents practice in the use of the method. For genuine problem solving to take place throughout a series of tasks, each task of the series must be faced as a new problem-solving situation, as another occasion for decision making. In short, that a problem is solved does not imply that genuine problem solving, in the sense in which we employ the phrase, was necessarily involved.

The remarks about the relationship between E effects and genuine problem solving may be considered as an a posteriori speculation or as an induction drawn from observations of many studies. They are intended to state, not a full-blown conclusion, but a hypothesis to be tested. Here we want to show how aptly the hypothesis applies to the basic experiment and to many of the variations that extremized E effects in the criticals and/or the extinction task or that came close to doing so.

Earlier in this chapter we suggested that perseverance in a given act of behavior does not result from a fundamental tendency to persevere or to repeat, but is found under certain conditions and not under other conditions. Among the conditions conducive to perseverative, repetitive behavior, we now suggest, are those that operate against genuine problem solving and support uncritical application of a method to a problem. The basic experiment may readily give rise to conditions that hinder genuine problem solving. For example, the paradigm of the basic experiment—several similar-appearing problems all solvable by one method, followed by tasks that superficially appear to be similar—may give rise to the impression of a homogeneous, unitary series, homogeneous with respect to appearance as well as method of solution. E responses may be made to a test problem because this problem appears, "through the specific conditions of the experiment, as an equal part of a whole which is one unitary group, unitary also with regard to the applicability of the E method. As the tasks, so the responses build in such cases a quasi-rhythmical succession of parts in one underlying whole" (Luchins, 1942, p. 29). Viewing a test problem as a part of a homogeneous series, the subject may be inclined to apply uncritically to it the method that worked in other parts of this "unitary series," rather than to stop to examine the problem carefully and engage in decision-making processes with reference to its solution. What we are trying to bring out is that the situation of the basic experiment lent itself readily to mechanical repetition and contained forces of considerable strength that worked against the likelihood of genuine problem solving in the test tasks. Moreover, variations that maximized (minimized) E effects may be interpreted as having supported (or weakened) these forces.

Consider how the maximizing variations apparently influenced genuine problem solving. Under speed conditions, the tense social atmosphere was not conducive to careful examination of each problem and to decision making with reference to a mode of solution. The use of ten E tasks hindered genuine problem solving by enhancing the likelihood of uncritical application of a method, perhaps through fostering the impression of a homogeneous series; so many times did the E method work that the subject was taken out of a decision-making area and the problems became simply occasions in which to repeat a response (cf. Luchins, 1942, p. 85, for extended remarks). When the experiment was presented as an isolated-drill lesson, in which the E method was formulated as the rule to be practiced, the subjects were told in effect (although not explicitly) that they were not to engage in genuine problem solving but were simply to practice a method. When the subjects were told just before the experiment to try to generalize or discover a method or rule of solution, the main or sole problem for them seemed to be the discovery of the E method or rule; those who succeeded in discovering it had, as far as they were concerned, solved the primary problem and were no longer in a decision-making area; now they had merely to apply the method they had discovered. Here the problem of generalizing a rule became central while the water-jug tasks, as problem-solving situations, played more of a peripheral role in the subject's cognitive grasp of the situation. In a similar manner we could formulate what happened to most subjects under speed-test conditions by saying that the water-jug problems, as problem-solving situations, became peripheral while the central problem was that of the need for finishing quickly and for saving oneself from failure.

Maximum E effects were obtained in an elementary-school class in which the E method was $A + B - 4C$ and the direct method $B - A - C$, as well as in a high-school class in which the roles of these methods were reversed so that the method that solved the E tasks was $B - A - C$ while that needed in the extinction task was $A + B - 4C$. Here genuine problem solving may well have been hindered by the cognitive difficulty of the problems for these children. For the grade-school children, the $A + B - 4C$ procedure was so complex that, after it was demonstrated, they used it by rote without understanding or, once having mastered the method, they clung tenaciously to it. For the high-school students, to discover the $A + B - 4C$ method in the test tasks (the only method that solved all these tasks) was so difficult that, even if they had stopped to examine a test problem carefully, it is not likely that they would have discovered this complex method. What we are suggesting is that problems which are cognitively very difficult, relative to a given subject's ability, may not permit genuine problem solving.

Clarification methods, particularly when combined with the "Don't be blind" admonition, may have helped subjects to become aware of the dangers of blind repetition and of the need for facing each water-jug task as a new problem-solving situation, and thus may have encouraged genuine problem solving throughout the series.

Variations that yielded relatively little failure of the extinction task (less than 20 per cent) may also be interpreted as having enhanced opportunities for genuine problem solving. Giving a college class only one E task reduced the chances for uncritical application of the E method to the test tasks. Telling college students with each task that they did not necessarily have to use the largest jar may have encouraged them to examine each problem carefully in order to decide whether or not this jar was needed in the solution. Telling them this just before administration of the test tasks apparently helped them to see the test tasks as separate from the E tasks and thereby helped to destroy the impression of the tasks as constituting a homogeneous series. All other experimental attempts to reduce E effects by separating E tasks from test tasks (by the introduction, between E and test tasks, of an explanation, instructions, or intervals) apparently worked in a minimizing direction only for those subjects who did not see the two kinds of tasks as similar, who did not regard the series of problems as homogeneous in nature.

The use of superfluous jars in a task did not allow uncritical application of the E method to the task since, even if a subject were set to apply this method, he first had to examine the task in order to decide which three jars to select; that is, superfluous jars brought in their wake examination of the task and decision making, and thus encouraged genuine problem solving. That the addition of a fourth jar was more effective in reducing E effects when its placement was randomized, rather than when it was always before (or after) the usual three jars, may be accounted for on the ground that the randomized order called for still more careful examination of the task before the jars could be selected.

Alternation of E tasks with extinction tasks operated against formation of the impression of a unitary series, homogeneous with respect to method.

Stipulation of the fluid that could be wasted in each problem, and allowance of full credit for solution only if there was not undue wastage, encouraged the subject to examine each problem in the light of the stipulated wastage and to seek for economical methods, so that each task tended to be faced as a new problem-solving situation; but, when subjects were tense and "overmotivated," as when this variation was introduced as a college-entrance test, they were less capable of careful examination or of clearheaded decision making.

When, in the E tasks only, the end jars were written in red ink and the center jars in blue ink, one class showed less than 20 per cent failure of an extinction task. It is not clear how this finding fits our tentative hypothesis. Some subjects said that they were puzzled about the use of different inks; their reaction to the use of different colors may have led to careful examination of the tasks and may have hindered complacent, automatic repetition of the E method.

Turning to the variability experiments, we find that those subjects who were nonvariable with respect to the simplest available method, the filling of one jar, showed much less failure of an extinction task (the last problem, solvable only by a new method, $2A - C$) than those who were nonvariable with respect to the $B - A - 2C$ method. Subjects' comments suggested that the latter had not seen any method other than the $B - A - 2C$ procedure, whereas most of those who used the simplest available method were aware of other procedures but deliberately chose the simplest method. In other words, nonvariability with respect to the filling of one jar, usually followed examination of the task and represented a conscious choice or decision; and, when the filling of one jar was found inappropriate in an extinction task, this critical attitude evidently carried over and enabled most of the subjects to find a new method that would solve the task.

When opportunities were given to create water-jug problems prior to administration of the basic experiment, the lowest E effects were yielded among subjects who were free to determine the volumes to be found and/or the methods to be used in the preliminary problem-creation session; the provision for wider opportunities for decision making prior to administration of the experiment may have fostered decision making and genuine problem solving during its administration.

All this is admittedly *ad hoc* and a posteriori. Nonetheless, it seems worth while to interpret the experiments in terms of opportunities for genuine problem solving and to undertake more research on the proffered hypothesis. As a project pertinent to this hypothesis, we propose beginning with a situation that differs from the basic experiment in that it does not readily foster mechanical repetition but instead favors genuine problem solving. The project would consist in applying a variational approach to this situation in attempts to minimize and maximize genuine problem solving.

Suggestions for Controlling Mechanized Behavior

The experimental variations hint at how to control mechanized behavior under certain conditions. But *how* to control behavior is intimately linked with the *why* and the *what for* of the control (cf. Cantril, 1950). These in turn relate to questions of ethics and social philosophy that are beyond the scope of this monograph. Control of behavior, in its broadest sense, may be directed toward creation of a particular model of man. At the one extreme, the model of man may be *homo mechanicus*, a robotlike mechanism; at the other extreme, the model of man may be *homo sapiens*, a thinking, rational being. If those who attempt to control mechanized behavior or rigidity of behavior are aiming for *homo mechanicus*, they will presumably attempt to maximize mechanical habits in order to enhance automatic performance in man. Assuming that those who attempt to control rigidity of behavior are aiming for *homo sapiens*, should they attempt to minimize mechanical habits, to eliminate all automatic performances? An affirmative answer does not seem to us to be appropriate for the reasons stated below.

Mechanized habits have a place in the behavior of *homo sapiens*; indeed, living would be difficult, exhausting, perhaps impossible without them. They can serve as tools to facilitate personality and social functioning. Mechanized habits equip an individual with ready, quick responses to recurring everyday situations so that he does not have to devote much thought or energy to these situations or trouble himself to find responses to them each time they occur. They permit him to develop facility in dealing with his environment. If a person had to stop to think about each of his responses, and to make a decision in every situation, he would be much like the centipede who stopped to analyze his leg movements and ended up immobile in a ditch. There are some unhappy individuals who find it agonizing to make a decision, who fret and fume in every choice situation, and who often make choice situations out of what others deal with effectively in an automatic or semiautomatic manner.

By providing the individual with ready responses to certain aspects of his environment, habits allow him more time and energy to devote to other aspects. The reader of this page presumably has made so automatic the habits involved in reading that he can devote himself to concentrating on the meaning conveyed by the print. He who is taking notes while reading, can concentrate on his task without having to focus on how to form the particular letters put down. An individual who does his creative work while pacing in his study is fortunate indeed that he does not have to concentrate on how to move his legs. Thus, by developing certain mechanical habits, one has greater freedom to expand his mental horizons. Such habits, then, are not necessarily the foes of, or restraints on, thinking, but may free one for creative activity. Hence, the concept of *homo sapiens* is not inherently incompatible with mechanized responses.

We underscore this point, lest our emphasis on the possible blinding effects of mechanized habits be interpreted as depreciating the importance or positive value of habits in general. What occurred in the Einstellung situation for those subjects who were blinded to the method of solving the extinction problem by their attempts to apply the E method to it, may be characterized as indiscriminate application of a mechanized response (or of an assumption or generalization). Indiscriminate applications of habits are likely to produce difficulties anywhere. Suppose, to take a rather farfetched example, that an individual, in learning to read or to write, were to apply the habits that serve him in walking; clearly, they would not serve in these contexts or for these functions. For effective functioning, habits require contextual selection and discrimination. What our findings suggest is that, under certain conditions, a habit may cease to be a tool discriminately applied and become a Procrustean bed to which the situation must conform. Such conditions ought to be avoided by those who believe in a *homo sapiens* model of man. The experimental variations hint at ways to avoid such conditions, but the concrete forms the hints take depend in part on who is attempting to control the rigidity of behavior, whose behavior is involved, and what kind of behavior is in question. Moreover, the fruitfulness of the suggestions will, of course, have to be tested empirically.

To limit the discussion, let us consider what the schools might do to avoid indiscriminate application of habits. Educators ought perhaps to keep in mind the distinction between problem solving and sheer exercise or application of a method or process. A problem-solving situation, by its very nature, is a decision-making situation; if there were no decision to be made, there would be no problem. Telling students to apply a designated method or process in a "problem" reduces the problem-

solving aspect by removing an opportunity for decision making. Moreover, if he is told to apply a particular method or to repeat the same
response, the student may be less likely to study the context in which
the method is used or the response is made and, hence, less likely to
learn to distinguish between situations to which the method or response
applies and those to which it does not at all apply (or does not apply as
well as other responses). This failure to relate method or response and
context is all the more likely to occur if the assignment is to repeat the
same response (method, procedure, or formula) in a series of tasks, as
in isolated drill. Emphasis on isolated drill, frequently employed in
teaching arithmetical skills, may help to account for the fact that some
children and adults know the individual arithmetical processes (they
know how to add, subtract, multiply, and divide), but are at a loss to
know which process to apply unless the problem explicitly indicates
the process to be used. It might be said that they have not grasped the
relationship between the arithmetical process and the context or area
of applicability. One implication of our findings is that the limitations
of isolated drill ought to be recognized. While such drill may be of value
in teaching *how* a process, skill, or habit should be applied, it does not
serve to teach *where* it should be applied. Hence, in addition to being
given practice in the application of various processes, students should
be given more opportunities to select the process that is appropriate to
the task involved.

In a broader sense, the findings suggest that repetition may exert
deleterious influences. Emphasis on repetition in school teaching may
be in line with the ancient slogan, *Repetitio mater studiorum est.* But
the findings surveyed in this monograph suggest a revision of the shib-
boleth to: *Repetitio mater asinorum est.*

Related to emphasis on repetition is the dictum that only one thing
(skill, method, formula, fact) should be taught at one time since only
one thing can be efficiently learned at a time. This belief may help to
explain the prevalency of isolated drill, particularly in the initial learning period. The experiments in which various kinds of problems were
alternated (in the initial learning period), showed that even young
children were capable of learning several methods of solving jar problems; furthermore, they learned to apply the methods with more discrimination than did children of similar age and background who devoted the same period of time, in the initial learning period, to repetition
of one method. This suggests that a means of combating the possible
blinding effects of repetition is to teach more than one thing in a given
lesson and to allow practice in more than one response in a given practice period.

Provision should be made not only for more opportunities to select processes or methods but also for more opportunities to select data to be used in solving problems. This is suggested by the experiments involving superfluous jars. These experiments yielded little E effects but they also showed how unaccustomed many subjects were to discarding any of the given data or "givens" in a problem. (Reluctance to do so may be a partial explanation of E effects, even in the basic experiment.) In problems that arise in life, in the sciences, and in the professions, selection of data to be used in solving problems is often part and parcel of the problem-solving process. But in the teaching of most school subjects this opportunity for decision making is neglected entirely. In some classes (for example, occasionally in the teaching of algebra), a few problems are given that either lack sufficient data for solution or that contain more data than are needed, but usually the missing or superfluous data are so obvious (particularly when they are met with in a familiar type of problem) that little decision is required to detect them. Wider employment of extraneous as well as missing data to help students learn to survey and select data to be used in solving problems in many school subjects, is suggested as a means to prevent indiscriminate application of habits and to encourage decision making.

Many of our subjects were surprised to learn that there was more than one method of solving a critical problem. Their experience in school had apparently been limited solely or mainly to problems each of which was presented as solvable by one and only one method. Yet, outside of the classroom, it is not uncommon to find a problem that can be solved by more than one method (that is, several methods may lead to the same answer or end product) or one that has nonunique solutions (in the sense that a method or methods may lead to several answers or end products) or one that has no known solution. Experience in school with problems that have nonunique solutions or that are solvable by various methods may help the student to become concerned with the distinction between methods and the solutions to which they lead and with the conscious selection of a method as one of the steps in problem solving. It may help the student to realize that there may be several ways of resolving a problem and that one method may require more steps, take longer, and be more or less "elegant" than another method. Schools should perhaps show more interest in processes as contrasted with the end products of the processes. Emphasis on the end product is characteristic of certain so-called "objective tests" in which one's score or grade is based, not on the process that led to the answer, but merely on the answer, the end product; yet, an essentially suitable process may, through a minor error, lead to an incorrect final answer while a correct final answer may conceivably be obtained through incorrect or invalid reasoning (see Luchins and Luchins, 1946, for elaboration). It may even be worth while to acquaint the student with unsolved problems as well as with problems that have been proved to be unsolvable in order to help combat the assumption that to each problem there is one and only one solution.

It was found that little E effect was obtained when, prior to administration of the basic experiment, subjects created water-jug problems in which they were free to determine the method of solution and the volume to be obtained. Our schools, at least those below the graduate level, rarely provide a student with opportunities to discover, create, and formulate problems, but instead hand ready-made problems to him. Yet such opportunities can readily be included at all educational levels. Thus, in addition to requiring the student to solve problems and to answer questions in order to afford practice in or to test what was taught, the student should be encouraged to devise exercises and problems pertaining to the subject matter that was taught; what he devises may reveal to the teacher whether or not he understands what was taught. More generally, a student should be permitted to participate in creative problem-solving experiences—to discover, formulate, and then attempt to solve his brain child—rather than always being confined to the problems that others have created. Such experiences may give the student the "feel" of creativity, may help him to understand how problems are formulated and clear up some of the mystery surrounding the origin of problems proposed by textbooks and teachers. Furthermore, such experiences may give the student a deeper understanding of the relationship between what is given in the statement of a problem and what has to be found as well as of the relationship between the problem and the method or methods, if any, of solving it.

It is noteworthy that opportunities to create water-jug problems were more effective in minimizing E effects when subjects were permitted to decide on the volume to be obtained and the method to be used, than when the volume or method was stipulated by the experimenter. In other words, the problem-creating experiences were more effective when the subjects had more opportunities for decision making. This is further experimental evidence that decision making may operate against arbitrary application of a response. It suggests that schools may profitably provide a student with more and varied opportunities for decision making. By this we do not intend to imply that all decisions should be up to the students. It is important (but by no means a simple matter) to teach a student the distinctions among situations (1) that permit a decision made solely by himself, (2) that call for him to act as one of the members of a group reaching a group decision, (3) that call for decisions which he can best make after consulting references or authorities (dictionary, encyclopedia, parent, teacher, etc.), and (4) that do not belong to his domain of decision making. The last may be situations that can be effectively dealt with in an automatic manner; or they may be situations over which the student has no authority; or they may be situations in which he is not prepared to assume the responsibilities and consequences involved in a decision by him; or they may be situations that involve areas wherein he is not sufficiently expert to help formulate a decision. Where feasible, the student should be given the reasons why he may or may not participate in the decision making pertaining to a given problem.

Experimental evidence (see Luchins, 1942, pp. 28-31 and pp. 87-93, for elaboration) suggests that certain attitudes and certain conditions of work were more conducive to indiscriminate application of the E method than others. Some children exhibited absolute confidence in the teacher, a kind of blind trust akin to unthinking submission, an attitude which in extreme cases amounted to the belief that what the teacher said (or seemed to say) was correct, that one should do just what the teacher did, and that there was no reason for individual initiative. Such an attitude, when transferred to the experimenter (who was apparently regarded as a teacher by most children), may have fostered E effects, with the children blindly copying the illustrated E method or reasoning that they must use this method because the experimenter had demonstrated it or because they thought the experimenter wanted them to use it or wanted them to use all three jars, etc. We think that a distinction should be drawn between respect for authority, on the one hand, and unquestioning submission and sheeplike following, on the other, and that the latter ought to be avoided if genuine problem solving is the objective.

Experiments in which the allowable wastage was stipulated, suggest that either extreme in motivation, either little interest in the problems or intense interest stemming from considerable ego involvement, favored large E effects. The findings suggest that extremes in motivation ought to be avoided in order to avoid indiscriminate application of a response to a problem. That many subjects did not keep a record of or did not heed the amount of available fluid, but were satisfied with "getting the answer," underscores their interest in the final answer as contrasted with the means to this end. That most subjects kept and heeded the record only when failure to do so was linked with loss of credit on the test, makes us wonder whether there has perhaps not been an undue emphasis in schools on motivations extrinsic to problem solving—motivations stemming from the desire to get a good score or to do better than others or to please the teacher. We think that more intrinsic motivation—a desire to solve a problem for the sake of solving it rather than for the sake of "one's dear ego"—could be fostered by our schools and that it would be conducive to genuine problem solving.

"Speed test" experiments indicate the possible deleterious influences on thinking of extreme ego involvement and of social conditions that make for tenseness or fear. The findings point to a need for re-evaluation of the speedy, instantaneous responses demanded in some classrooms and on many tests. They imply that the nature of the prevailing social atmosphere may be a powerful determinant of whether an individual meets problems with robotlike habituation, even when inappropriate to a problem, or whether he faces problems freely and engages in reasoned decision making.

Suggestions for controlling mechanized behavior drawn for school situations, can be adapted to other contexts. (Both in school situations and in other contexts their fruitfulness will, of course, have to be tested by observation and research.) The experimental findings suggest that the home can help to combat indiscriminate application of habits by not demanding of the child blind obedience, by not putting a premium on speedy responses, by avoiding a tense social asmosphere, by providing varied opportunities for genuine problem solving, and by explaining to the child the distinction between situations that are or are not in his domain of decision making. In industrial plants, there may be situations that call for mechanized, unthinking behavior, and the experimental variations that maximized E effects may here be of suggestive value; but, if the objective is to encourage problem solving, then many of the suggestions made for the schools seem to be in order. In this connection, it is noteworthy that opportunities for employees to engage in decision making, through suggestions to management and through membership on joint employer-employee committees, have at times paid off for industry in terms of better employer-employee relationships as well as improved industrial processes or equipment. The experimental variations can even be adapted to psychotherapy. Illustrations are furnished by the various methods used by one of the writers to encourage participation of patients in decision making in certain problems that pertained to their welfare in the hospital (see Luchins, 1955) ; some of these methods have apparently been successful in combating lethargy and extreme tendencies toward repetitive activities and in shaking some patients out of set ways of perceiving and reacting to the world about them.

In summary, the experimental variations may be interpreted as offering suggestions (or tentative hypotheses) as to what can be done to control mechanized behavior or rigidity of behavior and to maximize the advantages of habits while minimizing their disadvantages in personal and social functioning. Educators, parents, industrialists, psychologists, psychiatrists—all can play roles in developing an individual who will face problems constructively rather than act from blind force of habit, who will use habits as tools without becoming a slave to habits, and who will so well master habits that they do not master him.

CHAPTER XXII

FRONTIERS OF RESEARCH ON THE
SELECTED CASE

W E WOULD CONSIDER it unfortunate if the reader gained the impression that the story of the selected case of mechanized behavior has been completely told or that research on this case has come to an end. Years of research apparently have not yet revealed all that there is to know about this apparently simple instance of mechanized behavior. Nor have the many experimental variations exhausted the possible research paths that converge on the selected case. It seems to us that the water-jug problems have not yet been "worked to death." As a demonstration of their viability, we shall describe some research trails that we have been following in recent months and that are still in the process of being explored. It is noteworthy that we began to explore some of these trails many years ago (cf. Luchins, 1939) but abandoned them for other research trails.

GROUP PROBLEM SOLVING

Unless otherwise specified, it is to be understood that the experiments discussed in this section were conducted in 1957 in Eugene, Oregon.

Problem Solving by Pairs of Subjects

In the usual administration of the water-jug problems, each subject works individually and independently on the problems. What would happen to E effects if two subjects were asked to work together on the problems, if the solutions to the problems were arrived at through group decisions? Would two heads prove to be better than one, in the sense that the two subjects would show less or no E effects? To answer this question, the experiment was administered to pairs of subjects. Two subjects, seated at a table, were told, in addition to receiving the usual instructions, that they were to work together on each problem and to tell each other their thoughts concerning the problems. They were further told that, while each subject, if he wanted to, might use scratch paper to make independent calculations, the final solution was to be agreed upon by both; it was to represent their joint decision. Moreover, while each subject had his own sheet of paper for scratch work, only one sheet of paper was furnished to both subjects on which to write the solutions of the problems. Each problem was typed on a card

[536]

that was placed on the table where it could be seen by both subjects. As each problem was presented, the two subjects were again reminded to work together on it.

In this manner, with a two-and-one-half-minute maximum time allotment per problem, the usual problems through Critical 4, followed by two additional problems, were presented to ten pairs of college students and to ten pairs of junior-high-school students (J.H.S. 1). In order to study the effect of the time factor, for ten other pairs of junior-high-school students (J.H.S. 2), the same procedure was used, but with no time limit for the solution of the problems.

The results in the usual test problems were as follows:

College .... C_1: 100% E C_2: 100% E Ext.: 20% F C_3: 30% E C_4: 30% E
J.H.S. 1 .... C_1: 70% E C_2: 80% E Ext.: 20% F C_3: 40% E C_4: 30% E
J.H.S. 2 .... C_1: 80% E C_2: 50% E Ext.: 20% F C_3: 30% E C_4: 20% E

The high percentages of E solutions to Criticals 1 and 2 indicate that joint solution of problems by two people does not prevent a set from developing. However, a striking feature of the results is the 20 per cent failure of Problem 9, the extinction task. This is significantly less failure than was found in the many experiments wherein subjects worked independently on the problems. It, therefore, seems that two heads were better than one on the extinction problem (even if not on the first two criticals). Also, E solutions of the last two criticals, on the average, were substantially less than under the customary method of administration. Thus, solving the problems in pairs did not prevent the development of a set but did foster recovery from the set.

A word is in order concerning the absence of timing for the J.H.S. 2 group. In the four critical problems, the pairs in this group generally required less than the two and one-half minutes ordinarily allotted per problem. More time was used in the extinction task, but unlimited time did not save two pairs in this group from failing this task. One pair announced after four minutes, and the other pair after six minutes, that they could see no way of solving this problem and that they wanted to stop working on it and go on to the next problem.

After Critical 4, all subjects received a problem that was solvable by the E method, by $A - C$, and by the simple method of filling one jar. The one-jar solution was given by 60 per cent of the college pairs, by 50 per cent of J.H.S. 1 pairs, and by 60 per cent of J.H.S. 2 pairs; in each case the percentage was higher than that usually obtained when subjects worked independently on the problem. As the last task, each pair received a problem solvable only by a new method, $2A - C$. Of the college pairs, 60 per cent solved this problem, a percentage that was somewhat higher than that obtained under customary administration. While the

J.H.S. 1 pairs showed only 20 per cent solution of this final problem, which was within the range obtained when subjects worked independently, the J.H.S. 2 pairs showed 60 per cent solution of it, which was higher than that obtained under the customary administration. The six J.H.S. 2 pairs solving this problem required an average of five minutes for it. Thus, the extra time available to them was important in the discovery of the new method. That extra time was not available to the J.H.S. 1 pairs may help to explain why so few of these pairs solved the final problem.

As noted, the opportunity for subjects to work in pairs substantially reduced E effects in the extinction task and the two subsequent criticals. But the opportunity to work in pairs did not invariably reduce E effects. This was seen in results obtained when the problems through Critical 4 were administered in the manner described above to ten pairs of sixth-grade children. Here, where the classroom teacher served as the experimenter, eight of the ten pairs did not use the direct method at all. The ten pairs as a whole showed very high E effects, within the range for sixth-grade children who worked independently on the problems.

$$C_1 : 90\%\ E \quad C_2 : 80\%\ E \quad \text{Ext.} : 80\%\ F \quad C_3 : 80\%\ E \quad C_4 : 80\%\ E$$

Comments. How can we understand these results? Why is it that working in pairs reduced E effects below the usual level for the college and junior-high-school subjects, at least beginning with the extinction problem? Perhaps the instruction to communicate with one another concerning their solutions helped to make the E method a less automatic, unreflective response than when subjects worked individually. Moreover, the members of a pair were able to confirm each other's observations that the E method did not work in the extinction problem and therefore may have had greater certainty concerning the need to reject this method than did a subject who worked alone. Also, the probability was higher that two subjects would discover the direct method than would one working independently.

There still remains the question: Why is it that the opportunity to work in pairs was not effective for the elementary-school subjects? Possible contributory factors include the following:

(1) Factors of age and educational level may have favored the junior-high-school and college pairs. The younger children apparently found it more difficult than the older ones to work together on the problems and to communicate with one another concerning the problems.

(2) The fact that the classroom teacher served as the experimenter for the sixth-grade subjects may have caused the subjects to regard the experimental situation as a school-test situation. We know that a test atmosphere may foster E effects.

The experimenters had the impression that subjects found it somewhat awkward to work with someone else on the problems. This seemed
especially true for the elementary-school pairs but seemed true to some
extent for the junior-high-school and college pairs. The writers had
gained the same impression in 1937-39 when they administered
arithmetical problems and word-block (anagram) problems to pairs of
elementary-school children and told them to work together. It is an interesting commentary that, in the experiments reported on above (done
in 1957), the subjects still behaved as if they were quite unaccustomed
to cooperating on the solution of the problems despite the passage of two
decades during which there has been considerable emphasis in the
schools on affording children opportunities to work together. Perhaps
these classroom opportunities for cooperative work have not involved
arithmetic problems or perhaps the experimental situation did not
allow for the transfer of school-fostered attitudes toward joint under-
takings.

A major question in the study of problem solving is what thought
processes underlie a particular mode of solution. Group problem solving,
in which subjects work together on a problem and communicate with
one another concerning their thoughts and feelings during the problem-
solving session, seems to provide a rather natural setting in which the
processes that underlie a solution may be revealed; the situation is certainly less artificial than that in which the subject is asked to "think
aloud" as he works alone on a problem. It was therefore hoped that,
when one member of a pair told the other member his thoughts about
the water-jug problems (as he had been instructed to do), we would
gain clues concerning the underlying thought processes. In actual fact
we learned little in this respect. Subjects generally did not verbalize the
thoughts or processes that led them to decide on a solution but confined
their communications largely to the proposal of a solution or to agreement with a proposal; that is, the communications were generally confined to the end products of the processes. Moreover, the communications between members of a pair were generally rather skimpy. This
may be related to the afore-mentioned apparent awkwardness in working together. There is also the possibility that a subject was not consciously aware of the processes that led to a solution or that he was not
able to verbalize the processes.

We are presently conducting research concerning the nature of the
members of pairs and their relationship to one another. The age, educational level, mathematical ability, sex, intelligence, and other characteristics of members of pairs are being varied in order to see what effect
variation of these factors has on E effects and on communication between members. Other factors that are being varied are the prestige

and the roles (e.g., a teacher and a pupil, a mother and a child) of the two members. We are also interested in the operation of suggestion and imitation as revealed, for example, in the acceptance by one member of a pair of a method offered by the other.

Recently we have undertaken research on problem solving by pairs of psychotic patients. Such patients are allegedly deficient in their inter-personal relations. We are interested in finding out how they compare with normals in their behavior in group problem solving and in whether or not conditions can be created under which their behavior in group problem solving will be similar to that shown by normals.

Suggested Research on Group Problem Solving

It would be of interest to give pairs of subjects experience in work-ing together on different kinds of tasks during which they are to com-municate verbally with one another concerning their thoughts and feelings. Will such experience help to develop facility in working to-gether and/or in communicating the thoughts and feelings that in-fluence their decisions with respect to the tasks? If the pairs, after such experience, are given the water-jug problems to work on together, what will happen to E effects and to the manner in which the members of the pair work together and communicate with one another? A related but broader problem for research is how to develop facility in an indi-vidual in recognizing and verbalizing his problem-solving processes, whether he is working alone or with others.

Another problem for research in group problem solving concerns the size or numerosity of the group (cf. Georg Simmel's ideas on the role of numerosity in group behavior, as formulated in Wolff, 1950). We have seen that, for some groups of two, E effects were lower in the extinction problem and subsequent criticals than they usually were for individuals. Will an increase in the size of the group further decrease E effects? Will a group of three be less likely to develop an Einstellung than a pair or than a group of four? Is there an optimum group size above or below which there is a greater tendency for group members to develop an Einstellung or to be blinded by an Einstellung to more direct methods? These questions are facets of the broader question how the size of a group is related to its behavior and efficiency in problem solving, a question that is of both theoretical and practical importance in con-temporary small-group research. Specifically, the question for small-group research suggested here is as follows: What is the relationship between the size of a group and the likelihood that its members will become mechanized and blinded by the habits of work that develop in their interaction?

Another problem that awaits study is the effect of the homogeneity or heterogeneity of the group's members. There is also the need to study the influence on group problem solving and, specifically, on E effects, of the characteristics (age, sex, intelligence, etc.) of the group's members and of the relationship among its members.

When the E method is adopted by a group of subjects as the method to be used in the water-jug problems, it can be regarded as the rule of behavior or "norm" of the group in the particular problem-solving situation. This norm is appropriate for some of the problems but not for all; that is, to solve all of the tasks, certain objective requirements have to be met by the norm. Group solution of the water-jug problems offers a possibility of studying the development and influence of group normative behavior or social norms in a situation wherein the norm is rather objectively determined. It can serve in a small way to supplement the experimental study of the development of group normative behavior or social norms in situations wherein the norm is less objectively determined but instead more subjectively determined. For example, in Sherif's (1936) pioneer study of social norms which utilized the autokinetic phenomenon (the apparent movement to a subject of a stationary light on which he fixates), the group norm was rather subjectively determined. In the Sherif study, the problem confronting the group, that of judging the distance that the stationary light had (apparently) moved, was solved as well by one norm that the group decided upon as by another; for example, the problem was solved as well by a group norm of two inches as by a group norm of twenty inches. But the problem of solving the extinction task was not at all met if the group norm was the E method. Life situations in which group norms form and operate vary with respect to the extent to which these norms must meet certain objective requirements. Group problem solving, through judicious choice of the kinds of problems to be solved (for example, through inclusion of a problem with a unique solution, a problem with no solution, a problem with a multiplicity of equally appropriate solutions, a problem with several solutions that vary in their appropriateness), may be useful in studying group normative behavior in situations that vary with respect to the extent to which the norm is objectively or subjectively determined.

Attempts to Maximize E Effects in Group Problem Solving

Studies are being conducted in which attempts are made to maximize E effects in group problem solving through the introduction of factors that apparently were successful in enhancing E effects under the usual mode of administering the water-jug problems. Here we report on the "maximizing" experiments that have been done to date.

Speed and Competition. An experiment involving speed conditions was administered to ten pairs of University of Oregon freshmen. In addition to being instructed to work together on each water-jug problem and to tell each other their thoughts with regard to the solution of the problems, the members of the pairs were informed that they were being timed to see how quickly they could solve the problems. They were further told to let the experimenter know when they were finished with the series of problems. The usual series of problems, through Critical 4, had been written on the blackboard beforehand. As in the speed experiments described previously in this monograph, the experimenter noted the passage of time on the blackboard and commented at intervals that the subjects were taking more time than had elementary-school children.

Verbal communications between the members of a pair tended to be less frequent and less leisurely than had been the case when college pairs had been allowed a maximum of two and a half minutes per problem. Usually one subject took the lead and did all the writing—possibly to save time—while the other hastily gave his consent to the solution. Several pairs, when they did not immediately discern the solution to the extinction problem, left it and went on to Critical 3. Some wanted to return to the extinction problem after solving the subsequent criticals but this was not permitted. The ten pairs worked very rapidly and showed very high E effects:

$$C_1C_2: 100\% \, E \quad \text{Ext.}: 80\% \, F \quad C_3C_4: 80\% \, E$$

In another speed experiment two pairs of University of Oregon freshmen were tested simultaneously in the same room. Each pair was seated at a table, with the tables separated by the width of the room. The tables were placed so that all the subjects could read the problems on the blackboard. For each pair the instructions were the same as those used in the speed experiment just described. In addition, the experimenter said that this was a test to see which pair would finish the problems first; that is, the experimenter tried to introduce competition between the groups. This procedure was used with twenty pairs of subjects (ten administrations). Communications between members of a group were infrequent and tended to be whispered—perhaps because of the presence in the room of the other couple. Subjects worked very rapidly and, with the exception of one pair, showed complete E effects. The results for the twenty pairs were as follows:

$$C_1C_2: 100\% \, E \quad \text{Ext.}: 95\% \, F \quad C_3C_4: 95\% \, E$$

Comments on Speed Experiments. Let us first compare the results in these speed experiments with those obtained when college pairs were allowed a maximum of two and a half minutes per problem. When two and one half minutes were allowed per problem, only two out of ten pairs *failed* the extinction task. In the speed test, only two out of ten pairs *solved* the extinction task and, in the speed-plus-competition situation (where pairs competed against each other), only one pair out of twenty solved this task. Thus, results with respect to E and direct solutions were reversed in the extinction task. Results in Criticals 3 and 4 were also strikingly different under speed conditions as compared with results when two and a half minutes were allotted per problem. It would seem that speed conditions vitiated the positive benefits of working together insofar as E effects were concerned. Moreover, we saw that under speed conditions subjects tended to communicate less with each other than when the two-and-one-half-minute maximum time allotment prevailed and that one member of the pair tended to do all the writing. Thus, speed conditions seemingly affected the very act of working together; apparently such conditions not only brought about a change in the subjects' perception of the problem but also created a different group structure and process. The subjects apparently considered the task of finishing as rapidly as possible to be more important than the task of working together. Their perception of what constituted the central task may explain the low level of intercommunication.

The question arises: What will happen under speed conditions if different subjects are used—say, subjects younger or older than the college students? It also is of interest to study the influence of speed conditions on the solution of the problems and on intercommunication when more than two subjects are asked to work together. Will the level of intercommunication tend to be inversely proportional to the size of the group and will the patterns of communication tend to be different for groups of various sizes?

Instructions to Generalize a Rule. An experiment involving instructions to generalize a rule was administered to pairs of sixth-grade children. In addition to being instructed to work together on each water-jug problem and to tell each other their thoughts concerning the problems (with a maximum of two and a half minutes allowed per problem), each pair was told, before any of the problems were given, "While solving the subsequent tasks, try to generalize or discover a method of solution or a rule to solve these problems." After the experiment was completed, subjects were asked whether or not they had generalized a rule. The results were fractionized on the basis of whether the members of a pair claimed that they had generalized a rule (thirteen pairs) or whether they claimed that they had not generalized a rule (three pairs).

Generalized a rule ....13 pairs C_1C_2: 100% E Ext.: 92% F C_3C_4: 96% E
Did not generalize a rule......3 pairs C_1C_2: 33% E Ext.: 0% F C_3C_4: 0% E
Total   ....16 pairs C_1C_2: 93% E Ext.: 81% F C_3C_4: 78% E

It was clear from the answers to the question asked at the end of the session that, for those children who had generalized a rule, the rule was the E method. We see that those who claimed to have generalized a rule had strikingly more E effects than those who did not make the claim. Once the rule had been generalized, members of the pairs often began to work new problems without even glancing at the volume that was required to be obtained; only after their attempted utilization of the E method had been completed, did they look to see if their answer matched the required volume. Two pairs of subjects told the experimenter that the answer they obtained to the extinction problem was 42 and not 25 and said that the volume required in the extinction task should be 42 instead of 25. Three other pairs asked the experimenter if he was sure that he wanted 25 quarts; when the experimenter confirmed that 25 quarts was the desired quantity, they spent the remaining time allowed to solve this problem in checking their arithmetical computations, clearly puzzled as to why the rule did not work here.

In most cases the members of the pairs seemed to be constrained in their behavior and did not raise their voices above a whisper when communicating with each other, even though they had been told to work and talk together and were reminded to do so with each problem.

With the assistance of Ray Lewis, the same procedure was used with ten pairs of undergraduate students at the University of Oregon. By the second or third E problem, subjects generalized that the E method was or seemed to be the rule. Three pairs showed complete E effects, failing the extinction task and using the E method in every critical. The seven other pairs used the E method in Criticals 1 and 2 but discovered the direct method in the extinction problem and used it thereafter. Thus, the results for the ten pairs were as follows:

$$C_1C_2: 100\% \ E \quad \text{Ext.}: 30\% \ F \quad C_3C_4: 30\% \ E$$

The seven pairs that found the direct method seemed to be somewhat suspicious of the rule, even in the E problems; some comments suggested that most of them thought it would be too simple just to apply the rule each time and suspected that they might be tricked or that they might be given tasks wherein the rule would not work.

After Critical 4, the ten college pairs received two additional problems. In the first of these two problems, 30 per cent used the one-jar solution; 50 per cent, the two-jar solution, $A - C$; and 20 per cent, the E solution. The last problem, which required the $2A - C$ method, was solved by 50 per cent of the college pairs.

With the assistance of James Whitman, the same procedure recently has been used with ten pairs of adult male psychotics hospitalized in Roseburg, Oregon. Patterns of interaction between the members of the pairs here seemed to be more varied than was the case for the normal subjects. The members of some pairs of psychotic patients actively co-operated in working on the problems; in other pairs, one member did all the work while the other made no suggestions; in others, one patient took the lead and did all or most of the calculations and writing while the other patient—apparently somewhat slower in coming to grips with the problems—agreed with the first but at times did not seem to understand what was going on; in still others, it appeared that the "slower" member did most of the writing, while his partner told him what to write or offered suggestions and criticisms. Although too few pairs have been studied to permit generalizations, it seemed that active co-operation in working on the problems tended more often to yield direct solutions than did the other patterns of interaction.

The psychotic subjects had also been instructed to try to discover or generalize a method or a rule of solution. Although they used the E method in the E tasks, none of them spontaneously verbalized the E method as the rule of solution, whereas all of the ten college pairs quickly generalized that method of solution. A few psychotic patients, when questioned at the end of the session as to whether they had followed a rule, claimed that they had not. Their answers included these: "No rule—it always changed"; "Didn't see rule—it changed several times"; "None." From the remaining comments (the majority), it was not apparent whether a rule had been generalized or, if it had, whether the rule was the E method; ambiguous replies given in response to the question whether a rule had been followed included the following: "Two of these and one of those"; "Fill this once and this twice"; "Add them up until you get an even number"; "I did the first thing that came to my head"; "Just arithmetic"; "Mostly subtraction—some addition."

It was therefore decided not to fractionize the results on the basis of whether subjects claimed to have generalized a rule. For the ten pairs of psychotic patients, the results in the usual test problems were as follows:

$$C_1 C_2 : 80\% \, E \quad \text{Ext.}: 30\% \, F \quad C_3 C_4 : 40\% \, E$$

Note that these quantitative results are not very different from those yielded by the college students, despite the fact that all of the college students spontaneously verbalized the E method as the rule of solution during the E problems whereas none of the patients did.

In the problem that followed Critical 4, 20 per cent of the patient pairs used the one-jar method; 60 per cent, the two-jar method, $A - C$; and

20 per cent, the E method. Only one pair of patients solved the last problem that required the $2A - C$ method as compared with 50 per cent of the college students.

Instructions to Generalize a Rule Plus Additional E Problems. Into the group-problem-solving situation for pairs, we introduced both the initial instructions to generalize a rule and three additional E tasks given prior to the criticals. The expectation was for high E effects since, under the administration of the problems to individuals, the instruction to generalize a rule and the use of additional E tasks had each tended to maximize E effects. This expectation was borne out by the results obtained with ten pairs of sixth-grade children. Only one pair claimed not to have generalized a rule (this pair discovered the direct method in Critical 2 and used it thereafter); the other pairs showed almost complete E effects. The results for the ten pairs were as follows:

C_1: 100% E C_2: 90% E **Ext.:** 90% F C_3: 90% E C_4: 90% E

The expectation was, however, not upheld by the results obtained with ten pairs of undergraduates at the University of Oregon. These subjects, who were tested with the assistance of Thomas Hurley, had no difficulty in formulating the E method as the method which seemed to be the rule and in all cases did so by the second or third E problem. The outstanding characteristic of these pairs was a suspicion that the E method would not solve all the subsequent problems. Thus, while working on the additional E tasks, subjects offered comments such as these: "I'll bet they're not all like this"; "When do these get different?"; "This is too easy"; "Doesn't seem like it [the E method] should work every time"; "One of these isn't going to work"; "He [the experimenter] is going to slip us up on one of these." Despite this anticipation of a change in method, all pairs used the E method in Criticals 1 and 2. But in the extinction problem all of them realized, usually after an attempt to apply the E method, that the method did not work here. All pairs discovered the direct method and used it thereafter. It is interesting to compare the time required by these college students to solve the extinction task with the time required to solve the preceding critical. In Critical 2, wherein all the ten pairs used the E method, the time of solution ranged from three to ten seconds with a mean of seven seconds; in the succeeding extinction task, the time of solution ranged from eighteen to sixty-three seconds with a mean of thirty-three seconds. Thus, although the subjects anticipated some change in method, the direct method was not immediately evident to them.

Comments on Generalization Experiments. Why is it that the instructions to generalize a rule, alone or in conjunction with additional

E tasks, yielded very high E effects for the elementary-school pairs but not for the college pairs? The answer would seem to lie in attitudinal differences. The children seemed to regard the experiment as a school learning or testing situation and were quite serious about their work. The college students were more suspicious and at the same time more jovial; they regarded the experiment as child's play, as too easy. Most of the college pairs (although they did not put it in just these words) seemed to have the attitude that the rule which they were asked to discover was so apparent in the early problems that it did not require two college students working together to discover it; they suspected that the experimenter (a college student) was not interested solely in seeing them apply this rule over and over again and must be out to "use psychology" on them by tricking them, perhaps by giving a problem where they should not use the method they had formulated as the rule. The use of the additional E tasks seemed to strengthen this attitude. In the group-problem-solving situation, attitudes of suspicion of trickery and expectation of change on the part of one member of a pair usually aroused or reinforced similar attitudes on the part of the other; and, in talking to one another (for example, in reminding one another to be skeptical), members of a pair often seemed to keep such attitudes operating longer than was the case when college subjects worked individually.

It is interesting that suspicion of the rule and anticipation of change did not alert any college pair to the direct method in the first two criticals—that is, apparently did not prevent them from developing a set—but had positive results only when there was obvious proof that the rule had failed. It seems that suspicion is not the most adequate attitude with which to meet the critical problems.

> To view freely, to look directly at the merits of the problem situation, not negatively suspicious, but facing positively the actual requirements of the problem—these appear to us, to be important. . . . Of course, if one is inclined toward blind mechanization, the suspicion of some trick may aid him, but the more favorable conditions seem to be not to be concerned with trickery but to go straight and productively forward with each task. (Luchins, 1942, p. 30 n.)

The pairs of psychotic patients did not manifest overt suspicion or anticipation of change. Yet their quantitative results are similar to those shown by the college students. The patients, it will be recalled, did not spontaneously verbalize the E method as the rule of solution during the E tasks. It is not known whether this was because they were not aware that they were using the E method or because they felt no need (or were reluctant) to communicate such awareness or because they had difficulty in expressing or communicating their thoughts under the experimental conditions.

Experiments are now in progress in which pairs of psychotic patients are being assisted in generalizing and verbalizing the E method in the E tasks. Experiments are contemplated in which, prior to the water-jug problems, pairs of psychotic patients will be given other kinds of problem-solving situations in which they will receive guidance intended to facilitate their discovery and communication of the rationale underlying their problem-solving processes.

Conformity in Group Problem Solving

Conformity Experiments Involving the Water-Jug Problems. How would a subject's responses to the water-jug problems be influenced if he overheard another person's responses to these problems. Preliminary studies done by one of the writers in 1940 with pairs of New York City sixth-grade children were concerned with this question. The problems were administered to pairs of subjects; in each problem, one subject responded first while the other looked on and then the second subject gave his answer to the problem. The same subject responded first throughout the series of problems. In the small number of pairs that were studied in this manner, both subjects generally showed strong E effects but it was not clear whether or not one subject was copying the other.

In order to have better control over the overheard responses, we stabilized the situation by taking one member of the pair into our confidence beforehand and instructing him with regard to the responses he was to give; that is, one member of the pair was the experimenter's confederate while the other was a naive subject. Some confederates were instructed to use or to attempt to use the E method in every task, including the extinction task, while others were instructed to use the E method in the E tasks (if they were given the E tasks), but the direct method in the test problems. In some instances, the problems up to Critical 1 or up to the extinction task were administered to the naive subject only; at this point the confederate was called into the room and the remaining problems were administered to the pair with the confederate responding first. In still other instances, all the water-jug problems were administered to the pair, with the confederate again responding first.

When the confederate used the E method in the criticals, most naive subjects also used this method. Of course, it is likely that they would have done so even if they had not overheard the confederate's responses. When the confederate persisted in applying the E method to the extinction task, where it does not yield the desired answer, a few subjects agreed with him while most subjects said that he was wrong; however, only a few gave the direct response.

When the confederate used the direct method, there were exclamations of surprise or dramatic gestures on the part of some subjects that suggested that the confederate's answer had made them aware of the direct method. Usually the subjects then shifted to the direct method but a few subjects continued to use the E method in the criticals even though the confederate had used the direct method. Questioning after the experimental session revealed that some of the latter subjects were reluctant to "copy" the confederate's reply or thought that it might be regarded as cheating to give the same answer as the confederate gave in every problem. Indeed, most subjects seemed somewhat uncomfortable because they had to respond after the confederate and, in some cases, requested permission to go first; permission was not granted.

The question arose: Suppose two subjects working together on the problems have generalized the E method as the rule of solution; and suppose further that someone enters the room during the presentation of the test problems and gives a direct response to a critical. Will the pair of subjects relinquish the E method and adopt the direct method? If the E method is regarded as the rule or the norm, the question may be rephrased: Will the pair give up its norm and adopt the direct method? If the individual who enters the room during the presentation of the test problems is a naive subject and not a confederate, and if he responds after the pair makes its responses, then there arises also the question: Under what conditions will he conform to the group norm? In attempts to answer such questions, experiments have been conducted and are still in progress. We report here on some of these experiments (done in Eugene, Oregon in 1957).

After a trio of elementary-school children was given the usual illustrative water-jug problems, one member of the trio, selected at random, was asked to leave the room. The remaining dyad was then given the instructions described in the section of the present chapter entitled "Instructions to Generalize a Rule" (p. 543). The usual E problems and test problems were then presented, one at a time, with a maximum allotment of two and a half minutes per problem. Half of the groups worked under what will be called Condition 1 and the others under Condition 2.

Under Condition 1, the member of the trio that had been sent out of the room—henceforth called the control subject since he did not receive the E tasks—was recalled just as the dyad was about to receive Critical 1. The control subject was told to watch while the other two subjects solved this problem, then to make remarks, if he wished to do so, concerning their solution, and, finally, to solve the problem. The same procedure was followed in each of the remaining test problems; that is, first the dyad solved the problem while the control subject looked on and then the latter gave his remarks and his solution.

Under Condition 2, the control subject was recalled after the dyad had solved Critical 1 and just as Critical 2 was about to be presented. The control subject was allowed to solve Critical 2 first while the other two looked on. The two onlookers were then told to comment on the solution if they cared to and, after this, they were told to solve the problem together. The same procedure was used with each of the three subsequent test problems; that is, the control subject solved the problem first while the members of the dyad looked on and then the latter gave their comments and their solutions.

Ten trios of sixth-grade children were tested, half of them under Condition 1 and the others under Condition 2, with the assistance of Ray Lewis. For ten other trios of similar subjects, the classroom teacher was the experimenter; again half of the trios were studied under Condition 1 and the others under Condition 2.

Consider first what happened under Condition 1 when the classroom teacher was the experimenter. Although the five control subjects saw the E method illustrated by the experimenter, and although they saw the dyads solve Critical 1 by the E method, they invariably solved every test problem in the direct manner, presumably because they had not received any of the E problems other than the illustrative one. In other words, under Condition 1, when the classroom teacher was the experimenter, the control subjects did not "conform" to the group norms. The members of the dyads expressed surprise at the use of the direct method and usually asked the teacher whether it was all right to use it or whether one should stick to the rule. When the teacher replied that they should solve the problem by whatever method they considered best, most dyads shifted to the direct method in Critical 2 and all used it in the extinction task and the subsequent tasks. In short, observation of the E method, as illustrated by the experimenter and as used by the dyads in Critical 1, did not lead the control subject to adopt this method; instead, most dyads adopted the fresh point of view that the control subject introduced.

Quite different results were obtained under Condition 1 when a university student (a stranger to the children) was the experimenter. Now four of the five control subjects in Critical 1 chose the E method used by all dyads in that critical; that is, four control subjects "conformed" to the norms of their respective groups (dyads). One of these four dyads discovered the direct method in Critical 2 and used it thereafter, with the control subject also doing so. But the direct method was never used by three of the five groups, not even in the extinction task. Here, then, the control subjects tended to conform to what their respective dyads were doing. The only exception, a control subject who gave the direct method in Critical 1 after witnessing the dyad's E solution, was an intellectually superior pupil with an I.Q. of 143 (the highest of any subject tested under either Condition 1 or 2) as compared with I.Q.'s of 112 and 123 for the members of the corresponding dyad; the members of the dyad apparently regarded her as the brightest of the three and were willing to let her take the lead as soon as she came in.

Consider now what happened under Condition 2 when the classroom teacher was the experimenter. Here, where the control subjects preceded the dyads in giving their solutions to Critical 2, they invariably used the direct method. This evoked surprise on the part of the dyads who usually questioned the teacher as to the permissibility of this method. When the teacher replied that they should use what they thought was the best method, most dyads shifted to the direct method in Critical 2 and all dyads used it in the extinction task and in the subsequent criticals. Here, again, we did not find conformity to a group norm.

When, under Condition 2, the experimenter was a university student (a stranger to the children), all five control subjects also offered the direct solution to Critical 2. Now four of the five dyads immediately adopted the direct method. However, one dyad, insisting that the direct method was "wrong," persisted in using the E method in the remaining problems even though it led them to failure in the extinction problem. It may be noteworthy that the control subject whom the dyad would not follow was a very bright pupil (with an I.Q. of 133 as compared with I.Q.'s of 98 and 117 for members of the dyad) but also a stout and rather homely girl who, according to the teacher, was not popular with the other children. Can it be that the two subjects would not give up the E method and accept the direct method offered by the control subject— and thereby failed the extinction task—simply because they did not like the control subject? This raises an interesting point as to the role played by interpersonal relationships in group problem solving. It is possible, of course, that the pair who insisted that the direct method was "wrong" may have regarded the rule that they had generalized as "right" and any other response as "wrong," irrespective of who offered the other response.

Comments on Conformity Experiments. The results do not permit any clear-cut conclusion to be drawn concerning conformity experiments involving the water-jug problems. Clearly there is a need for further research in this area, particularly since relatively few pairs have been studied. The social atmosphere, attitudinal and personal factors, the relationship between the subjects and the experimenter, the relationships among members of the group (dyad) and between the group and the control subject—all these require further study in order to see what influences they have on conformity behavior. In particular, we do not know at present why it was that, under Condition 1 (where the control subject responded after the dyad), the results were strikingly different when the experimenter was the classroom teacher than when the experimenter was a university student and a stranger to the children. It is of interest that conformity to the group norm (that is, adoption by the control subject of the E method used by the dyad) was found only under Condition 1, and then only in the case where the experimenter was a university student. Under Condition 1, when the experimenter was the classroom teacher, and under Condition 2, regardless of whether the experimenter was the classroom teacher or a university student, every control subject used the direct method in the first critical solved by him and most dyads were influenced to the extent that they used the direct method in subsequent problems. It could be said that most dyads conformed to the responses made by the control subject.

The procedure used in the experiments just described was quite different from the usual procedure followed in conformity studies (cf. Asch, 1952; Luchins, 1944; Luchins and Luchins, 1955b). In the usual conformity procedure, the subject overhears a response to a task and then offers his response to the same task; the experimenter's concern is with whether the subject's response conforms with the overheard response. Results obtained in the present experiments suggest that conformity behavior should also be studied (1) when a confederate offers a response to a particular task *after* the subject has already given his response to the same task and (2) when the overheard response may influence responses to subsequent tasks. Such experimentation is in progress at the University of Miami with judgments of lines and also with incomplete test problems which are given to two subjects after one has developed a set for a method and the other a set for a goal. Such studies may throw light on various questions. For instance, under what conditions will a subject comply with the confederate's response to the extent that he changes the response he has already given so that it agrees with the confederate's? (Note that the dyads did not do this; that is, they did not say that they wanted to change to a direct response the E response that they had given to Critical 1, perhaps because to have done so would have appeared to be cheating or copying or perhaps because they did not think it was permissible to change their response.) Under what conditions will the subject's responses to succeeding tasks show the influence of the confederate's responses? (The dyads who used the direct method after the control subject used it presumably reflected such influence.) In order for such influence to prevail, the succeeding tasks must of course be related in some way to the confederate's past responses.

We think that it is of value, in conformity studies, to vary (1) the structure of the series of tasks and their interrelationships, (2) the appropriateness of the confederate's response to a particular task, and (3) the degree to which the confederate's response in one task can serve as a cue to the response he will give in the next task. This last point may become of particular concern to the subject if the experimenter evaluates the subject's response as "wrong" unless it agrees with the response that the confederate gives subsequently to the same task. It is of interest to study what happens to conformity behavior—particularly if the subject can be motivated to want to have his response evaluated as right—when mere imitation or repetition by the subject of the response that the confederate gave last is the basis for being adjudged "right," or when imitation or repetition does not suffice but one can infer or generalize from the confederate's responses the response that he will give subsequently, or when the confederate's responses do not permit the subject to determine a basis for being "right." The extent to which the response that is called "right" fits the requirements of the task is another factor to be varied.

There are many life situations in which an individual—perhaps because he desires to be "right"—wants to conform to certain standards or to certain behavior that he thinks someone else expects of him or that someone else would show in these situations. But the individual may not know just what constitutes conforming behavior in a particular situation. Perhaps he has to act before he can see how others behave. He may not be able to imitate or repeat someone else's response to a situation but perhaps must infer from other experiences with people what would be their response to the situation. Thus, there are life situations that involve conformity behavior but that are not patterned after the usual experiment on conformity where one has overheard responses which he may copy. We are, therefore, suggesting the study of conformity behavior (both with the water-jug problems and with other material) in a variety of situations that more closely approximate the variety of life situations in which compliant behavior is shown.

Other Conformity Studies. It may not be out of place to refer here to conformity studies with material other than the water-jar problems. The paradigm of the Einstellung experiment has been used by the writers with word blocks. The word blocks are composed of twenty-five letters of the alphabet arranged in a square. In the *E* tasks, a word is obtained by reading diagonally from right to left. In the critical tasks, this method yields a word while other words result from reading horizontally from left to right or diagonally from left to right. Only the latter two methods yield words in the extinction task. In the conformity experiments, the *E* tasks and the first critical are presented to one subject or to a pair of subjects; just before the second critical, another subject (either the experimenter's confederate or a naive person) enters and responds to each of the remaining tasks before (or after) the subject or subjects that received the *E* tasks.

Similar experiments are being conducted with series of drawings involving gradations of structure. For example, the face-bottle series (Luchins, 1950a) pictures the gradual disintegration of a face and the gradual emergence of a bottle. The beginning drawings of the face-bottle series are presented to a subject who often develops a set or Einstellung for a face so that he overlooks features of the emerging bottle. Later in the series, another individual (sometimes a confederate, sometimes a naive person) is brought into the room and allowed to respond to each of the remaining drawings before (or after) the subject who has received all the drawings.

Preliminary work done with the word blocks and the face-bottle series, using elementary-school children in New York City and in Montreal as subjects, has yielded the following observation. When the confederate gave a non-*E* response to a critical word block (i.e., gave a word obtained by reading horizontally or diagonally from left to right), subjects who overheard the response sometimes gave both the non-*E* response and the *E* response. Similarily, when a confederate reported seeing a bottle in a drawing in which both a bottle and a face could be discerned, subjects who overheard this response sometimes reported seeing both the bottle and face or features of both. Contrast these findings with what happened in the critical water-jar problems where subjects were less prone to give both the *E* and direct responses.

It is interesting to speculate on the reasons for the difference in results. Subjects were probably aware that a drawing may contain more than one object and an array of letters more than one word, but they may have assumed that a water-jar problem—or perhaps any arithmetical problem—has only one method of solution. Having given one method, they may not have looked for another. Or they may have assumed that it suffices to give one method. Moreover, subjects who reported more than one word in a word block or both a face and a bottle in a picture probably considered that they were giving several answers, whereas a subject may have been aware of both the *E* and the direct methods and yet not have regarded them as distinct "answers" since both led to the same amount of water. In other words, if the subject considers his answer to be the end product of the process, then the *E* and the direct methods, although distinct processes, yield the same "answer." Methods of teaching arithmetic which emphasize the end product of the process rather than the process itself may have influenced the results in this respect.

Another possible explanation may be found in the relative evaluations subjects gave of the E and non-E methods in the conformity experiments involving water-jar problems. At the end of these experiments, subjects sometimes referred to the direct method as "better" or "nicer" or "shorter" than the E method. Subjects were less prone to evaluate the face response as better or worse than the bottle response, and in the word blocks they did not evaluate one word as better or worse than another. In short, a subject who overheard the confederate give a direct response to a critical and who himself then gave this response instead of the E method, may have felt that he was using the better of two methods, whereas a subject who gave both the overheard and the E response in the word blocks or the picture series, may have felt that he was giving two equally good answers.

We have also been studying conformity behavior in experiments involving the formation of impressions of personality. The material employed consists of a series of eleven paragraphs which describe the behavior of a person named Jim in different situations and at different times. The first paragraph describes rather extroverted behavior; the eleventh paragraph describes rather introverted behavior. From the first paragraph to the sixth paragraph, the described behavior gradually becomes less extroverted in nature until it reaches rather "average" or "neutral" behavior in the sixth paragraph. From this paragraph to the eleventh paragraph, the described behavior gradually becomes more introverted in nature. Studies using these paragraphs have been conducted with high-school and college subjects both in Montreal, Canada and in Eugene, Oregon. In some studies (nonconformity studies), the paragraphs are given to only one subject; he is given one paragraph at a time to read and, after each, is asked to write his impression of Jim or to list adjectives that best describe Jim. Most subjects in nonconformity studies who received the series of paragraphs (from the first through the eleventh) developed a kind of Einstellung in the sense that they initially developed an impression of Jim as an extrovert and this initial impression influenced their interpretation of the behavior described in subsequent paragraphs. Thus, they tended to describe Jim as an extrovert after reading a paragraph which, when read in isolation (not in the series), presents Jim as "average" or even as somewhat introverted.

In the conformity studies, a newcomer (either a naive subject or the experimenter's confederate) was brought in at the showing of the fifth, sixth, or seventh paragraph. The paragraph was placed on the table before both individuals and the newcomer was allowed to read the paragraph and give his impression of Jim before the other subject did so. The same procedure was followed for all subsequent paragraphs. After the first paragraph that he read, the newcomer usually described Jim as an average or a somewhat introverted person. It is interesting that this description usually was not accepted by the subject who described Jim as somewhat extroverted, as he had after reading previous paragraphs. In other words, the subject generally did not conform to the overheard response to the fifth, sixth, or seventh paragraph. In the later paragraphs, which depicted behavior that was more strikingly introverted, subjects did agree more often with overheard responses that portrayed Jim as introverted.

It was noticed that subjects, in responding to a paragraph, did not give both the overheard response (that described Jim as average or somewhat introverted) and the response fostered by the Einstellung (that portrayed Jim as somewhat extroverted). Why did they not give both responses as subjects sometimes did to a critical word block or drawing? The answer may be that the subject may have conceived of Jim (as he might any person) as having a unity or consistency of some sort, a personality from which stemmed certain characteristic behavior; to have described Jim as average or somewhat introverted and also as somewhat extroverted would have been to overlook this unity or consistency.

Why did subjects not conform to the overheard response in the middle paragraphs of the series? Why were they less prone to adopt the overheard response here than were subjects who overheard the direct response to a test problem? The answer may lie in part in the appropriateness of the overheard response. While subjects not infrequently described the direct method as "better" or "shorter" or "nicer" than the E method, they never evaluated the overheard response (the impression of Jim) as better than their own. Related to this is the fact that the appropriateness of the direct method is quite objectively determined (thus, one can see that it involves less steps than the E method or that it leads to solution of the extinction problem whereas the E method does not), whereas the relative appropriateness of two impressions of a person may be more difficult to determine, particularly if the impressions are based on the behavior described in the middle paragraphs of the series which are somewhat ambiguous in nature, not so clear-cut as the paragraphs toward the beginning or end of the series. Moreover, the subject may have felt that, since he had read the preceding paragraphs, which the newcomer into the experimental situation had not read, he had more information about Jim than the newcomer and therefore was better able to give an accurate description of Jim.

It seems to us that the structure of the "Jim" experiment differs fundamentally from that of the water-jar experiment and that the difference may help account for the differing results. In the Jim experiment, the various items (paragraphs) are explicitly given common-class membership; that is, it is indicated that they all pertain to Jim. Moreover, the subject is told that his task is to characterize Jim; in other words, his task is to characterize the class to which the items in the series pertain. But in the water-jar experiment the various items (problems) are not explicitly given membership in a common class and the assigned task is not to characterize a class but to deal with each item. Thus, in the Jim experiment, after reading each paragraph, the subject's task is not to report what he has read therein but to describe the kind of person Jim is; in the water-jug experiment, the task is to respond to each problem. It can be said that the Einstellung process in the water-jar experiments involves the attribution (by the subjects) of a common class of membership to the discrete items; that is, the problems are treated as if they belonged to the class of problems solvable by the $B - A - 2C$ method. In the Jim experiment, the Einstellung process may be said to involve the characterization of the class (Jim) in terms of one of its properties (extroverted behavior in certain situations).

The word-block and face-bottle experiments are similar to the water-jar experiment in that the various items are not explicitly given common-class membership and the task is to respond to each item rather than to characterize a class. There is a need to study further the dynamics of the Einstellung process in the water-jar experiment (and in the word-block and face-bottle experiments) and to compare the dynamics here with the dynamics of the Einstellung process when one is explicitly given the class to which the items in the series belong. Perhaps the processes that underlie stereotypes and prejudices against an individual or a group are more similar in dynamics to the processes in the Jim experiment than to those in the water-jug experiment.

The most adequate way of dealing with a water-jug problem may be to treat it as a separate, discrete entity and not to be concerned over the class to which it belongs. But, in reading about a person's behavior, in an attempt to form an impression of the person, the most adequate approach may not be to react to an item of behavior as a discrete, isolated item since the behavior may take on a different role and meaning depending on the person who performs the behavior, that is, depending on the class to which the item of behavior belongs. It is of interest to see what happens to E effects and to conformity behavior when experiments are conducted in attempts to vary systematically the extent to which it is appropriate or adequate to respond to a particular item in the series in terms of its class membership.

It should be noted that conformity studies have also been done in which the series of paragraphs describing Jim's behavior have been given in reverse order; that is, from the eleventh to the first, from descriptions of the most introverted behavior to descriptions of "neutral" behavior and, finally, to descriptions of the most extroverted behavior.

Finally, we want to note that the results obtained in the Jim experiments with subjects in Oregon were somewhat different from those obtained with subjects in Montreal. The preliminary findings hint that introverted behavior was regarded as more abnormal or atypical behavior by the Oregon subjects than by the Montreal subjects. Differences between Montreal and Oregon subjects were noted whether the paragraphs were presented in order from the first through the eleventh or in reverse order. For example, under the reverse order of presentation, some of the Oregon subjects were quicker than most Montreal subjects to detect extroverted behavior, which they often interpreted as a sign that Jim was getting "adjusted." Also, some Oregon subjects, under the reverse order of presentation, agreed earlier in the series than did most Montreal subjects with a confederate who reported that Jim was average or extroverted; other Oregon subjects seemed to develop a stronger Einstellung than Montreal subjects for viewing Jim as introverted and did not agree anywhere in the series with a confederate who reported that Jim was average or extroverted. Preliminary as these results are, they point to differences in E effects, in conformity behavior, and in personality evaluation between Oregon and Montreal subjects. One wonders what contributed to the differences.

E Effects and Experimentally Induced Conflict in Group Problem Solving

What would happen if two subjects, each of whom had practiced a different method, received a task that could be solved by either of the practiced methods? Would they respond differently to this task on the basis of previously developed sets? If so, how would they react to the differences and how would they resolve the conflict? Summaries of our experimental attempts to answer these questions are given below. Each of the experiments was administered to two subjects who were seated at opposite ends of a table in a classroom or in classroom seats at opposite ends of the room. Unless otherwise indicated, it is to be understood that the subjects worked independently on the tasks. Experiments 1 through 3 were done in 1937-38 and Experiments 4 and 5 in 1957-58.

Experiment 1. This experiment involving water-jug problems was administered to twenty-four pairs of New York City sixth-grade children. An index card with a water-jug problem printed on it was presented to each of two subjects. The next card was presented to a subject after two and one half minutes or sooner if he indicated that he had completed the previous problem. For each subject, the first and second cards contained the first and second problems respectively of the basic experiment; as usual, the experimenter illustrated answers to these on the blackboard. For one subject of each pair, the next four cards contained the usual subsequent problems: the last four E tasks. For the other subject of each pair, however, the four cards contained different tasks, each of which involved three jars but was solvable only by the $A - C$ method. Thus, we were attempting to develop an Einstellung for the $B - A - 2C$ method in one child but an Einstellung for the $A - C$ method in the other child.

The next card presented to each child contained the usual Critical 1. After both subjects had indicated that they had completed this problem, the experimenter asked them to sit near each other at a table. A card containing Critical 1 was then placed on the table so that both subjects could see the problem, and the experimenter asked them to read aloud the solutions they had written to it. Generally the subject who received the usual problems reported an E solution of Critical 1 while the other subject reported an $A - C$ solution. Both subjects generally expressed surprise at the difference in solutions. In about one third of the pairs, the subject who had given an E solution spontaneously remarked that the $A - C$ solution was preferable to his own.

The card containing Critical 2 was then placed so that both subjects could see it. Each subject was told to write his answer to this problem on his own sheet of paper. After both had indicated that they had completed the problem, each was asked to read his answer. The same procedure was followed for the remaining test problems of the basic experiment.

The $A + C$ method was used in Critical 2 by every child who had practiced the $A - C$ method and by over half of the children who had practiced the $B - A - 2C$ method. Every child solved the extinction task and the subsequent criticals in the direct manner.

After Critical 4, the experimenter again presented a card containing Critical 1 and asked each subject to indicate what solution to it he preferred. With few exceptions subjects said that they preferred the $A - C$ solution. When asked why some had not originally offered this solution to the task, the children (in some cases, only after hints by the experimenter) surmised that they had not all practiced the same method.

Similar studies are planned, using the incomplete test problems (p. 427), where the conflict is between sets for a method and sets for a goal (cf. p. 432).

Experiment 2. A procedure similar to that of Experiment 1, but involving word blocks (arrays of twenty-five letters of the alphabet arranged in a square) was used with eighteen pairs of New York City sixth-grade children. The experimenter demonstrated on the blackboard various methods of solving the first word block, that is, methods of obtaining five-letter words composed of successive letters in the array. For one subject, each of the next five tasks was solvable by one and only one method: by reading diagonally downwards from the upper left-hand corner to the lower right-hand corner. For the other subject of the pair, each of the five corresponding tasks was solvable only by a different method: by reading diagonally downwards from the upper right-hand corner to the lower left-hand corner. (The experimenter walked over to each subject while he was working on the first of these five tasks and assisted him, if necessary, in finding the solution to it, speaking in low tones so as not to be overheard by the other subject.) Thus, we were attempting to develop sets for two different methods of finding a word. Each of these methods solved the next word block, the first critical. As in Experiment 1, the children, following their solution of Critical 1, were asked to sit near one another and to read aloud responses to this problem which they had written on their papers. Invariably the children responded in accordance with their respective sets, one responding with the word "lemon" and the other with the word "woman." As in Experiment 1, they expressed surprise at the difference in their responses. With few exceptions, each subject then used both methods in the second critical and in each of the two criticals that followed the extinction task. The extinction task, wherein a word could be obtained by only one of the methods, was solved by every subject.

Unlike what had happened in Experiment 1, no child in the present study said that one solution to the first critical was better than the other, either spontaneously or when the question was raised by the experimenter at the end of the session. Almost half of the children spontaneously made remarks indicating that they thought both words ("lemon" and "woman") equally good and that they were surprised or chagrined that they had overlooked one of the words; similar remarks were made by most of the remaining children when they were questioned at the close of the session. When asked, after the experiment, why they had originally offered different solutions to the first critical, the children surmised (with hints required by most pairs) that they had not practiced the same method.

Experiment 3. This experiment, in which a face-bottle series of pictures was used (Luchins, 1945), was done with fifteen pairs of New York City fifth-grade children. Each child was told to write on his sheet of paper what he saw on every card. One child was given the first seven cards of the series, on which there appeared a picture of a face that gradually disintegrated. The other child was given the last seven cards of the series beginning with the last card, on which there appeared a picture of a bottle that gradually disintegrated. Thus, we were attempting to set one child to see a face but to set the other child to see a bottle. The eighth drawing of the series, which was rather ambiguous in nature, was presented at the same time to both subjects. When they were then told to sit near one another and to read aloud the response to this drawing which they had written on their papers, they invariably responded in accordance with their respective sets, one reporting that he saw a face and the other reporting that he saw a bottle. Not only did the children express surprise at the difference in responses, but usually they expressed doubt that the object reported by the other child was depicted in the drawing. However, after each child had traced the object he claimed to see in the drawing, or had pointed to features of this object, the other child generally admitted that both objects might be seen in the drawing. For each of the subsequent drawings (the ninth through the fourteenth of the series), almost every subject reported seeing both a face or a bottle.

The children did not refer to the response of face as better than the response of bottle, or vice versa, either spontaneously or when questioned at the close of the session. When asked why they had given different responses to the eighth drawing, which was now presented again, some children found it difficult to surmise that the reason lay in the fact that, prior to the original presentation of this drawing, they had been viewing different drawings. Instead, they said that they could not imagine why they had seen different objects or they responded with vague generalities such as "Different people see different things." But, after a sufficient number of broad hints, all the subjects saw the source of the differences.

Several of the picture series in the manual of rigidity (Luchins, 1950a) have been used for similar experiments. For example, the sailor-goblet series was administered to ten pairs of New York City high-school students. One subject received the first eight cards of the series, which depicted the gradual disintegration of the picture of a sailor; the other subject received the twenty-third card down through the sixteenth card of the series that depicted the gradual disintegration of the picture of a goblet. Thus, we were attempting to set one subject to see a sailor and the other subject to see a goblet. The ninth drawing of the series was shown to both subjects at the same time. When asked to read aloud the responses to this drawing which they had written on their papers, subjects always responded in accordance with their respective sets, with one reporting that he had seen a sailor and the other reporting that he had seen a goblet. Reactions to the differences were similar to those found in the experiment using the face-bottle series and, as therein, subjects reported both percepts in subsequent drawings presented (the tenth through the fifteenth of the series). An added point of interest was that subjects generally did not report seeing a human female form, which was the most striking feature of the ninth through the fifteenth drawings for subjects who were shown only these drawings. Thus, their resolution of their differences may have led them to ignore striking features of the drawings.

Experiment 4. This experiment, which involved the series of eleven paragraphs describing Jim, was administered to ten pairs of University of Oregon undergraduates. After reading each paragraph, the subject was told to write on his paper five adjectives that best described the person he had just read about. One subject received Paragraphs 1-4 of the series, which described decreasingly extrovertive behavior; the other subject of the pair received Paragraphs 11, 10, 9, and 8, which, in that order, described decreasingly introvertive behavior. Copies of Paragraph 6 of the series were then given to both subjects at the same time. (Paragraphs 5 and 7 were omitted in order to allow sharper differences between the two subjects' impressions of Jim.) The subjects were then asked to sit near one another and to read aloud the adjectives each had written after reading Paragraph 6, a copy of which was placed so that both could see it. Reactions varied considerably. A few pairs saw no conflict between the two lists of adjectives. In these cases, the experimenter tried to make the subjects aware of differences in their lists. Most subjects, however, were immediately aware of the differences and expressed surprise at them. In some cases one subject protested that the other subject's adjectives were inappropriate for Jim. No subject said that the other subject's list of adjectives was preferable to his own. In some pairs a rather heated discussion arose as to the relative appropriateness of the two lists of adjectives. In defense of their own lists, subjects pointed to (1) Paragraph 6, noting that it contained evidence to support their adjectives, (2) their own abilities as judges of human behavior and personality, and (3) the paragraphs they had previously read about Jim. The latter point, oddly enough, was usually the last to be mentioned and in some pairs was referred to only after a hint by the experimenter. But, eventually, the members of each pair surmised that they had read different paragraphs. The experimenter then told them that all the paragraphs referred to one person, and he asked each subject to read the paragraphs which had previously been received by the other subject. On the basis of all the information they now had about Jim, the two subjects were then asked to agree on a characterization of Jim and to express this by agreeing on five adjectives that best described Jim. The list that was jointly agreed upon was generally the product of compromise; for example, taking the place of the term "friendly" in one subject's list and of the term "unfriendly" or "shy" in the other subject's list was the phrase "somewhat friendly" or "somewhat shy" in the joint list.

Experiment 5. This experiment, in which the Jim paragraphs were used, was designed to ascertain the impact on the subjects' impressions (of the person about whom they had read) exerted by the resolution of the conflict between their initial impressions. One member of each of ten pairs of University of Oregon undergraduates received the first paragraph which described extrovertive behavior by Jim; the other member received the last paragraph of the series which described introvertive behavior by Jim. Immediately after reading the respective paragraphs, each subject was requested to fill out a detailed questionnaire about Jim (Luchins, 1957a, pp. 187-89); for example, in the questionnaire the subject was directed to write a paragraph portraying his impression of Jim, to select adjectives or adjectival phrases most apt for Jim, to describe Jim's physical features, and to predict his behavior in a variety of situations. After both subjects had completed the questionnaire and the questionnaires had been collected, the procedure followed was essentially that used in Experiment 4, with the exception that no further paragraphs about Jim were given to the subjects. Thus, each subject was asked (independently) to write a list of five adjectives that best described Jim; they were then asked to read the lists aloud; after they had discovered that they had read different paragraphs, each subject was asked to read the paragraph that the other subject had received previously; then they were requested, on the basis of all the information they now had about Jim, to agree on a characterization of Jim and to express this by agreeing on five adjectives that best described Jim. As in Experiment 4, the joint list was generally the product of compromise. After the joint list had been agreed upon, each subject received another copy of the same questionnaire that he had previously answered and was asked to respond to it on the basis of all the information he now had about Jim. We compared the two questionnaires for each subject. Usually answers were somewhat different, those in the second questionnaire reflecting some influence of the second paragraph the subject had read about Jim and the list of adjectives that had been jointly agreed upon. But, for a few subjects, responses to the questionnaire were virtually unchanged despite all that had intervened between the original presentation and the re-presentation of the questionnaire. The question arises: Was this because these latter subjects rigidly adhered to their initial impressions of Jim (perhaps having agreed with the other subject prior to the second presentation of the questionnaire only to appear to be accommodating) or was it because, even though their impression of Jim may have changed, they were reluctant to reveal that their opinions had been swayed to the extent that they would give different answers to the same questionnaire?

The experiment did not end with the second opportunity to respond to the questionnaire. Instead, each subject next received a paragraph describing the behavior of a girl named Joan. The paragraph received by one subject described Joan as manifesting anti-Negro, prosegregationist behavior in a number of situations; the paragraph received by the other subject described Joan as manifesting pro-Negro, antisegrationist behavior in a number of situations. The procedure followed was analogous to that used with the Jim paragraphs; that is, each subject filled out a questionnaire about Joan, wrote a list of five adjectives that best described Joan, read his list aloud, and, after discovering that the other subject had read a different paragraph (a discovery readily made after the experience with the Jim paragraphs), read the paragraph the other had read, and they then agreed on a characterization of Joan which they expressed by agreeing on five adjectives that best described her. Finally, each responded again to the questionnaire about Joan.

For ten other pairs of University of Oregon undergraduates, the procedure was reversed so that the experience with the Joan paragraphs preceded the experience with the Jim paragraphs. It was found that the resolution of conflicts generally took more time and involved a more heated and controversial discussion in the Joan part of the experiment than in the Jim part, regardless of which part was given first. After the Joan paragraphs had been responded to, the discussion tended to be dominated by the subjects' views on the issue of school segregation or integration and the social implications of Joan's behavior while the primary issue of Joan's personality tended to fade into the background. While responses to the questionnaires concerning Joan have not yet been fully analyzed, a preliminary survey of responses suggests that subjects tended to respond to the questionnaire about Joan, the first time it was given, in terms of social stereotypes ascribed to the pro-segregationist or antisegregationist. Results also suggest that differences in a subject's initial and second responses to the questionnaire tended to be more striking when Joan was involved than when Jim was involved, regardless of whether the Joan paragraphs preceded or followed the Jim paragraphs. In short, it seems that the resolution of the conflict concerning Joan, when it finally occurred, tended to have a greater impact on the subject's impression of Joan than did the corresponding resolution of the conflict concerning Jim. The task of analyzing the data in more detail and of collecting new data has been undertaken with the assistance of William J. Meyers.

Comments. The described procedures appear to be rather fruitful experimental modes of exploring the induction and resolution of conflicts. The results to date suggest that subjects' reactions to differences in their responses to the same task as well as their preference for one or another response, may vary with different kinds of tasks. For example, we found that subjects usually stated that the $A - C$ response was better than the $B - A - 2C$ response to a critical water-jug problem and that the other subject's response to a critical word block was as good as their own, that they were willing to accept the other person's response to an ambiguous picture once supporting evidence for the percept was pointed out to them in the picture, but that they did not state that the other subject's initial response concerning an impression of a person (Jim or Joan) was more appropriate or even as appropriate as their own response. It is interesting that this varied pattern of stated preference for a response follows the same general pattern found in the conformity studies reported upon in a previous section of this chapter, where, for example, subjects stated that the direct method was better than the E method for a critical water-jug problem but that their own and the overheard response to a critical word block were equally good. These results testify to the role that the objective evidence may play in situations that involve differences of opinions.

The described procedures, which have been used with relatively few subjects, ought to be repeated with more subjects. Various experimental variations also might be attempted. It should be of interest to investigate the induction and resolution of conflict, with a given pair of subjects, first using one kind of material (for example, the word blocks) and then using another kind of material (for example, the paragraphs dealing with Jim or Joan) in order to study the transfer which occurs from one kind of material to another.

Another area for experimental variation concerns the introduction, into a situation involving the induction and resolution of conflicts, of the factors that tended to maximize or minimize E effects with the water-jug problems. What would happen if we sought to maximize (or minimize) the set for both subjects, or sought to maximize the set for one subject but to minimize it for the other, or introduced factors to extremize (maximize or minimize) the set for one subject but did not introduce extremizing factors for the other subject? What would be the influence of such factors on the resolution of the conflict? And would a given factor that is introduced to extremize the set vary in influence with different kinds of material? Such experimentation may yield further information about the domain of influence of the various factors that tended to extremize E effects with the water-jug problems.

Still another area for experimentation concerns attempts to extremize the extent to which the objective evidence is taken into account by one or both subjects.

Still other variations might focus on studying the impact on induction and resolution of conflicts which results from experimental variations of (1) the social atmosphere of the experimental situation, (2) the kinds of subjects used and the interpersonal relationships between the two members of the pair (for example, by varying subjects' ages, prestige, roles, etc.), (3) the numerosity of the group, and (4) subjects' attitudes toward the task or material (by using subjects for whom these attitudes are known—for example, by giving the Joan paragraphs to subjects whose attitudes toward school segregation are known—or by seeking to foster certain attitudes toward the task or various degrees of ego involvement on the part of one or both subjects).

It might be found that certain factors in the social atmosphere, factors relating to the size and the composition of the group, and various personal and attitudinal factors tend to extremize the conflict. It should prove of interest to attempt experimentally to pit such factors against factors that tend to extremize the extent to which objective evidence is taken into account in an attempt to determine the relative strength of various factors in the induction and resolution of conflicts. Such experimentation, it seems to us, would be particularly valuable because, in current discussion of the resolution of conflicts or tensions in group situations, the emphasis tends to be on social factors, interpersonal relationships, and "feelings," to the relative neglect of the role played by objective evidence.

The Artificiality of the Selected Case

The introduction of this monograph, which contains some examples of habituation and rigidity manifested by individuals and groups in "real life" situations, may have developed an expectation in the reader that definitive answers would be given regarding the operation and control of rigidity in these life situations. At the risk of disappointing the reader, we might say that scientific research does not have to lead to practical applications. However, we believe that it behooves researchers, particularly when they try to enlist interest in their research, as we have done, by using examples from life, to be concerned with the relevancy of their findings to life situations. That the case selected for intensive study is in some respects a rather artificial laboratory situation is recognized. But this does not mean that knowledge derived from study of the selected case is necessarily devoid of relevancy to instances of more natural habituation and rigidity operating outside of the laboratory. Certainly physicists, biologists, and other scientists have in artificial situations discovered and formulated laws that proved adequate to account for events occurring in more natural situations.

The problem of the practical application of laboratory findings is a problem in its own right which must, we believe, be met anew in each study. Throughout this monograph we have tried to indicate implications of a practical nature that seemed to stem from or to be related to the research findings. But we are far from satisfied with the practical applications thus far made of the results. Careful observation and research are needed to determine, for example, whether or not factors that were found to maximize (or minimize) E effects in the water-jar problems operate similarly outside of the laboratory. In general, after a laboratory study is completed, there still remains the need to study the applicability of the findings to more natural conditions as well as the need to determine the kind of changes that should be introduced in conclusions based on laboratory findings so that the conclusions may be applicable to more natural conditions. The study of how to vary conclusions or formulations derived from laboratory research so as to maximize their practical applicability may be regarded as in keeping with (or at least an extension of) the variational approach to research. Such study may in turn lead to the discovery of crucial variables involved in the phenomena and add to the body of knowledge that the laboratory studies have yielded.

In the attempt to bridge the gap between laboratory conditions and more natural conditions, another approach may be explored; namely, one may take a close look at the particular laboratory situation with which one is dealing in an endeavor to ascertain what experimental variations should be introduced in order to approximate the situation to more natural situations. Such variations can be introduced without vitiating the benefits of experimental control and systematic manipulation of variables that are the advantages of laboratory studies. As an example, let us turn to the selected case and ask: How do conditions here differ from "real life" situations in which habituation and rigidity are manifested? Perhaps several differences occur to the reader. We mention one difference that occurred to us and illustrate how this difference may suggest research via a variational approach.

Experimental Attempts to Modify the Homogeneous and Serial Nature of the Selected Case

It is characteristic of the selected case that the events (E tasks) in which the Einstellung develops follow one another in immediate succession. But is this characteristic of all life situations in which habituation and rigidity are observed? Certainly not. Events in which a habit or a set develops may be (and usually are) separated by a variety of other events. Similarly, the events in which habituation and rigidity operate do not necessarily come one after another in immediate succession as do the test problems. Indeed, events in which other habits develop and operate usually are intermingled among events in which a particular habit develops and operates. In short, the selected case has a homogeneous and serial nature—similar-appearing events occurring in immediate succession—while "real life" situations in which habits or sets develop and operate may lack the homogeneous or serial quality.

With this in mind, we were interested in what a variational approach to the selected case can do to approximate more closely in the laboratory to "real life" conditions that do not have a homogeneous or a serial quality. A few preliminary steps that have already been taken will be sketched.

There are activities that an individual performs just once (or perhaps twice) a day that have become habituated. He may get out of bed in the morning or prepare for bed in a ritualized manner or follow set patterns in eating breakfast or in leaving for work, etc. As a rough attempt to approximate to conditions that prevail when a habituated way is developed of dealing with events that occur once or perhaps twice daily, the water-jar E tasks were presented so that the subject received only one or two a day (rather than receiving them in immediate succession).

In 1937, a classroom teacher presented the tasks to a New York City sixth-grade class. On Wednesday, the class received the first illustrative problem and the first E task, the solutions to which were illustrated as usual; on Thursday and Friday, the second and third E tasks respectively; on the following Monday and Tuesday, the two remaining E tasks; and, on Wednesday, all the test problems. An attempt was made to present the problems at about the same time each day. The usual maximum of two and a half minutes was allowed per problem. Failures to solve the E tasks were more frequent than under the usual method of administration; of the thirty-six pupils in the class, only twelve solved all the E problems. A few pupils were absent on certain days and did not receive all of the E problems, but even those who received all of them showed more failures than were usually found under the customary mode of administration. The twelve who solved all the E tasks showed E effects that were within the range found in the basic study:

$$C_1C_2: 83\% \ E \quad \text{Ext.}: 67\% \ F \quad C_3C_4: 67\% \ E$$

Of the twelve, eight solved all the criticals in the E manner and failed the extinction task. Comments of these eight subjects indicated that most of them had generalized a rule, thought that they were practicing a rule, or thought that they had learned a method which they were to practice.

Two decades later, in 1957, through the cooperation of Martin Elle, a graduate student of the School of Education at the University of Oregon, it was arranged to have two teachers present the problems over a period of several days to their classes in Springfield, Oregon. To a fifth-grade class, the teacher presented the E tasks and the test tasks in the usual manner and order but at the rate of one a day. Of thirty-two pupils, only nine solved all the E tasks. E effects for these nine pupils were less than those usually obtained under the customary mode of administration:

$$C_1C_2: 60\% \ E \quad \text{Ext.}: 0\% \ F \quad C_3C_4: 30\% \ E$$

It is not known why these nine Springfield pupils showed so much lower E effects in the extinction task and subsequent criticals than did subjects in the afore-mentioned New York City sixth-grade class who solved all the E problems that were received over a period of days. Perhaps the fact that only one problem per day was given to the Springfield pupils influenced the results. One wonders whether differences in methods of teaching arithmetic that have developed during the past two decades may also have influenced the results.

To a fourth-grade class in the same Springfield school, another classroom teacher presented the water-jar problems in the usual manner and order but at the rate of one or two a day. Of thirty-one pupils, twelve solved all the E tasks and these twelve showed somewhat lower E effects than were usually obtained but not as low as the fifth-grade class:

$$C_1C_2: 67\% \ E \quad \text{Ext.}: 17\% \ F \quad C_3C_4: 37\% \ E$$

We mention in passing that here the experiment had been planned originally so that only one problem a day would be given but the fourth-graders' clamor for more problems led the classroom teacher to give them two on most days. Such is the stuff of which experimental variations are born.

An exploratory experiment was concerned with what happens when events in which one Einstellung develops are intermingled with events in which another Einstellung develops. Based on the paradigm of the water-jar experiment, a series of two-jar problems was devised in which the E method was a two-jar method and the direct method was the filling of one jar. The E problems of this new series were interspersed among the usual E problems, and the new test problems were interspersed among the usual test problems. The resulting "interlaced" series was presented by one of the writers to a New York City sixth-grade class with a maximum time allotment per problem of two and one half minutes. All the problems were given in one session. Of forty-eight pupils in the class (all of them with I.Q.'s above 110), only twenty solved all the E problems in both series. E effects for these twenty were as follows:

Usual series ....C_1C_2: 90% E Ext.: 80% F C_3C_4: 90% E
New series ....C_1C_2: 75% E Ext.: 55% F C_3C_4: 60% E

Here we see that two rather strong sets developed and operated in an "interlaced" manner.

Another experiment involved the "interlacing" of the face-bottle series of pictures with the lady-in-the-bathtub series (Luchins, 1950a). Twenty-four Oregon adults to whom the "interlaced" series was presented tended to develop two sets, but the sets were somewhat weaker (that is, the emerging percepts were reported earlier) than when the component series were presented separately to similar subjects.

Subjects who participated in the interlacing experiments were questioned after the sessions. Comments of those who showed E effects implied that many of them had categorized the problems (or the pictures) as belonging to certain classes or types (e.g., the two-jar class and the three-jar class; the face type and the lady-in-the-bathtub type) and had responded to each problem (or picture) in terms of the class or type to which it belonged.

Comments. Comments made by subjects who showed E effects in the interlacing variations and in the variations wherein one or two problems were given daily suggest that usually they categorized the problems or pictures as belonging to particular types or classes. This implies that categorization may lead to mechanization and may not be the most adequate way of facing the problems or the pictures; one may become blinded by categories and by concepts based on categorization or classification. This is a point that merits attention since some psychologists regard categorization and classification as the essence of concept formation and of thinking while others do not. (Cf. our discussion of thinking in Chapter VI.)

When the problems were presented over a period of several days, the 1957 results (but not the 1937 results) suggested that it might be more difficult to develop an Einstellung than when the problems followed one immediately after another. Perhaps if more E tasks were given at daily intervals, stronger E effects would be found; that is, more repetitions may be needed to foster a set when the problems are given at daily intervals. Perhaps if subjects were directed to generalize a rule, more E effects would result under the one-problem-daily routine. Further studies along these lines, using water-jar problems as well as other material in the rigidity manual (Luchins, 1950a), and using adults as well as children as subjects, may reveal the relationship between the development of E effects and the length of the interval between set-inducing tasks. We are particularly interested in whether or not factors that were found to work in a maximizing or minimizing direction when the problems were given in one session will be found to operate similarly when an interval of a day (or more) intervenes between presentation of the problems. Such studies possibly may throw light on the selected case as well as on what happens when habituation develops in activities that occur once or twice daily (or at less frequent intervals).

Experiments are planned in which three or more picture series are interlaced or in which water-jug problems are interspersed among a picture series and/or the "Jim" series having to do with the formation of impressions of personality. We are interested in such questions as these: Is the strength of Einstellung developed in each series a function of the *number* of interlaced series? Is it a function of the *similarity* of the various series? If the number of E tasks in one series is increased, while the numbers in the other interlaced series are left invariant, will a stronger Einstellung develop for the series that has the most E tasks? What happens when an interlaced series is presented under the one-problem-daily routine? What factors maximize and minimize E effects in the interlaced series? How do these compare with factors that maximize and minimize E effects in the basic experiment? And will factors that work in a minimizing or maximizing direction in the selected case influence results in interlaced-series experiments?

Similarity of the Basic Experiment
to Studies of Judgment Scales

The Einstellung phenomenon is in many respects similar to phenomena studied under the rubrics of judgment scales and frames of ref-

erence. In fact, the basic experiment was originally viewed as an out-
growth of research on judgment scales and was seen against the historical background of such psychophysical studies as those mentioned
below (Luchins, 1939).

Müller and Schumann (1898) performed an experiment on the judgment of weights wherein the subject had the task of lifting two weights
and stating which was the heavier. The subject first compared the standard weight, 676 grams, with various other weights, the heaviest of which
was 876 grams. He then compared the standard weight thirty times
with a weight of 2,476 grams. After this, he compared the standard
weight once with each of the following weights: 926, 876, and 826
grams. In the last three comparisons, the hand that held the variable
weight flew up in the air in an exaggerated fashion and the subject reported (erroneously) that each of the variable weights was lighter than
the standard weight. Müller and Schumann concluded that the subject,
in comparing the standard weight with the weight of 2,476 grams, had
developed a motor adjustment, which they called an Einstellung, and
that the subject carried the Einstellung over to the last three comparisons.

Fernberger (1931), using the method of single stimuli (one weight
was lifted at a time), asked a subject to give an "absolute" judgment of
each of a series of seven weights, ranging from 84 to 108 grams, in
terms of whether it was light, intermediate, or heavy. After the subject
had judged each weight many times, he was asked to lift, first, a standard
weight of 100 grams and, then, one of the weights in the first series, and
to state whether the latter weight was lighter than, equal to, or heavier
than the standard weight (relative judgment). Fernberger found that
"a definition of judgment [was] carried over to the relative judgment
from the absolute judgment" (1931, p. 578).

Using the method of single stimuli, Wever and Zener (1938) repeatedly presented a series of weights in random order, followed by
another such series. Each weight was to be described as heavy or light.
When a weight, such as 96 grams, occurred in a series ranging from 84
to 100 grams and then appeared in a heavier series ranging from 92 to
108 grams, the subject, in the latter series, persisted for a while in judging the weight with reference to the first series and therefore referred to
it as "heavy."

Pratt (1933), employing the method of single stimuli, asked a subject to judge the intensities of sounds in terms of one of a series of nine
values. When a series of "loud" intensities were followed by a series
of "soft" intensities, it was found that the subject's judgment of a
stimulus was influenced by his experience with the preceding stimuli.
Pratt concluded that "a general level of reference built up in the past

... serves as the basis of the alignment of all impressions constituting a more or less homogeneous mass" (1933, p. 808).

It may be said that in each of these experiments the subject developed a judgment scale or frame of reference (or Einstellung) that carried over and influenced subsequent judgments. (Correspondingly, in the basic experiment, the subject may be said to have developed a frame of reference in the E problems which carried over to the test problems and influenced his judgment of them.) Characteristic of each of these experiments is the serial quality that was noted as characteristic of the selected case; that is, stimuli of a particular kind follow one immediately after another in the development and functioning of a judgment scale or frame of reference. This serial quality characterizes much of the experimental work dealing with judgment scales and frames of reference. But judgment scales and frames of reference (whether or not they have the character of an Einstellung) are developed in life situations that do not necessarily consist of homogeneous events that follow one another in immediate succession or even at regular intervals. It is conceivable that an incomplete picture is being obtained when experimentation is restricted (or largely restricted) to homogeneous events that occur in series. From such restricted experimentation, we do not necessarily learn enough about how judgment scales develop and operate when events are not homogeneous or are not in series.

We are suggesting that a variational approach should be used in conducting experimental variations of judgment studies. One research task might be to change the homogeneity characteristic of most of these studies (for example, by "interlacing" weights with sounds and odors, all of which have to be judged, rather than using only weights or only sounds or only odors). This might be a step in the direction of approximating in the laboratory to the more natural conditions under which frames of reference and judgment scales operate in "real life" situations. To approximate in the laboratory to the more natural conditions of "real life" judgment situations seems particularly important since concepts derived from laboratory judgment studies are being applied to "real life" judgment situations. In recent years such concepts have also been applied increasingly to varied social phenomena. Sherif and Cantril (1947) and Volkmann (1951) have pointed out some implications of scales of judgment for social psychology. And Sherif and Sherif (1956) have utilized concepts stemming from judgment studies as cores around which to organize phenomena of social psychology. Finally, to note but one more example, the literature on conformity behavior has been integrated and organized (by Mouton and Blake, 1957) in terms of Helson's concept of adaptation level (1947, 1948), a concept intimately related to judgment scales.

Conclusion

In this chapter we have led the reader into various research trails that lie in or are connected with the frontiers of research on the selected case. This was done with the hope that some of our readers will help to explore these trails and will seek new ones. We are well aware that more questions have been raised than have been answered. But this, we believe, is not necessarily a shortcoming. It is our conviction that the virtue of scientific endeavor is not so much that it finds answers but that it searches for answers. If this monograph will stimulate others to search, then one of its purposes will have been fulfilled.

CHAPTER XXIII

PSYCHOLOGICAL RIGIDITY COMPARED WITH ELASTIC DEFORMATIONS IN PHYSICS

A THOROUGHGOING variational approach should not be confined to one branch of psychology or even to psychology proper, but should include examination of other disciplines to see what they may have to offer concerning the investigation and interpretation of the psychological phenomenon under consideration. There are sound grounds for such a broadening of the approach: communication between disciplines is desirable; the concepts of other disciplines can sometimes be utilized with considerable benefit in one's own field; it is advantageous for psychologists to become acquainted with what is happening in other sciences.

Turning to physics, we found that the phenomena with which physicists deal under the heading of "elasticity" bear striking analogies to the phenomena with which psychologists deal under the heading of "rigidity." Although we are aware of the possible danger of being misled by analogies, it seems to us that the study of the elasticity of substances by physicists provides a rich storehouse of germinal ideas for the development of concepts and methods in the psychological study of rigidity.

RIGIDITY, ELASTICITY, AND PLASTICITY

Rigidity

In discussing elastic phenomena, the physicist sometimes employs the term "rigidity," referring to the resistance of a body to the influence of applied forces.* This is similar to the definition of rigidity offered by some psychologists. Thus, Lewin (1936, p. 218) writes that the greater the forces necessary to overcome boundaries (barriers, walls), the more rigid the boundaries are. He defines "fluidity," the obverse of rigidity, in these terms: the smaller the forces necessary (other conditions being equal) to produce a certain change in a thing or medium, the more fluid the thing or medium is (1936, p. 218). Similarly, Cattell and Tiner state that, "so long as we adhere to standard English, rigidity must

---

* In mechanics, that branch of physics which deals with the motions of bodies and the causes of changes in these motions, the physicist is also concerned with *rigid* bodies. A "rigid body" may be defined as a body which does not change its shape or size as it moves in space. We are not here directly concerned with this conception of rigidity.

[575]

be used to mean stiffness, i.e., a resistance to forces attempting to produce change" (1949, p. 321). On the other hand, there are definitions
of rigidity offered by psychologists, e.g., Goldstein's definition of rigidity in terms of concrete rather than abstract behavior (1941), which
do not seem similar to the physicist's conception of rigidity as resistance
to the effects of applied forces.

It is interesting to note that physicists consider that nothing known
in nature is completely rigid, that solid bodies invariably distort under
the influence of applied forces, although sometimes the distortions are
so small as to require extremely sensitive instruments for their detec-
tion. But some psychologists speak of "rigid" persons or of "nonrigid"
persons as if rigidity were an absolute which one either possesses or
lacks.

Elasticity

"Elasticity" has been defined in physics texts as that property of
matter by virtue of which a body endeavors to return to its original
shape when strained, the recovery taking place when the disturbing
forces are removed (Duncan and Starling, 1922, pp. 153-57), or as the
tendency of a body to return to its original shape or size after having
been stretched, compressed, or deformed (Chambers, 1940, p. 284),
or, more briefly, as simply the tendency to recover from distortion
(Duff, 1909, pp. 106-15). Similar definitions have been offered in
some psychological writings. For example, Lewin defines "elasticity"
as the "tendency of a changed region to return to its original state"
(1936, p. 217). Cattell and Tiner (1949, p. 322) note that, when there
is a tendency to return to an original position after change has been
produced, then the concept of elasticity must be invoked.

Plasticity

"Plasticity," as used in the natural sciences, has been defined as that
property of a material which enables its shape to be changed by a slight
pressure or tension and the changed shape to be retained when the
pressure or tension is released (Miall, 1940). Plasticity, so defined,
involves two distinct properties: (1) a readiness to be changed by
applied forces, which may be considered as low rigidity or as the obverse of rigidity, and (2) a tendency to retain the change (not to recover completely), which may be considered as low elasticity or as the
obverse of elasticity. An analogous definition of "psychological plasticity" has been offered by Lewin. He writes that the plasticity of a psychological region "corresponds to the ease of producing a relatively
lasting and stable change in its structure" (1936, p. 216) and notes that

plasticity involves both fluidity (the obverse of psychical rigidity) and elasticity.

It is clear, from the manner in which plasticity has been defined in the natural sciences and by Kurt Lewin, that it cannot be regarded as simply the obverse of rigidity, since plasticity involves not only a tendency to change under the influence of applied forces but also a tendency for the change to be retained when the forces are removed. But other psychologists have used the term "plasticity" as precisely the opposite of rigidity. Thus, Cattell (1950, p. 208) refers to plasticity as a lack of rigidity, and Werner (1940, p. 55) employs the term as the obverse of rigidity.

Nature and Measurement of Stresses, Strains, and Stress-Strain Ratios

In physics the term "strain" has been used to denote a change or distortion which occurs in the form or in the dimensions of a body when external forces are applied to it. Stretching of a wire, bending of a beam, compression of a gas into a smaller volume or expansion into a larger volume, constitute some examples of strains. A body is said to be in a state of "stress" due to the action of external forces on it, if there are internal forces between the contiguous parts of the body in addition to whatever internal forces there may have been before the external forces were applied. The ratio of the magnitude of the stress to the accompanying strain, a ratio which is called a "modulus" (or measure or coefficient) of elasticity, is employed in analyzing elastic deformations.

A possible analogy for psychology suggests itself. If "stress" is regarded as related to the intensity of the external force that is intended to produce change and if "strain" is interpreted as the extent of the accompanying psychological change (say, the change in the individual's behavior or in his personality structure), then "rigidity," at least as studied by some psychologists, may be interpreted as involving a stress-strain relationship. For a given external force or for a given "stress," the psychologist is concerned with determining the concomitant psychological change or "strain." The lower the extent of the strain for a given intensity of external force or of stress, the greater the rigidity. We shall pursue this analogy further in order to derive some implications for psychology from the manner in which the physicist studies stress-strain relationships.

Stresses and External Forces

In Physics. One of the problems in the theory of elasticity is that of developing methods for predicting the state of stress which results when specified forces are applied to a body of specified form. In some cases, e.g., the stretching of a wire by an attached weight, the stress is equal to the external force per unit of area; in other cases, e.g., the bending of a beam by a weight that acts at some point, the stress does not bear a simple relation to the external force (Duff, 1909, pp. 106-15). It should be remembered that moduli of elasticity refer to *stress-strain* relationships and not to *external force*–strain relationships.

In Psychology. The psychologist who is concerned with studying psychological change or resistance to change might do well to study the relationship of the change (strain) to the *stress* induced by the external force rather than the relationship of the change to the external force itself. But what is to constitute the psychological analogue of what the physicist describes as stress? We suggest that one might equate the "external force" to the force in the "geographical world" (Koffka, 1935) while regarding "stress" as the corresponding force in the individual's "behavioral world." That two individuals show different changes (strains) under the influence of presumably equal external forces (e.g., certain directions issued by the experimenter) may in part be due to the fact that the external forces have set up different stresses in them. Attempts to determine the relationship of strain to stress would therefore have to be preceded by a determination of what kind and degree of stress have been induced. Psychologists would thus be faced with a problem analogous to that involved in the theory of elasticity; namely, the development of methods for determining the state of stress which results when specified external forces are applied to a given individual.

Perhaps an illustration will help to clarify our point. The numerous investigations concerned with the effects on rigidity of psychological stress, tension, frustration, etc., have utilized various kinds of external forces, including interpolated unsolvable tasks, the experimenter's hostile attitude, unfavorable interpretation of test results, etc. In some studies it was assumed that these external forces necessarily produced psychological stress so that all individuals who were subjected to these external forces were considered as a group manifesting (presumably equal) stress, while individuals who were subjected to external forces of a contrary nature (e.g., interpolated solvable tasks, the experimenter's friendly attitude, favorable interpretation of test results) were all considered as a group manifesting little or no psychological stress. Here psychological stress was more or less equated with external force. But it was noted by some of the investigators that not all subjects who received the forces intended to produce stress necessarily reacted in the same way to these forces, while some of those who were in the so-called "nonstress group" actually seemed upset, frustrated, etc. In other words, there did not always seem to be a simple relationship between applied force and induced stress. Utilization of a rating scale to measure the degree of frustration (Christie, 1949) may be interpreted as an attempt to determine induced stress in the individual case rather than to rest content with equating external force and resulting psychological stress.

Perhaps greater progress may be made in the investigation of rigidity when psychologists substitute for the study of external force–change relationships the study of stress-change relationships, a substitution that is contingent on the discovery and application of methods of determining the kind and intensity of stress induced in an individual by a given external force.

Classification of Stresses and Strains

In Physics. A distinction is drawn among different kinds of strains depending on the nature of the change produced in the substance. For example, a strain that consists in a change of shape only without any change of volume is called a "shear" or "shearing strain"; a strain that consists in a change of volume only without any change of shape is described frequently as "volume strain" or "volumetric strain"; more common are strains involving changes of both volume and shape. Strains are also classified as homogeneous or heterogeneous depending on whether or not the nature and magnitude of the strain are the same at all points in the body. Examples of homogeneous strains are found in the stretching of a wire, the compression of a rod, or the subjection to pressure of a liquid or gas. Examples of heterogeneous strains are found in the twisting of a rod where the strain is greatest at the surface and least at the center and in the bending of a beam which is accompanied by stretching on the convex side and compression on the concave side.

Stresses are often classified in terms of the kind of change or strain they produce. For example, a "shearing stress" is one which produces a shearing strain. Stress is said to be uniform if equal areas at every part of the body on which the external forces act sustain equal stress; otherwise, the stress is said to be varying or variable.

In Psychology. It seems to us that there is an interesting implication here for psychologists. Consider firstly how psychologists tend to classify external forces which they usually employ in place of stresses. Sometimes it is the *order* of the forces which is the main concern, e.g., whether two skills or habits or forces occur in alternation or in succession, and the effect on behavior of a difference in order. At times the concern is with the similarity between forces, or with the differences between forces, or with the interference of forces. Psychological research on rigidity may conceivably become more fruitful if we distinguish among external forces in terms of the *changes* or *strains* they produce. Does the external force (or, better yet, the stress it induces) tend to change a habit or a process or a personality region? What is the nature, direction, and intensity of the change? Is the change homogeneous in the sense that all aspects of the habit (or process or personality region) are equally affected or would it be better described as heterogeneous? Attention to such questions may conceivably yield greater insight into the stress-strain relationships involved in psychological rigidity.

Elastic Limit

In Physics. There are strains from which a body completely recovers in the course of time in the sense that, gradually or rapidly, it returns to its original form; that is, to the form it had prior to the strain. The greatest intensity of strain which a body may undergo and completely recover from is called the body's "elastic limit" for that kind of strain; corresponding stress is called the "limiting stress." The elastic limit for any given kind of strain may differ widely for different substances. Thus, rubber may be greatly extended and still completely recover its original form, while the limit of elasticity for the extension of glass and ivory is much smaller. For stresses beyond the elastic limit, a given substance fails to recover completely. To use the physicist's terminology—which here shows a striking similarity to the psychologist's—stresses beyond the elastic limit always result in a "permanent set" from which complete recovery never occurs.

In Psychology. The greatest intensity of strain which an individual may undergo and completely recover from might be considered as the psychological analogue of a body's elastic limit for a certain strain. Determination of the existence and meaningfulness of the psychological counterpart of an elastic limit requires attention to problems such as these: How is one to measure recovery from "strain" or psychological change? How long a period of time should be permitted to elapse before it is determined whether or not the individual has recovered completely? Does every psychological change, no matter how low its intensity, leave some permanent effects, some degree of "permanent set"? If this last question is answered affirmatively, then complete recovery from strain would be a meaningless concept in psychology and the psychological analogue of the elastic limit would be nonexistent. One might seek to cope with this difficulty by modifying "complete recovery" so as to allow for some minimum effects of the strain. The psychological analogue of the elastic limit would then be the greatest or maximum intensity of a given kind of psychological change which an individual may experience and still not show any aftereffects from other than the (previously stipulated) minimum effects.

Once the psychological analogue of the elastic limit is defined and its existence granted, there remains the problem of measuring intensity of psychological change along a gradient in order to determine the greatest intensity of a particular kind of strain from which an individual "recovers completely" in the sense that he shows only the (previously stipulated) minimum effects. For example, in the case of the Einstellung phenomenon, we might be interested in determining the largest number of set-inducing problems which can be given to an individual and from which he still recovers, in the sense that he employs a direct method in a subsequent critical or extinction task. It may turn out that there is no consistent relationship between the number of set-inducing problems given to an individual and the degree of recovery which he manifests. More generally, it may be found, upon investigation, that recovery from psychological change or strain is not necessarily an increasing, decreasing, or monotonic function of the intensity of the strain. It is conceivable that an individual may recover from one intensity of strain and yet fail to recover from a lower intensity of the same kind of strain, a finding which of course would complicate the problem of the nature and meaningfulness of the "elastic limit" for this kind of strain. Nonetheless, it seems to us that some provocative research may be stimulated by attempts to face problems that concern the existence and meaningfulness of the psychological counterpart of the elastic limit.

Elastic Aftereffect

In Physics. From strain within the elastic limit the strained material recovers in the course of time and there is no permanent set. But frequently the removal of the force is not accompanied by immediate recovery. Rather, after removal of the external force, there remains what the physicist refers to as a small "temporary set" from which the substance only gradually recovers. This slow recovery from temporary set is called an "elastic aftereffect" or *"Nachwirkung."* It is shown by rubber, glass, and other substances consisting of mixtures of diverse molecules, whereas crystals and quartz threads do not show it.

In Psychology. As an example of a psychological phenomenon analogous to what the physicist calls a "temporary set," one might consider an Einstellung or other momentary set, as opposed to habits which are

more permanent and enduring in nature. Slow recovery from temporary set, or the elastic aftereffect, may be said to have its analogue in
such phenomena as afterimages and figural aftereffects (Köhler and
Wallach, 1944) in perception and in retroactive-inhibition phenomena
in learning. Numerous other examples could also be cited.

Again, an existence problem may be regarded as involved: Is it possible, in psychological phenomena, to have only a *temporary* set from
which one *completely* recovers in the course of time? Modification of the
criterion of complete recovery may be needed before we can assume
the existence of a "temporary" set. This issue aside, it seems to us that
there may be some value in systematically investigating the kinds and
intensities of psychological stresses and strains which seem to lead to
phenomena analogous to what the physicist describes as temporary sets
and elastic aftereffects.

Relationship of Strain to Stress

In Physics. In 1678 Robert Hooke enunciated his famous law of the
proportionality of stress and strain. Hooke's law states that, *within the
elastic limit,* stress is proportional to strain; that is, within the elastic
limit, the ratio of the magnitude of the stress to the accompanying strain
is constant, the exact value of the constant being dependent on the
particular substance and on the particular kind of strain; but, beyond
the elastic limit, this proportionality of stress and strain no longer holds.

As an illustration of what happens when a substance is strained beyond the elastic limit (beyond the range for which Hooke's law holds),
consider the stretching of wire. Let a force be applied to the wire which
stretches it beyond its elastic limit. If this force is increased, the wire
will be elongated in *greater proportion* for each successive *equal increase* in the force; the ratio of the stress to the strain, in other words,
will no longer be constant. Should the force be decreased somewhat
once the elastic limit is passed, the strain will nonetheless continue to
increase but at a diminished rate. When the force is weakened sufficiently, the strain will cease to increase and, when the applied force is
removed entirely, the wire will contract somewhat but will retain a
large permanent set. Thereafter it will act like a different wire with a
new elastic limit.

Suppose that the applied force, after stretching the wire beyond its
elastic limit, continues to increase in intensity. The strain will then increase rapidly. Once a certain intensity of strain, called the "yield
point," is surpassed, the strain will continue to increase even if the
force is not increased until at last the wire "necks in" and breaks. Beyond the yield point, the wire flows much like a very viscous fluid.

In Psychology. As a task for psychologists we propose the investigation of whether an analogue of Hooke's law holds for psychological phenomena. Within limits, does the resulting psychological change tend to be proportional to the magnitude of the stress or to the intensity of the external force? As in physics, the exact nature of the proportion may vary for different individuals and for different kinds of psychological change.

Even more general than the task of determining whether an analogue of Hooke's law holds is the task of investigating the effect on psychological change of increments or decrements in the intensity of the applied force or in the intensity of the induced stress. This would require systematic variations of the intensity of the applied force or of the induced stress along a more or less continuous gradient. At various points along this gradient, does an increment lead to an increase or decrease in psychological strain, to no apparent psychological effect, or to a qualitative change in the nature of the psychological change? For example, as the intensity of anger-arousing stimuli is increased, an individual may grow increasingly angry; but, with still greater increases in the intensity of the stimuli, he may calm down or manifest behavior qualitatively distinct from anger.

Investigation of stress-strain relationships by varying the intensity of the stress (or, at least, of the external force) may reveal the existence of the psychological analogue of the "yield point" (the point beyond which the specimen of wire, for example, necks in and breaks). There are cases in which it would seem that only a small additional force—akin to the proverbial straw on the camel's back—suffices to lead to great increases in psychological reaction, to "neurotic breakdowns" or other severe reactions. Perhaps the reason for the remarkable psychological strain which is seemingly produced by a small increment in applied force may be explained on the ground that the increment comes at a time when existing psychological strain has reached the "yield point" or has passed it.

Stress-Strain Ratios

In Physics. As noted, within the elastic limit, the ratio of the magnitude of the stress to the accompanying strain has been found to be constant. This ratio is called the modulus or measure or coefficient of elasticity and, for a given substance, depends upon the particular kind of strain involved. Since there is a large variety of forms of strain, there is a correspondingly large number of moduli of elasticity. We cite three examples of these moduli. The "bulk modulus," involved when the strain is one of volume only, is the ratio of the stress per unit of area to the change of volume per unit of volume. The "rigidity modulus" (also called the "shear modulus"), applicable when the strain is one of shape only, is the ratio of the intensity of the shearing stress to the shear (change of shape) corresponding to this stress. "Young's modulus" pertains to the stretching of a uniform wire or rod; it is the ratio of the measure of the stress (the pull per unit of area) to the measure of the stretch (the extension per unit of length).

What we wish to emphasize is that there is no *one* stress-strain relationship which is generally characteristic of a given substance. A substance may have one bulk modulus, a completely different shear modulus, an unrelated Young's modulus, etc.

In Psychology. It is tempting to draw possible analogies for psychology. If the relatively simple substance with which the physicist deals is not characterized by one stress-strain ratio (even within its elastic limits), then it may well be that the far more complex human being does not have a stress-strain ratio which is generally characteristic of him. Perhaps the human individual, like the substances with which the physicists deal, shows various unrelated stress-change ratios and not one constant stress-strain ratio. In other words, he may not show what has been called a "general factor of rigidity," a factor necessarily characteristic of all or much of his behavior. That psychologists who have been searching for such a general rigidity factor do not seem to have been very successful in locating it, may perhaps be due to the fact that such a factor simply does not exist.

There remains the problem of determining the psychological analogues, if any, of the various moduli of elasticity. Tentatively, one might consider as analogues the various rigidities and rigidity factors which have been proposed by psychologists. The list is long and varied. It includes structural rigidity, disposition rigidity, perceptual rigidity, motor rigidity, ideational inertia, ego rigidity, superego rigidity, and numerous others. Some of the proposed rigidities and rigidity factors seem to be based on so-called *psychological processes* such as motor, nonmotor, perceptual, and ideational processes; some seem to be based on various *abilities*, e.g., the ability to form new habits; still others seem to pertain mainly to different "compartments" of the individual, e.g., ego, superego. It is difficult to distinguish among them on the basis of the *kind of psychological change* produced in the individual. If such a distinction could be drawn, it might help us to determine which of the proposed rigidities and rigidity factors may be considered as distinct rigidity "moduli" in the sense that they constitute distinct stress–psychological change ratios (or, at least, external force–psychological change ratios), which fail to meet this criterion at all, and which may be subsumed under the same modulus.

The thesis that for any one individual there may exist a variety of psychological stress-strain relationships, a variety of rigidity moduli, may prove a means of reconciling apparent discrepancies resulting from different approaches to the study of rigidity. One may refer here to the controversy between Werner (1946a) and Kounin (1948). Perhaps one could get to the roots of this controversy, as well as of other controversial discussions concerning rigidity, by considering what kind of psychological stress-strain relationship, what kind of rigidity modulus, is involved in a particular approach to the study of rigidity. From this point of view, the approach of Lewin (1935) and Kounin (1941a and 1941b) may be interpreted as concerned with the change or resistance to change of personality *structures* or *regions*. Werner (1940, 1946b) and others who regard rigidity as a lack of adaptability or a lack of variability of response, may be considered to be dealing with the resistance to change of various *responses* or *performances*. Those who deal with rigidity in terms of habit interference, who are concerned with so-called "creative effort rigidity" (e.g., Cattell and Tiner, 1949), may be regarded as dealing with resistance to change of various *habits*. And, to give a final illustration, those concerned with sensory rigidity or with "process-momentum rigidity" may be considered to be dealing with resistance to change of various *processes*. Each of these approaches may actually be concerned with different rigidity moduli. That the various approaches have yielded some apparently contradictory results (e.g., that rigidity as dealt with by Lewin and Kounin seems to increase with age, while rigidity as dealt with by Werner seems to decrease with age) can perhaps best be understood by considering the different approaches to be dealing with different, not necessarily related, stress-strain relationships or rigidity moduli. That an individual does not necessarily show similar results as measured by the different approaches —that he shows what appears to be a lack of consistency—may simply mean that the individual's various rigidity moduli have different values. But this is no more cause for controversial discussion than, say, the fact that a substance with which the physicist deals has a bulk modulus which differs from its shear modulus and from its Young's modulus, etc.

At the present time we are not prepared to defend the thesis that the various approaches to rigidity are tapping (or at least attempting to tap) different rigidity moduli. We are suggesting that each of the approaches be studied with the aim of determining whether it is concerned with a rigidity modulus or a set of moduli and, if so, how the modulus (or moduli) compares with that involved in another approach. Investigation along these lines may conceivably yield some insights into each of the approaches and point to the fundamental bases of controversies among the proponents of the various approaches.

Determination of Stress-Strain Ratios

In Physics. In order to determine a substance's modulus for a given
kind of strain, the physicist varies the intensity of stresses *for that substance* and measures the resulting strain. He does not, it should be
noted, seek to keep the stress constant while varying the kinds of substances studied.

In Psychology. Psychologists in their study of rigidity tend to keep
the external force or test situation more or less constant while varying
the populations to whom the force is applied. If they are to follow a procedure analogous to that used by the physicist, psychologists will have
to concentrate on the individual and subject him to various intensities
of stress or of external force and note the resulting effects. Their task,
then, will not be that of comparing an individual's "rigidity score" on
a given test or test situation with the scores made by other individuals
but, rather, that of comparing the "rigidity score" or the stress-strain
ratio an individual shows in one situation with the scores or ratios which
the same individual shows as the situation is systematically varied. In
brief, it will call for systematic experimentation and investigation of the
individual case, for what we have called a variational approach to the
individual case.

We recall that in physics strains of sufficient intensity—beyond the
elastic limit for a given substance—may so affect the substance, e.g., a
wire, as to change it for all purposes into a new substance with a new
elastic limit and new stress-strain ratios. The psychologist who is
searching for rigidity moduli can draw a possible moral: psychological
strains or experiences of one kind or another may so affect the individual as to render him a "new person," in the sense that they change his
stress-strain ratios or rigidity moduli and possibly change the psychological analogues of the elastic limits. In brief, the moduli of elasticity
of the wire (or similar substances) are not immune from the effects
of the strains or "experiences" to which the wire is subjected. Analogously, the rigidity moduli of an individual may be affected by various
experiences to which he is subjected. One of the psychologist's tasks,
then, is to determine the kinds of experiences which affect a given individual's rigidity moduli and to determine the magnitude and direction
of the effects. This means that the psychologist must suspend the assumption that rigidity is an invariant of the individual, that rigidity is
not influenced by situational factors.

Comparison of Two Substances

In Physics. A physical substance is not often described as generally
more or less elastic than another. But two substances may be compared

with respect to a particular kind of stress-strain relationship or a particular modulus of elasticity.

In Psychology. Psychologists frequently compare two individuals, two groups, or two stages of development. Thus, they may describe one person as more rigid than another, an ethnocentric person as more rigid than a nonethnocentric person, a child as more rigid than an adult, mental patients as more rigid than normals, one race as more rigid than another, or one species as more rigid than another that is higher on the phylogenetic scale. The analogue that may be drawn from physics is that such comparisons should be made with respect to a particular stress-strain relationship or a particular modulus of rigidity. We have already suggested that subjection of two individuals to the same external force (e.g., the same test situation) does not mean that they are being subjected to the same stress. It is undoubtedly difficult to be certain that two individuals are being compared with respect to the same stress-strain relationship, and the difficulties increase when one compares two groups or two stages of ontogenetic or phylogenetic development. Caution dictates that, in making comparative statements, psychologists should at least specify the particular standard or criterion they are using for defining and measuring rigidity, the range of conditions under which the relative comparative status prevails, and the evidence or lack of evidence for the comparison. Exercise of such caution may make for fewer sweeping comparisons of rigidity.

Concerning Value Judgments

In Physics. Physicists' discussions of elasticity, as might be expected, are devoid of value judgments. To have a larger bulk modulus, for example, is not considered as "better" or "worse" or more or less "adequate" than to have a smaller bulk modulus. True, for certain industrial processes, it may be advisable to use substances with certain elastic properties rather than others, but, to the physicist, there is nothing inherently bad or good or inherently adequate or inadequate about any elastic properties.

In Psychology. Psychologists' discussions of rigidity are replete with value judgments. Opprobrium tends to be associated with the term. Consider the oft-cited definitions of rigidity as lack of shift in behavior when shift is needed or as adherence to behavior that is inadequate in the present situation. Who or what determines that shift is needed or that the behavior is inadequate? For example, some investigators who accept these definitions have used E solutions of the criticals as the criterion of rigidity; but shift from the E method is not needed for solution of the criticals and, as far as the subject is concerned, the E method here may be wholly adequate. Clearly, then, the judgment of inadequacy —and hence of rigidity—may depend on who is making the judgment. An illustration of how judgments concerning criteria of rigidity may differ, is furnished by the fact that, using the same test, one investigator interprets as evidence of rigidity precisely the same response that another interprets as lack of evidence; cf. utilization by Cattell and Tiner (1949) and by Horwitz (1951) of the Luchins' hidden-word Einstellung test.

Getting away from Einstellung situations, let us note that what one individual considers as rigidity in the sense of adherence to inadequate behavior, may strike another as admirable concentration on one task, as unswerving pursuit of a task or a goal, as constant, steadfast, and reliable behavior, as an instance of not being deflected or distracted and not being at the mercy of changes in the environment, etc. Whether or not behavior is considered as rigid may also depend on the time span in which the judgment is made. Thus, lack of shift in behavior today, when judged at a later date, may turn out not to have been rigidity, since shift actually was not needed to accomplish a particular task or achieve a particular goal; that is, in the light of history, the behavior was adequate. Or what seems at present to be adherence to behavior that is adequate, may later be evaluated, by the performer or others, as stubborn adherence to an inadequate response; that is, history may show that the behavior was maladaptive. When others think that change in behavior is called for, the performer may see no need for change. A soldier's persistence in maladaptive behavior or in showing symptoms of mental illness, may be regarded by others as rigidity, but may be considered by the soldier as adequate behavior since it takes him out of the horrors of battle. Rigid behavior caused by mental illness, may be adjudged by society in general and by the treating psychiatrist in particular as inadequate and as requiring change; but the rigid behavior may play a positive role in the behavioral world of the patient and help him to achieve and maintain a stable equilibrium.

In short, these definitions of rigidity (and indeed most definitions) are associated with negative values and may be difficult to apply in an objective manner. The negative values probably arise from the conception that rigid behavior connotes a lack of adjustment and flexibility—to conform, to adjust is to be flexible and "good." But here again we run into the problem of value judgments, since what is called adjustment and flexibility when judged from one frame of reference may be called maladjustment and inability to persevere when judged from another frame of reference.

For whatever it is worth, we note that high rigidity sometimes is associated with "name-calling" traits and low rigidity with so-called glittering generalities or "virtues." For example, the ethnocentric, prejudiced, authoritarian individual is said to be rigid, while the democratic, tolerant personality is described as less rigid or nonrigid (Frenkel-Brunswik, 1949).

Taking a clue from physicists' treatment of elasticity, we suggest that psychologists seek to develop methods of defining, studying, and measuring rigidity that are relatively divorced from value judgments. Just as certain elastic properties of physical substances are particularly suited for certain industrial processes, so the needs of certain situations or institutions may be better met by certain kinds or levels of rigidity—but the scientist's definitions of rigidity and his methods of studying and measuring rigidity should not be inherently linked with these needs. A variational approach to rigidity, particularly when it uses the individual as the base line for comparison of his processes of change, may allow for relatively value-free treatment of rigidity. The investigator can study under what conditions the individual shows one or another degree of change, or under what conditions the changes tend to be maximized or minimized, without having to evaluate one degree or one extreme as "better" or "worse," or as more or less "adequate" or "needed" than another. *In view of the negative connotations of the term "rigidity," perhaps it would be best to characterize such research, not as the study of "rigidity," but as the study of "differential processes of change."*

Information produced by variational research may be utilized by those who wish to control and change behavior; and how it is utilized will undoubtedly depend on the value judgments of those attempting to control or to change behavior. *But such value judgments do not have to enter into the definition, study, and measurement of changes in behavior in relation to changes in conditions.*

CHAPTER XXIV

THE NEED FOR A PHENOMENON-CENTERED
VARIATIONAL ORIENTATION

OUR ORIENTATION to research, characterized as a "phenomenon-centered variational approach" or simply as "phenomenon-centered" or as "variational," focuses on a specific phenomenon (situation, event, problem, issue) and studies it under a variety of conditions. It seeks to explore the variables in the phenomenon under a wide range of conditions. As is often done in mathematics, we consider a constant as "the special case of a variable whose 'domain of variation' consists of a single element only" (Courant and Robbins, 1941, p. 275). If a variable involved in the phenomenon turns out not to change, but to remain invariant as conditions are changed, then it is considered as constant within the particular range of conditions (or within the "domain of variation"). Thus, variational research is capable of yielding not only the variables in behavior but also the invariants or constants. In brief, such research is concerned with what happens to a specific case under a given range of conditions, with what remains invariant, with what changes, and with the direction, extent, and quality of the changes in the phenomenon in relation to changes in the conditions.

It might be said that the object of variational research is to discover both the invariants and the nonconstant variables through processes of variation or through differential processes of change as internal and external conditions are changed. To discover constants is quite different than to assume that a particular factor is constant, is independent of conditions. "Projecting" constants into phenomena is not uncommon; for example, rigidity is considered by some as a constant, invariant factor for a given individual although its invariance has not been established.

We have applied a variational approach not only to the Einstellung phenomenon but to some other psychological phenomena and problems (Luchins, 1957b). The findings seem to testify to the versatility and fruitfulness of the approach. We advocate a wider adoption of a variational outlook—not as a replacement of other orientations—but as a potentially productive approach to research. It therefore seems in order to discuss the proposed phenomenon-centered variational approach and to compare it with the orientation which seems to be predominant in contemporary psychology and which, for purposes of comparison, we shall characterize as theory-centered.

Scientific Status of Phenomenon-Centered Research

Is phenomenon-centered research scientific? The answer to this question depends in part on what one regards as the method or methods of science and as the objectives of science, matters on which, we shall see, there exist considerable differences of opinion.

Scientific Status of Methods Used in Phenomenon-Centered Research

Theory-centered research generally aims at (but does not always succeed in) using what has been called the hypothetico-deductive or postulational-deductive method in science, while phenomenon-centered research does not necessarily aim at using this method. The hypothetico-deductive or postulational-deductive method in science has been characterized as consisting of the following steps: setting up of postulates or conceptual beliefs; making logical deductions from them; controlled testing of the deductions; and, finally, consequent confirmation, rejection, or modification of the initial postulates. There are psychologists who accept this procedure as characterizing *the* method of science and endorse it as the most "adequate approach to knowing" (Blake, Ramsey, and Moran, 1951, p. 4). Stevens writes of the hypothetico-deductive method that "there can be no doubt that this is the method of science at its best" (1939, p. 40). But other psychologists state that "this is not the way most scientists actually work" (Skinner, 1950, p. 195) and that he who claims it is, is taking his clues from the logician rather than from the empirical scientist. Still other psychologists insist that the scientific method "is at some time or other all things to all scientists. There is no such thing as THE scientific method" (Klein and Krech, 1951, p. 14). Since phenomenon-centered research need *not* use the hypothetico-deductive method, whether or not such research is regarded as using a scientific method (or the best scientific method) may depend on whether or not one insists that the hypothetico-deductive method is the sole (or the best) scientific method.

Some psychologists' insistence on the hypothetico-deductive method can probably be traced to the belief that this is the method of mathematics and of the natural sciences. It is therefore of interest to note that not all mathematicians and natural scientists insist on using this method, or attribute their discoveries to this method, or consider that the use of the method necessarily has advanced their science's progress. Einstein, for example, states that he did not do his original thinking along a hypothetico-deductive path and that the axiomatic form in which his matured thinking may appear in print is a much later state of development (in Wertheimer, 1945, pp. 183-84, n.). Discussing the nature of mathematics, Courant and Robbins (1941) write that the weight of the Greek geometric tradition, with its emphasis on a deductive-postulational approach, probably retarded for almost two thousand years the evolution of the number concept and of algebraic manipulation which later formed the basis of modern science. They note: "There seems to be a great danger in the prevailing overemphasis on the deductive-postulational character of mathematics" (1941, p. xvii). Likewise, it seems to us that there is danger in the prevailing insistence that psychology should have a deductive-postulational character. In particular, methods used in phenomenon-centered research should not be regarded as unscientific simply because they may not be postulational-deductive in nature.

In conducting our research, we often varied conditions without knowing what influence the variations would have on the phenomenon. Sometimes we did not stipulate expectations before conducting the research; after it was done, we speculated about why it yielded the obtained results. Some psychologists might frown on such research, preferring what they call a priori specification to a posteriori speculation. But why should these adjectives not be reversed? After all, when one has conducted an experiment and has the findings, he has some grounds for specification and is less likely to be merely speculative. Yet the same statement when made before the description of the experiment tends to be elevated to the rank of specification whereas, when made afterwards, it is considered mere speculation.

A false sense of security may sometimes be associated with a priori specifications. All too often what is being tested is not a logical deduction from a hypothesis, deduced from it by means of valid reasoning, but merely a suggestion gleaned from it. Suggestions of this nature do not enjoy the immunities and privileges attendant on logical deductions. Moreover, as any elementary-logic student should know, one cannot confirm or establish the truth of a logical deduction but can only establish its falsity. Working with a priori specifications, the investigator may sometimes be lulled into an erroneous belief that he has confirmed a hypothesis or verified a theory. Such a belief may bestow on his report that sense of finality which is bestowed on a proof in mathematics when the final Q.E.D. is announced. Q.E.D.'s are rare in the social sciences. At least a posteriori speculations have an open, unfinished character about them; they call for future experimentation and do not regard issues as settled.

Scientific Status of Objectives of Phenomenon-Centered Research

Theory-centered research is generally concerned with developing a theory (or defending or attacking a theory) or establishing general laws. On the other hand, the objective of phenomenon-centered variational research is to obtain facts about the phenomenon under consideration by empirical observations and by measurements where possible. The facts are in the nature of empirical relationships between the phenomenon and conditions, and these relationships may eventually yield empirical laws. But variational research is *not necessarily* concerned with the establishing of general laws based on its findings or with the development of (or defense of or attack on) a theory. Whether this is regarded as a scientific objective depends on one's views concerning the tasks or objectives of science. There are psychologists who agree with Marx (1951) that direct empirical measurement is the fundamental task of science, while others agree with Rosenblueth and Wiener (1945) that the primary goal of science is the development of theories and systems of formal models.

The concern of variational research with empirical observations may be frowned upon by those psychologists who maintain that the scientist finds it necessary to reject as untrustworthy direct knowledge gained through raw or sense perception and that the scientific method has replaced the "empiricism of the prescientific era with its emphasis on 'fact finding' through reliance on raw sense perceptions" (Blake, Ramsey, and Moran, 1951, p. 4). To substantiate this claim, Blake, Ramsey, and Moran quote Barnett's remark in *The Universe and Dr. Einstein*: "In accepting a mathematical description of nature, physicists have been forced to abandon the ordinary world of our experience, the world of sense perceptions" (1949). But compare this statement with Einstein's own remarks that physics treats directly with sense experiences and the understanding of the connection between these experiences, that the only thing which differentiates science from a logical but empty scheme of concepts is the totality of connection of scientific concepts with "complexes of sense experience," and that a scientific system must be "compatible with the observations made by our senses" (1950, pp. 60-63). Concern in psychology with sense experiences, with empirical observations, it seems to us, need be no less scientific than a corresponding concern in physics.

The Role of Theory in Psychological Research

The Question Whether Research Must Stem from Theory; Variety of Referents for the Term "Theory"

Some psychologists contend that research must begin with a theory or a hypothesis. Referring to those social scientists who suggest that one should dispense with all theories and just get the facts, Miller states that "some selection must inevitably be made among the *infinite* number of facts that could be observed. ... It is impossible to avoid selecting data on the basis of some sort of a hypothesis" (1951, p. 86). "*Some* theoretical guide is necessary as a principle of selection," Hebb states, noting that there are an infinite number of relationships and aspects of behavior that the psychologist can record, and that "we must recognize the positive value even of 'wrong' theories as guides to observation" (1951, p. 47). Asserting that we all have models in the back of our heads when we collect systematic sets of data, Tolman suggests that we make these models explicit to ourselves and others since "conscious, even though bad theory is better than unconscious theory" (1949b, p. 49). In sharp contrast to these viewpoints is that advocated by Koch, who frowns on the prevalent belief that "*any* theoretical assumption, no matter how foolhardy the inductive leap (assuming that there is something to leap *from*) is better than none at all" (1951b, p. 297).

Admittedly our research on the Einstellung phenomenon was guided by certain hunches that led to varying certain factors and not other factors. Since hunches are equated by some psychologists with theories, it could therefore be said that we were using theories. This raises a problem as to the referents of the term "theory." There is considerable disagreement among psychologists concerning the proper meaning of the term. For example, while Tolman equates the terms "theory" and "model," Allport (1946) differentiates between the two terms. Dallenbach (1953) notes that the term "theory" has been given distinctly different meanings and has also been used as if it were synonymous with such terms as "conjecture," "speculation," "doctrine," and "hypothesis"; he contends that these terms have been used interchangeably, loosely, and indiscriminately. While some psychologists distinguish between "theory" and "speculation" (Marx, 1951, p. 5), others maintain that "theories are always speculative" (Klein and Krech, 1951, p. 20). There are psychologists who apply the term theory to a limited hypothesis or hunch or suggestion while others do not consistently do so. For example, Miller writes that a system of symbols "can properly be called a model or theory if, and only if, one can use it to make rigorous deductions ... It is obvious that many current 'theories' or 'models' in psychology fail to meet this criterion" (Miller, 1951, pp. 82-83). Brown (1936) and Hull (1943) state that a "scientific theory" necessarily involves the hypothetico-deductive method. Spence (1944) writes that, unless constructs are introduced in some such precise manner as Hull introduces them in his hypothetico-deductive conceptual system, one really does not have a theory, and laments that much of what has passed for theory in psychology has failed to meet this criterion with regard to constructs.

That the meanings given the word may vary in the same report and that the evaluation of theory may depend on the associated meaning seem to be illustrated in a report by Dallenbach (1953). First, he warns against "theory-blindness," against being so blinded by a specific theory as to be unable truly to see the facts. Referring to Titchener's admonition to "carry your theories lightly," he explains that Titchener meant, "Do not rush to their attack or to their defense but go about your own proper work of gathering facts. They and they alone verify or disprove theory" (p. 34). Then, on a later page, Dallenbach notes that doing something without a theory is not a scientific experiment; it constitutes mere busywork (p. 39). The term "theory" has different meanings in the two contexts.

Thus, whether the use of hunches or suggestions in conducting experimental variations is described as the use of theories, depends on how the term "theory" is defined. Some of the controversy concerning the value of theories and theorizing in psychology may be traced to different referents of the word. As indicated above, one of the arguments raised against empiricists is that, in eschewing theory, they overlook the fact that some theory is necessary in selecting data for study. But the "theory" necessary for selecting data may be a hunch, an intuition, or a limited hypothesis, and not the avowedly formal conceptual system eschewed by the empiricist.

The Role of Theory Compared in Phenomenon-Centered and Theory-Centered Research

Regardless of how the term "theory" is defined, a distinction can be drawn between the roles played by theories in phenomenon-centered and theory-centered research. The latter usually involves the testing of a theory or of deductions or suggestions derived from a theory. The former may involve experimentation suggested by theories (as in some of our work on the Einstellung phenomenon), but the primary emphasis is not on the testing of a hypothesis or theory. If a suggestion for experimentation derived from a theory should prove fruitful (e.g., should succeed in extremizing E effects), so much the better; but, whether or not it does, the investigator does not have to become involved in defending, refuting, or modifying theories to which the suggestion for experimentation may relate. In short, in phenomenon-centered research the focus of interest is the phenomenon. Theories serve as tools rather than as objectives. In theory-centered research the focus of interest is a theory or hypothesis while the phenomenon may be of interest only insofar as it provides a possibility of testing the theory or hypothesis.

Moreover, in variational research, an appeal to a theory does not imply that the investigator accepts the theory. Hence, he is more likely to vary the theories to which he turns for suggestions, whereas in theory-centered research there is a more monistic tendency. In other words, a variational approach encourages a multitheoretical outlook on the part of the investigator rather than the unitheoretical outlook prevalent today. A shift from one theoretical view to another is considered by some as akin to repudiation of one religious faith and conversion to another (cf. Mowrer's apology (1951) for changing from a monistic to a dualistic learning theory). But in variational research shifts are encouraged since the investigator regards theories as research tools and not as creeds or articles of faith.

Differing Opinions on Merits of Research That Is Not Theory-Centered

There have been differences of opinion as to the merits of research that stems from or does not stem from a theory. Hebb predicts that "without theory of some kind, somewhere, psychological observation and description would at best be chaotic and meaningless" (1951, p. 39). But Skinner, perhaps the most outspoken of the critics of theory-centered research, questions the supposition that research would be aimless and disorganized without a theory to guide it. He suggests that research not designed to test theory "will lead more directly to the kind of information that a science usually accumulates" (1950, p. 195). While Spence (1948) regards theories as an aid in discovering the unknown variables in the process or system under study, Skinner claims that, "instead of prompting us to search for and explore relevant variables, they [theories] frequently have quite the opposite effect" (1950, p. 194). One of the virtues of theories is said to be the research to which they lead; on this score also Skinner is skeptical:

> Research designed with respect to theory is also likely to be wasteful. That a theory generates research does not prove its value unless the research is valuable. Much useless experimentation results from theories, and much energy and skill are absorbed by them. Most theories are eventually overthrown, and the greater part of the associated research is discarded. (1950, p. 194.)

The Relative Productivity of Phenomenon-Centered and Theory-Centered Orientations Toward the Selected Case

In view of the controversies over the relative merits of research that stems from or does not stem from a theory, it is of interest to turn to a specific case on which there has been both phenomenon-centered and theory-centered research in an attempt to evaluate the relative productivity, in this case, of the two orientations. The selected case allows such evaluation. One of the points in favor of phenomenon-centered research on the Einstellung phenomenon is the fact that most of the experimental variations that extremized E effects were suggested by empirical observational analysis rather than by theories of rigidity or learning. Also in its favor is the fact that a survey of research done by investigators who have used the selected case or variations of it to test deductions from a theory, did not reveal even one variable in the Einstellung phenomenon, or any factors or conditions that influence E effects, that had not already been discovered through phenomenon-centered variational research. For this case, at least, no new knowledge was yielded by theory-centered research despite the claim that such research may aid in discovering the variables in the process or system under study. Another merit sometimes attributed to theory-centered research is that the findings can be used to support one rather than another theory. It is therefore of interest that theory-centered research on the water-jug problems has not yielded findings that definitely supported one theory rather than another and, in particular, that the same findings have been used to support conflicting theories; for example, Kendler (1952) and Tresselt (1951) have used the Einstellung phenomenon to support conflicting theories of mental set.

One of the criticisms sometimes leveled against phenomenon-centered research is that study of a specific case cannot add to systematic knowledge and that the results of such study can have no broad, general applicability. Yet not only has research centered on the Einstellung phenomenon contributed to systematic knowledge about this case but the findings of that research have had broad applicability. The findings have proved relevant to many concepts, issues, and theories of rigidity and learning. Moreover, we saw that the variations which extremized E effects in the water-jug problems also extremized rigidity in other situations. These variations therefore suggest hypotheses with reference to conditions that tend to maximize or enhance rigidity and conditions that tend to minimize or prevent rigidity. Experimentation pertinent to these hypotheses—ranging from studies of rigidity in the perception of a series of pictures to studies of rigidity in adhering to an impression one forms of another person—has rather consistently yielded data supporting the hypotheses.

Thus, a variational approach, focused on one example of behavior, may serve to yield hypotheses concerning a broad class of behavior. To the extent that these hypotheses are supported by research, they may be regarded as empirical relationships or as principles applicable to a broad area of psychology. Our phenomenon-centered investigation may even be considered as a "miniature system." Other miniature systems have been developed in psychology, notable among them being the hypothetico-deductive system of Hull and his colleagues (1943). In

Hull's miniature system, theorems or principles are derived from axioms that involve various logical constructs. In contrast to this hypothetico-deductive miniature system, a phenomenon-centered investigation may be characterized as an empirical, experimental miniature system. In place of the logical constructs is the one case selected for investigation; in place of the formulation of axioms is the systematic experimental (and theoretical) exploration of the case; in place of the content of the axioms are the insights concerning the phenomenon which result from the investigations; and in place of the derived theorems or principles there may be hypotheses, yielded by the investigation, which are pertinent to a broader class of behavior than the specific case under investigation. It seems to us that phenomenon-centered studies which serve as miniature systems (and, in particular, the present study) can be regarded as adding to systematic knowledge and as having applicability beyond the one specific case that was the focus of attention. In short, one of the criticisms sometimes raised against phenomenon-centered research may not be justified.

It seems justified to say that the phenomenon-centered research on the Einstellung phenomenon has been more productive and has added more to systematic knowledge than has theory-centered research using this phenomenon. The implication, for those who wish to draw it, is that there is nothing inherently unfruitful about a phenomenon-centered orientation. For that matter, there is nothing inherently unfruitful about a theory-centered orientation. But we think that there are certain potential dangers in the latter orientation against which the investigator must be on guard, such as the danger that an emphasis on a particular theory may lead the investigator to overlook certain aspects of the phenomenon and other and perhaps more suitable methods of treating and interpreting the data, and may even cause him to discard a considerable portion of the data because it does not happen to fit into the categories suggested by his theory.

The Need for Phenomenon-Centered as Well as Theory-Centered Orientations

Despite the finding that phenomenon-centered variational research was more productive than theory-centered research for the selected case, we recognize that there may be merits in research geared to testing or promulgating theories. Theories are valuable so long as they do not usurp the whole stage of psychological investigation and discussion. The important point, it seems to us, is that psychologists should not insist on one orientation to the exclusion of any other. Discoveries in mathematics have resulted both from a formal hypothetico-deductive approach and from a constructive, intuitive, empirical approach (cf. Courant and Robbins, 1941). Use of more than one orientation to research has fostered discoveries in the natural sciences. A compelling illustration was furnished in nuclear research by the discovery within the past few years of about a dozen elementary particles hitherto unknown; Oppenheimer (1956) has pointed out that the existence of any one of these particles was not deduced from existing theories and, in fact, was not deducible from them. Yet the discovery of these particles is not ignored or treated as unimportant or as unscientific because it was not derived from theories. Instead, the discovery of the particles has led to speculation concerning the need for revision of nuclear theories.

The moral we hope to point out to psychologists is patent. It seems to us that psychological discoveries may be enhanced if both phenomenon-centered and theory-centered research are encouraged, particularly if the findings of both are coordinated.

RELATION BETWEEN FACTS AND THEORIES IN PSYCHOLOGY

The Question of Overabundance of Facts or of Theories

There has been some controversy as to whether psychology is in need of more facts or more theories. Psychology has been said to have too much theory and insufficient facts (Brown, 1936) and, on the other hand, to have sufficient facts but not enough theory (Leeper, 1948). We are told of the "usefulness of speculation for psychological theory" (Krech, 1950, p. 346) and assured that "it is never too early for speculation and theory in science" (Klein and Krech, 1951, p. 20). On the other hand, Lewin writes that theorizing and formalizing should be done "only to the degree that the maturity of the material under investigation permits at a given time" (1951, p. 9); Marx admonishes those psychologists "whose speculations too often tend to outstrip their empirical foundations" (1951, p. 126); and Koch disapproves of the "continued spinning" of psychological theories (1951b, p. 298), claiming that we still "lack basic areas of empirical knowledge of the sort necessary for adequate theory" (1951a, p. 148).

Certain areas, it is undoubtedly true, are characterized by many theories about which psychologists disagree and by little empirical knowledge and few empirical laws about which they agree. For example, after surveying over a dozen theories of learning, Hilgard (1948) concludes that there is not one law of learning which we can teach our students with confidence—this, in one of the most intensively investigated areas of psychology.

There are those who object to the plethora of facts in psychology and who regard the further collection of facts, through empirical investigations, as mere dust collecting. But there are others who object to the growing plethora of psychological theories and theorettes and who are annoyed by the heat and smoke generated by many theoretical pipe dreams and controversies, which, they say, seem to serve no useful function and seem to lead to no decisive conclusions and no new knowledge. It seems to be a question whether one prefers smoke or dust in his eyes.

The Need for Interrelated Facts and Empirical Relationships

Perhaps the issue should not pertain to whether psychology has too many facts or too many theories but to the quality of existing facts and theories. While there are many isolated facts, there are relatively few interrelated, integrated facts and still fewer empirical relationships or empirical laws. And, while there are numerous theories, there are few theories adequate to account for the phenomena which they encompass. We see the need for more interrelated facts, empirical relationships, and empirical laws, as well as the need for more adequate theories, closely geared to available empirical knowledge and serving as explanations of phenomena and, to use Dallenbach's expression (1953), as bridges to span gaps in our knowledge.

Variational research, it should be stressed, does not yield scattered, isolated facts. Rather, the facts are organized around a phenomenon (problem, situation, event, issue); variational research involves systematic fact collecting. Facts gathered in variational research may also be considered as organized around what we called an empirical, experimental miniature system.

It may be contended that zeal in collecting facts can be overdone. This is true. We certainly do not advocate that contemporary theory fever be replaced by fact-finding fever. However, in psychology at least, systematic fact finding has a long way to go before it reaches a feverish level. To change the metaphor, there seems to be little danger at present of systematic fact collecting becoming a malignant growth on the psychological body.

In short, we think that psychology needs more systematic fact collecting as well as more cautious theory building closely geared to available facts. A variational phenomenon-centered approach may be valuable in meeting these needs. Knowledge collected through this approach may be of interest in its own right and may also have value for the theorists or system builders in psychology.

Disputes over Facts Compared with Disputes over Theories

We recognize that the "facts" set forth by one investigator who is doing phenomenon-centered research may be disputed by another investigator who is doing research on the same phenomenon. But such disputes may possibly be settled more readily than theoretical disputes. In phenomenon-centered research one is interested in observing what occurs under certain experimental conditions; hence, two experimenters, engaged in such research, who get conflicting answers, may be willing to compare and check their experimental work, to repeat their experiments under similar and different conditions. In so doing, they may discover the reason for the original discrepancy in their findings and perhaps achieve greater understanding of the relationships between the phenomenon and various conditions.

In theoretical disputes, however, since particular facts and observations of what occurs under various experimental conditions are of secondary concern while theories are of primary concern, it is less likely that two disputants will be willing to repeat and check their experimental work. Indeed, it is not farfetched to say that some contemporary theoretical arguments continue because opponents of a particular theory ignore the experiments conducted by adherents of this theory but instead cling to their own experimental setups. When they do give recognition to an opponent's experiments, it may be to dismiss them as improper on one ground or other. And, when they offer refutation of those experiments, it is often based on other experiments or on modifications of the disputed experiments. Modifications may indicate originality on the part of psychologists, but they do not necessarily help to settle the theoretical argument under consideration. If the concern is not with theories but with a certain specific phenomenon, it may be possible more readily to reach agreement. Moreover, two or more theories may be experimentally equivalent in the sense that, because of the limitations imposed by existing knowledge and methods, it is not possible to decide which theory is more adequate. It may be well if some of the time and energy presently expended in disputes over certain theories which are experimentally equivalent, were instead invested in phenomenon-centered studies. These latter studies might lead to new knowledge and new methods which in turn might perhaps end the deadlock among certain theories.

Fact Finding and Theory Building Need Not Be by the Same Investigator

Everyone who conducts an experiment must link it with a theory lest it be called mere busywork. Concomitantly, everyone who promulgates a theory must conduct experiments to establish it, lest his paper be called top-drawer stuff. Perhaps the hyphen in experimental-theoretical has not left enough space between the two terms. (Luchins, 1957b, p. 107.)

He who is interested in conducting experiments should be allowed to do so without having to hedge the experiments in with theoretical considerations. He who is interested in theory building should be permitted (indeed, should be expected) to use experiments conducted by others and existing facts established by others. There has perhaps been too much insistence in psychology that the function of establishing facts and the function of theory building should be done by the same individual. There has perhaps also been undue emphasis on the suggestive or deductive power of a theory (or hypothesis). While it is a virtue for a theory to suggest new research or new facts, or to account for new findings, it is also a virtue for a theory to account for existing facts. That the former virtue has been stressed more than the latter, and that the same psychologist has been expected to link experiment and theory, may help to account for what amounts to a virtual obliviousness to the literature on the part of some investigators. Some investigators are primarily interested in demonstrating that a particular theory has generated or suggested a new experiment, or that it can account for the findings of a new experiment, or that the findings of a new experiment were deduced from or predicted by the theory, with these experimental findings interpreted as supporting the validity of the theory. But the investigator may fail to examine the literature in order to see: (1) whether other studies have been reported upon which are relevant to his study; (2) in particular, whether an experiment identical with or similar to his "new" experiment has already been reported upon and, if so, how the results compare with the results he has obtained, whether the other experiment was described as suggested by or deduced from a theory or hypothesis (perhaps one which has since been discarded), and how this theory or hypothesis compares with the one that suggested his own experiment; (3) whether results closely akin to the results he has obtained have perhaps been interpreted differently in the literature, say, interpreted as explained by or as supporting the validity of a theory different from the theory he offers, perhaps even conflicting with it; (4) whether there are other experimental findings or facts reported in the literature which the theory he advances can account for; and (5) whether there are other experimental findings or facts which run counter to the theory he advocates.

Illustrations of what we have been talking about are found in some reports on the Einstellung phenomenon. There are reports of research on the water-jug problems which seem to be quite oblivious to the literature that has accumulated around these problems. This obliviousness may extend even to research work that is in the same area and that deals with the same relationship. Thus, some of the reports on anxiety in relation to E effects fail to mention other research dealing with just this relationship. Investigators who use the Einstellung phenomenon to support a particular theory (e.g., of rigidity or of anxiety or of learning or of the acquisition of mental sets), usually do not discuss different theoretical explanations that have been offered for essentially similar findings. The same issue of a journal (the *Journal of Abnormal and Social Psychology*, 1953, vol. 48, no. 4) contains two reports on studies of ethnocentrism in relation to rigidity that use water-jug problems and yield conflicting findings and diverse theoretical explanations; yet no attempt is made, in this issue or, as far as we know, in any subsequent issue, to relate one study to the other.

We do not intend to imply that the failure to relate studies or to co-ordinate findings or the failure in other ways to pay adequate heed to the literature are due entirely to the insistence that the same investi-gator link theory and experiment and to the insistence that a "good" theory should generate new research. But we do think that these may be factors contributing to inadequate attention to the literature, even if only by emphasizing new research at the expense of research already reported upon in the literature. If there is less insistence along these lines—if those who promulgate theories are encouraged to use findings established by others, and if those who conduct experiments are not expected to link them to theories and, specifically, are not expected to show that the experiments or experimental findings were deduced from or support a particular theory—then there may be less obliviousness to the literature, less tendency to add to the plethora of inadequate theories, and more chance that worth-while research may be preserved even when theories with which they are associated are overthrown.

Theories as Filing Systems

It is tempting to draw an analogy between theories and filing systems. A business concern usually finds that it requires a filing system and filing cabinets in order to keep its collection of records in usable order. Psychological theories, in the broad sense of the term, may be regarded as serving the functions of filing cabinets and systems. They may be employed to relate, integrate, and order data. If data consist of scattered facts, then some theory in the sense of a filing system is essential so that we may know where to file (and to find) the facts.

If the data are organized around phenomena or empirical miniature systems, then the data are ready for filing under the particular phe-nomenon or empirical miniature system to which they pertain. But theories may still be employed both to relate various phenomena and empirical miniature systems and to help explain why a given change of experimental conditions is concomitant with a certain change in the experimental findings. Data organized around a particular phenomenon or empirical miniature system may be cross-indexed under an explanatory theory.

A theory, in the sense of a filing system, may suggest certain gaps in the data filed under it and thus instigate research. But this is not the only research needed. The danger in psychology is that our filing systems too often are allowed to dictate the kinds of questions we ask, the kinds of problems we deal with, the kinds of experiments we conduct, and the aspects of the data which we analyze or which we discard.

Kinds of Problems to Be Investigated in Psychological Research

The Question Whether Problems Must Be Linked to Theories or Specific Methods

We have noted that there is a danger that psychological theories (or filing systems) may dictate the kinds of problems dealt with in psychology. It is not uncommon to find the demand imposed upon psychologists that they deal with problems linked to psychological theory: journal articles, projects for research grants, and suggestions for doctoral dissertations have been rejected on the ground that they were not linked with or did not contribute to psychological theory. The situation is quite different in mathematics and in the natural sciences. Many journal articles dealing with mathematics, biology, physics, and chemistry, do not support or refute a general or even a specific theory. Moreover, graduate students in these disciplines are often permitted to deal with problems that are not linked with theories or that are not of general theoretical significance; an example is chemical analysis of a specific substance. Perhaps psychology ought to emulate mathematics and the natural sciences in this respect. Careful, intensive investigation of one phenomenon or problem, whether or not it contributes directly to theory or to theoretical decisions, may be a worthy project. If the research may add to knowledge of the facts or variables relevant to a specific case, demonstrate some of the obstacles in the way of furthering this knowledge, or pave the way for new research, then it seems to us that graduate students and research workers in psychology should be encouraged to undertake it.

One sometimes hears the complaint, from social scientists as well as from laymen, that the social sciences have not dealt with fundamental problems of society, that they have concerned themselves with trivial issues. Hilgard (1948) comments on the trivial nature of much of the research in learning and the neglect of problems that are of intense concern to educators; he implies that this state of affairs is due in part to the tendency to allow learning theories and accepted methods and techniques to dictate problems that are investigated. Ackoff (1952) attributes the triviality of much social research to the fact that social scientists are discouraged from deviating from techniques and methods set by universities and professional organizations.

It seems to us that, while theories or specific techniques may suggest research, they should not be allowed to tyrannize over research. One should not study *only* those problems which are suggested by or happen to conform with certain methods, techniques, or theories. In phenomenon-centered research one begins with a particular phenomenon (problem, situation, event, issue) and it continues to be the center of interest. Hence, in such research, vital, practical problems and issues have at least as good a chance to be investigated as relatively trivial ones.

In suggesting that psychology should not neglect important, practical problems, we do not intend to imply that only those problems should be dealt with which are of immediate utilitarian significance or which are of interest to a large segment of the public. Even a phenomenon which does not seem to have immediate practical or widespread or "scientific" significance, which is perhaps but a curiosity, nonetheless deserves to be studied. The curiosities of yesterday often turn out to have very practical uses today, as the history of science well reveals. In mathematics, imaginary and complex numbers were introduced long before it was known that they would prove of value in mathematical analysis of the flow of current in electrical circuits; and, to cite but one more of many other possible examples, when Riemann's non-Euclidean geometry was devised, it was not known that it would be useful in Einstein's thinking on relativity.

The Need for an Analogue of Hilbert Problems in Psychology

The problems to be investigated by a variational approach, we reiterate, need not be very grandiose or very general. Humble, modest problems, capable of formulation in elementary terms, should not be scorned. We are reminded here of the problems proposed by the mathematician, David Hilbert, in 1900, in an address to the international congress of mathematicians at Paris (Courant and Robbins, 1941, p. 107). Most of these problems were formulated in elementary terms; none seemed capable of solution at the time they were proposed. But most of them have since been solved, with consequent enrichment of mathematical knowledge and technique.

As an example of the specific, apparently nongeneral problems formulated by Hilbert, consider the following problem: Is $2^{\sqrt{2}}$ an algebraic number, a number which is the root of a polynominal equation with integral coefficients, or is it a transcendental (nonalgebraic) number? Note that Hilbert did not ask whether $a^{\sqrt{a}}$ or $a^{\sqrt{b}}$, where a and b are integers, is a transcendental number. He selected a very specific problem, seemingly trivial in nature. And yet consideration of whether or not $2^{\sqrt{2}}$ is a transcendental number has led to the discovery of methods of proving the transcendental nature not only of this number but of any number a^b where a is an algebraic number other than 0 or 1 and b is any irrational algebraic number (Courant and Robbins, 1941, p. 107).

We can use a Hilbert in psychology to formulate problems, not solved at present, perhaps seemingly not even capable of solution by existing methods. If each of these problems, however specific or humble its nature, becomes the center of investigation by an individual or by a team of psychologists or other social scientists, then we may gain insight not only into the particular problem but also into broader problems and we may possibly enrich our techniques.

THE NEED FOR A VARIATIONAL ORIENTATION FOR NONPSYCHOLOGISTS

A variational orientation is valuable, we believe, not only in psychology but in every field of inquiry. Moreover, we believe that such an orientation is also valuable for the general public. We envision a variational outlook, in a wide sense, as an outlook that the nonpsychologist should adopt in order that he may realize the true nature of the scientific attitude—doubting, questioning, and searching. In the teaching of all sciences, as well as in popular scientific writings, we suggest there be adopted a variational approach and, in particular, a multitheoretical approach. A theory should not be presented as the established truth, the universal and eternal law of nature, or as a directive for conduct akin to a law decreed by the legislature. A scientific formulation should be presented as tentative, as subject to re-evaluation in the light of further knowledge and hence as subject to revision or rejection, and as possibly only one of several proposed explanations.

While all scientists can help to foster a variational outlook on the part of the public, social scientists and particularly psychologists seem to us to have a special responsibility in this regard. This is because social scientists are to some extent both interpreters and arbiters of human behavior. Laws, principles, doctrines, and theories promulgated in the social sciences, readily transmitted to the public by modern methods of communication, may directly or indirectly influence the very objects to which they pertain. For example, theories of economics may influence the management of business and, in turn, the economic activity of a society. Because of the public's interest in psychology and in human behavior, psychological theories and concepts advanced to explain human behavior have a ready audience. It is not unusual to find psychological theories and concepts accepted as creeds for belief and as guides for action (which in turn creates evidence to substantiate them). The history of education reveals that a particular theory of learning may exert considerable influence on methods of teaching. At the present time an educator who adheres to Gestalt principles of learning (e.g., Stern, 1949), when given the opportunity, would run a school quite differently than one who adheres to, say, stimulus-response principles of learning. Psychoanalytic and other theories of personality functioning and development, when imparted to parents and educators, lead to practices which may influence child development and perhaps personality functioning. The writers believe that theories and concepts of adolescence and "teen-agers" have influenced parents and others in contact with adolescents, as well as adolescents themselves, and have had a considerable share in molding contemporary youth. It is apparent that theories of psychopathology may influence hospital administration and therapy and thereby influence the behavior of the patients. In short, formulations in the social sciences in general and in psychology in particular, can mold and change the objects to which they pertain.

Harold Lasswell, in discussions with one of the writers, made the point that this potential influence of the social sciences on human behavior could be used to maximize human freedom—to develop new horizons, new possibilities for human thought and action. We think that it also places an awesome responsibility on social scientists and, in particular, on psychologists. That is why we regard with skepticism the rather widely accepted thesis among psychologists that even a "bad" theory or a "wrong" theory is better than no theory at all, because a "bad" or "wrong" theory may have an adverse influence on human behavior. That is one of the reasons why we suggest that the psychologist does not have freedom to invent arbitrary axiomatic systems or conceptual schemes relating to human behavior without regard to their relation to empirical knowledge, but should instead attempt to keep his formulations closely geared to empirical knowledge.

It must be kept in mind that the layman who hears of a psychological theory may not have the orientation of a scientist who may view the theory as tentative. Nor does the layman generally see his task to be that of doubting or of testing the correctness of the theory. But, if a variational orientation were encouraged on the part of laymen and were used in presentations of psychological information to them, it might help to forestall erroneous conceptions on the part of laymen, help them to view theories as provisional explanations, and foster a questioning attitude toward psychological issues. Such an outlook on the part of the public would be more in keeping with the spirit of inquiry characteristic of psychology as a science than acceptance of psychological theories and concepts as creeds for belief or as guides for action.

In summary, we suggest that a variational approach would be useful in all fields of inquiry, that scientific information should be presented both to scientists and to laymen via such an approach, and that the development of a variational outlook with regard to science on the public's part, while not solely the responsibility of the psychologist, is a function in which he should participate.

BIBLIOGRAPHY

Ach, N. 1905. *Über die Willenstätigkeit und das Denken.* Göttingen: Vanderhoeck & Ruprecht.

Ach, N. 1910. *Über den Willensakt das Temperament.* Leipzig: Quelle & Meyer.

Ackoff, R. L. 1952. Scientific method and social science—East and west. *Sci. Monogr.,* 75: 155-60.

Adler, A. 1927. *Understanding human nature.* New York: Greenberg.

Adler, A. 1930. *The education of children.* London: George Allen & Unwin.

Adler, A. 1931. *What life should mean to you.* New York: Grosset & Dunlap.

Adler, A. 1938. *Social interest: A challenge to mankind.* London: Farber & Farber.

Ainsworth, L. H. 1950. Rigidity as manifestation of insecurity. Unpublished Master's thesis, Univer. of Toronto.

Alexander, F. 1951. *Our age of unreason.* (Rev. ed.) Philadelphia: J. P. Lippincott.

Allport, G. W. 1930. Change and decay in the visual memory image. *Brit. J. Psychol.,* 21: 134-48.

Allport, G. W. 1937. *Personality.* New York: Henry Holt.

Allport, G. W. 1946. Scientific models and human morals. *Psychol. Rev.,* 54: 182-92.

Allport, G. W., & Postman, L. 1947. *Psychology of rumor.* New York: Henry Holt.

Ames, A. 1949. *Nature and origin of perceptions.* (Mimeographed laboratory manual.) Hanover, N.H.: Hanover Institute.

Apostolatos, R. 1951-52. Unpublished research, McGill Univer.

Aronoff, L. L. 1951. Unpublished research, McGill Univer.

Asch, S. E. 1952. *Social psychology.* New York: Prentice-Hall.

Avery, J. 1951-52. Unpublished research, McGill Univer.

Barnett, L. K. 1949. *The universe and Dr. Einstein.* New York: William Sloane.

Becker, H., & Schwartz, E. 1950-51. Unpublished research, McGill Univer.

Bernstein, E. 1924. Quickness and intelligence. *Brit. J. Psychol. Monogr. Suppl.,* 3, No. 7.

Blackham, H. J. 1952. *Six existentialist thinkers.* London: Routledge & Kegan Paul.

Blake, R. R., Ramsey, G. V., & Moran, L. J. 1951. Perceptual processes as basic to an understanding of complex behavior. In R. R. Blake and G. V. Ramsey (Eds.), *Perception: An approach to personality.* New York: Ronald Press. C. 1.

Blake, R. R. *See also* Mouton, J. S. 1957.

Bochner, R., & Halpern, F. 1945. *The clinical application of the Rorschach test.* New York: Grune & Stratton.

Brogden, W. J. 1951. Animal studies in learning. In S. S. Stevens (Ed.), *Handbook of experimental psychology.* New York: Wiley. C. 16.

Brown, J. F. 1933. Die dynamischen Eigenschaften der Realitäts und Irrealitätschichten. *Psychol. Forsch.,* 18: 1-28.

Brown, R. W. 1951. Personal communication.

Brown, W. 1936. Facing the facts. *Proc. 25th Anniv. Celebr. Monogr. grad. Stud.* (Los Angeles: Univer. of Southern California Press), 116-21.

Brugmans, H. J. T. W. *See* Heymans, G. 1913.

Bruner, J. S., & Postman, L. 1948. An approach to social perception. In W. Dennis et al. (Eds.), *Current trends in social psychology*. Pittsburgh: Univer. of Pittsburgh Press. Pp. 71-118.

Burnett, A. 1951-52. Unpublished research, McGill Univer.

Burri, C. 1934. Individual differences in ability to alternate activities. *J. gen. Psychol.*, 10: 344-63.

Burri, C. 1935. The present status of the problem of individual differences in alternating activities. *Psychol. Bull.*, 32: 113-39.

Burt, C., & Stephenson, W. 1939. Alternative views on correlations between persons. *Psychometrika*, 4: 269-81.

Cameron, D. E., & Caunt, T. G. B. 1933. Studies in perseveration. *J. ment. Sci.*, 79: 735-45.

Cantril, H. 1950. *The "why" of man's experience*. New York: Macmillan.

Cantril, H. *See also* Sherif, M. 1947.

Carr, H. A. 1931. The laws of association. *Psychol. Rev.*, 38: 212-28.

Cathecart, E. P., & Dawson, S. I. 1928. Persistence: A characteristic of remembering. *Brit. J. Psychol.*, 18: 262-75.

Cattell, R. B. 1935. On measurement of perseveration. *Brit. J. educ. Psychol.*, 5: 76-91.

Cattell, R. B. 1936. *Guide to mental testing*. London: Univer. of London Press.

Cattell, R. B. 1946. *Description and measurement of personality*. Yonkers-on-Hudson: World Book.

Cattell, R. B. 1950. *Personality*. New York: McGraw-Hill.

Cattell, R. B., & Malteno, E. V. 1940. Contributions concerning mental inheritance: II. Of temperament. *J. genet. Psychol.*, 57: 31-47.

Cattell, R. B., & Tiner, L. G. 1949. The varieties of structural rigidity. *J. Pers.*, 17: 321-41.

Caunt, T. G. B. *See* Cameron, D. E. 1933.

Chamber's technical dictionary. (C. F. Tweney & L. E. C. Hughes, Eds.) 1940. New York: Macmillan.

Christie, R. 1949. The effects of frustration upon rigidity in problem solving. Unpublished doctoral dissertation, Univer. of California.

Chu, Y. J. *See* Huang, I. 1936.

Clarke, H. J. 1951. The Rosenzweig picture frustration study. In H. H. Anderson & G. L. Anderson (Eds.), *Projective techniques*. New York: Prentice-Hall. Pp. 312-23.

Combs, A. W. *See* Snygg, D. 1949.

Constant, L. 1952. Unpublished research, McGill Univer.

Constantine, E. 1951-52. Unpublished research, McGill Univer.

Courant, R., & Robbins, H. 1941. *What is mathematics?* New York: Oxford Univer. Press.

Cowen, E. L. 1950. A study of the influence of varying degrees of psychological stress on problem solving rigidity. Unpublished doctoral dissertation, Syracuse Univer.

Cowen, E. L., & Thompson, G. 1951. Problem solving rigidity and personality structure. *J. abnorm. soc. Psychol.*, 46: 165-76.

Cowen, E. L., Wiener, M., & Hess, J. 1953. Generalization of problem solving rigidity. *J. consult. Psychol.*, 17: 100-03.

Dallenbach, K. M. 1953. The place of theory in science. *Psychol. Rev.*, 60: 33-39.

Dawson, S. I. *See* Cathecart, E. P. 1928.

Deitcher, S. 1953. Einstellung-effect and effortfulness of task. Unpublished Master's thesis, McGill Univer.

Dembo, T. 1931. Der Ärger als dynamisches Problem. *Psychol. Forsch.*, 15: 1-44.

Deutsche, J. M. 1943. The development of children's concepts of causal relation. In R. G. Barker, J. S. Kounin, & H. F. Wright (Eds.), *Child behavior and development*. New York: McGraw-Hill. Pp. 129-46.

Dollard, J. *See* Miller, N. E. 1941.

Dudek, F. J. *See* Kleemeier, R. W. 1950.

Duff, A. W. 1909. *A textbook of physics*. Philadelphia: P. Blakiston's Sons.

Duncan, J., & Starling, S. F. 1922. *A textbook of physics for the use of science and engineering*. London: Macmillan.

Duncker, K. 1945. On problem solving. (Translated by L. S. Lees.) *Psychol. Monogr.*, 58, No. 5 (Whole No. 270).

Ehrlich, G. 1943. The relation between the learning of a motor skill and measures of strength, ability, educability, and capacity. *Res. Quart. Amer. phys. Educ. Ass'n*, 14: 46-59.

Einstein, A. 1950. *Out of my later years*. New York: Philosophical Library.

Elle, M. 1957. Unpublished research, Univer. of Oregon.

Ellis, W. D. (Ed.) 1938. *A source book of Gestalt psychology*. New York: Harcourt, Brace.

Ericksen, S. C. 1942. Variability of attack in massed and distributed practice. *J. exp. Psychol.*, 31: 339-45.

Fenichel, O. 1945. *The psychoanalytic theory of the neurosis*. New York: Norton.

Ferguson, G. A. *See* Oliver, J. A. 1951; Scheier, I. H. 1952.

Fernberger, S. W. 1931. On absolute and relative judgments in weight lifting experiments. *Amer. J. Psychol.*, 43: 560-78.

Finkel, R., & Notkin, J. 1951-52. Unpublished research, McGill Univer.

Fisher, S. 1950. Patterns of personality rigidity and some of their determinants. *Psychol. Monogr.*, 64, No. 1 (Whole No. 307).

Forgus, R. H. 1950. Unpublished research, McGill Univer.

Forgus, R. H. 1951. An investigation of the relationship between the Einstellung effect and variability. Unpublished Master's thesis, McGill Univer.

Forgus, R. H. *See also* Luchins, A. S. 1955.

Frenkel-Brunswik, E. 1949. Intolerance of ambiguity as an emotional and perceptual personality variable. *J. Pers.*, 18: 108-43.

Frenkel-Brunswik, E. 1951. Personality theory and perception. In R. R. Blake and G. V. Ramsey (Eds.), *Perception: An approach to personality*. New York: Ronald Press. Pp. 356-420.

Freud, S. 1918. *Totem and taboo*. New York: Dodd, Mead.

Freud, S. 1922. *Beyond the pleasure principle*. London: Hogarth.

Freud, S. 1930. *Civilization and its discontents*. New York: Johnathan Cape & Harrison Smith.

Freud, S. 1933. *New introductory lectures*. New York: Norton.

Freud, S. 1949. *An outline of psychoanalysis*. New York: Norton.

Freud, S. 1953. *Collected papers*. Vols. 2, 3, 4. (J. Strachey, Ed.) London: Hogarth.

Friedman, L. 1951-52. Unpublished research, McGill Univer.

Fromm, E. 1941. *Escape from freedom*. New York: Farrar & Rinehart.

Fromm, E. 1947. *Man for himself*. New York: Rinehart.

Fuchs, W. 1921. Unterschung über das Sehen der Hemianopiker und Hemiambly-
    opiker, II Dietotalisierende Gestaltauffassung. *Z Psychol.*, 86: 1-143. Con-
    densed in Selection 29 in W. D. Ellis (Ed.), 1938, *A source book of Gestalt
    psychology.* New York: Harcourt, Brace.

Galler, B. 1951-52. Unpublished research, McGill Univer.

Gebhard, N. *See* Meer, B. 1950.

Gibson, J. J. 1929. The reproduction of visually perceived forms. *J. exp. Psychol.*,
    12: 1-39.

Gill, M. *See* Rapaport, D. 1945.

Goldberger, L. 1950-52. Unpublished research, McGill Univer.

Goldstein, K. 1939. *The organism.* New York: American Book.

Goldstein, K. 1943. Concerning rigidity. *Charact. & Pers.*, 11: 209-26.

Goldstein, K., & Scheerer, M. 1941. Abstract and concrete behavior. *Psychol.
    Monogr.*, 53, No. 2 (Whole No. 239).

Gottschaldt, K. 1926. Über den Einfluss der Erfahrung auf die Wahrnehmung von
    Figuren I; Über den Einfluss gehäufter Einprägung von Figuren auf ihre
    Sichtbarkeit und umfassenden Konfigurationen. *Psychol. Forsch.*, 8: 261-317.

Gross, O. 1902. *Die cerebrale Sekundaerfunction.* Leipzig: Vogel.

Gruenberg, A. *See* Kendler, H. H. 1952.

Guetzkow, H. 1951. An analysis of the operation of set in problem solving be-
    havior. *J. gen. Psychol.*, 45: 219-44.

Guthrie, E. R. 1935. *The psychology of learning.* New York: Harper.

Guthrie, E. R. 1940. Association and the law of effect. *Psychol. Rev.*, 47: 127-48.

Guthrie, E. R. 1942. Conditioning: A theory of learning in terms of stimulus, re-
    sponse and association. *41st Yearb. nat. Soc. Stud. Educ.*, Part II, 17-60.

Guthrie, E. R. 1952. *The psychology of learning.* (Rev. ed.) New York: Harper.

Guthrie, E. R., & Horton, G. P. 1946. *Cats in a puzzle box.* New York: Rinehart.

Guyer, M. F. 1941. *Animal biology.* New York: Harper.

Halpern, F. *See* Bochner, R. 1945.

Halprin, E. 1951-52. Unpublished research, McGill Univer.

Hamilton, J. A., & Krechevsky, I. 1933. Studies in the effect of shock upon be-
    havior plasticity in the rat. *J. comp. Psychol.*, 16: 237-53.

Hargreaves, H. L. 1927. The "faculty" of imagination. *Brit. J. Psychol. Monogr.
    Suppl.*, 8, No. 10.

Harlow, H. F. 1949. The formation of learning sets. *Psychol. Rev.*, 56: 51-56.

Harman, H. H. *See* Holzinger, K. J. 1941.

Harris, R. A. 1951. The effects of stress on rigidity of mental set in problem solu-
    tion. Unpublished doctoral dissertation, Harvard Univer.

Hartley, D. 1791. *Collected works.* London: J. Johnson.

Hebb, D. O. 1949. *Organization of behavior.* New York: Wiley.

Hebb, D. O. 1951. The role of neurological ideas in psychology. *J. Pers.*, 20: 39-55.

Hebb, D. O., & Thompson, W. R. 1954. The social significance of animal studies.
    In G. Lindsey (Ed.), *Handbook of social psychology.* Cambridge: Addison-
    Wesley. Pp. 532-62.

Heglin, H. J. 1955. Problem solving set in different age groups. Unpublished doc-
    toral dissertation, Univer. of Florida.

Heidigger, M. 1950. *Time and being.* New York: Philosophical Library.

Helson, H. 1947. Adaptation-level as frame of reference for prediction of psycho-
    physical data. *Amer. J. Psychol.*, 60: 1-29.

Helson, H. 1948. Adaptation-level as a basis for a quantitative theory of frames of reference. *Psychol. Rev.*, 55: 297-313.

Henle, M., & Hubble, M. B. 1938. "Egocentricity" in adult conversation. *J. soc. Psychol.*, 9: 227-34.

Herbart, J. F. 1891. *A textbook in psychology.* New York: Appleton.

Hess, J. *See* Cowen, E. L. 1953.

Heymans, G., & Brugmans, H. J. T. W. 1913. Intelligenzprüfungen mit Studieren-den. *Z. Psychol.*, 7: 317-31.

Hilgard, E. R. 1948. *Theories of learning.* New York: Appleton-Century-Crofts.

Hilgard, E. R., & Marquis, D. G. 1940. *Conditioning and learning.* New York: D. Appleton-Century.

Hobbes, T. 1839. *Leviathan.* In Sir Wm. Molesworth (Ed.), *The English works of Thomas Hobbes.* London: J. Bohn. Vol. 3.

Hoffman, H. 1952-53. Unpublished research, McGill Univer.

Holzinger, K. J., & Harman, H. H. 1941. *Factor analysis.* Chicago: Chicago University. Press.

Horney, K. 1937. *The neurotic personality of our times.* New York: Norton.

Horney, K. 1939. *New ways in psychoanalysis.* New York: Norton.

Horney, K. 1945. *Our inner conflicts.* New York: Norton.

Horton, G. P. *See* Guthrie, E. R. 1946.

Horwitz, L. 1951. An investigation of the nature of rigidity. Unpublished doctoral dissertation, New York Univer.

Hovland, C. I. 1951. Human learning and retention. In S. S. Stevens (Ed.), *Handbook of experimental psychology.* New York: Wiley. C. 17.

Huang, I., & Chu, Y. J. 1936. The social function of the children's language. *Chung Hun educ. Rev.*, 23: 69-94.

Hubble, M. B. *See* Henle, M. 1938.

Hull, C. L. 1935. Mind, mechanism, and adaptive behavior. *Psychol. Rev.*, 42: 219-45.

Hull, C. L. 1943. *Principles of behavior.* New York: D. Appleton-Century.

Hume, D. 1896. *A treatise of human nature.* Oxford: Clarenden Press.

Hume, D. 1939. *An enquiry concerning human understanding.* In E. A. Burtt (Ed.), *The English philosophers.* New York: Modern Library. Pp. 585-689.

Humphrey, G. 1951. *Thinking: An introduction to its experimental psychology.* London: Methuen.

Hunter, W. S. 1920. The temporal maze and kinaesthetic sensory processes in the white rat. *Psychobiology*, 2: 1-17.

Hurley, T. 1957. Unpublished research, Univer. of Oregon.

Husserl, E. 1952. *Ideas.* (Translated by W. R. B. Gibson.) New York: Macmillan.

Immergluck, L. 1952. The role of set in perceptual judgment. *J. Psychol.*, 34: 181-89.

Irion, A. L. *See* McGeoch, J. A. 1952.

Jacobi, J. 1942. *The psychology of C. G. Jung.* London: Kegan Paul, Trench, Trubner.

James, W. 1890. *Principles of psychology.* London: Macmillan.

Jasper, H. A. 1930. Is perseveration a functional unit participating in all behavior processes? *J. soc. Psychol.*, 2: 29-51.

Jeffries, L. A. 1948. The nature of human abilities. *Amer. J. Psychol.*, 61: 107-11.

Jensen, F. *See* Murphy, G. 1932.

Joad, C. E. M. 1934. Herbert Spencer. In *Encyclopaedia of the social sciences.* New York: Macmillan. Pp. 295-96.

Johnson, E. C., & Josey, C. C. 1931. A note on the development of thought forms of children as described by Piaget. *J abnorm. soc. Psychol.,* 26: 338-39.

Jones, H. M. *See* Mowrer, O. H. 1943.

Jones, L. W. 1915. Perseveration. *Rep. Brit. Ass'n Adv. Sci.,* 85: 698.

Jones, L. W. 1929. Individual differences in mental inertia. *J. nat. Inst. industr. Res.,* 4: 282-94.

Josey, C. C. *See* Johnson, E. C. 1931.

Judd, C. H. 1908. The relation of special training to general intelligence. *Educ. Rev.,* 36: 28-42.

Jung, C. G. 1915a. On psychological understanding. *J. abnorm. soc. Psychol.,* 10: 385-99.

Jung, C. G. 1915b. The theory of psychoanalysis. *Nerv. ment. Dis. Monogr. Series,* No. 19.

Jung, C. G. 1920a. *Collected papers on analytical psychology.* (2nd ed.) London: Balliere, Tindall & Cox.

Jung, C. G. 1920b. *Psychological types.* New York: Harcourt, Brace.

Jung, C. G. 1928. *Contributions to analytical psychology.* New York: Harcourt, Brace.

Jung, C. G. 1939. *The integration of the personality.* New York: Farrar & Rinehart.

Kahn, A. 1951-52. Unpublished research, McGill Univer.

Kallen, H. M. 1934. Psychoanalysis. In *Encyclopaedia of the social sciences.* New York: Macmillan. Pp. 580-88.

Kelley, T. L. 1928. *Crossroads in the mind of man.* Stanford: Stanford Univer. Press.

Kelley, T. L. 1935. *Essential traits of mental life.* Cambridge: Harvard Univer. Press.

Kendler, H. H. 1952. "What is learned?"—A theoretical blind alley. *Psychol. Rev.,* 59: 269-77.

Kendler, H. H., Gruenberg, A., & Richman, H. 1952. The influence of massed and distributed practice on the development of mental set. *J. exp. Psychol.,* 43: 21-25.

Kenna, J. C. *See* Walker, K. F. 1943.

Kingsmill, D. 1951-52. Unpublished research, McGill Univer.

Kleemeier, R. W., & Dudek, F. J. 1950. A factorial investigation of flexibility. *Educ. psychol. Measmt.,* 10: 107-18.

Klein, G. S. 1951. The personal world through perception. In R. R. Blake & G. V. Ramsey (Eds.), *Perception: An approach to personality.* New York: Ronald Press. Pp. 328-55.

Klein, G. S., & Krech, D. 1951. The problem of personality and its theory. *J. Pers.,* 20: 2-22.

Klineberg, O. 1935. *Race differences.* New York: Harper.

Koch, S. 1951a. The current status of motivational psychology. *Psychol. Rev.,* 58: 147-57.

Koch, S. 1951b. Theoretical psychology, 1950: An overview. *Psychol. Rev.,* 58: 295-301.

Koffka, K. 1925. *Growth of the mind.* New York: Harcourt, Brace.

Koffka, K. 1935. *Principles of Gestalt psychology.* New York: Harcourt, Brace.

Köhler, W. 1925. *Mentality of apes.* London: Kegan Paul, Trench, Trubner.

Köhler, W. 1937. Psychological remarks on some questions of anthropology. *Amer. J. Psychol.*, 50: 271-88.

Köhler, W. 1938. *The place of value in a world of facts.* New York: Liveright.

Köhler, W. 1941. On the nature of associations. *Proc. Amer. phil. Soc.*, 84: 489-502.

Köhler, W., & Wallach, H. 1944. Figural after-effects: An investigation of visual processes. *Proc. Amer. phil. Soc.*, 88: 269-357.

Kolber, N. 1951-52. Unpublished research, McGill Univer.

Kopin, R. Brownstein. 1950-52. Unpublished research, McGill Univer.

Kounin, J. S. 1941a. Experimental studies of rigidity: I. The measurement of rigidity in normal and feebleminded persons. *Charact. & Pers.*, 9: 251-72.

Kounin, J. S. 1941b. Experimental studies of rigidity: II. The explanatory power of rigidity as applied to feeblemindedness. *Charact. & Pers.*, 9: 273-82.

Kounin, J. S. 1943. Intellectual development and rigidity. In R. G. Barker, J. S. Kounin, and H. F. Wright (Eds.), *Child behavior and development.* New York: McGraw-Hill. Pp. 179-97.

Kounin, J. S. 1948. The meaning of rigidity: A reply to Heinz Werner. *Psychol. Rev.*, 55: 157-66.

Krech, D. 1950. Dynamic systems as open neurological systems. *Psychol. Rev.*, 57: 345-61.

Krech, D. *See also* Klein, G. S. 1951.

Krechevsky, I. 1932. Hypotheses in rats. *Psychol. Rev.*, 39: 532-76.

Krechevsky, I. 1937a. Brain mechanisms and variability: I. Variability within a means-end-readiness. *J. comp. Psychol.*, 23: 121-38.

Krechevsky, I. 1937b. Brain mechanisms and variability: II. Variability when no learning is involved. *J. comp. Psychol.*, 23: 139-63.

Krechevsky, I. 1937c. Brain mechanisms and variability: III. Limitations of the effect of cortical injury upon variability. *J. comp. Psychol.*, 23: 351-64.

Krechevsky, I. *See also* Hamilton, J. A. 1933.

Kuo, Z. Y. 1922. The nature of unsuccessful acts and their order of elimination in animal learning. *J. comp. Psychol.*, 2: 1-27.

Lankes, W. 1915. Perseveration. *Brit. J. Psychol.*, 7: 387-419.

Leeds, D. S. *See* Tresselt, M. E. 1951.

Leeper, R. W. 1948. The experiments by Spence and Lippitt and Kendler on the sign-Gestalt theory of learning. *J. exp. Psychol.*, 38: 102-06.

Lepley, W. M. 1954. Variability as a variable. *J. Psychol.*, 37: 19-25.

Levinson, D. J., & Sanford, R. N. 1944. A scale for the measurement of anti-Semitism. *J. soc. Psychol.*, 17: 339-70.

Lewin, C. 1951. The effect of failure in similar and dissimilar tasks on the continuation of a problem solving set. Unpublished doctoral dissertation, New York Univer.

Lewin, K. 1922a. Das Problem der Willensmessung und das Grundgesetz der Assoziation I. *Psychol. Forsch.*, 1: 191-302.

Lewin, K. 1922b. Das Problem der Willensmessung und das Grundgesetz der Assoziation II. *Psychol. Forsch.*, 2: 65-140.

Lewin, K. 1926. Vorsatz, Will und Bedürfnis (mit Vorbemerkungen über die psychischen Kräfte und Energien und die Struktur der Seele). *Psychol. Forsch.*, 7: 294-385. Condensed in Selection 24 in W. D. Ellis (Ed.), 1938, *A source book of Gestalt psychology.* New York: Harcourt, Brace.

Lewin, K. 1935. *A dynamic theory of personality.* New York: McGraw-Hill.

Lewin, K. 1936. *Principles of topological psychology*. New York: McGraw-Hill.

Lewin, K. 1938. *The conceptual representation and measurement of psychological forces*. Durham, N.C.: Duke Univer. Press.

Lewin, K. 1951. *Field theory in social science*. New York: Harper.

Lewis, R. 1957. Unpublished research, Univer. of Oregon.

Lillie, R. S. 1945. *General biology and philosophy of organism*. Chicago: Univer. of Chicago Press.

Loevinger, J. 1951. Intelligence. In H. Helson (Ed.), *Theoretical foundations of psychology*. New York: Van Nostrand. C. 12.

Lowie, E. 1951-52. Unpublished research, McGill Univer.

Lubin, S. 1951-52. Unpublished research, McGill Univer.

Luchins, A. S. 1939. The Einstellung effect in learning by repetition. Unpublished doctoral dissertation, New York Univer.

Luchins, A. S. 1942. Mechanization in problem solving. *Psychol. Monogr.*, 54, No. 6 (Whole No. 248).

Luchins, A. S. 1944. On agreement with another's judgment. *J. abnorm. soc. Psychol.*, 39: 97-111.

Luchins, A. S. 1945. Social influences on perception of complex drawings. *J. soc. Psychol.*, 21: 257-74.

Luchins, A. S. 1947. Proposed methods of studying degrees of rigidity in behavior. *J. Pers.*, 15: 242-46.

Luchins, A. S. 1948. *Examination for rigidity of behavior*. New York: N.Y.R.O. Veterans Admin.

Luchins, A. S. 1949. Rigidity and ethnocentrism: A critique. *J. Pers.*, 17: 449-60.

Luchins, A. S. 1950a. *An examination for flexibility-rigidity*. Montrose, N.Y.: FDR VA Hospital.

Luchins, A. S. 1950b. Restructuring social perceptions: A group psychotherapy technique. *J. consult. Psychol.*, 14: 446-51.

Luchins, A. S. 1951a. Patients view the therapist: A training and research device. *J. consult. Psychol.*, 15: 24-31.

Luchins, A. S. 1951b. On recent usage of the Einstellung effect as a test of rigidity. *J. consult. Psychol.*, 15: 89-94.

Luchins, A. S. 1951c. The Einstellung test of rigidity: Its relation to concreteness of thinking. *J. consult. Psychol.*, 15: 303-10.

Luchins, A. S., 1952. Toward an experimental clinical psychology. *J. Pers.*, 20: 440-56.

Luchins, A. S. 1954. The autokinetic effect and gradations of illumination of the visual field. *J. gen. Psychol.*, 50: 29-37.

Luchins, A. S. 1955. A social-experimental approach to group psychotherapy. *J. soc. Psychol.*, 46: 121-27.

Luchins, A. S. 1957a. Experimental attempts to minimize the impact of first impressions. In Carl I. Hovland (Ed.), *The order of presentation in persuasion*. New Haven: Yale Univer. Press. C. 5.

Luchins, A. S. 1957b. A variational approach to phenomena in social psychology. In M. Sherif and M. O. Wilson (Eds.), *Emerging problems in social psychology*. Norman: Univer. Book Exchange, Univer. of Oklahoma. C. 5.

Luchins, A. S., & Forgus, R. H. 1955. The effect of differential post-weaning environment on the rigidity of an animal's behavior. *J. genet. Psychol.*, 86: 51-58.

Luchins, A. S., & Luchins, E. H. 1946. Towards intrinsic methods in testing. *J. educ. Psychol.*, 37: 142-48.

Luchins, A. S., & Luchins, E. H. 1948. Children's attitudes toward homogeneous groupings. *J. genet. Psychol.,* 72: 3-9.

Luchins, A. S., & Luchins, E. H. 1950. New experimental attempts at preventing mechanization in problem solving. *J. gen. Psychol.,* 42: 279-97.

Luchins, A. S., & Luchins, E. H. 1954a. The Einstellung phenomenon and effortfulness of task. *J. gen. Psychol.,* 50: 15-27.

Luchins, A. S., & Luchins, E. H. 1954b. Variables and functions. *Psychol. Rev.,* 61: 315-22.

Luchins, A. S., & Luchins, E. H. 1955a. Previous experience with ambiguous and nonambiguous perceptual stimuli under various social influences. *J. soc. Psychol.,* 42: 249-70.

Luchins, A. S., & Luchins, E. H. 1955b. On conformity with true and false communications. *J. soc. Psychol.,* 42: 283-304.

Luchins, E. H. *See* Luchins, A. S. 1946, 1948, 1950, 1954a, 1954b, 1955a, 1955b.

Lyman, B. 1951. Concrete mindedness and rigidity. Unpublished Master's thesis, McGill Univer.

MacBride, T. 1950-51. Unpublished research, McGill Univer.

MacLeod, R. B. 1947. The phenomenological approach to social psychology. *Psychol. Rev.,* 54: 193-210.

Maier, N. R. F. 1930. Reasoning in humans: I. On direction. *J. comp. Psychol.,* 10: 115-43.

Maier, N. R. F. 1933. An aspect of human reasoning. *Brit. J. Psychol.,* 24: 144-55.

Maier, N. R. F. 1937. Reasoning in rats and human beings. *Psychol. Rev.,* 44: 365-78.

Maier, N. R. F. 1938. A further analysis of reasoning in rats: III. The influence of cortical injuries on the process of "direction." *Comp. psychol. Monogr.,* 15: 44-80.

Maier, N. R. F. 1939. The specific processes constituting the learning process. *Psychol. Rev.,* 46: 241-52.

Maier, N. R. F. 1949. *Frustration.* New York: McGraw-Hill.

Malteno, E. V. *See* Cattell, R. B. 1940.

Markus, K. Z. 1951. Unpublished research, McGill Univer.

Marquart, D. I. 1948. The pattern of punishment and its relation to abnormal fixation in adult human subjects. *J. gen. Psychol.,* 39: 107-44.

Marquis, D. G. *See* Hilgard, E. R. 1940.

Martin, S. 1951-52. Unpublished research, McGill Univer.

Marx, M. H. (Ed.). 1951. *Psychological theory: Contemporary readings.* New York: Macmillan.

McCarthy, D. 1930. Language development of the preschool child. *Inst. of Child Welf. Monogr. Series,* 4. Minneapolis: Univer. of Minnesota Press.

McCarthy, D. 1946. Language development in children. In L. Carmichael (Ed.), *Manual of child psychology.* New York: Wiley. C. 10.

McGeoch, J. A. 1942. *The psychology of human learning.* New York: Longmans, Green.

McGeoch, J. A., & Irion, A. L. 1952. *The psychology of human learning.* New York: Longmans, Green.

McNemar, O. W. *See* Taylor, D. W. 1955.

Meer, B., & Gebhard, N. 1950. Personal communication.

Merling, S. S. 1951-52. Unpublished research, McGill Univer.

Messer, A. 1906. Experimentalle-psychologische Untersuchungen über das Denken. *Arch. ges. Psychol.,* 8: 1-224.

Meunzinger, K. 1954. Unpublished manuscript on factor analysis, Univer. of Colorado.

Meyers, W. J. 1957. Unpublished research, Univer. of Oregon.

Miall, S. 1940. *New dictionary of chemistry*. London: Longmans, Green.

Mill, J. 1869. *An association of ideas in analysis of the phenomena of human nature*. London: Longmans, Green, Roeder, Dyer.

Miller, N. E. 1951. Comments on theoretical models illustrated by the development of a theory of conflict. *J. Pers.*, 20: 82-100.

Miller, N. E., & Dollard, J. 1941. *Social learning and imitation*. New Haven: Yale Univer. Press.

Moran, L. J. *See* Blake, R. R. 1951.

Morgan, C. T. 1951. The psychophysiology of learning. In S. S. Stevens (Ed.), *Handbook of experimental psychology*. New York: Wiley. C. 20.

Mortimer-Maddox, J. 1951-52. Unpublished research, McGill Univer.

Mouton, J. S., & Blake, R. R. 1957. *The Psychology of conformity*. (Mimeographed ed.) Austin: Univer. of Texas Press.

Mowrer, O. H. 1948. Learning theory and the neurotic paradox. *Amer. J. Orthopsychiat.*, 18: 571-610.

Mowrer, O. H. 1951. Two-factor learning theory: Summary and comment. *Psychol. Rev.*, 58: 350-54.

Mowrer, O. H., & Jones, H. M. 1943. Extinction and behavior variability as functions of effortfulness of task. *J. exp. Psychol.*, 33: 369-86.

Mullahy, P. 1948. *Oedipus myth and complex*. New York: Hermitage.

Müller, G. E., & Pilzecker, A. 1900. Experimentelle Beiträge zur Lehre vom Gedächtniss. *Z. psychol. Ergbd.*, 1.

Müller, G. E., & Schumann, F. 1898. Über die psychologischen Grundlagen der Vergleichung gehobener Gewichter. *Pflüg. Arch. ges. Physiol.*, 45: 37-112.

Murphy, G., & Jensen, F. 1932. *Approaches to personality*. New York: Coward-McCann.

Murray, H. A. 1938. *Explorations in personality*. Cambridge: Harvard Univer. Press.

Neisser, C. 1894. 66 Sitzung des Vereins ostdeutscher Irrenärtze zu Breslau. *Allg. Z. f. Psychiat.*, 51: 1016.

Nishio, R. 1951-52. Unpublished research, McGill Univer.

Nordenskiöld, E. 1936. *The history of biology*. New York: Tudor.

Notcutt, B. 1943. Perseveration and fluency. *Brit. J. Psychol.*, 28: 200-08.

Notkin, J. *See* Finkel, R. 1951-52.

Oliver, J. A. 1950. An analysis of some new tests of disposition rigidity. Unpublished Master's thesis, McGill Univer.

Oliver, J. A., & Ferguson, G. A. 1951. A factorial study of tests of rigidity. *Canad. J. Psychol.*, 5: 49-59.

Oppenheimer, R. 1956. *The constitution of matter*. (Condon Lecture Publication, Oregon State System of Higher Education.) Eugene: Univer. of Oregon Press.

Ovsiankina, M. 1928. Wiederaufnahme unterbrochener Handlungen. *Psychol. Forsch.*, 11: 302-79.

Owens, W. A., Jr. 1942. A note on the effects of practice upon trait differences in motor skills. *J. educ. Psychol.*, 33: 144-47.

Pally, S. 1952. The effect of self-esteem threat upon the rigidity of thought processes. Unpublished doctoral dissertation, Univer. of Pennsylvania.

Paquet, R. 1952. Etude expérimentale sur la rigidity. Unpublished Master's thesis, Univer. of Montreal.

Peretz, F. 1951-52. Unpublished research, McGill Univer.

Perkins, F. T. 1932. Symmetry in visual recall. *Amer. J. Psychol.*, 44: 477-90.

Perkins, F. T. *See also* Wheeler, R. H. 1932.

Piaget, J. 1930. *The child's conception of physical causality.* (Translated by M. Gabin.) New York: Harcourt, Brace.

Pierce, I. 1951. Personal communication.

Pilzecker, A. *See* Müller, G. E. 1900.

Pinard, H. W. 1932. Tests of perseveration: Their relation to certain psychopathic conditions and introvertism. *Brit. J. Psychol.*, 23: 114-26.

Postman, L. *See* Allport, G. W. 1947; Bruner, J. S. 1948.

Potampa, L. 1954. Unpublished research, Univer. of Oregon.

Pratt, C. C. 1933. Time errors in the method of single stimuli. *J. exp. Psychol.*, 16: 798-814.

Rabin, M. J. 1951-52. Unpublished research, McGill Univer.

Rabinowitz, H. S. 1951. A study of rigidity and abstraction in brain injury. Unpublished Master's thesis, McGill Univer.

Ramsey, G. V. *See* Blake, R. R. 1951.

Rangachar, C. 1932. Differences in perseveration among Jewish and English boys. *Brit. J. educ. Psychol.*, 2: 199-211.

Rapaport, D., Gill, M., & Schafer, R. 1945. *Diagnostic psychological testing.* Vol. 1. Chicago: Yearbook Publishers.

Ray, J. J. 1936. The generalizing ability of dull, bright, and superior children. *Peabody Cont. Educ.*, No. 175.

Reich, W. 1945. *Character analysis.* New York: Orgone Press.

Reicher, E. 1951-52. Unpublished research, McGill Univer.

Reid, J. W. 1951. An experimental study of analysis of the goal in problem solving. *J. gen. Psychol.*, 44: 51-69.

Richardson, M. 1941. *Fundamentals of mathematics.* New York: Macmillan.

Richman, H. *See* Kendler, H. H. 1952.

Rickers-Ovsiankina, M. *See* Ovsiankina, M. 1928.

Robbins, H. *See* Courant, R. 1941.

Robinson, E. S. 1932. *Association theory today.* New York: D. Appleton-Century.

Rohrlick, R. 1951-52. Unpublished research, McGill Univer.

Rokeach, M. 1947. Generalized mental rigidity as a factor in ethnocentrism. Unpublished doctoral dissertation, Univer. of California.

Rokeach, M. 1948. Generalized mental rigidity as a factor in ethnocentrism. *J. abnorm. soc. Psychol.*, 43: 259-78.

Rosen, B. 1951-52. Unpublished research, McGill Univer.

Rosen, N. 1950-51. Unpublished research, McGill Univer.

Rosenblueth, A., & Wiener, N. 1945. The role of models in science. *Phil. Sci.*, 12: 316-21.

Rosenzweig, S. 1944. An outline of frustration theory. In J. M. Hunt (Ed.), *Personality and the behavior disorders.* Vol. 1. New York: Ronald Press. Pp. 379-88.

Rosenzweig, S. 1945. The picture-association method and its application in a study of reactions to frustration. *J. Pers.*, 14: 3-23.

Ross, V. M. 1952. A comparison of the effect of Einstellung in different age groups. Unpublished doctoral dissertation, McGill Univer.

Rotstein, M. 1951-52. Unpublished research, McGill Univer.

Rotter, J. B. 1942. Level of aspiration as a method of studying personality. *J. exp. Psychol.*, 31: 410-22.

Ryans, D. G. 1939. Changes in variability in "digit-symbol substitution" performance measured at the beginning and at the end of practice, *J. genet. Psychol.*, 54: 461-65.

Sanford, R. N. *See* Levinson, D. J. 1944.

Saul, R. 1951-52. Unpublished research, McGill Univer.

Schafer, R. *See* Rapaport, D. 1945.

Scheerer, M. *See* Goldstein, K. 1941.

Scheier, I. H. 1950. Unpublished research, McGill Univer.

Scheier, I. H. 1951. Further factorial studies of tests of rigidity. Unpublished Master's thesis, McGill Univer.

Scheier, I. H., & Ferguson, G. A. 1952. Further factorial studies of tests of rigidity. *Canad. J. Psychol.*, 6: 18-30.

Schnaiberg, L. 1951-52. Unpublished research, McGill Univer.

Schrödinger, E. 1945. *What is life?* New York: Macmillan.

Schumann, F. *See* Müller, G. E. 1898.

Schwartz, E. *See* Becker, H. 1950-51.

Schwartzben, M. 1951-52. Unpublished research, McGill Univer.

Schwartzman, A. 1952. The relationship between Einstellung-effect and psychical rigidity. Unpublished Master's thesis, McGill Univer.

Shapiro, L. 1950. Unpublished research, McGill Univer.

Sherif, C. W. *See* Sherif, M. 1956.

Sherif, M. 1936. *The psychology of social norms.* New York: Harper.

Sherif, M., & Cantril, H. 1947. *The psychology of ego involvement.* New York: Wiley.

Sherif, M., & Sherif, C. W. 1956. *An outline of social psychology.* (Rev. ed.) New York: Harper.

Shevach, B. J. 1936a. Studies in perseveration: VI. Methods for the study of sensory perseveration. *J. Psychol.*, 3: 381-402.

Shevach, B. J. 1936b. Studies in perseveration: VII. Experimental results of tests for sensory perseveration. *J. Psychol.*, 3: 403-27.

Shevach, B. J. 1938. A note on racial difference in perseveration. *J. Psychol.*, 5: 271-79.

Shulman, R. 1950. Unpublished research, McGill Univer.

Shulman, R. 1951. On some factors influencing mechanization in problem solving. Unpublished Master's thesis, McGill Univer.

Simak, M. 1950-51. Unpublished research, McGill Univer.

Simcoe, L. 1951-52. Unpublished research, McGill Univer.

Simpson, G. G. 1949. *The meaning of evolution.* New Haven: Yale Univer. Press.

Singerman, C. 1950-51. Unpublished research, McGill Univer.

Skinner, B. F. 1938. *The behavior of organisms.* New York: D. Appleton-Century.

Skinner, B. F. 1950. Are theories of learning necessary? *Psychol. Rev.*, 57: 193-216.

Skinner, B. F. 1953a. *Science and human behavior.* New York: Macmillan.

Skinner, B. F. 1953b. Some contributions of an experimental analysis of behavior to psychology as a whole. *Amer. Psychologist*, 8: 69-78.

Snygg, D., & Combs, A. W. 1949. *Individual behavior: A new frame of reference.* New York: Harper.

Solomon, N. D. 1953. A comparison of rigidity of behavior manifested by a group of stutterers compared with "fluent" speakers in oral and other performances as measured by the Einstellung-effect. Unpublished Master's thesis, Univer. of Michigan.

Solomon, R. L. 1948. The influence of work on behavior. *Psychol. Bull.*, 45: 1-40.

Spearman, C. 1927. *The abilities of man: Their nature and measurement.* New York: Macmillan.

Spearman, C. 1929. The tenth Maudsley lecture: The psychiatric use of the methods and results of experimental psychology, *J. ment. Sci.*, 75: 365-67.

Spence, K. W. 1944. The nature of theory construction in contemporary psychology. *Psychol. Rev.*, 51: 47-68.

Spence, K. W. 1948. The postulates and methods of "behaviorism." *Psychol. Rev.*, 55: 67-78.

Spence, K. W. 1951. Theoretical interpretations of learning. In S. S. Stevens (Ed.), *Handbook of experimental psychology.* New York: Wiley. C. 18.

Sproule, J. A. 1951-52. Unpublished research, McGill Univer.

Staines, R. G. *See* Walker, K. F. 1943.

Starling, S. F. *See* Duncan, J. 1922.

Stearns, E. 1952-54. Unpublished research, McGill Univer.

Stephenson, W. 1932a. Studies in experimental psychiatry: II. Some contacts of P-factor with psychiatry. *J. ment. Sci.*, 78: 315-30.

Stephenson, W. 1932b. Studies in experimental psychiatry: III. P-score and inhibition for high-P praecox cases. *J. ment. Sci.*, 78: 908-20.

Stephenson, W. 1934. An introduction to so-called motor perseveration tests. *Brit. J. educ. Psychol.*, 4: 186-208.

Stephenson, W. 1936. Foundations of psychometry: Four factor systems. *Psychometrika*, 1: 195-210.

Stephenson, W. *See also* Burt, C. 1939.

Stern, Catherine. 1949. *Children discover arithmetic: An introduction to structural arithmetic.* New York: Harper.

Stevens, S. S. 1939. Psychology and the science of science. *Psychol. Bull.*, 36: 221-63.

Strauss, A. A., & Werner, H. 1942. Experimental analysis of the clinical symptom 'perseveration' in mentally retarded children. *Amer. J. ment. Defic.*, 47: 185-88.

Sullivan, H. S. 1953. *The interpersonal theory of psychiatry.* New York: Norton.

Szasz, T. S. 1952. On the psychoanalytic theory of instincts. *Psychoanalytic Quart.*, 21:25-49.

Tannenbaum, L. 1951-52. Unpublished research, McGill Univer.

Taylor, D. W., & McNemar, O. W. 1955. Problem solving and thinking. *Annu. Rev. Psychol.*, 6: 455-77.

Thompson, C. 1950. *Psychoanalysis: Evolution and development.* New York: Hermitage.

Thompson, G. *See* Cowen, E. L. 1951.

Thompson, W. R. *See* Hebb, D. O. 1954.

Thomson, G. H. 1939. *The factorial analysis of human ability.* London: Univer. of London Press.

Thomson, G. H. 1946. *The factorial analysis of human ability.* (Rev. ed.) Boston: Houghton Mifflin.

Thorndike, E. L. 1913. *Psychology of learning.* (Vol. 2 of *Educational psychology.*) New York: Teachers College, Columbia Univer.

Thorndike, E. L. 1922. *The psychology of arithmetic.* New York: Macmillan.

Thouless, R. 1935. The tendency to certainty in religious beliefs. *Brit. J. Psychol.,* 26: 16-31.

Thurstone, L. L. 1944. *A factorial study of perception.* Chicago: Univer. of Chicago Press.

Thurstone, L. L. 1947. *Multiple-factor analysis.* Chicago: Univer. of Chicago Press.

Tiner, L. G. *See* Cattell, R. B. 1949.

Tolman, E. C. 1925. Behaviorism and purpose. *J. Phil.,* 22: 35-41.

Tolman, E. C. 1932. *Purposive behavior in animals and men.* New York: Appleton-Century.

Tolman, E. C. 1949a. Discussion. *J. Pers.,* 18: 48-50.

Tolman, E. C. 1949b. There is more than one kind of learning. *Psychol. Rev.,* 56: 144-55.

Tresselt, M. E. 1951. Personal communication.

Tresselt, M. E., & Leeds, D. S., 1951. Personal communication.

Trossman, S. 1951-52. Unpublished research, McGill Univer.

Turk, B. 1952. Unpublished research, McGill Univer.

Vineberg, R. 1951. The effect of massed and spaced practice upon different strength in mental set. Unpublished Master's thesis, New York Univer.

Voeks, V. W. 1950. Formalization and clarification of a theory of learning. *J. Psychol.,* 30: 341-62.

Volkmann, J. 1951. Scales of judgment and their implications for social psychology. In J. H. Rohrer & M. Sherif (Eds.), *Social psychology at the crossroads.* New York: Harper.

Walker, K. F., Staines, R. G., & Kenna, J. C. 1943. P-tests and the concept of mental inertia. *Charact. & Pers.,* 12: 32-42.

Wallach, H. *See* Köhler, W. 1944.

Warren, H. C. 1934. *Dictionary of psychology.* New York: Houghton Mifflin.

Watson, J. B. 1914. *Behavior: An introduction to comparative psychology.* New York: Henry Holt.

Watt, H. J. 1905. Experimentelle beiträge zu einer Theorie des Denkens. *Arch. ges. Psychol.,* 4: 289-436.

Werner, H. 1940. *Comparative psychology of mental development.* New York: Harper.

Werner, H. 1946a. Abnormal and subnormal rigidity. *J. abnorm. soc. Psychol.,* 41: 15-24.

Werner, H. 1946b. The concept of rigidity: A critical evaluation. *Psychol. Rev.,* 53: 43-52.

Werner, H. *See also* Strauss, A. A. 1942.

Wertheimer, M. 1912. Über das Denken der Naturvölker Zahlen und Zahlgebilde. *Z. Psychol.,* 60: 321-89. Condensed in Selection 22 in W. D. Ellis (Ed.), 1938, *A source book of Gestalt psychology.* New York: Harcourt, Brace.

Wertheimer, M. 1923. Untersuchungen zur Lehr von der Gestalt, II. *Psychol. Forsch.,* 4: 301-50. Condensed in Selection 5 in W. D. Ellis (Ed.), 1938, *A source book of Gestalt psychology.* New York: Harcourt, Brace.

Wertheimer, M. 1933. Zu dem Problem der Untersheidung von Einzelinhalt und Zeil, *Z. Psychol.,* 129: 353-58.

Wertheimer, M. 1945. *Productive thinking.* New York: Harper.

Wever, E. H., & Zener, K. 1938. Method of absolute judgment in psychophysics. *Psychol. Rev.,* 35: 457-76.

Wheeler, R. H. 1929. *The science of psychology*. New York: Crowell.

Wheeler, R. H. 1932. *The laws of human nature*. New York: Appleton.

Wheeler, R. H. 1940. *The science of psychology*. (2nd ed.) New York: Crowell.

Wheeler, R. H., & Perkins, F. T. 1932. *Principles of mental development*. New York: Crowell.

Whitman, J. 1957. Unpublished research, Univer. of Oregon.

Wiener, M. *See* Cowen, E. L. 1953.

Wiener, N. *See* Rosenblueth, A. 1945.

Wiersma, E. 1906. Die Sekundärfunktion bei Psychosen. *J. Psychol. Neur.*, 8: 1-24.

Witkin, H., *et al.* 1954. *Personality through perception*. New York: Harper.

Wolff, K. H. 1950. *The sociology of Georg Simmel*. Glencoe, Ill.: Free Press.

Woodworth, R. S. 1938. *Experimental psychology*. New York: Henry Holt.

Wulf, F. 1922. Über die Veränderung von Vorstellungen (Gedächtnis und Gestalt. *Psychol. Forsch.*, 1: 333-73. Condensed in Selection 10 in W. D. Ellis (Ed.), 1938, *A source book of Gestalt psychology*. New York: Harcourt, Brace.

Wylie, H. H. 1919. An experimental study of transfer of response in the white rat. *Behav. Monogr.*, 3, No. 16.

Yoshioka, J. G. 1929. Weber's law in the discrimination of maze distance by the white rat. *Univer. of Calif. Pub. in Psychol.*, No. 4: 155-84.

Yule, E. P. 1935. The resemblance of twins with regard to perseveration. *J. ment. Sci.*, 81: 489-501.

Zeigarnik, B. 1927. Über das Behalten von erledigten und unerledigten Handlungen. *Psychol. Forsch.*, 9: 1-85.

Zener, K. *See* Wever, E. H. 1938.

Zuckerman, C. 1951-52. Unpublished research, McGill Univer.

Zweig, J. 1952-53. Unpublished research, McGill Univer.